THE PORTABLE MATISSE

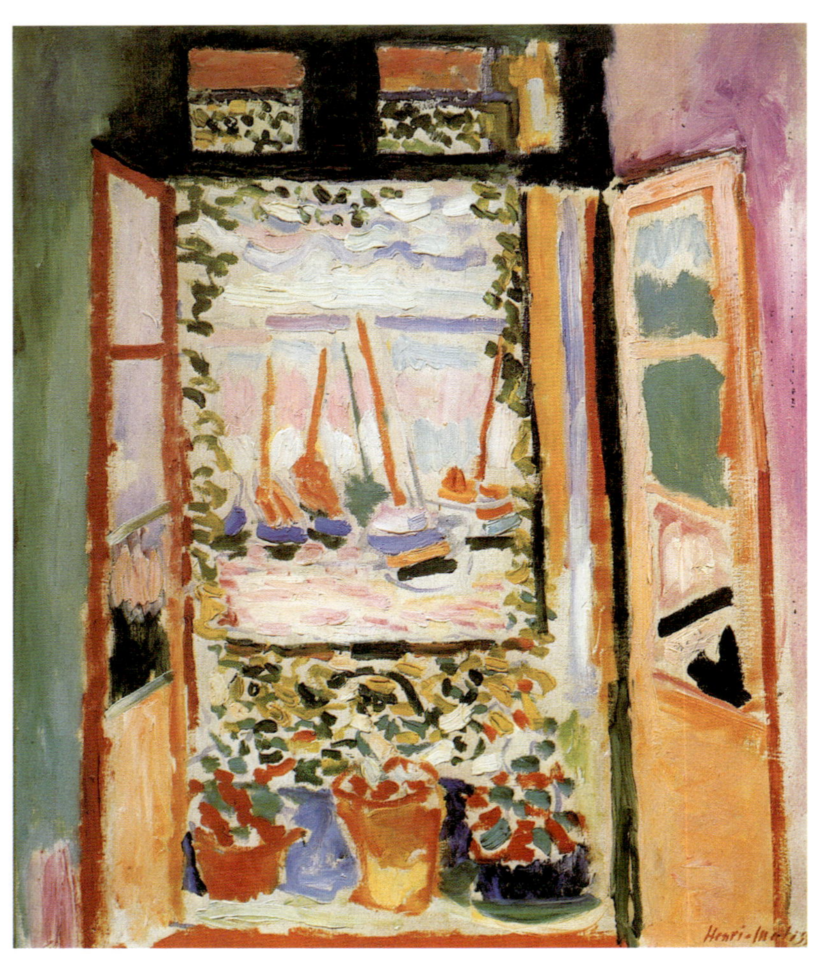

THE PORTABLE

MATISSE

with an essay by *Robert Hughes*

UNIVERSE

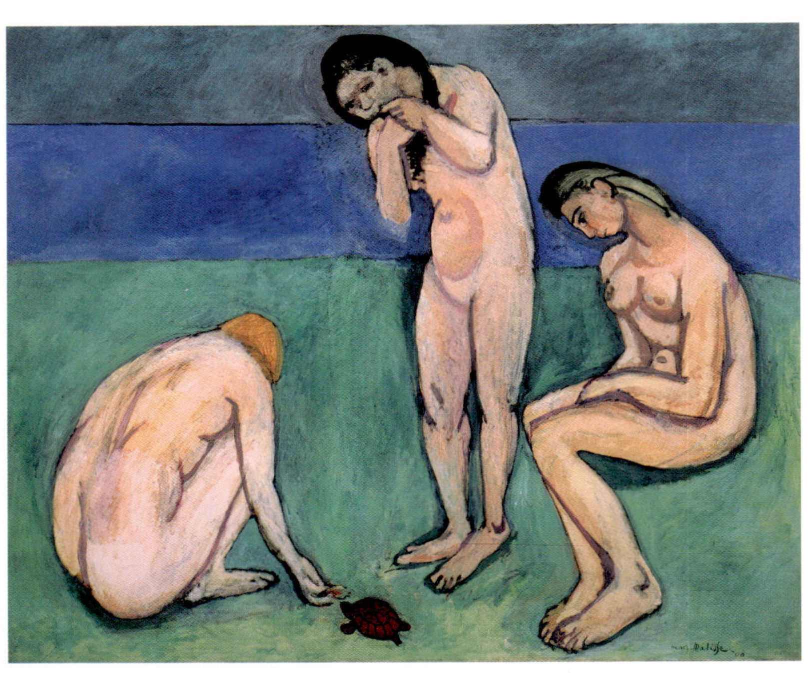

CONTENTS

Henri Matisse was born in 1869, the year the *Cutty Sark* was launched. The year he died, 1954, the first hydrogen bomb exploded at Bikini Atoll. Not only did he live on, literally, from one world into another; he lived through some of the most traumatic political events in recorded history, the worst wars, the greatest slaughters, the most demented rivalries of ideology, without, it seems, turning a hair. Matisse never made a didactic painting or signed a manifesto, and there is scarcely one reference to a political event — let alone an expression of political *opinion* — to be found anywhere in his writings. Perhaps Matisse did suffer from fear and loathing like the rest of us, but there is no trace of them in his work. His studio was a world within the world: a place of equilibrium that, for sixty continuous years, produced images of comfort, refuge, and balanced satisfaction. Nowhere in Matisse's work does one feel a trace of the alienation and conflict which modernism, the mirror of our century, has so often reflected. His paintings are the equivalent to that ideal place, scaled away from the assaults and erosions of history, that Baudelaire imagined in his poem *L'Invitation au voyage*:

"Furniture gleaming with the sheen of years would grace our bedroom; the rarest flowers, mingling their odors with vague whiffs of amber, the painted ceilings, the fathomless mirrors, the splendor of the East . . . all of that would speak, in secret, to our souls, in its gentle language. There, everything is order and beauty, luxury, calm and pleasure."

In its thoughtfulness, steady development, benign lucidity, and wide range of historical sources, Matisse's work utterly refutes the notion that the great discoveries of modernism were made by violently rejecting the past. His work was grounded in tradition — and in a much less restless and ironic approach to it than Picasso's. As a young man, having been a student of Odilon Redon's, he had closely studied the work of Manet and Cézanne; a small Cézanne *Bathers*, which he bought in 1899, became his talisman. Then around 1904 he got interested in the colored dots of Seurat's Divisionism. Seurat was long dead by then, but Matisse became friends with his closest follower, Paul Signac. Signac's paintings of Saint-Tropez Bay were an important influence on Matisse's work. So, perhaps, was the painting that Signac regarded as his masterpiece and exhibited at the Salon des Indépendants in 1895, *In the Time of Harmony*, a big allegorical composition setting forth his anarchist beliefs. The painting shows a Utopian Arcadia of relaxation and farming by the sea, and it may have fused with the traditional *fête champêtre* in Matisse's mind to produce his own awkward but important demonstration piece, *Luxe, calme et volupté*, 1904–1905. In it, Matisse's literary interest in Baudelaire merged with his Arcadian fantasies, perhaps under the promptings of Signac's table talk about the future Golden Age. One sees a picnic by the sea at Saint-Tropez, with a lateen-rigged boat and a cluster of bulbous, spotty nudes. It is not, to put it mildly, a very stirring piece of *luxe*, but it was Matisse's first attempt to make an image of the Mediterranean as a state of mind.

In 1905 Matisse went south again, to work with André Derain in the little coastal town of Collioure. At this point, his color broke free. Just how free it became can be seen in *The Open Window, Collioure*, 1905. It is the first of the views through a window that would recur as a favorite Matissean motif. All the color has undergone an equal distortion and keying up. The terracotta of flowerpots and the rusty red of masts and furled sails become a blazing Indian red; the reflections of the boats, turning at anchor through the razzle of light on the water, are pink; the green of the left wall, reflected in the open glazed door on the right, is heightened beyond expectation and picked up in the sky's tints. And the brushwork has a eupeptic, take-it-or-leave-it quality that must have seemed to deny craft even more than the comparatively settled way that Derain, his companion, was painting.

The new Matisses, seen in the autumn of 1905, were very shocking indeed. Even their handful of defenders were uncertain about them, while their detractors thought them barbaric. Particularly offensive was his use of this discordant color in the familiar form of the salon portrait — even though the "victim" was his wife, posing in her best Edwardian hat.

There was some truth, if a very limited truth, to the cries of barbarism. Time and again, Matisse set down an image of a pre-civilized world, Eden before the Fall, inhabited by men and women with no history, languid as plants or energetic as animals. Then, as now, this image held great appeal for the over-civilized, and one such man was Matisse's biggest patron, the Moscow industrialist Sergey Shchukin, who at regular intervals would descend on Paris and clean his studio out. The relationship between Shchukin and Matisse, like the visits of Diaghilev and the Ballet Russe to France, was one of the components of a Paris-Moscow axis that would be destroyed forever by the Revolution. Shchukin commissioned Matisse to paint two murals for the grand staircase of his house in Moscow, the Trubetskoy Palace. Their themes were "Dance" and "Music."

Even when seen in a neutral museum setting, seventy years later, the primitive look of these huge paintings is still unsettling. On the staircase of the Trubetskoy Palace, they must have looked excessively foreign. Besides, to imagine their impact, one must remember the social structure that went with the word "Music" in late tsarist Russia. Music pervaded the culture at every level, but in Moscow and St. Petersburg it was the social art *par excellence*. Against this atmosphere of social ritual, glittering and adulatory, Matisse set his image of music at its origins — enacted not by virtuosi with managers and diamond studs but by five naked cavemen, pre-historical, almost presocial. A reed flute, a crude fiddle, the slap of hand on skin: it is a long way from the world of first nights, sables, and droshkies. Yet Matisse's editing is extraordinarily powerful; in allotting each of the elements, earth, sky, and body, its own local color and nothing more, he gives the scene a riveting presence. Within that simplicity, boundless energy is discovered. *The Dance* is one of the few wholly convincing images of physical ecstasy made in the twentieth century. Matisse is said to have got the idea for it in Collioure in 1905, watching some fishermen and peasants on the beach in a circular dance called a *sardana*. But the *sardana* is a stately measure, and *The Dance* is more intense. That circle of stamping, twisting maenads takes you back down the line, to the red-figure vases of Mediterranean antiquity and, beyond them, to the caves. It tries to represent motions as ancient as dance itself.

The other side of this coin was an intense interest in civilized craft. Matisse loved pattern, and pattern within pattern: not only the suave and decorative forms of his own compositions but also the reproduction of tapestries, embroideries, silks, striped awnings, curlicues, mottles, dots, and spots, the bright clutter of over-furnished rooms, within the painting. In particular he loved Islamic art, and saw a big show of it in Munich on his way back from Moscow in 1911. Islamic pattern offers the illusion of a completely full world, where everything from far to near is pressed with equal urgency against the eye. Matisse admired that, and wanted to transpose it into terms of pure color. One of the results was *The Red Studio*, 1911.

On one hand, he wants to bring you into this painting: to make you fall into it, like walking through the looking-glass. Thus the box of crayons is put, like a bait, just under your hand, as it was under his. But it is not a real space, and because it is all soaked in flat, subtly modulated red, a red beyond ordinary experience, dyeing the whole room, it describes itself aggressively as fiction. It is all inlaid pattern, full of possible "windows," but these openings are more flat surfaces. They are Matisse's own pictures. Everything else is a work of art or craft as well: the furniture, the dresser, the clock, and the sculptures, which are also recognizably Matisses. The only hint of nature in all this is the trained houseplant, which obediently emulates the curve of the wicker chair on the right and the nude's body on the left. *The Red Studio* is a poem about how painting refers to itself: how art nourishes itself from other art and how, with enough conviction, art can form its own republic of pleasure, a parenthesis within the real world — a paradise.

This belief in the utter self-sufficiency of painting is why Matisse could ignore the Four Horsemen of the Apocalypse. When the war broke out in 1914, he was forty-five — too old to fight, too wise to imagine that his art could interpose itself between history and its victims, and too certain of his aims as an artist to change them. Through the war years, stimulated by a trip to North Africa, his art grew in amplitude and became more abstract, as in *The Moroccans*, 1916. In 1917 he moved, more or less permanently, to the south of France. "In order to paint my pictures," he remarked, "I need to remain for several days in the same state of mind, and I do not find this in any atmosphere but that of the Côte d'Azur." He found a vast apartment in a white Edwardian wedding cake above Nice, the Hôtel Régina. This was the Great Indoors, whose elements appear in painting after painting: the wrought-iron balcony, the strip of blue Mediterranean sky, the palm, the shutters. Matisse once said that he wanted his art to have the effect of a good armchair on a tired businessman. In the 1960s, when we all believed art could still change the world, this seemed a limited aim, but in fact one can only admire Matisse's common sense. He, at least, was under no illusions about his audience. He knew that an educated bourgeoisie was the only audience advanced art could claim, and history has shown him right.

— ROBERT HUGHES

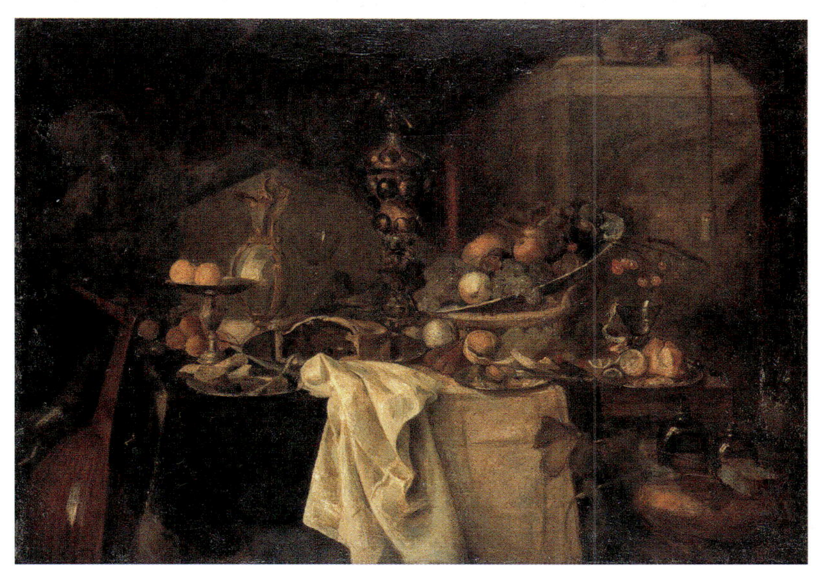

La Desserte (after Jan Davidsz de Heem) • 1893
Musée Matisse, Nice

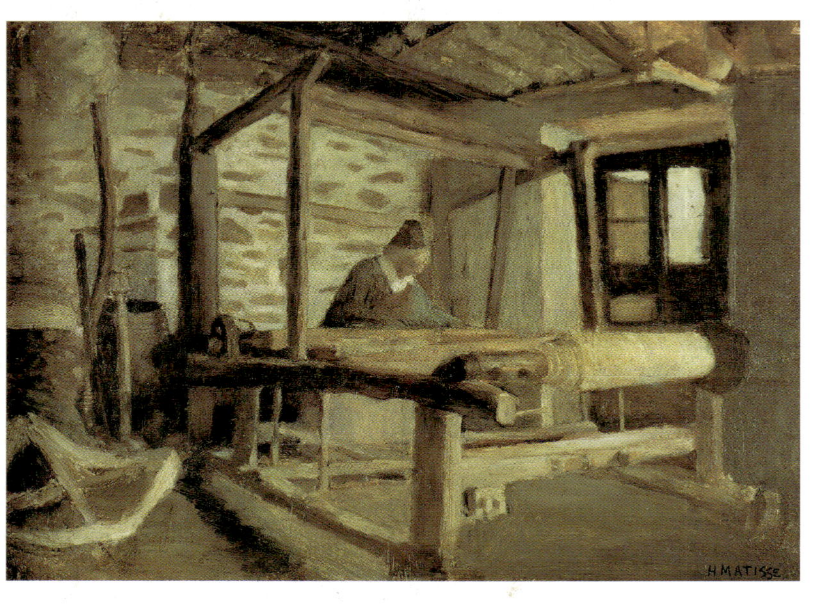

Studio of the Picard Weaver • 1895

Musée national d'art moderne, Paris

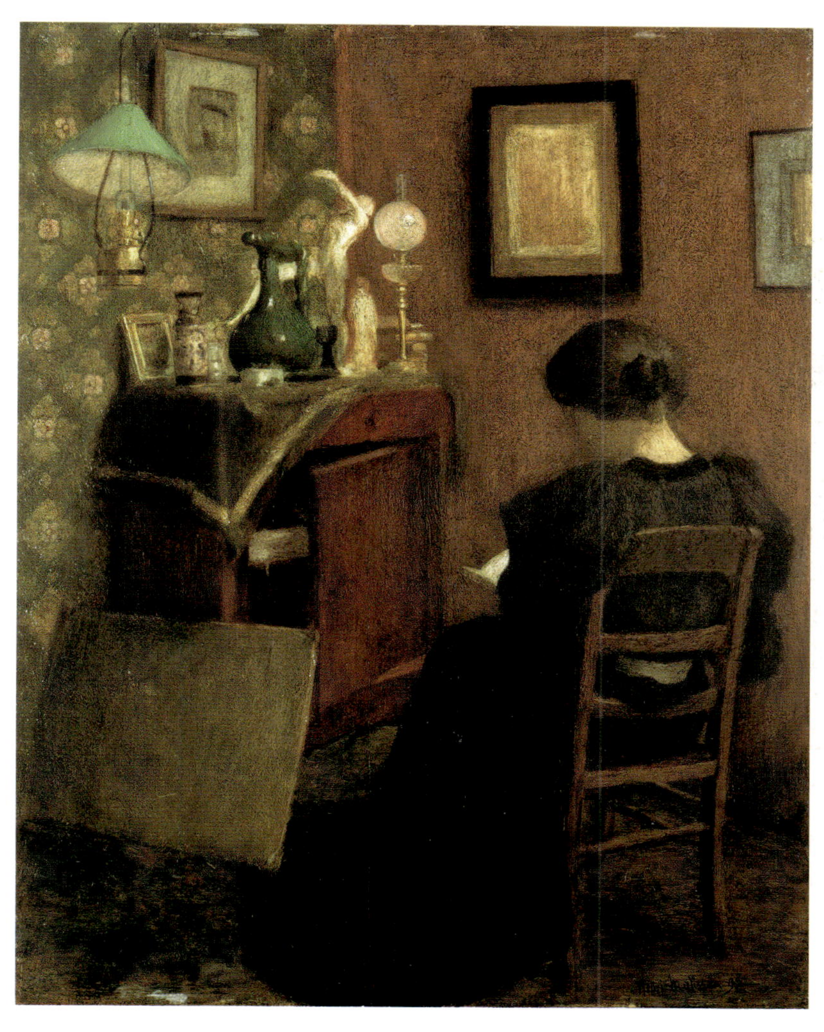

Woman Reading • 1895
Musée national d'art moderne, Paris

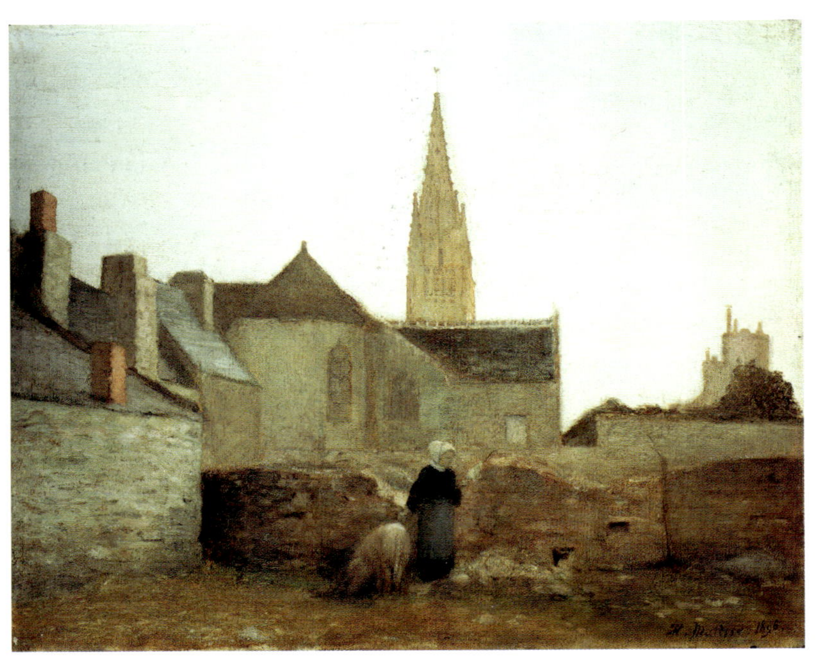

Village in Brittany · 1896

Musée Matisse, Nice

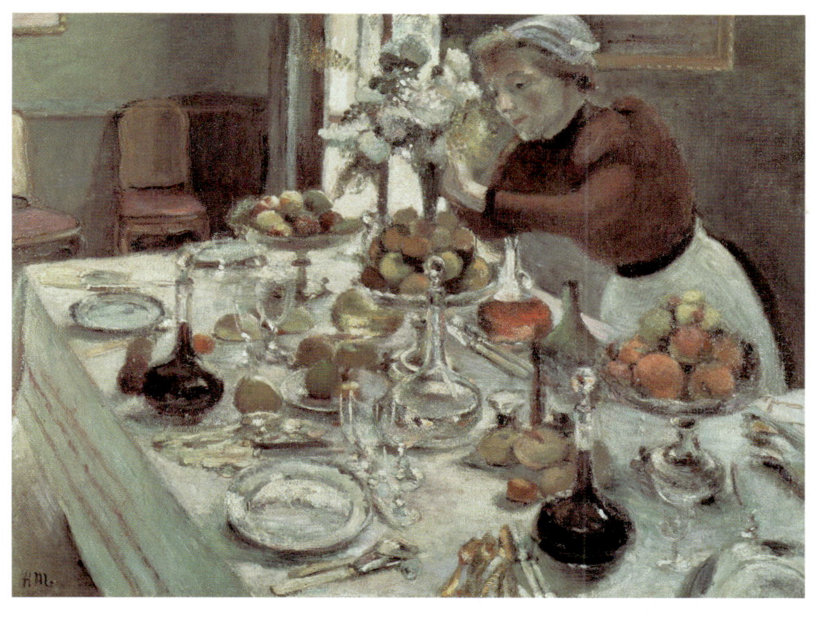

The Dinner Table · 1896–1897
Private collection

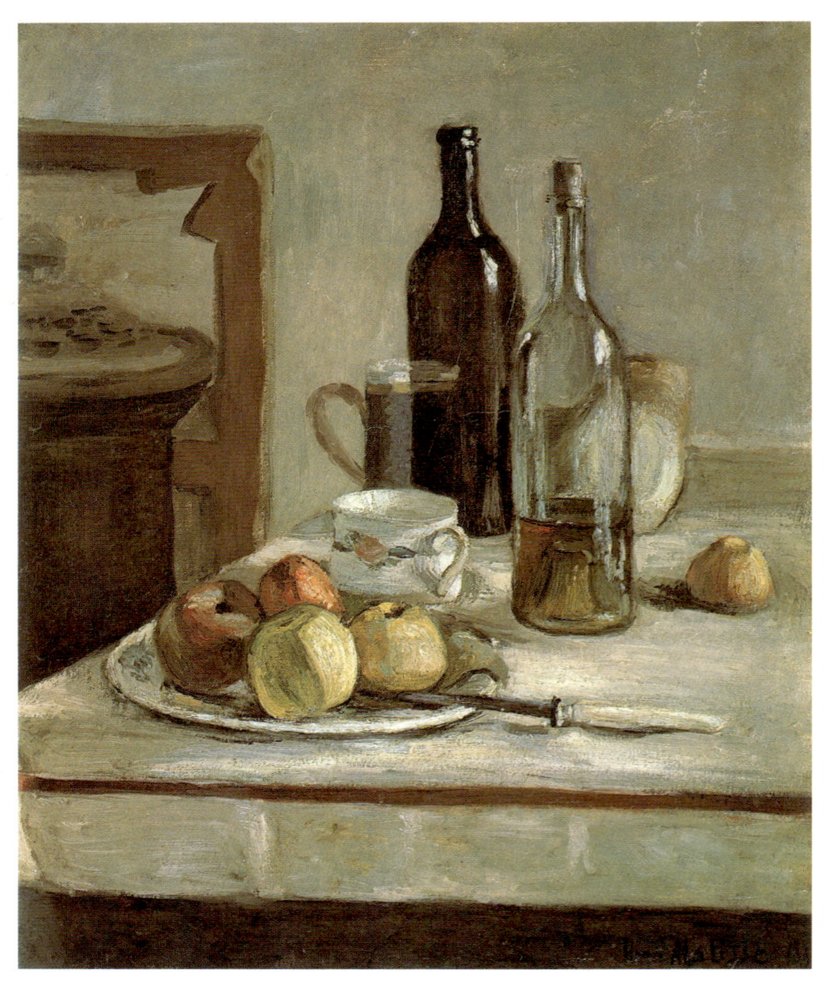

Still Life with Two Bottles · 1896

Private collection

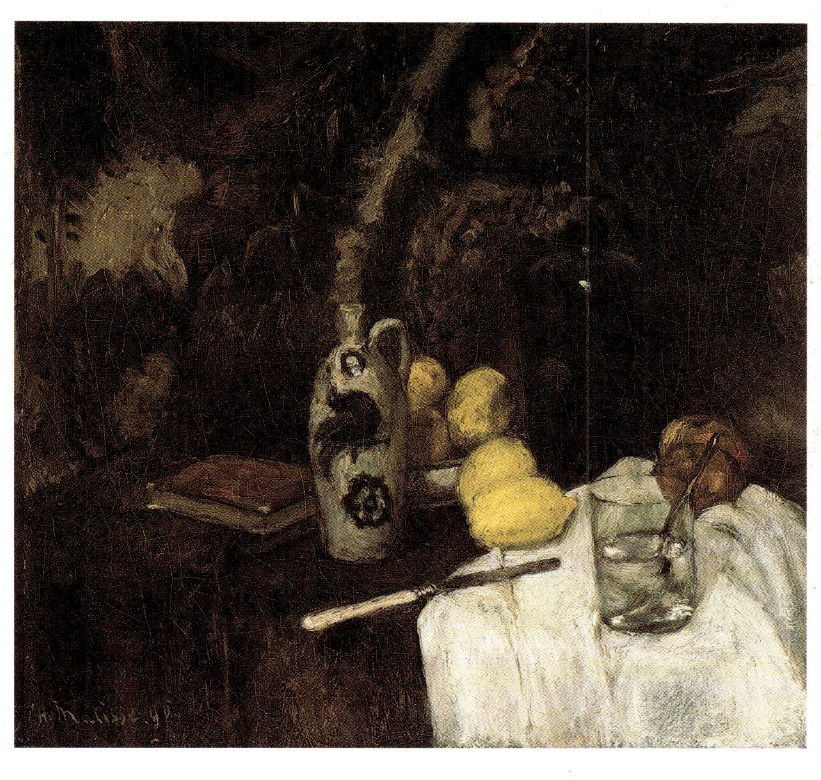

Still Life with Lemons and a Bottle • 1896
The Museum of Modern Art, New York, gift of Mr. and Mrs. Warren Brandt

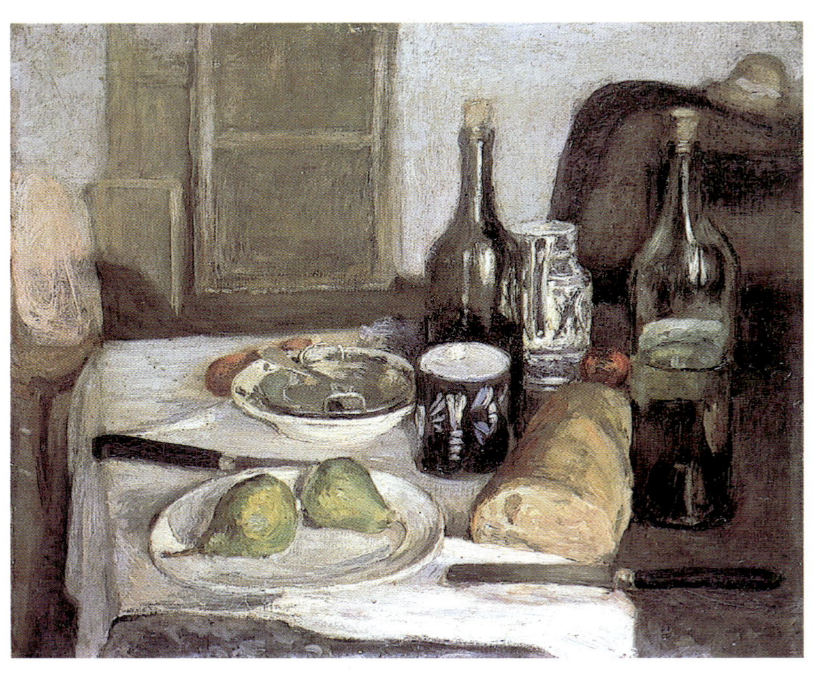

Still Life with Black Knives • c. 1896
Fonds national d'art contemporain, on deposit at Musée Fabre, Montpellier

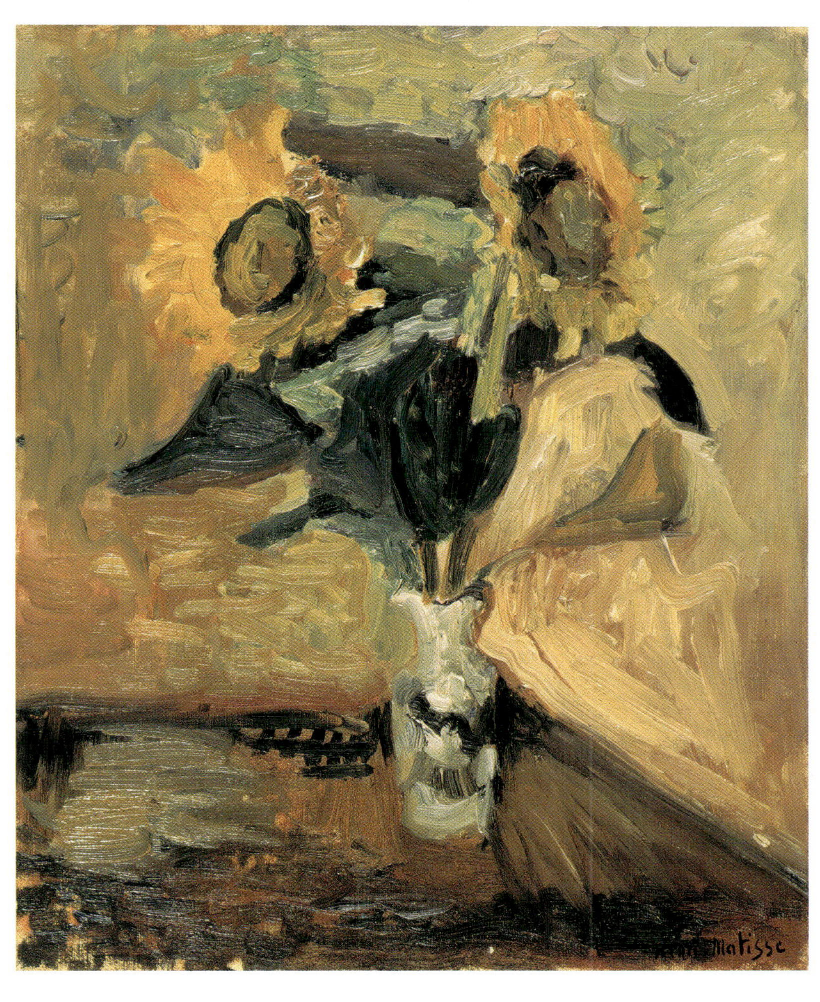

Vase with Sunflowers · 1898

Hermitage, Saint Petersburg

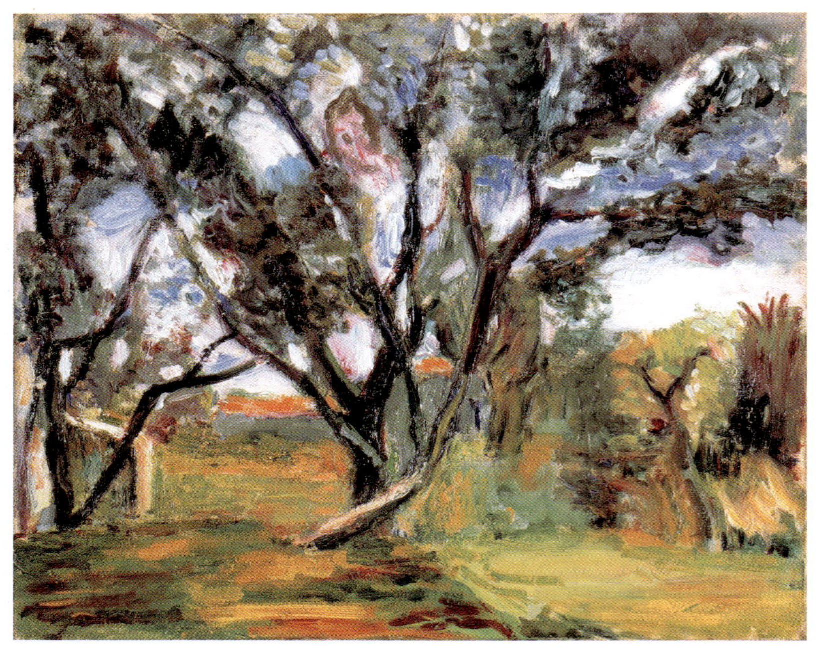

The Olive Tree • 1898
Private collection

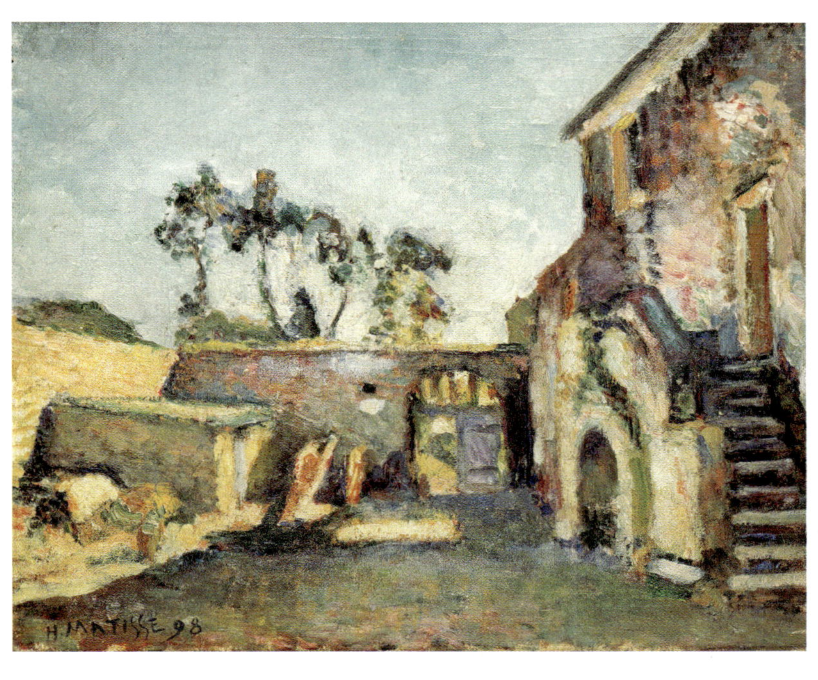

The Courtyard of the Mill · 1898

Musée Matisse, Nice

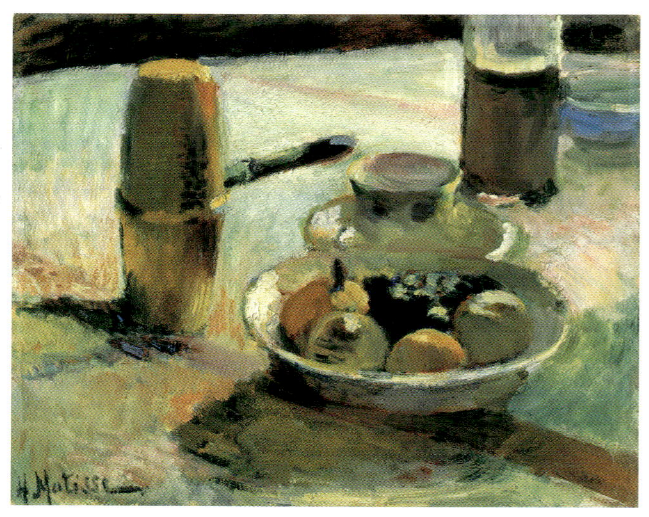

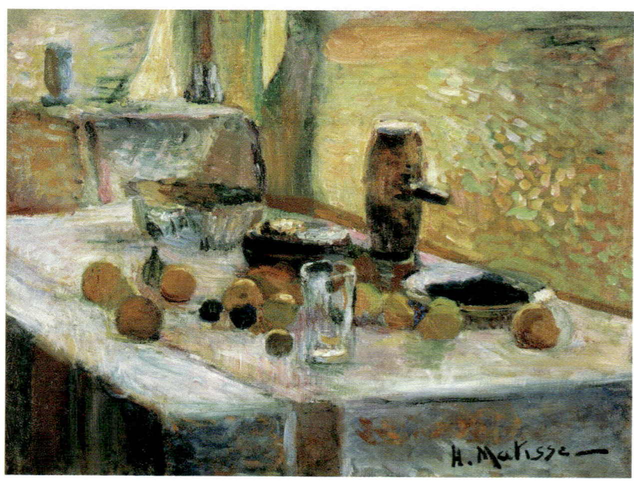

Fruit and Coffee-Pot · 1899
Hermitage, Saint Petersburg
First Orange Still Life · early 1899
Musée national d'art moderne, Paris

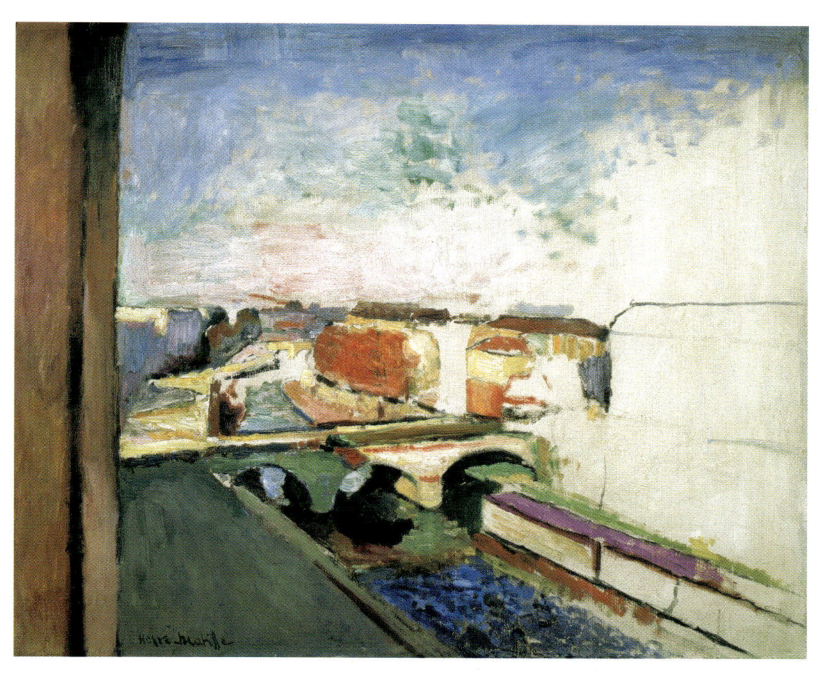

Pont Saint-Michel • c. 1900
Musée national d'art moderne, Paris

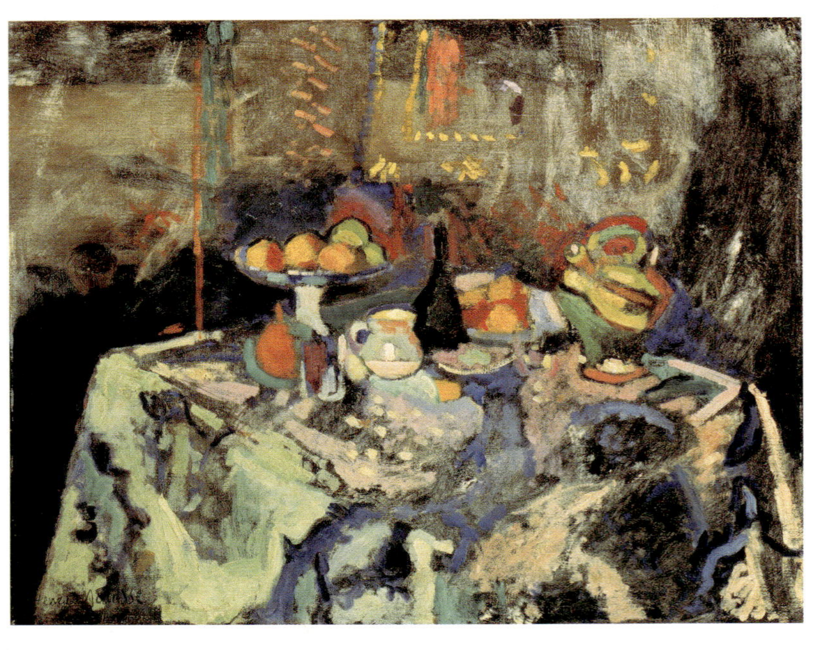

Still Life with Blue Tablecloth · c. 1900–1902

Hermitage, Saint Petersburg

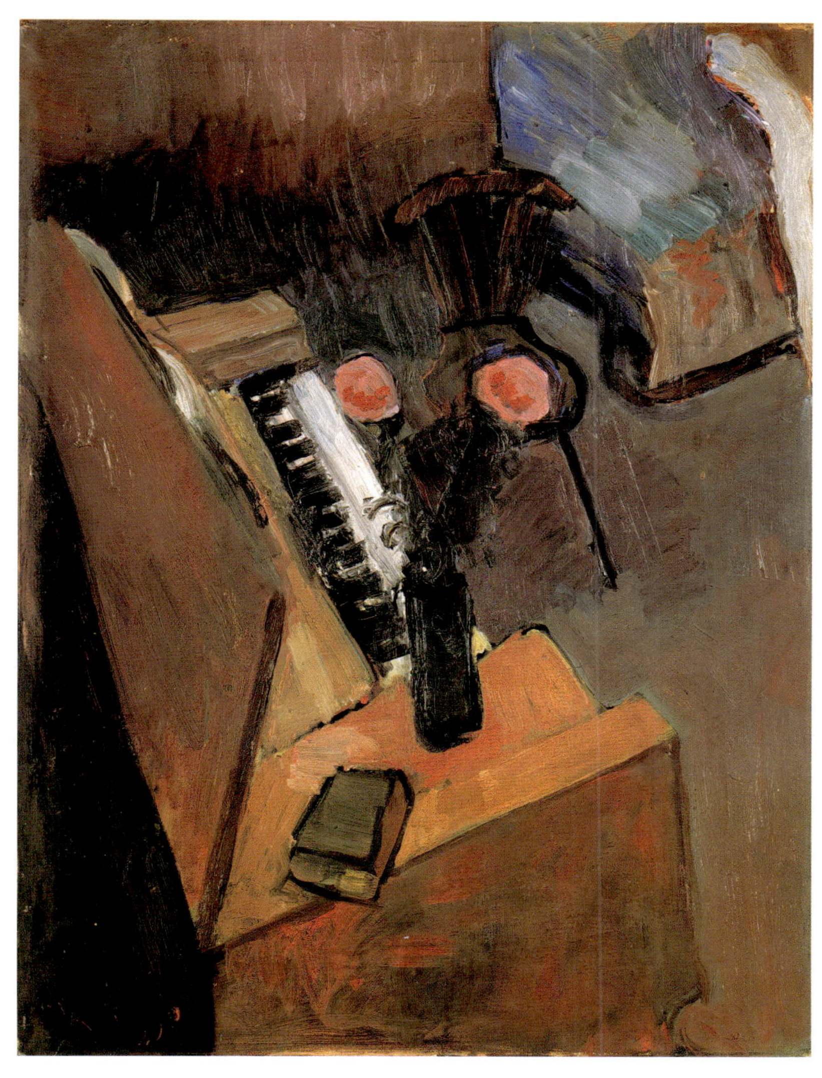

Interior with Harmonium • c. 1900

Musée Matisse, Nice

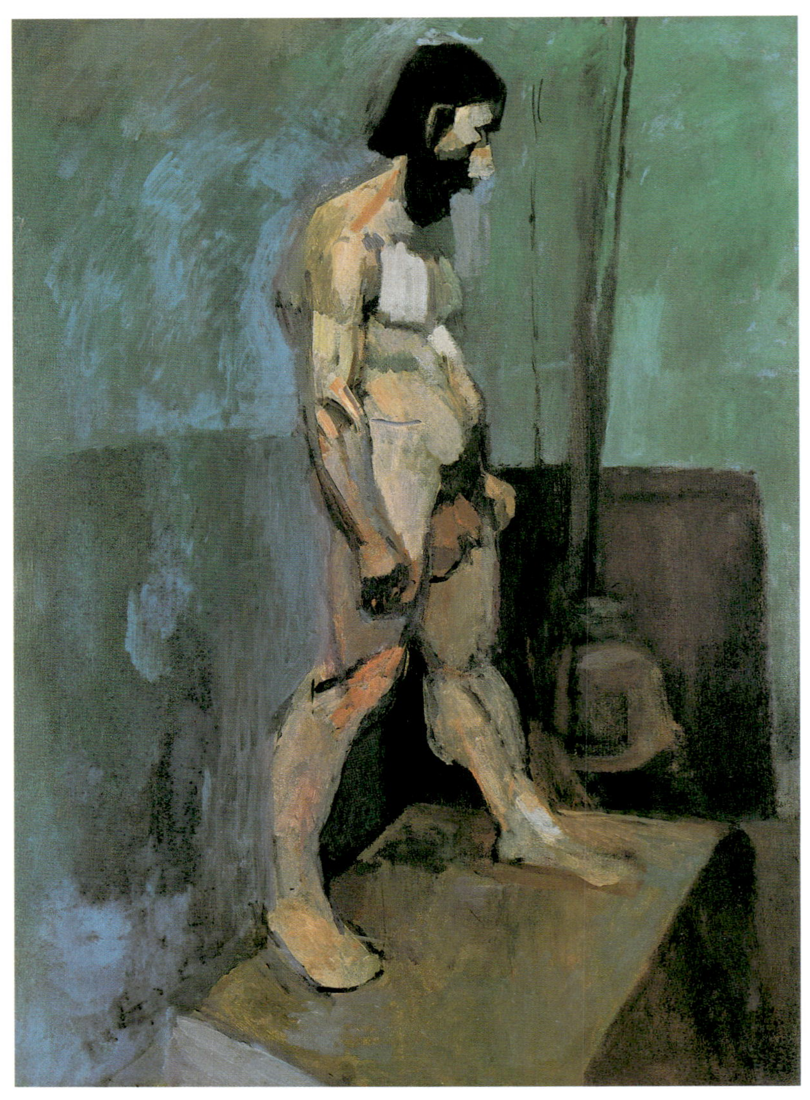

Male Model • c. 1900

The Museum of Modern Art, New York, Kay Sage Tanguy and Abby Aldrich Rockefeller Funds

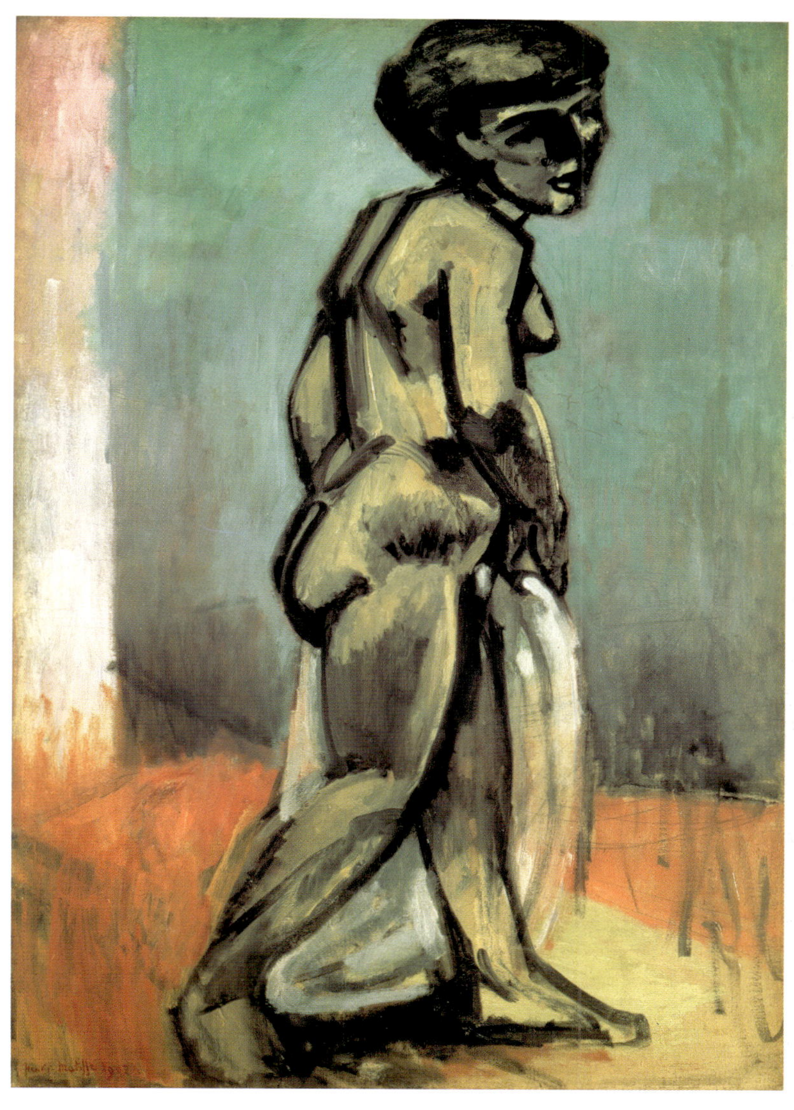

Standing Model / Nude Study in Blue · Autumn 1900–Spring 1901
Tate Gallery, London

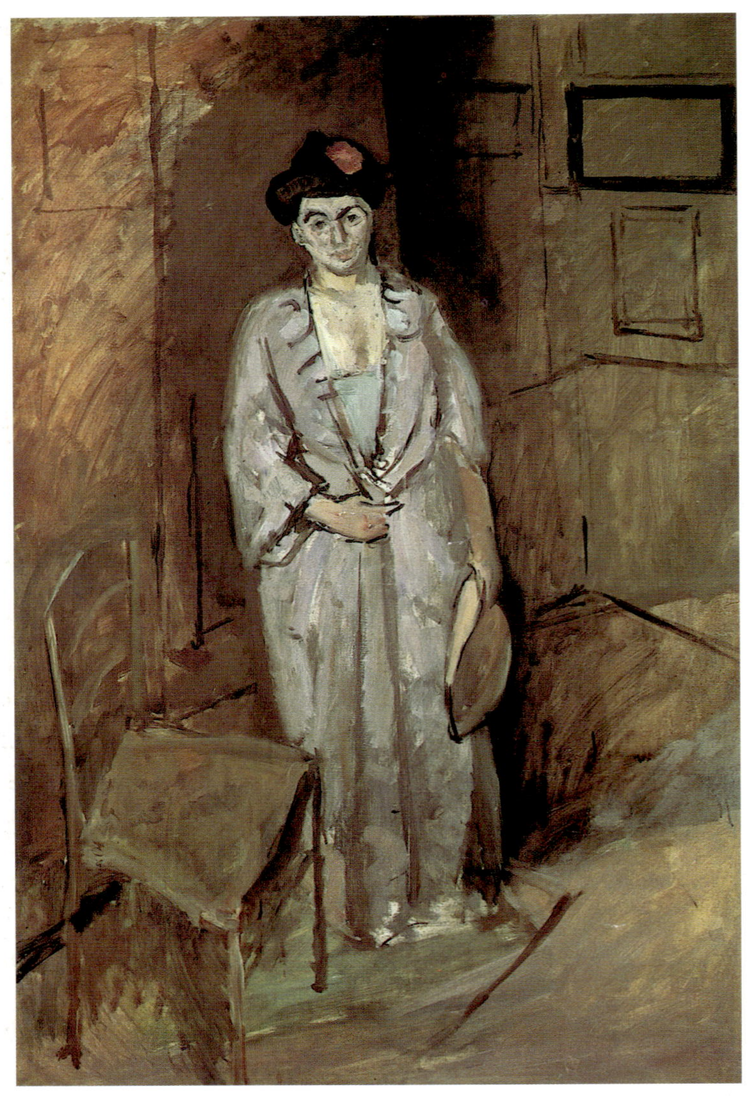

Mme Matisse in a Japanese Robe • c. 1901
Private collection

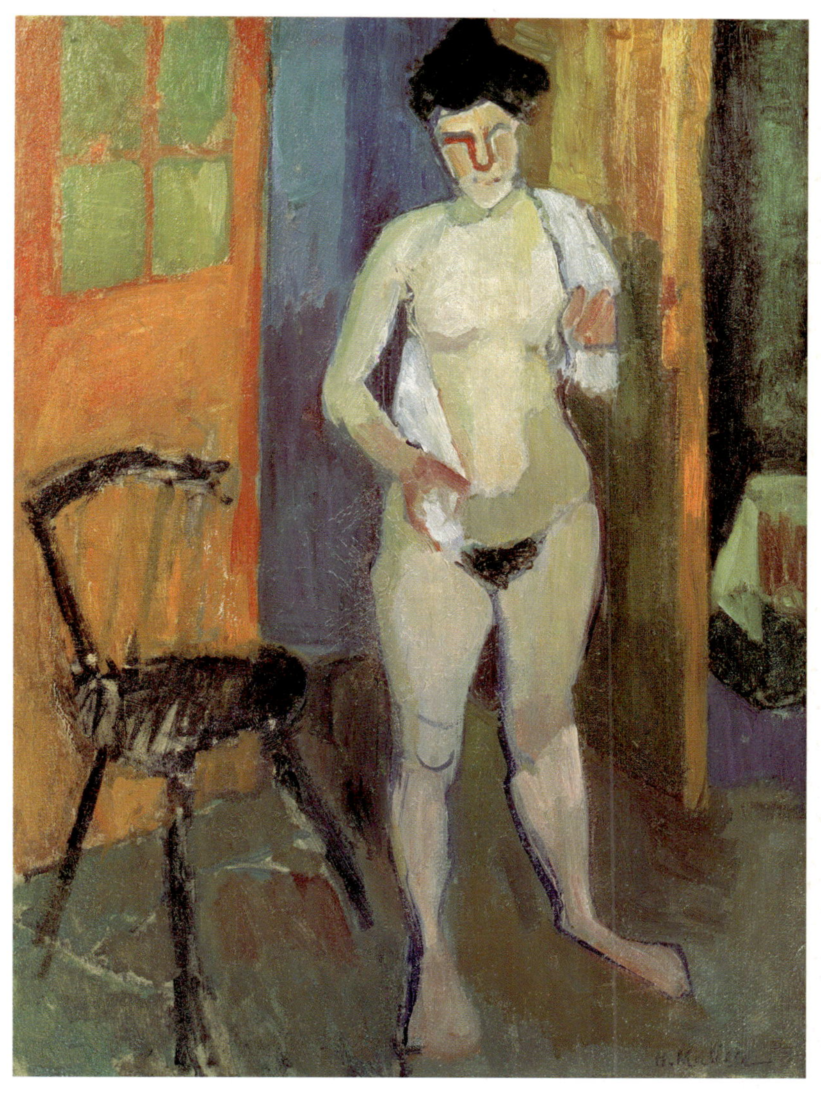

Nude with a White Towel • 1902–1903
Private collection

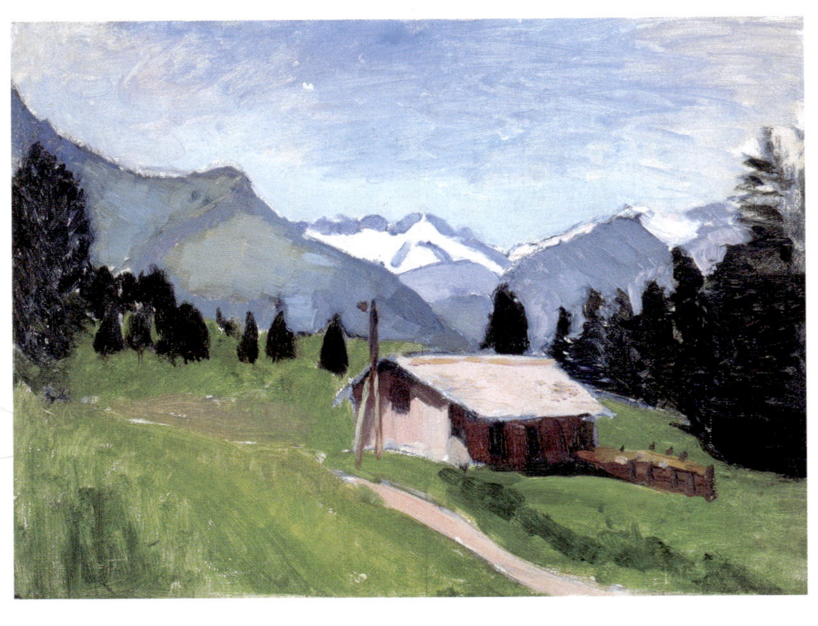

The Aiguilles vertes and the Croix de Javernaz · c. 1901

Musée Picasso, Paris

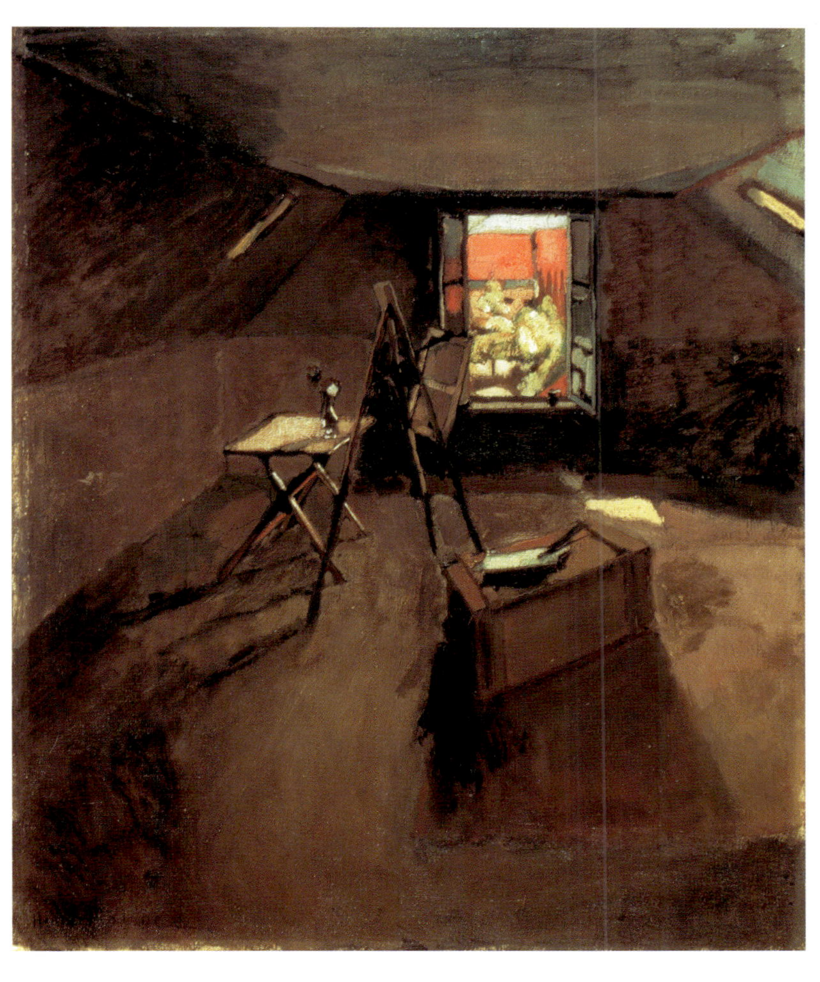

Studio Under the Eaves • 1901–1902
Fitzwilliam Museum, University of Cambridge

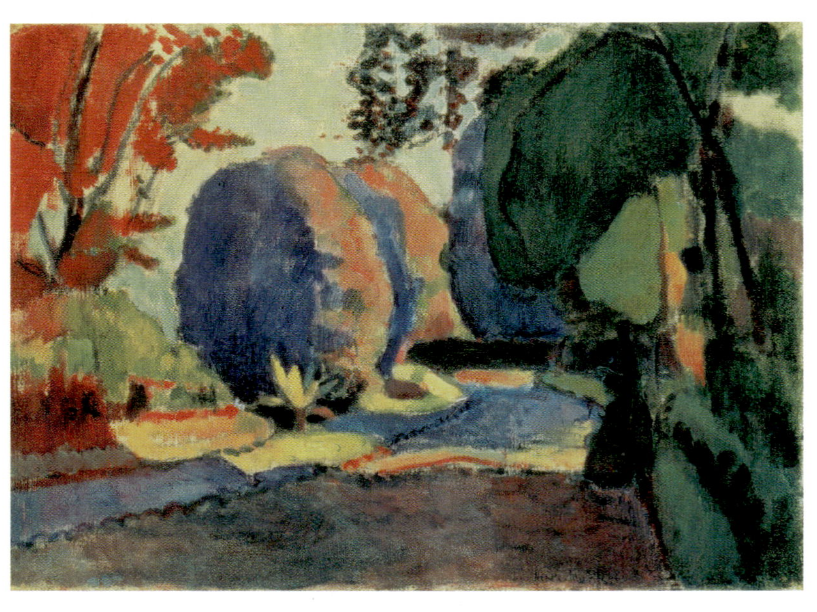

The Luxembourg Gardens • c. 1902
Hermitage, Saint Petersburg

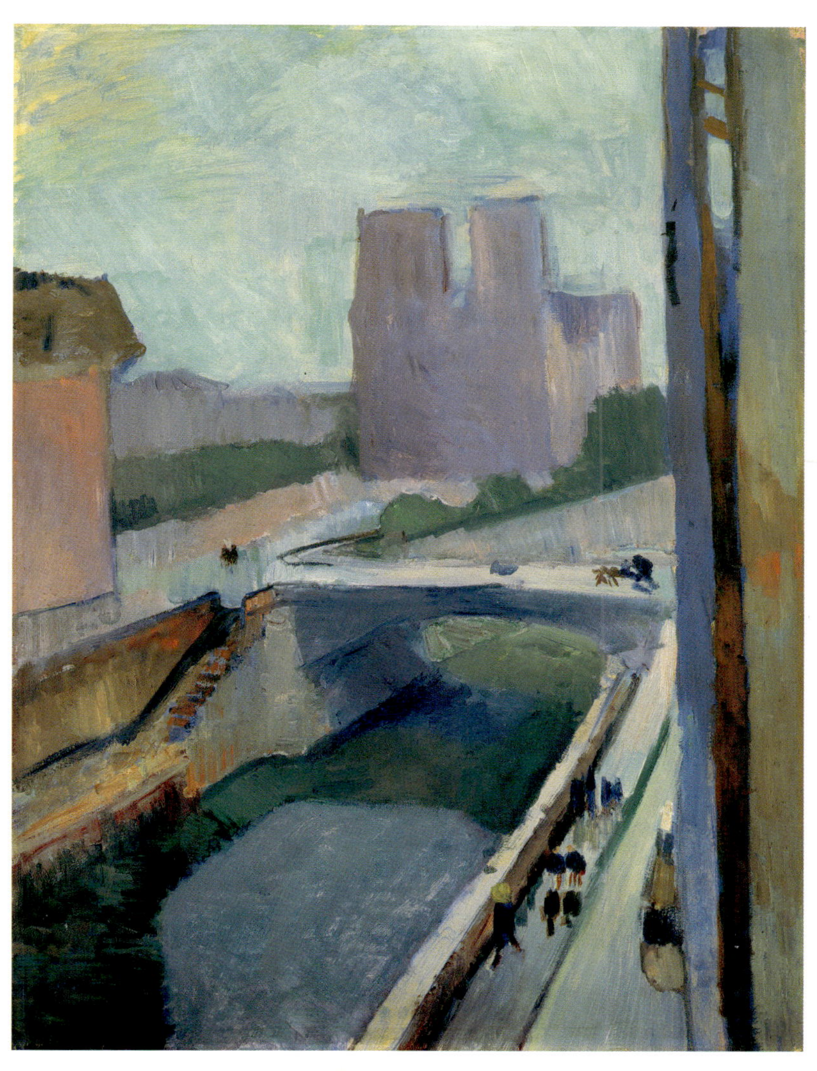

Notre-Dame in the Late Afternoon • 1902
Albright-Knox Art Gallery, Buffalo, New York, gift of Seymour H. Knox

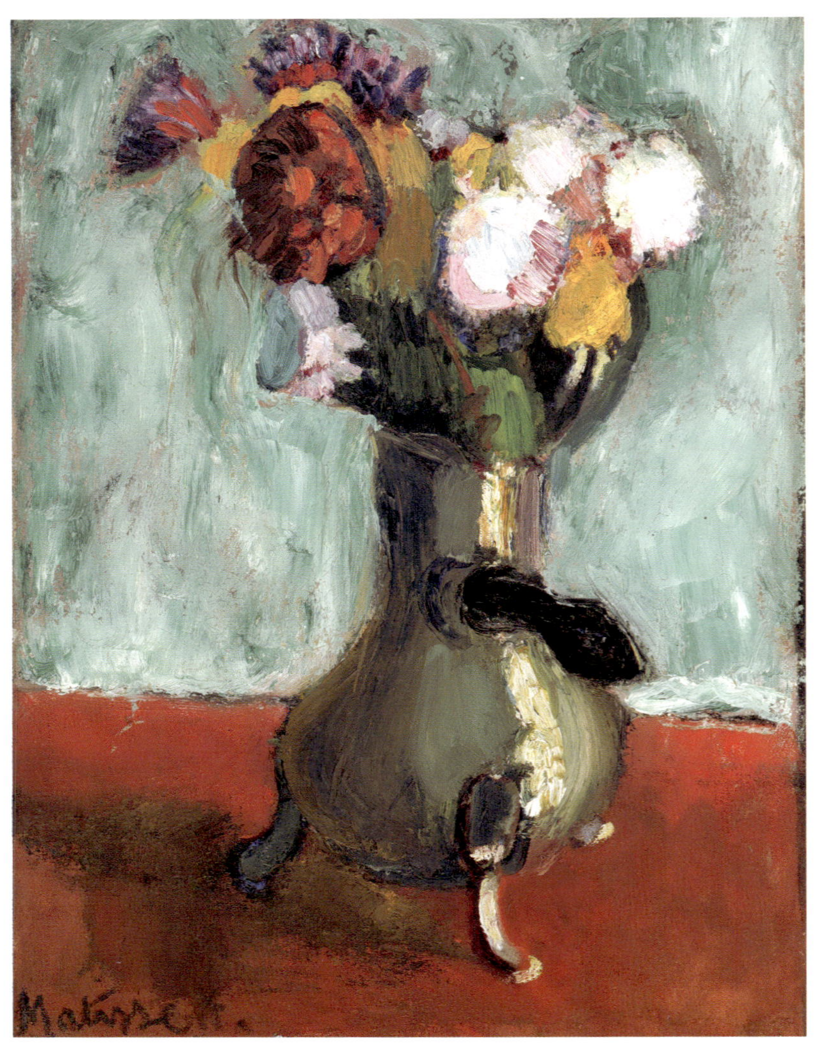

Bouquet of Flowers in a Chocolate Pot • 1902

Musée Picasso, Paris

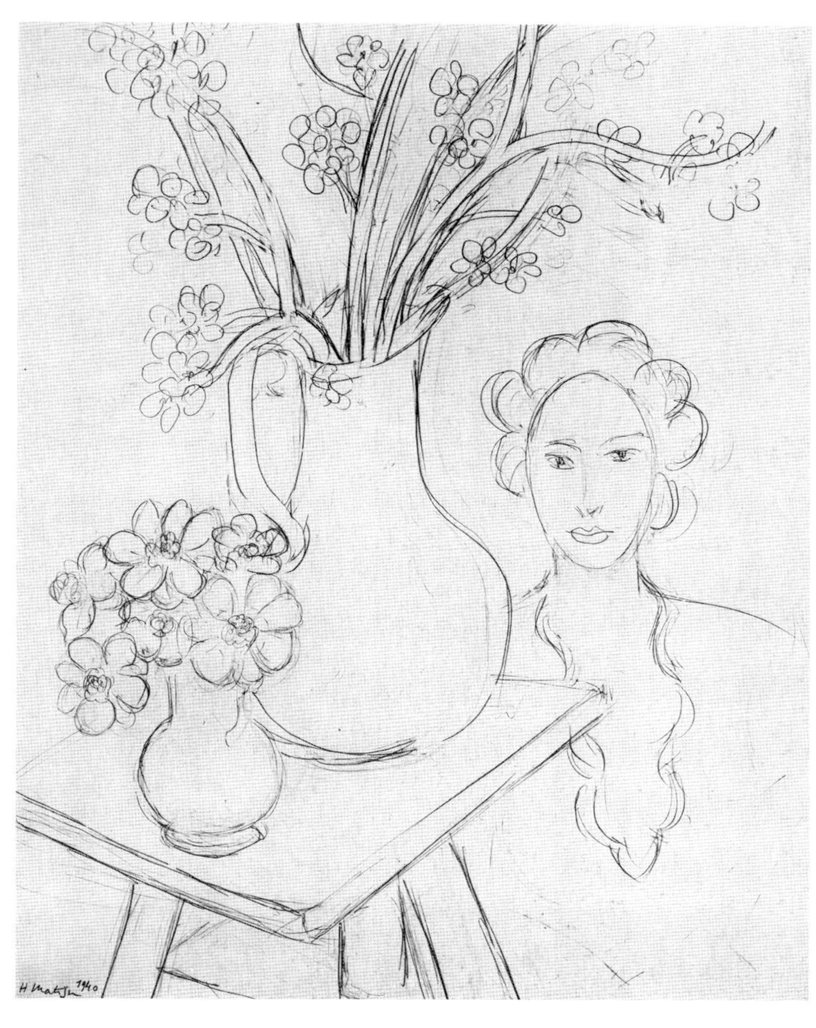

Life Study • c. 1903
Private collection

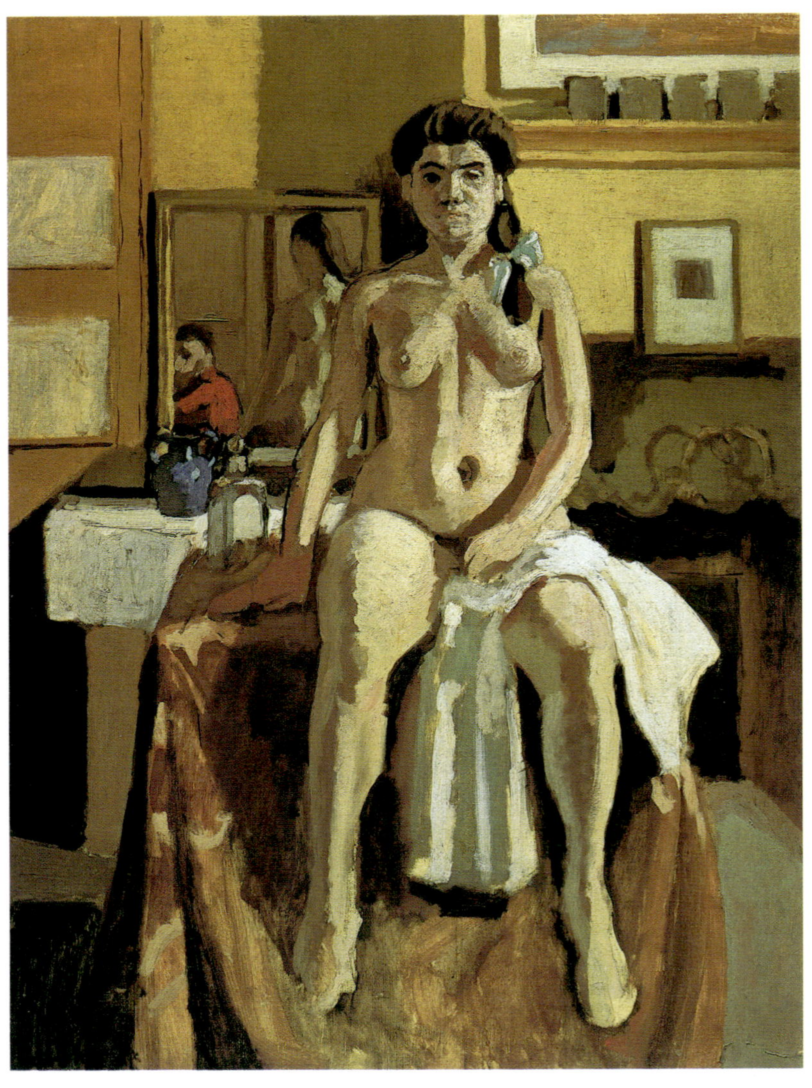

Carmelina • c. 1903–1904
Museum of Fine Arts, Boston, Tompkins Collection

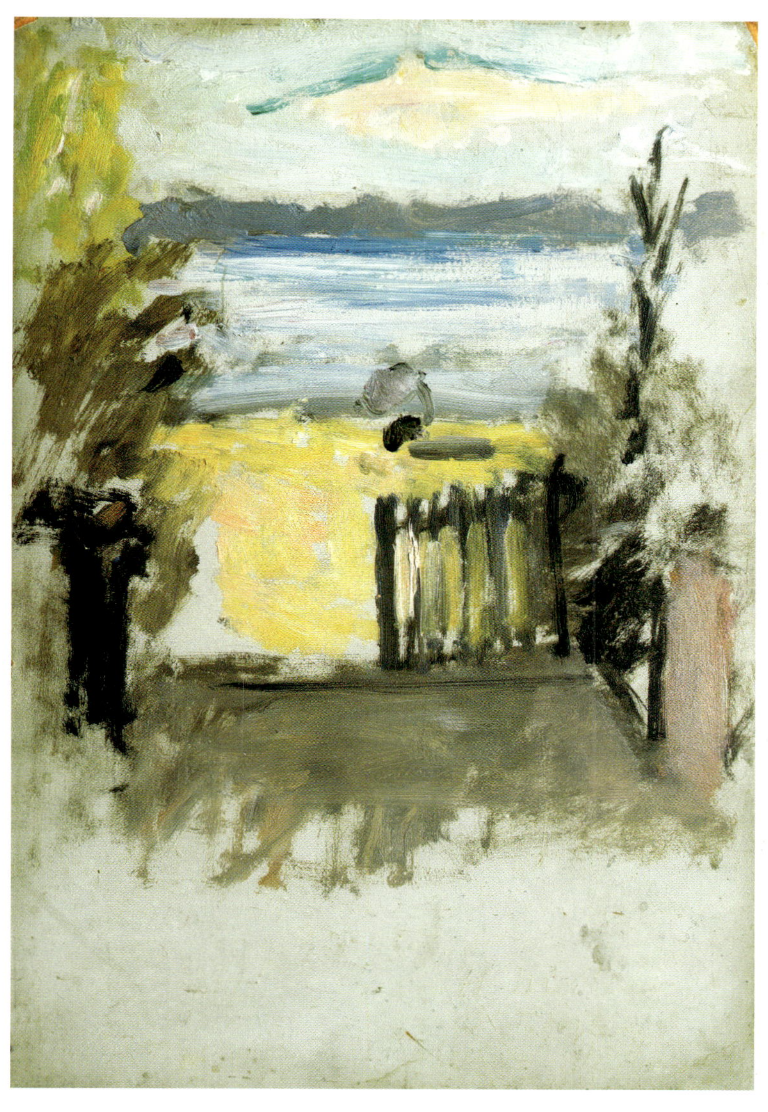

Entrance of Signac's Studio in Saint-Tropez · 1904
Private collection

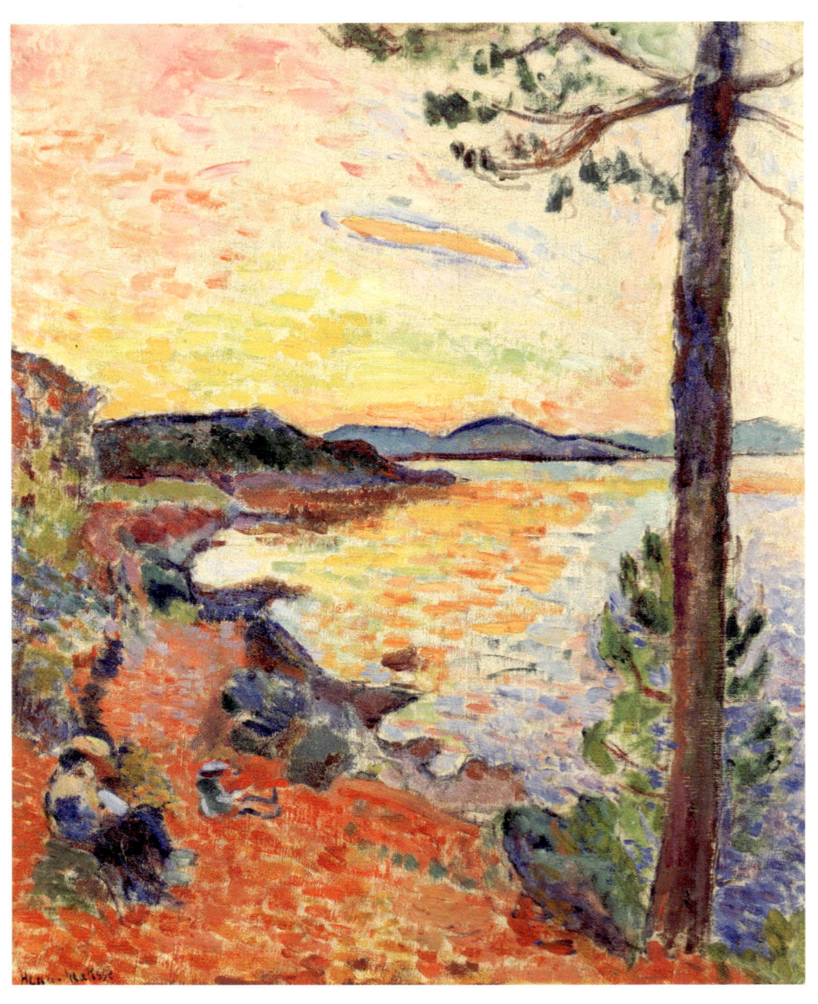

The Gulf of Saint-Tropez · Summer 1904
Kunstsammlung Nordrhein-Westfalen, Düsseldorf

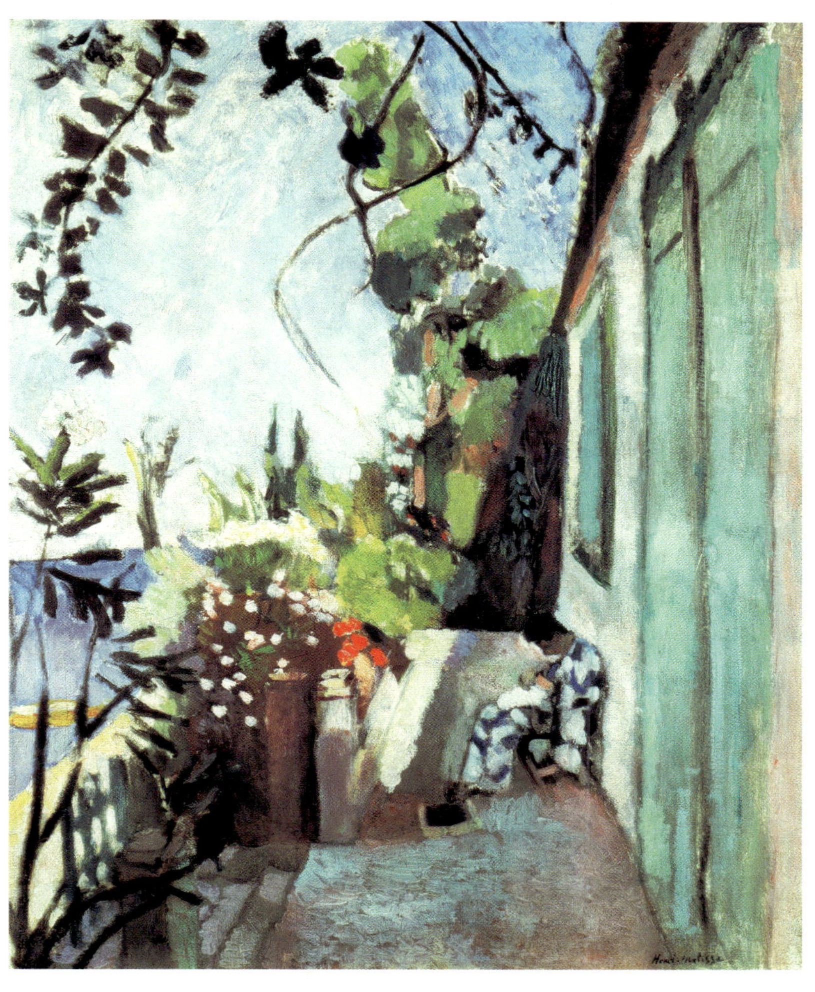

The Terrace, Saint-Tropez · Summer 1904
Isabella Stewart Gardner Museum, Boston, gift of Thomas Whittemore
> **Luxe, calme et volupté** · 1904–1905
Musée d'Orsay, Paris

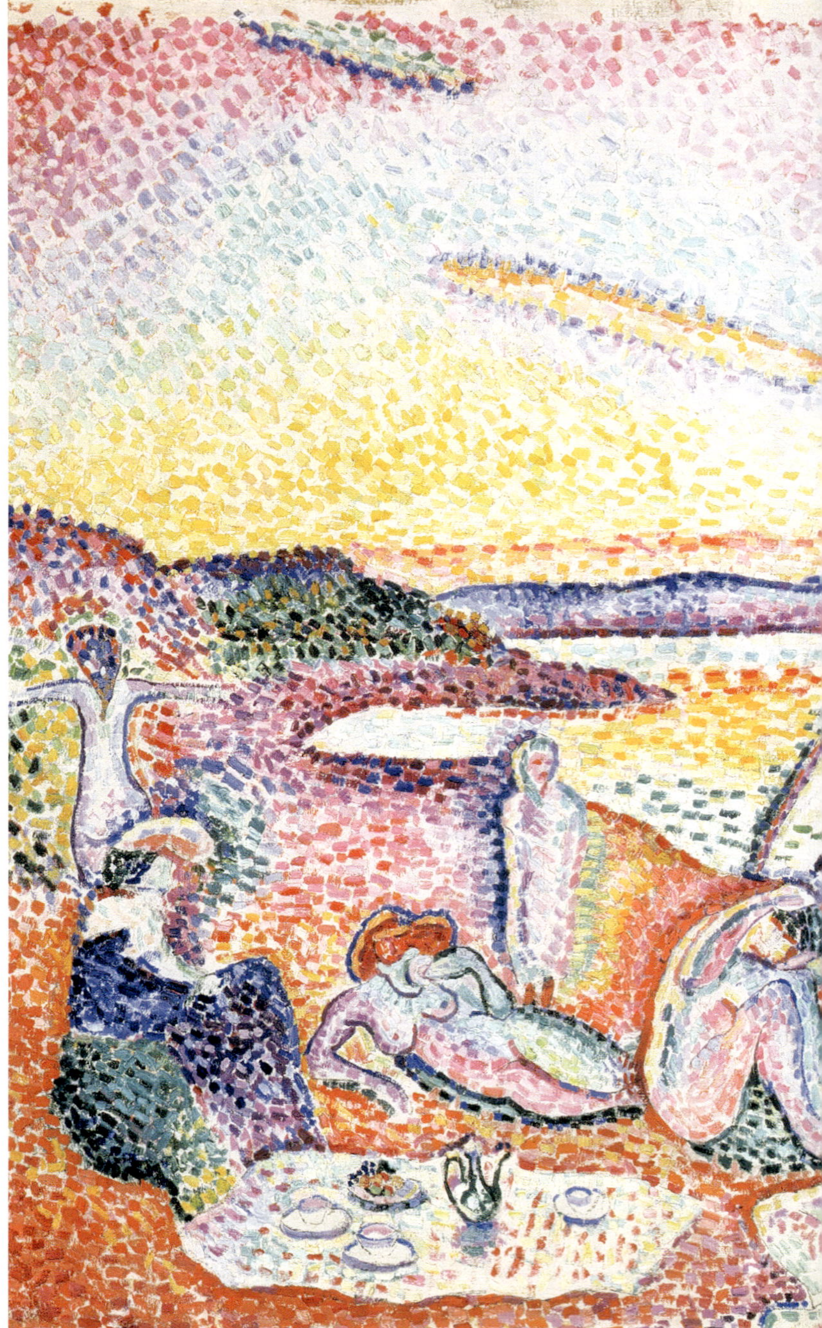

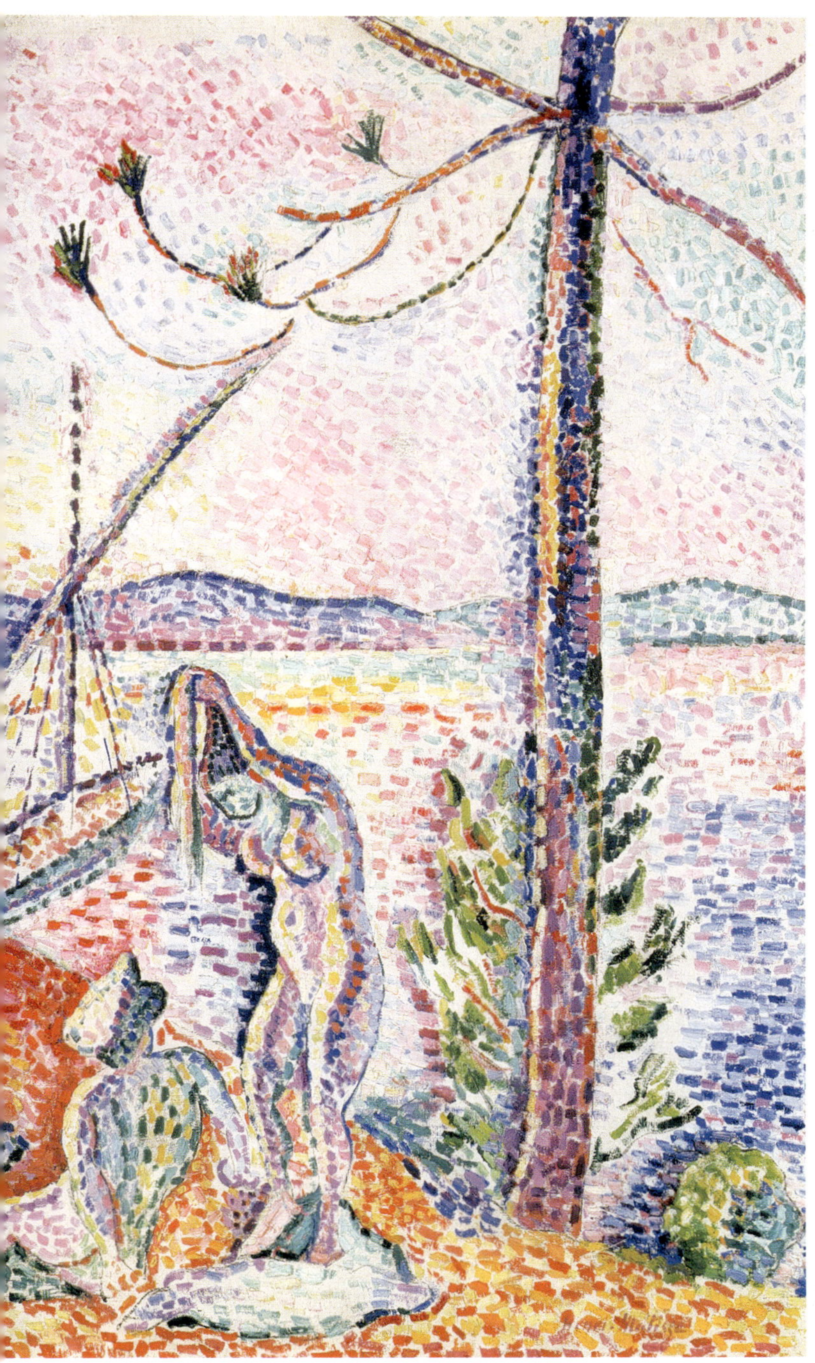

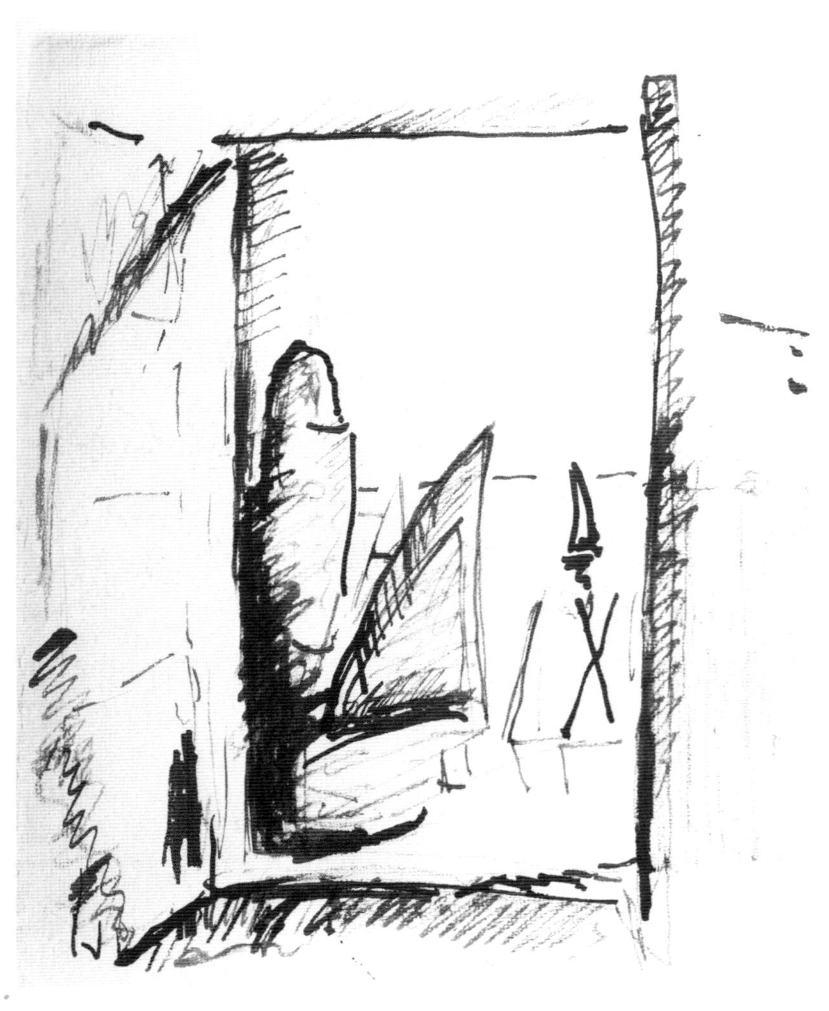

Collioure · 1905
Private collection

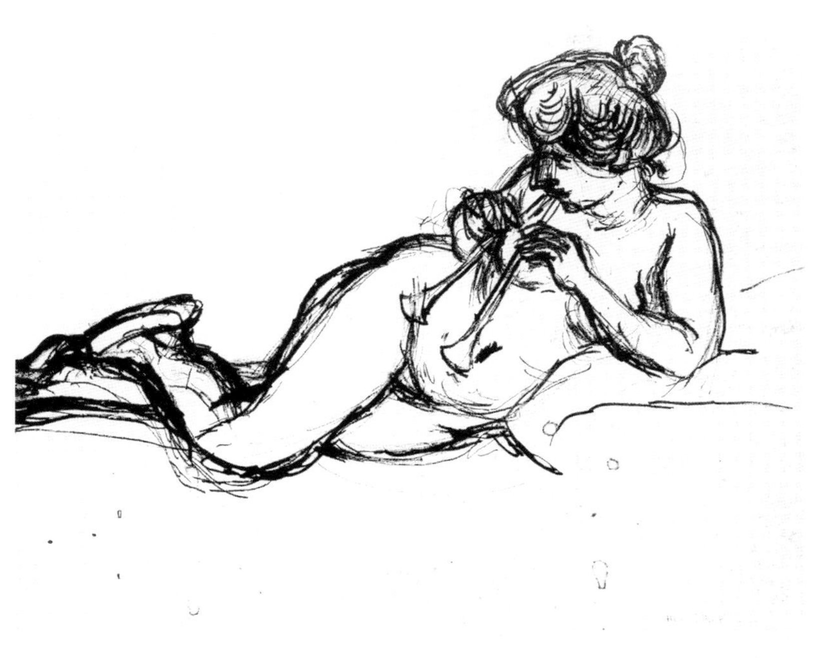

Reclining Nude Playing Pipes / Study for "Le bonheur de vivre" · 1905–1906
Private collection

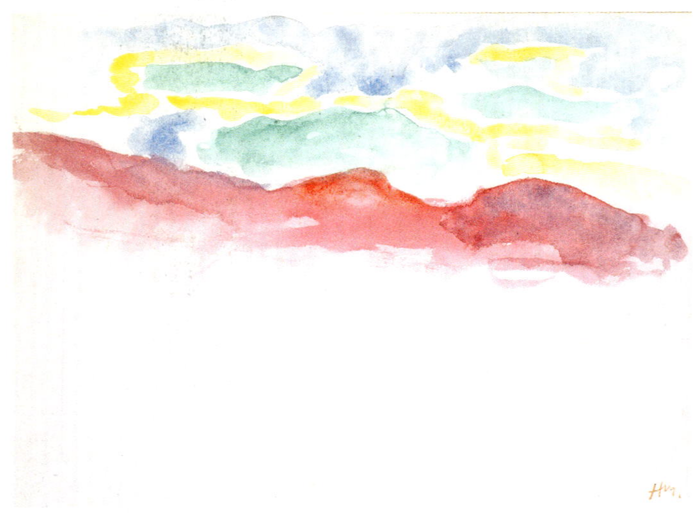

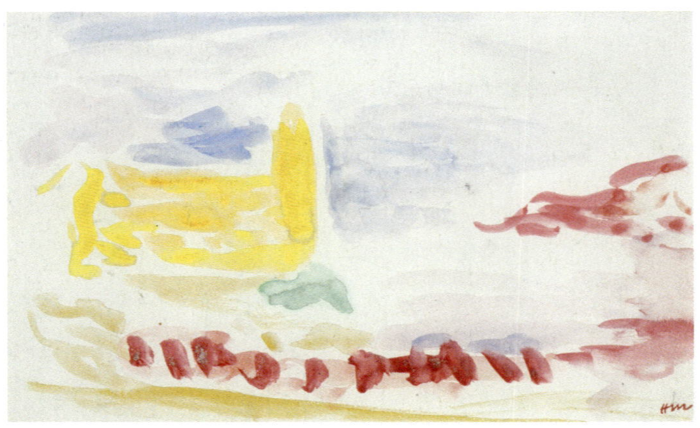

Mountains, Collioure · 1905
Private collection
The Bell Tower of Collioure · 1905
Private collection

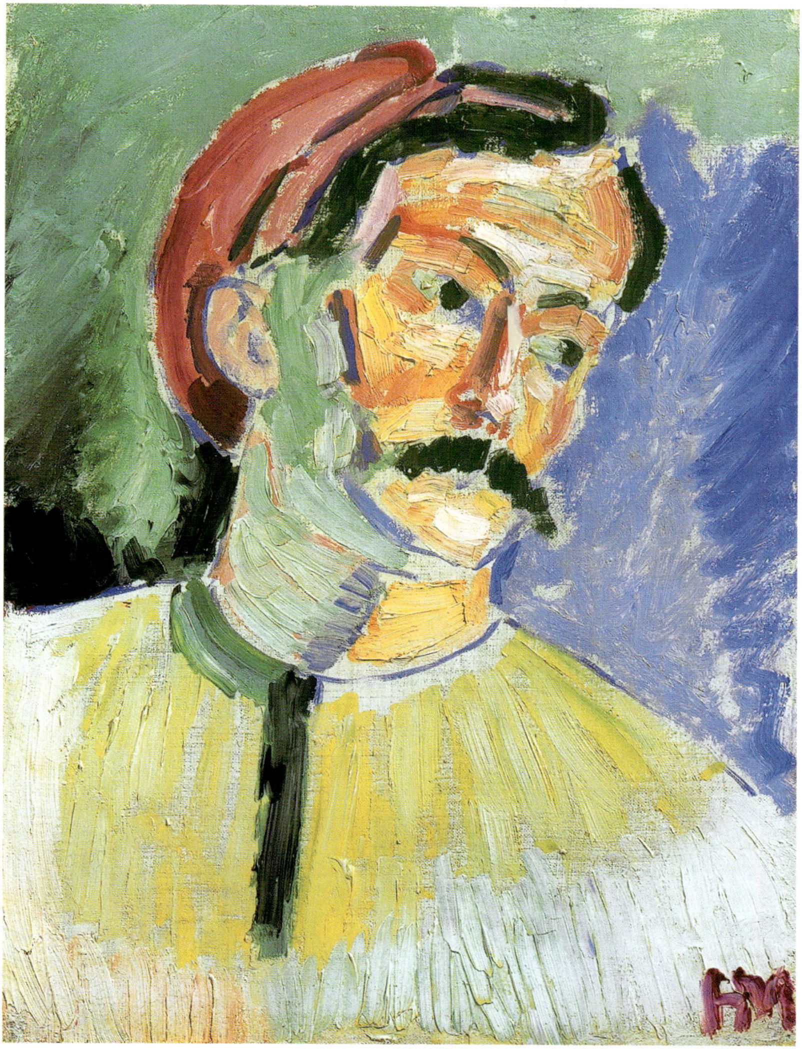

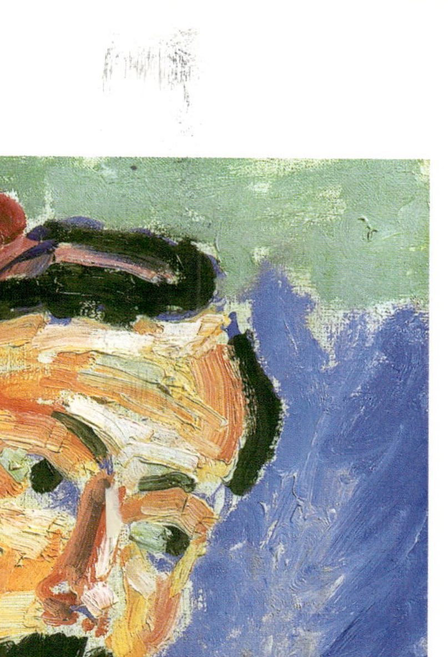

André Derain • Summer 1905

Tate Gallery, London

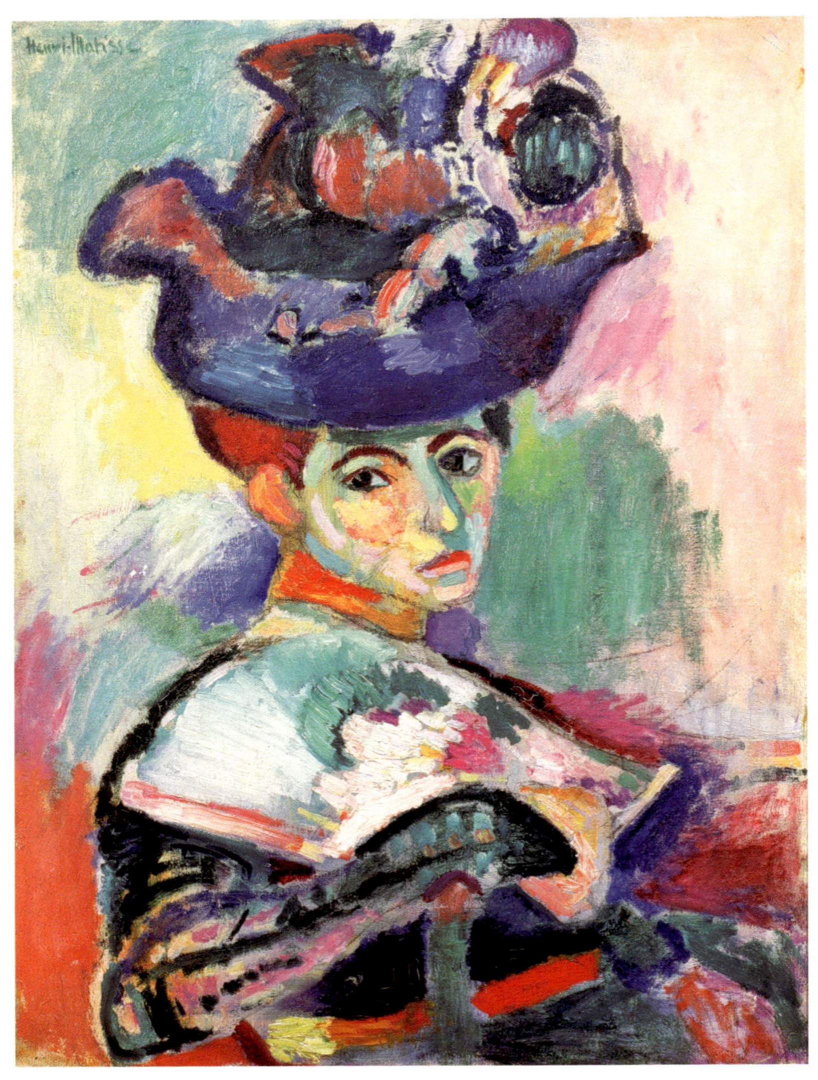

The Woman with the Hat • Autumn 1905

San Francisco Museum of Modern Art, bequest of Elise S. Haas

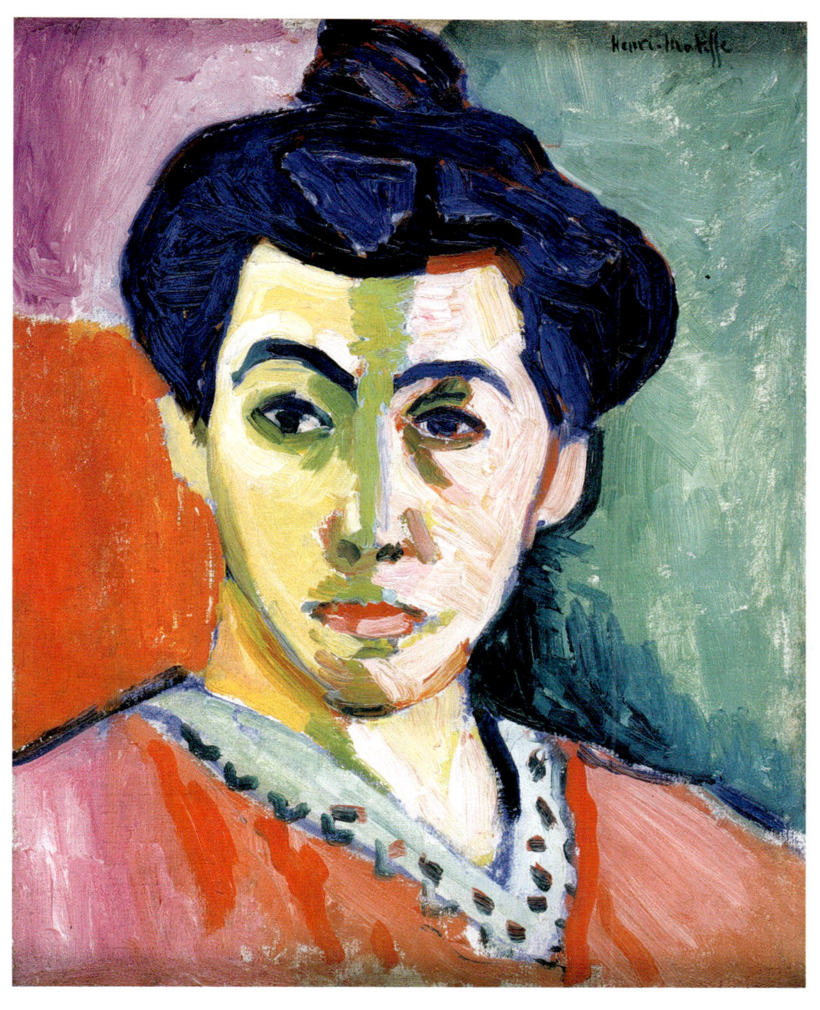

Portrait of Mme Matisse / The Green Line • 1905
Statens Museum for Kunst, Copenhagen

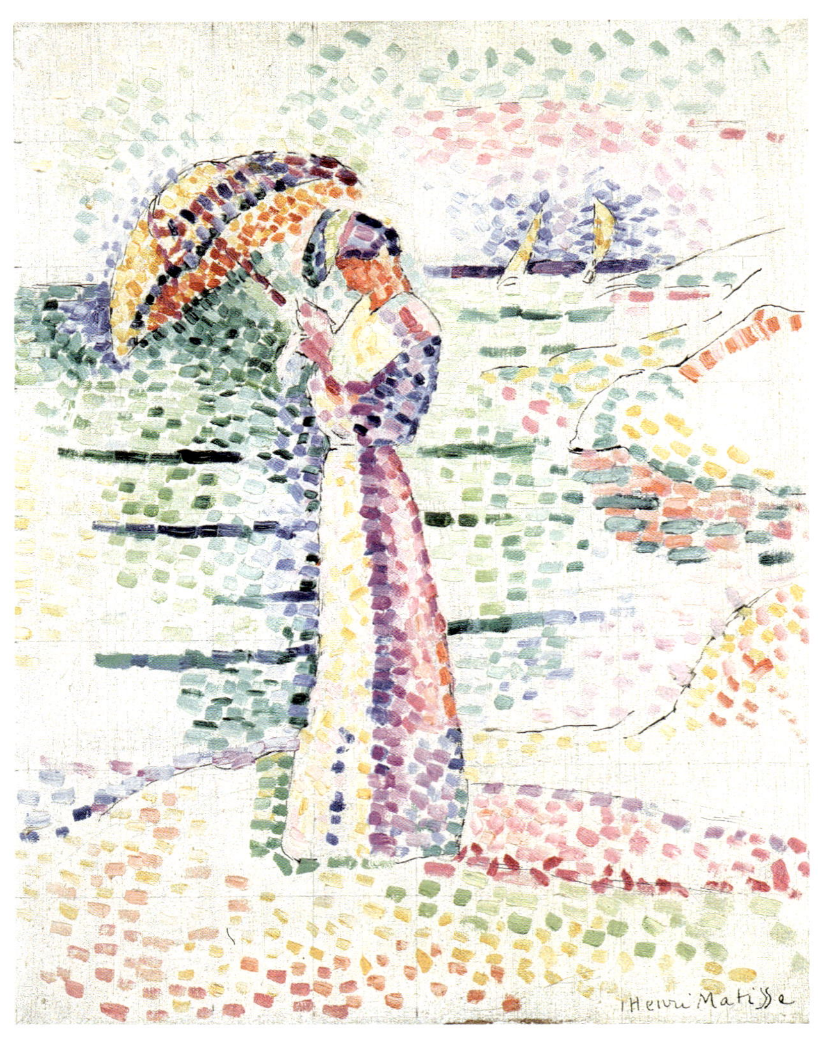

Figure with Parasol • 1905

Musée Matisse, Nice

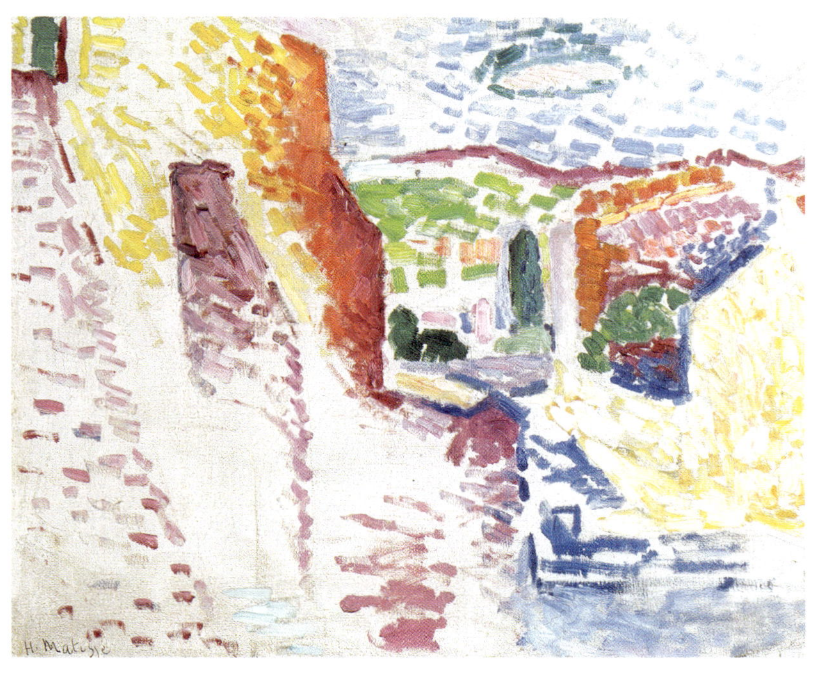

View of Collioure • Summer 1905

Musée Matisse, Le Cateau-Cambrésis

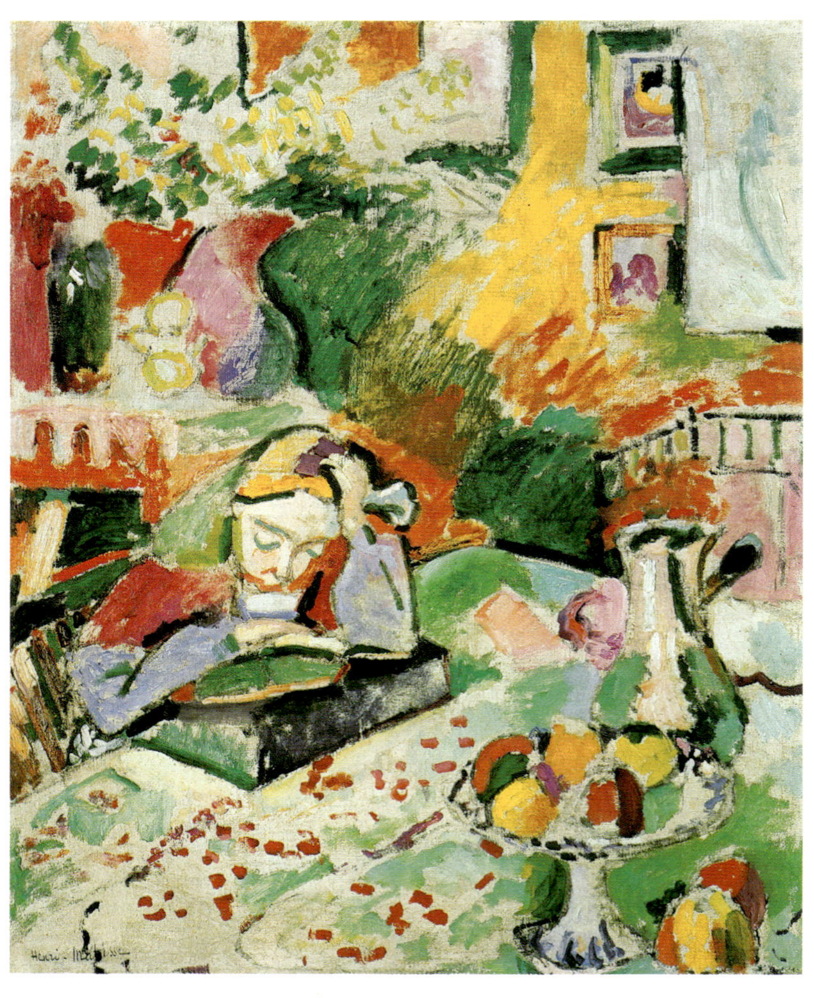

Interior with a Young Girl / Girl Reading • 1905–1906

Private collection

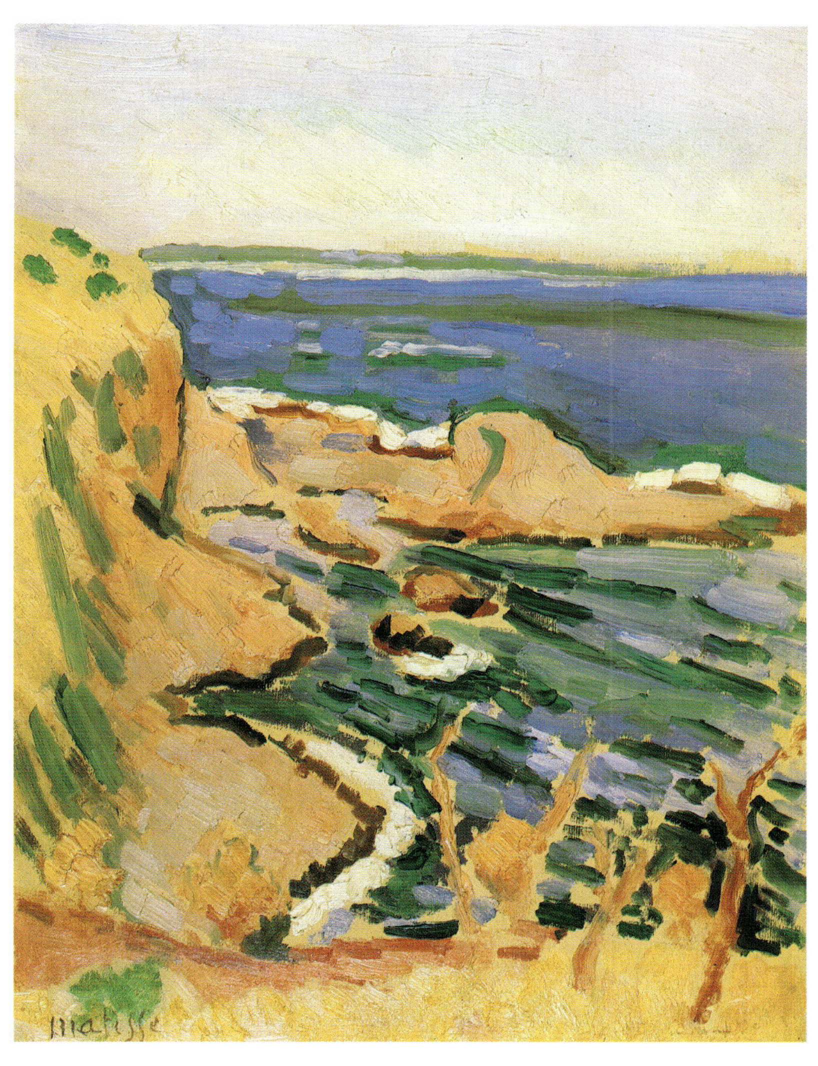

La Moulade, Collioure • 1905
Private collection

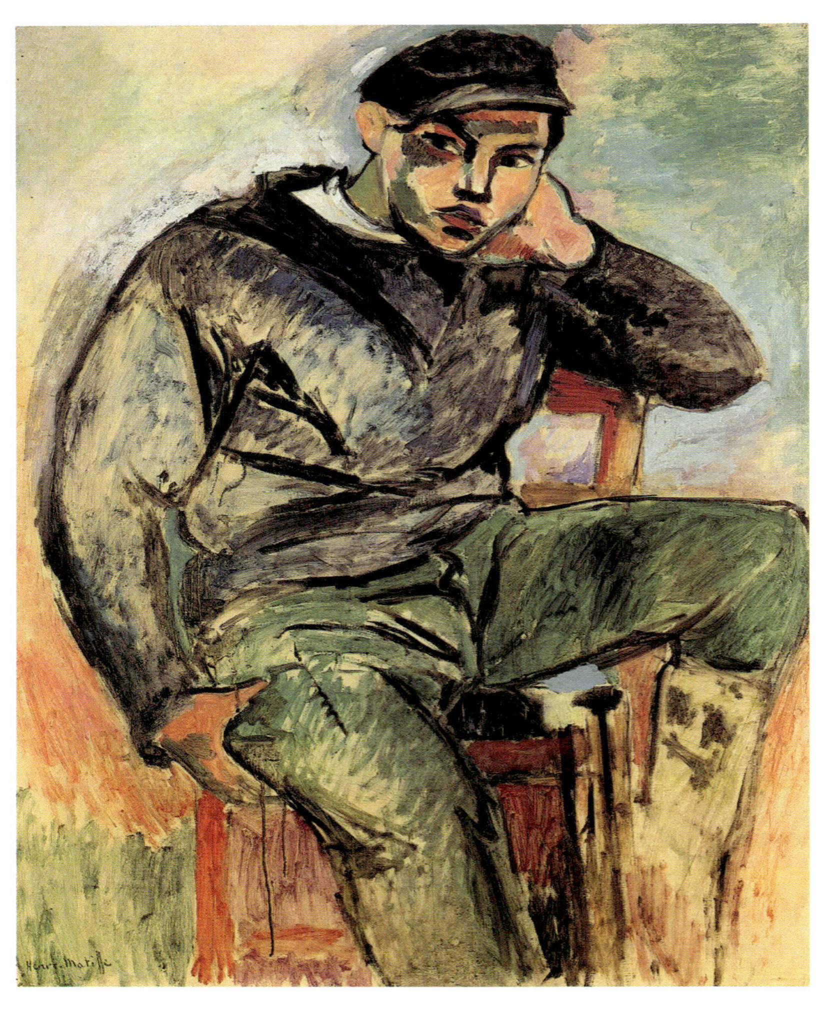

The Young Sailor (I) • 1906

Private collection

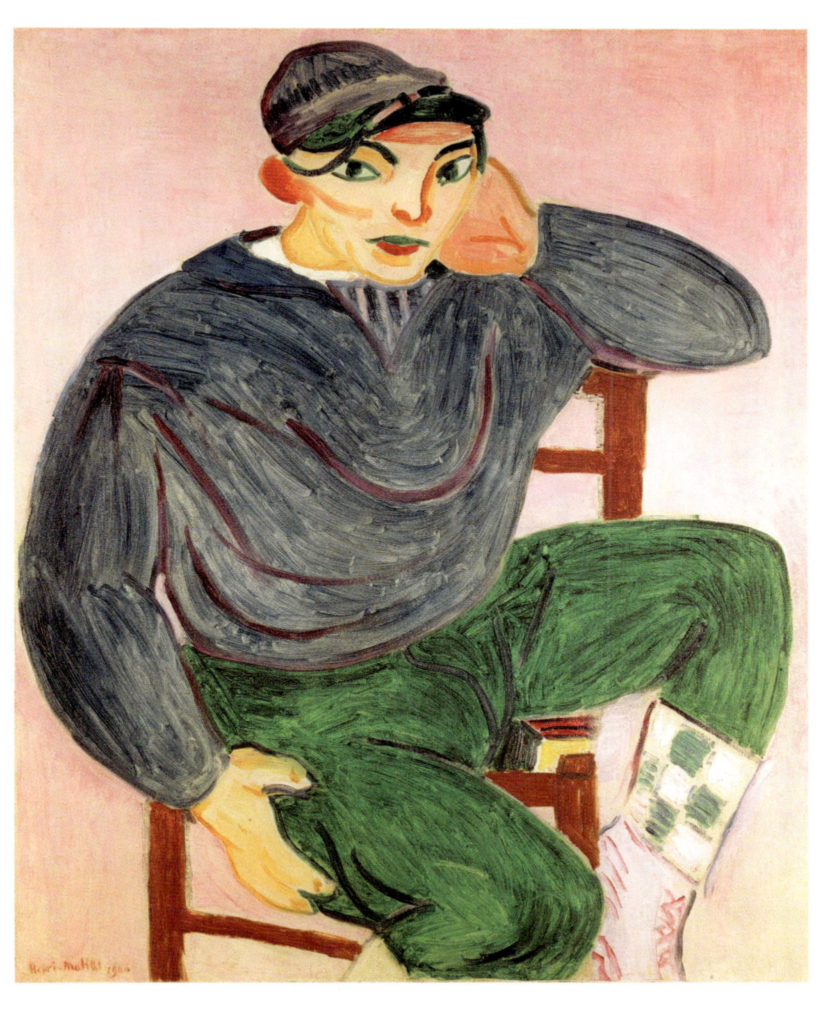

The Young Sailor (II) • 1906
The Metropolitan Museum of Art, New York

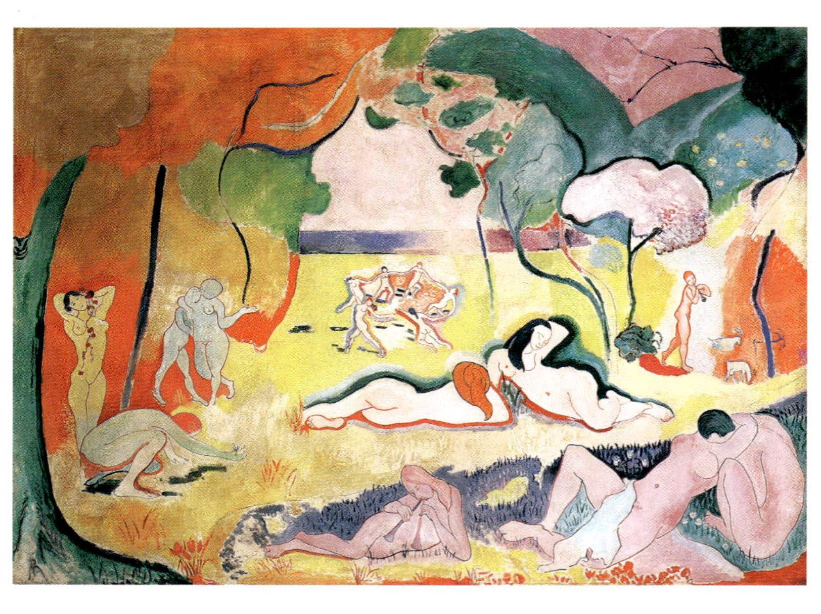

The Joy of Life • 1905–1906
The Barnes Foundation, Merion, Pennsylvania

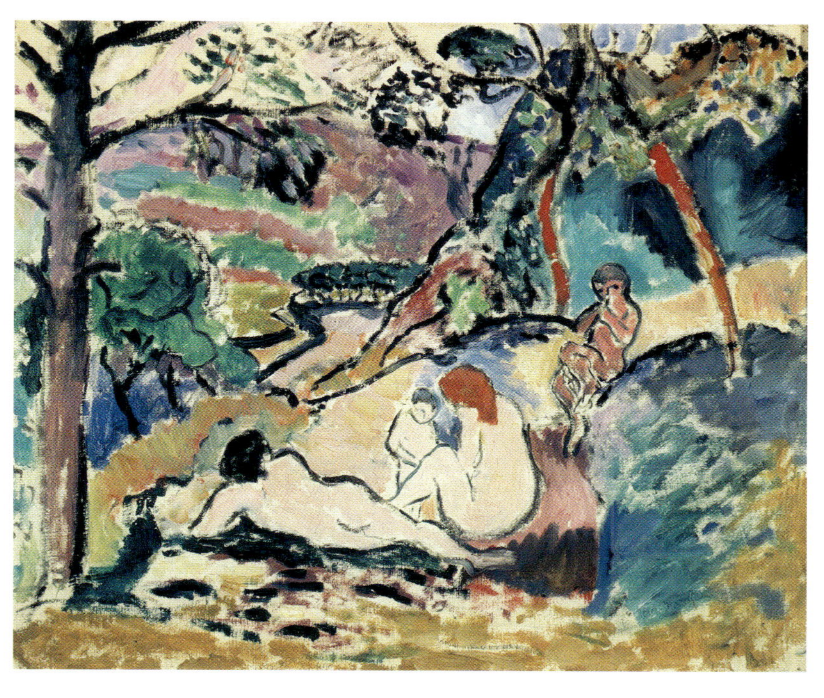

Pastoral · Summer 1906
Musée d'art moderne de la Ville de Paris

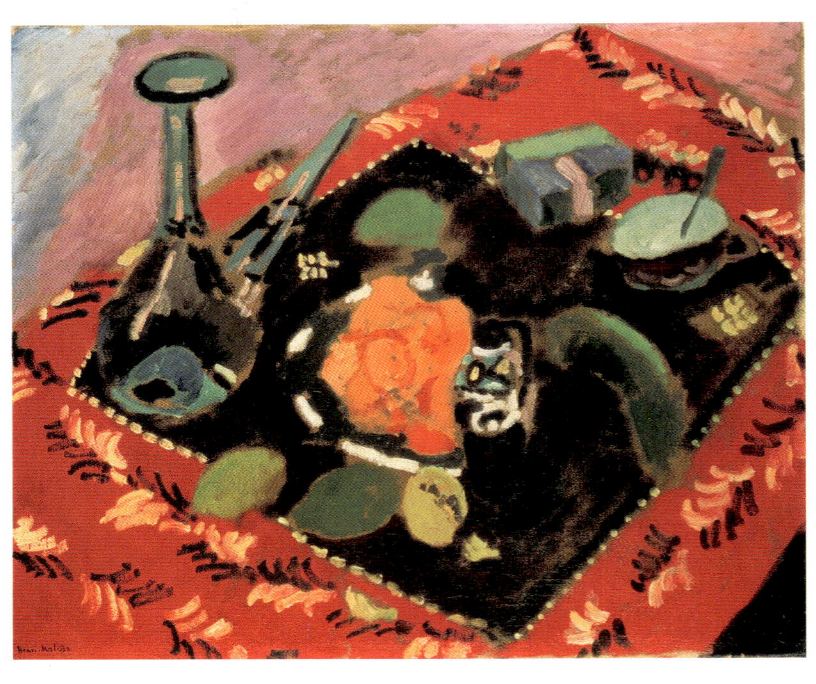

Still Life with a Black Rug • 1906

Hermitage, Saint Petersburg

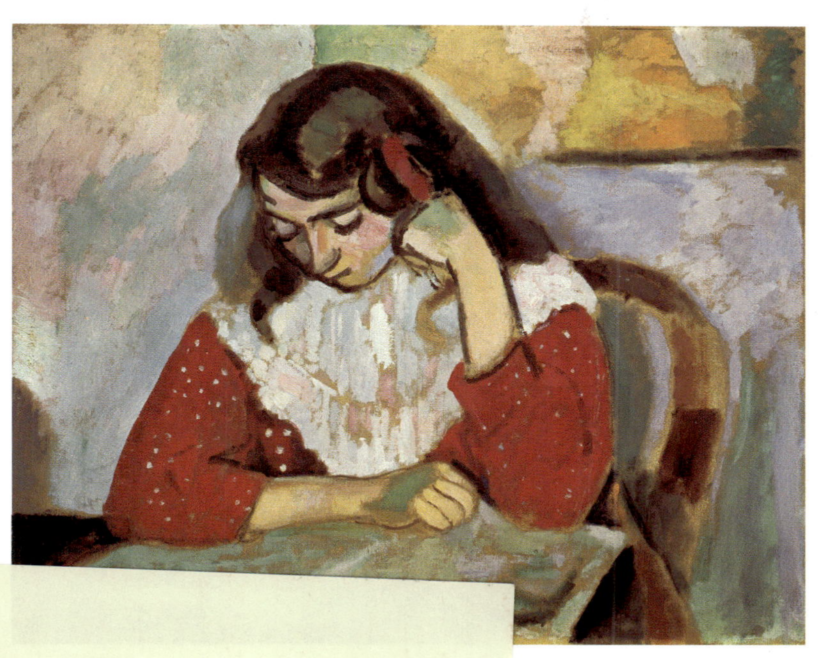

Marguerite Reading · Summer 1906
Musée de Grenoble

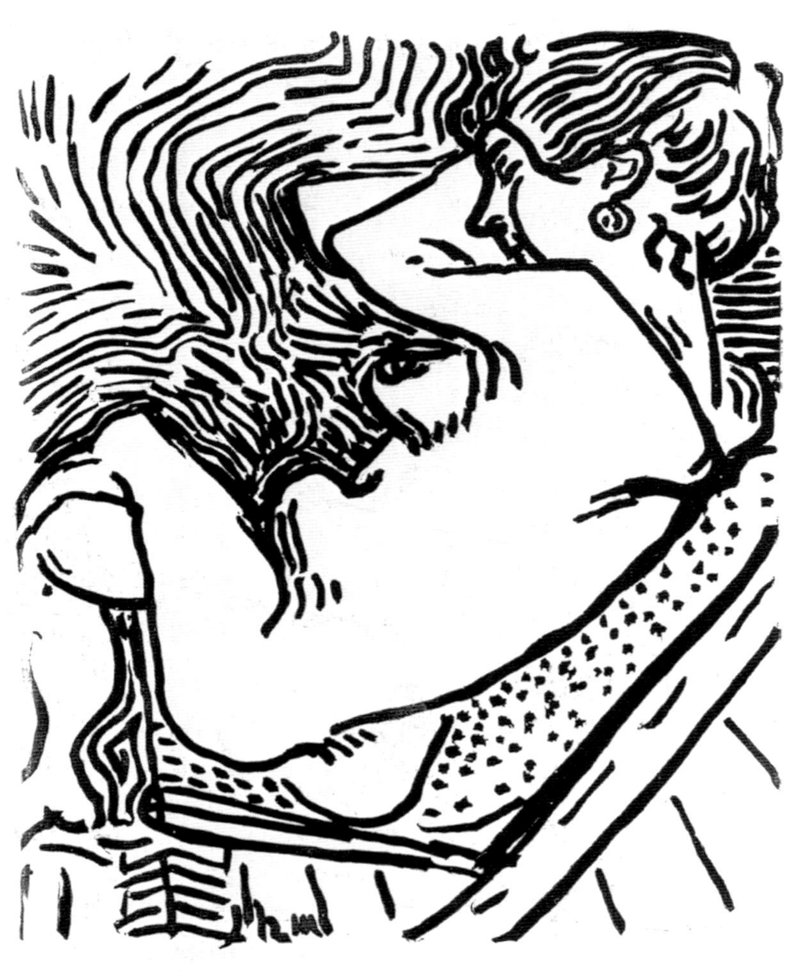

Seated Nude • early 1906
The Museum of Modern Art, New York, gift of Mr. and Mrs. R. Kirk Askew, Jr.

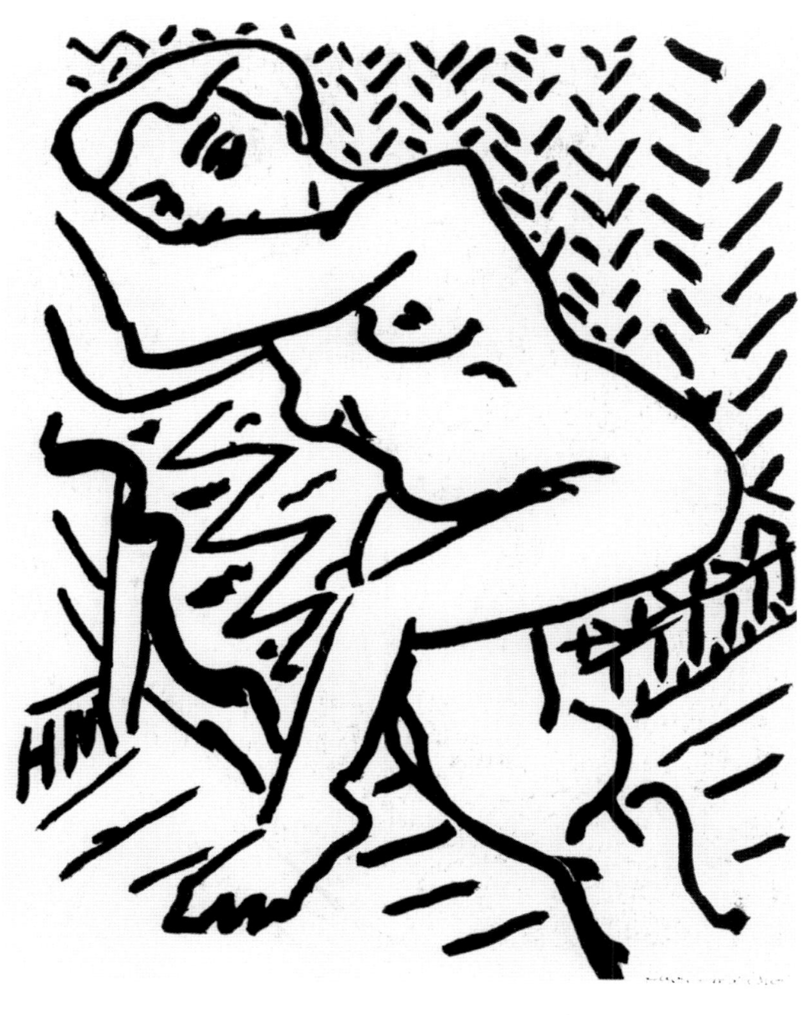

Seated Nude • early 1906
The Museum of Modern Art, New York, Abby Aldrich Rockefeller Fund

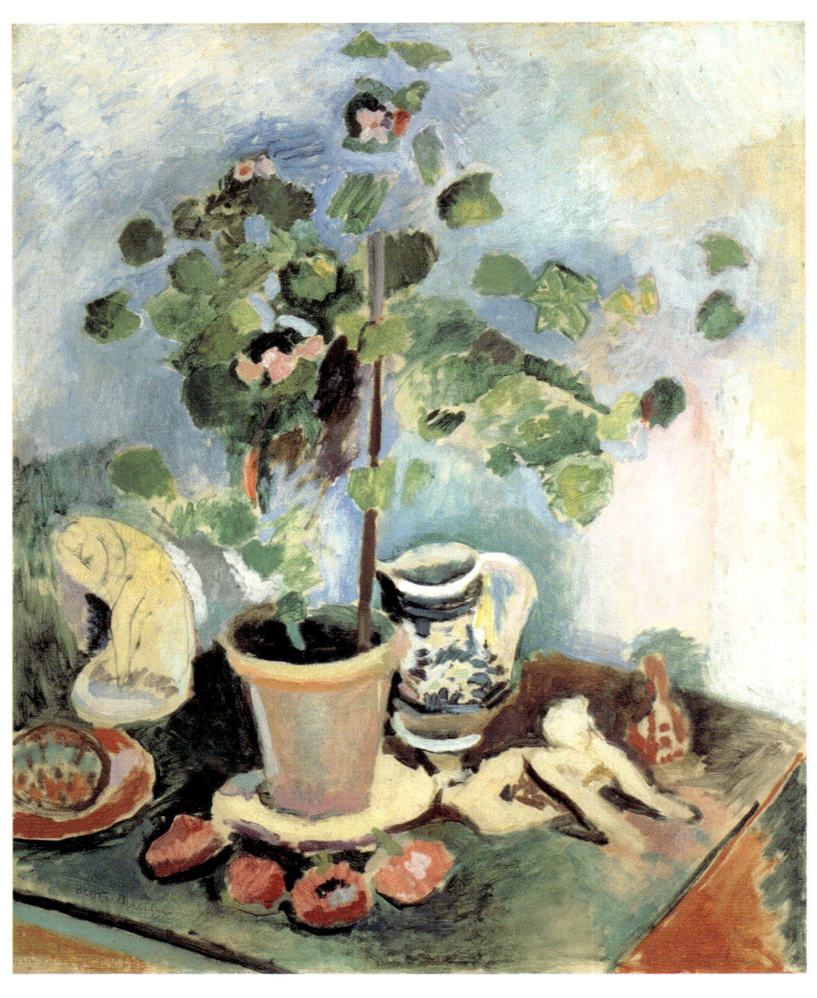

Still Life with a Geranium • Summer 1906
The Art Institute of Chicago, Joseph Winterbotham Collection

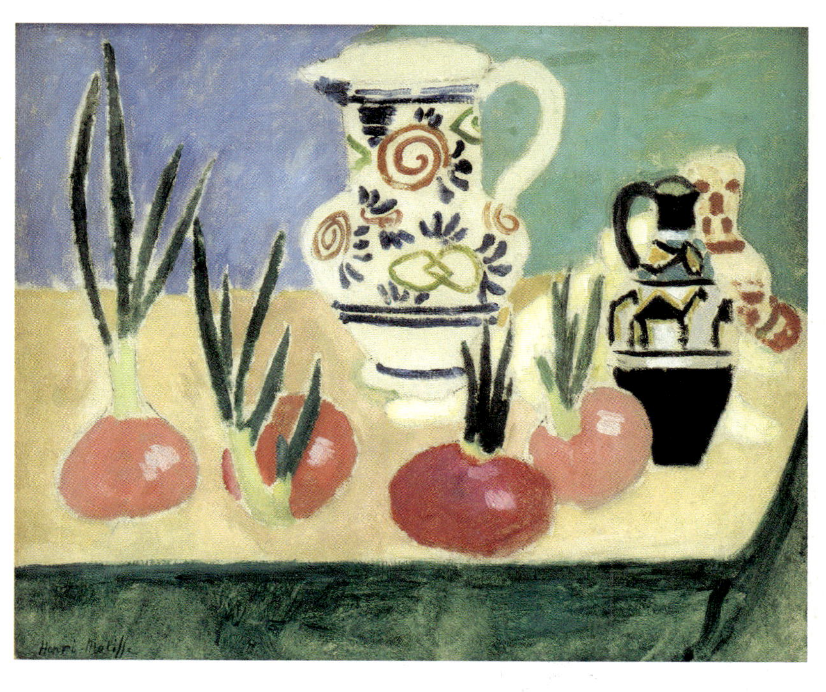

Pink Onions • Summer 1906?
Statens Museum for Kunst, Copenhagen

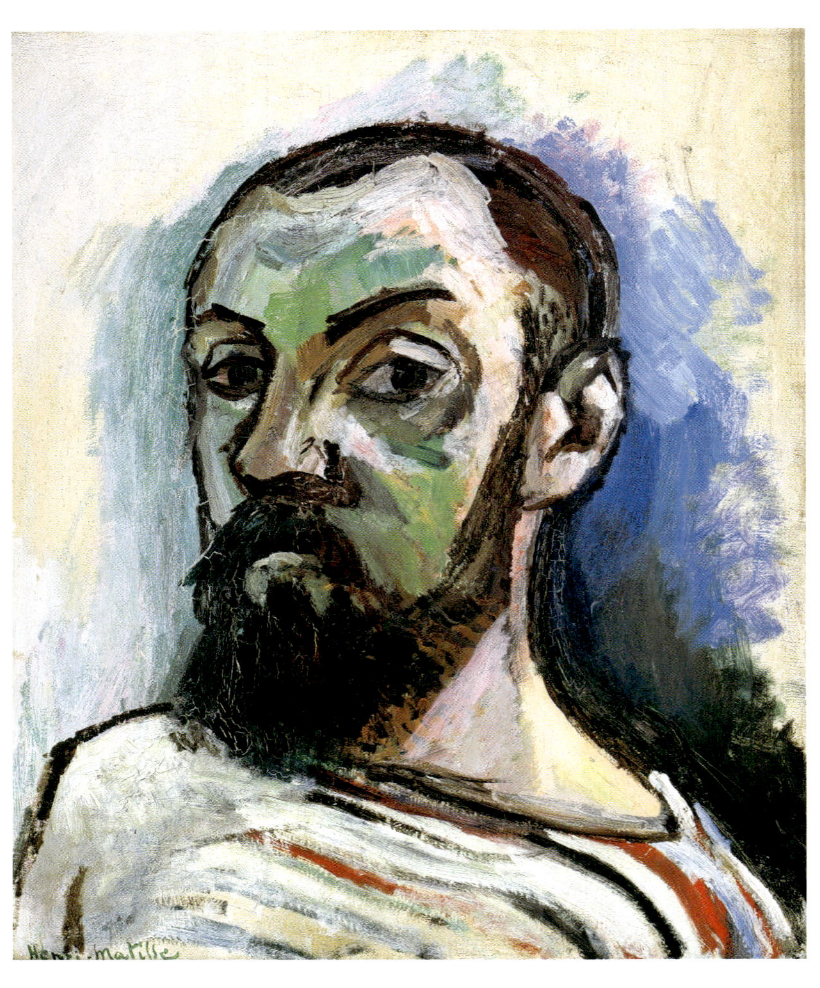

Self-Portrait · Summer 1906?

Statens Museum for Kunst, Copenhagen

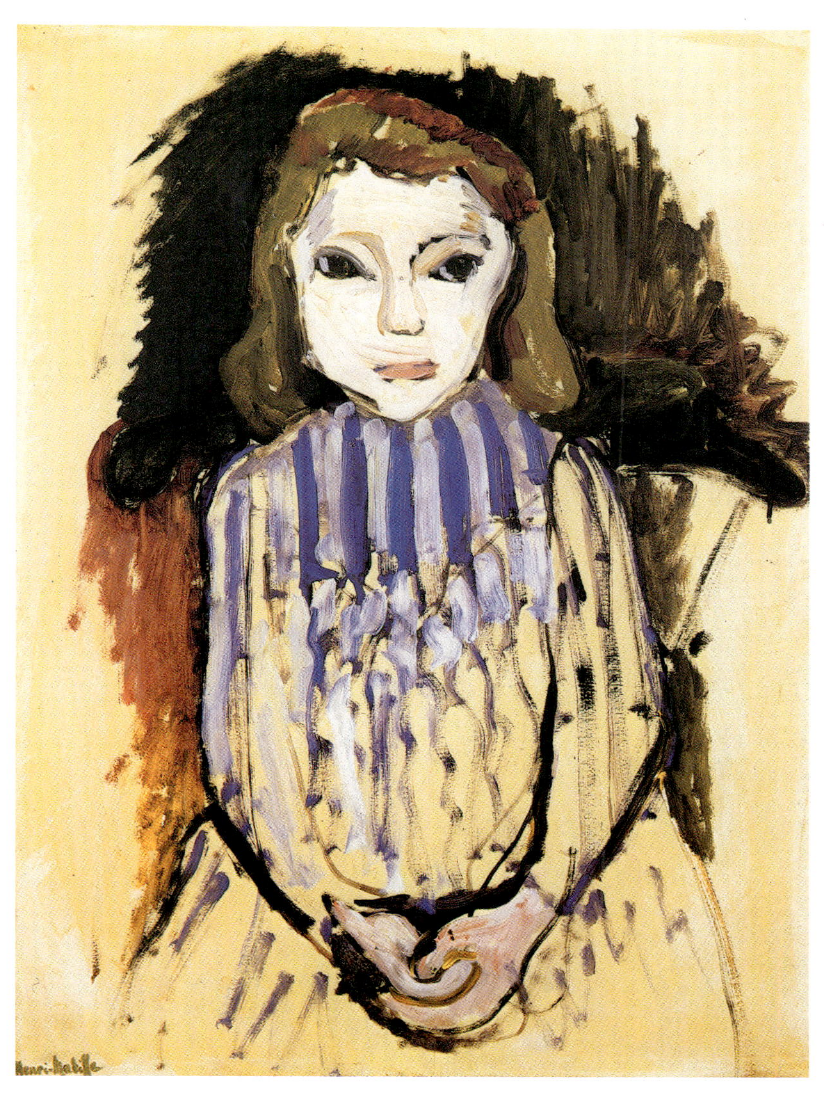

Marguerite • 1906
Private collection

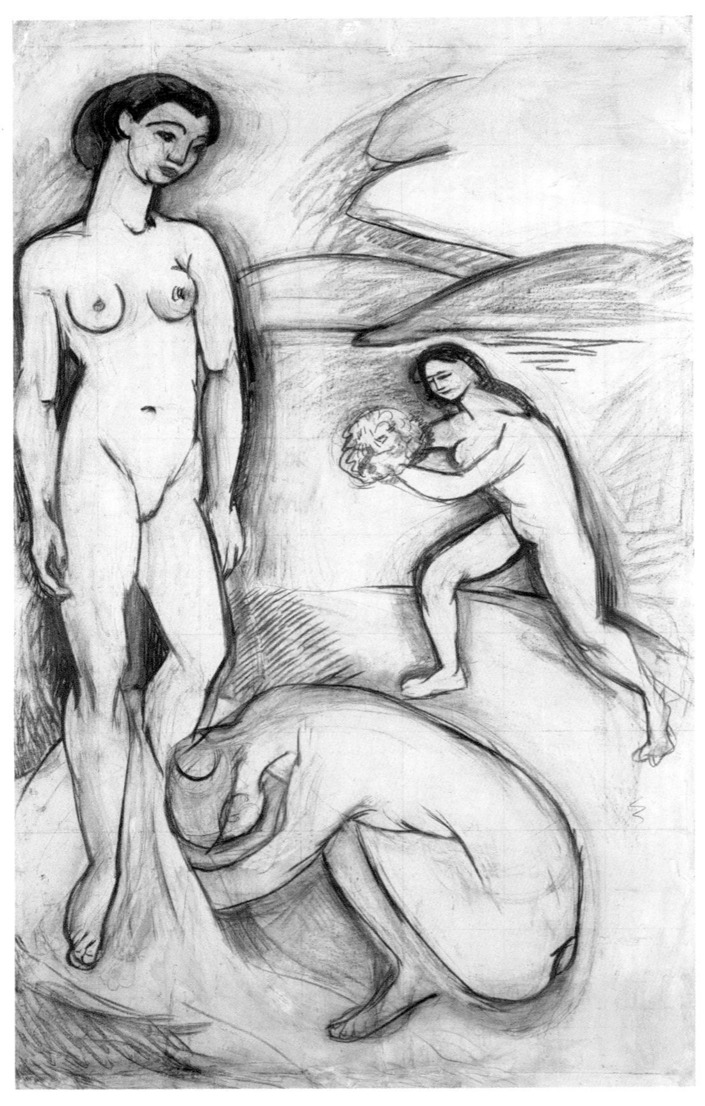

Study for Le Luxe (I) • 1907
Musée national d'art moderne, Paris

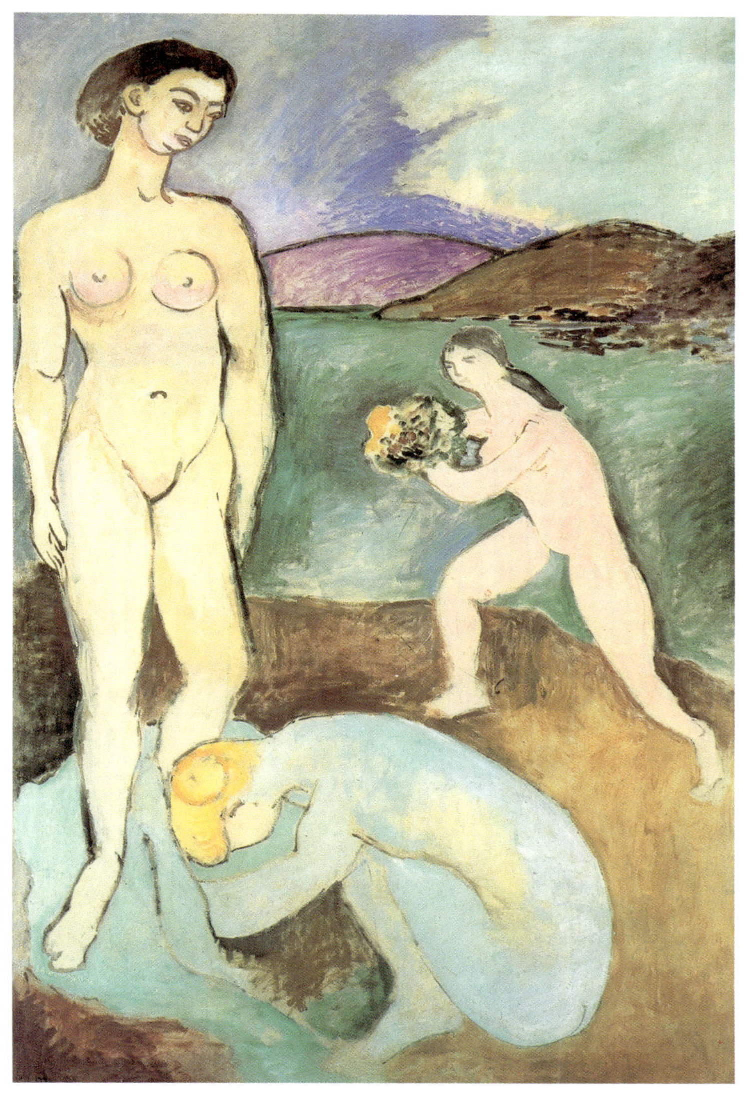

Le Luxe (I) • Summer 1907
Musée national d'art moderne, Paris

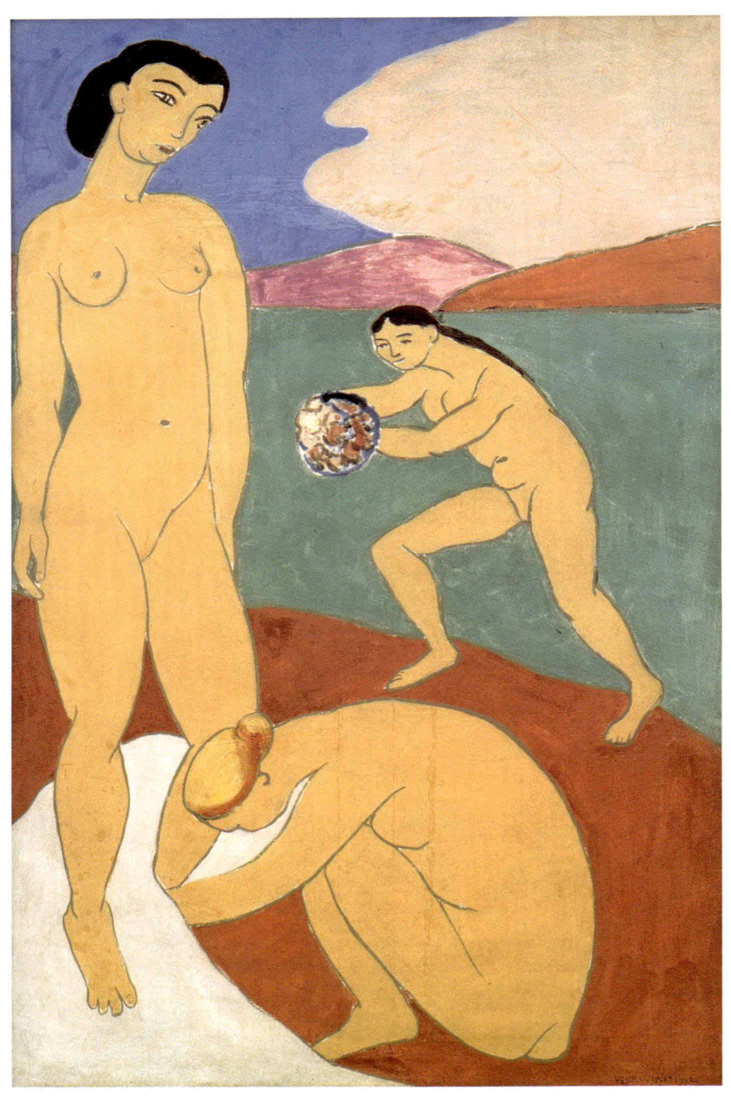

Le Luxe (II) • Summer 1907–1908
Statens Museum for Kunst, Copenhagen

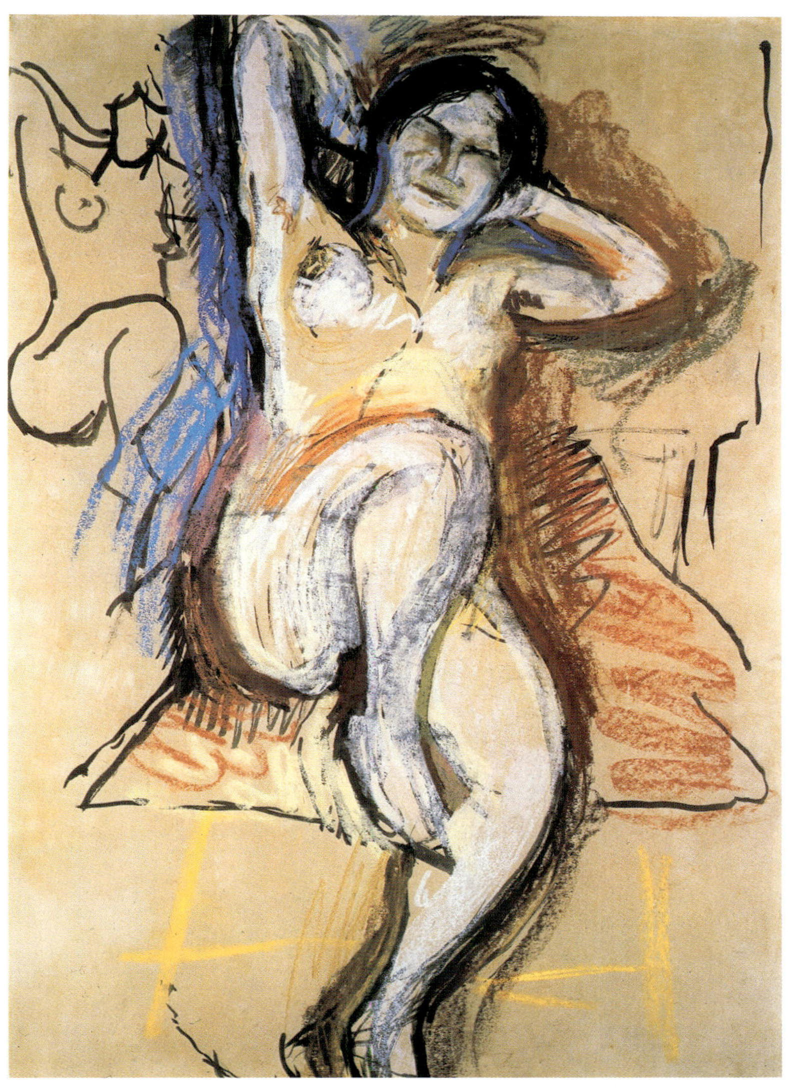

Seated Nude • 1906
Private collection

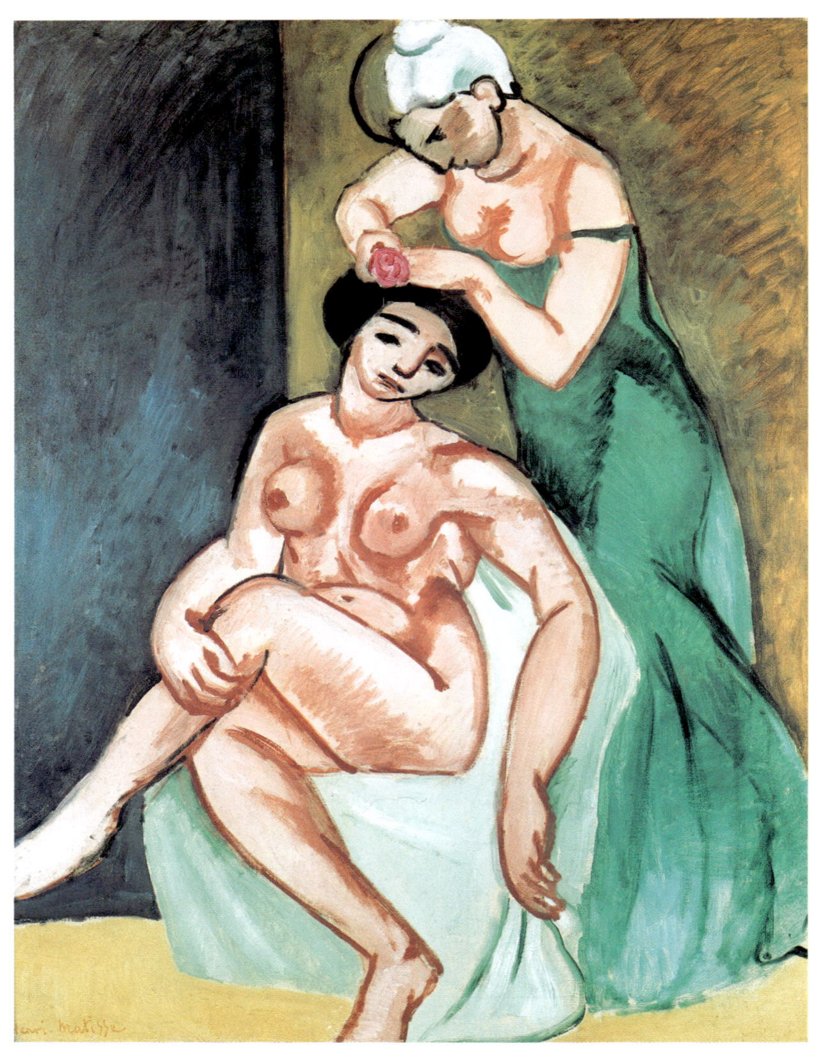

La Coiffure • 1907

Staatsgalerie, Stuttgart

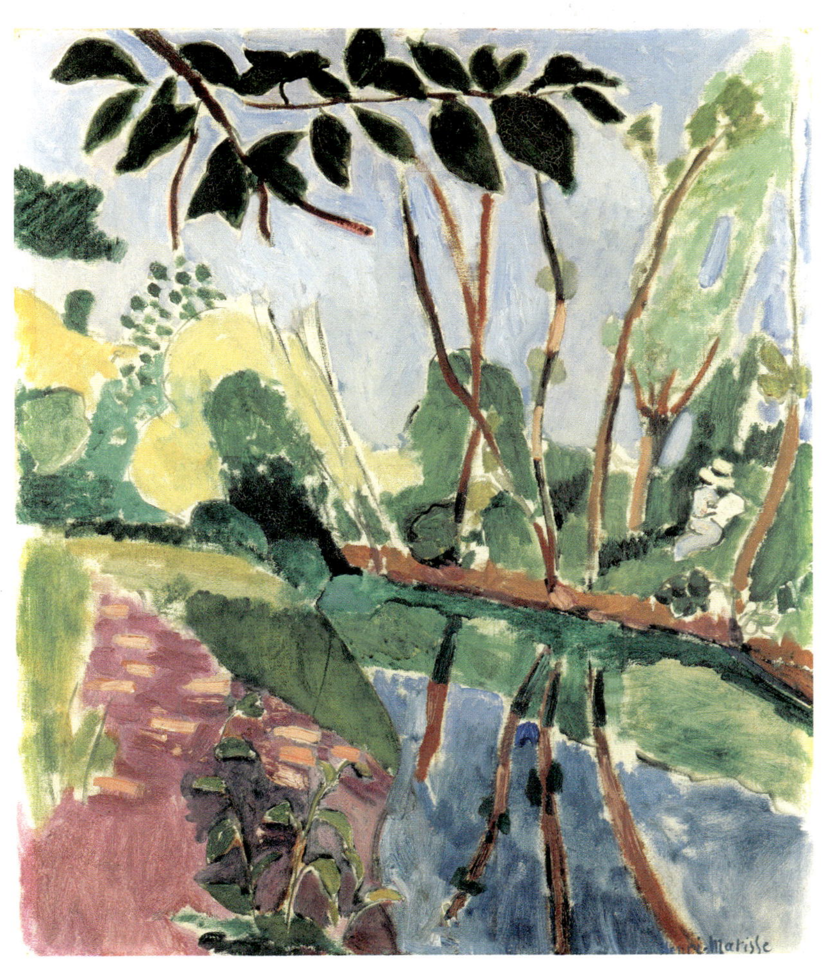

The Waterfront • 1907

Kunstmuseum, Basel

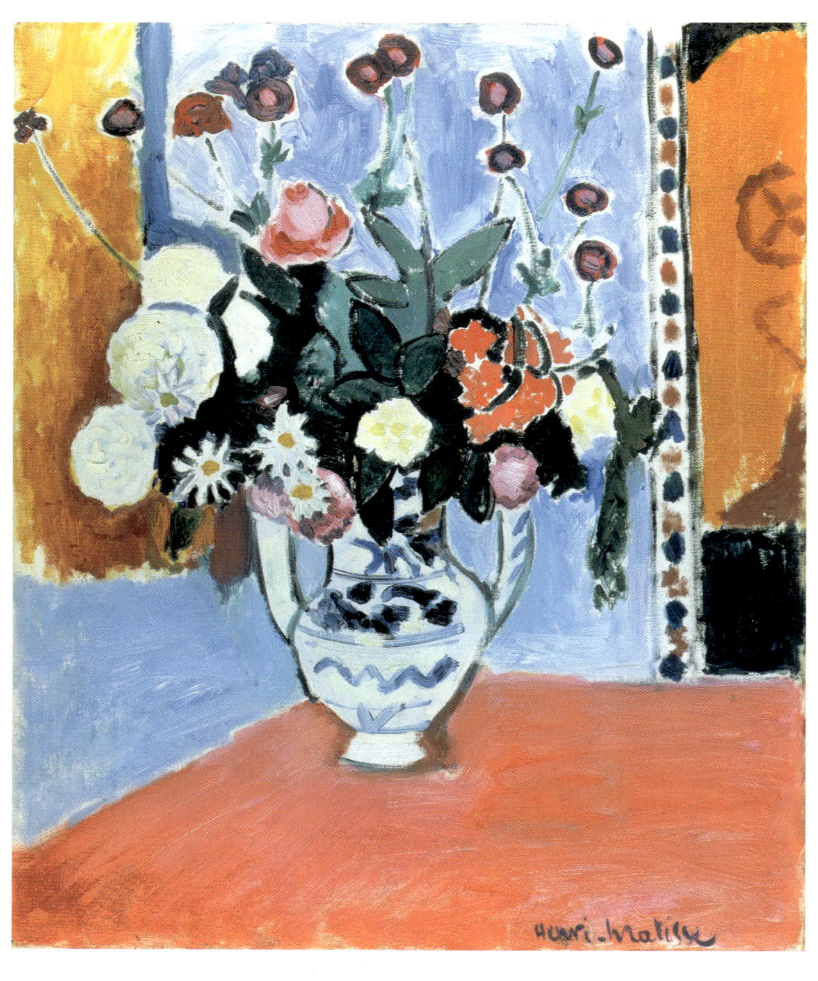

Vase with Two Handles · 1907

Hermitage, Saint Petersburg

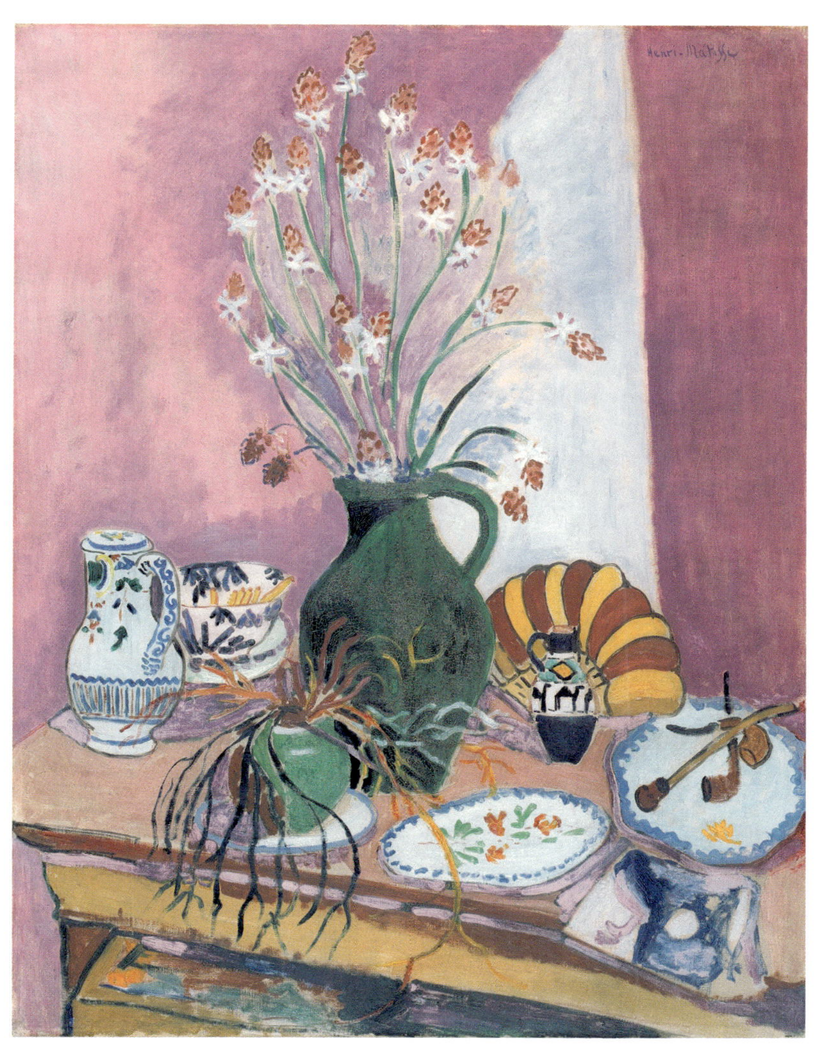

Still Life with Asphodels • 1907

Museum Folkwang, Essen

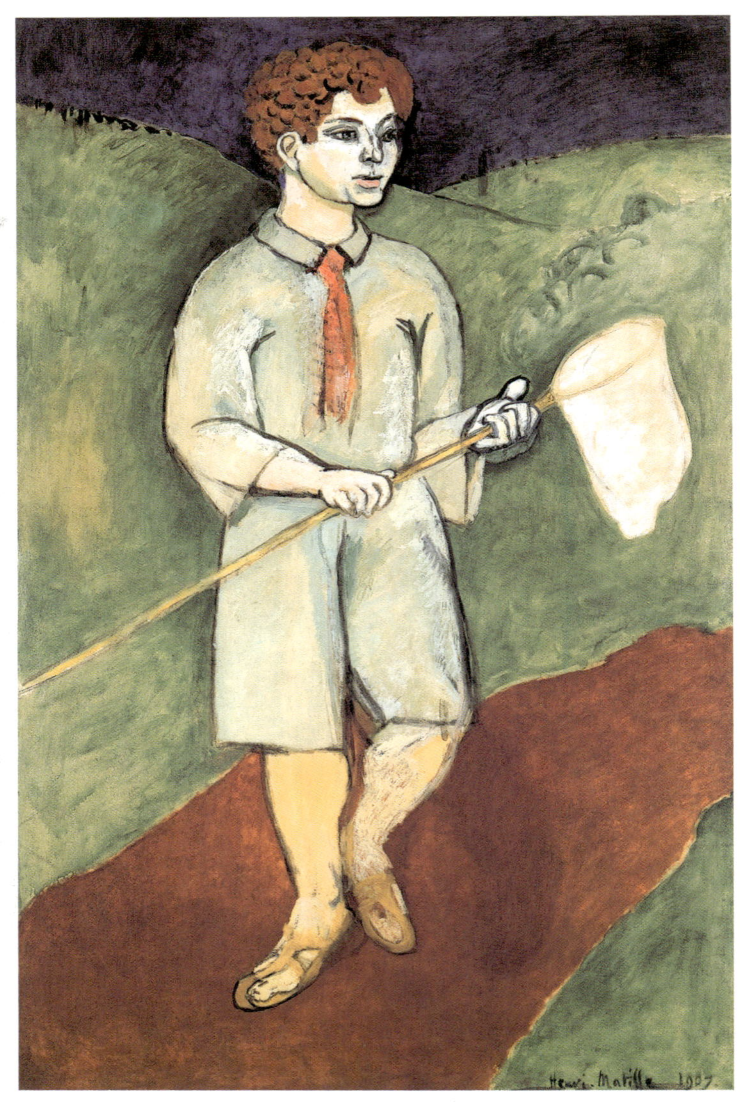

Boy with a Butterfly Net (Allan Stein) • 1907

The Minneapolis Institute of Arts, Ethel Morrison Van Derlip Fund

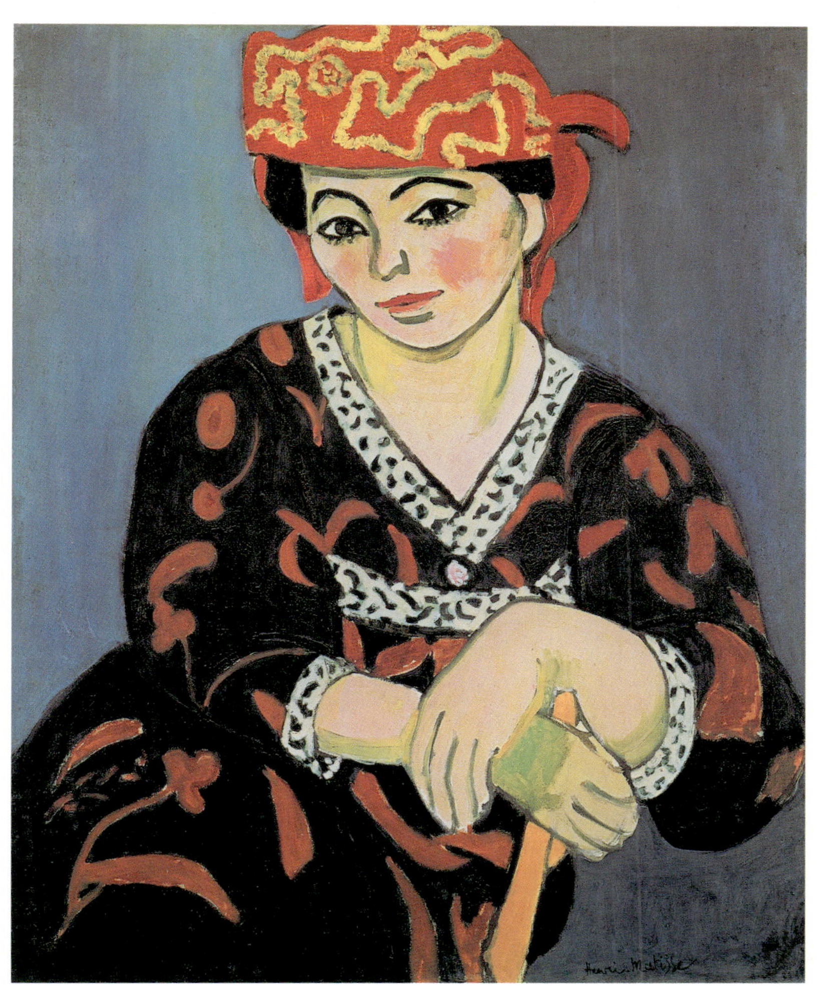

The Red Madras Headdress • 1907
The Barnes Foundation, Merion, Pennsylvania

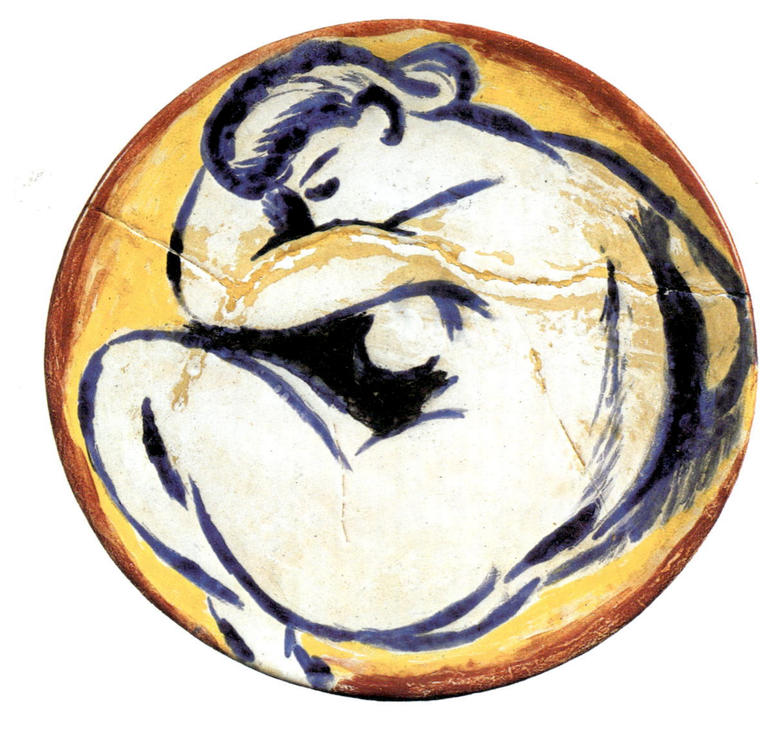

Plate with Nude • 1907

Private collection

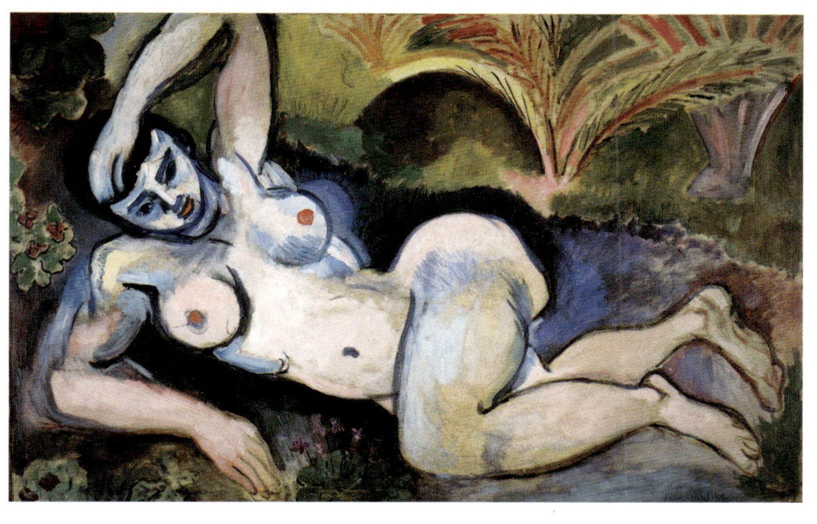

Blue Nude / Memory of Biskra • early 1907
The Baltimore Museum of Art, The Cone Collection
> **Harmony in Red / La Desserte** • 1908
Hermitage, Saint Petersburg

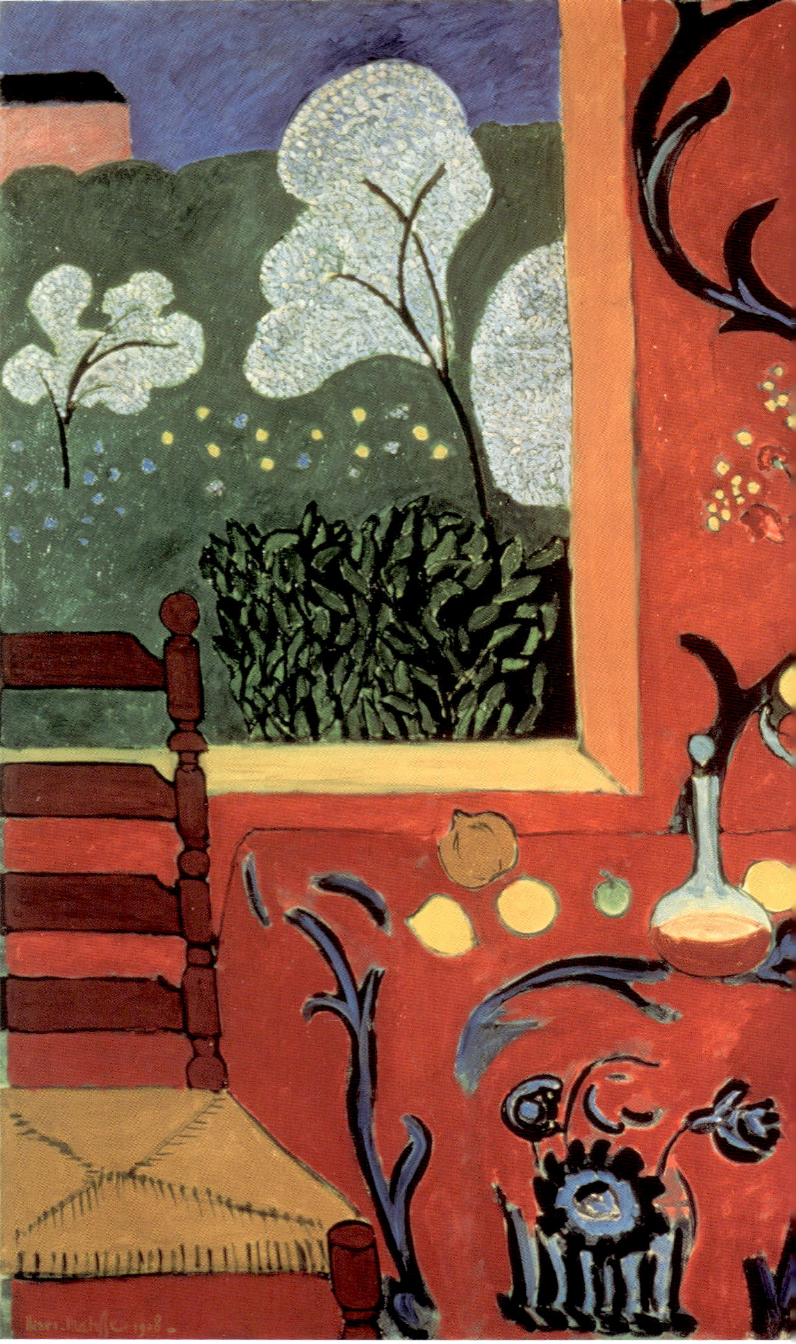

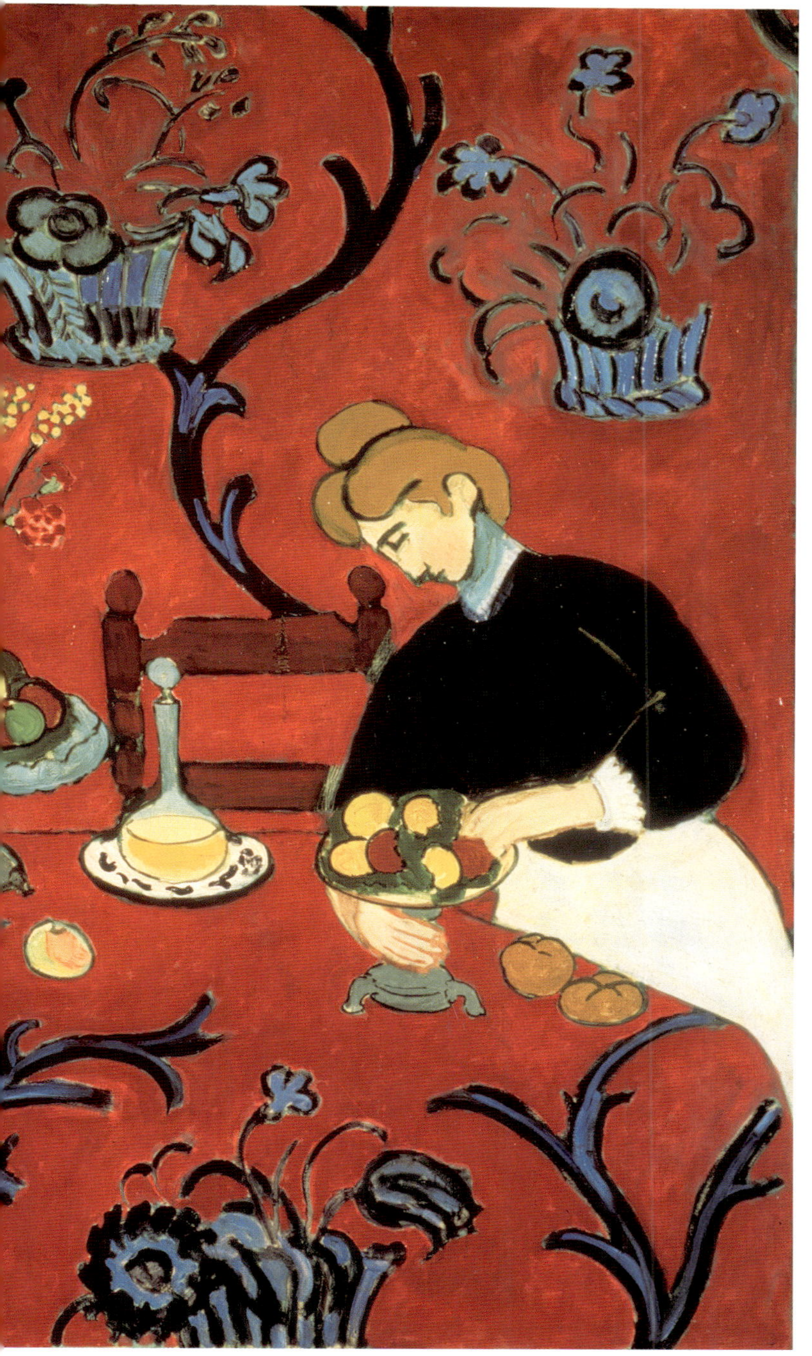

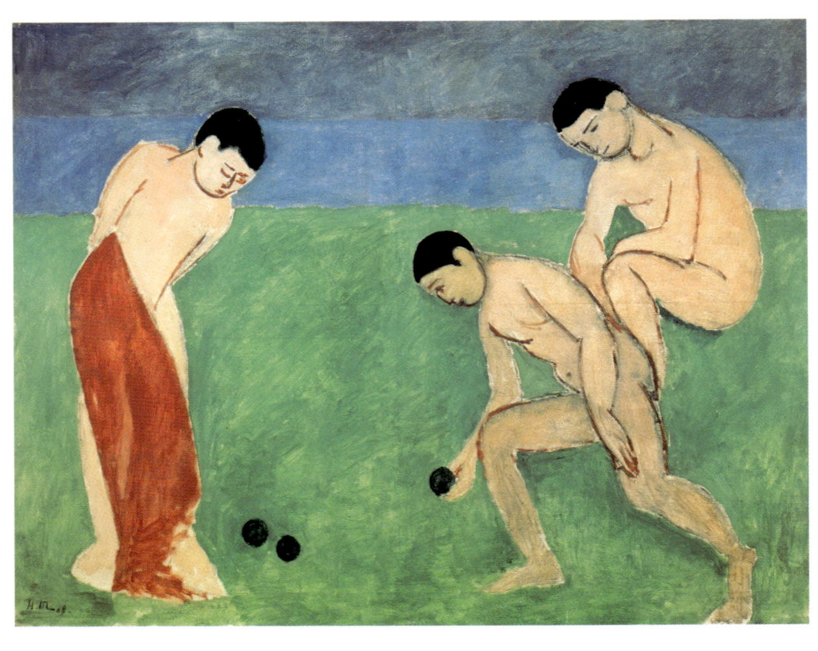

Game of Bowls · 1908
Hermitage, Saint Petersburg

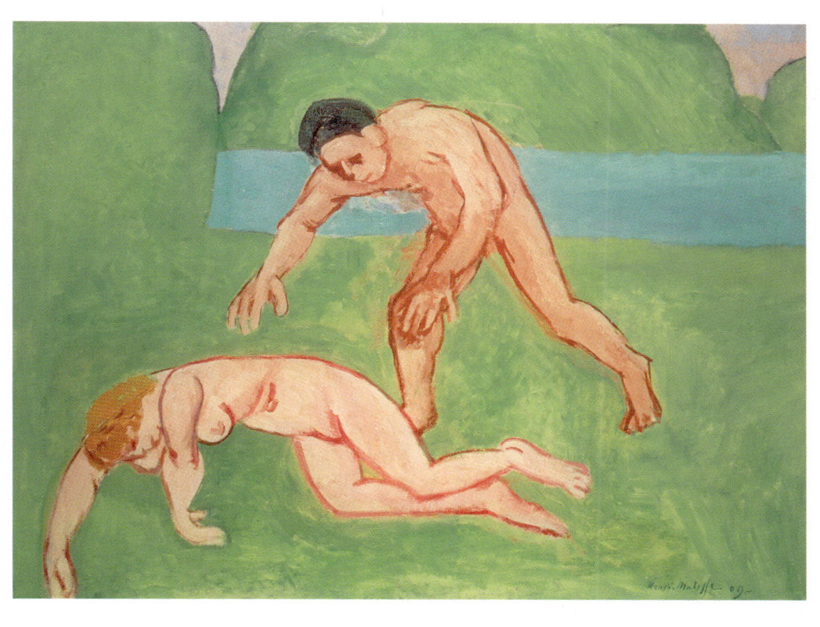

Nymph and Satyr • 1908–1909
Hermitage, Saint Petersburg

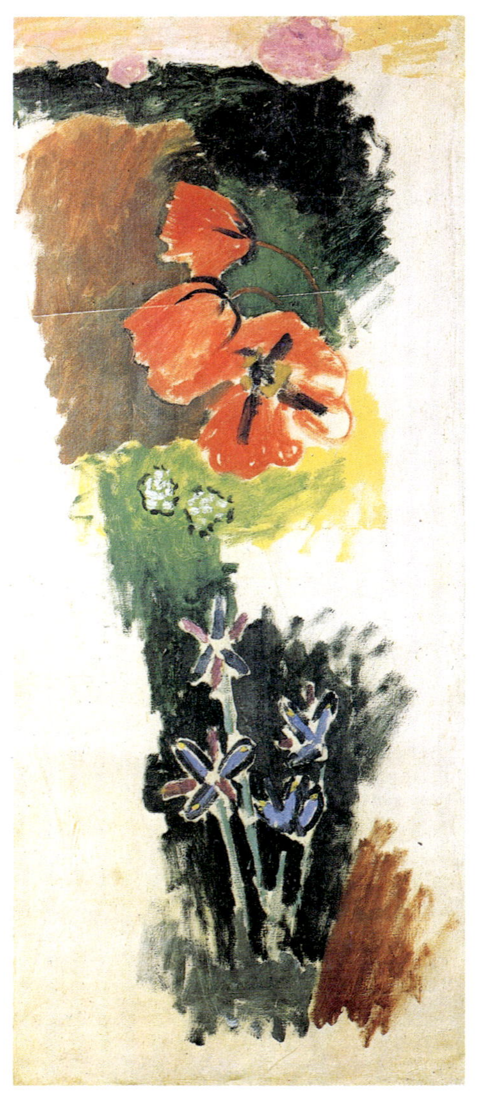

Poppies • 1908

Private collection

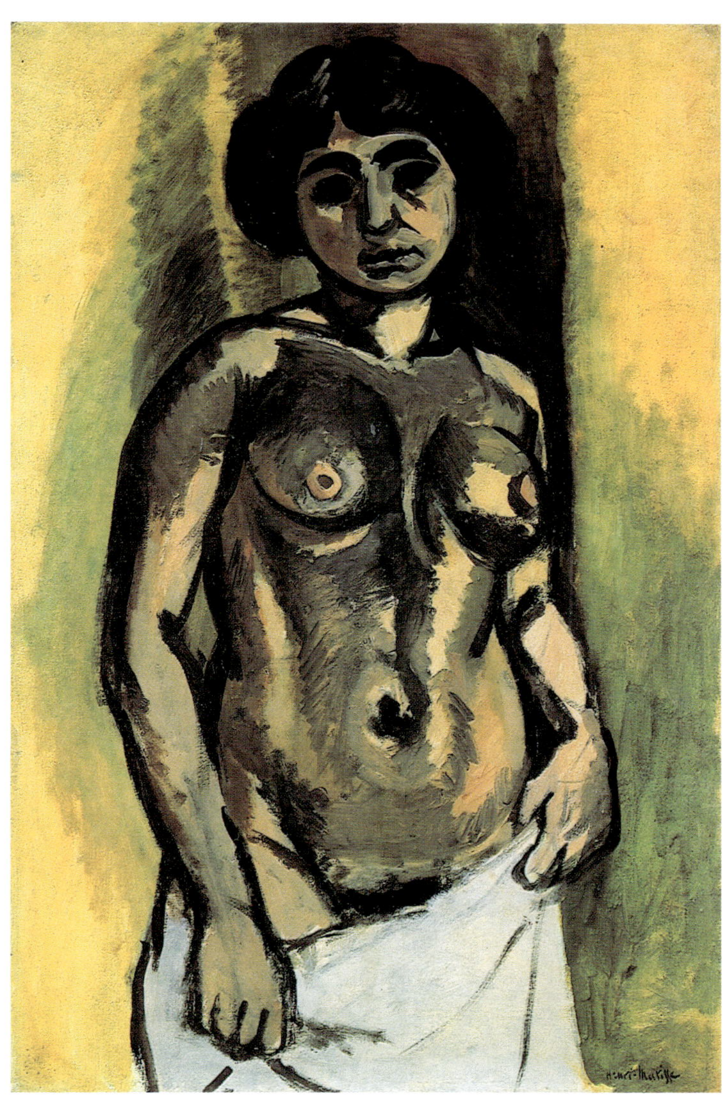

Nude, Black and Gold • 1908
Hermitage, Saint Petersburg

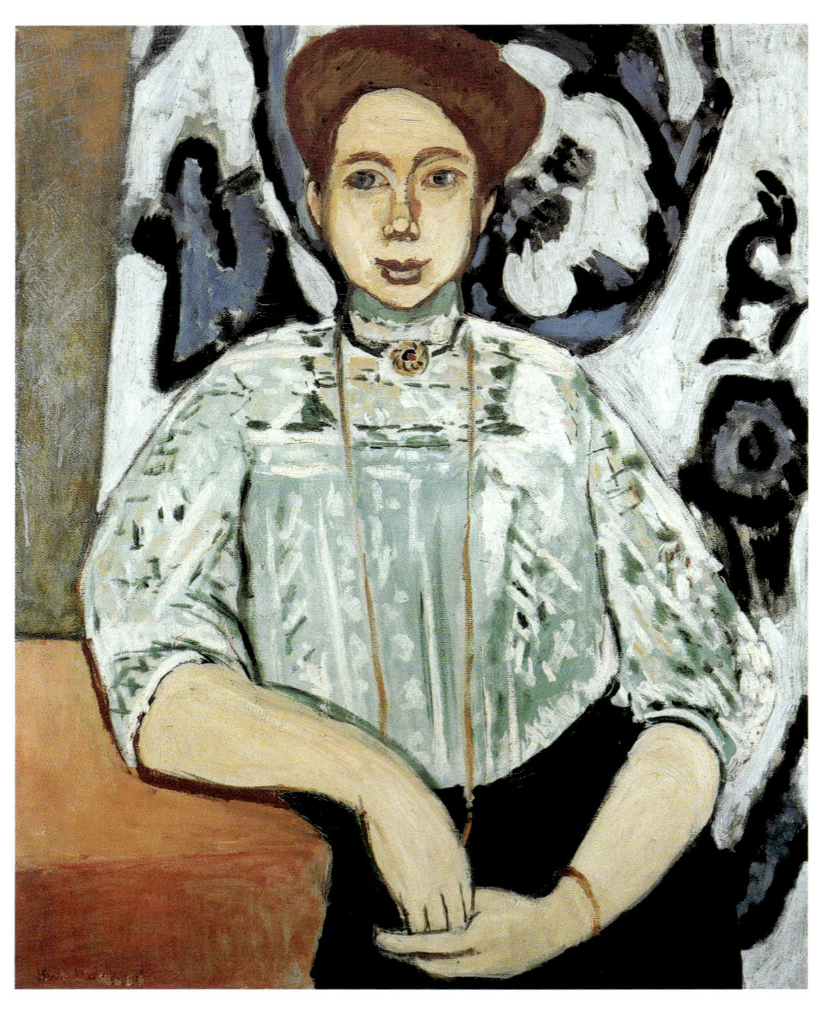

Portrait of Greta Moll • 1908
The National Gallery, London

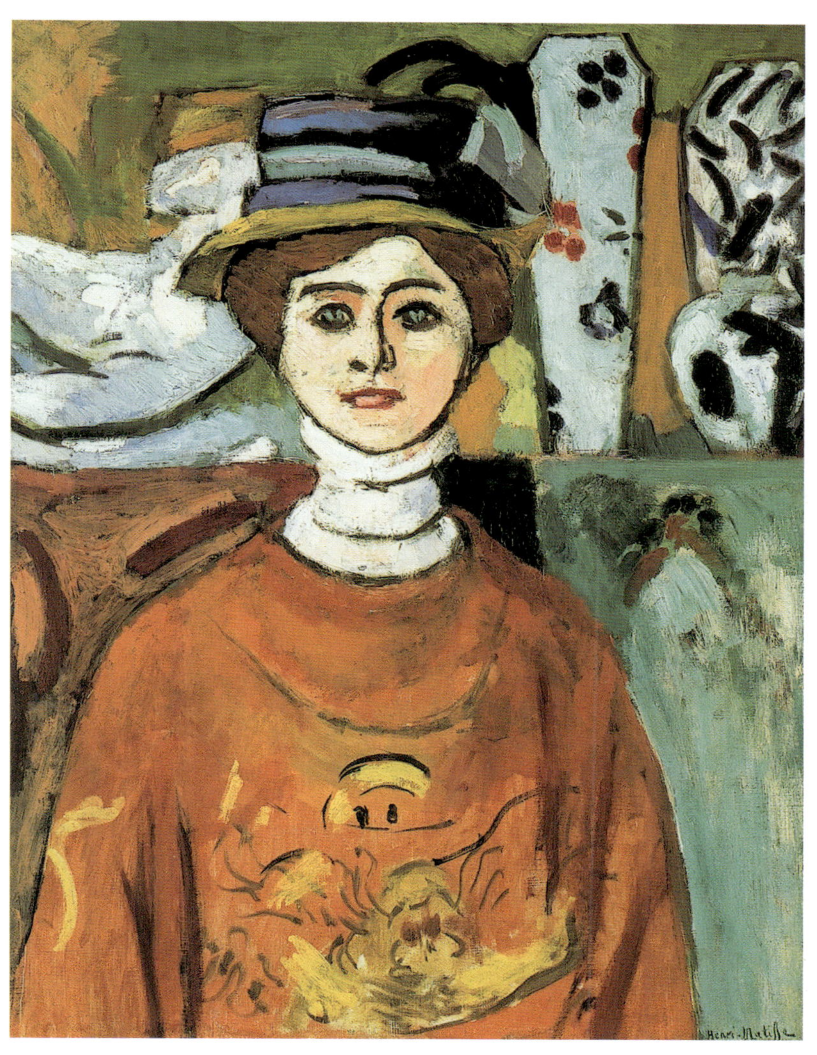

The Girl with Green Eyes • 1908
San Francisco Museum of Modern Art, bequest of Harriet Lane Levy

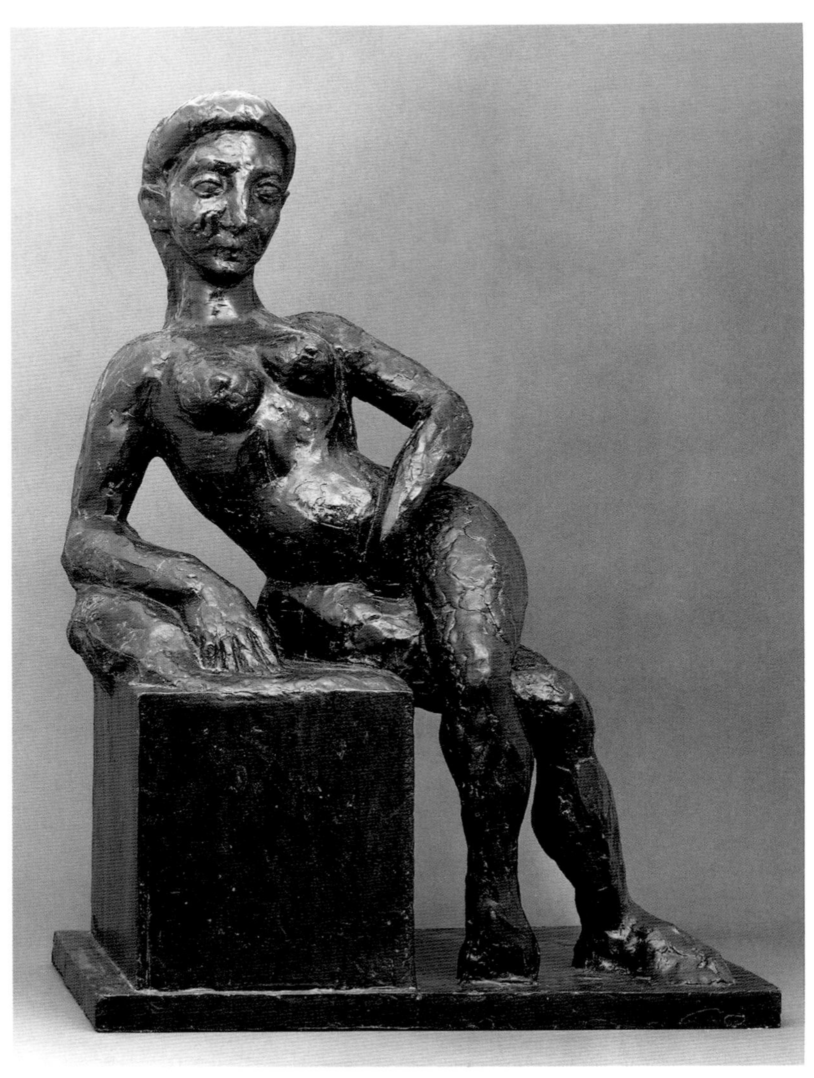

Decorative Figure • 1908
Collection of Patsy R. and Raymond Nasher, Dallas

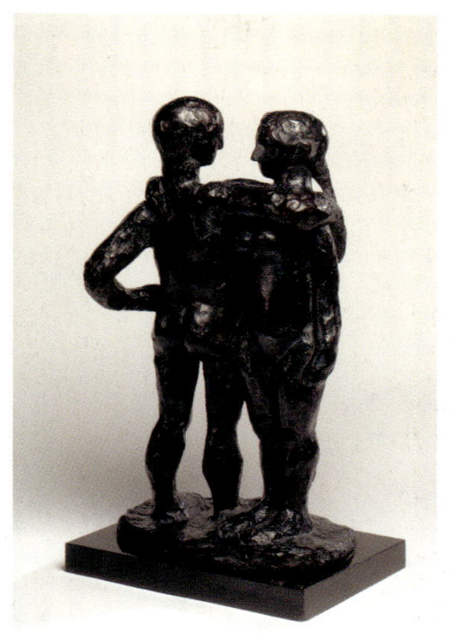

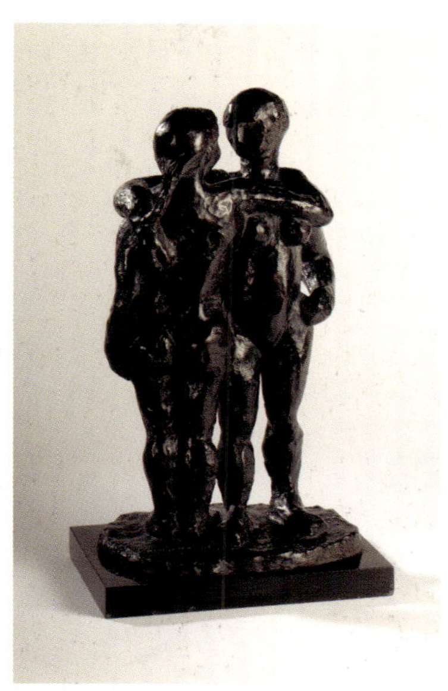

Two Women • 1908
Musée national d'art moderne, Paris

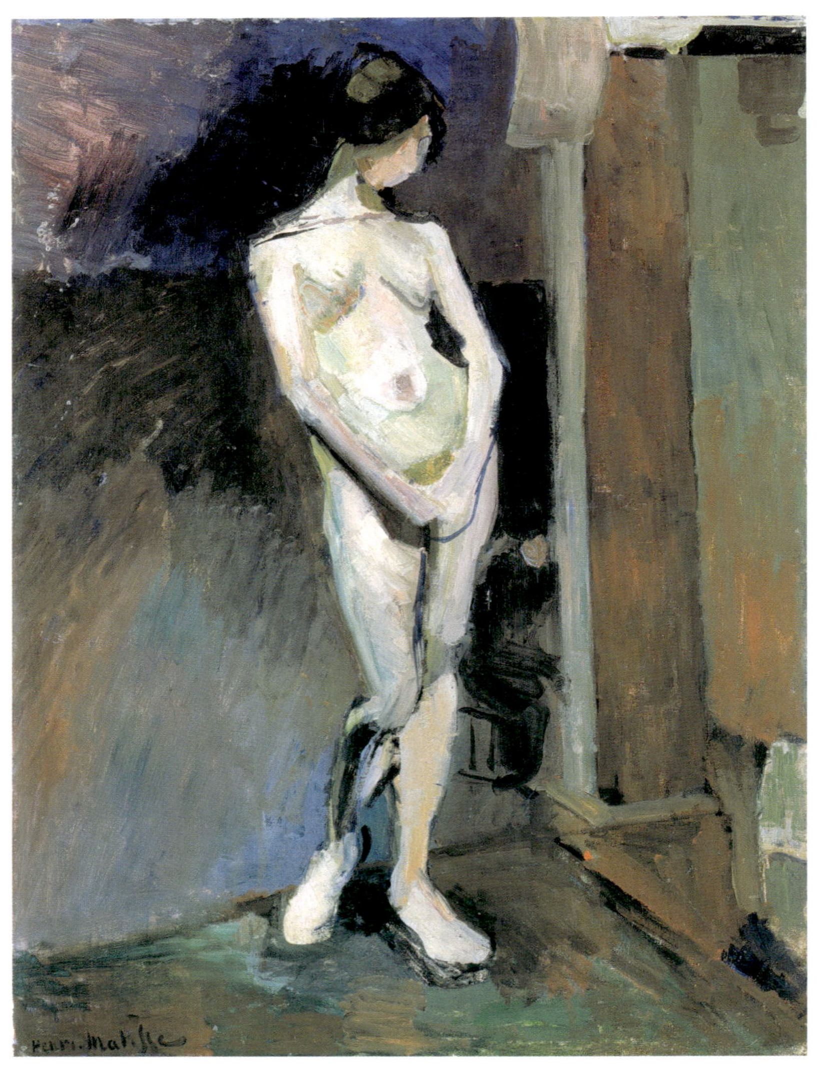

Standing Nude • late 1906–1907
Tate Gallery, London

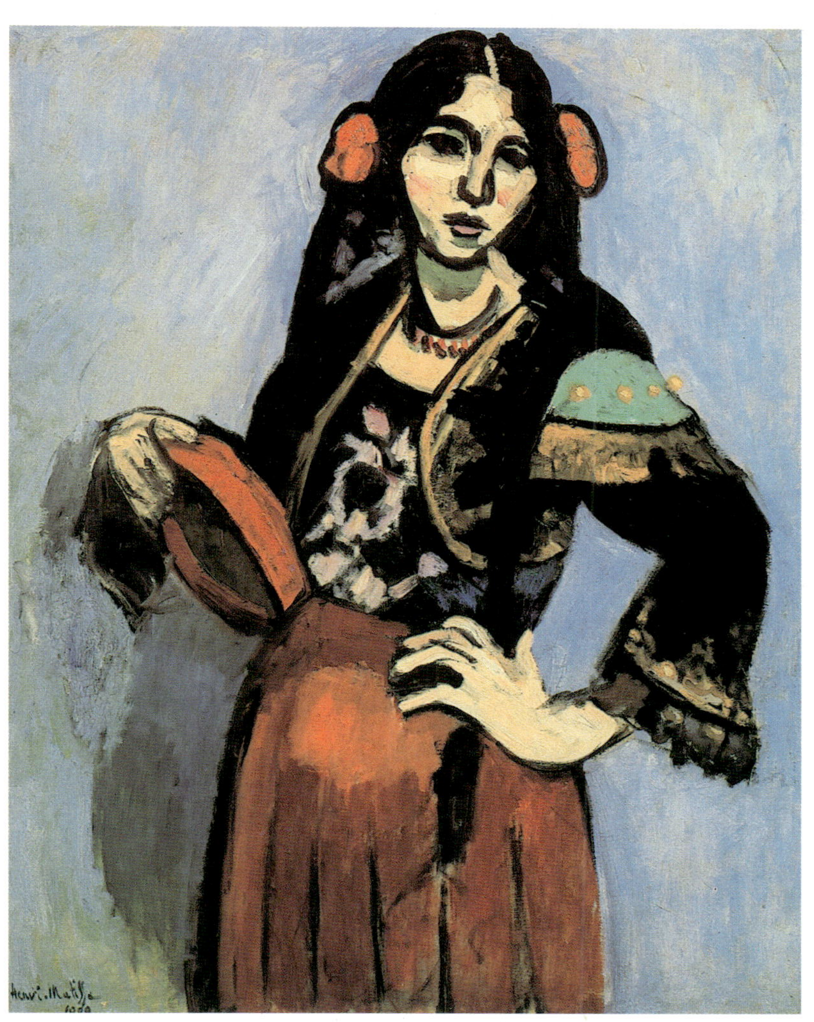

Spanish Woman with a Tambourine • early 1909
Pushkin Museum, Moscow

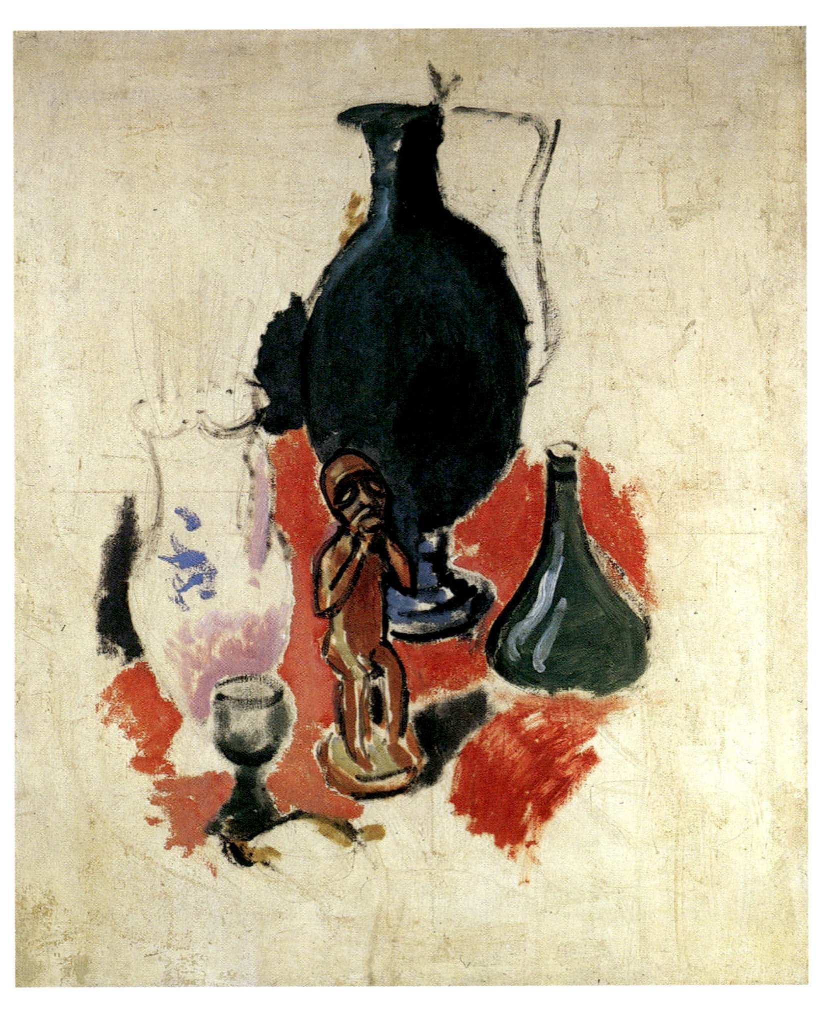

Still Life with Black Statuette • 1908–1909
Private collection

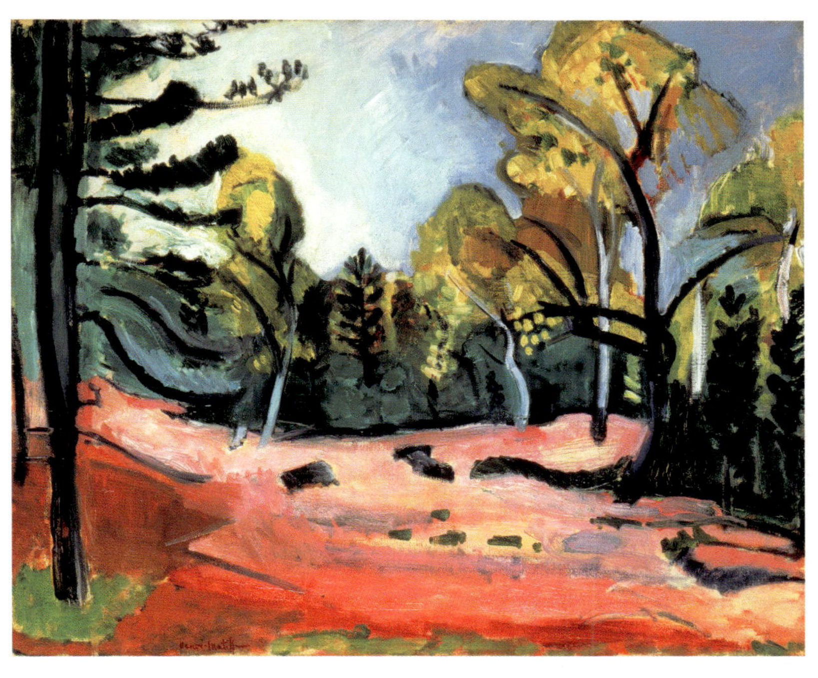

Clearing in the Woods of Fontainebleau · 1909
Private collection

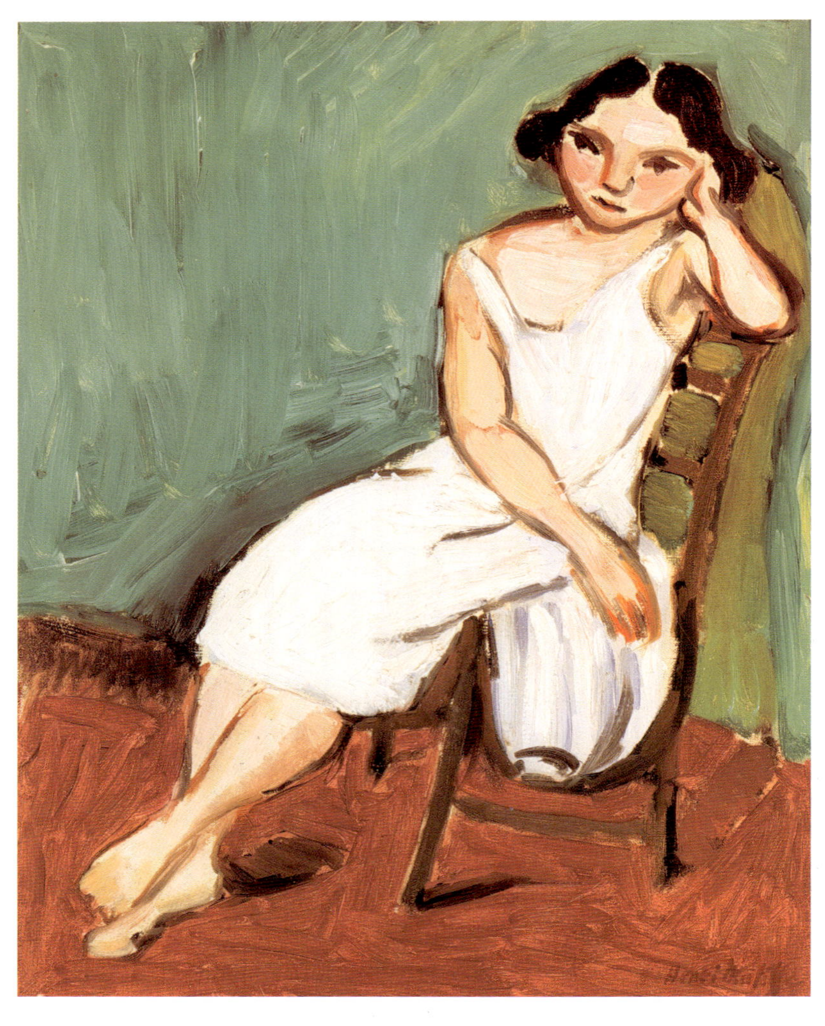

Seated Young Woman · 1909
Wallraf-Richartz Museum, Cologne

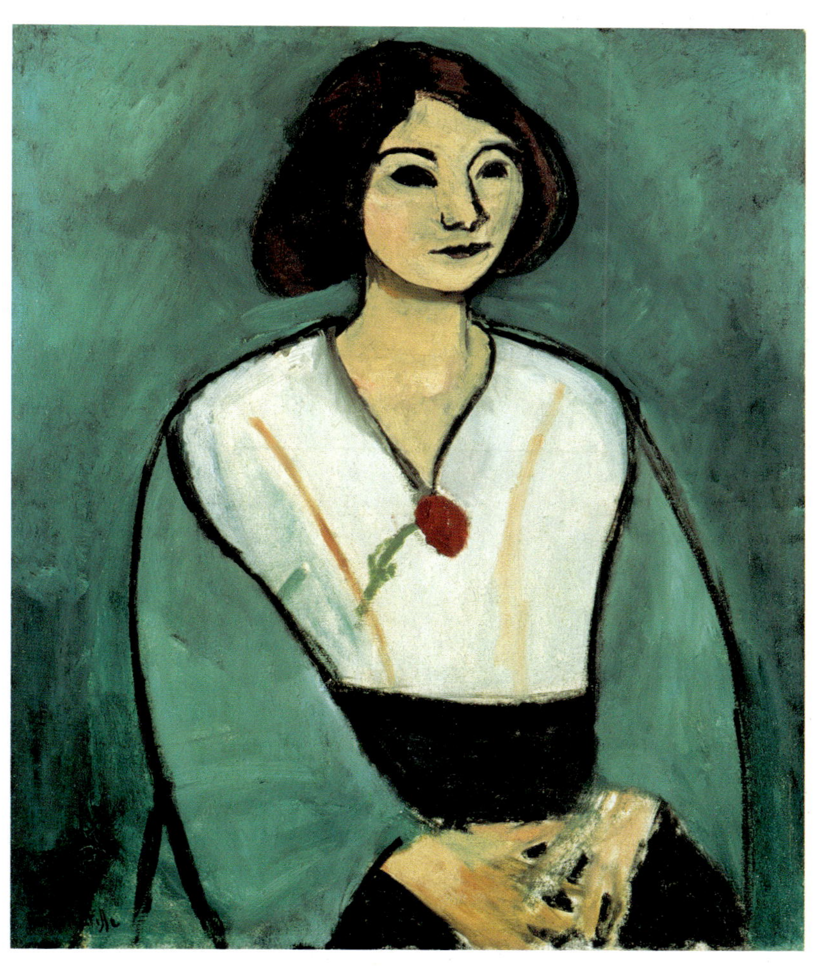

Lady in Green · 1909
Hermitage, Saint Petersburg
> **Music** · 1909–1910
Hermitage, Saint Petersburg
>> **The Dance (II)** · 1909–1910
Hermitage, Saint Petersburg

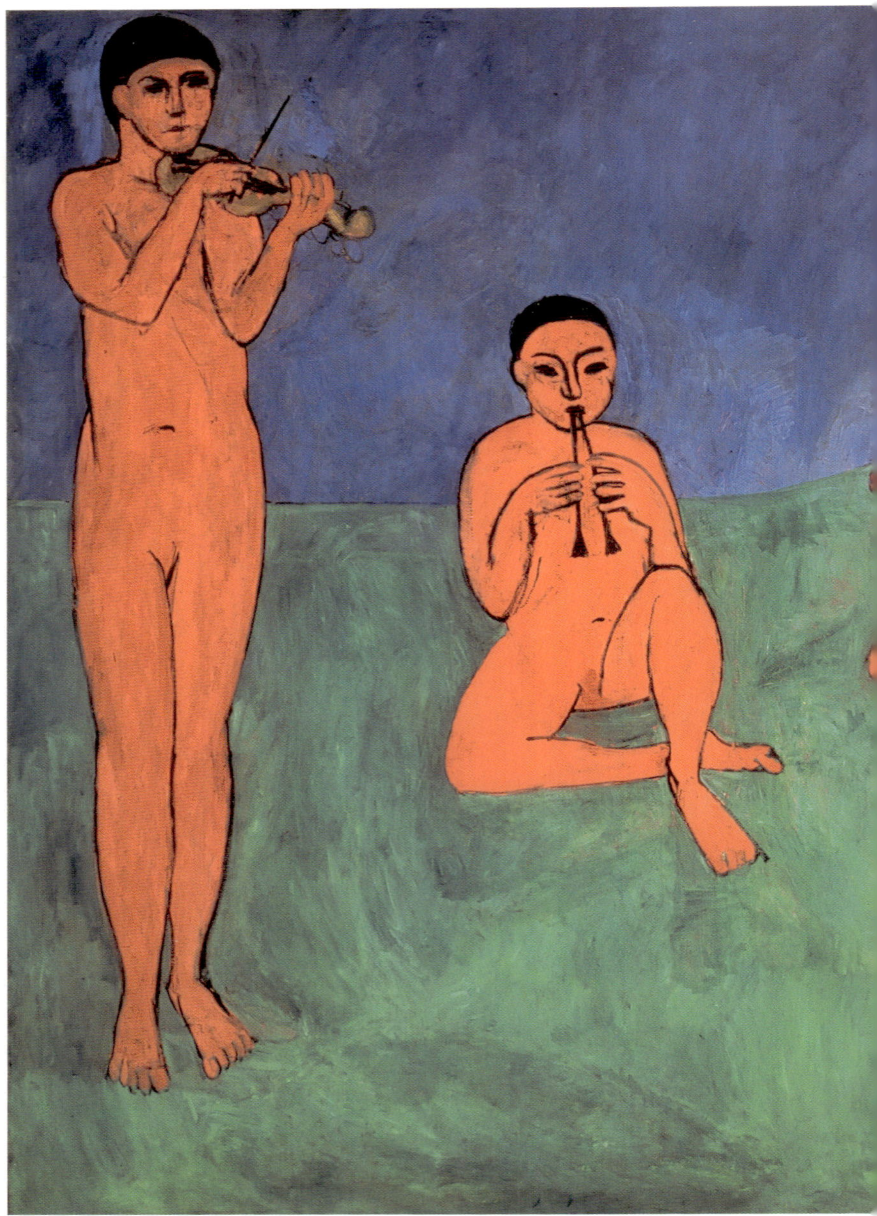

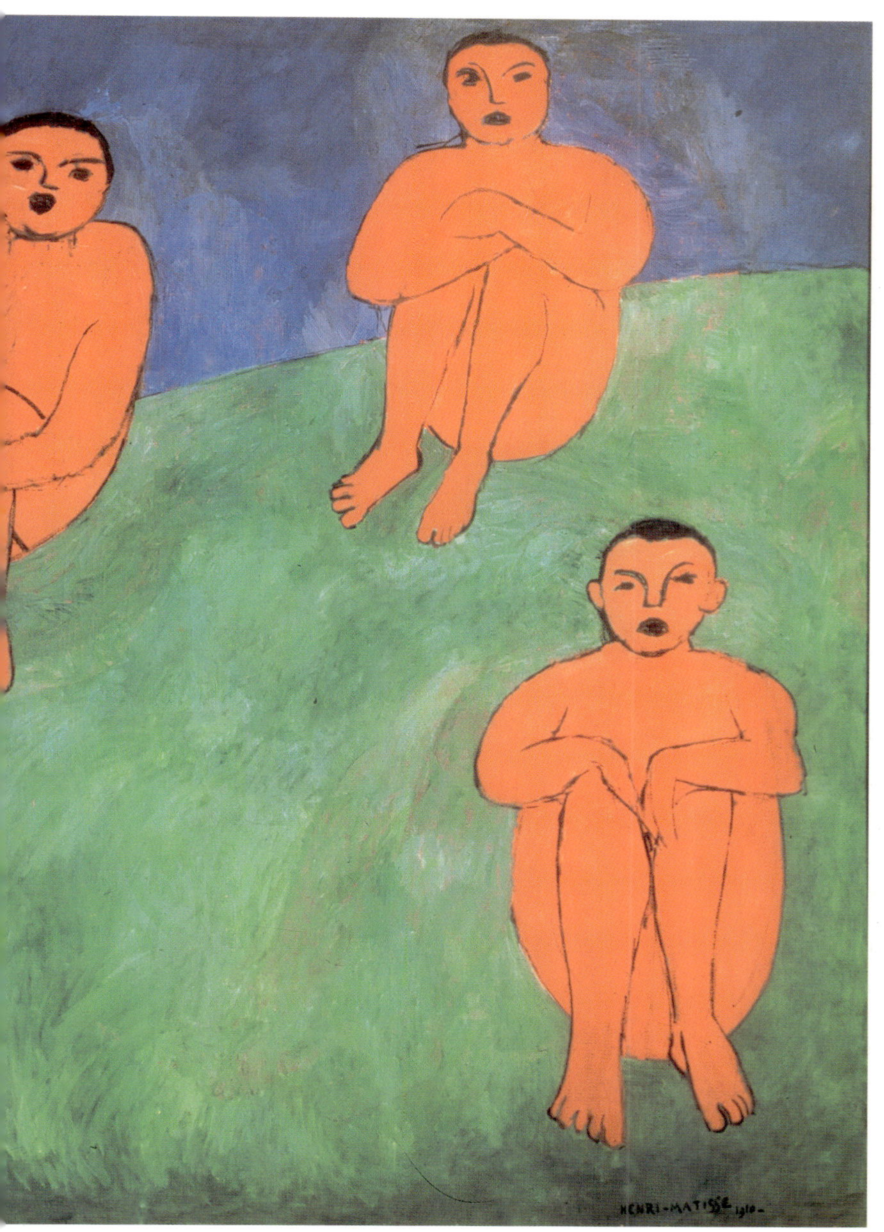
HENRI-MATISSE 1910

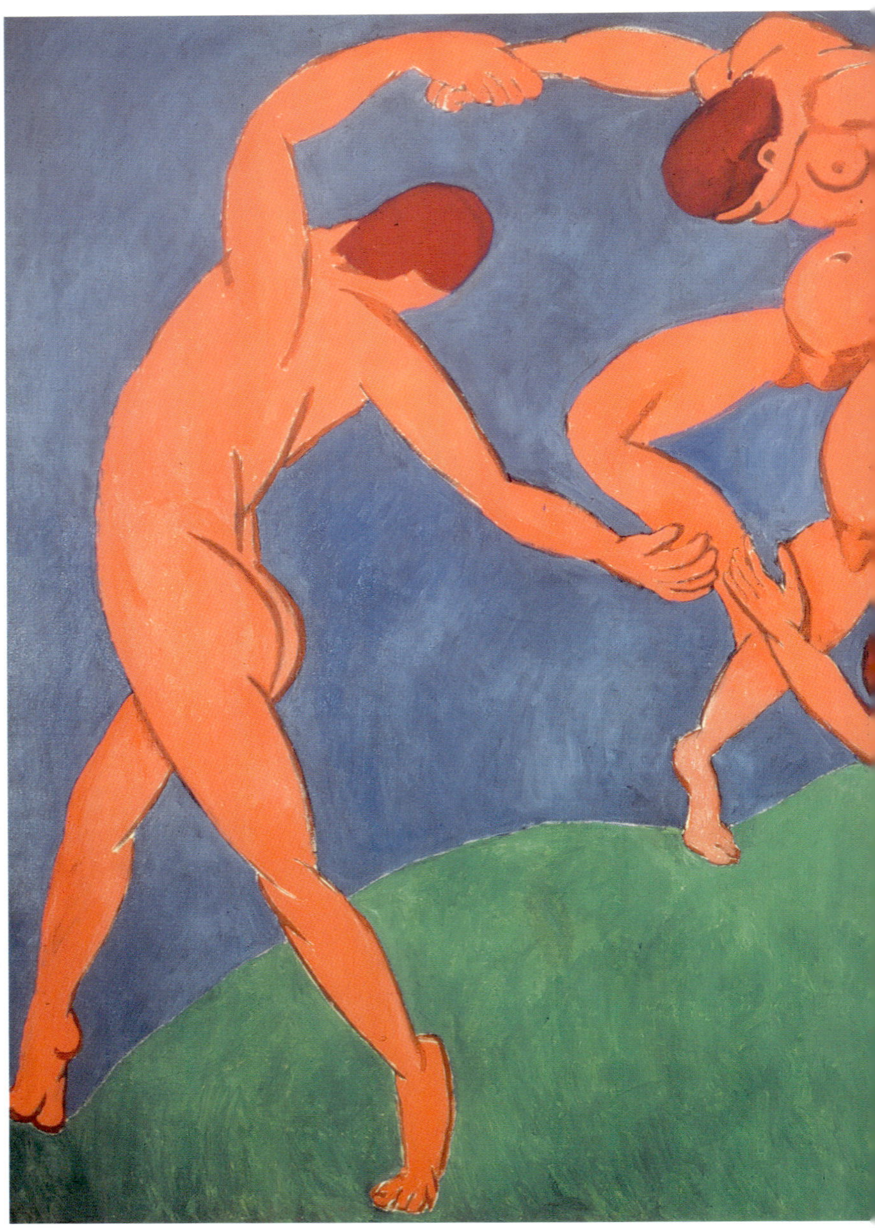

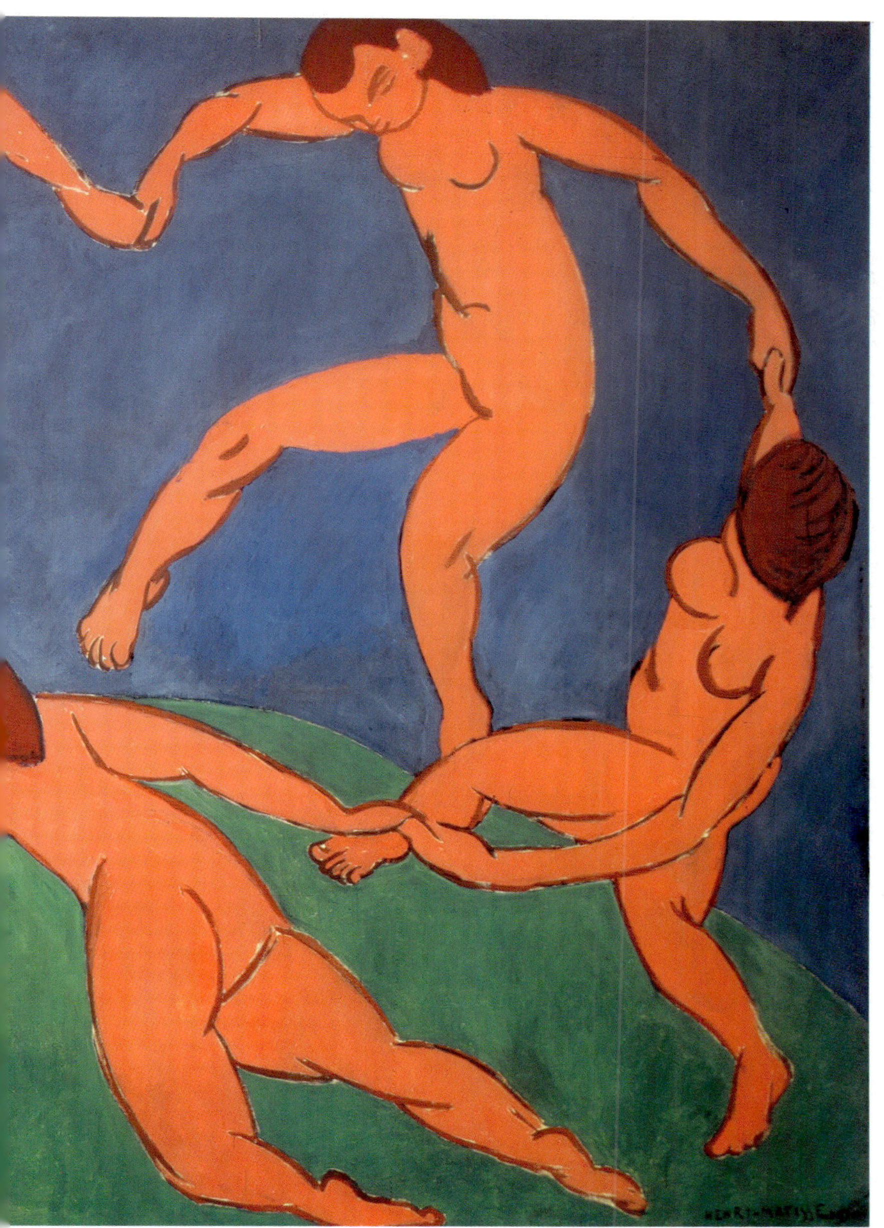

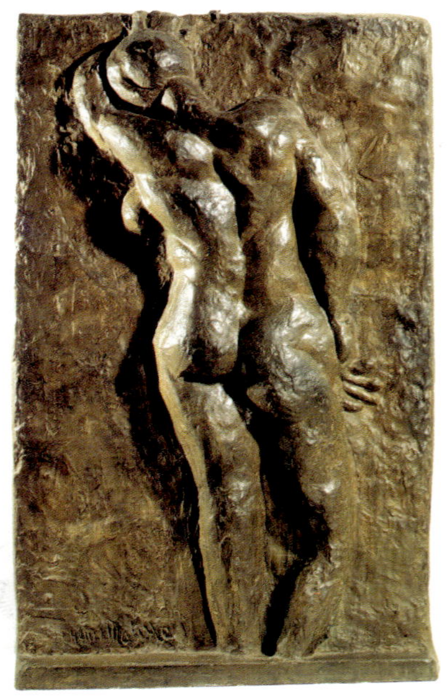

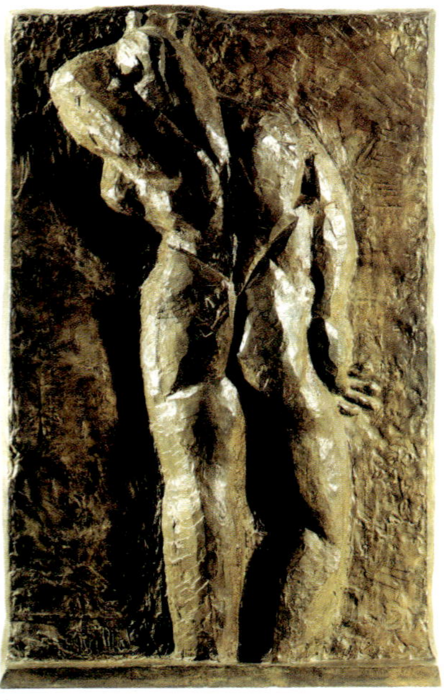

The Back (I) · 1913
Musée national d'art moderne, Paris
The Back (II) · 1909
Musée national d'art moderne, Paris

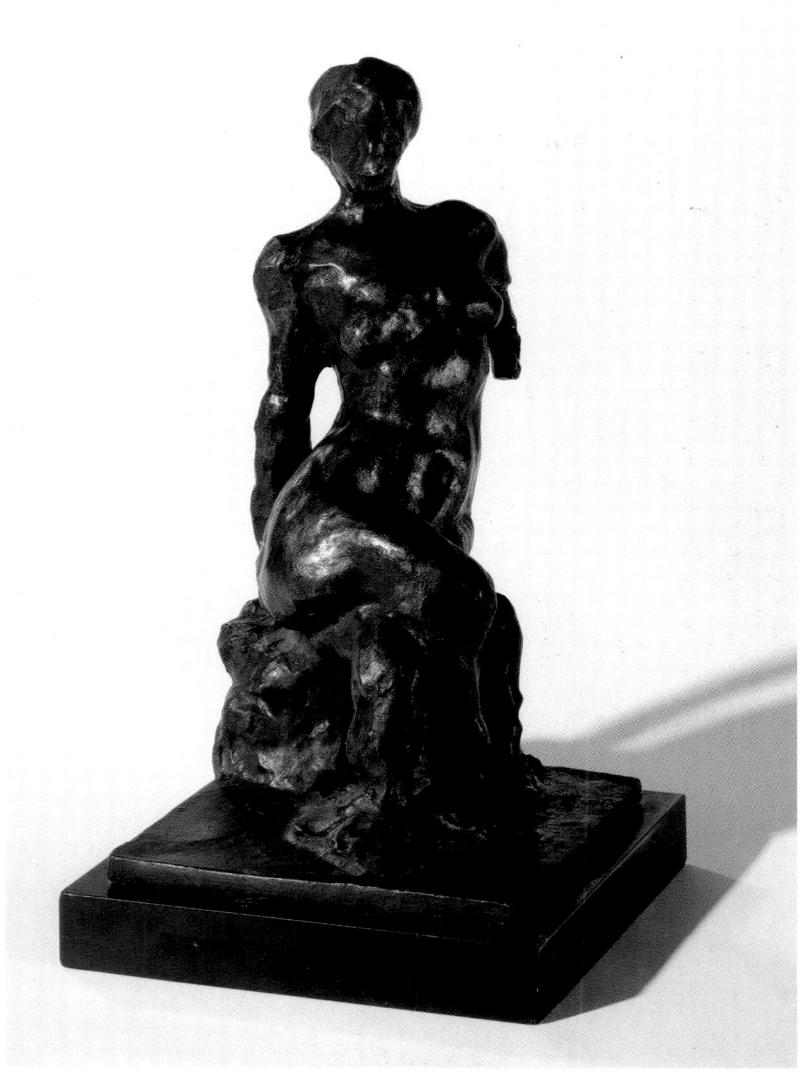

Seated Nude, Arm behind the Back · 1909
Musée national d'art moderne, Paris

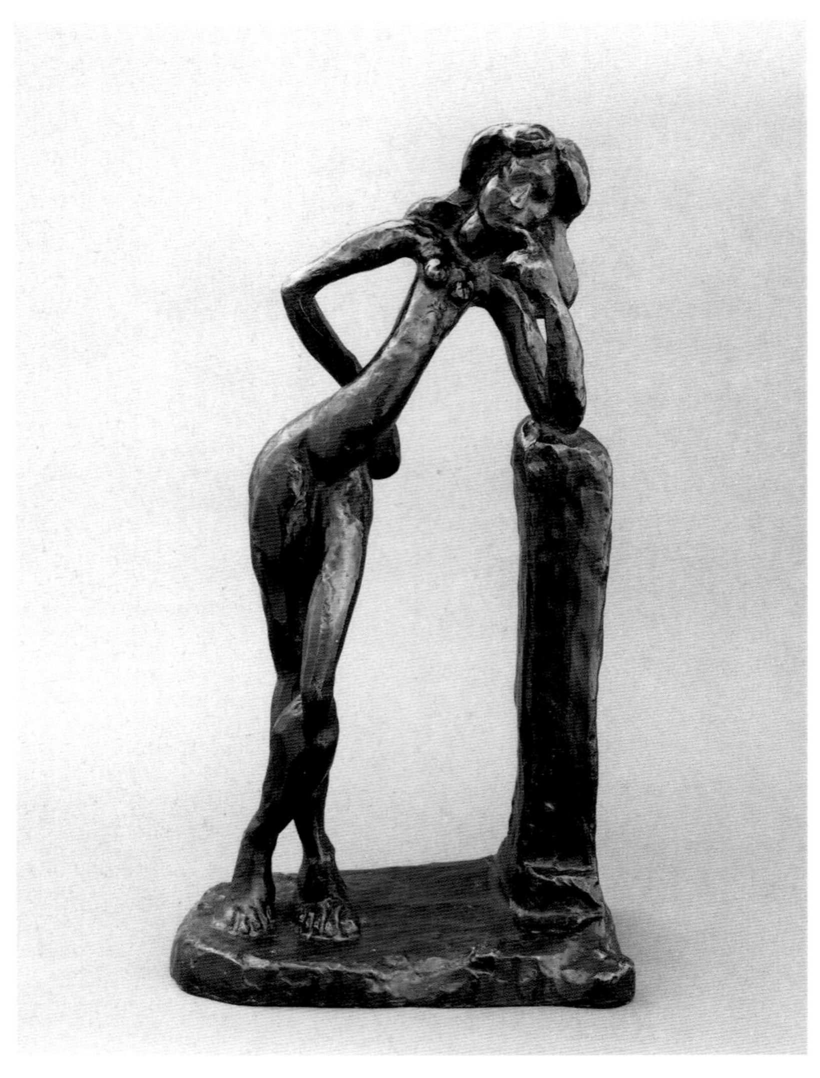

The Serpentine · 1909
Private collection

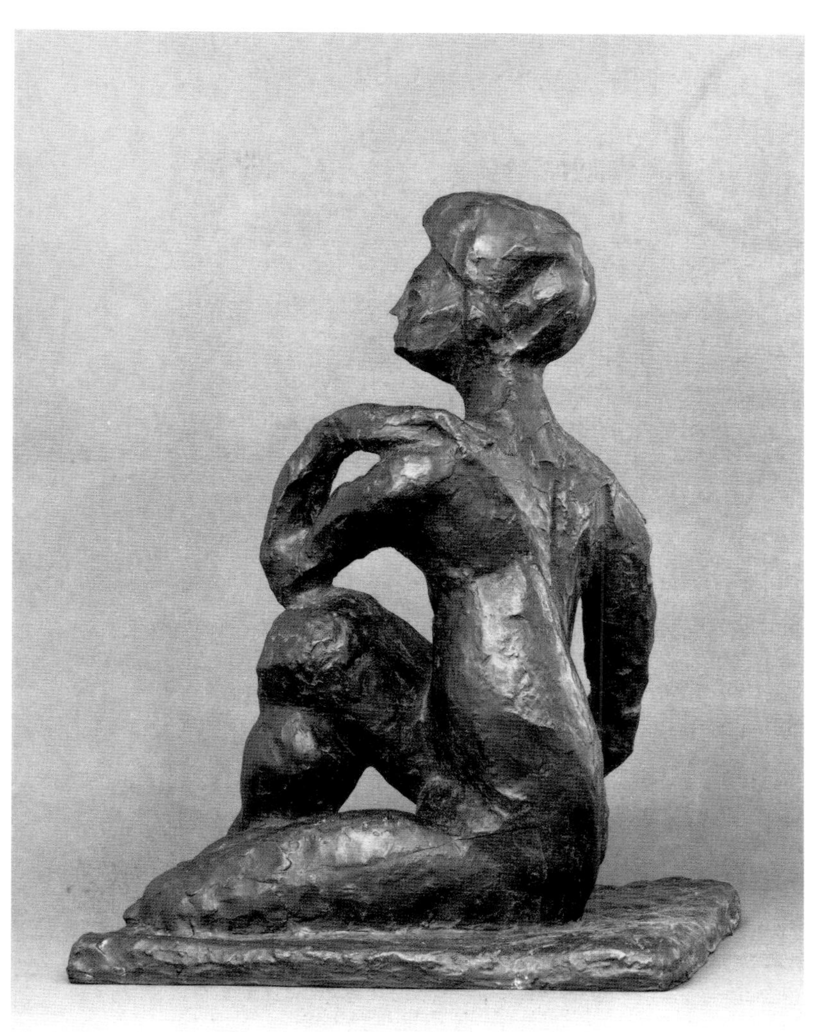

Seated Nude (Olga) • 1909–1910
Private collection

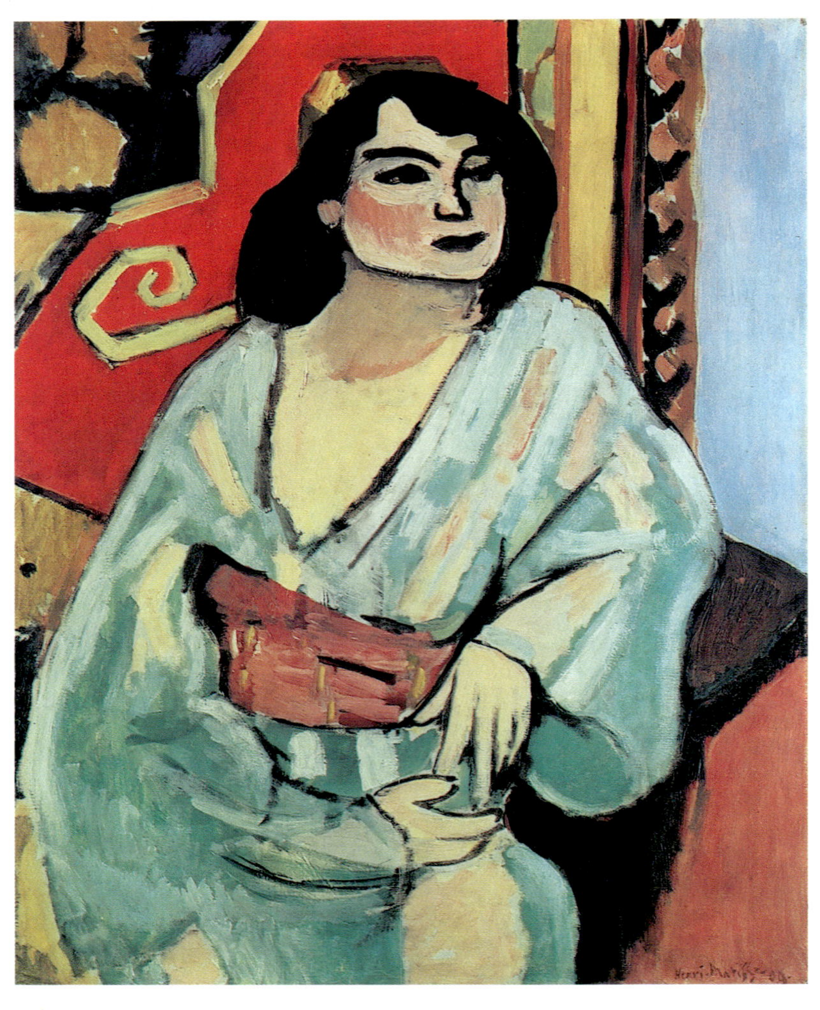

Algerian Woman • 1909
Musée des arts décoratifs, Paris

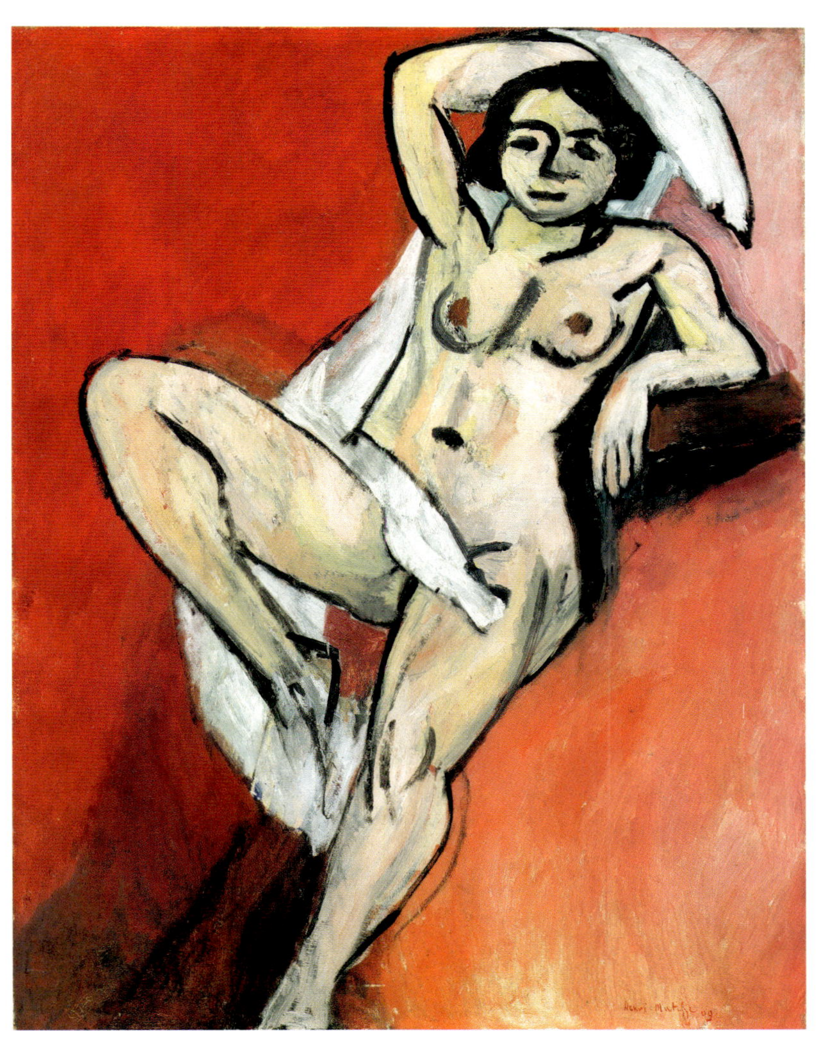

Nude with a White Scarf • 1909
Statens Museum for Kunst, Copenhagen

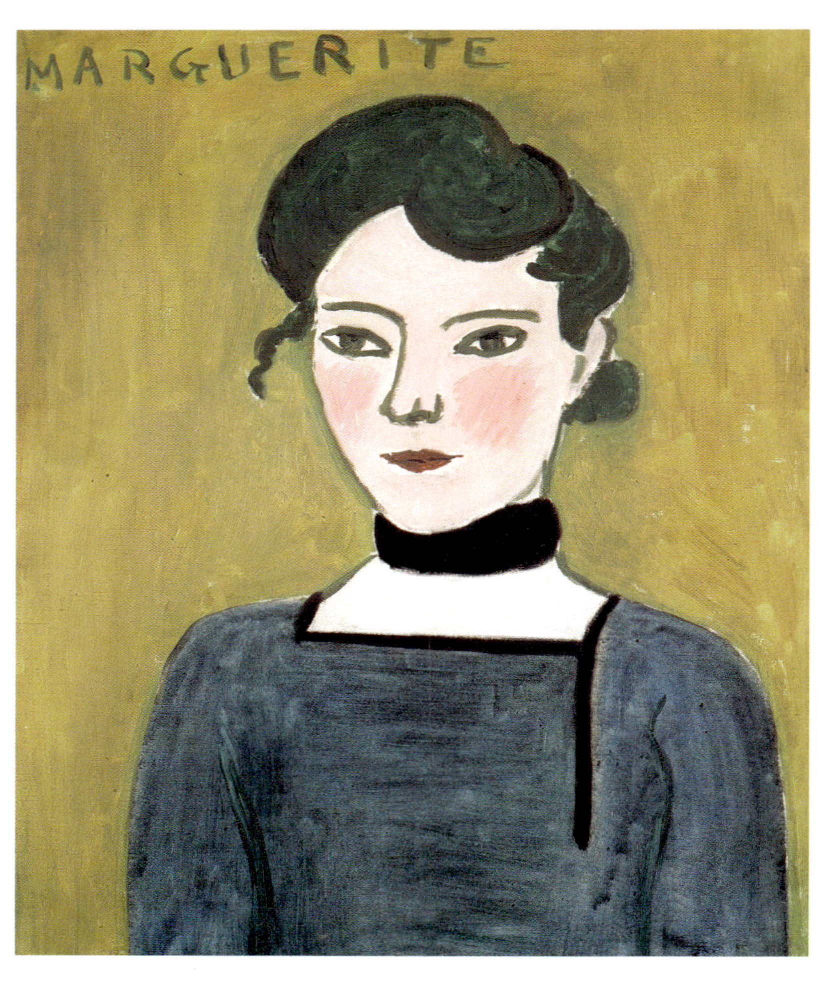

Marguerite • 1907

Musée Picasso, Paris

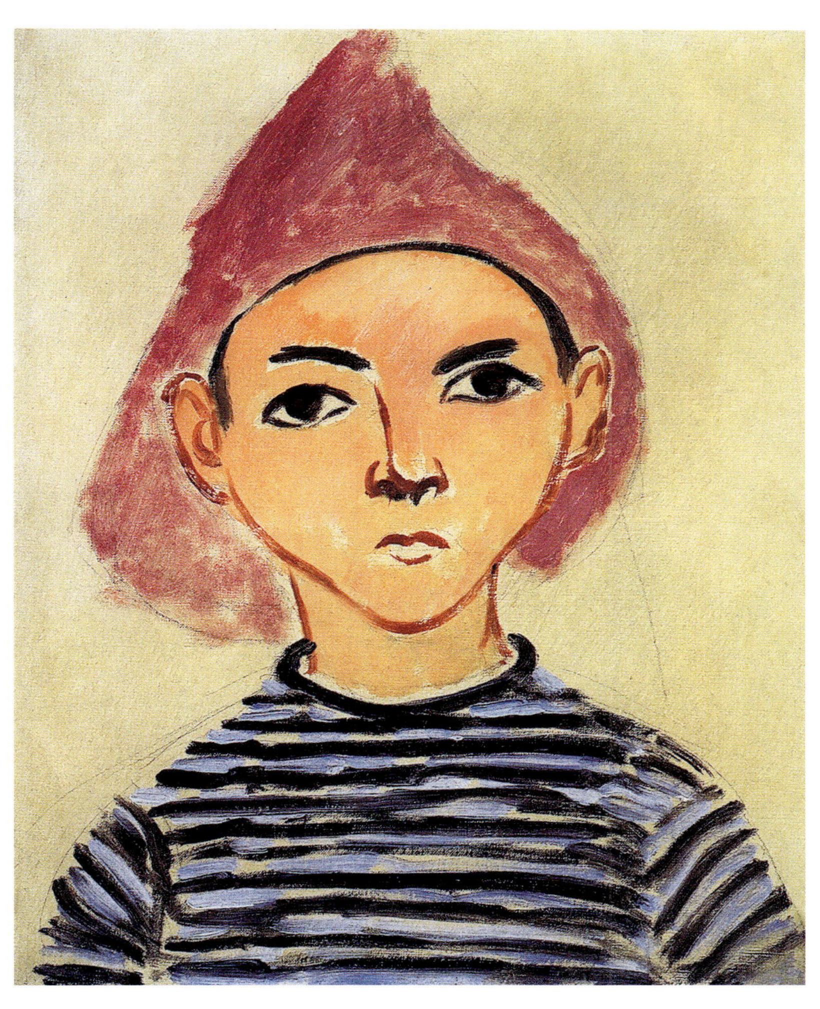

Pierre Matisse • 1909
Private collection
> **Still Life with Fruit** • 1910
Pushkin Museum, Moscow

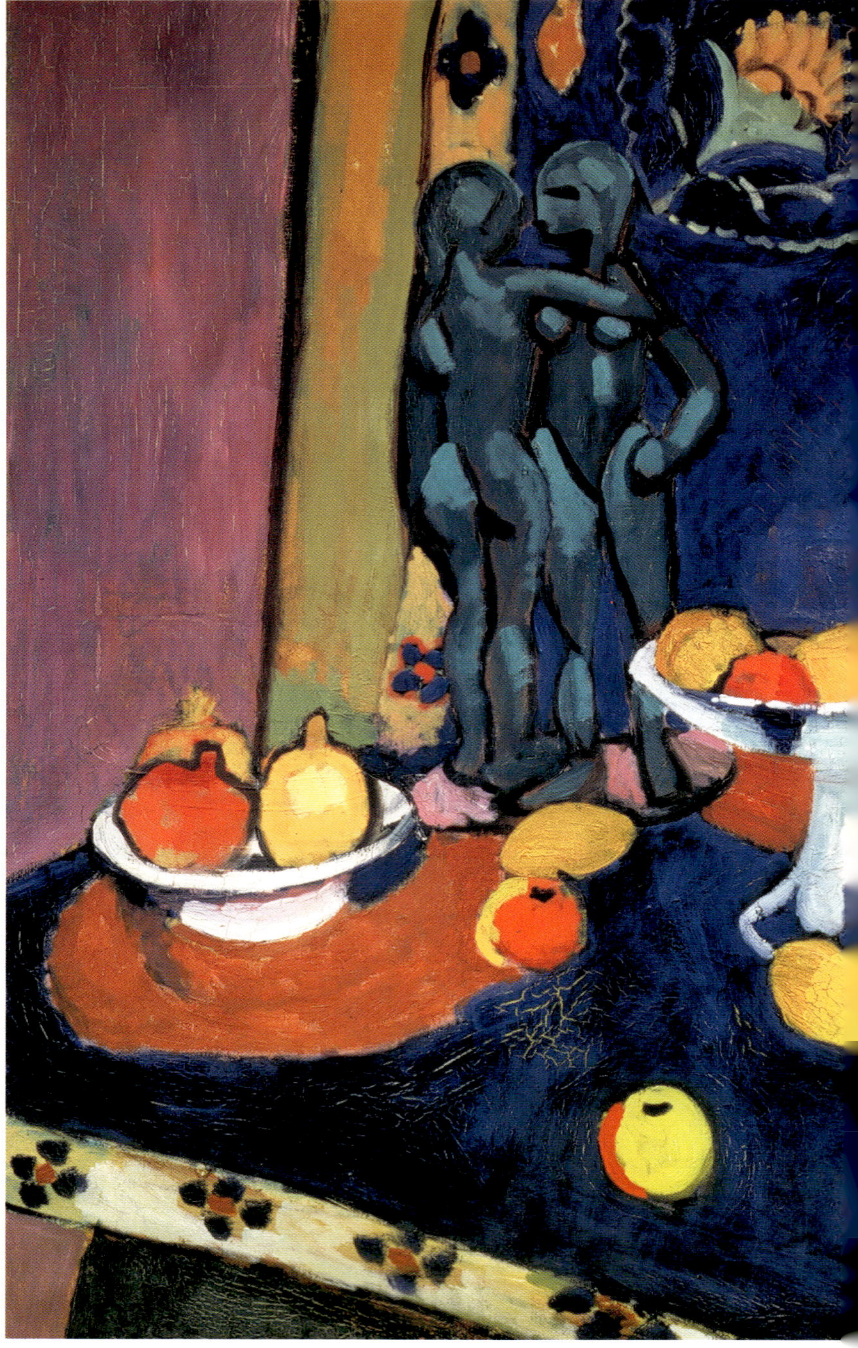

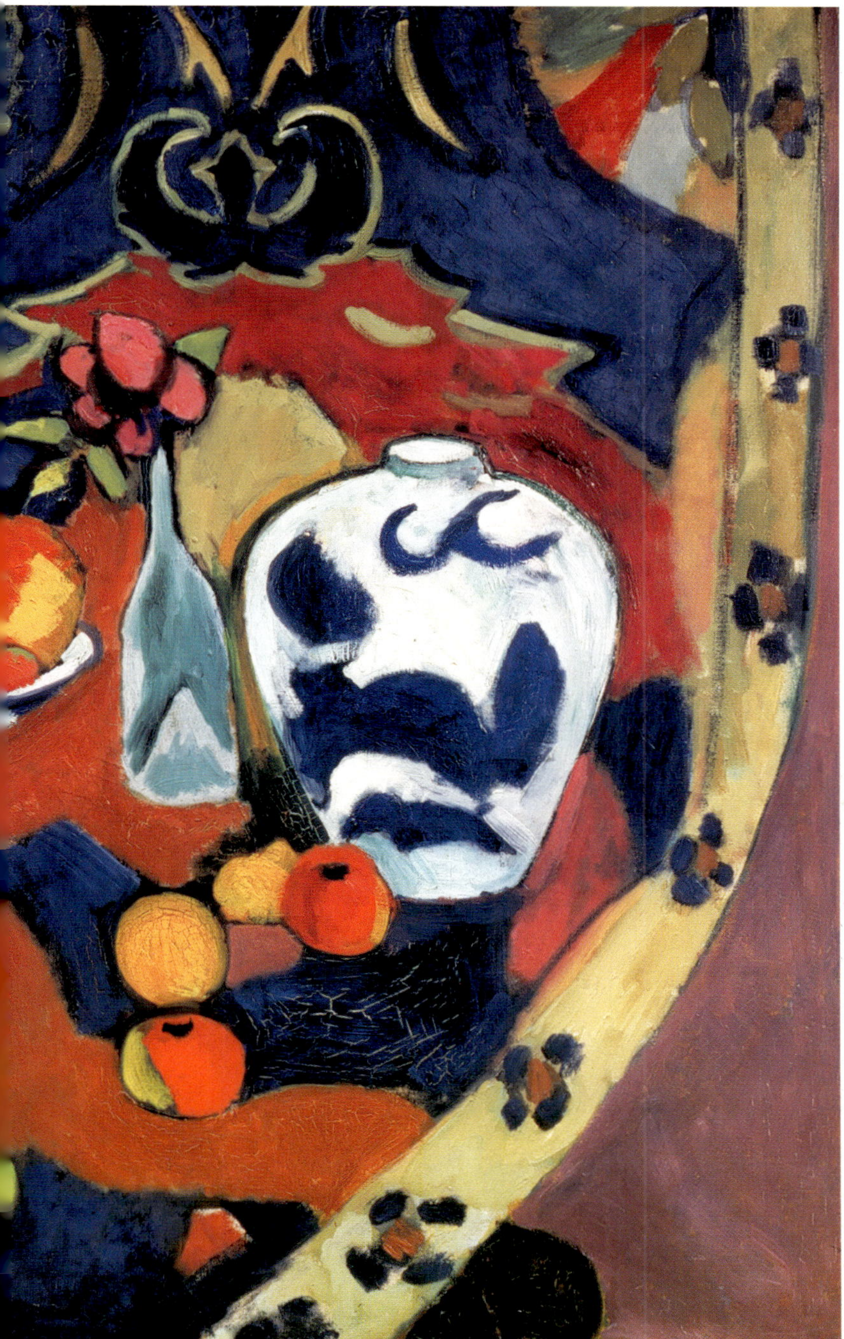

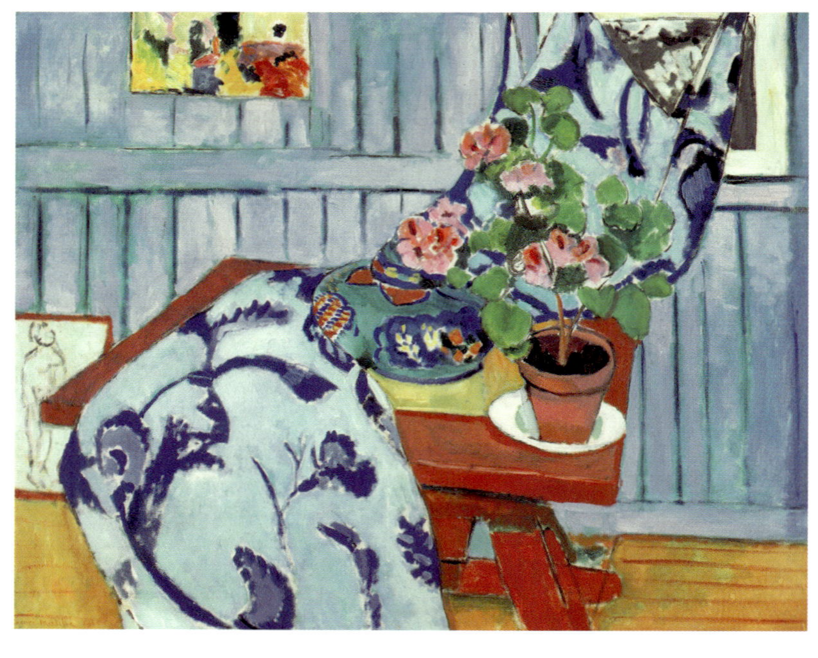

Still Life with Geraniums • 1910

Staatsgalerie moderner Kunst, Munich

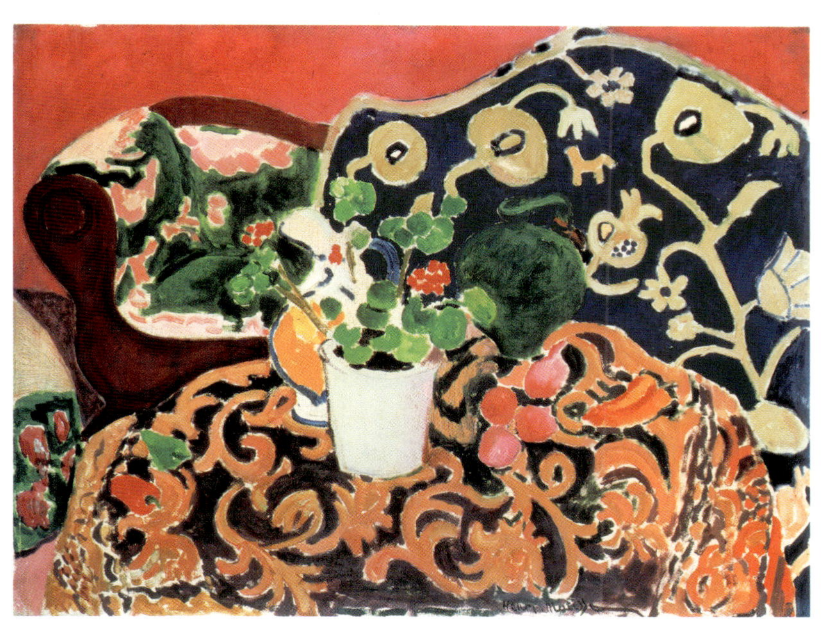

Spanish Still Life · 1910–1911
Hermitage, Saint Petersburg
> **Still Life with a Pewter Jug and Pink Statuette** · 1910
Hermitage, Saint Petersburg

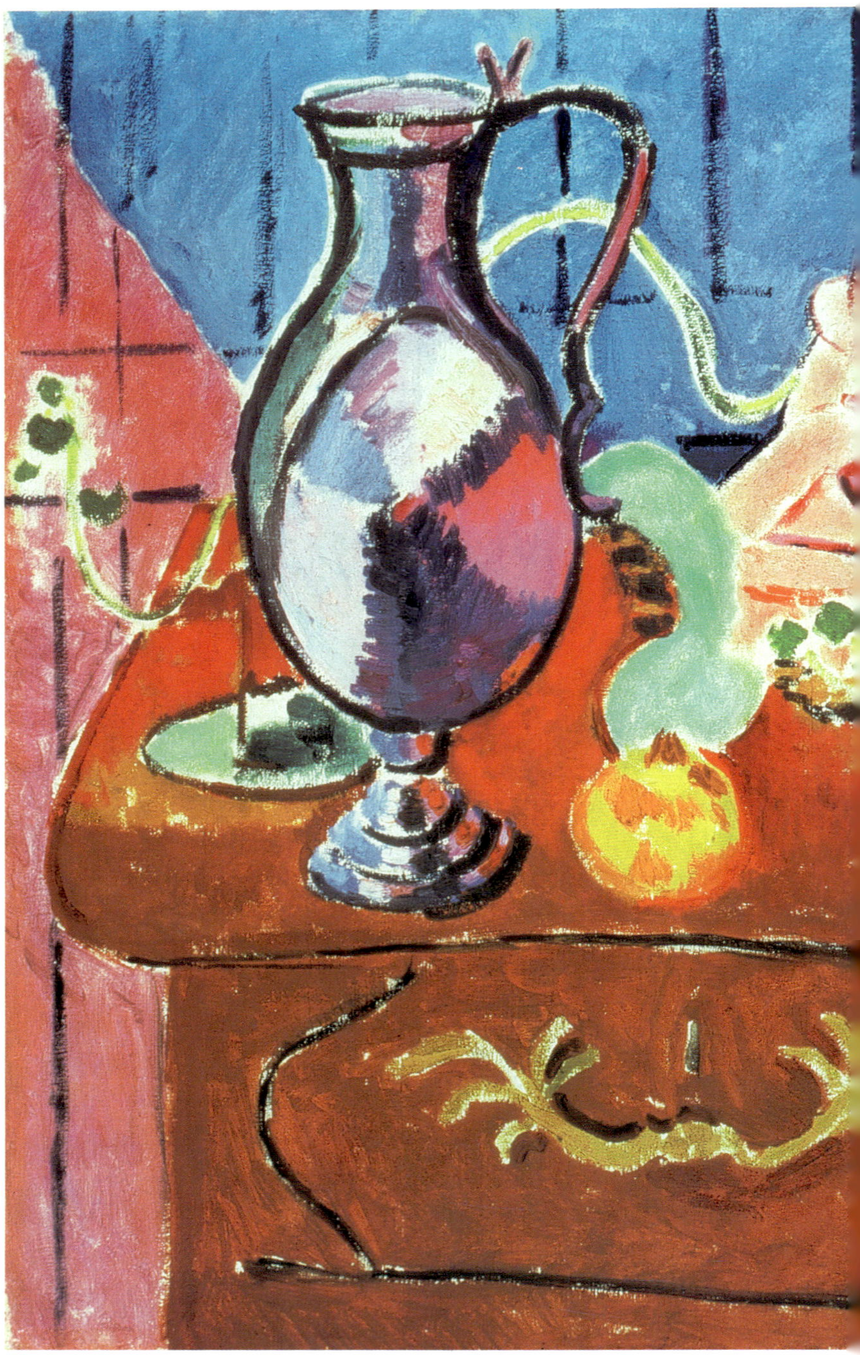

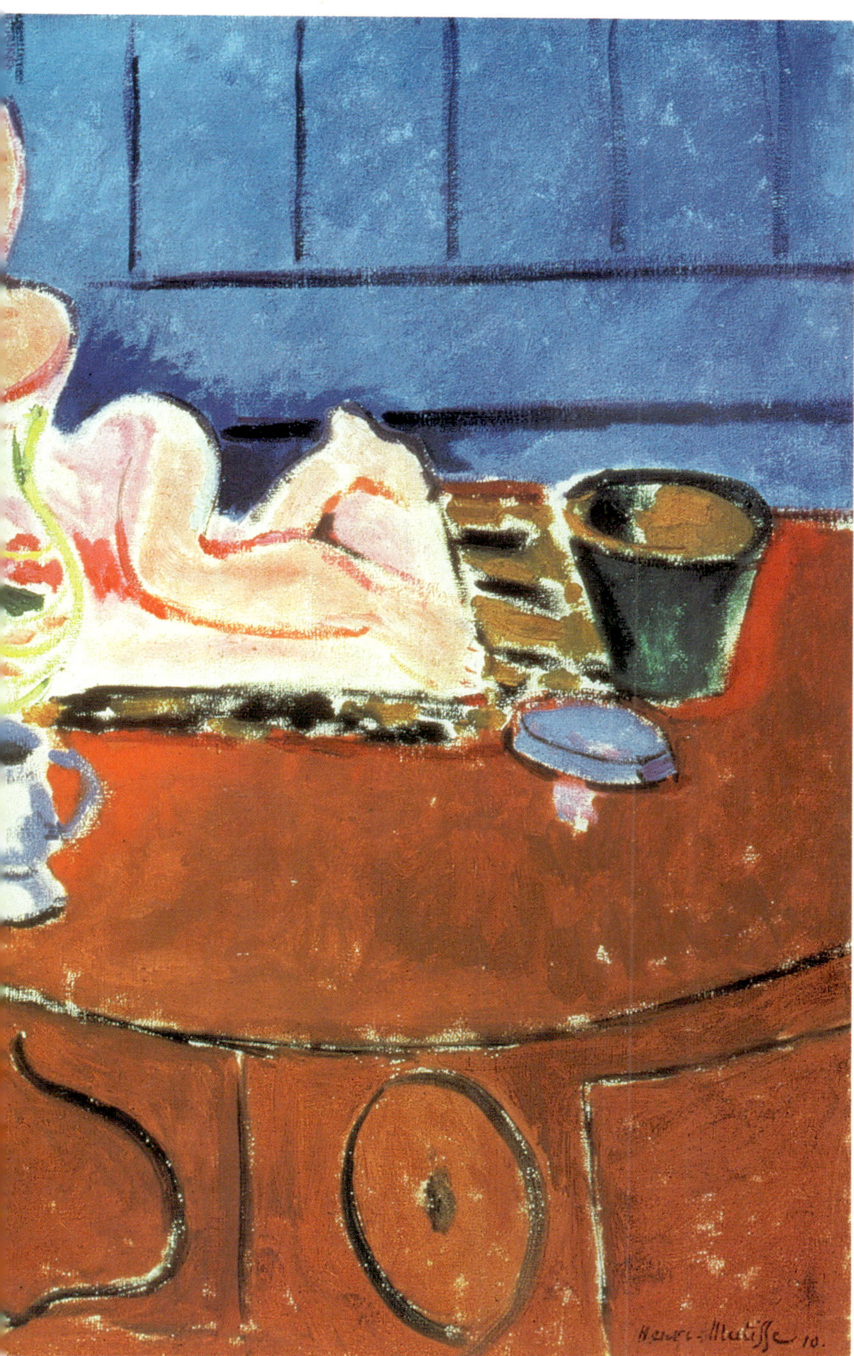
Henri-Matisse 10.

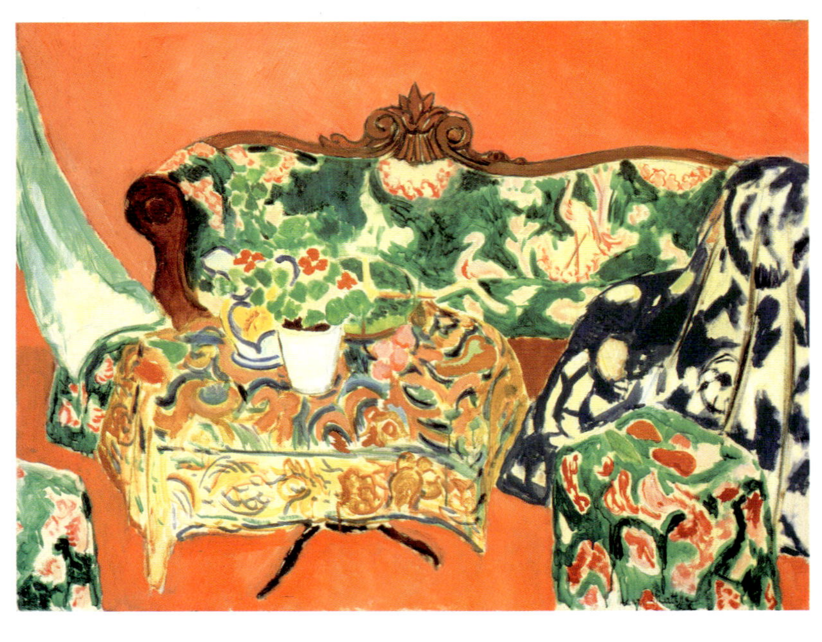

Seville Still Life · 1910–1911

Hermitage, Saint Petersburg

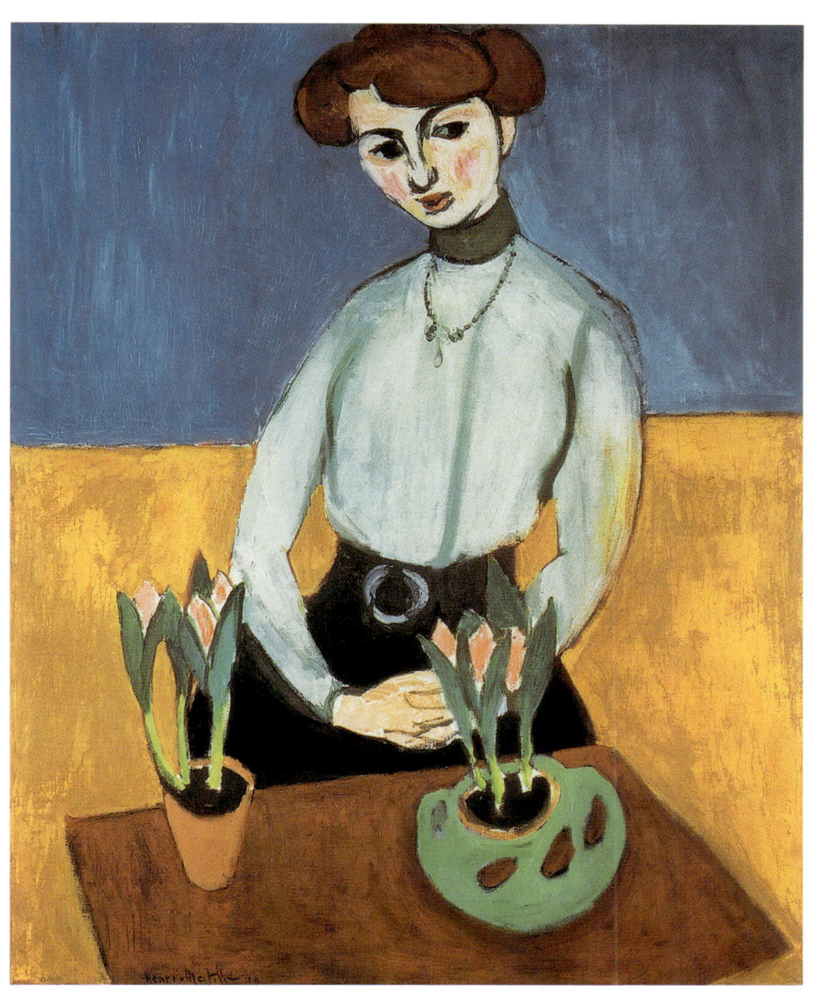

Girl with Tulips (Jeanne Vaderin) • 1910
Hermitage, Saint Petersburg

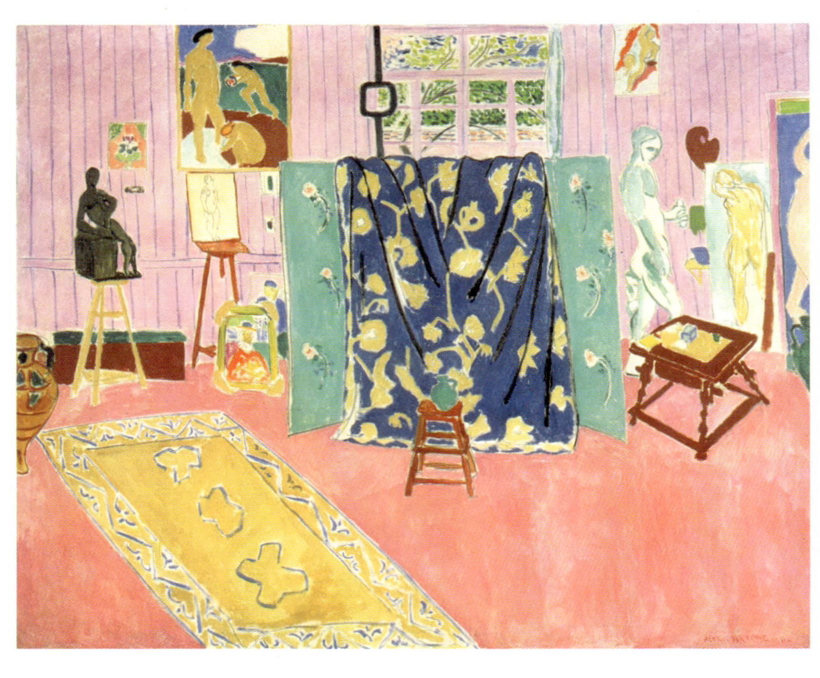

The Pink Studio · 1911

Pushkin Museum, Moscow

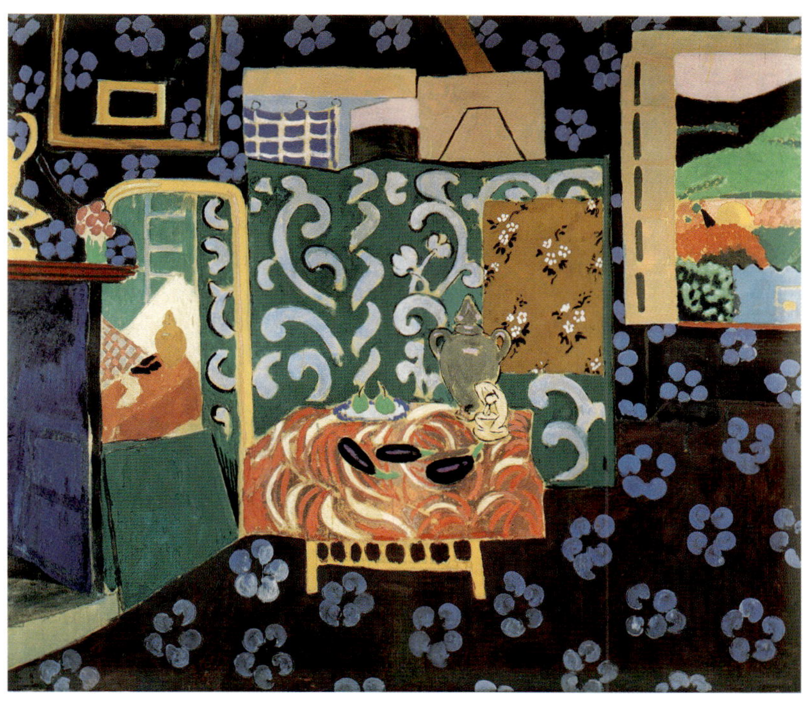

Interior with Aubergines · Summer 1911
Musée de Grenoble
> **The Red Studio** · Autumn 1911
The Museum of Modern Art, New York, Mrs. Simon Guggenheim Fund
>> **The Painter's Family** · Spring 1911
Hermitage, Saint Petersburg

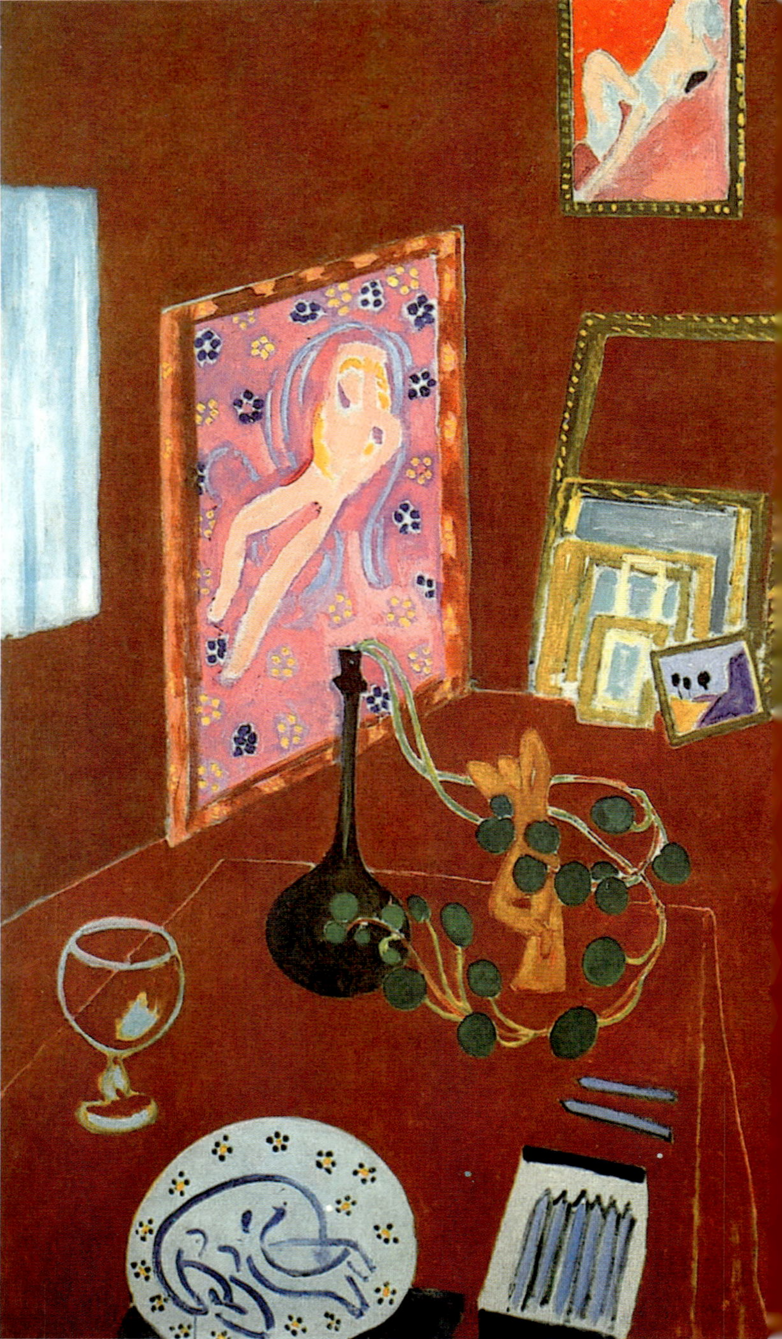

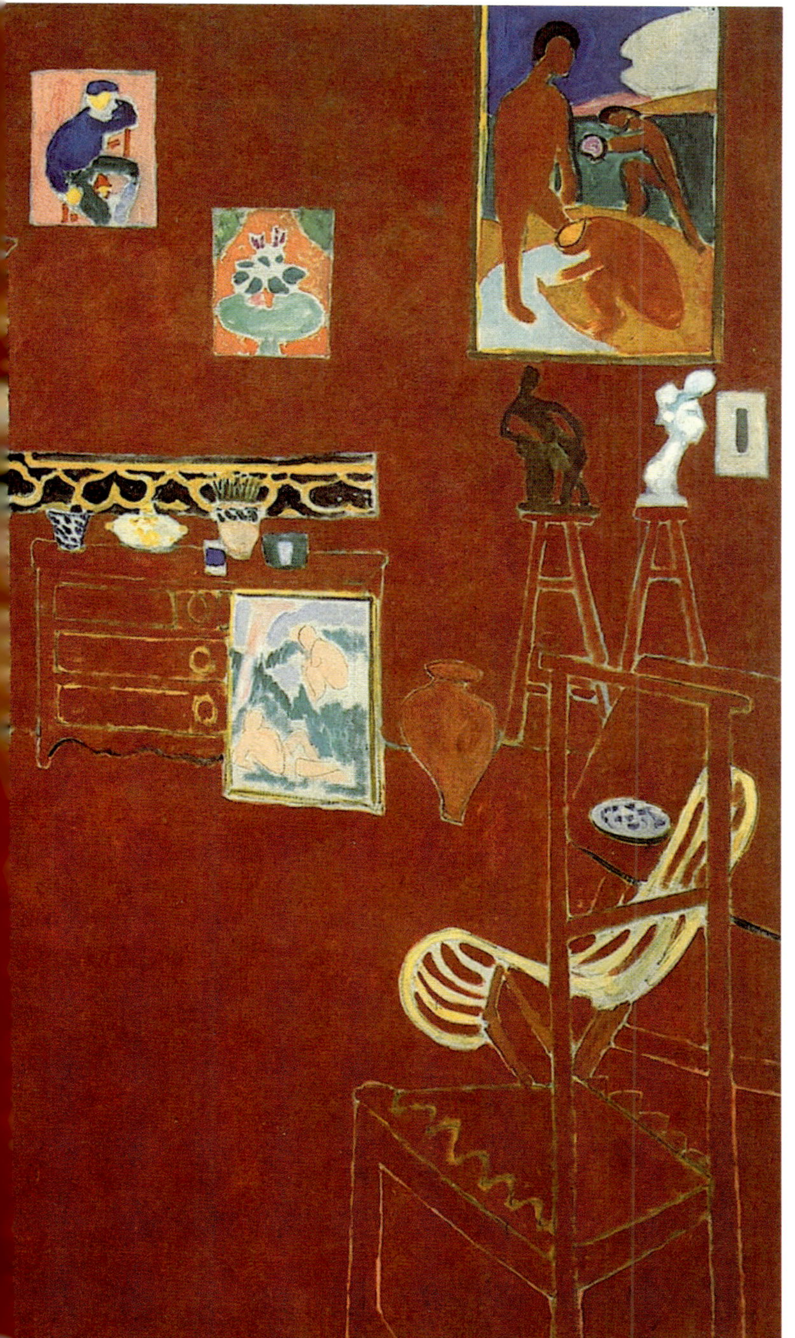

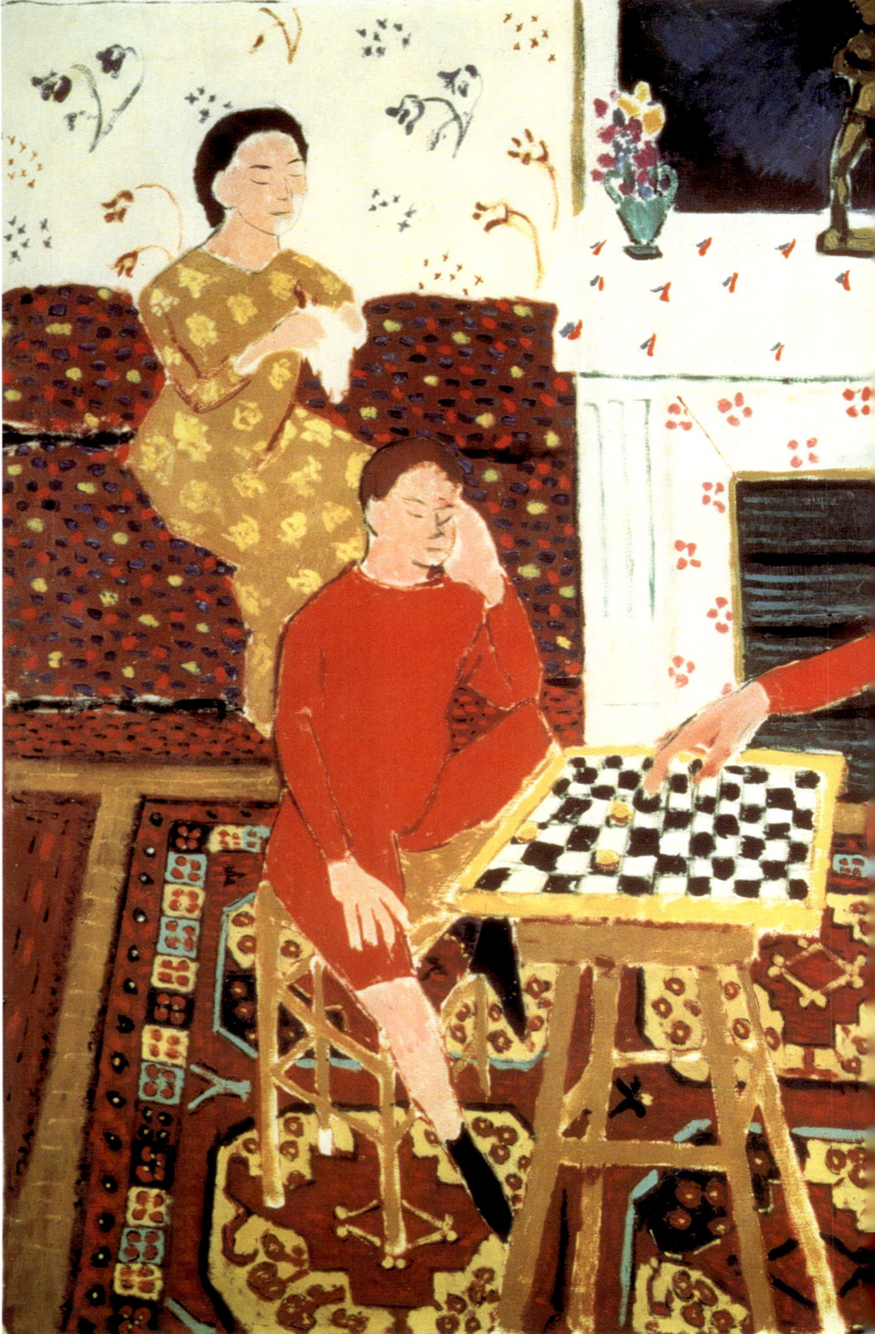

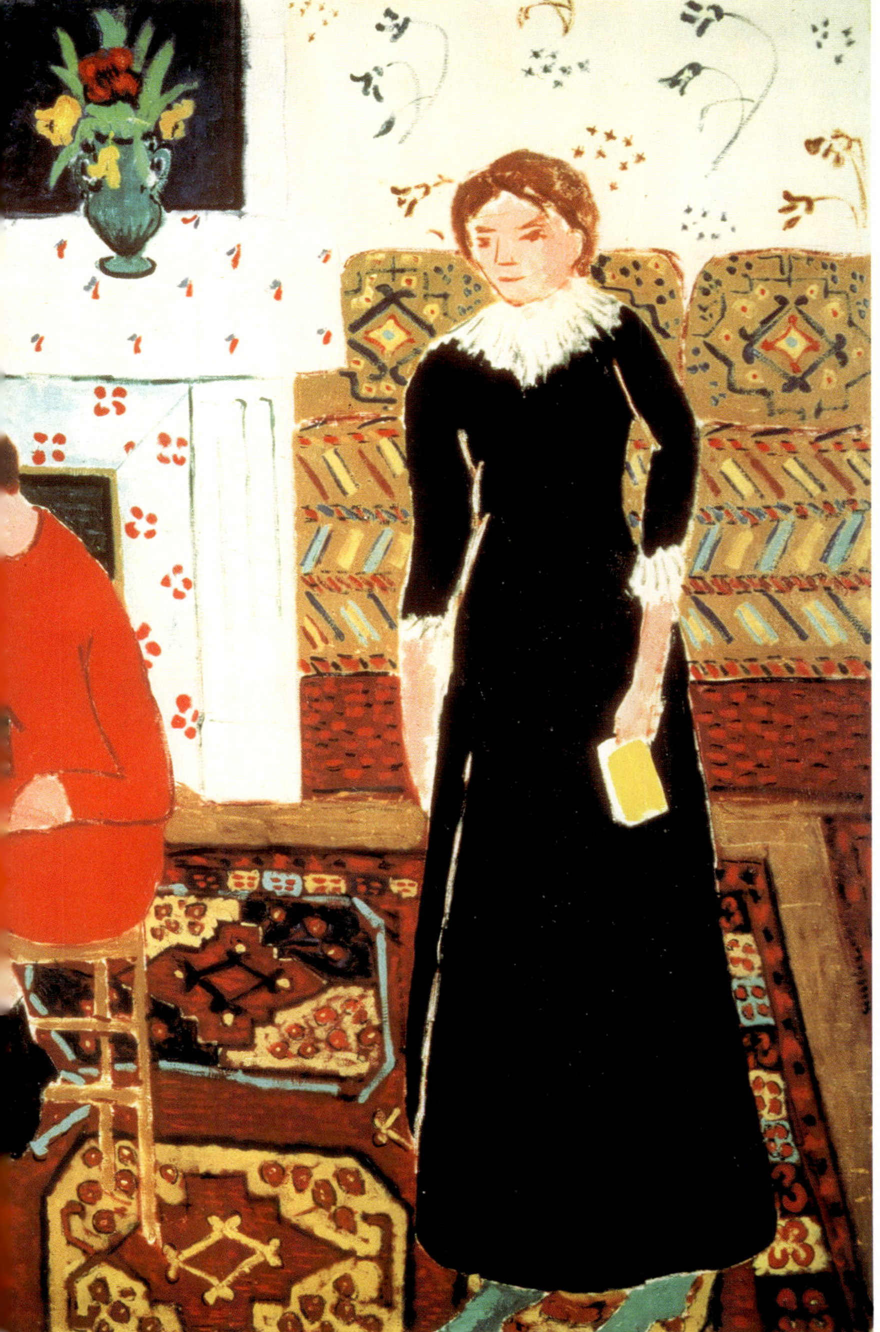

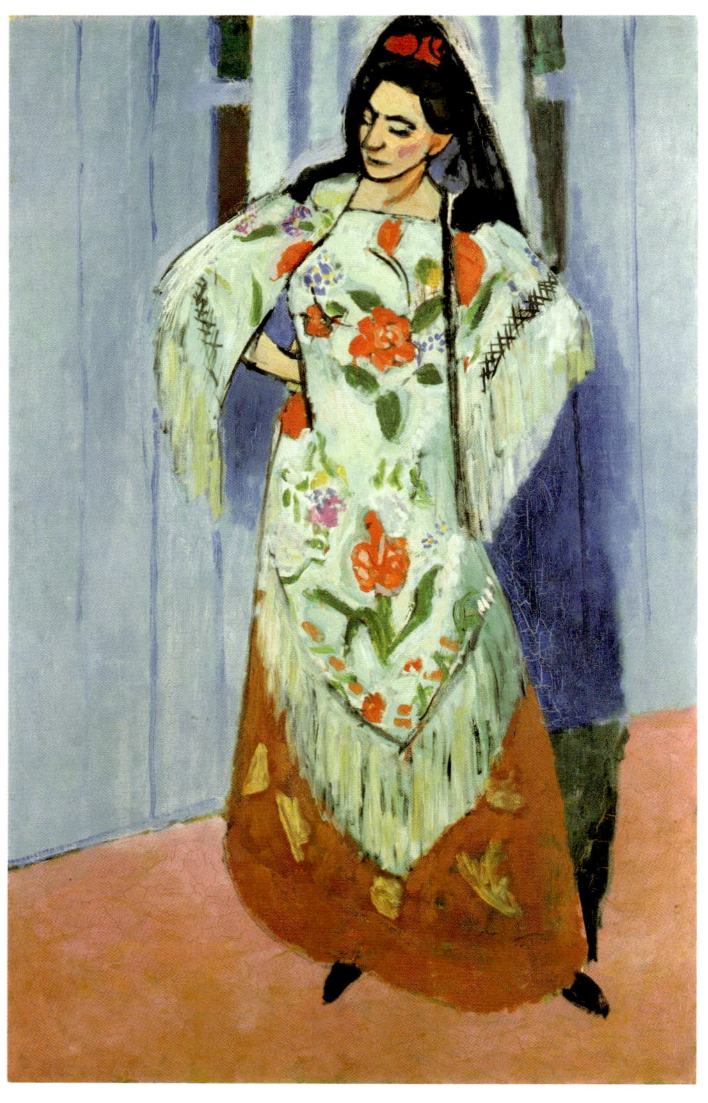

The Manila Shawl • 1911
Rudolf Staechelin Family Foundation, Basel

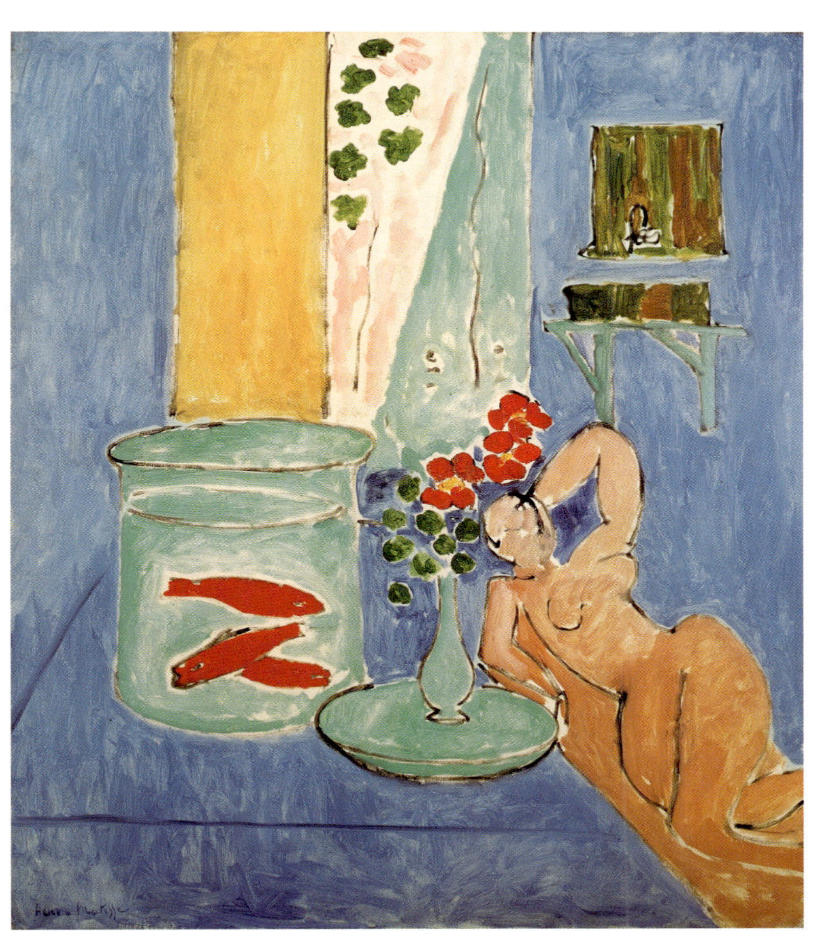

Goldfish and Sculpture • 1912
The Museum of Modern Art, New York

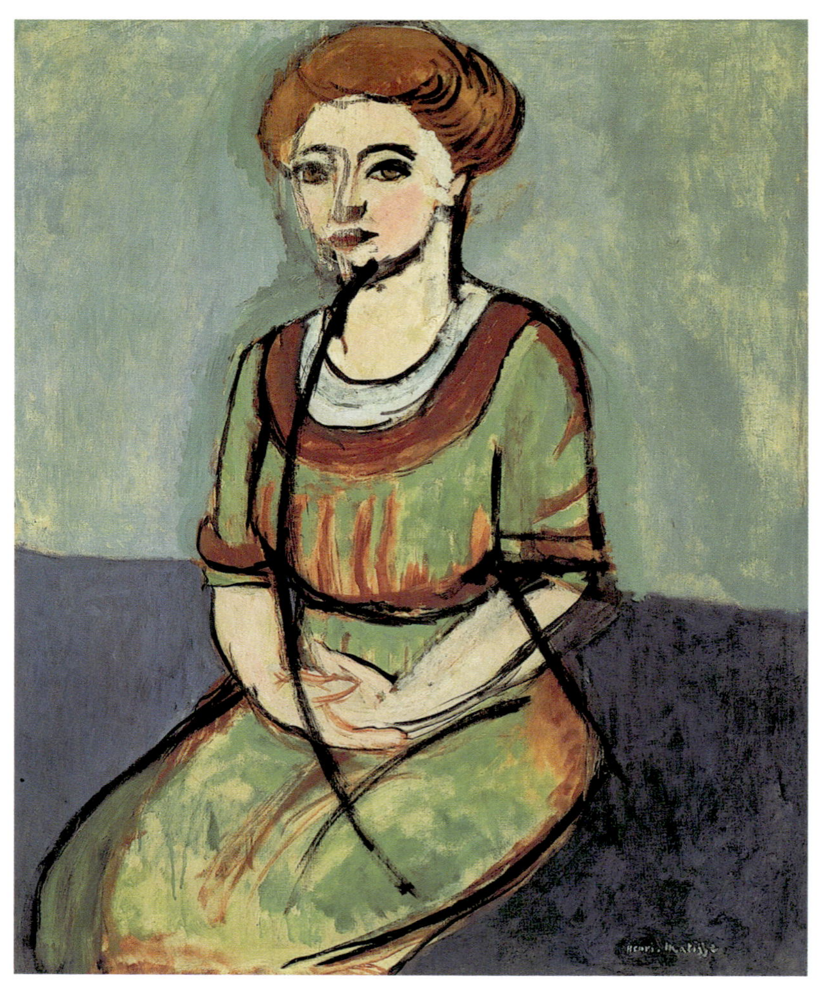

Portrait of Olga Merson · Summer 1911

The Museum of Fine Arts, Houston

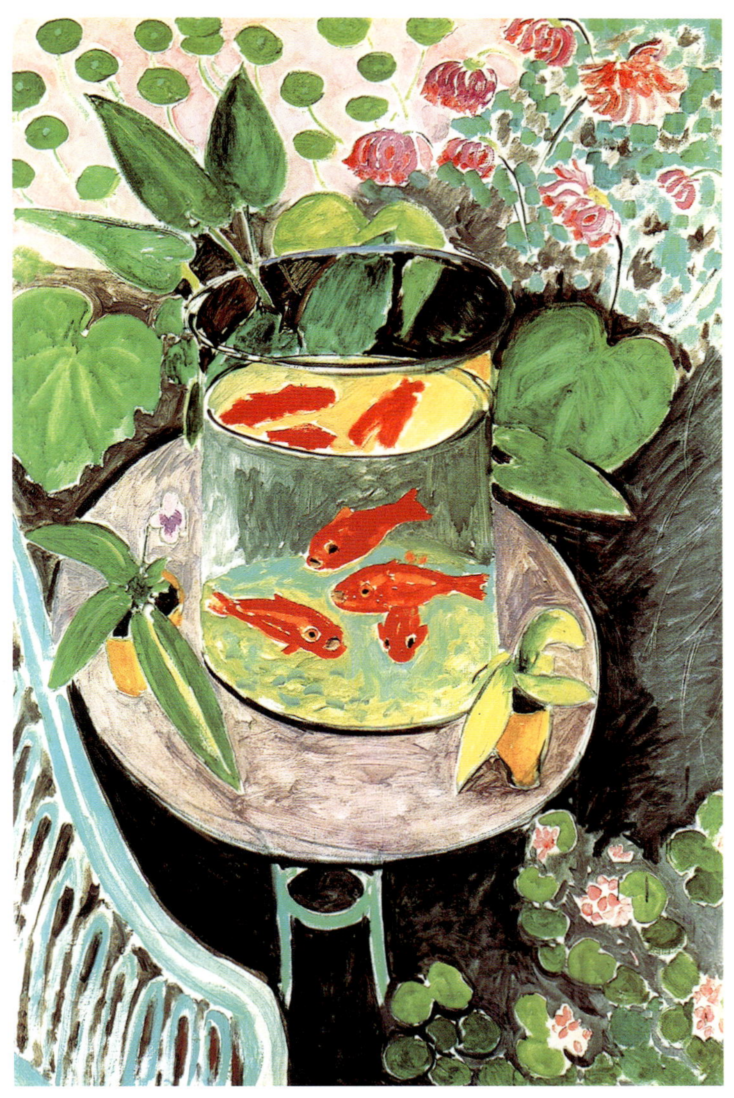

Goldfish • 1912

Pushkin Museum, Moscow

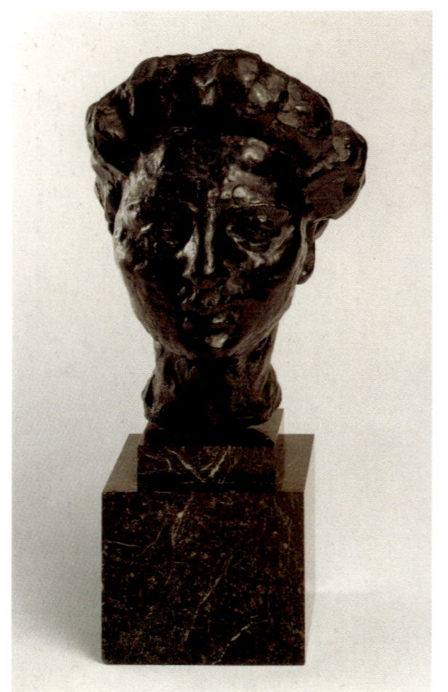

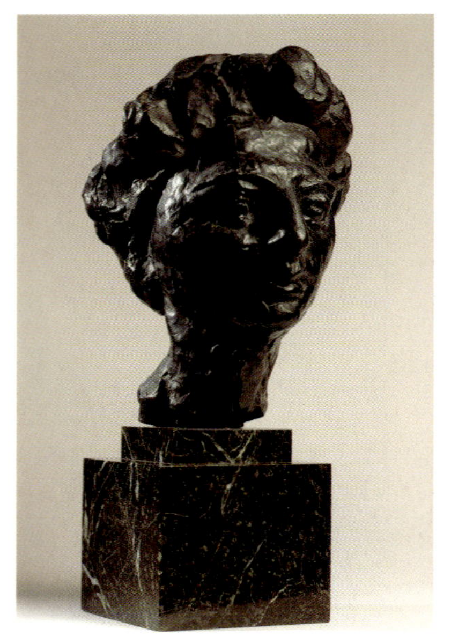

Jeannette I • 1910

Musée national d'art moderne, Paris

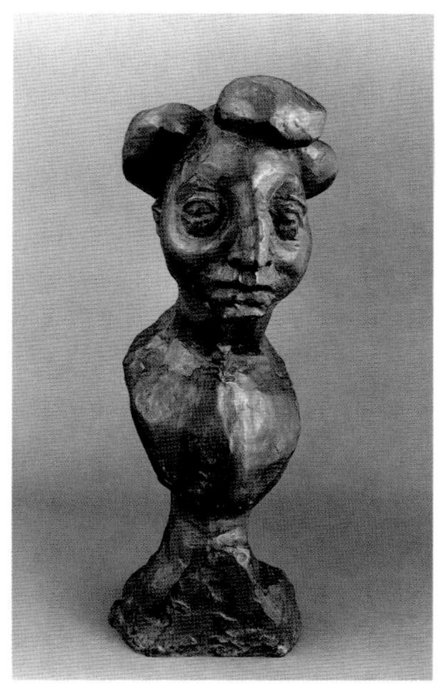

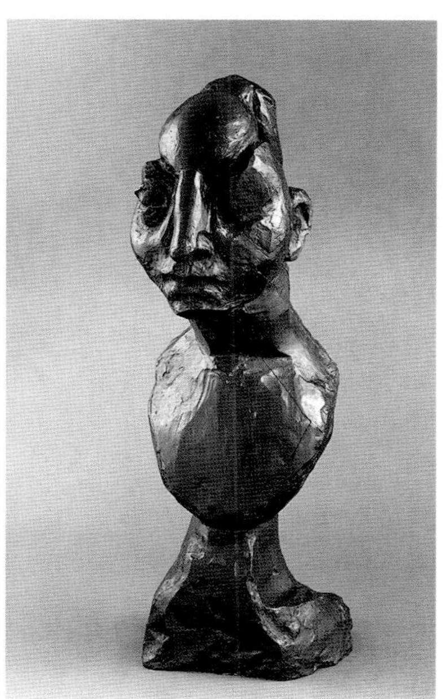

Jeannette III • 1911
Private collection
Jeannette V • Autumn 1913
Private collection

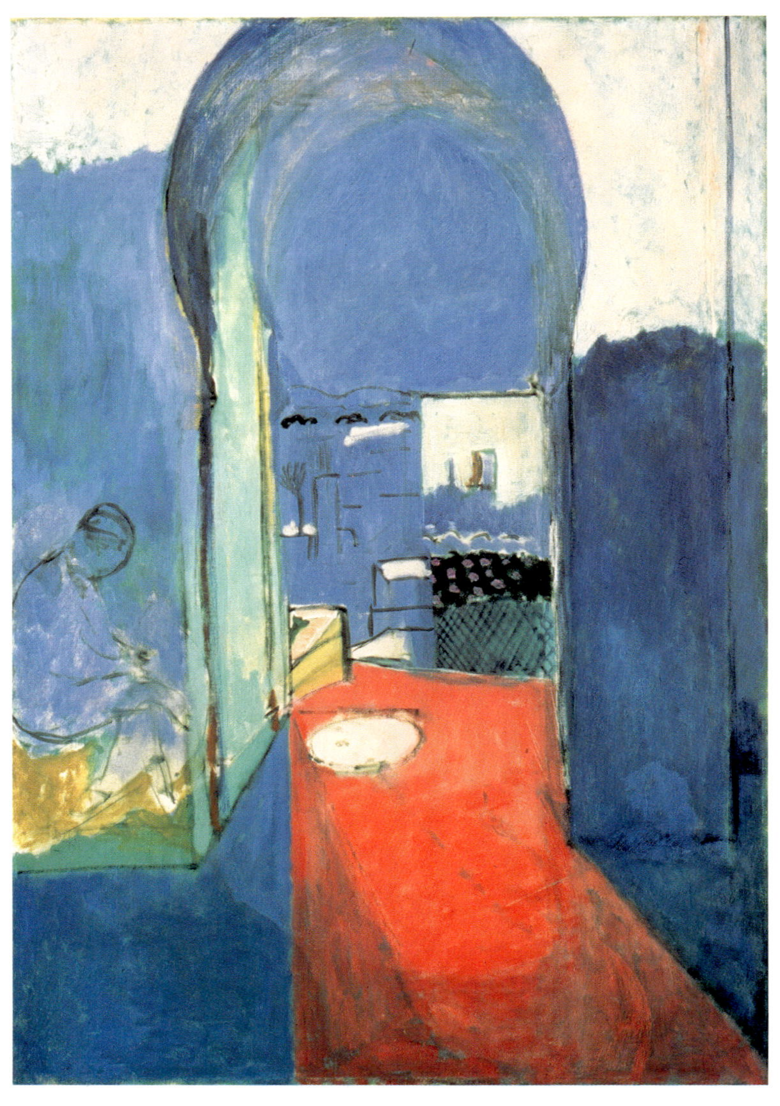

The Casbah Gate • 1912–1913
Pushkin Museum, Moscow

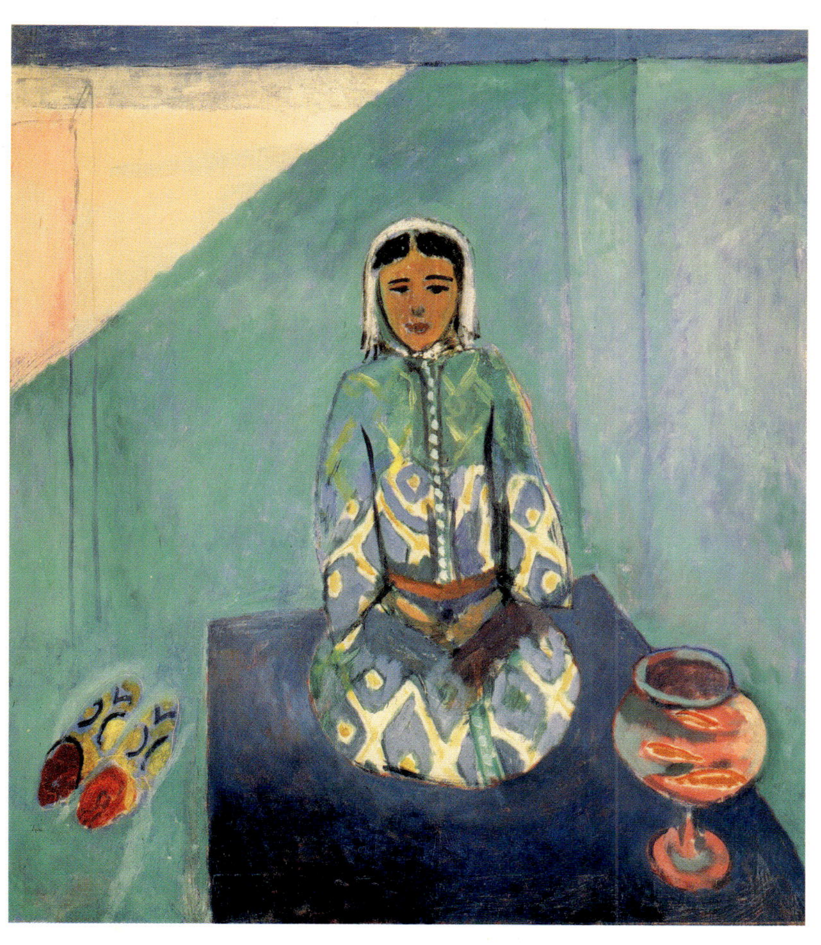

Zorah on the Terrace • 1912–1913
Pushkin Museum, Moscow

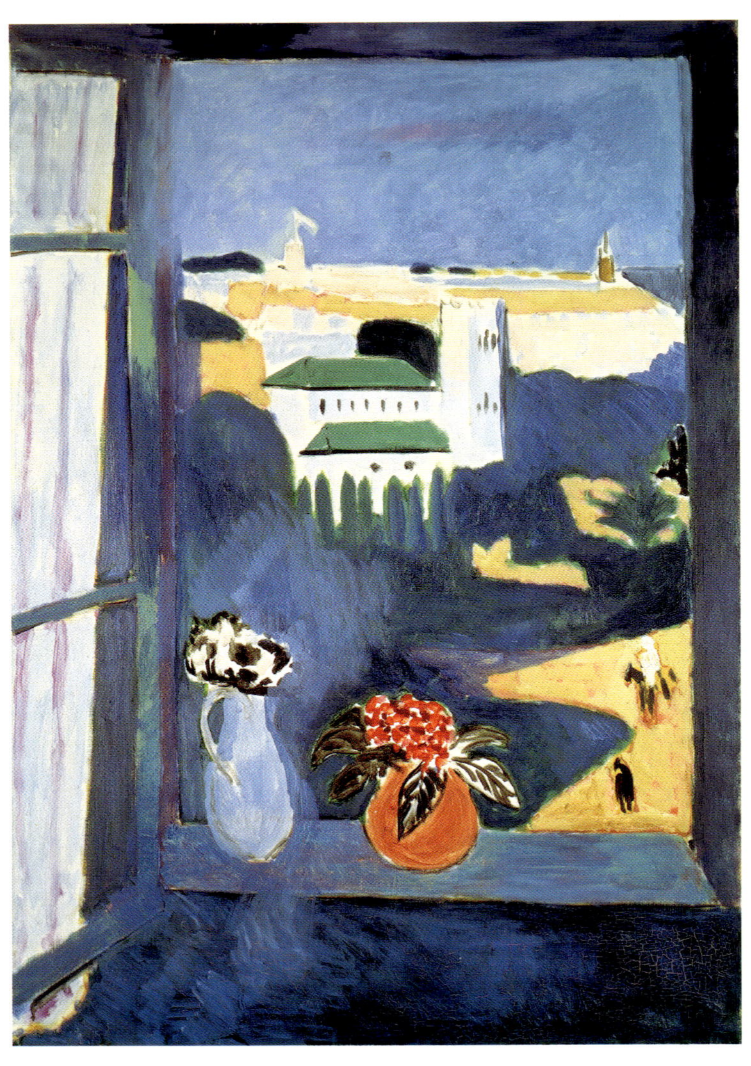

Landscape Viewed from a Window • 1912–1913
Pushkin Museum, Moscow

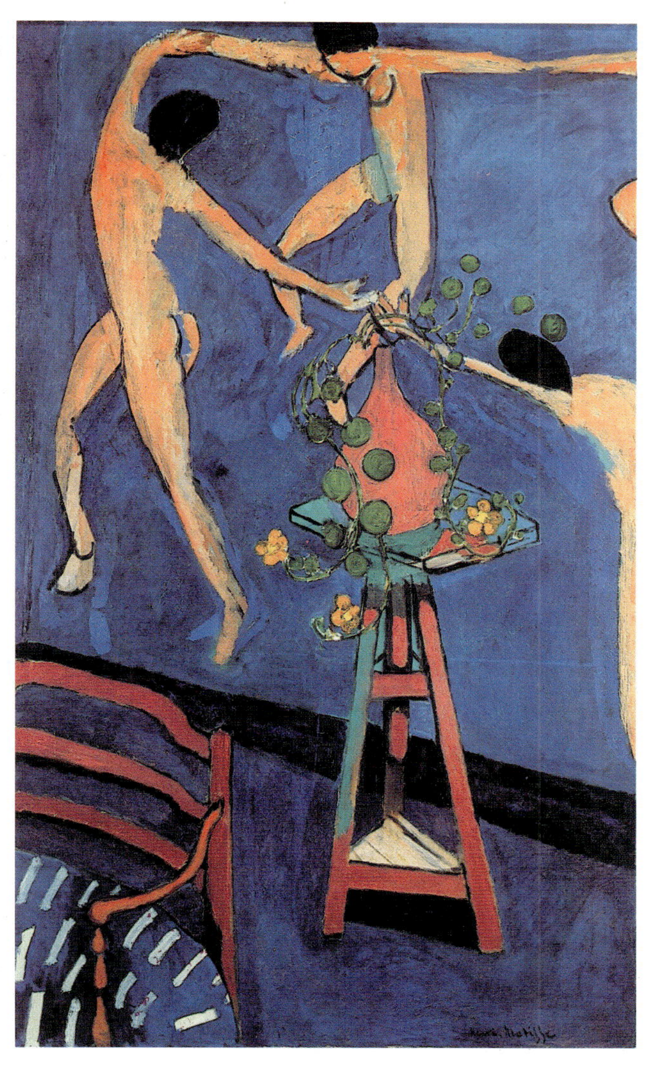

Nasturtiums with "Dance" (II) • 1912
Pushkin Museum, Moscow
> **Conversation** • 1908–1912
Hermitage, Saint Petersburg

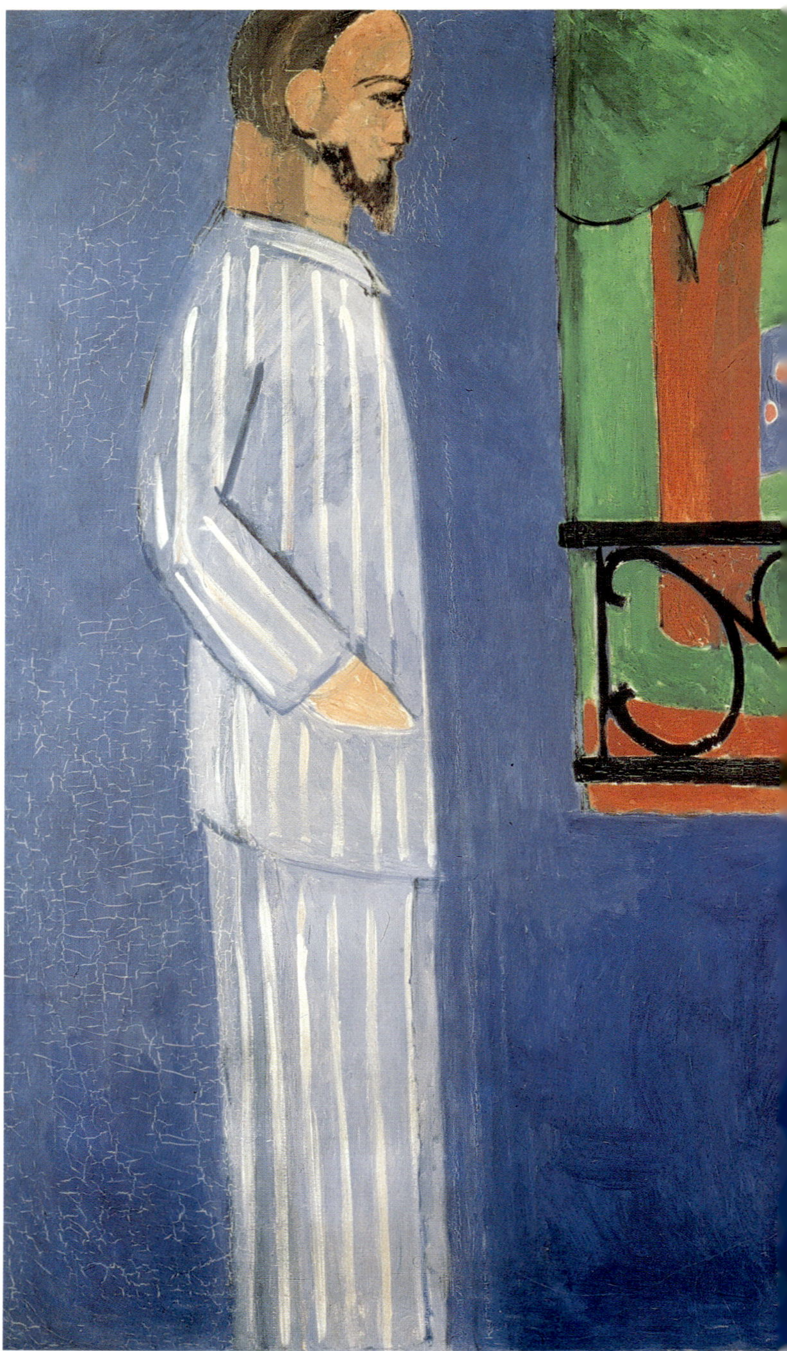

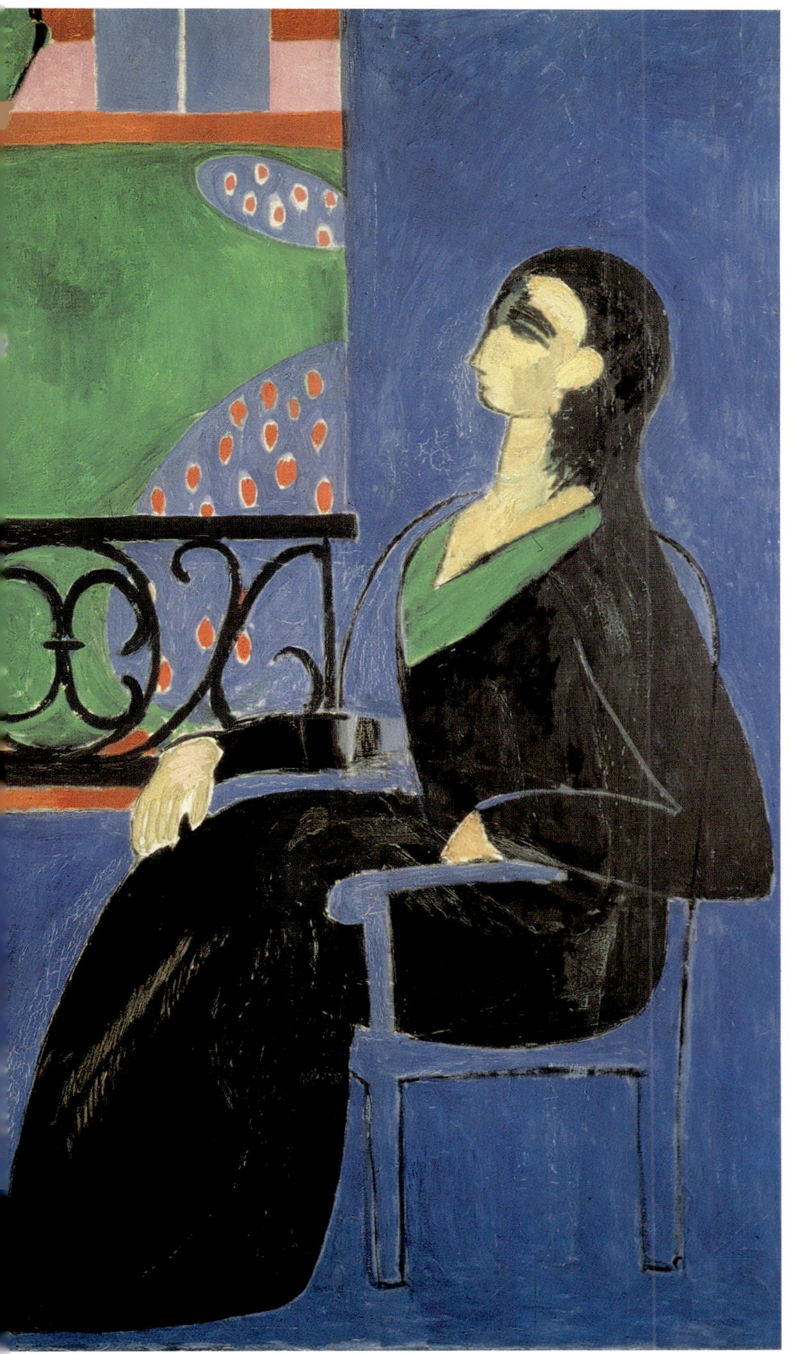

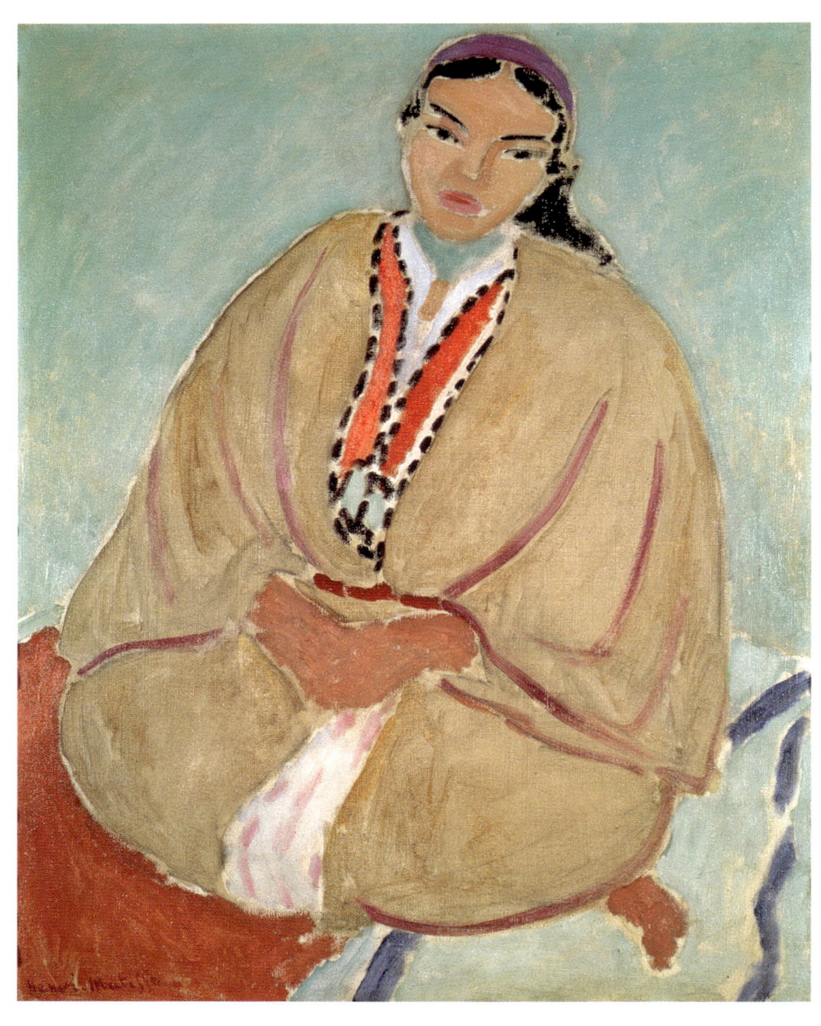

The Yellow Robe, Zorah • 1912
Cowles Collection, Lake Forest, California

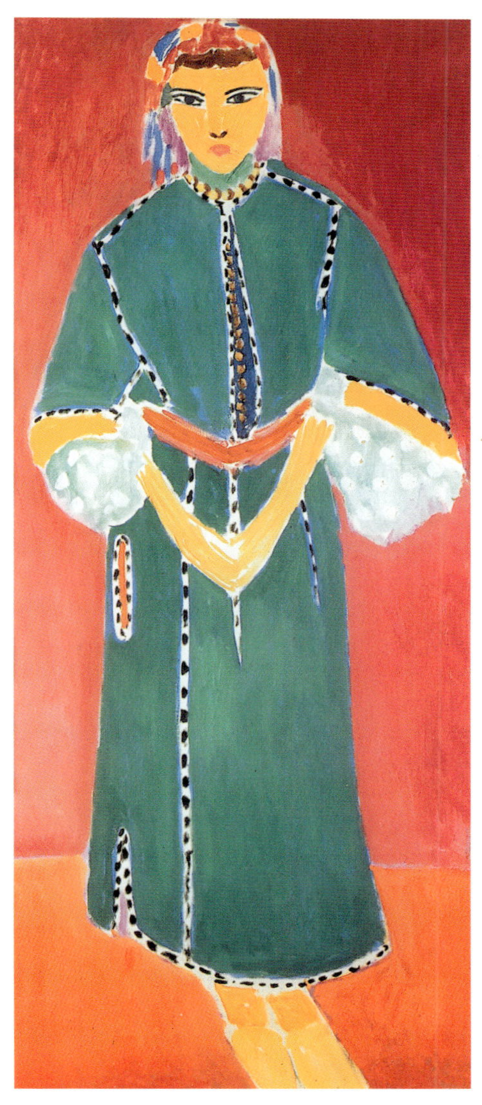

Zorah Standing • late 1912

Hermitage, Saint Petersburg

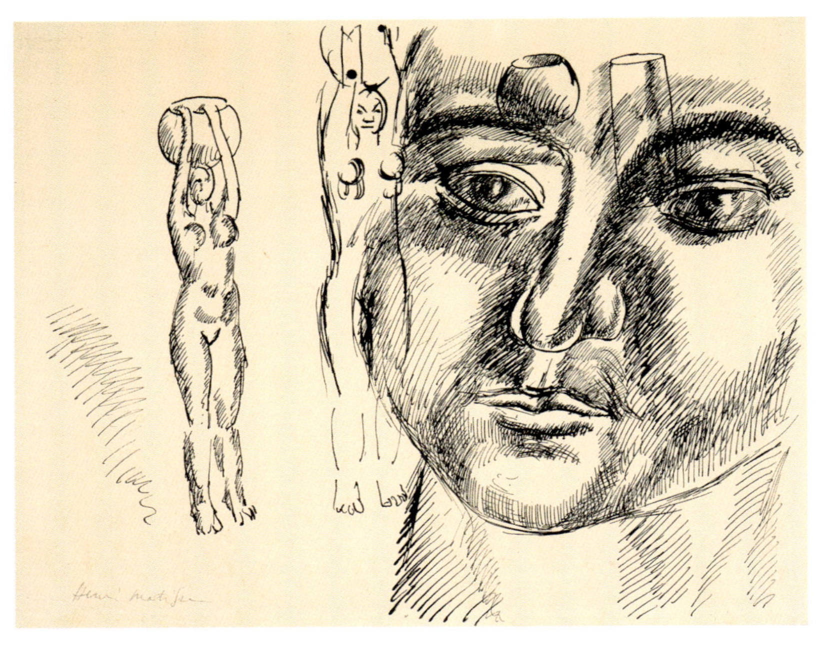

Face and Two Nudes with Calabash • 1912–1913
Musée national d'art moderne, Paris

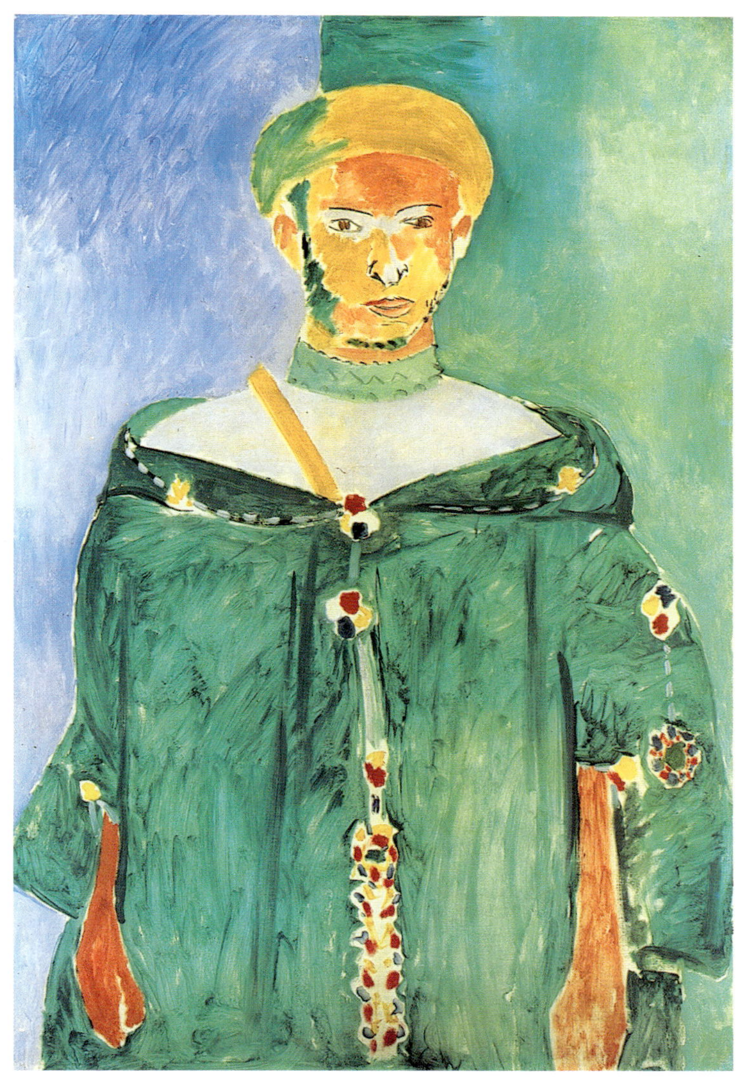

The Standing Riffian • late 1912
Hermitage, Saint Petersburg

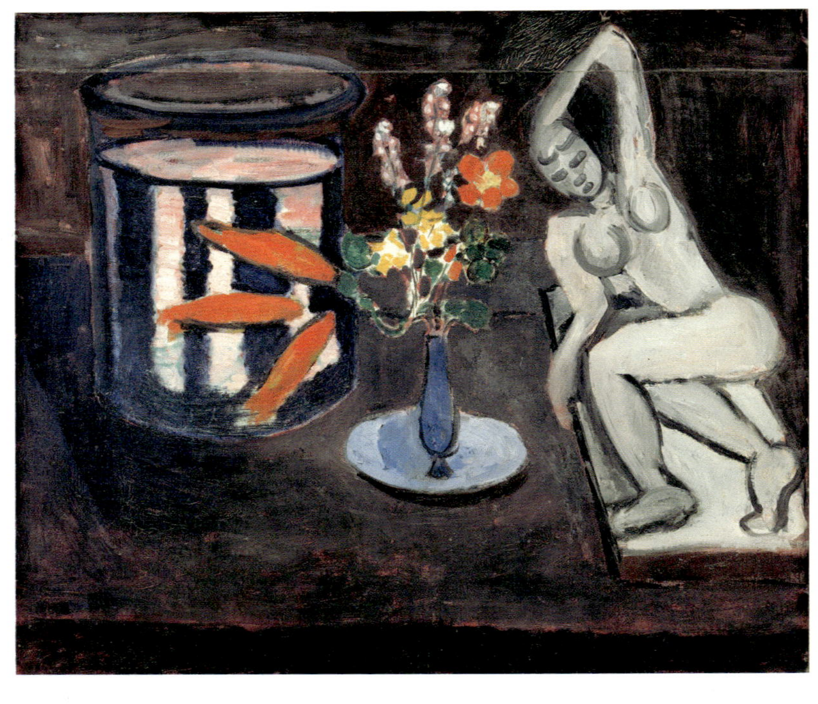

Goldfish • 1912

Statens Museum for Kunst, Copenhagen

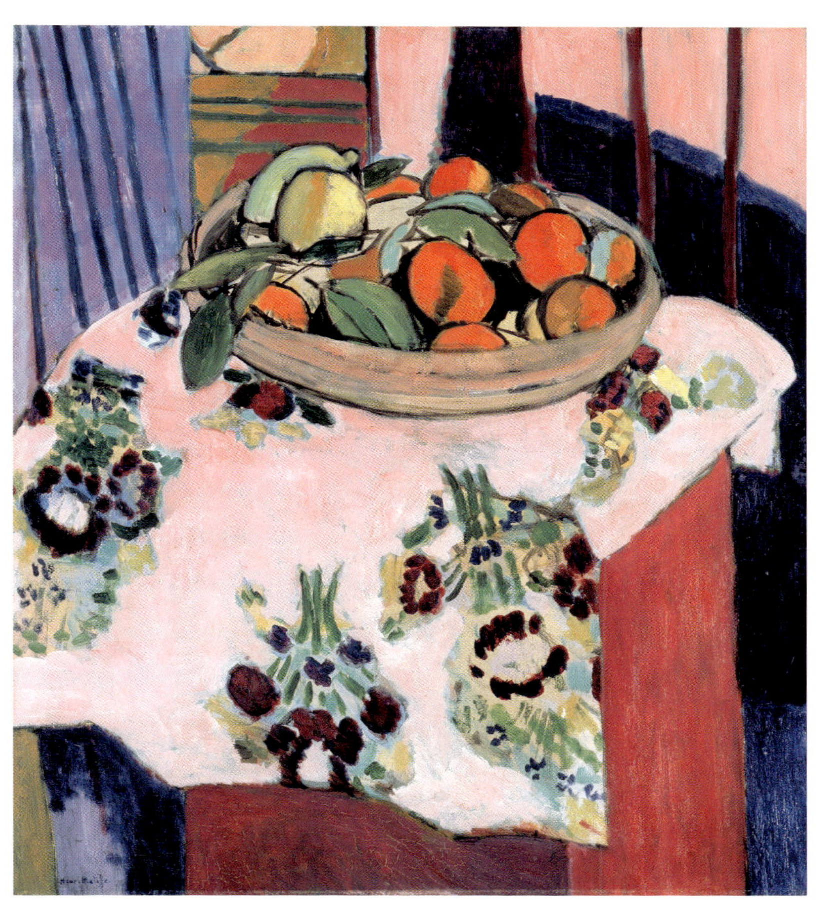

Basket of Oranges • 1912
Musée Picasso, Paris

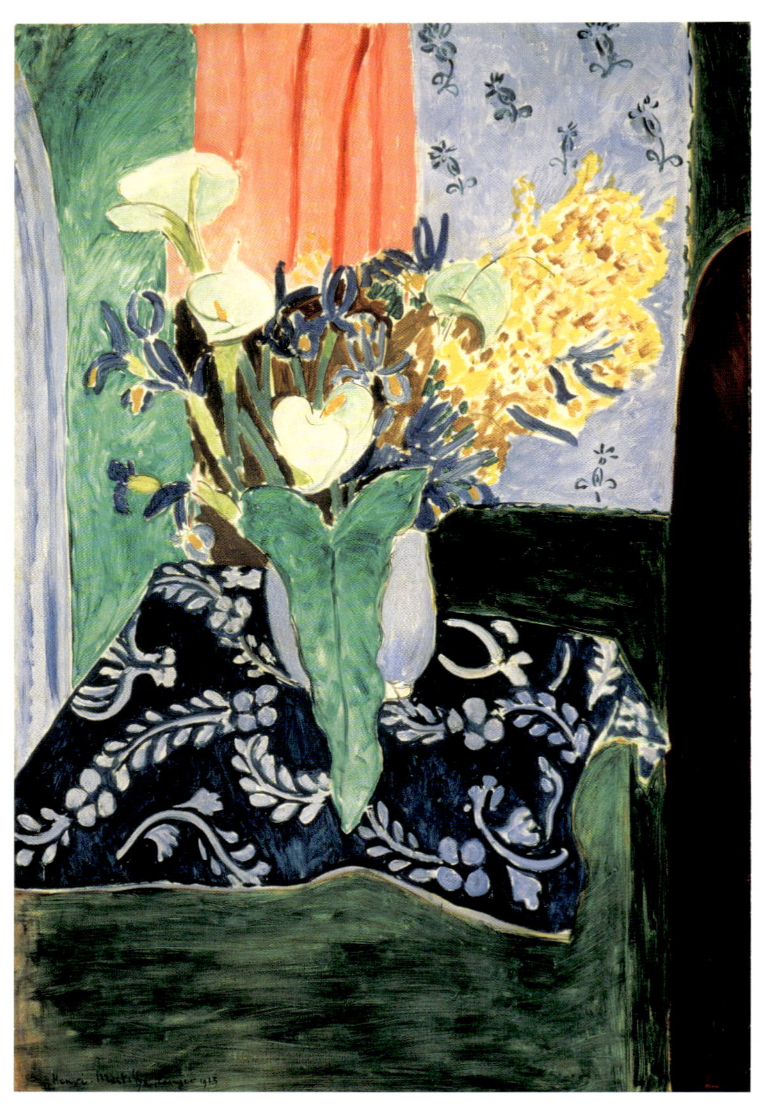

Calla Lilies, Irises, and Mimosas · early 1913
Pushkin Museum, Moscow

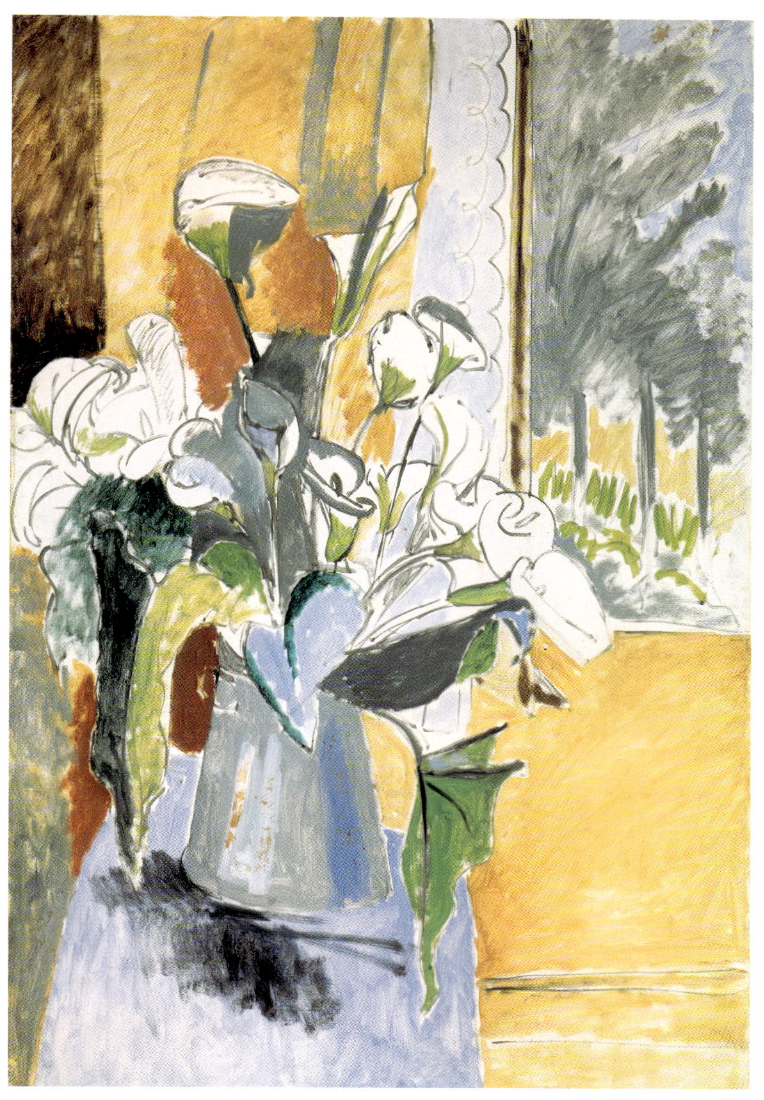

Bouquet of Flowers on a Veranda • 1912–1913
Hermitage, Saint Petersburg

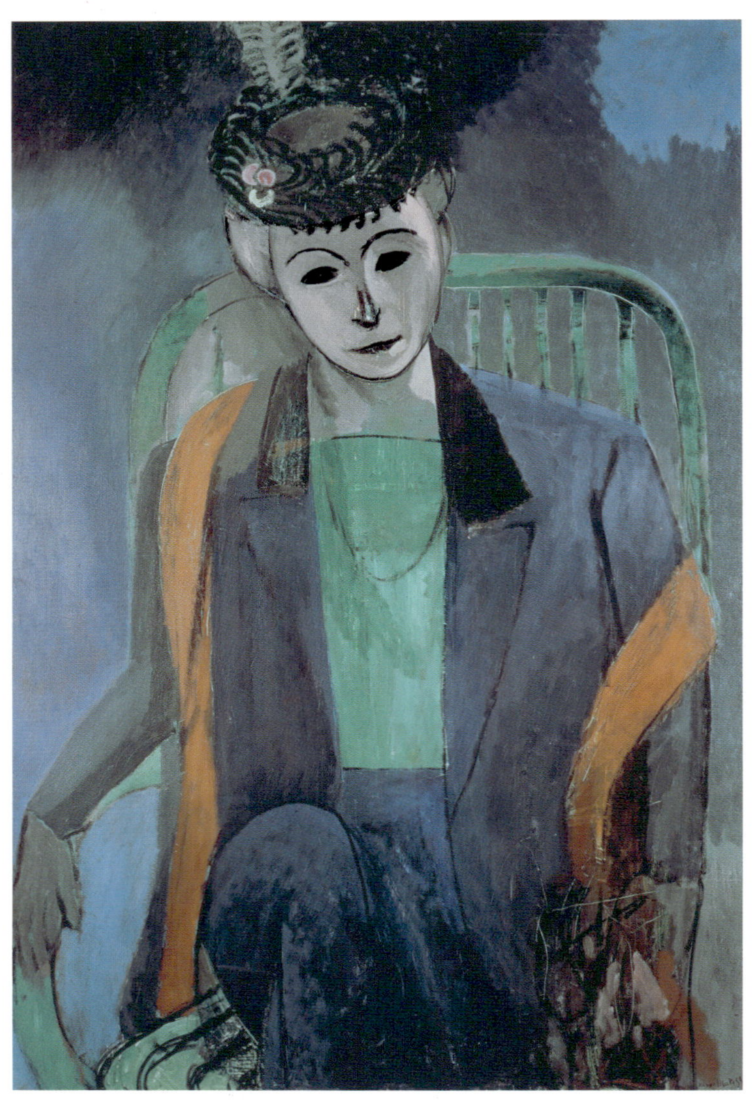

Portrait of Mme Matisse • 1913
Hermitage, Saint Petersburg

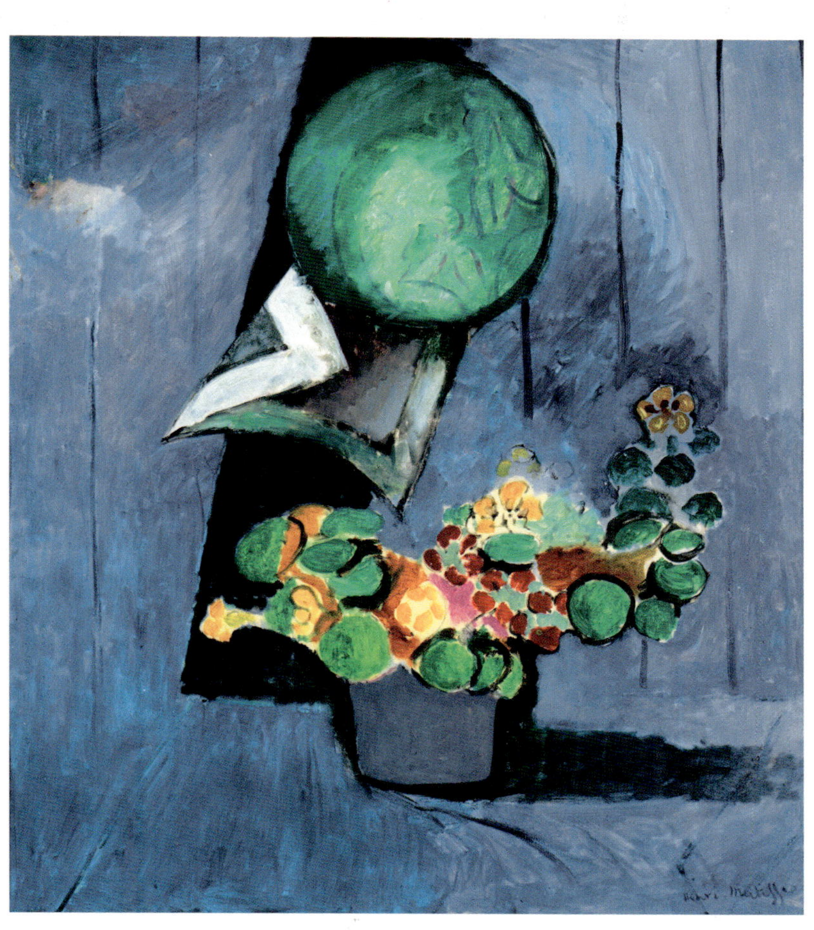

Flowers and Ceramic Plate · 1913
Städelsches Kunstinstitut und Städtische Galerie, Frankfurt am Main

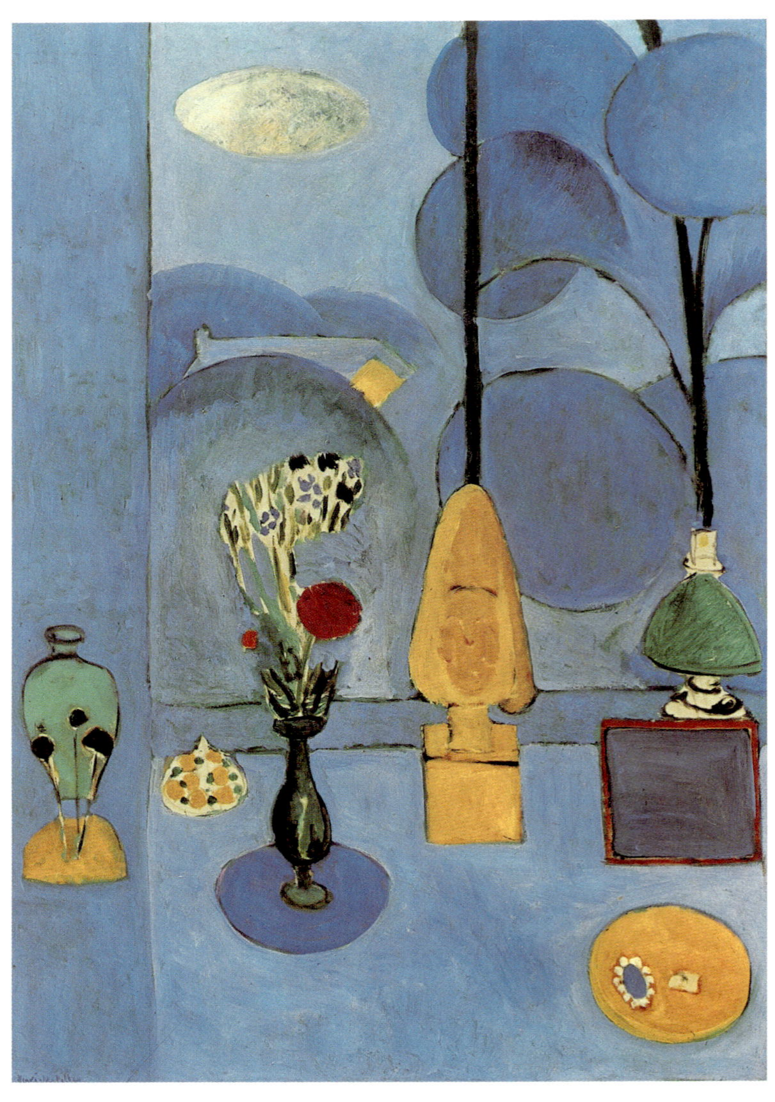

The Blue Window · 1913
The Museum of Modern Art, New York, Abby Aldrich Rockefeller Fund

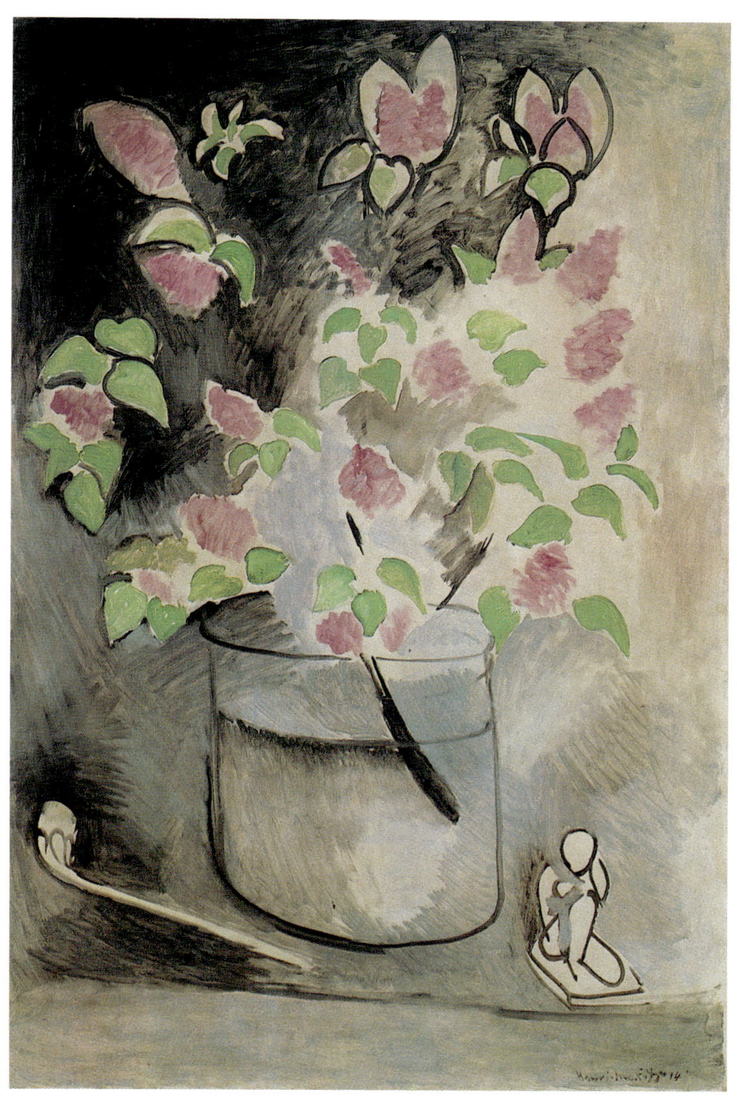

Branch of Lilacs • 1914
Private collection

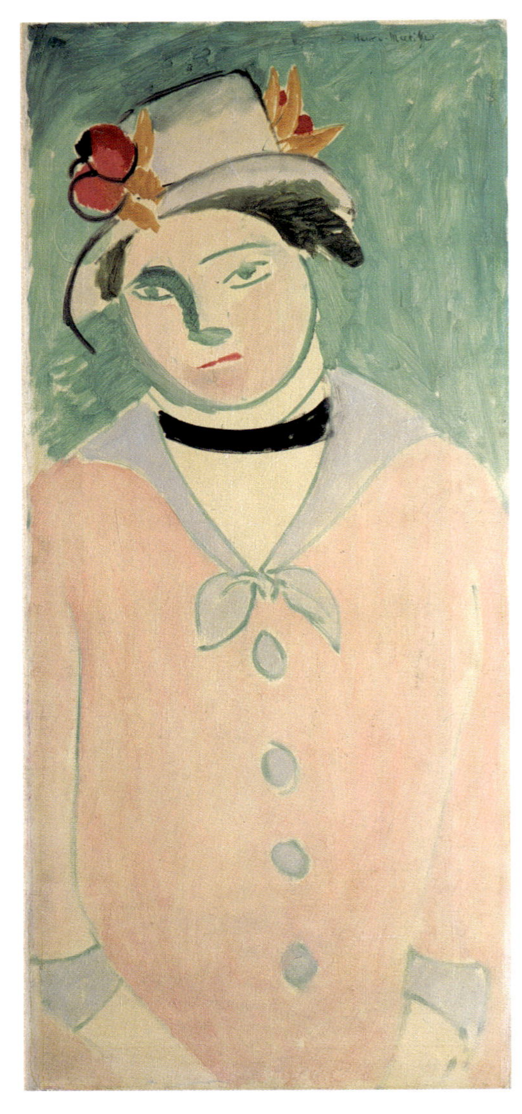

Marguerite with Hat with Roses • 1914
Private collection

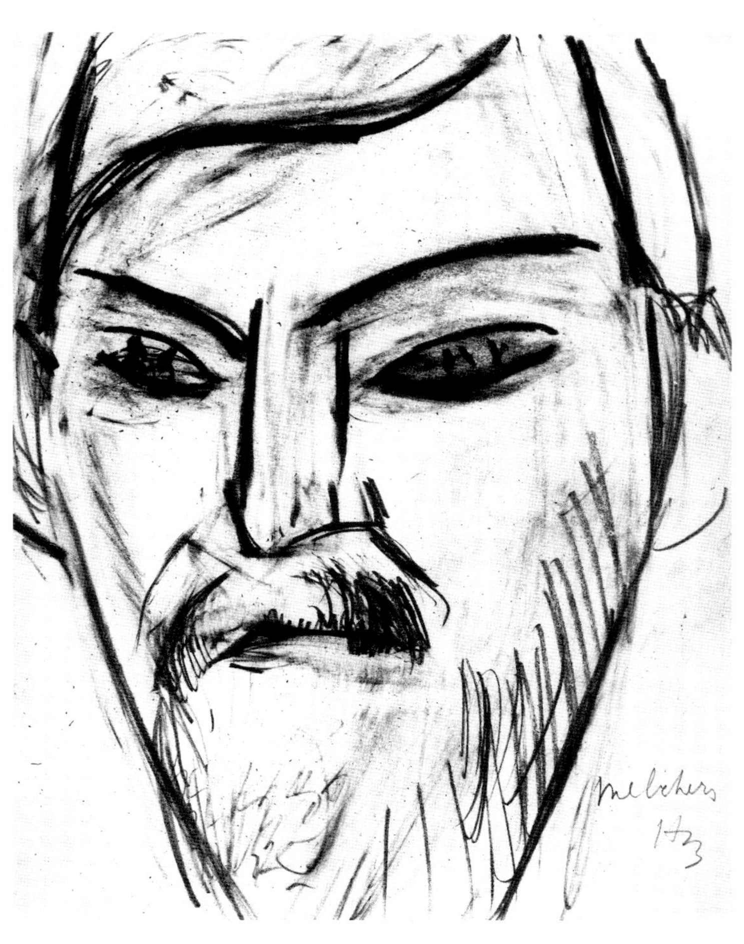

Melchers • 1914

Musée Matisse, Nice

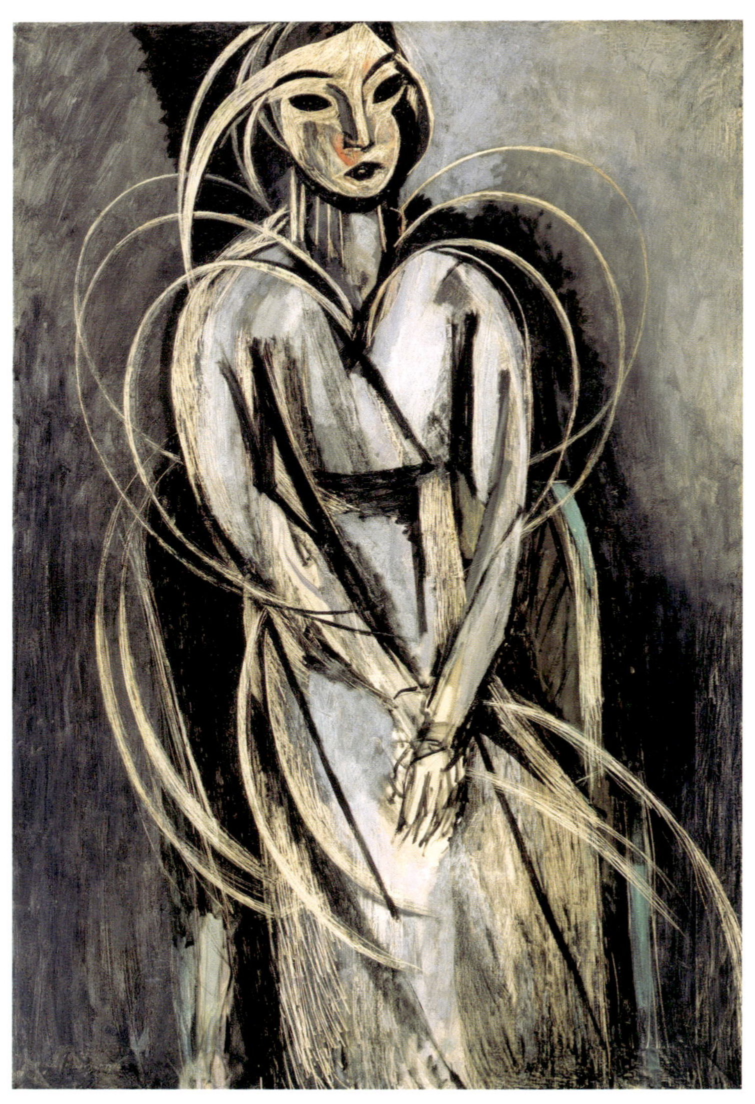

Portrait of Mlle Yvonne Landsberg • 1914
Philadelphia Museum of Art, The Louise and Walter Arensberg Collection

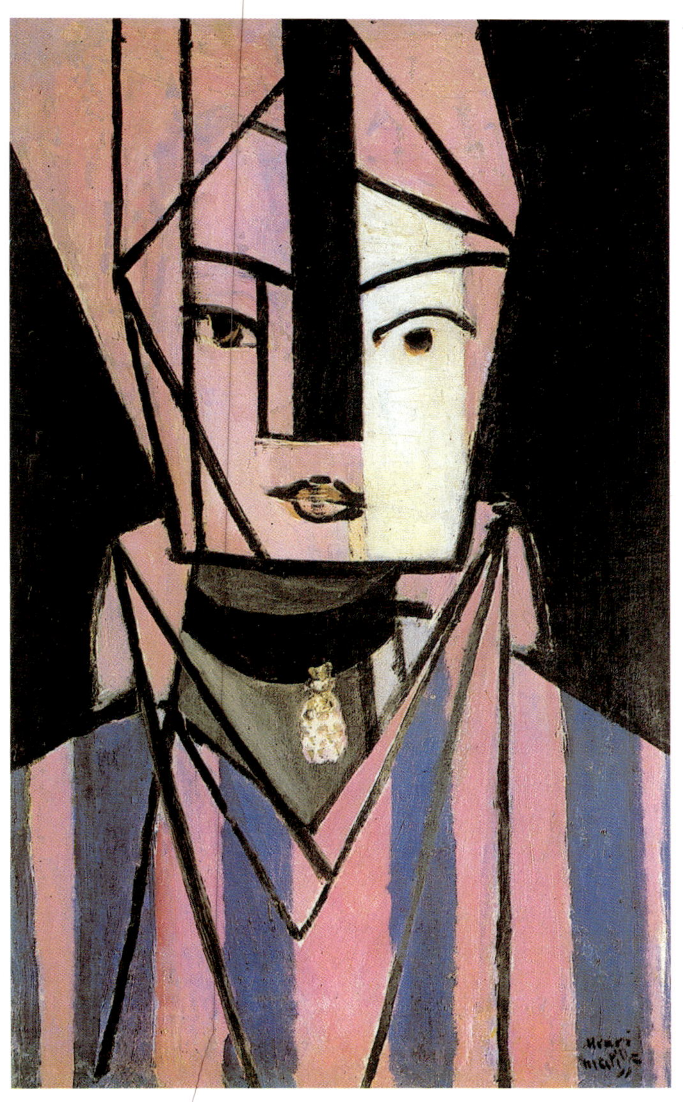

White and Pink Head • Autumn 1914
Musée national d'art moderne, Paris

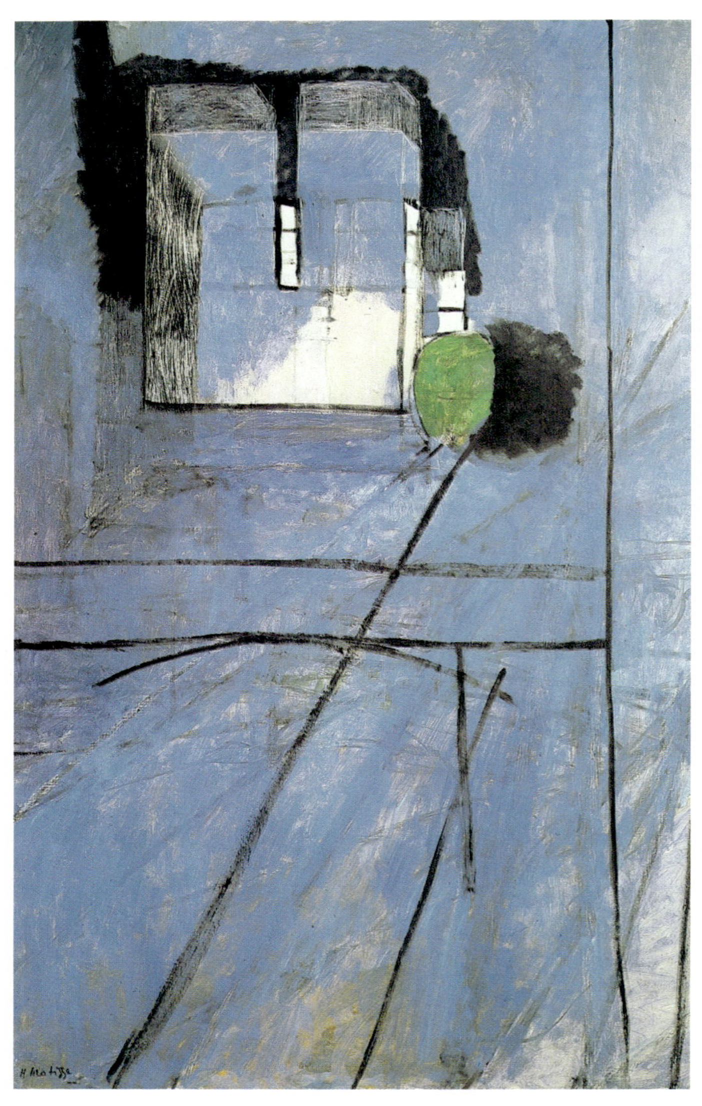

View of Notre-Dame • Spring 1914

The Museum of Modern Art, New York

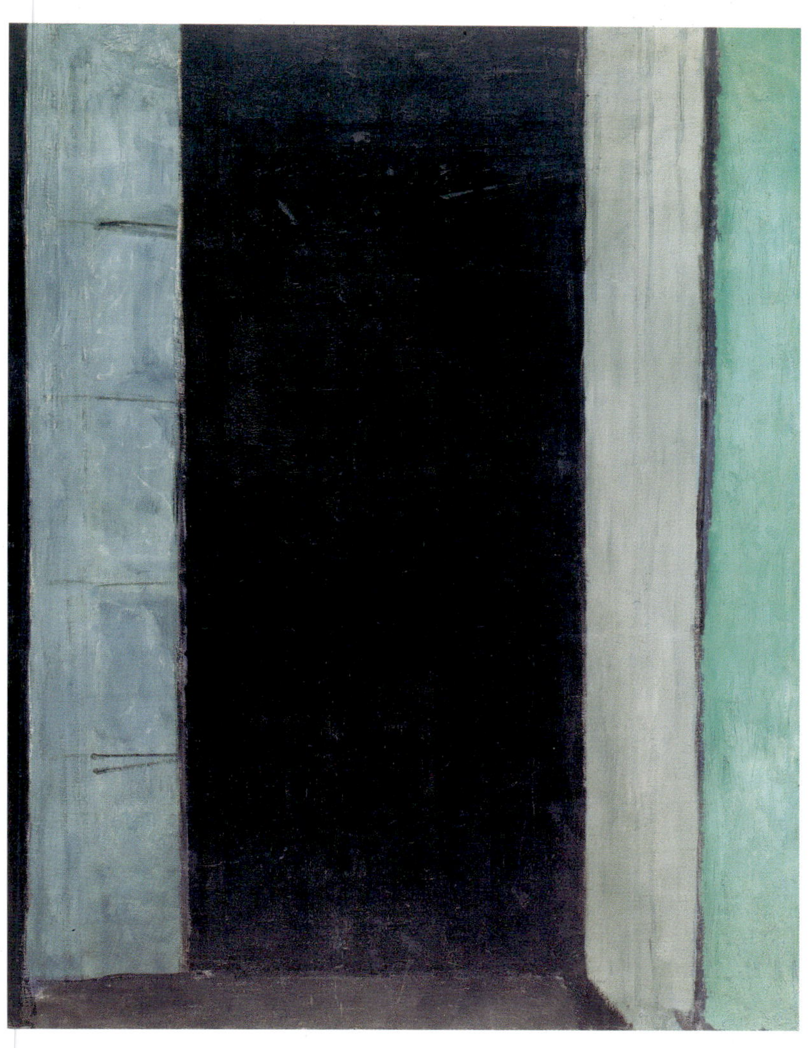

French Window at Collioure • September–October 1914
Musée national d'art moderne, Paris

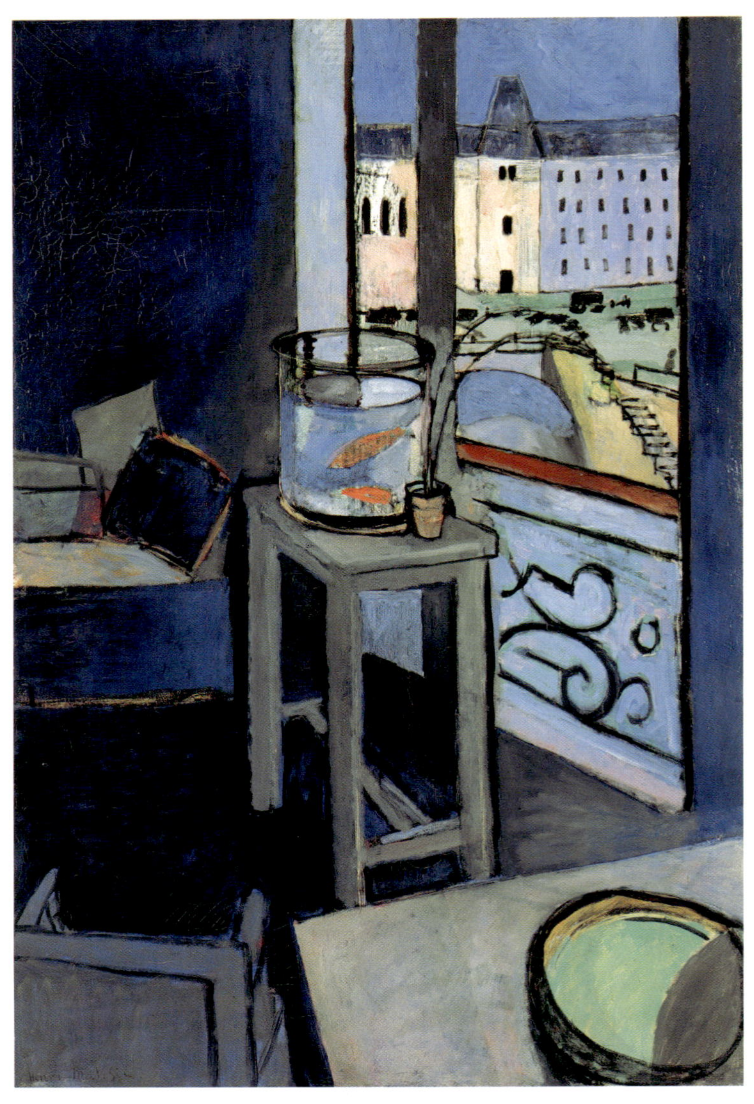

Interior with a Goldfish Bowl • Spring 1914
Musée national d'art moderne, Paris

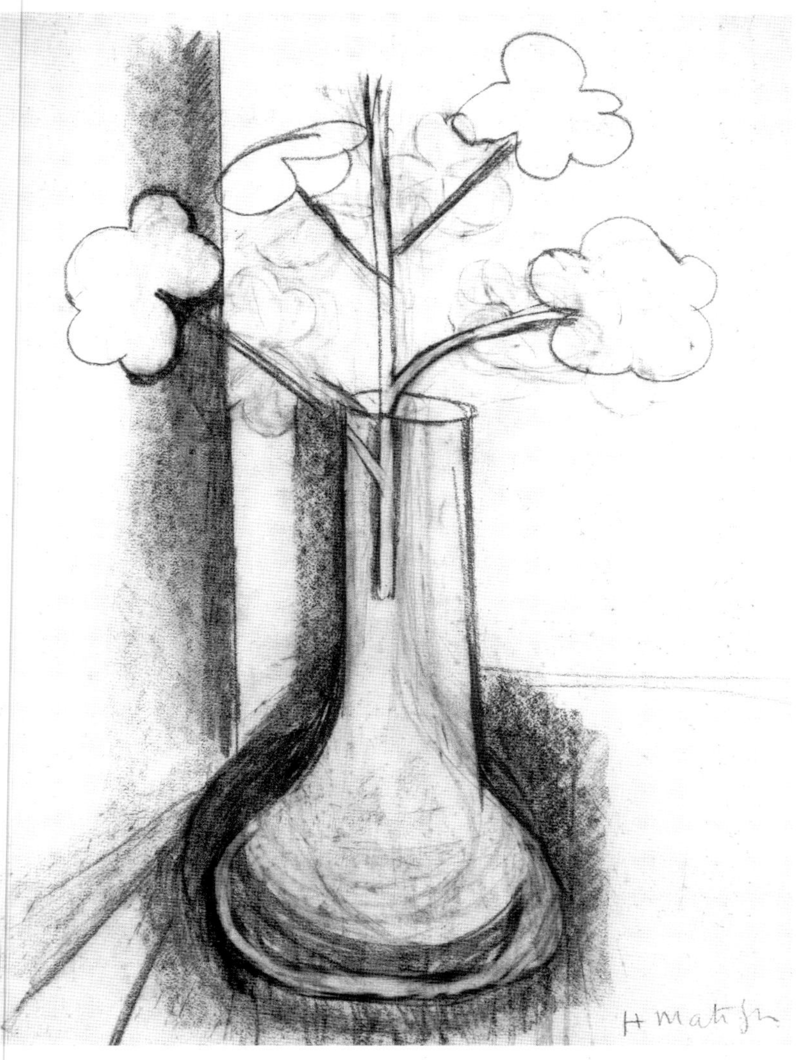

Vase with Geraniums • 1915–1916

Musée Matisse, Nice

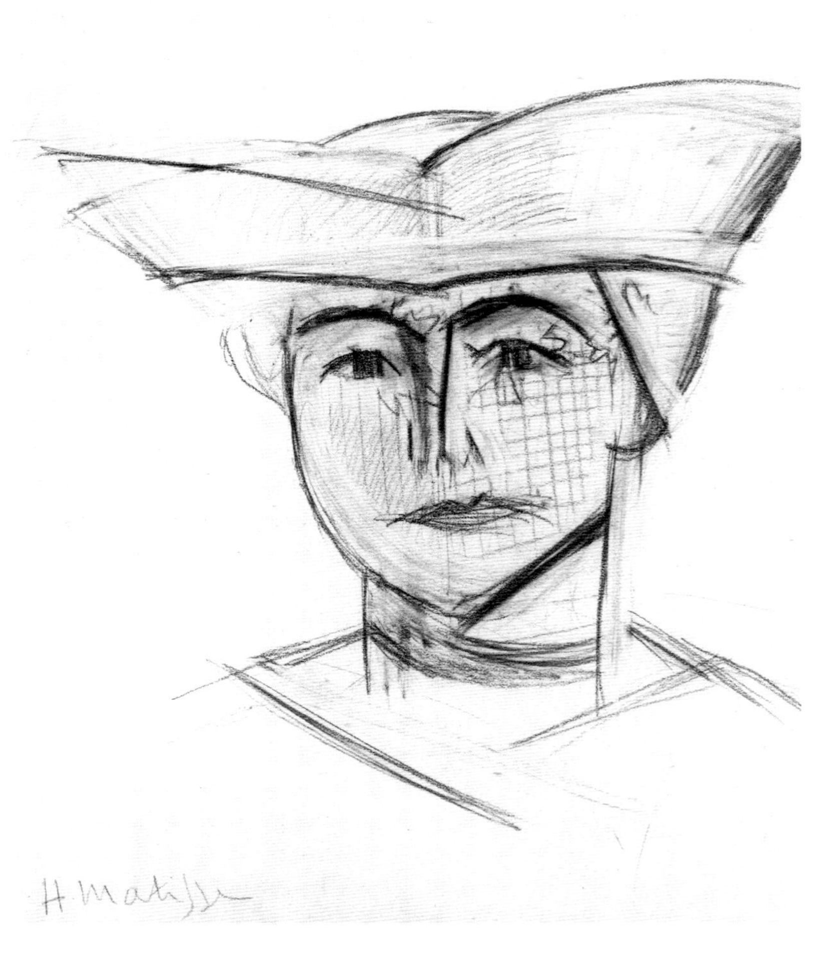

Portrait of Mme Matisse • 1915

Musée Matisse, Nice

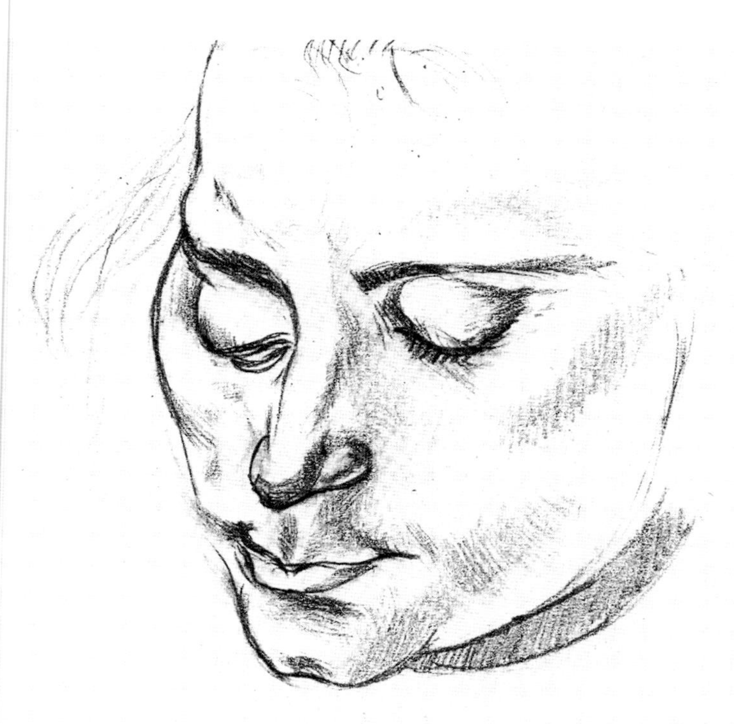

Marguerite • 1915
Private collection

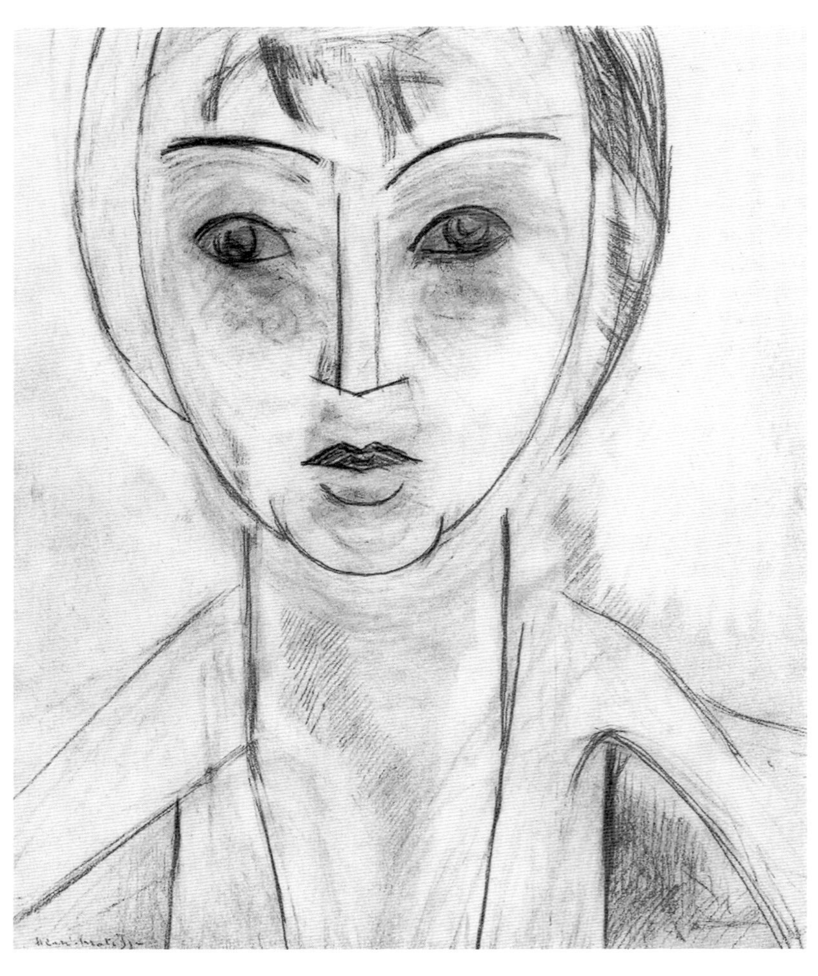

Josette Gris • 1915
Private collection

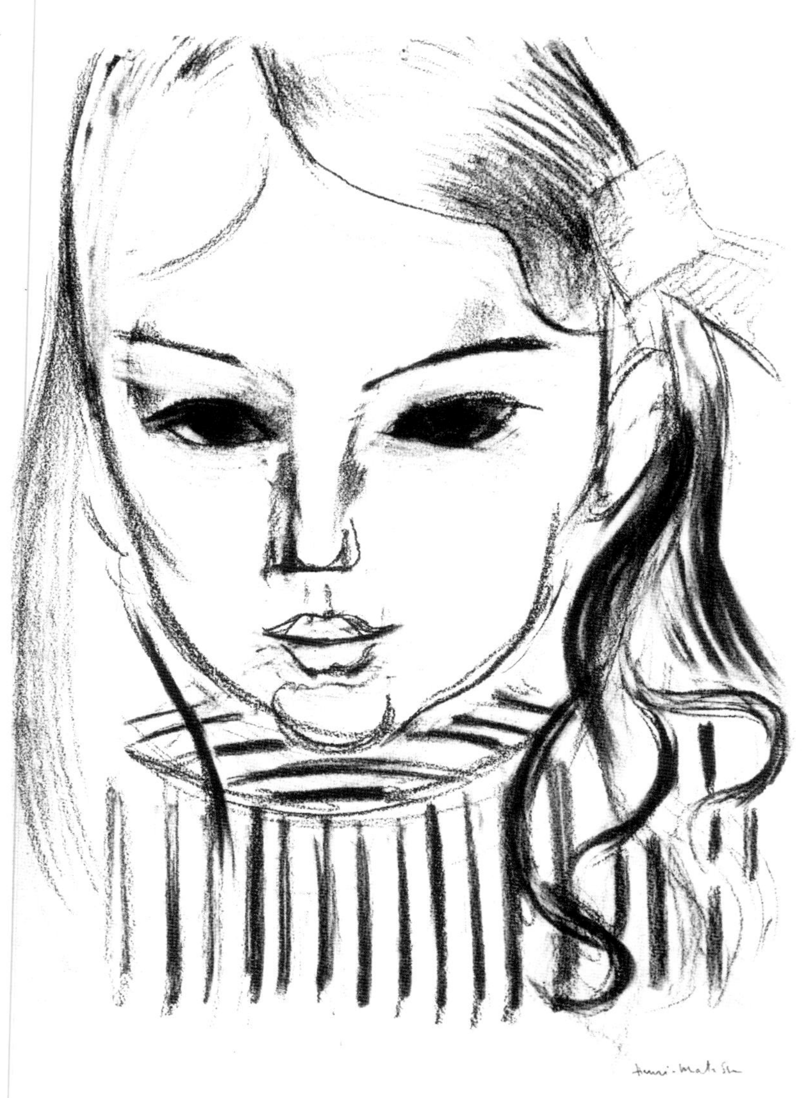

Young Girl • 1916–1917
Private collection

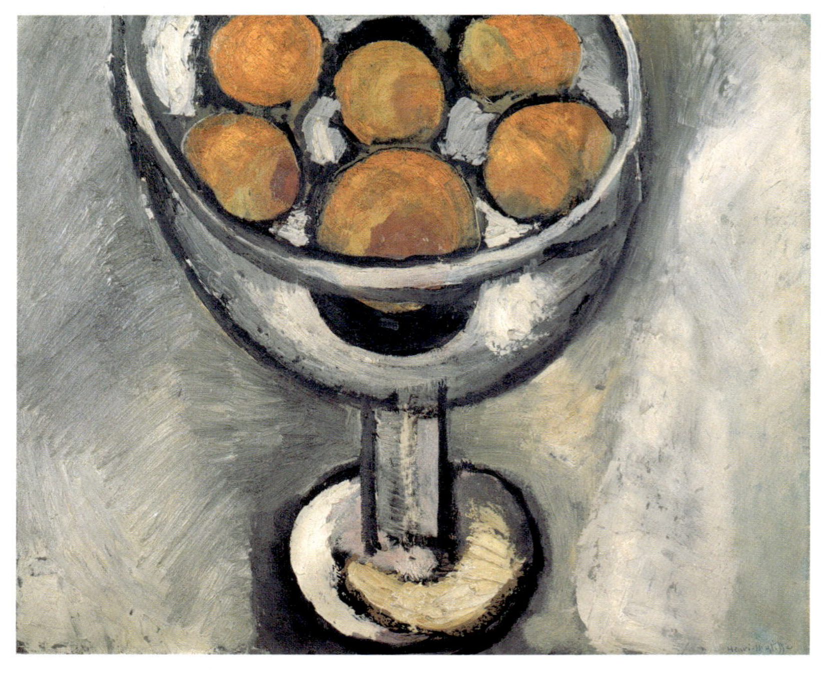

A Vase with Oranges • 1916
Private collection

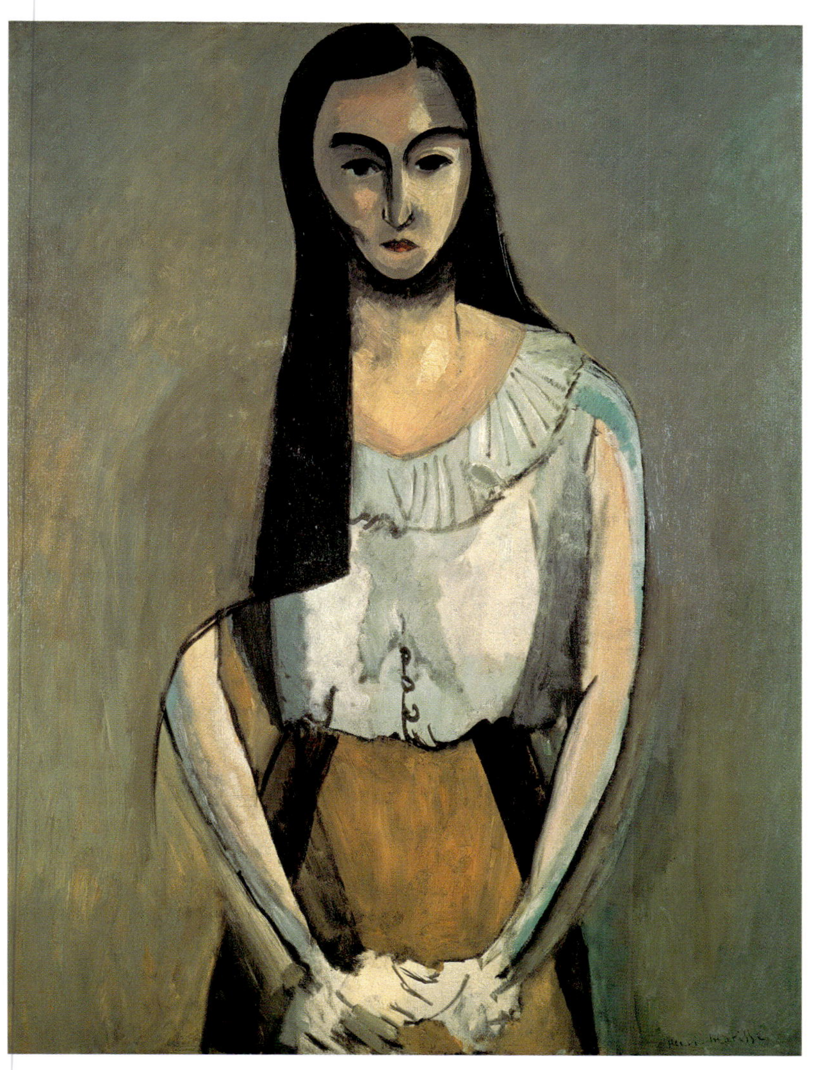

The Italian Woman • 1916
Solomon R. Guggenheim Museum, New York

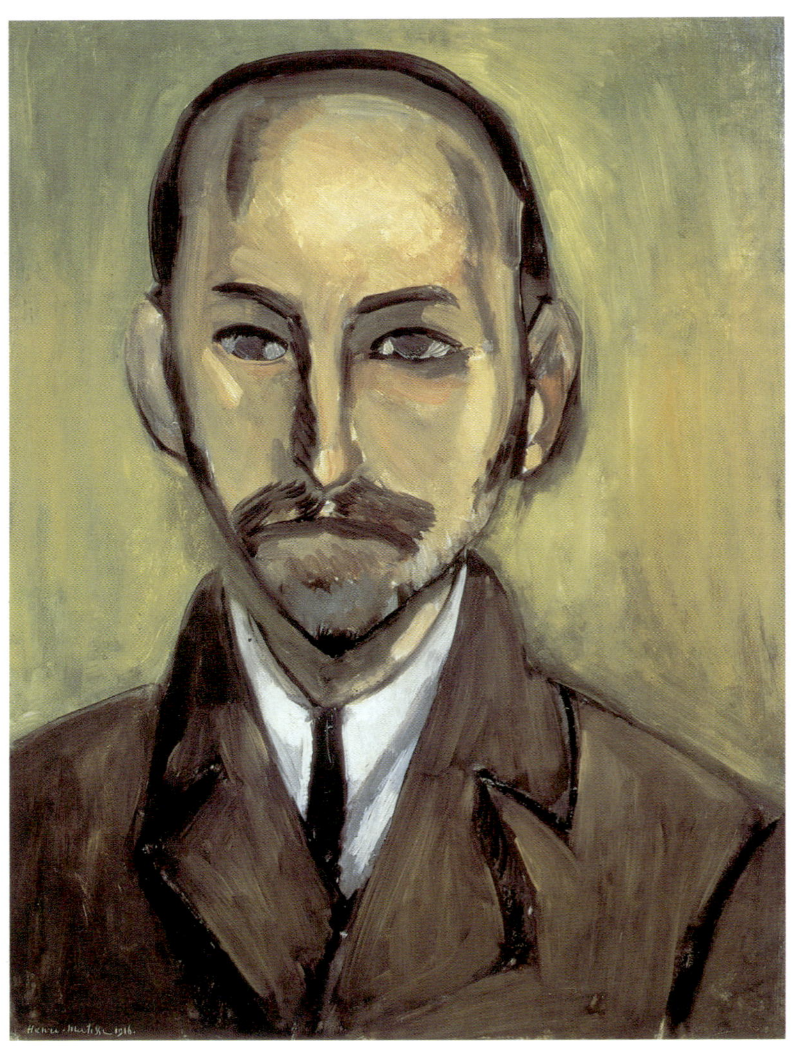

Portrait of Michael Stein • Autumn 1916
San Francisco Museum of Modern Art, Michael and Sarah Stein Memorial Collection, gift of Nathan Cummings

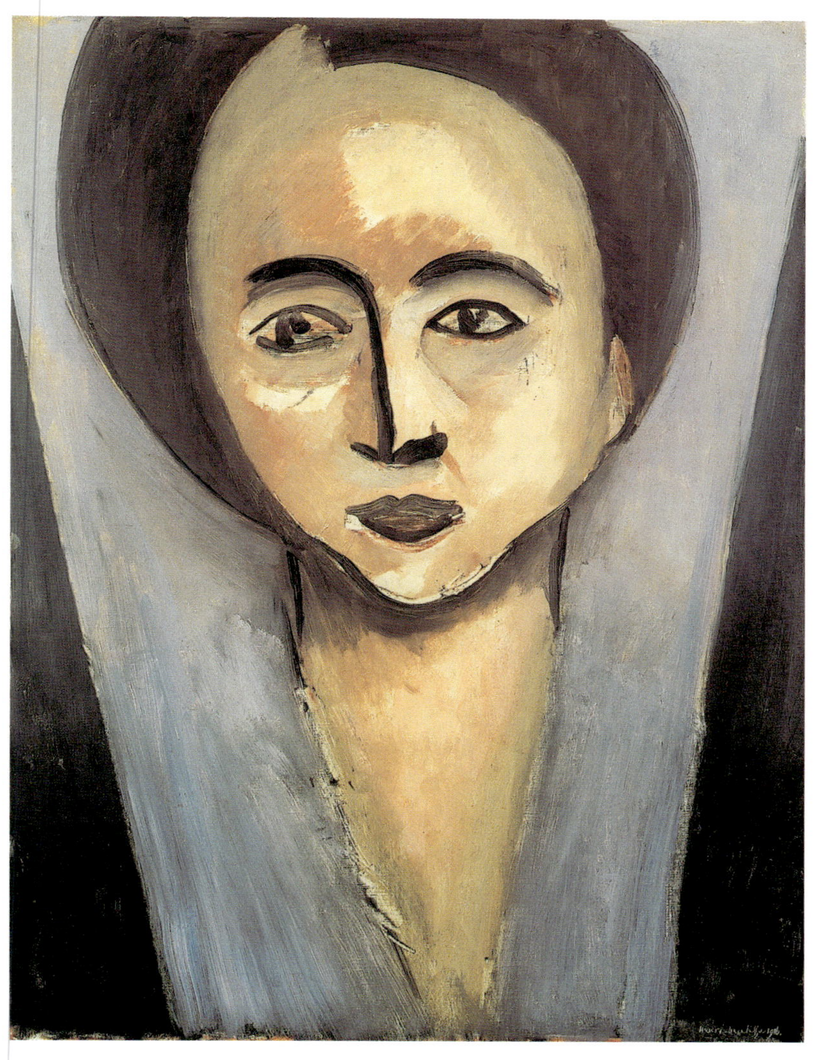

Portrait of Sarah Stein • Autumn 1916
San Francisco Museum of Modern Art, Michael and Sarah Stein Memorial Collection, gift of Elise S. Haas

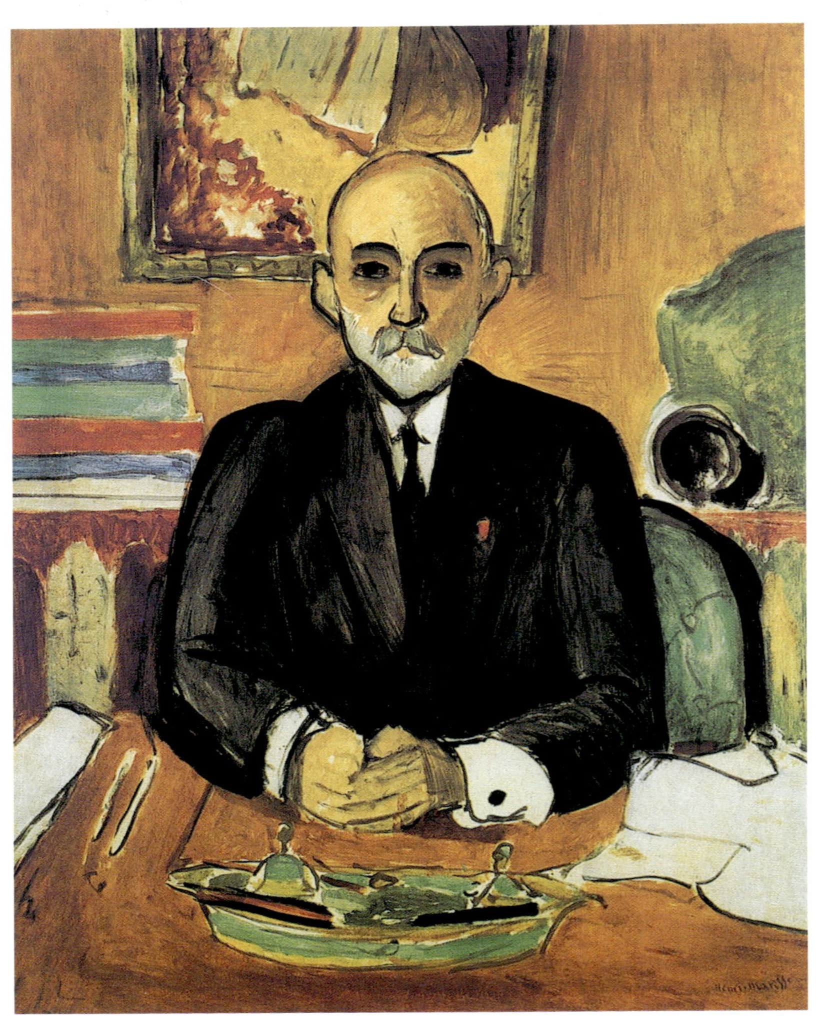

Portrait of Auguste Pellerin (I) · 1916
Private collection

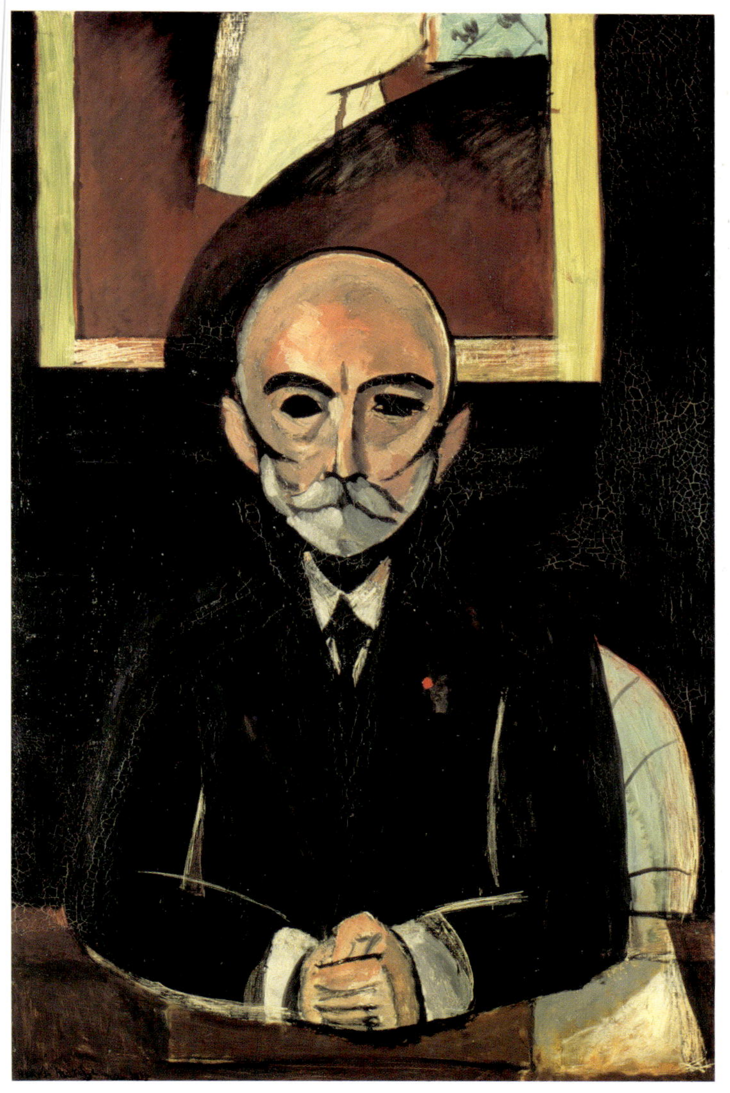

Portrait of Auguste Pellerin (II) • 1917
Musée national d'art moderne, Paris

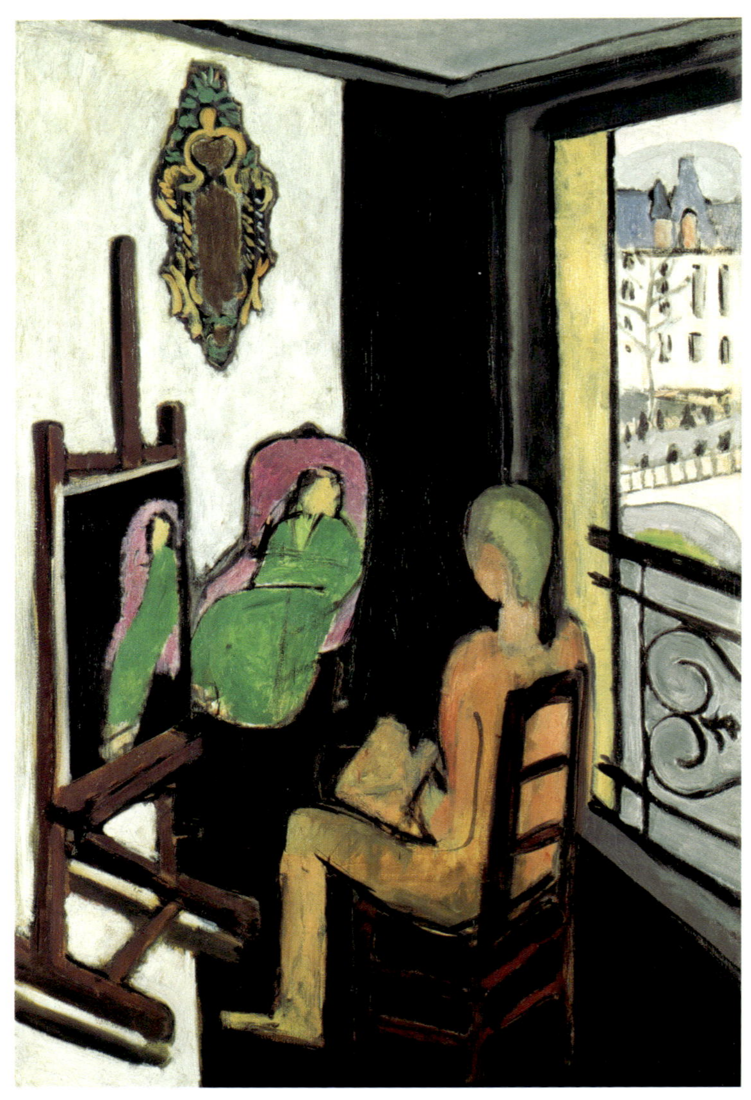

The Painter in His Studio • 1916
Musée national d'art moderne, Paris

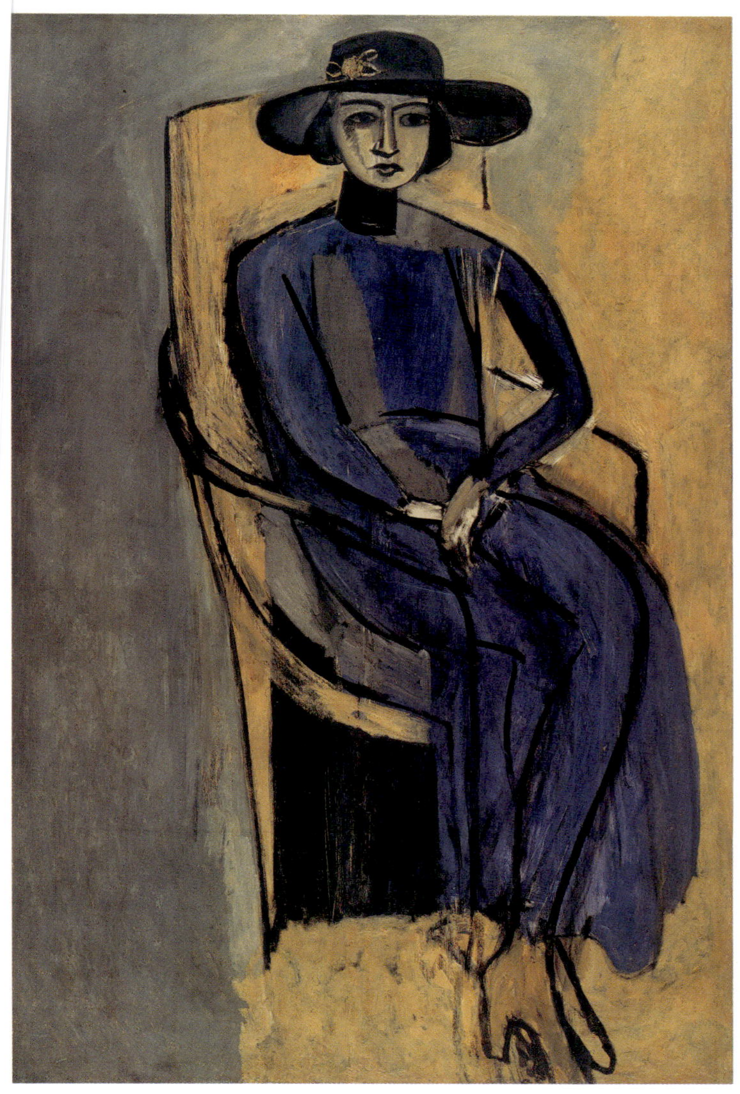

Portrait of Greta Prozor • late 1916
Musée national d'art moderne, Paris

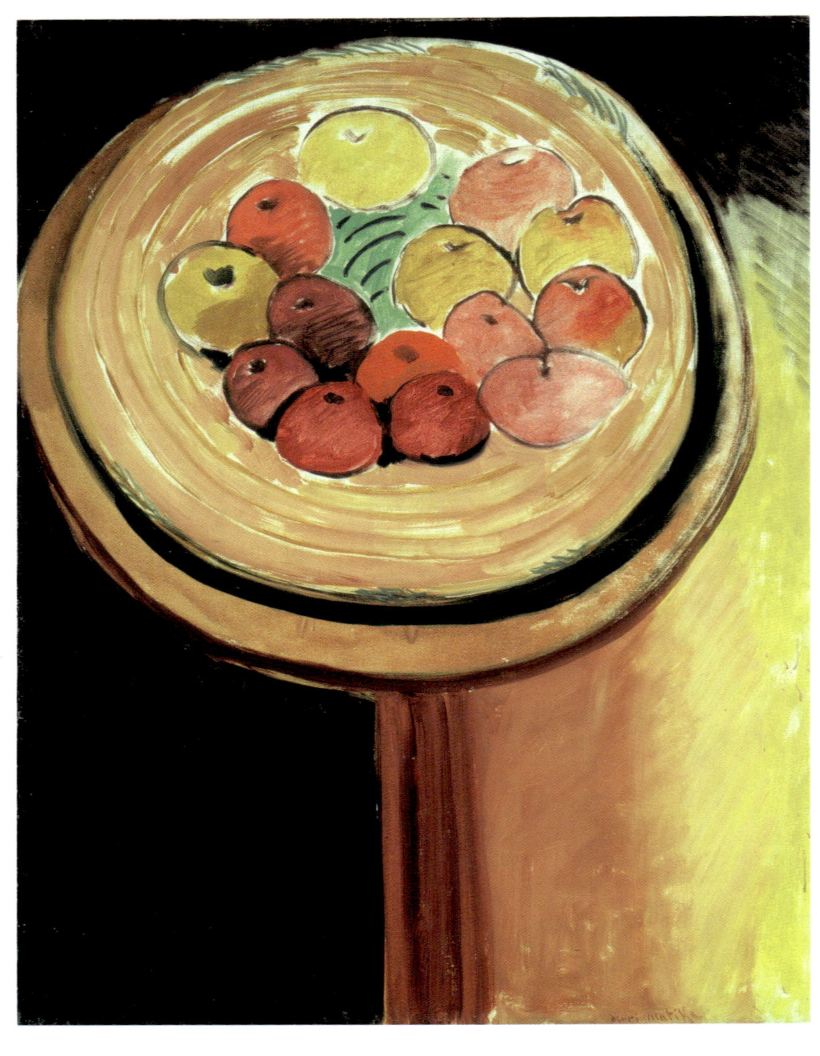

The Apples • 1916
The Art Institute of Chicago, gift of Florene May Schoenborn and Samuel A. Marx

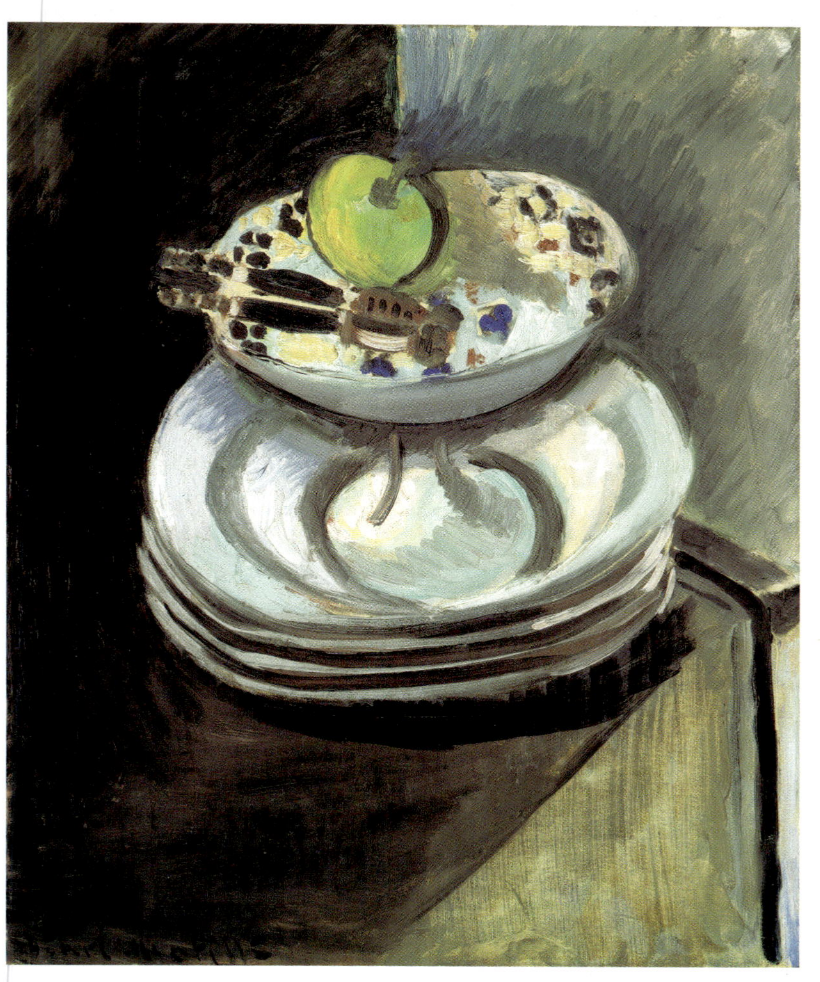

Compotier with Nutcracker • 1916
Statens Museum for Kunst, Copenhagen

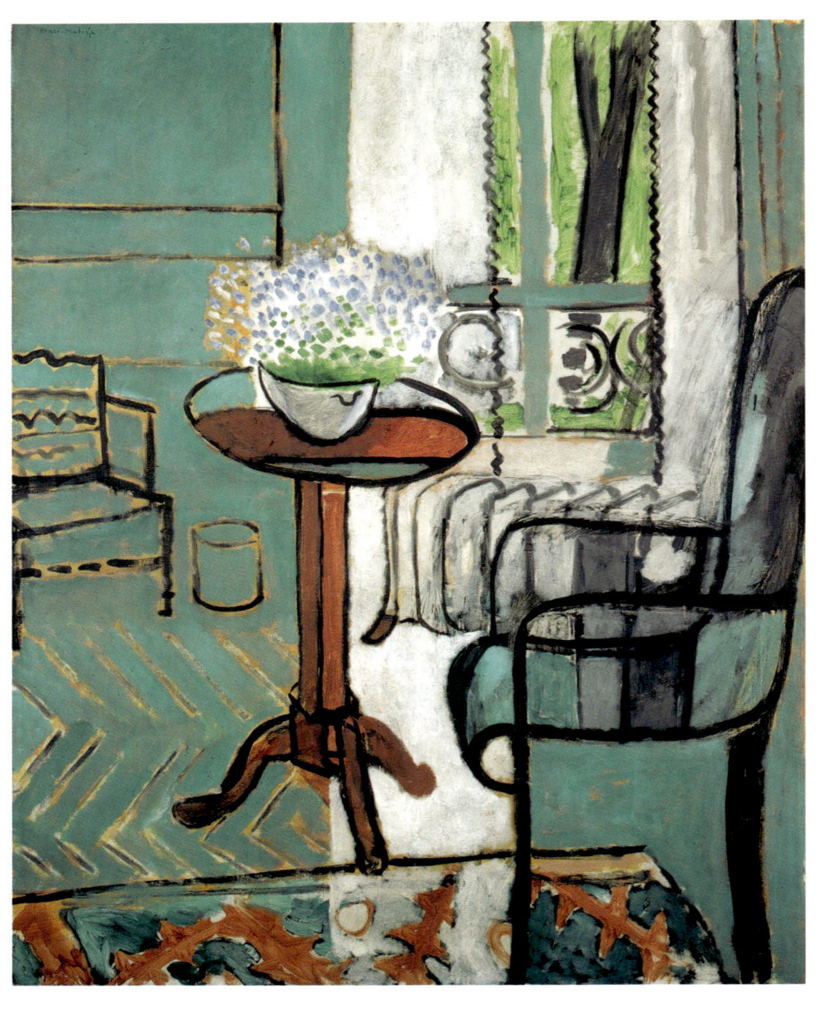

The Window • Spring 1916
The Detroit Institute of Arts

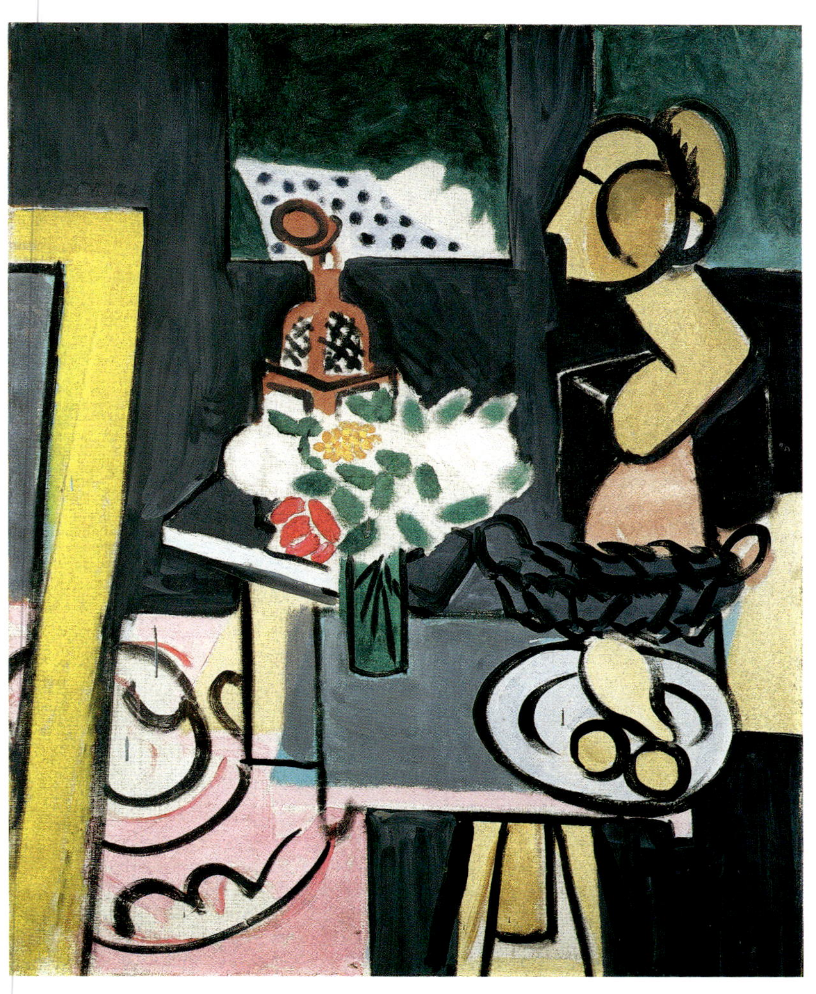

Still Life with a Plaster Bust • Spring 1916
The Barnes Foundation, Merion, Pennsylvania

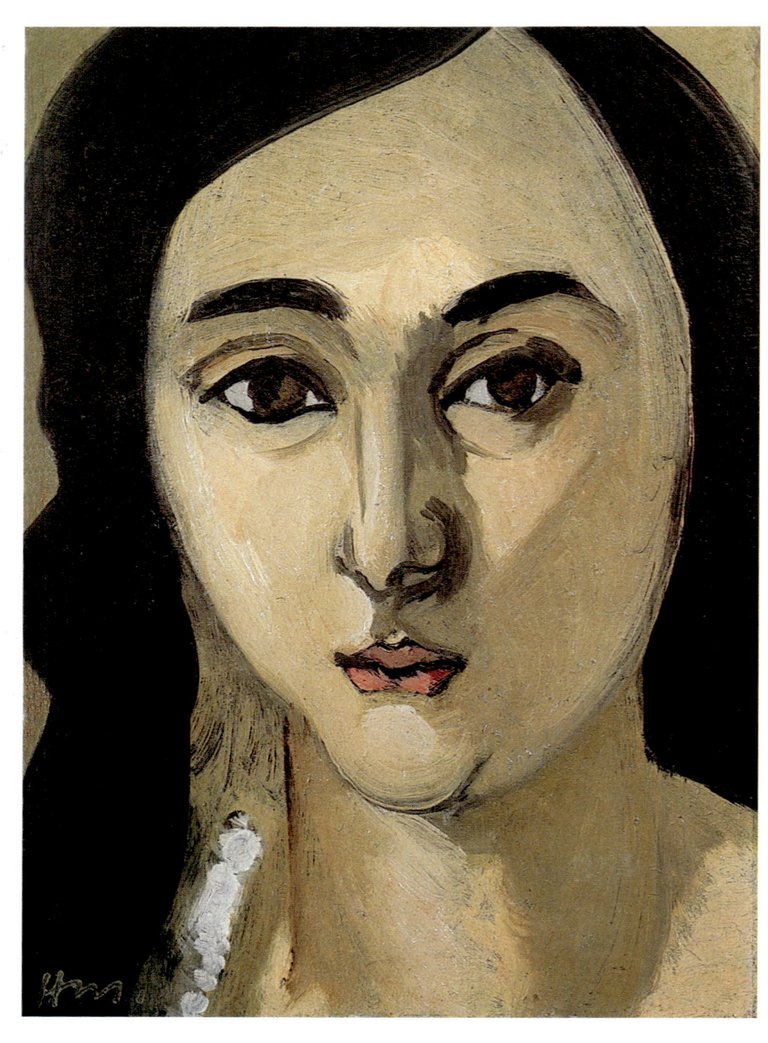

Laurette • c. 1916
Private collection

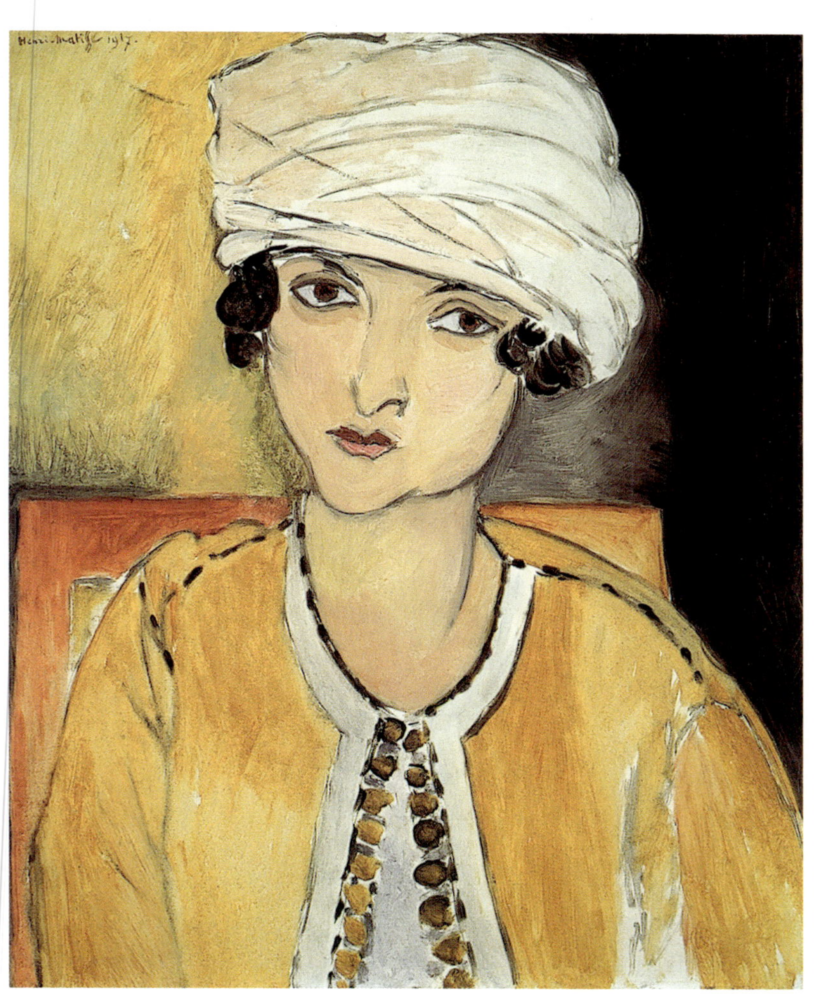

Laurette with Turban, Yellow Jacket • 1917
National Gallery of Art, Washington, Chester Dale Collection

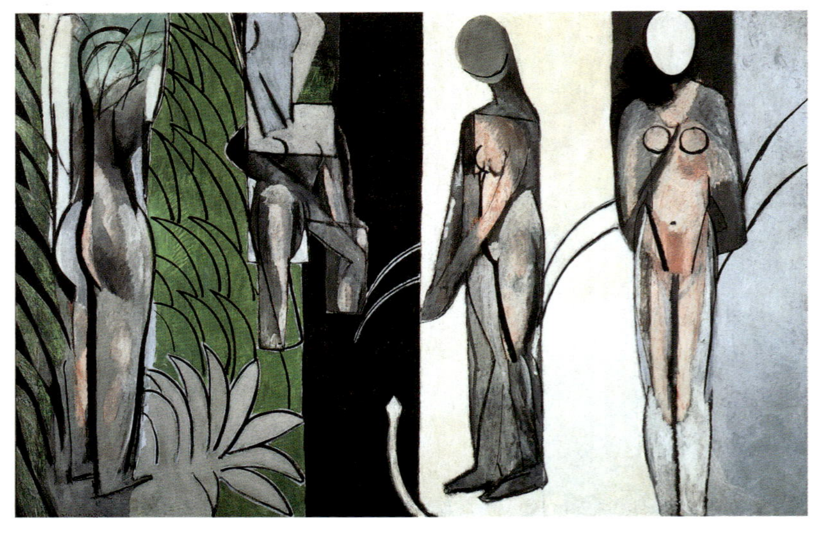

Bathers by a River • 1916

The Art Institute of Chicago, Charles H. and Mary F.S. Collection

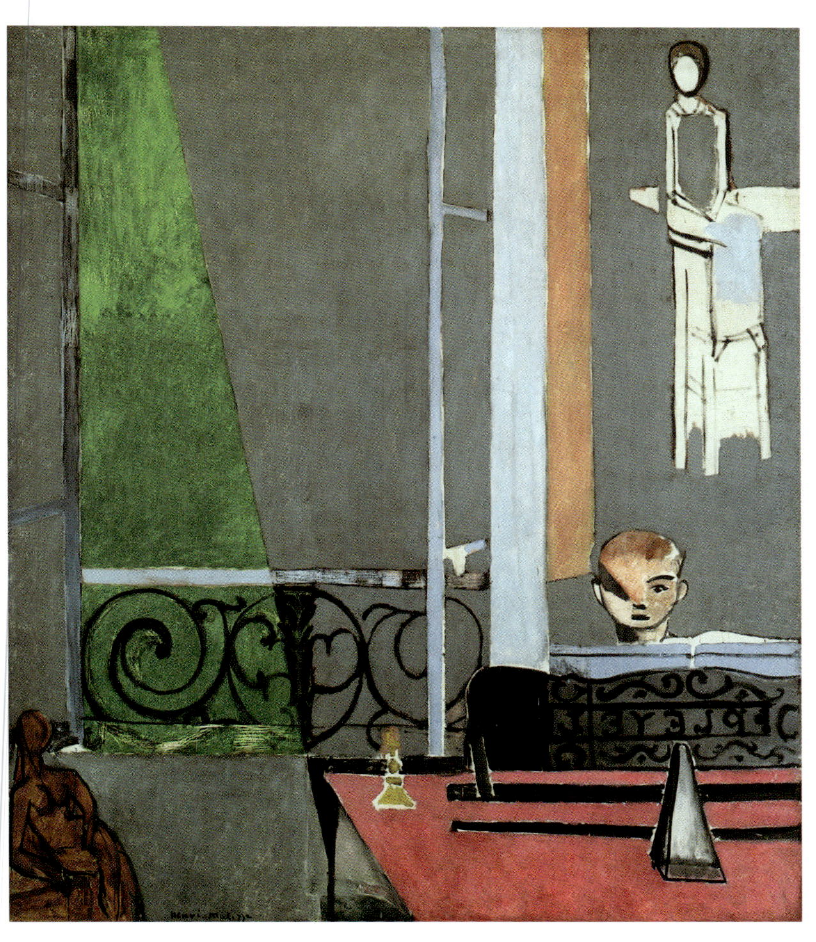

The Piano Lesson • Summer 1916

The Museum of Modern Art, New York, Mrs. Simon Guggenheim Fund

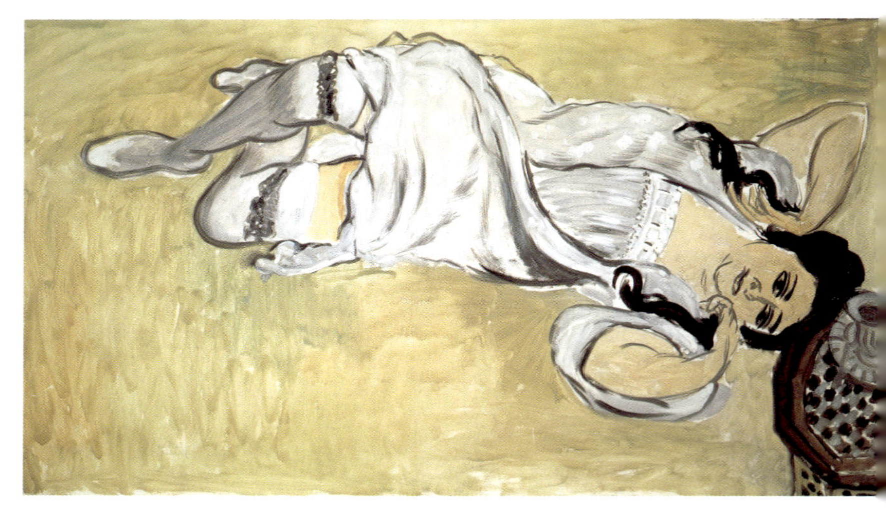

Laurette with a Cup of Coffee · 1917
Musée national d'art moderne, Paris

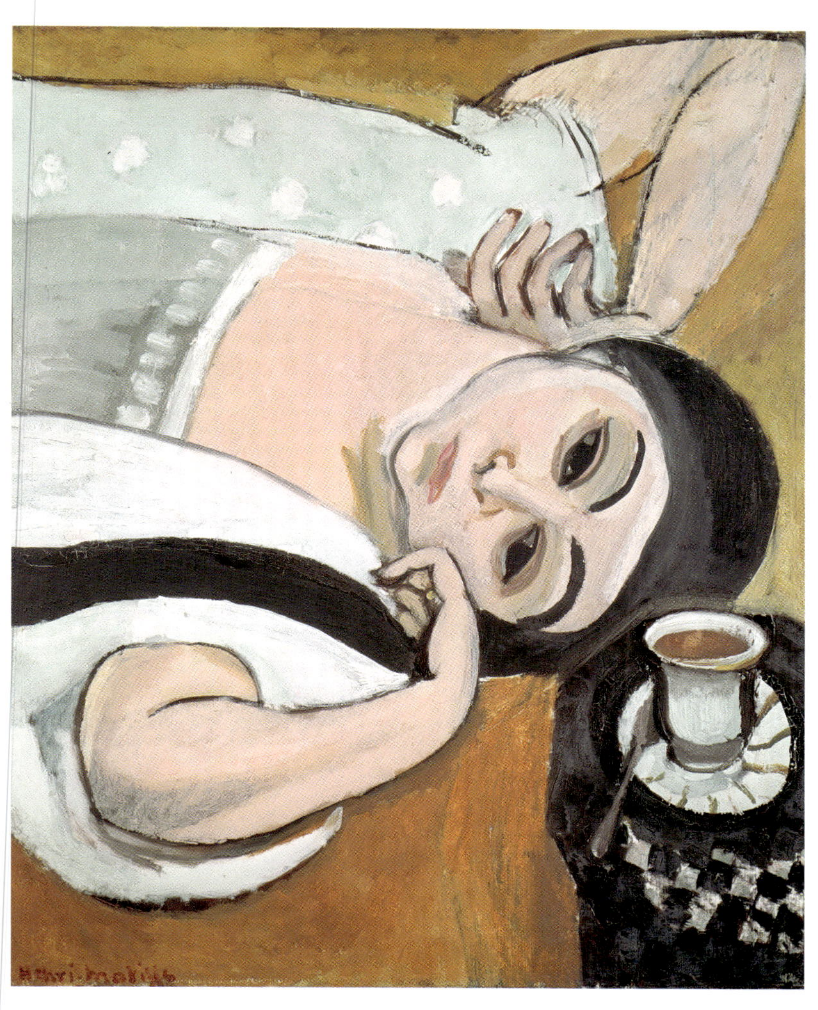

Reclining Laurette with a Cup of Coffee • 1917
Kunstmuseum, Solothurn

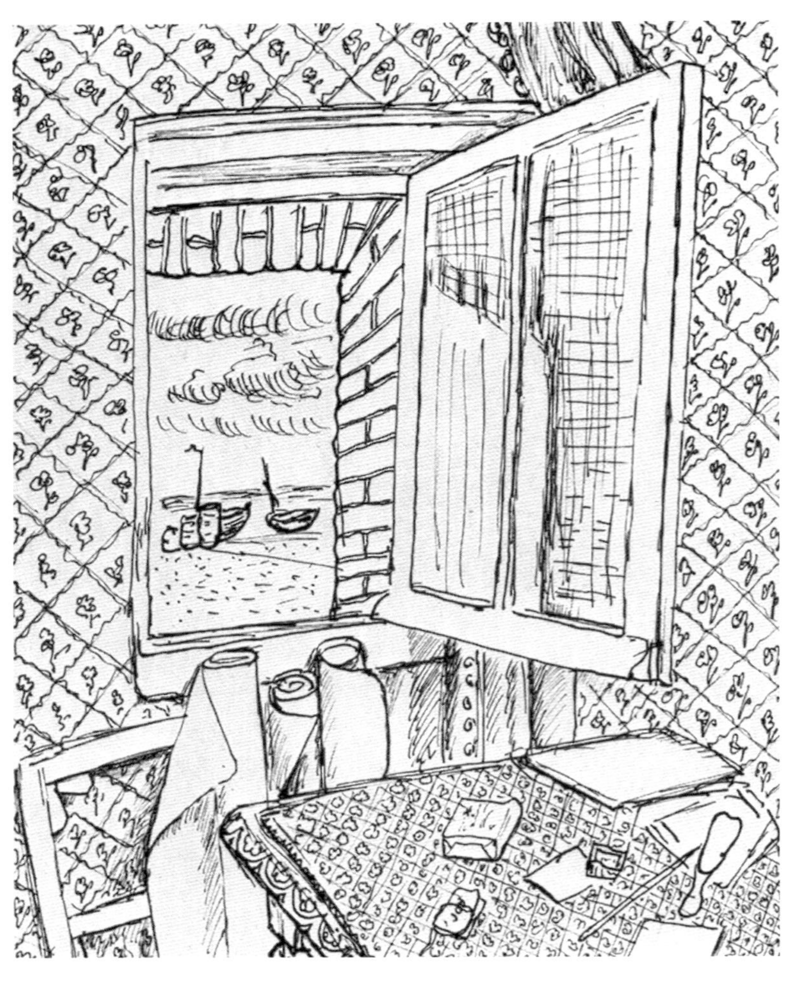

Window at Nice • 1917–1918
Musée national d'art moderne, Paris

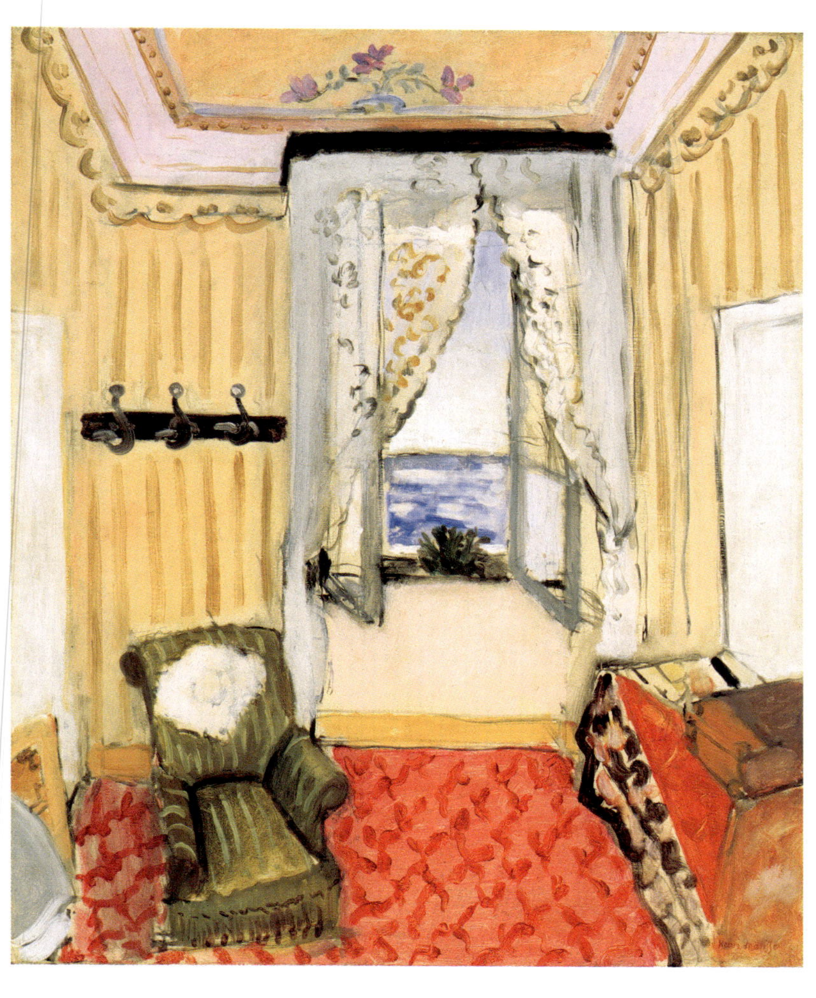

My Room at the Beau-Rivage • 1917–1918
Philadelphia Museum of Art, A. E. Gallatin Collection

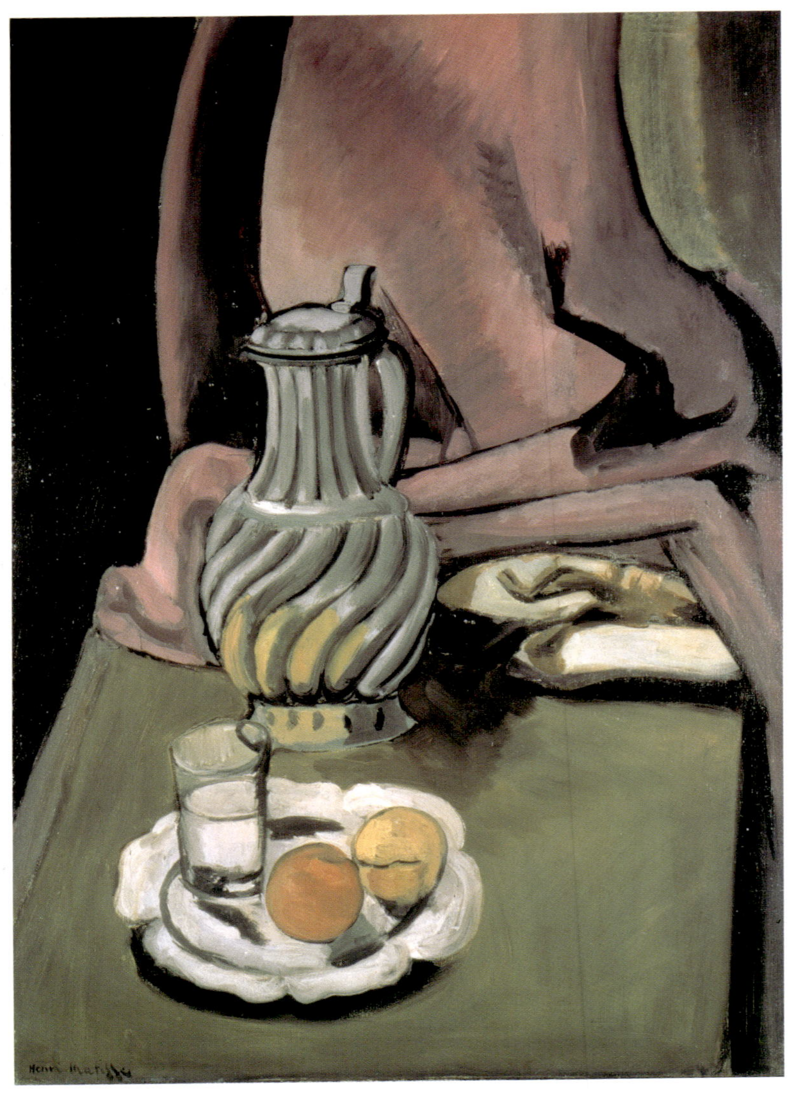

The Pewter Jug • c. 1917
The Baltimore Museum of Art, The Cone Collection

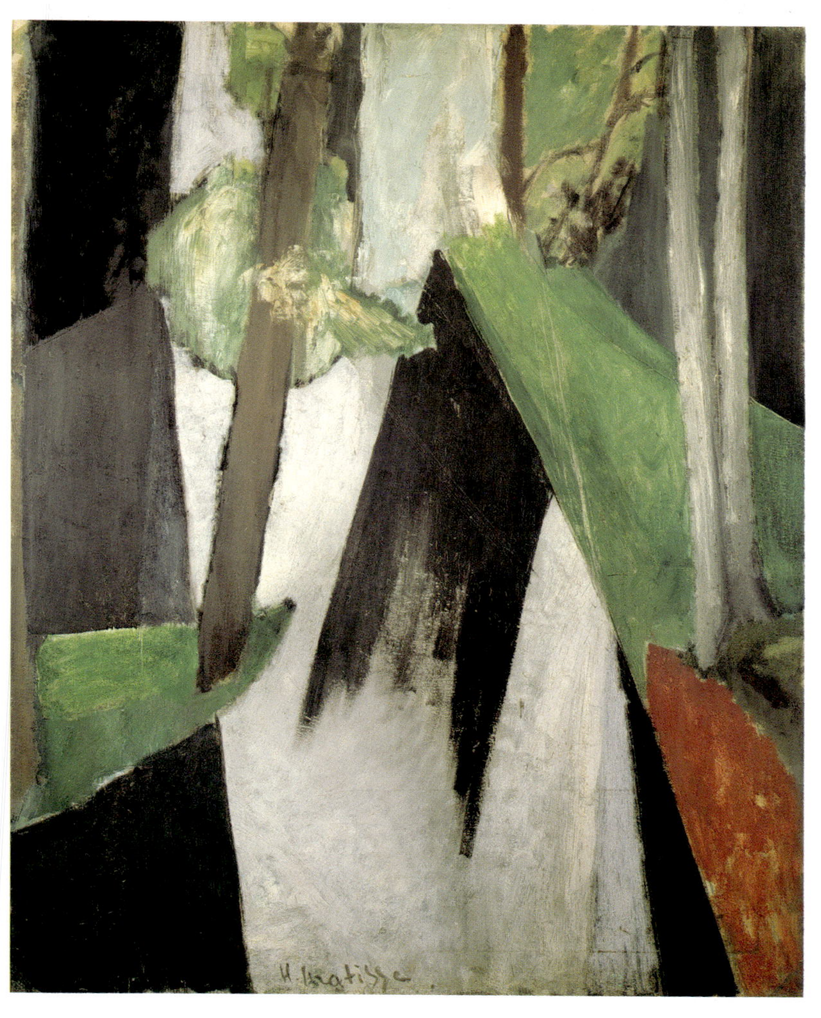

Shaft of Sunlight, the Woods of Trivaux • 1917
Private collection

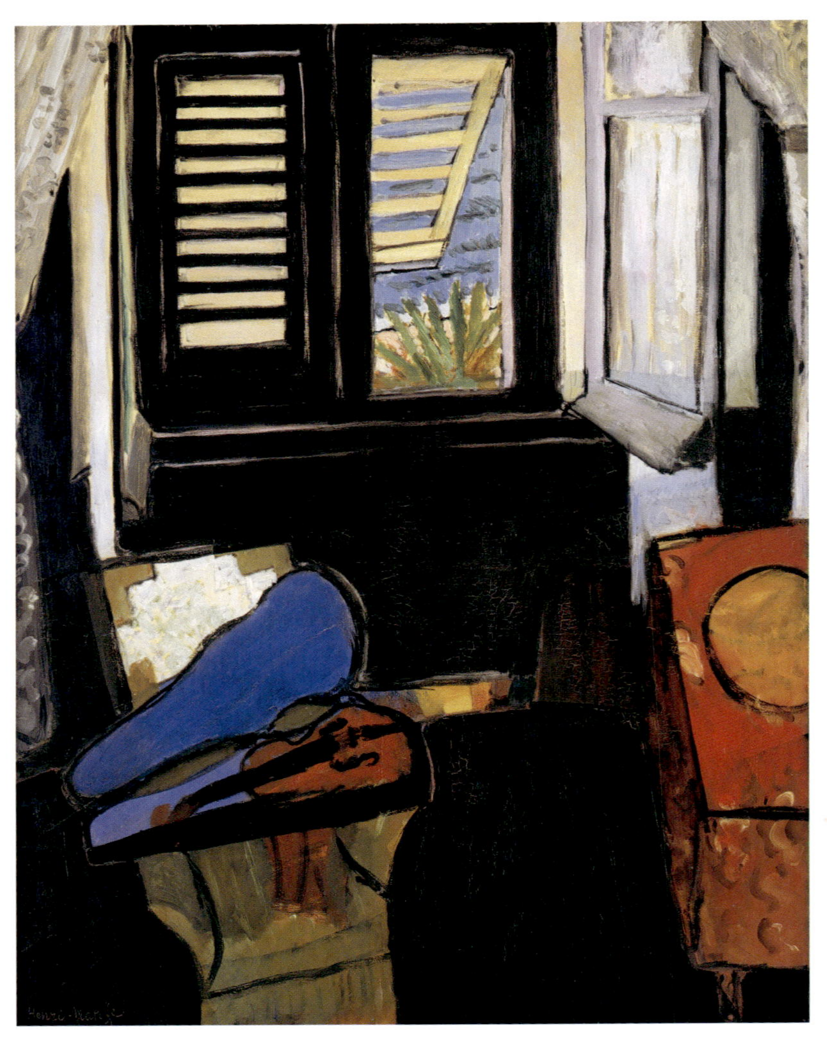

Interior with a Violin • 1917–1918
Statens Museum for Kunst, Copenhagen

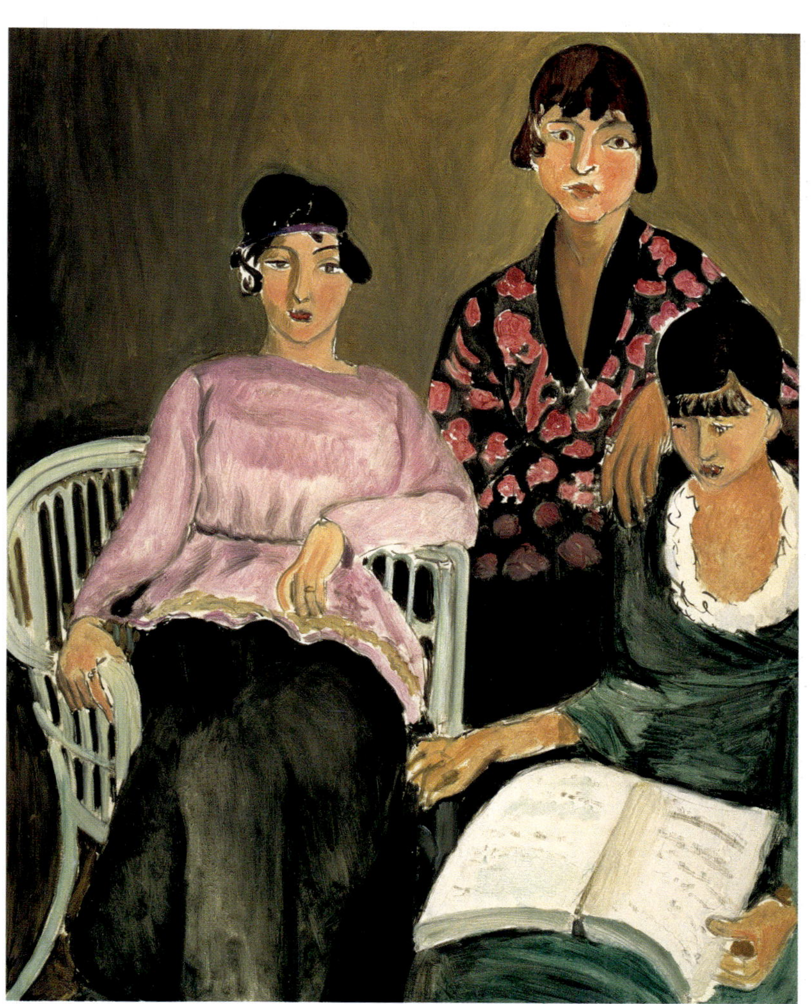

The Three Sisters • 1917
Musée de l'Orangerie, Paris

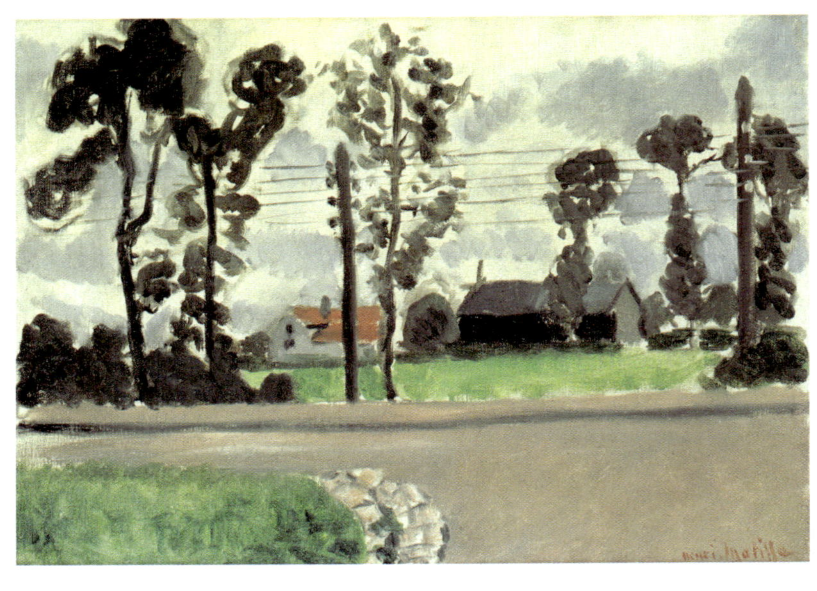

Road to Clamart · 1917
Musée national d'art moderne, Paris

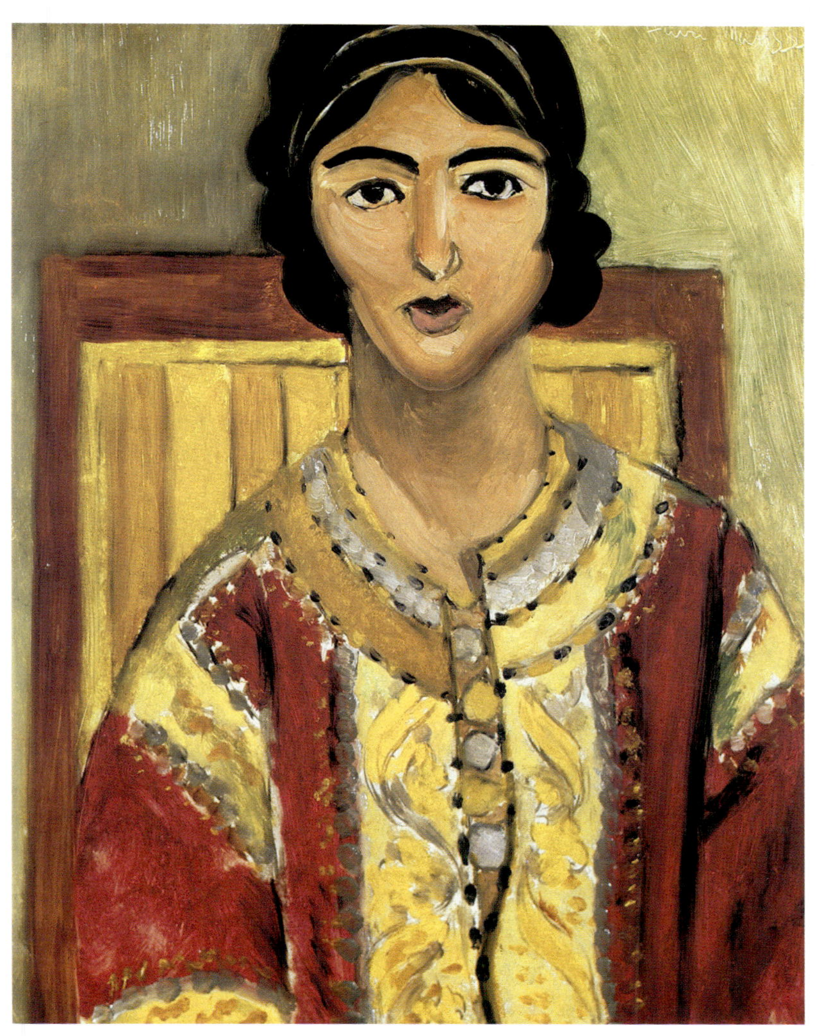

The Red Jacket • 1917
The Columbia Museum of Art, gift of Ferdinand Howald

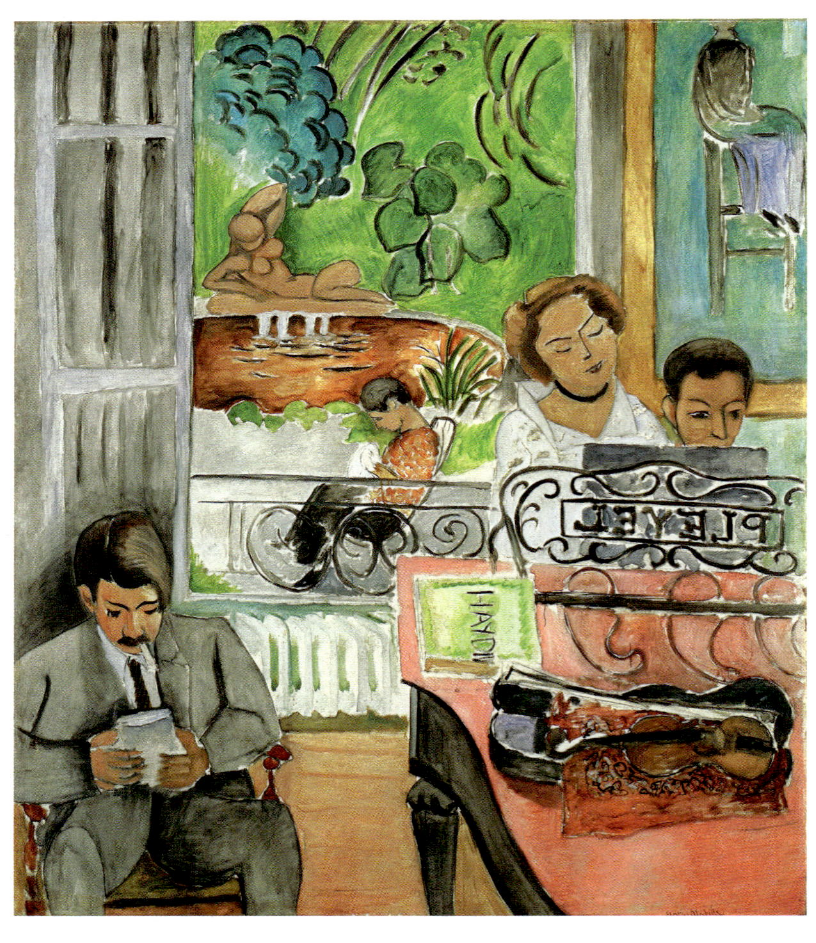

The Music Lesson · 1917
The Barnes Foundation, Merion, Pennsylvania

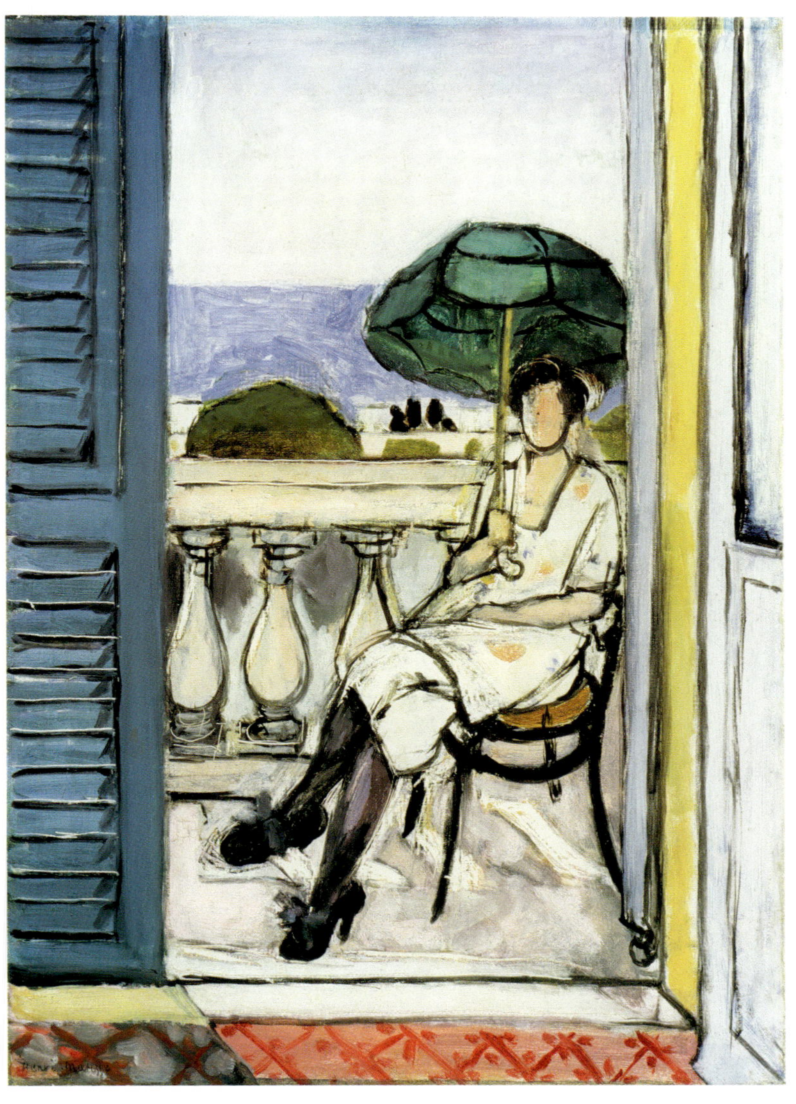

Woman with a Green Parasol on a Balcony • Winter 1918–1919
Private collection

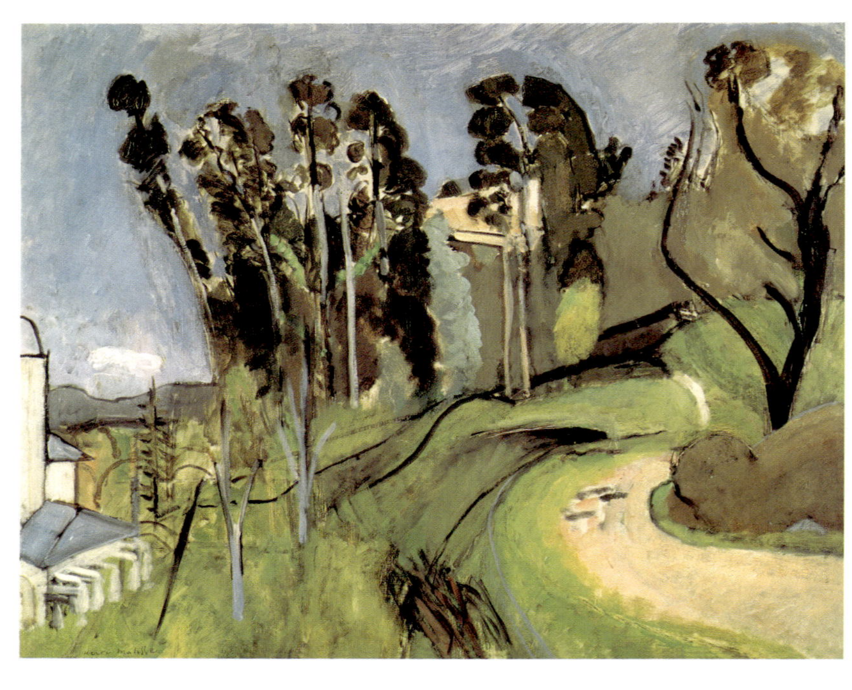

Large Landscape, Mont Alban · Spring 1918
Private collection

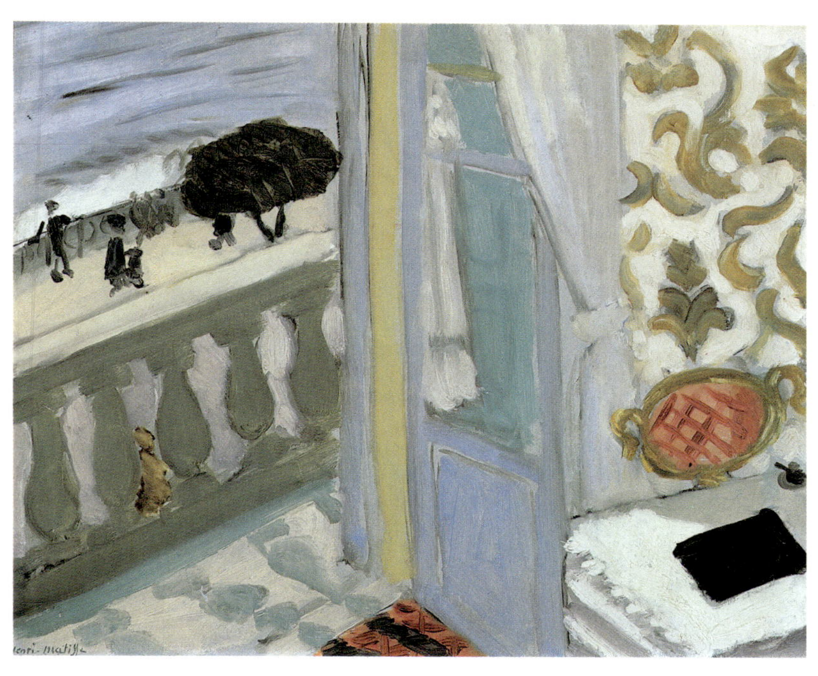

Interior with Black Notebook · 1918

Private collection

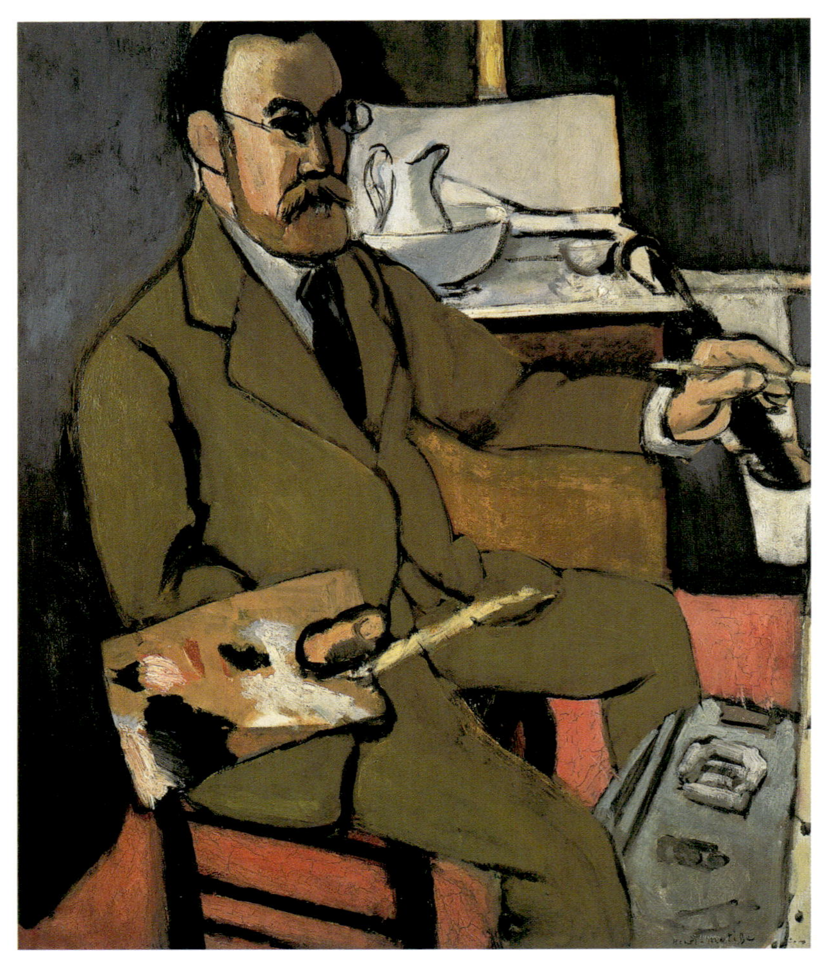

Self-Portrait · 1918
Musée Matisse, Le Cateau-Cambrésis

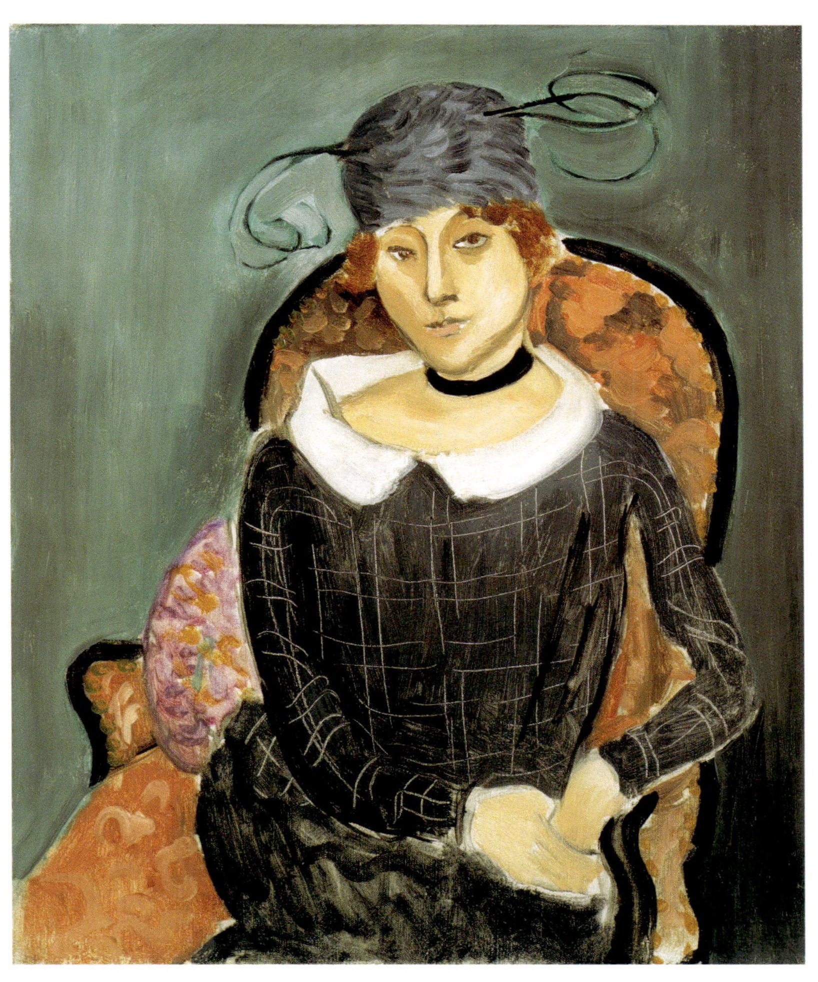

The Ostrich Feather Hat · Autumn 1918
Wadsworth Atheneum, Hartford, The Ella Gallup Sumner
and Mary Catlin Sumner Collection

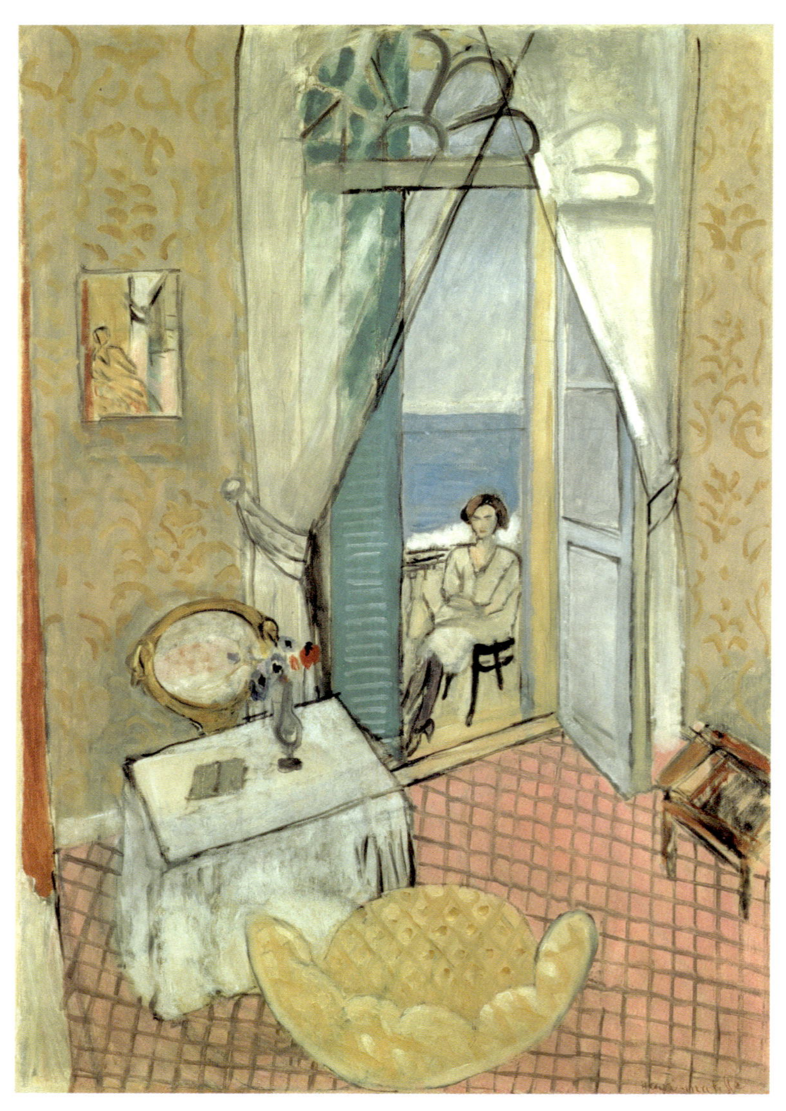

Large Interior, Nice • 1918–1919
The Art Institute of Chicago, gift of Mrs. Gilbert W. Chapman

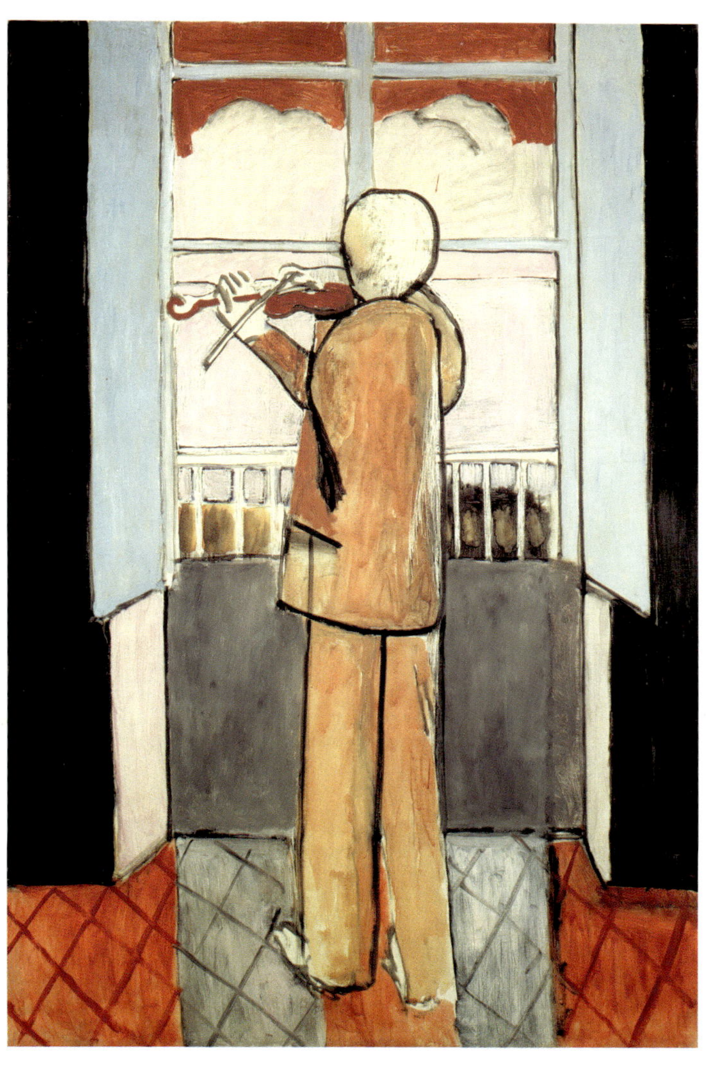

Violonist at the Window · Spring 1918
Musée national d'art moderne, Paris
> **The Painting Session** · 1918–1919
Scottish National Gallery of Modern Art, Edinburgh

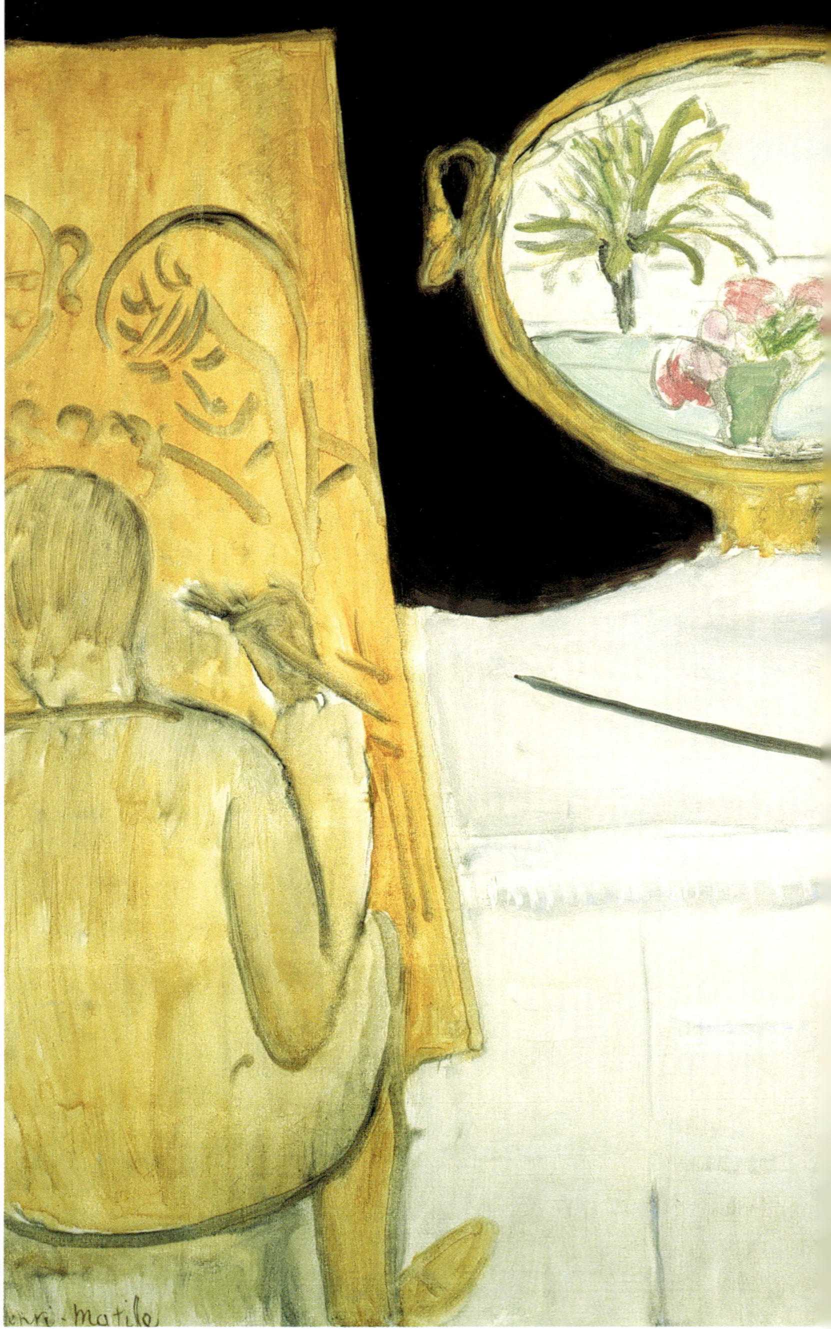

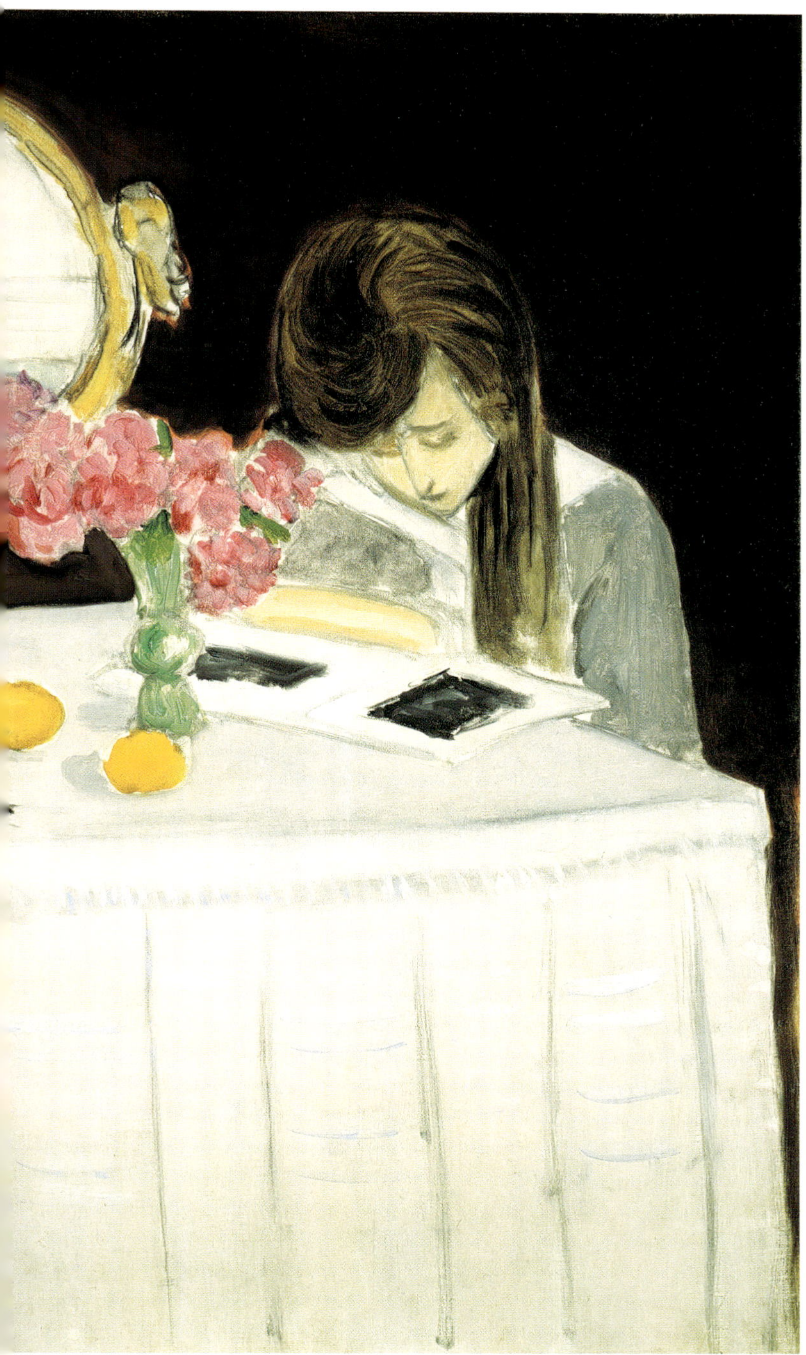

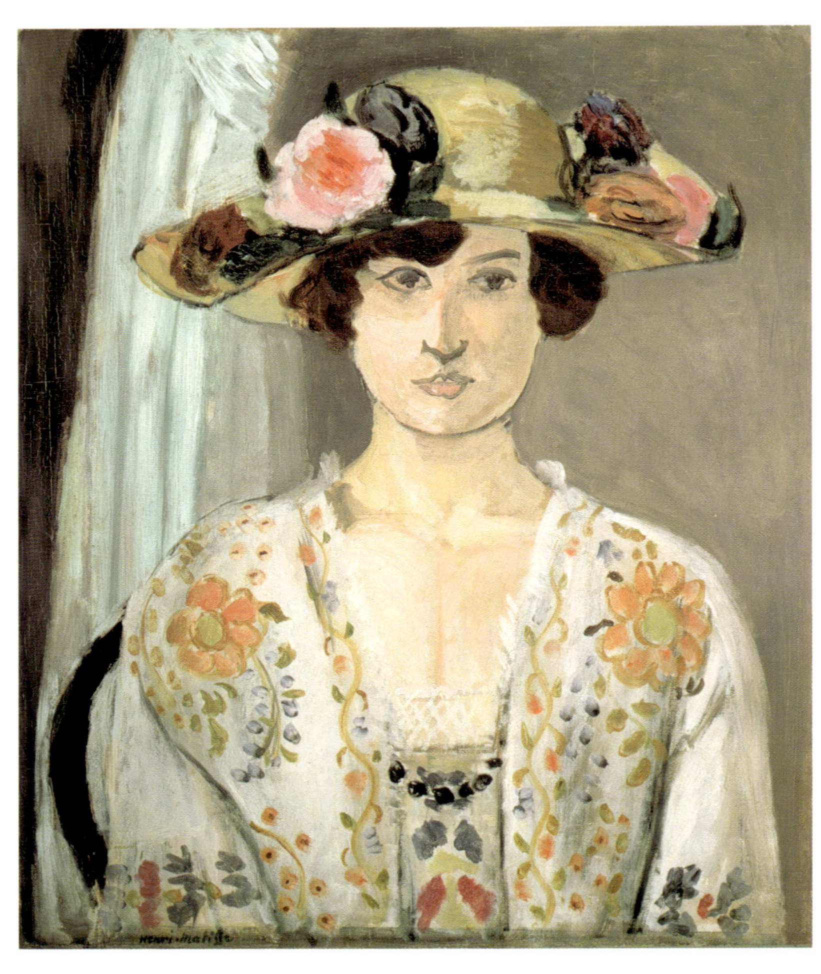

Woman in a Flowered Hat • 1919

Private collection

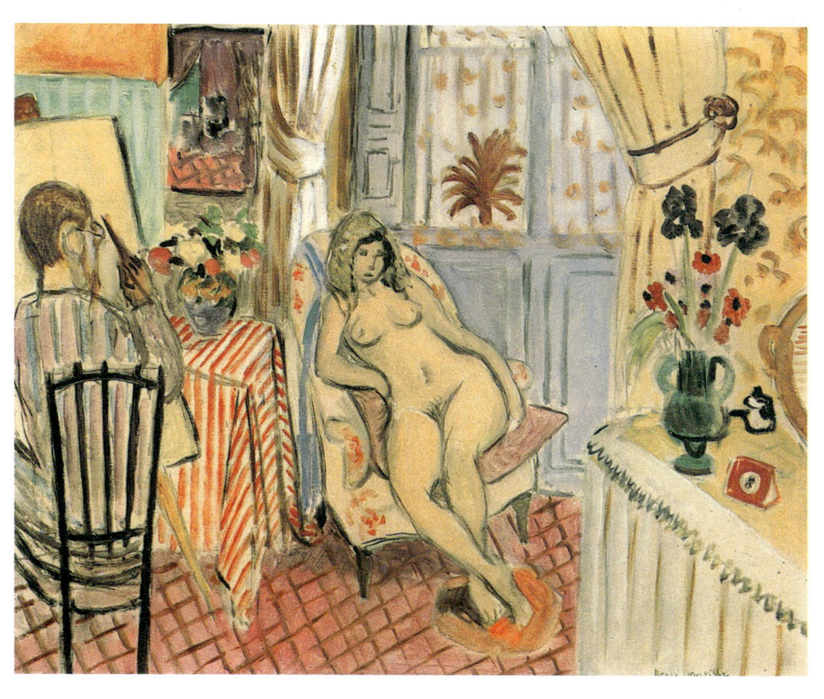

The Painter and His Model / Studio Interior

late 1918–Spring 1919 or late 1920–Spring 1921

Private collection

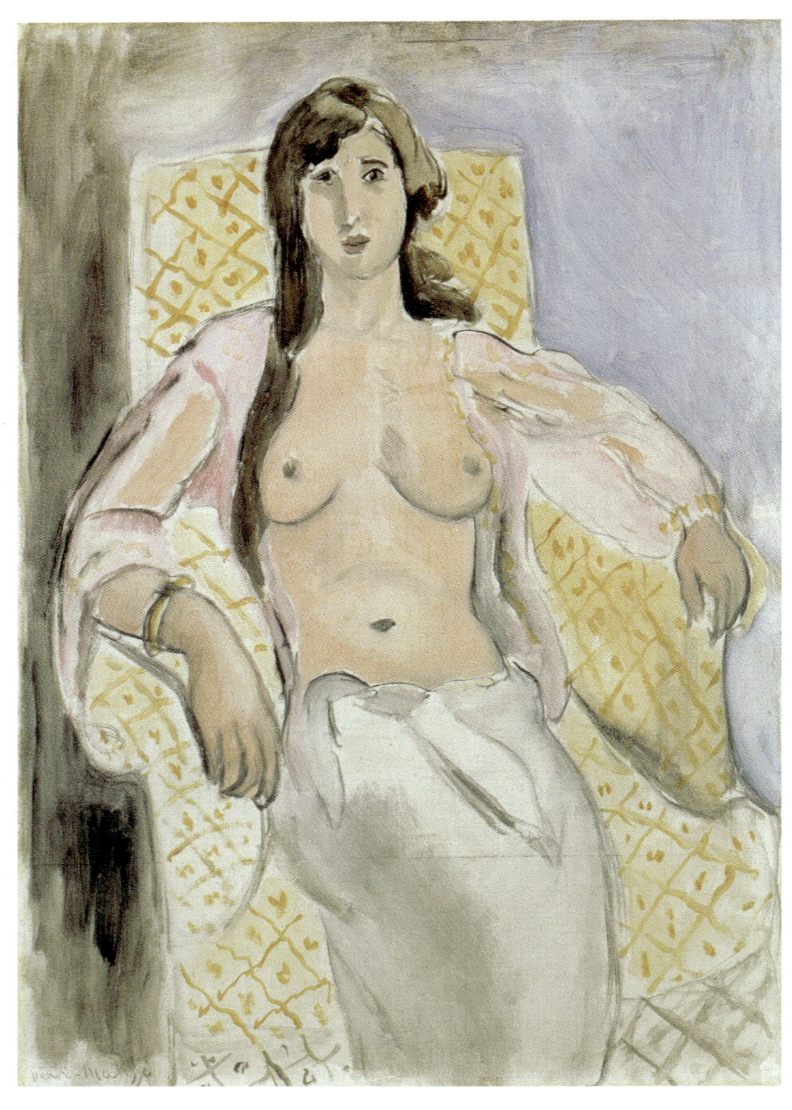

Woman in an Armchair, or Antoinette • 1919
Private collection

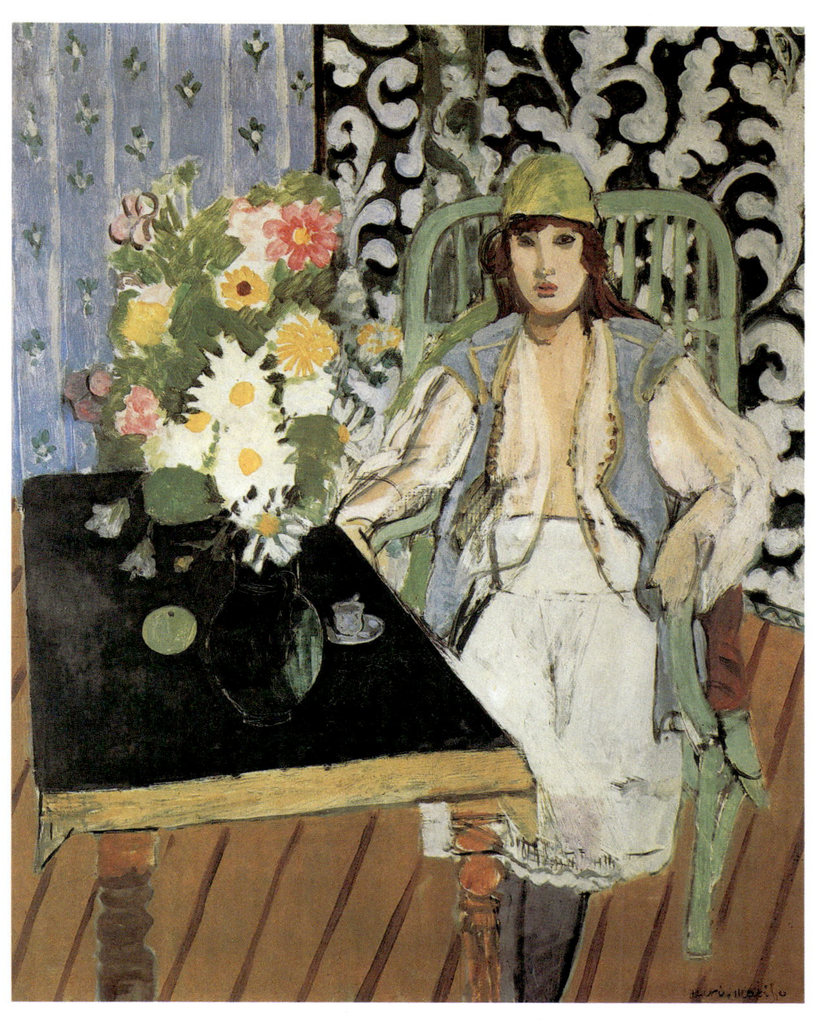

The Black Table • 1919
Private collection

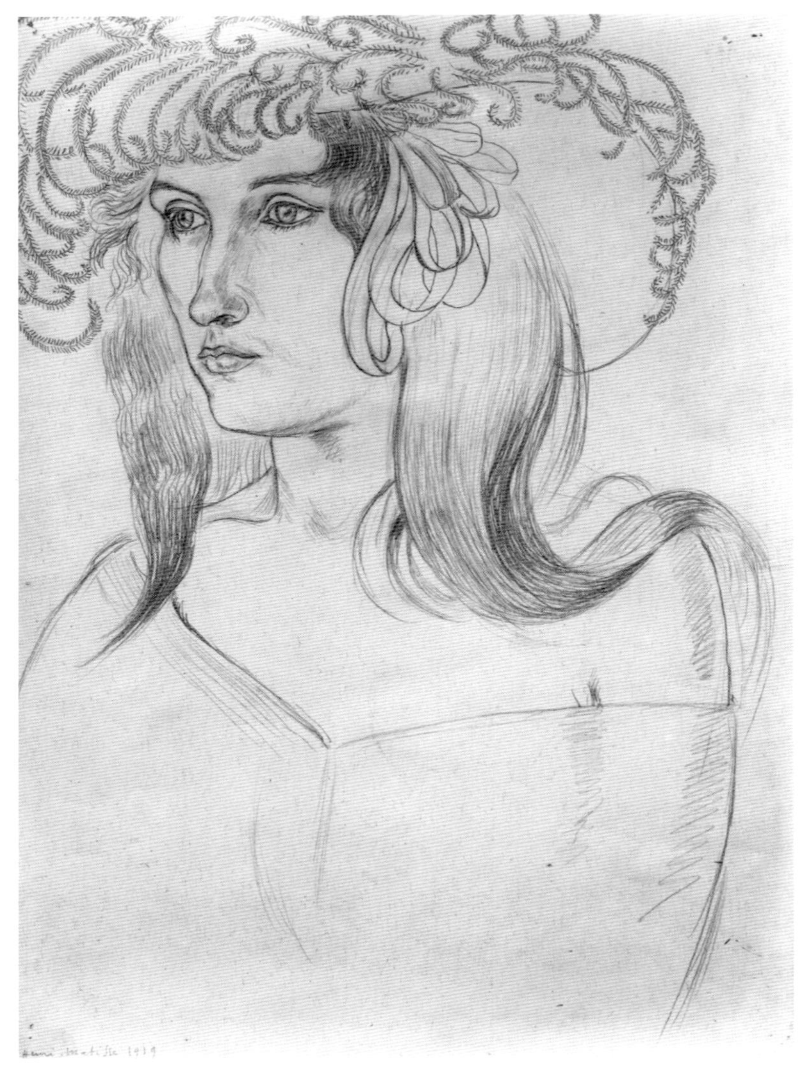

The Plumed Hat • 1919
Private collection

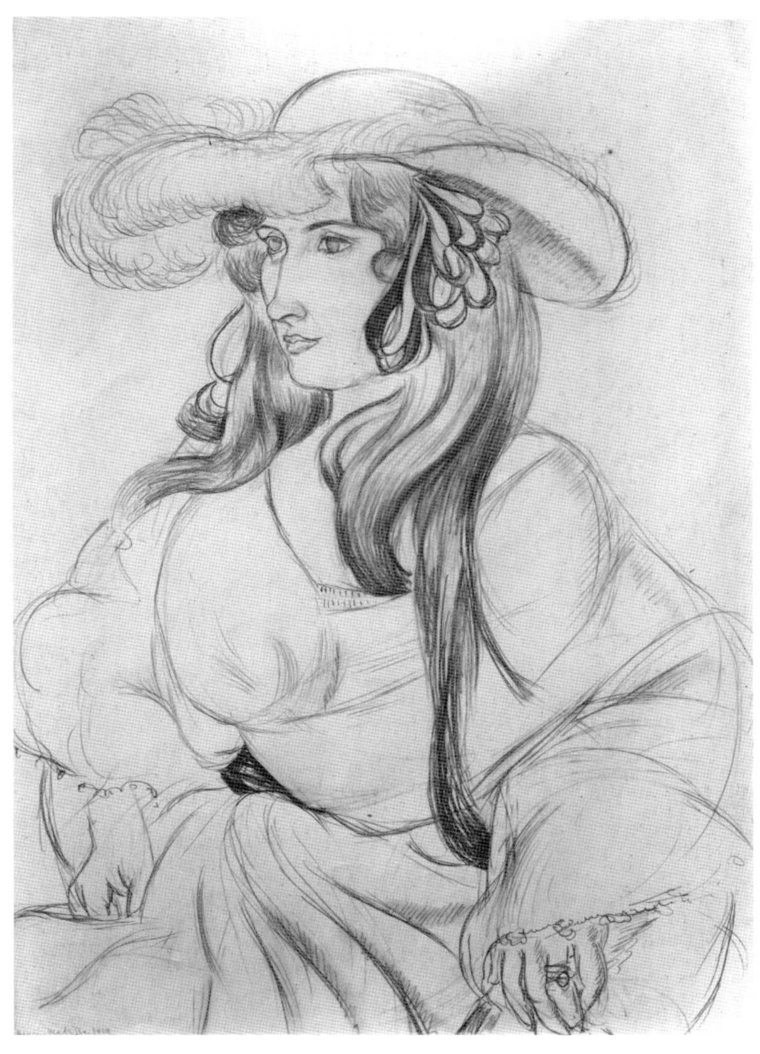

The Plumed Hat · 1919
The Detroit Institute of Arts, bequest of John S. Newberry

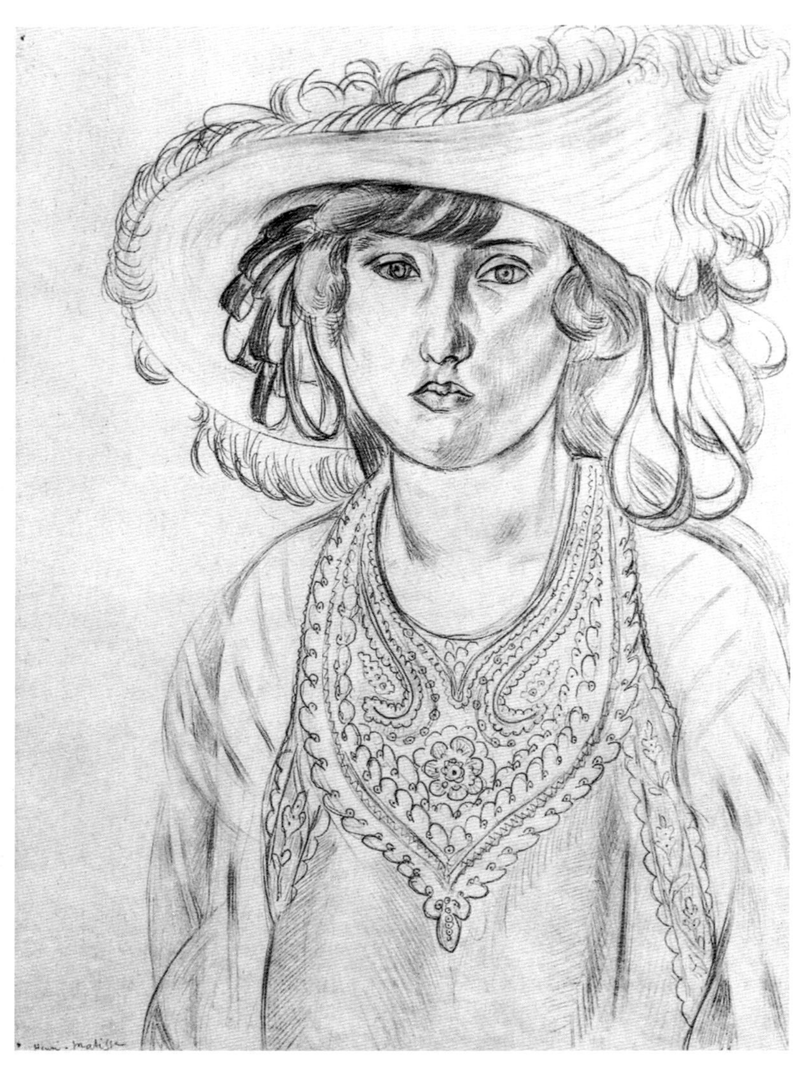

The Plumed Hat • 1919
The Baltimore Museum of Art, The Cone Collection

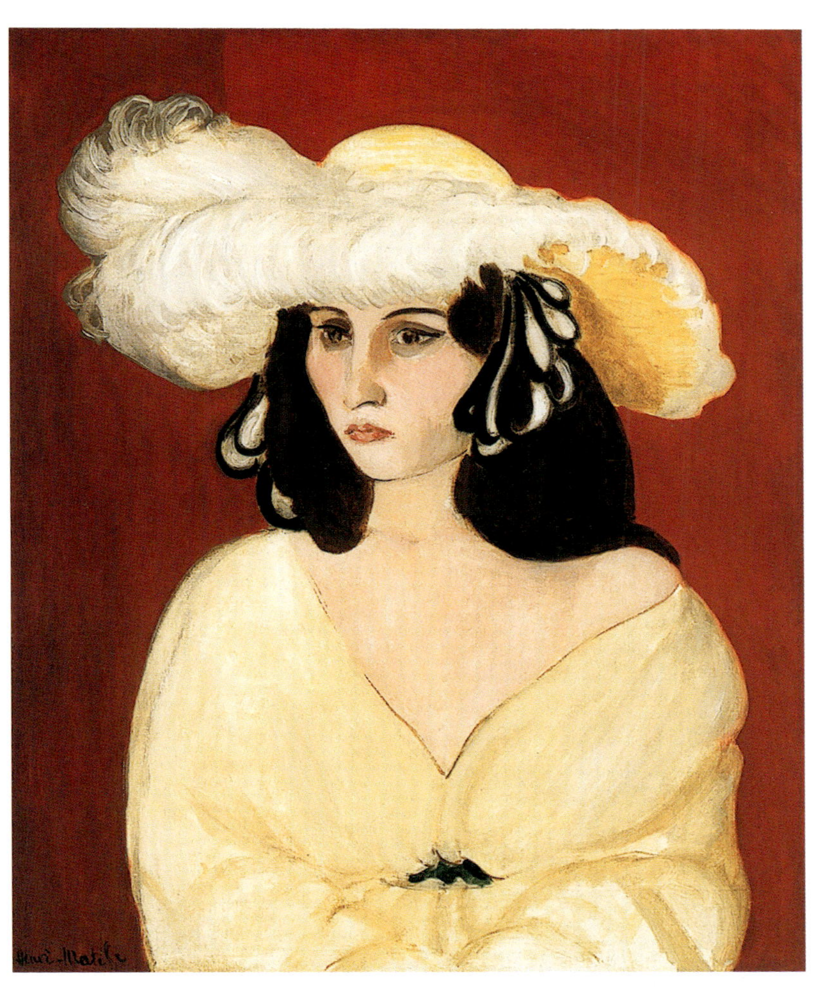

The White Plumes • early 1919

The Minneapolis Institute of Arts, The William Hood Dunwoody Fund

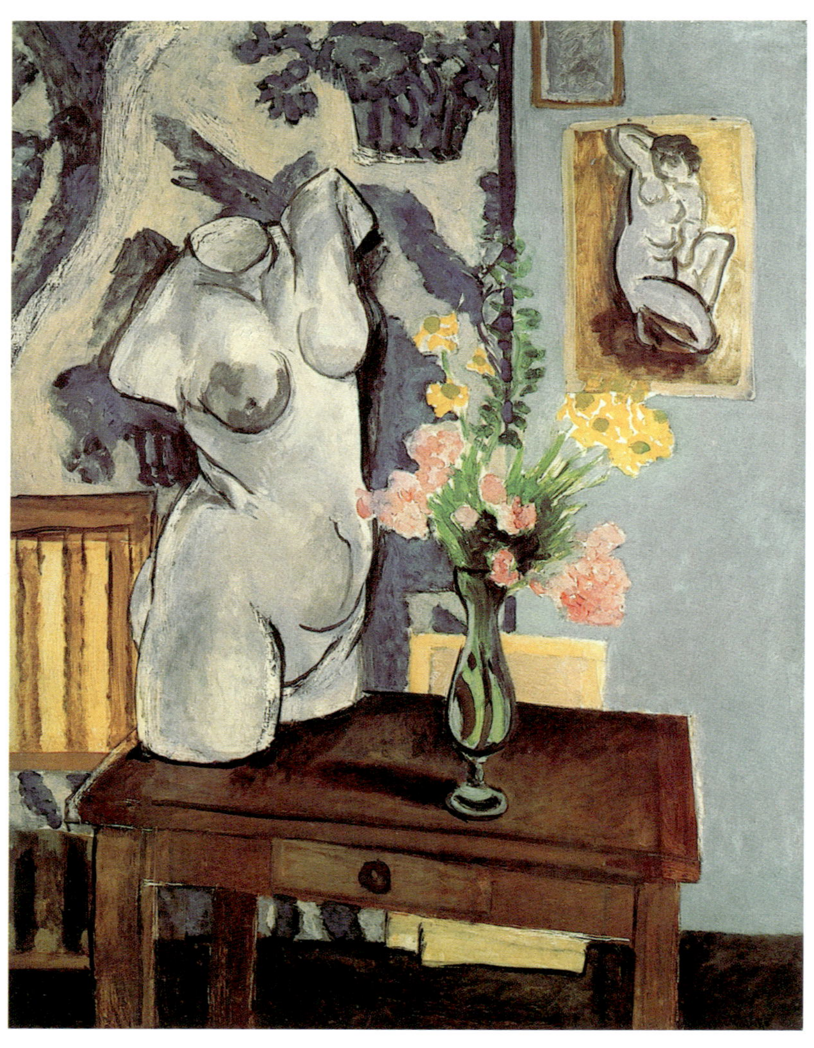

Plaster Figure, Bouquet of Flowers · Summer 1919

Museu de Arte, São Paulo

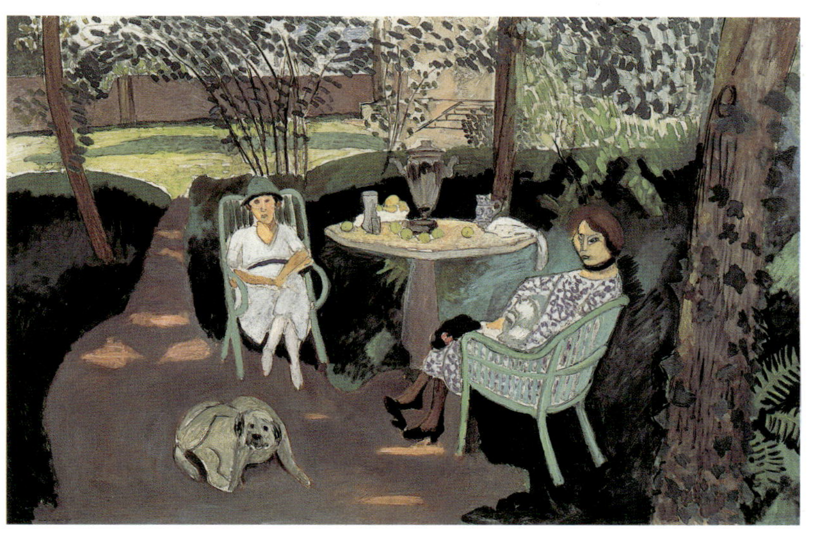

Tea in the Garden • 1919
Los Angeles County Museum of Art, bequest of David L. Loew
in memory of his father, Marcus Loew

> **Woman on a Sofa** • late 1920–Spring 1921
Kunstmuseum, Basel

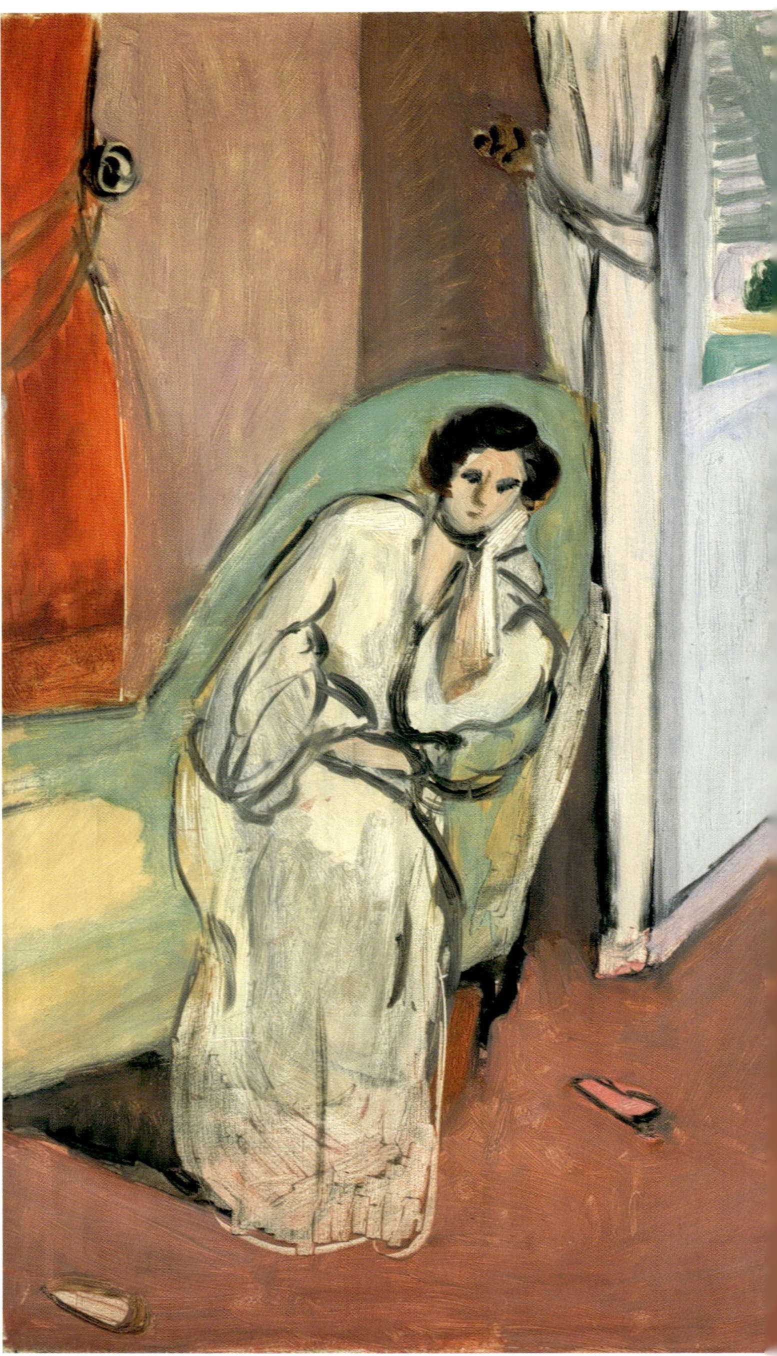

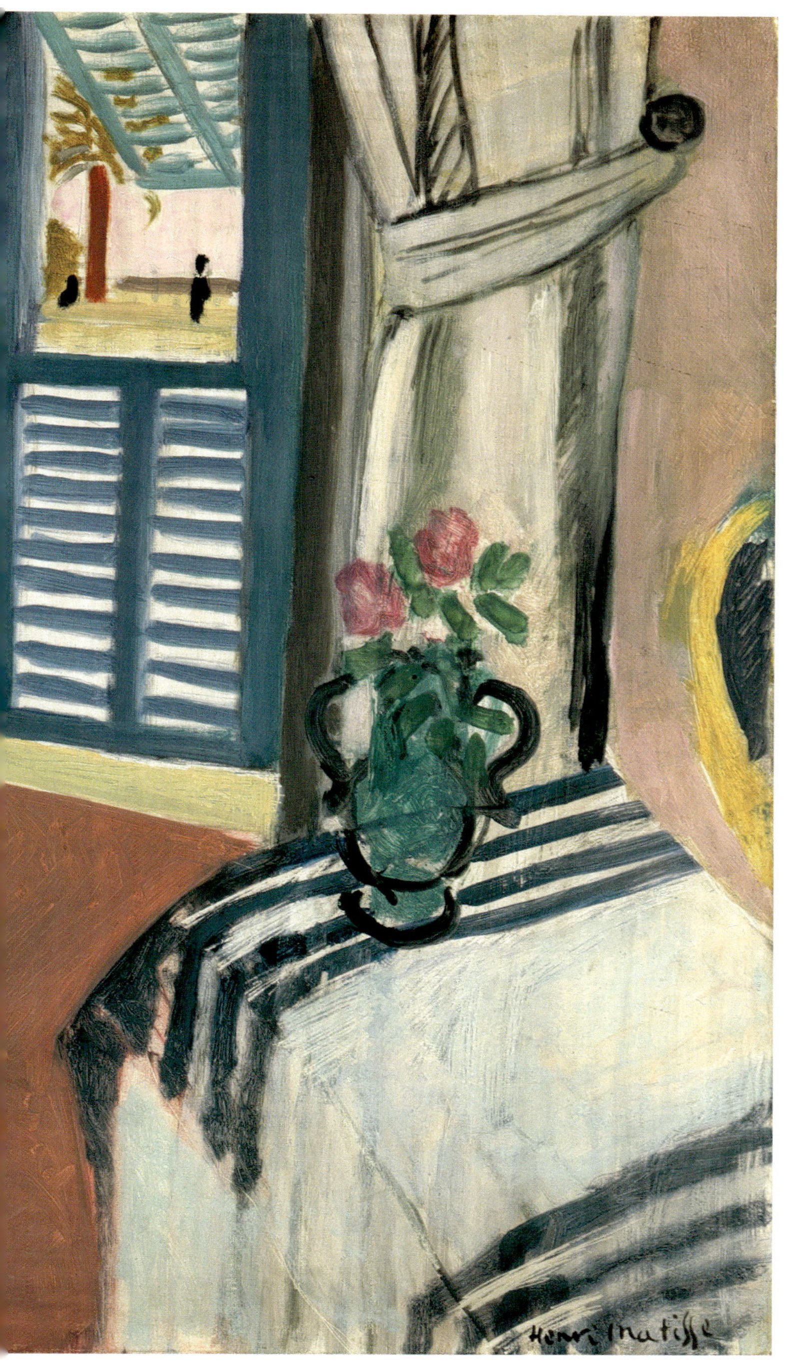
Henri Matisse

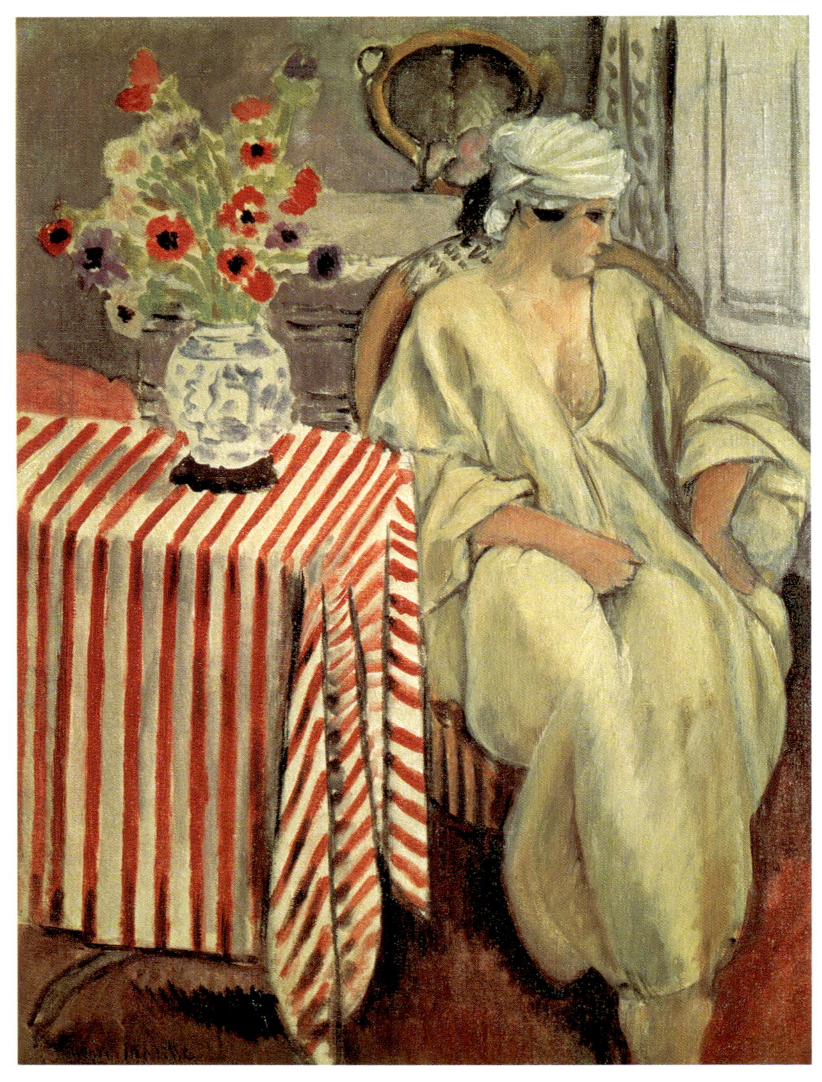

Meditation / After the Bath • late 1920–Spring 1921
Private collection

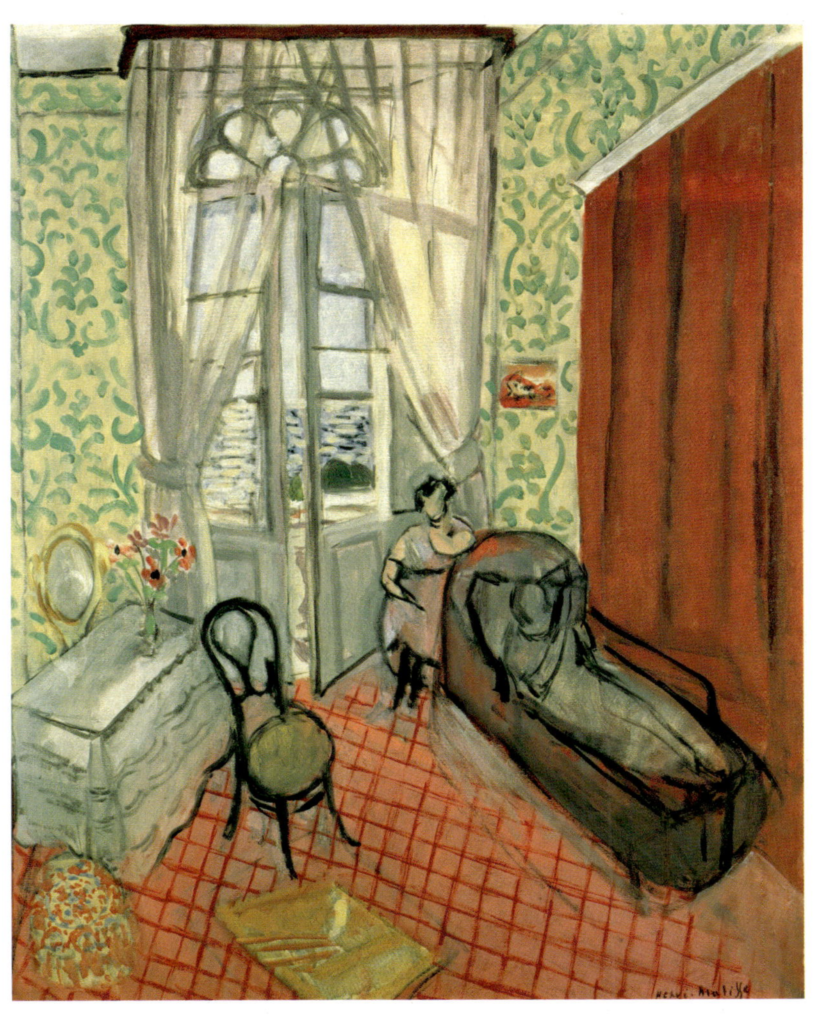

Two Women in an Interior • late 1920–Spring 1921
Musée de l'Orangerie, Paris

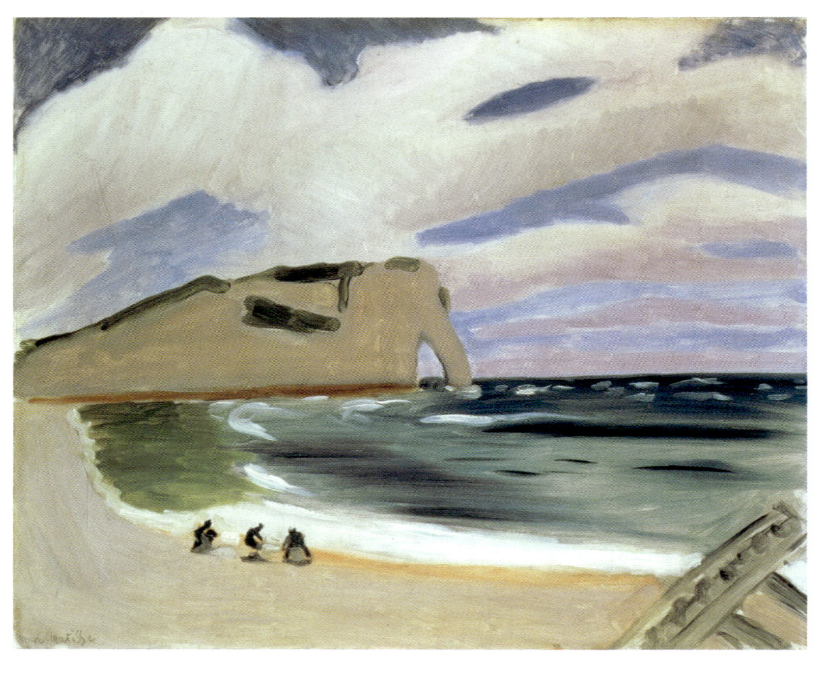

Etretat, Large Cliff • 1920

Fitzwilliam Museum, University of Cambridge

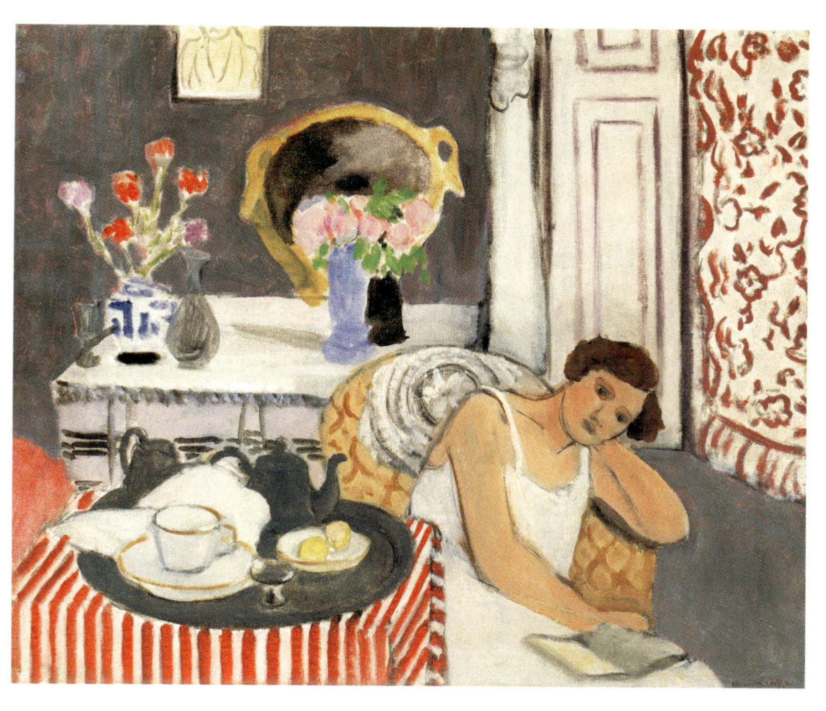

The Breakfast · late 1919–Spring 1920
Philadelphia Museum of Art, The Samuel S. White III and Vera White Collection

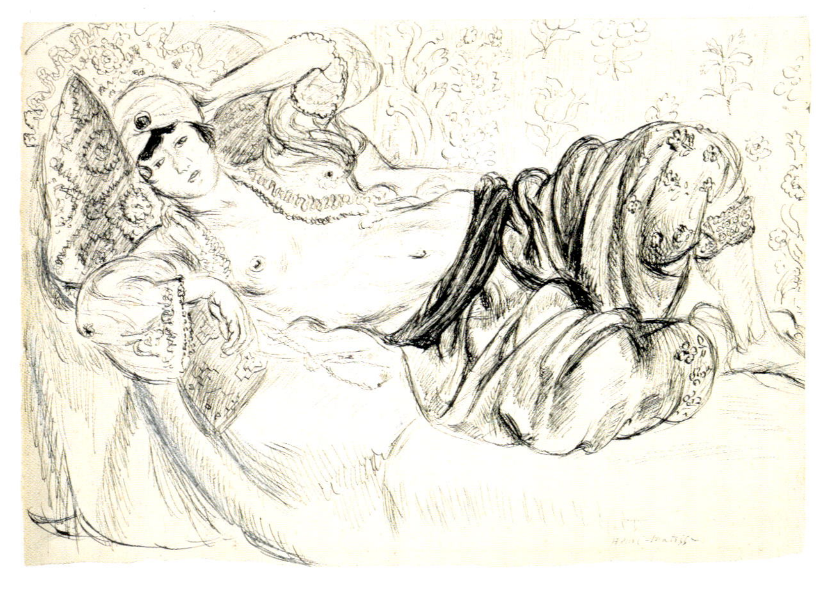

Odalisque with Turkish Trousers • 1920–1921
Musée national d'art moderne, Paris

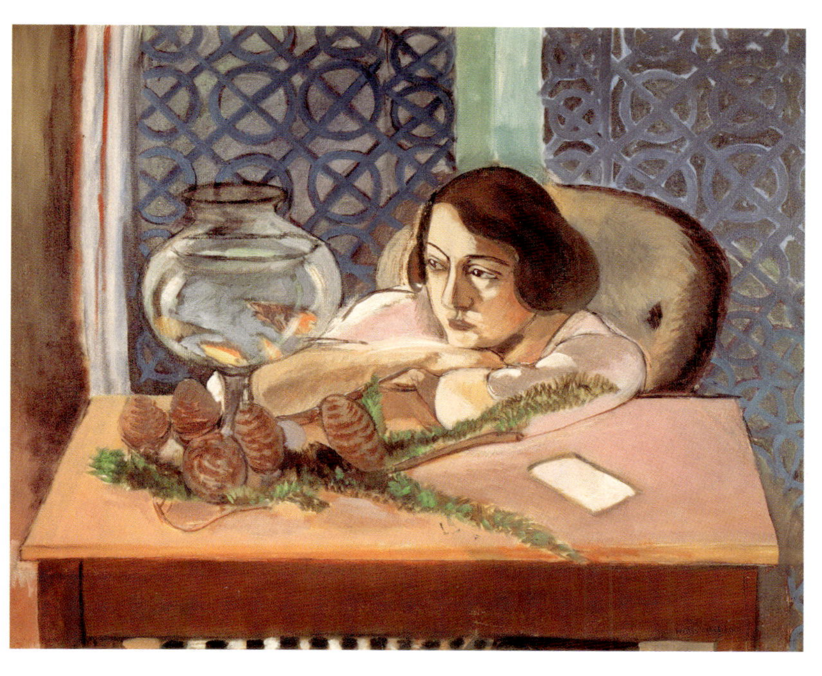

Woman Before an Aquarium • late 1921 or 1923
The Art Institute of Chicago, Helen Birch Bartlett Memorial Collection

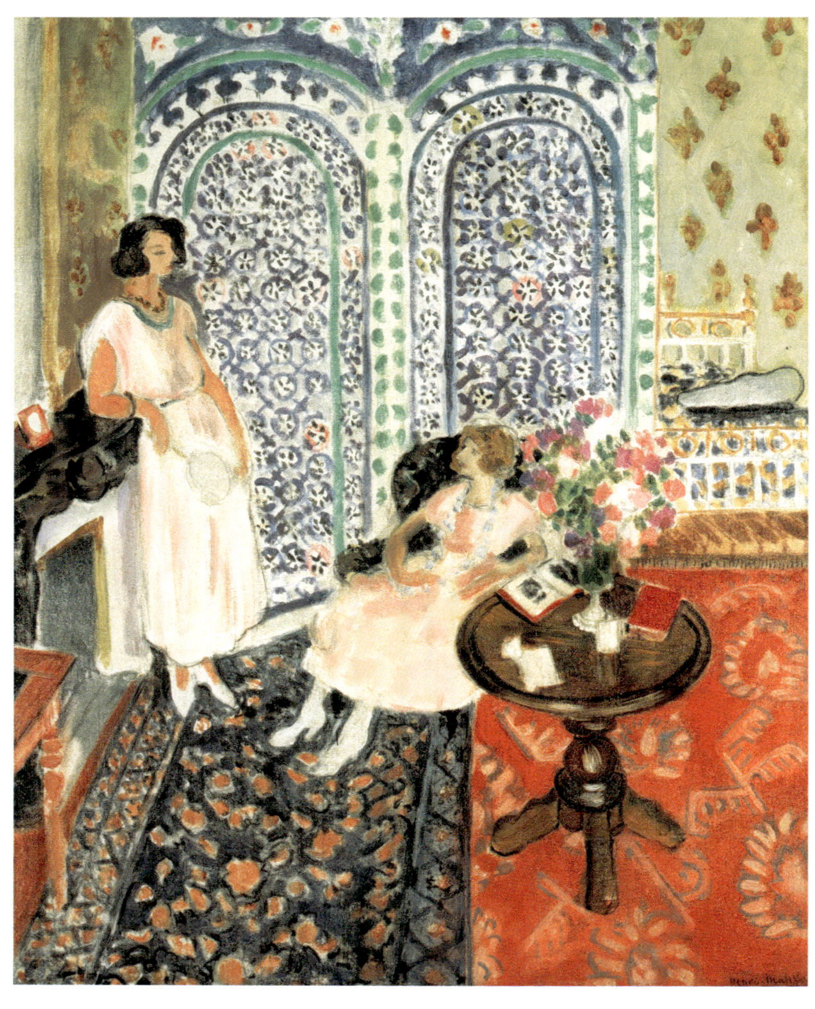

The Moorish Screen • late 1921

Philadelphia Museum of Art, bequest of Lisa Norris Elkins

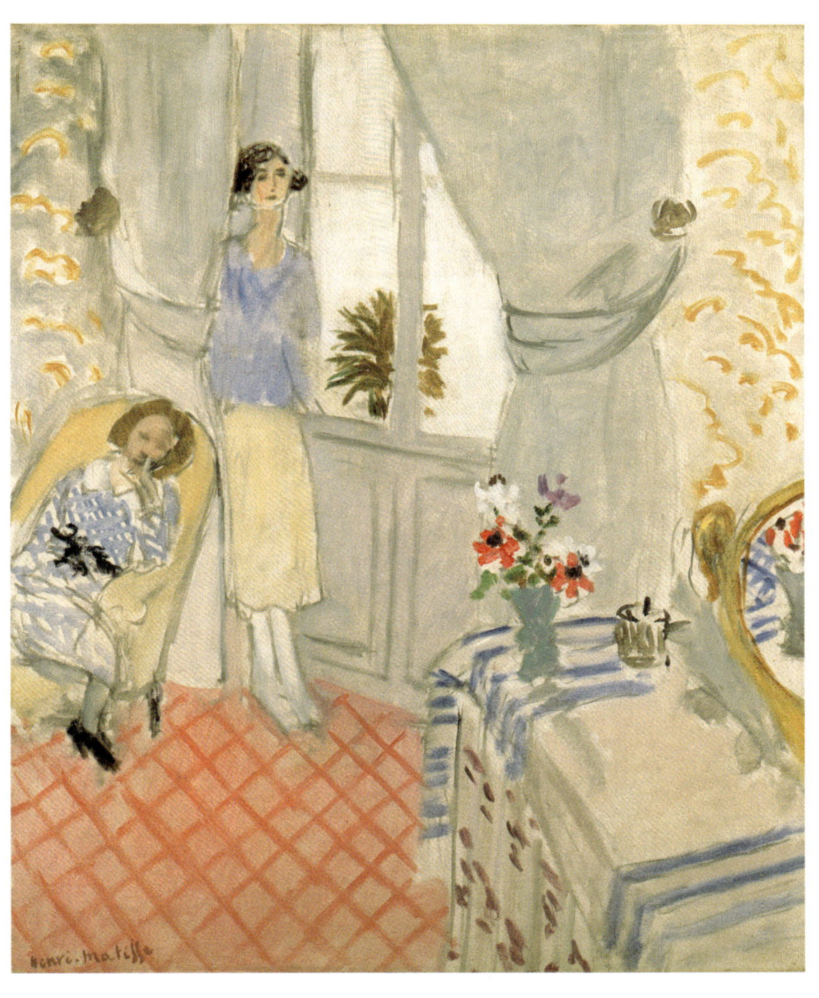

The Boudoir • 1921
Musée de l'Orangerie, Paris

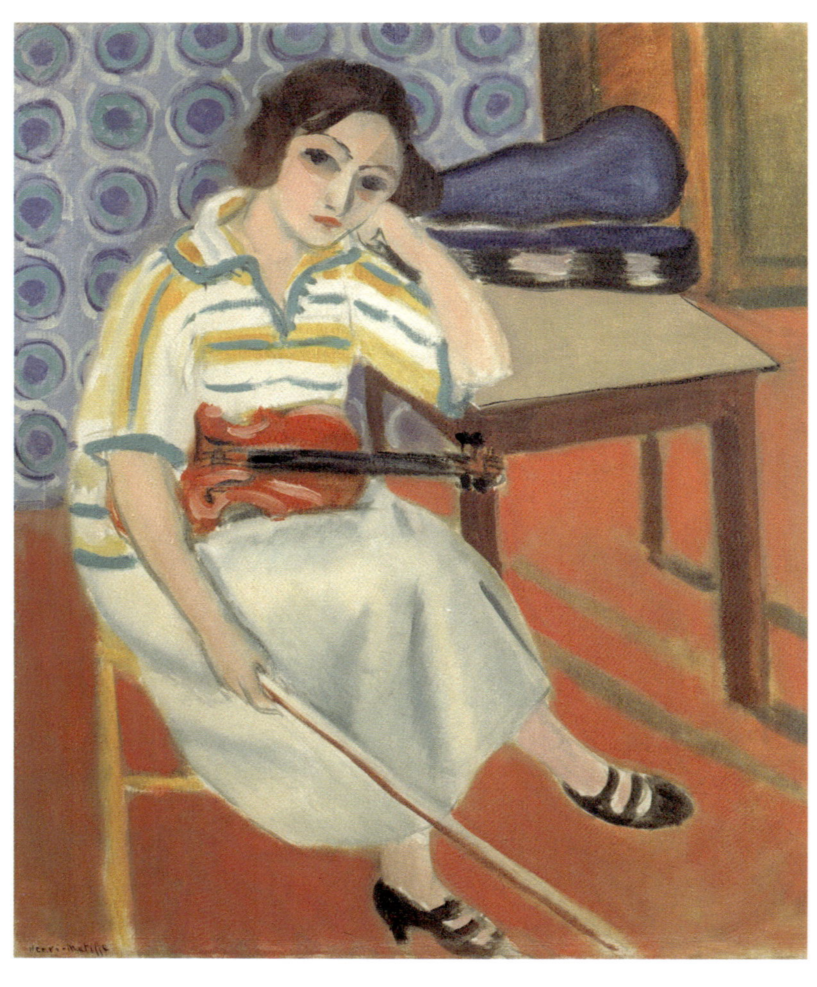

Woman with a Violin • 1921
Musée de l'Orangerie, Paris

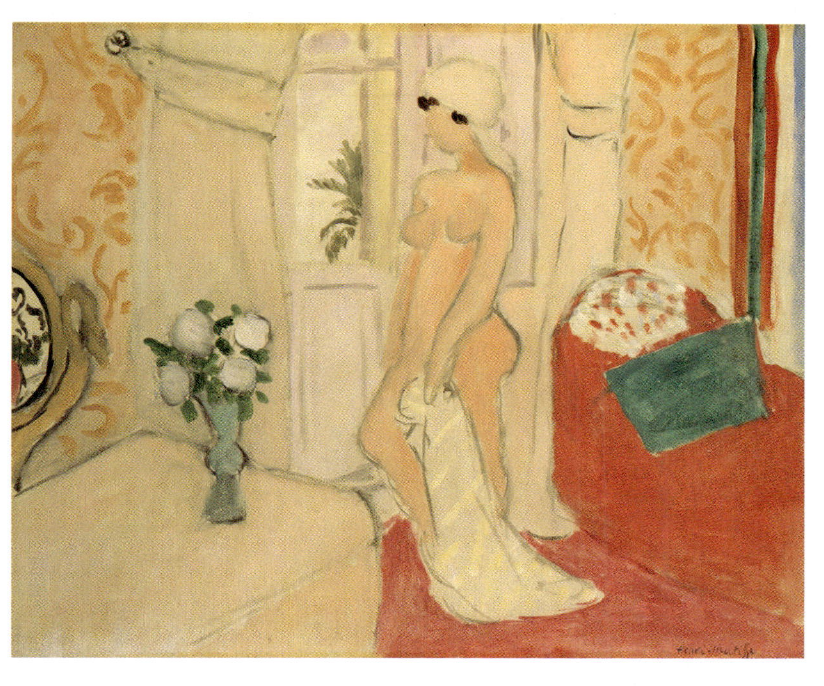

The Young Woman and the Vase of Flowers or The Pink Nude • date unknown
Musée de l'Orangerie, Paris

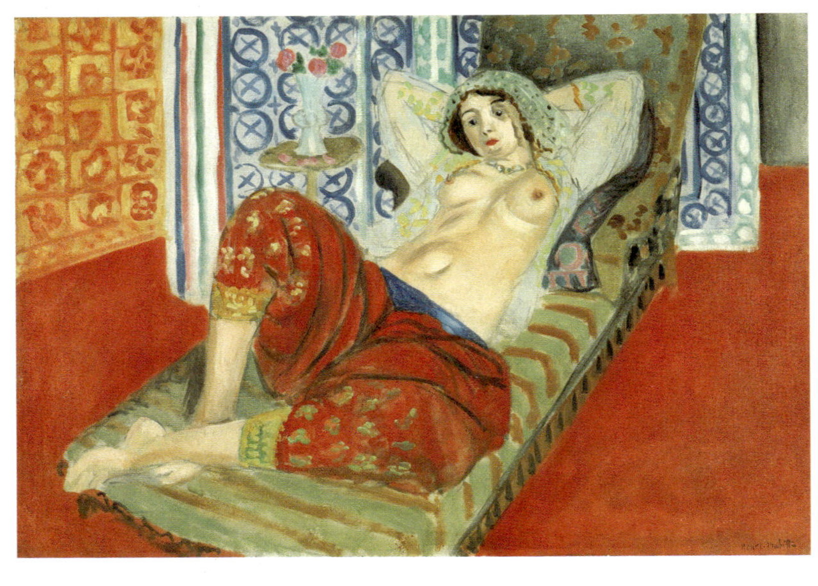

Odalisque with Red Culottes • Autumn 1921

Musée national d'art moderne, Paris

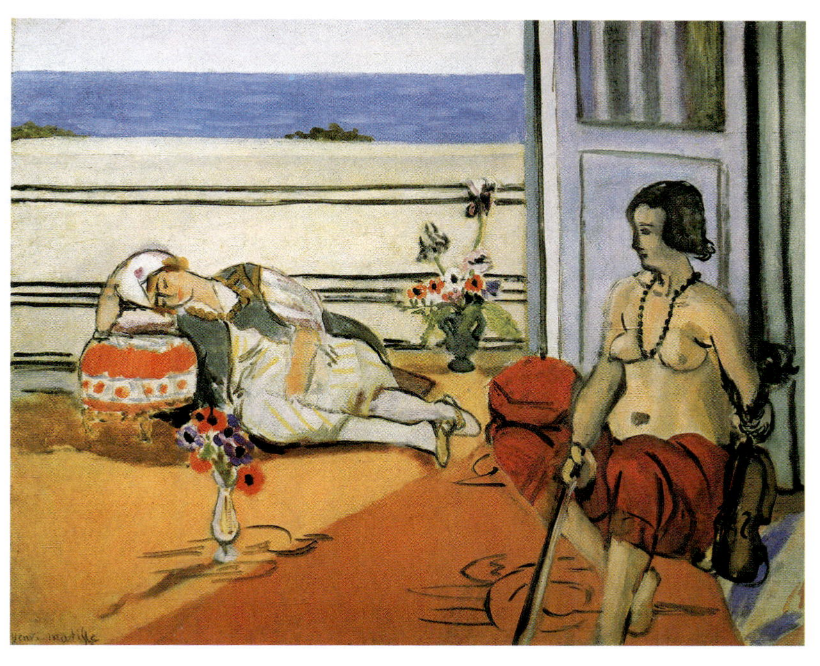

The Two Odalisques • 1921

Private collection

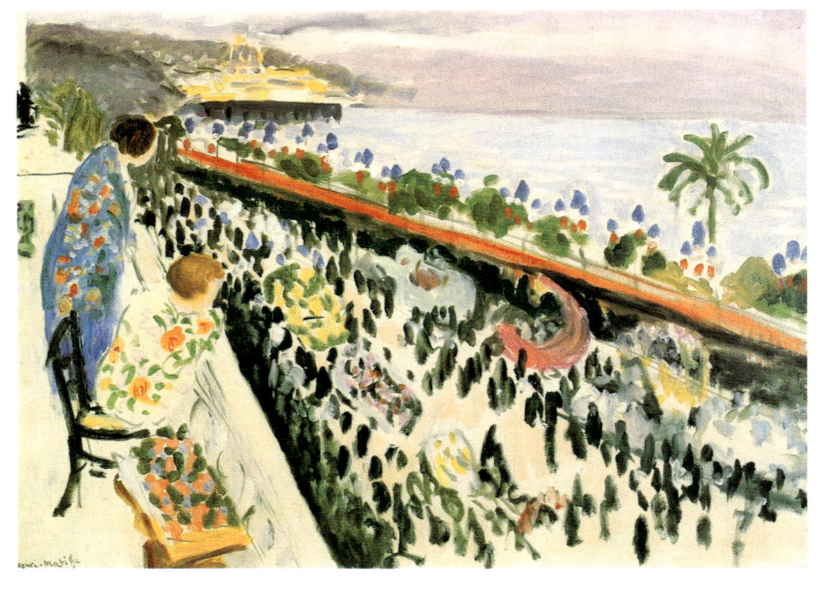

Festival of Flowers • 1921

Private collection

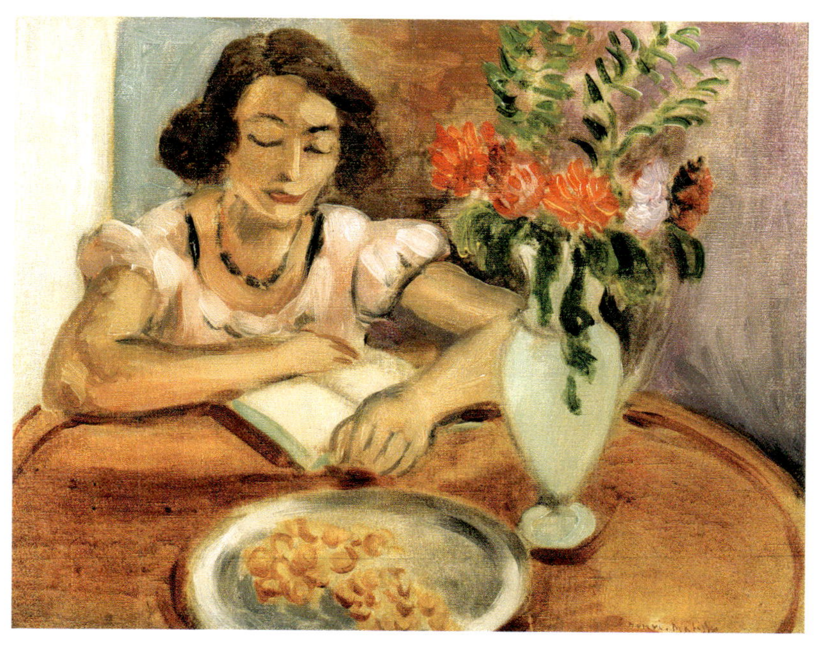

Woman Reading • c. 1922
Musée d'art moderne, Troyes

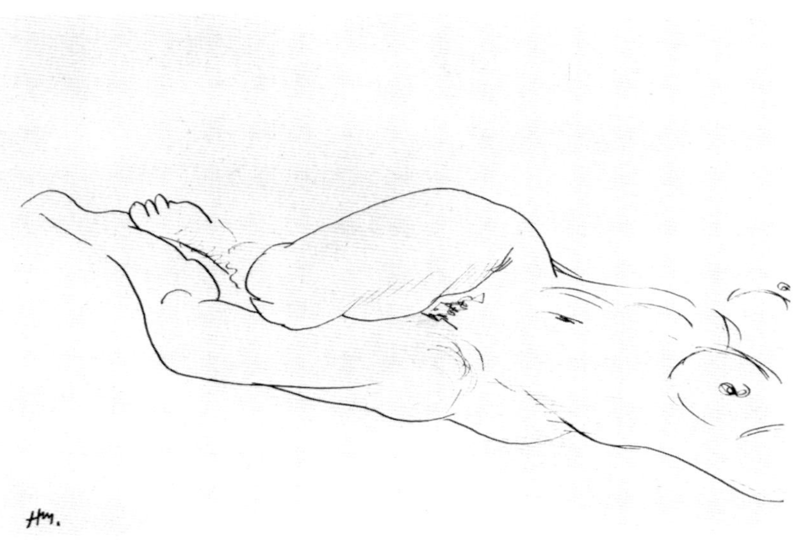

Reclining Nude • 1922
Private collection

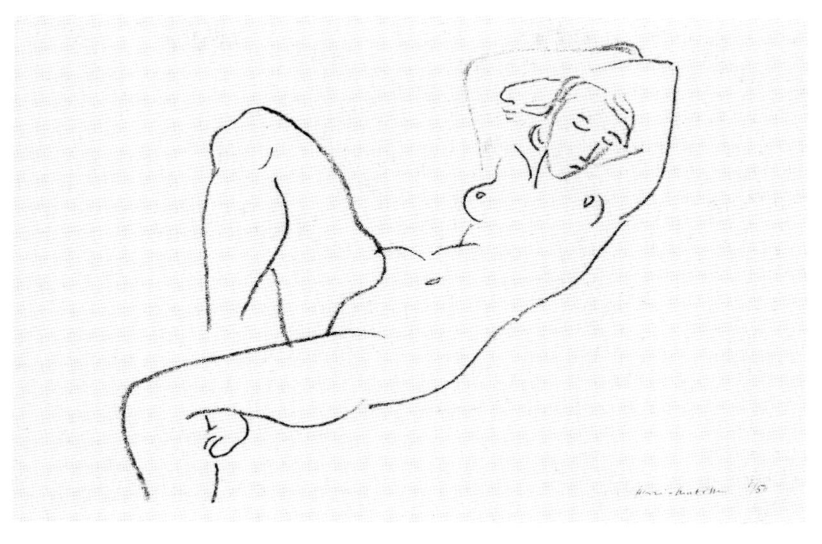

The Night • 1922
Private collection

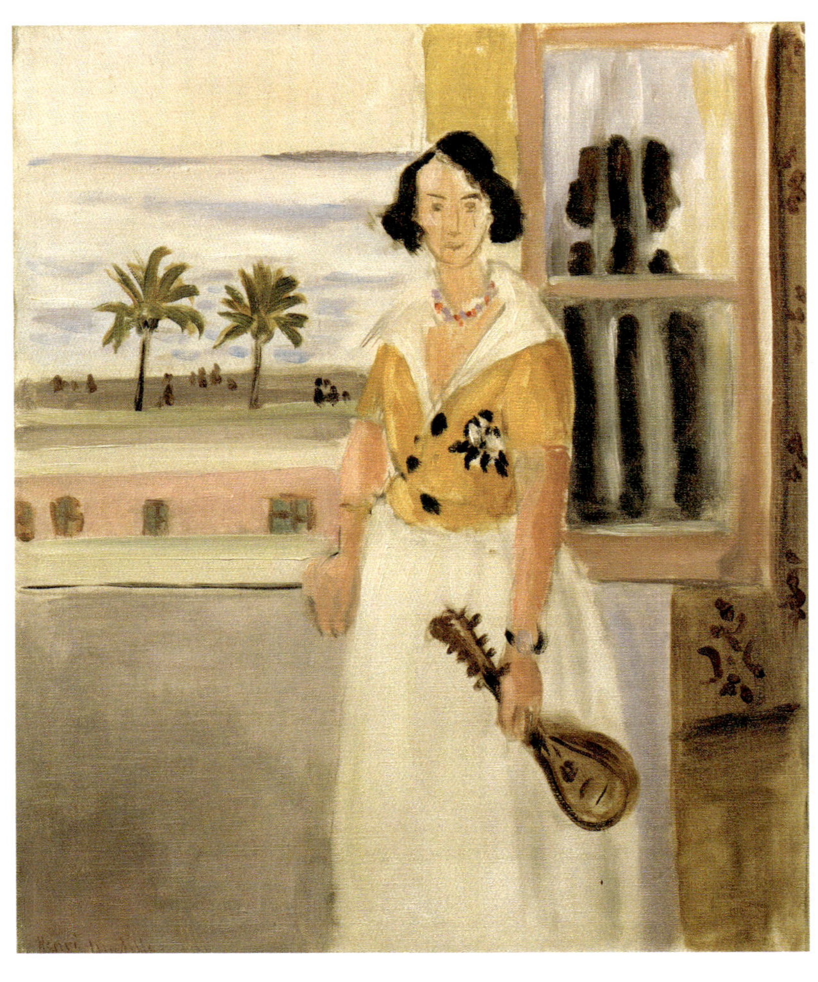

Woman with a Mandolin • c. 1922
Musée de l'Orangerie, Paris

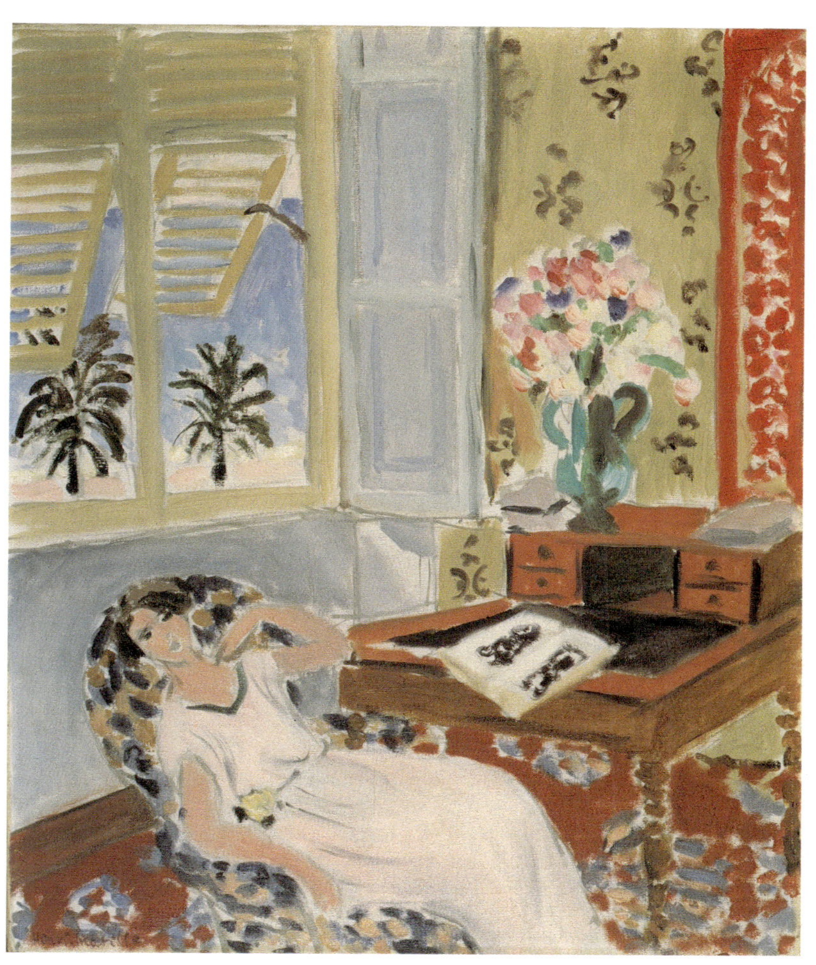

Siesta, Interior at Nice • 1922
Musée national d'art moderne, Paris

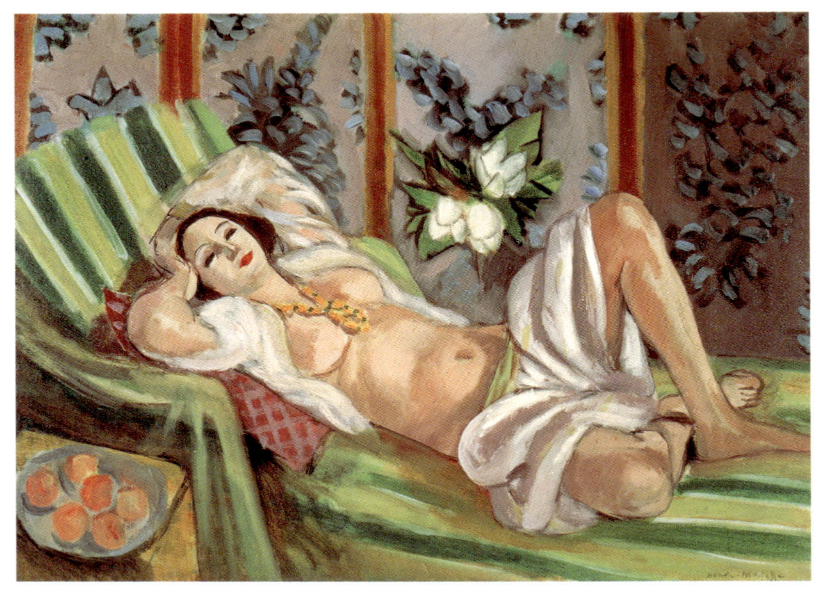

Odalisque with Magnolias • 1923 or 1924

Private collection

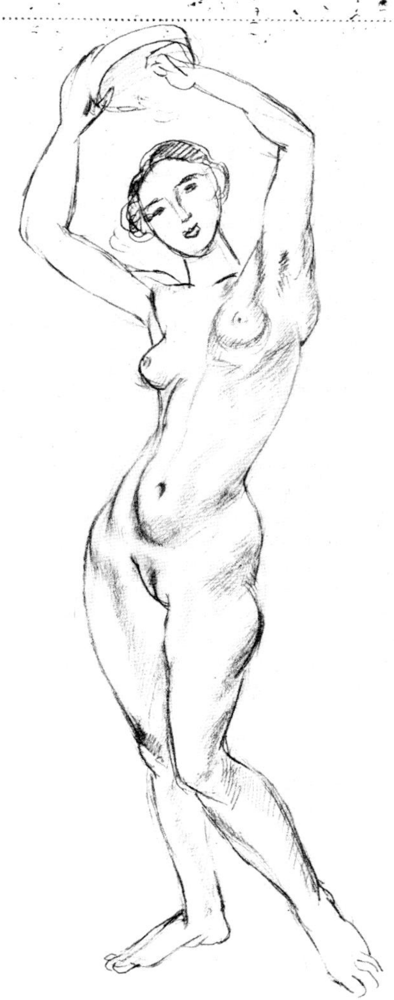

Odalisque with a Tambourine • 1923
Private collection
> **Odalisque with Red Culottes** • date unknown
Musée de l'Orangerie, Paris

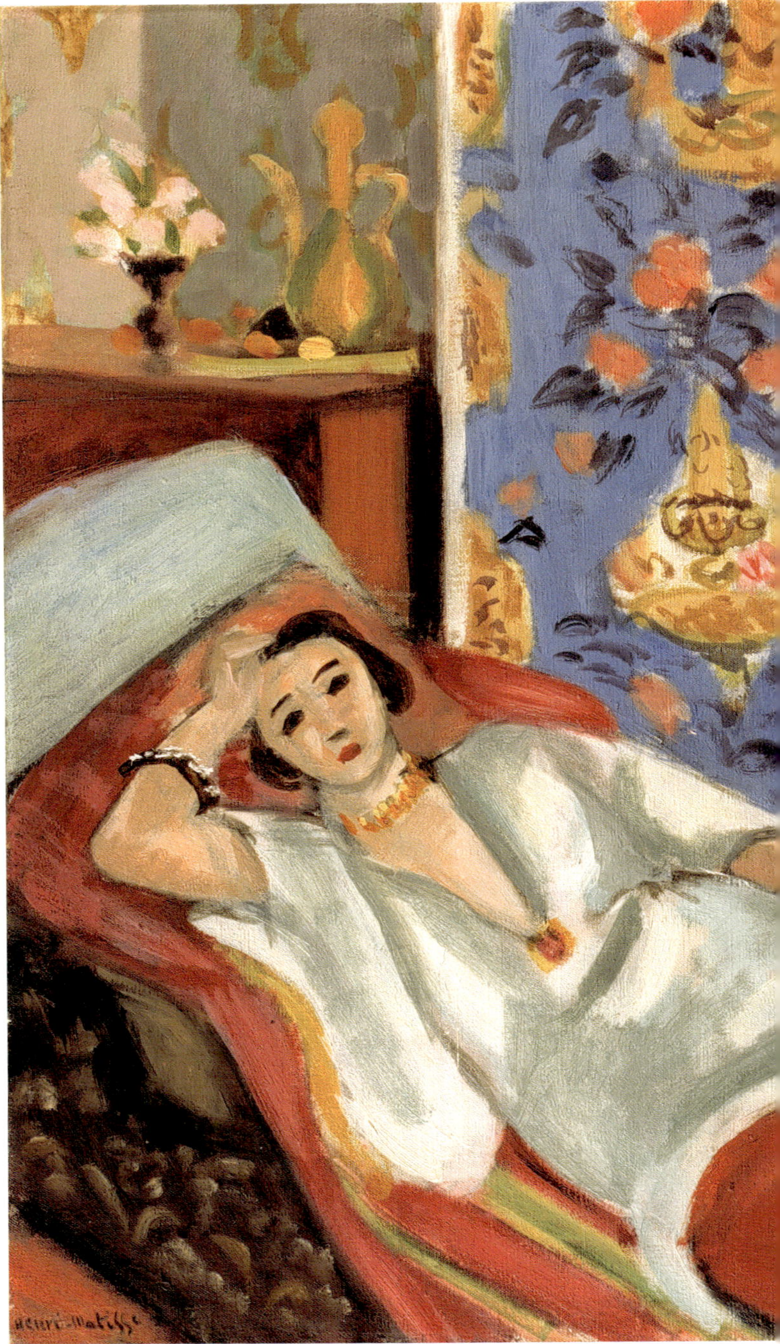
Henri-Matisse

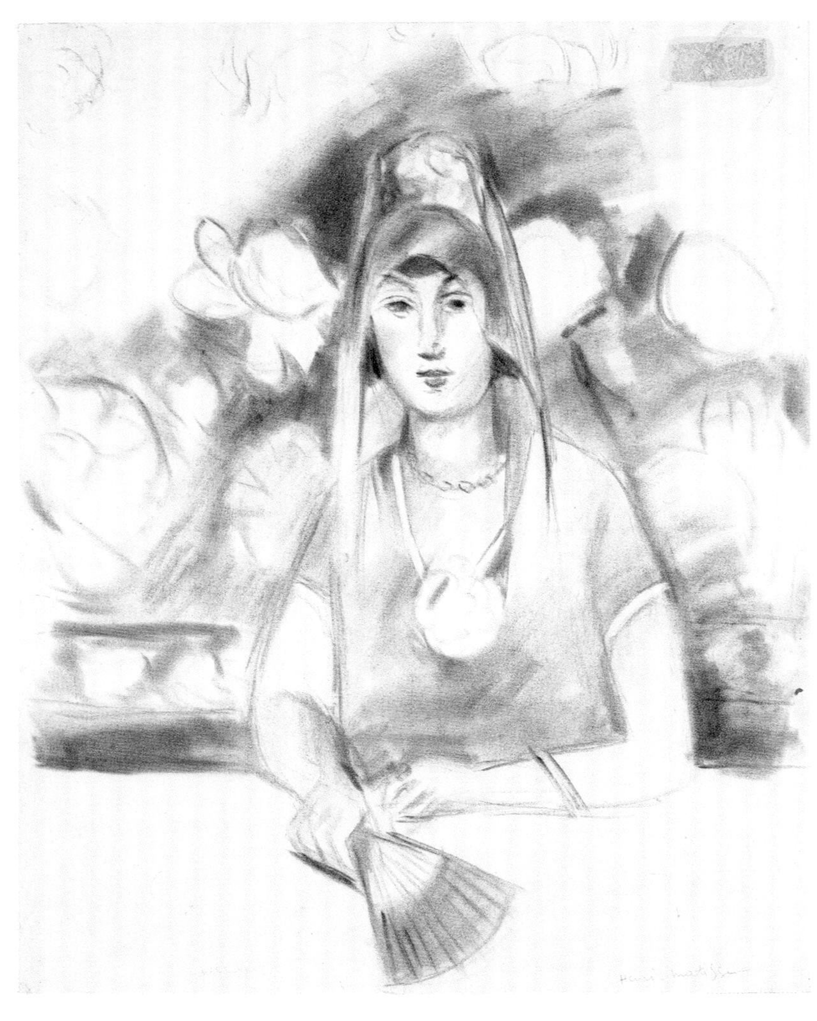

Spanish Woman with a Fan • 1923
Musée national d'art moderne, Paris

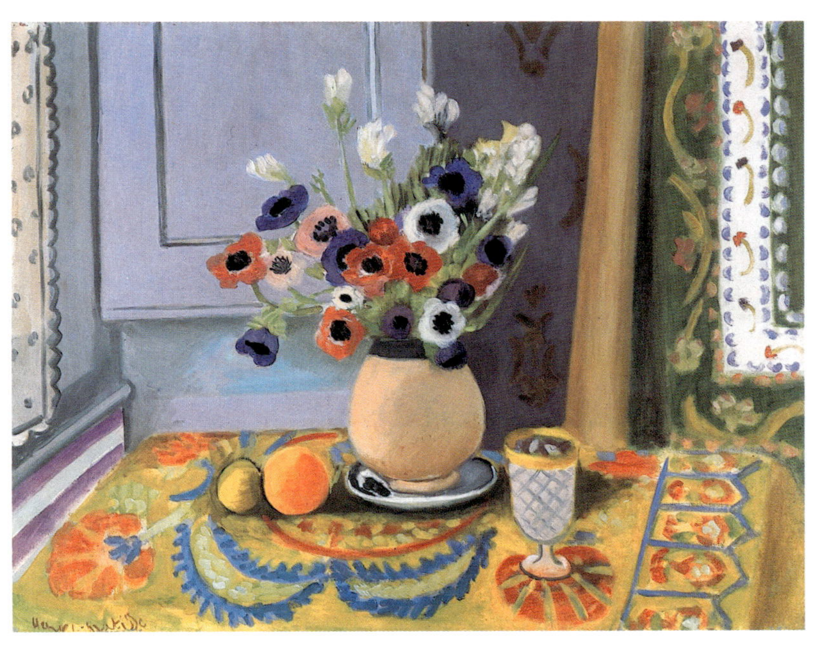

Anemones in an Earthenware Vase • 1924

Kunstmuseum, Bern

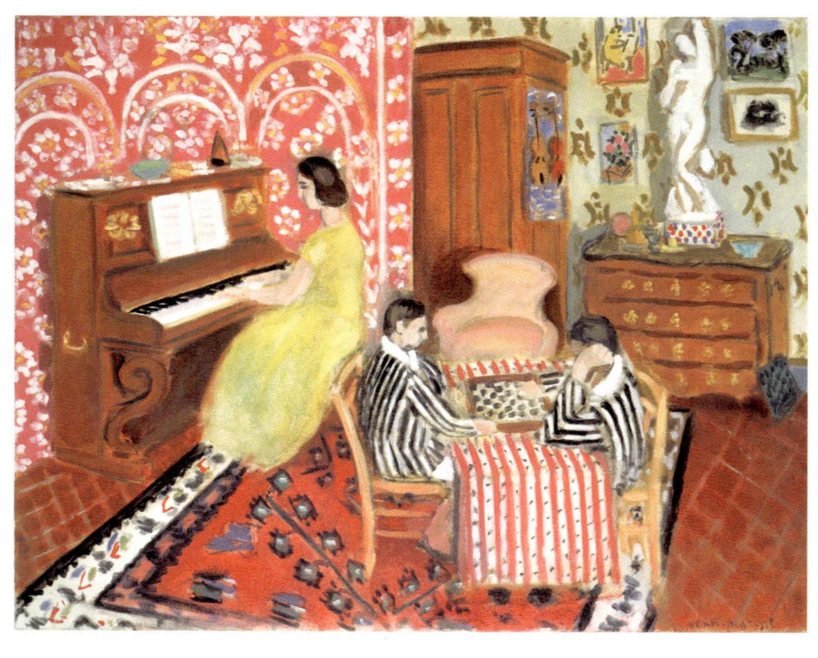

Pianist and Checker Players • early 1924
National Gallery of Art, Washington, Collection of Mr. and Mrs. Mellon

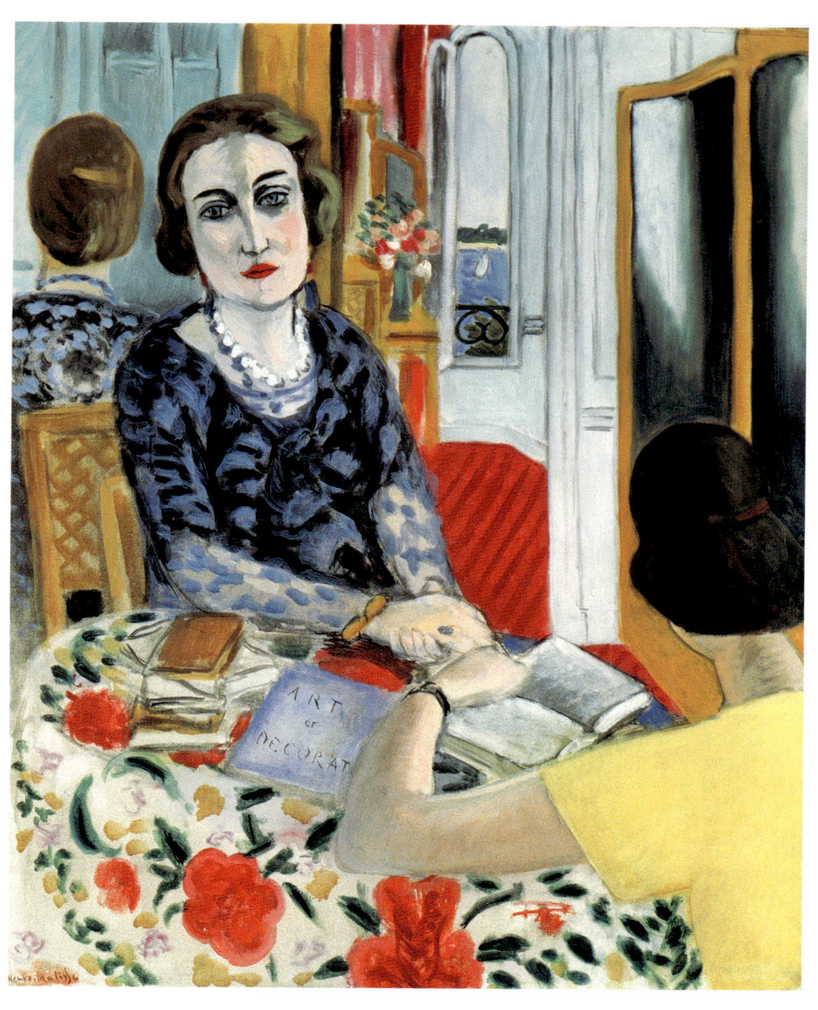

Portrait of Baroness Gourgaud • 1924
Musée national d'art moderne, Paris

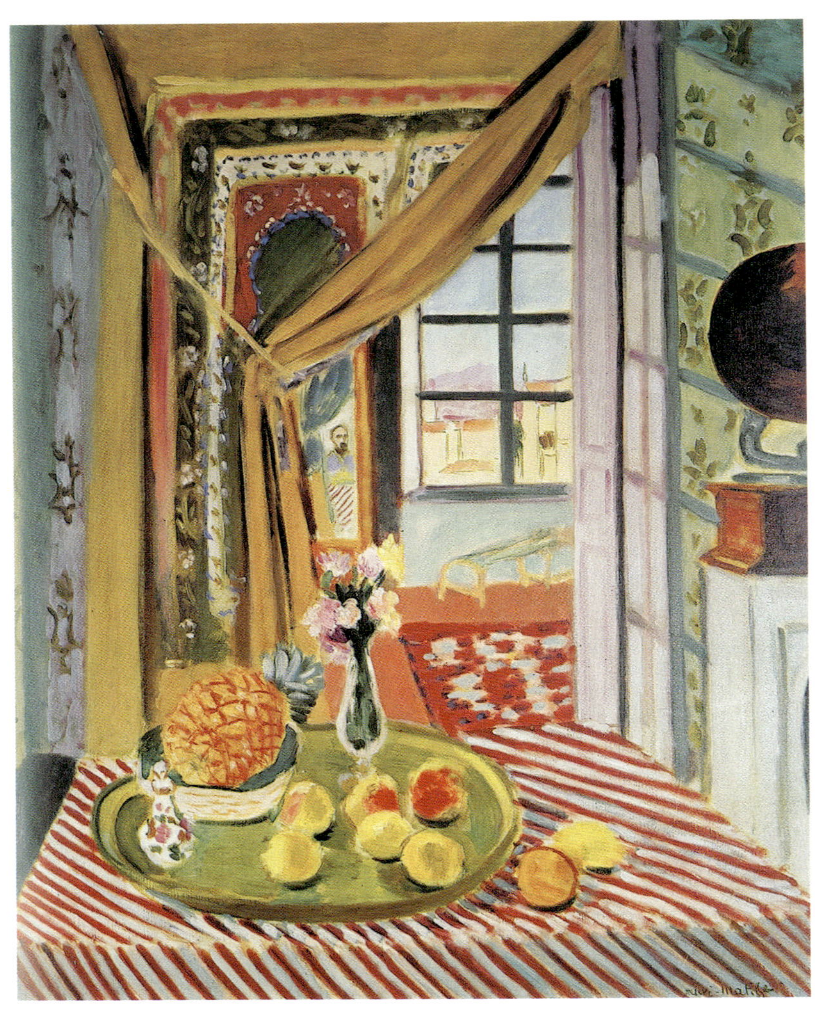

Interior with a Phonograph · 1924
Private collection

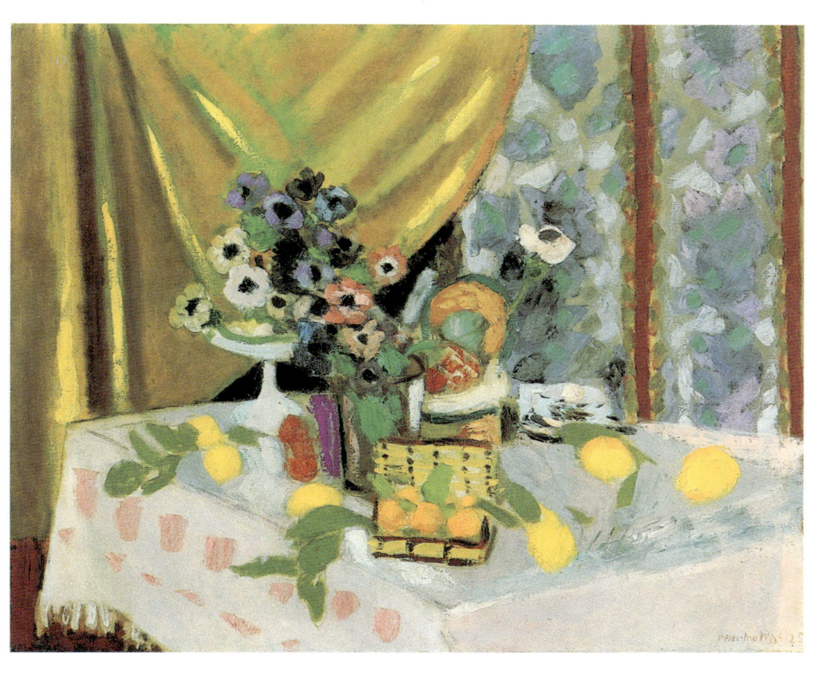

Still Life: Pink Tablecloth, Vase of Anemones, Lemons and Pineapple · 1925

Private collection

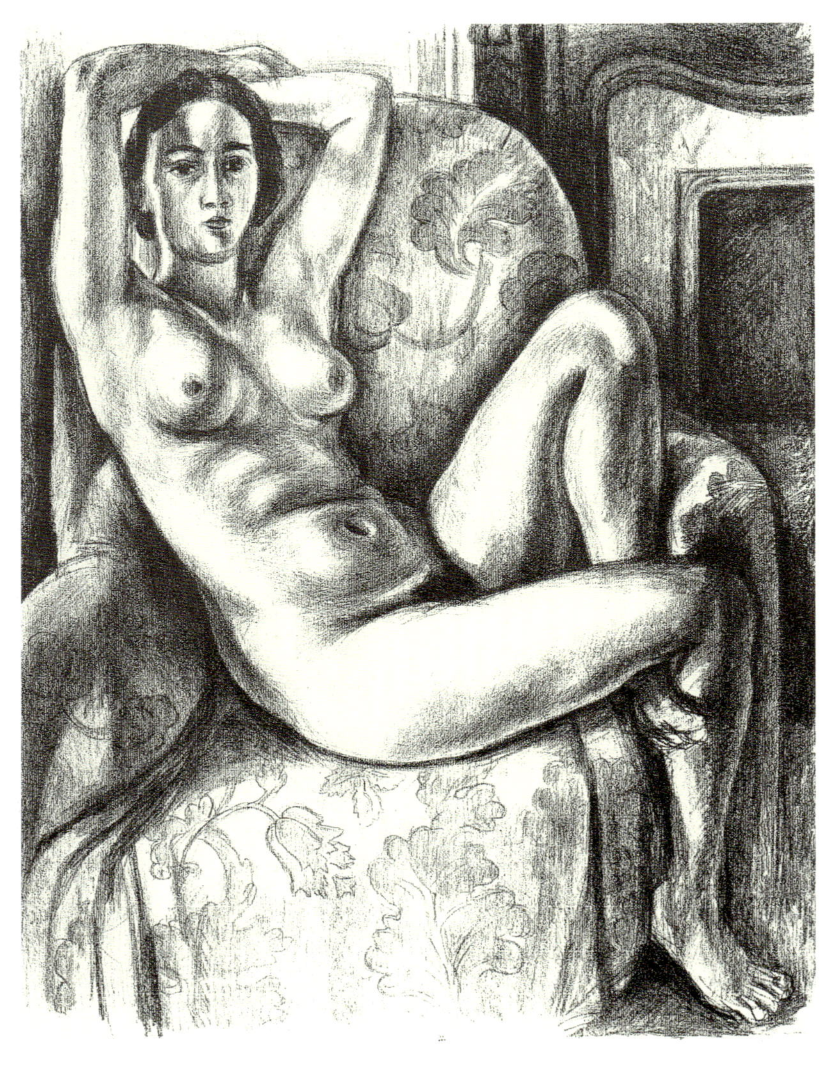

Nude with a Blue Cushion beside a Fireplace • 1925
Bibliothèque nationale, Paris

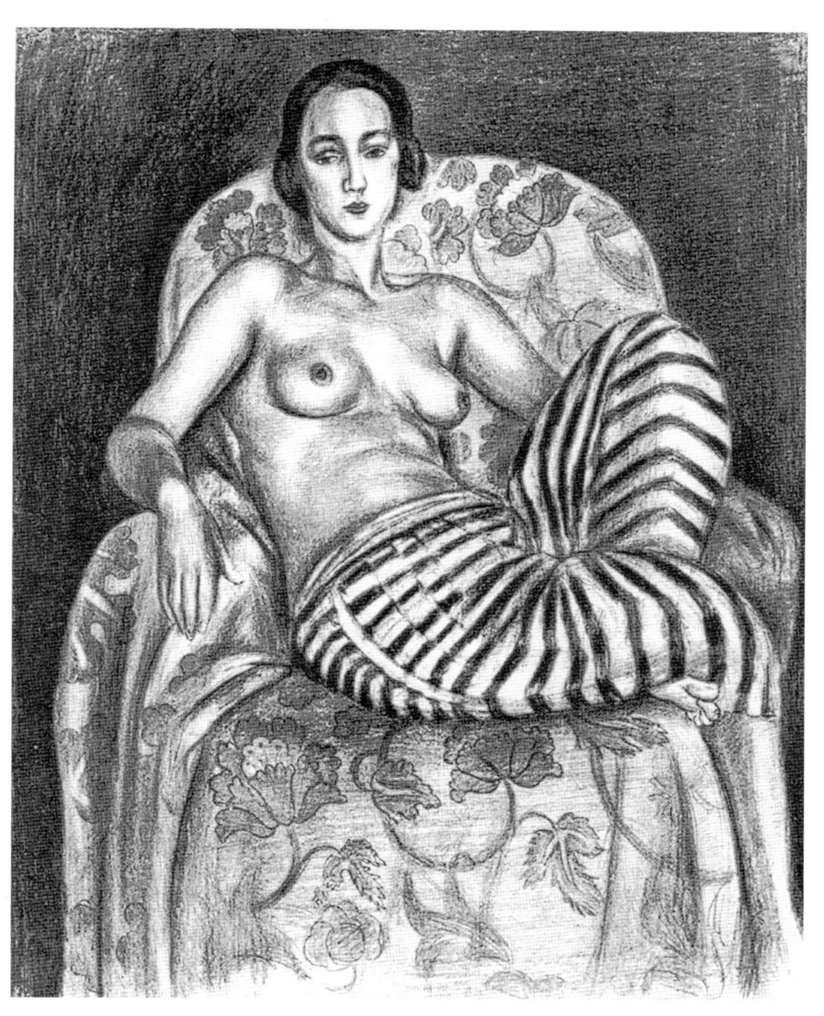

Large Odalisque with Bayadère Culottes · 1925
The Museum of Modern Art, New York, Nelson A. Rockefeller Bequest

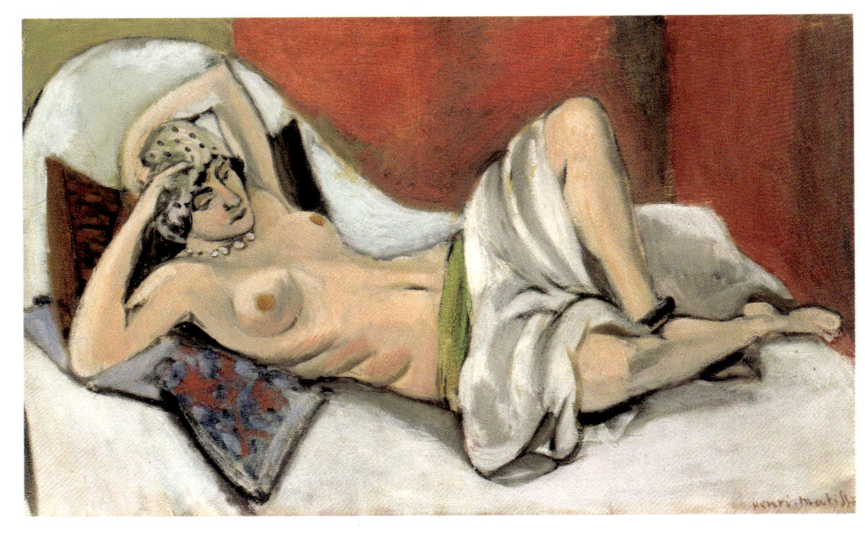

Reclining Nude with a Drape • date unknown

Musée de l'Orangerie, Paris

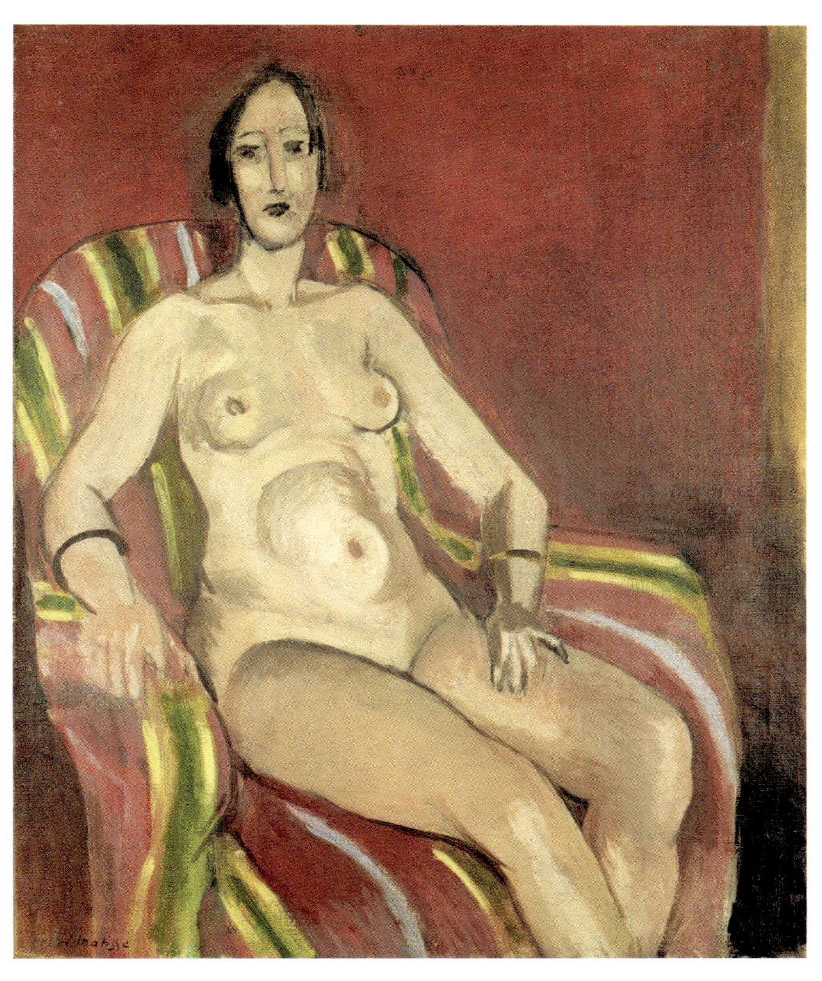

Seated Nude on a Red Background • 1925
Musée national d'art moderne, Paris

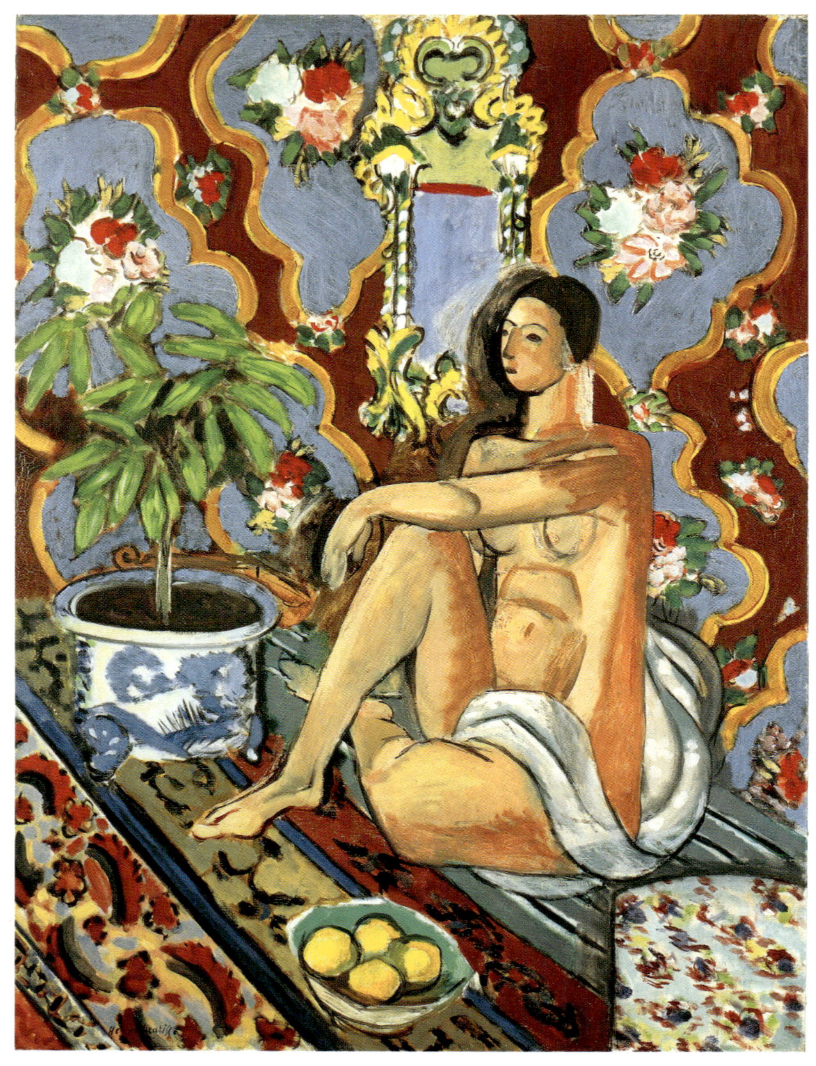

Decorative Figure on an Ornamental Ground • 1925–1926
Musée national d'art moderne, Paris

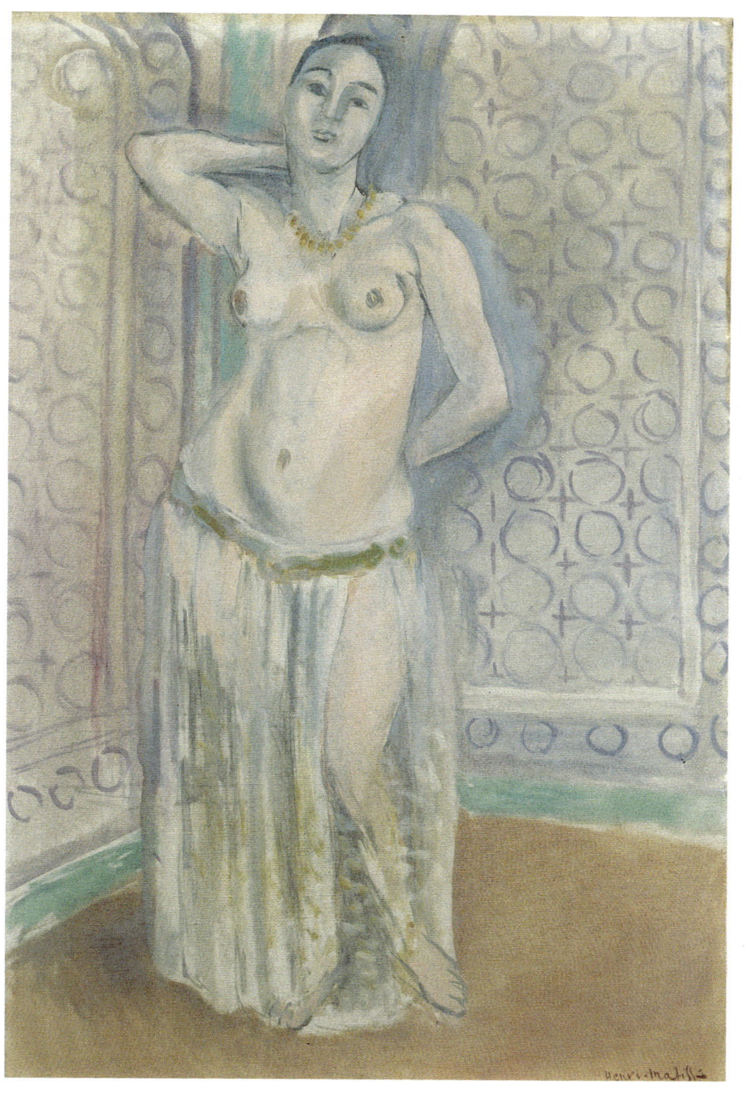

Odalisque or The White Slave • date unknown
Musée de l'Orangerie, Paris

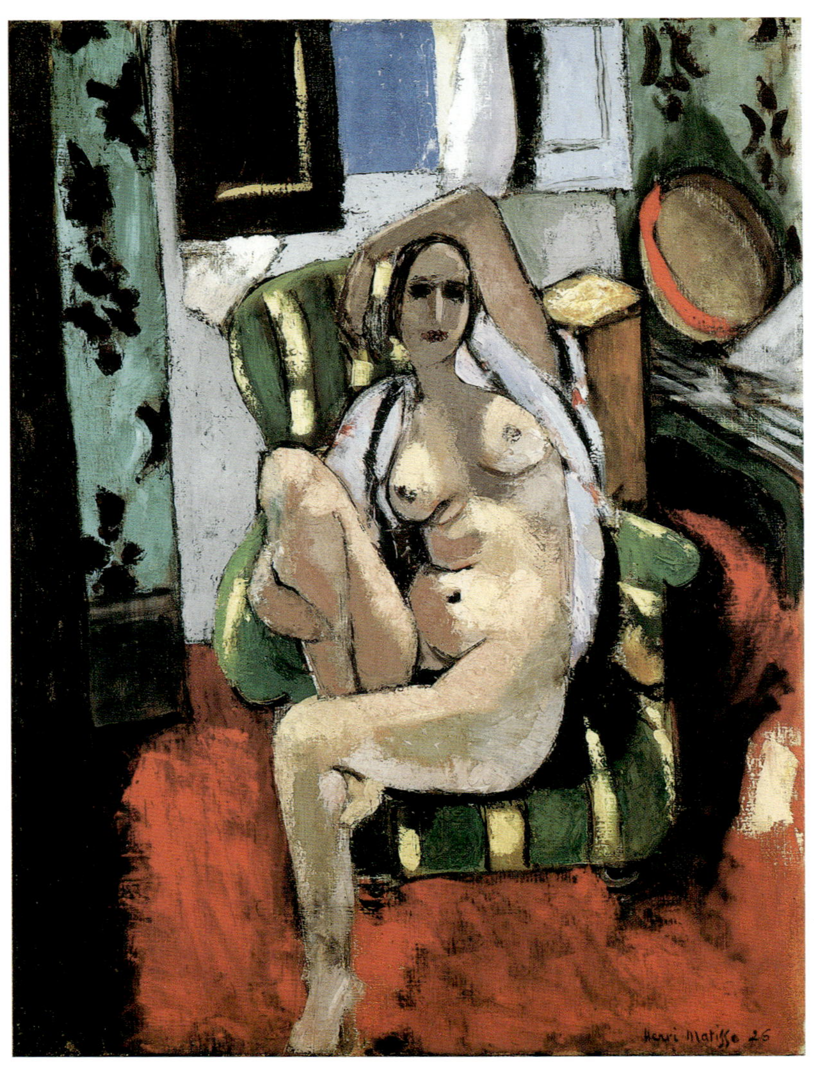

Odalisque with a Tambourine • 1926

The Museum of Modern Art, New York, The William S. Paley Collection

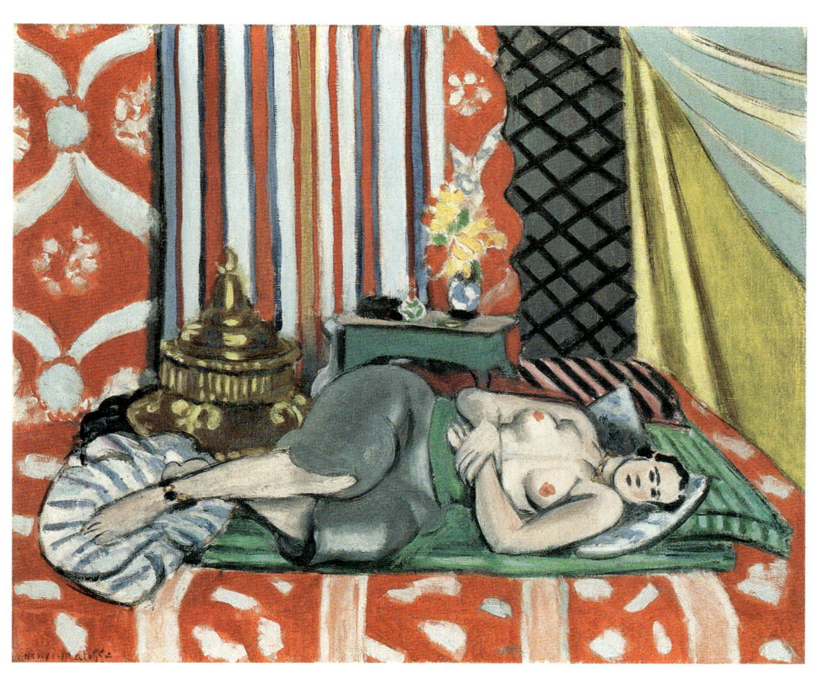

Odalisque with Gray Culottes • late 1926–Spring 1927
Musée de l'Orangerie, Paris

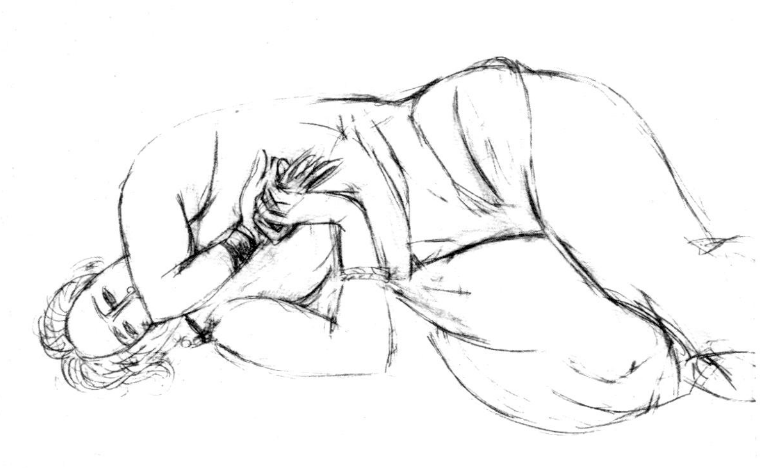

Woman Bending Her Arm • 1927
Private collection

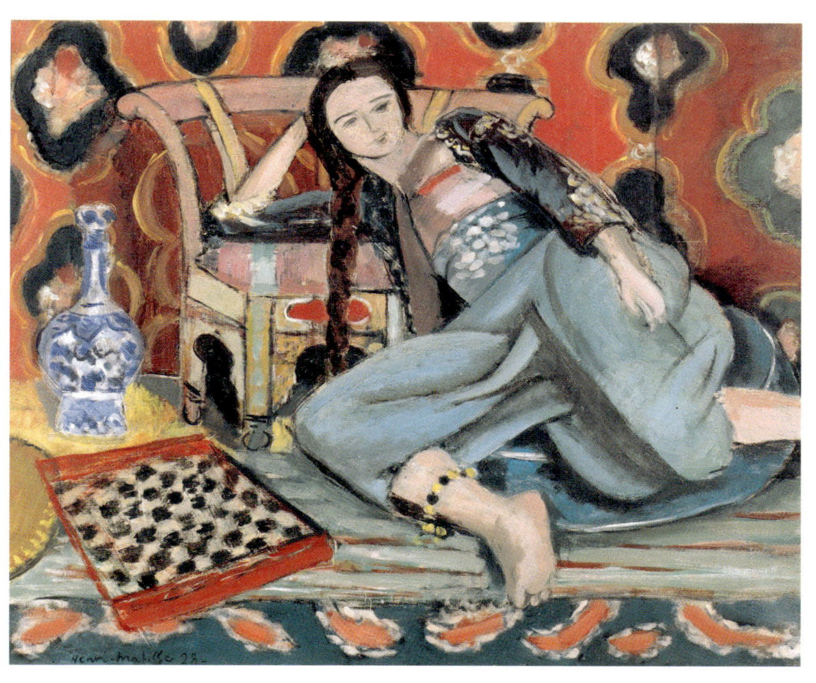

Odalisque with a Turkish Chair • late 1927–Summer 1928
Musée d'art moderne de la Ville de Paris
> **Still Life on a Green Sideboard** • 1928
Musée national d'art moderne, Paris

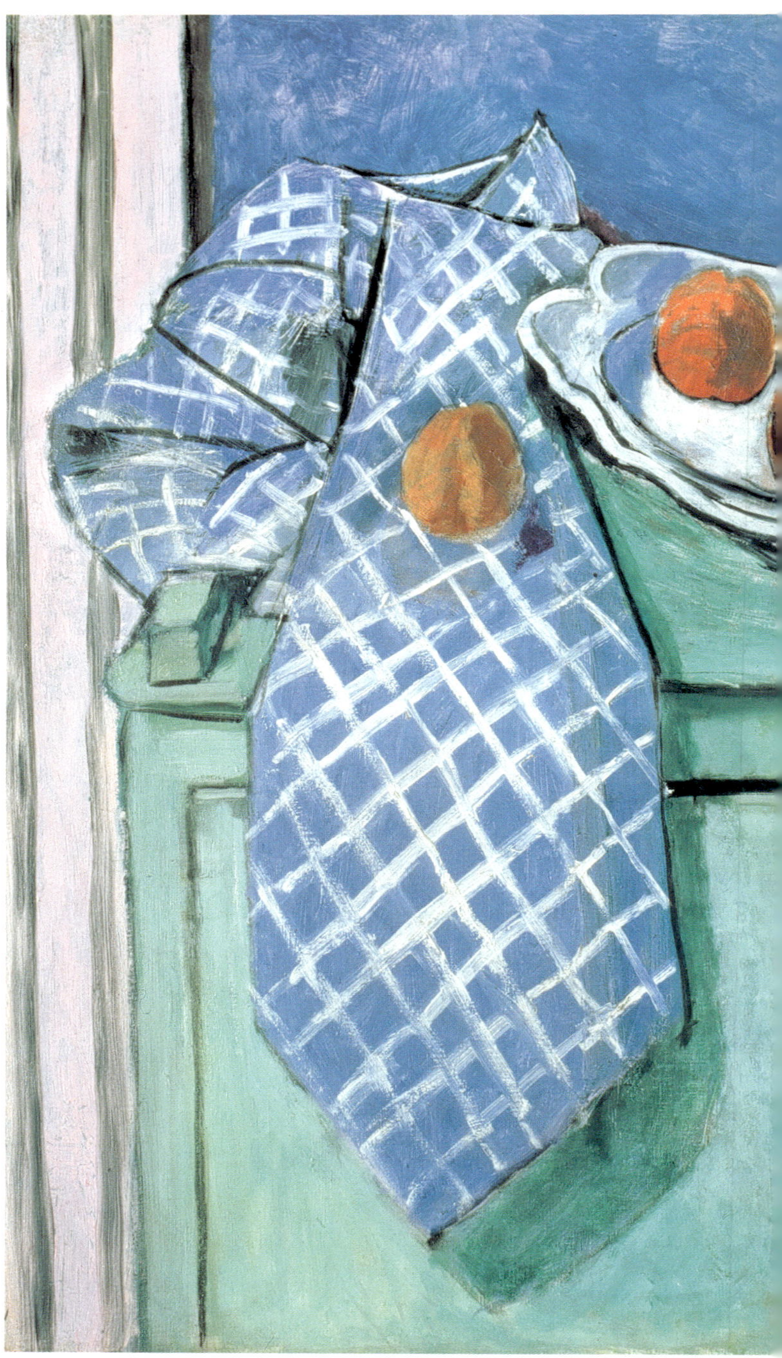

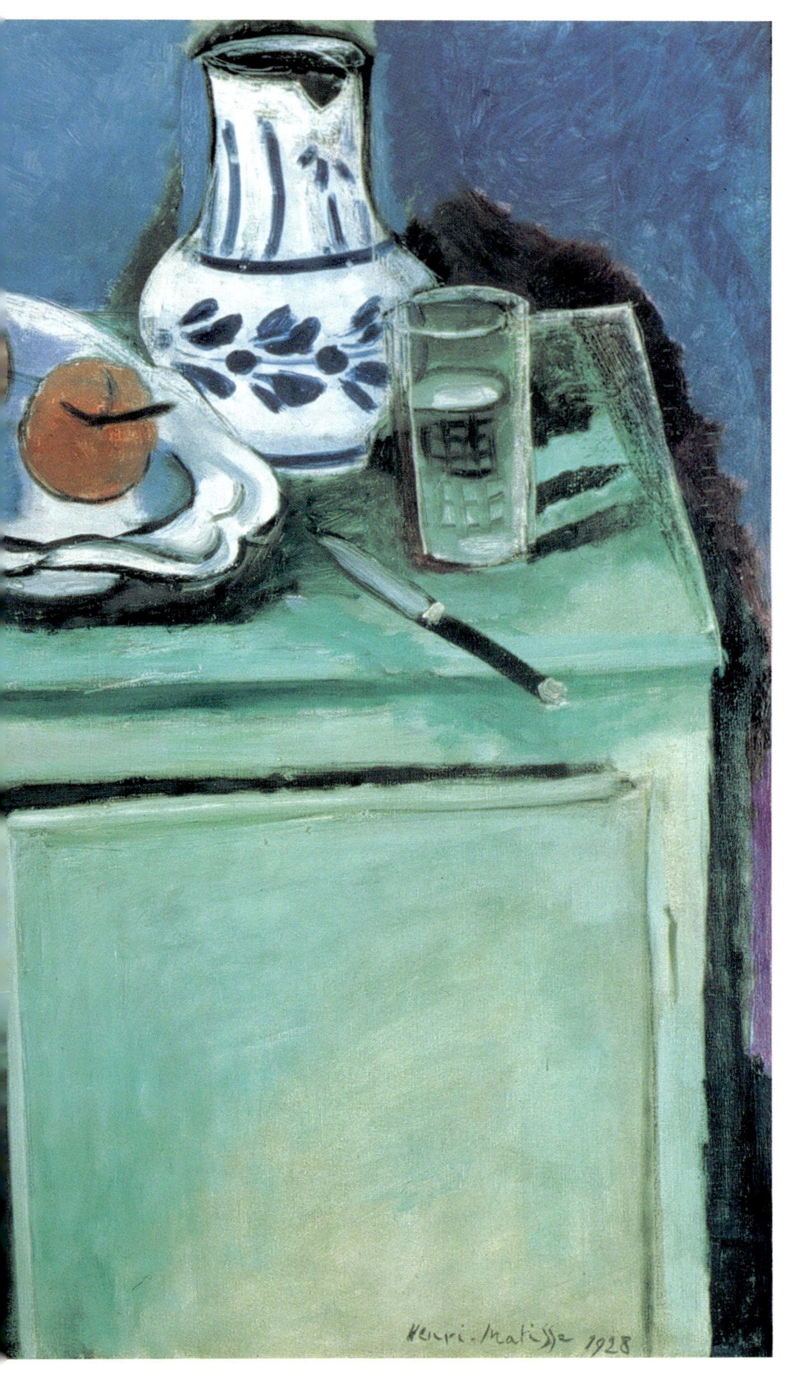
Henri-Matisse 1928

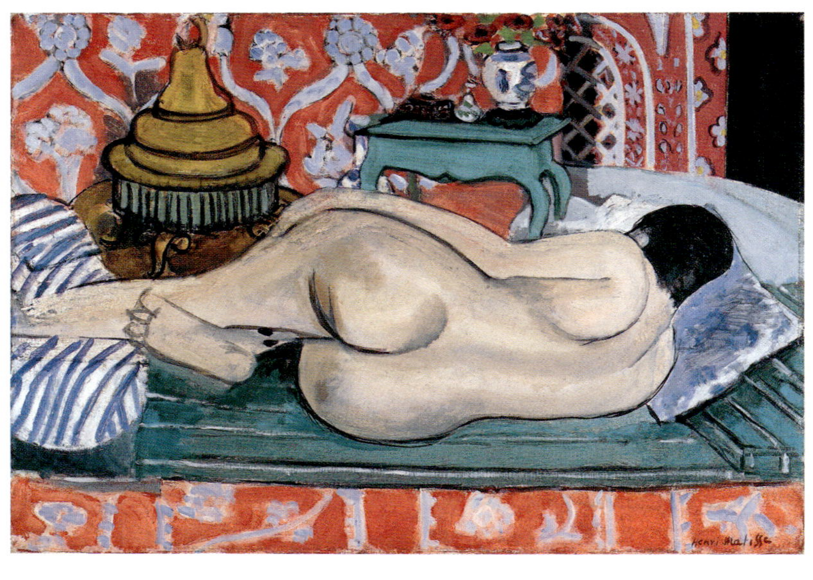

Reclining Nude Seen from the Back · Summer 1927

Private collection

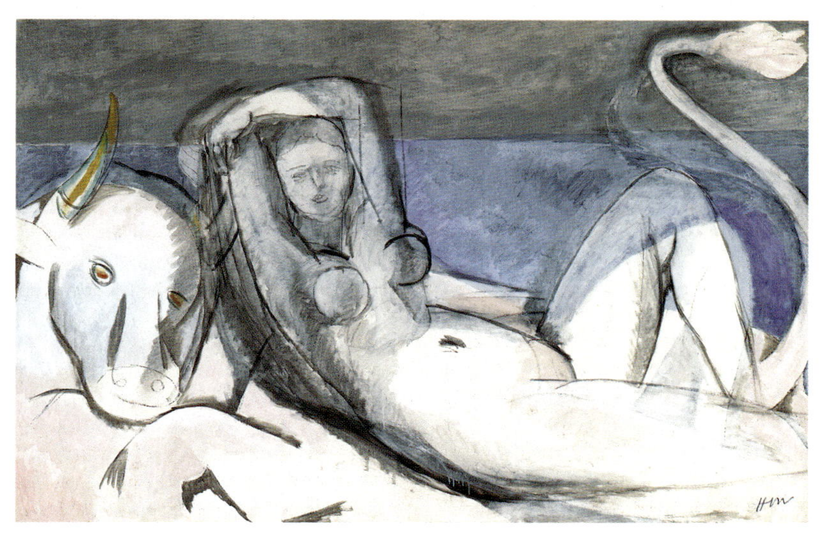

The Abduction of Europa • 1927–1929
National Gallery of Australia, Canberra

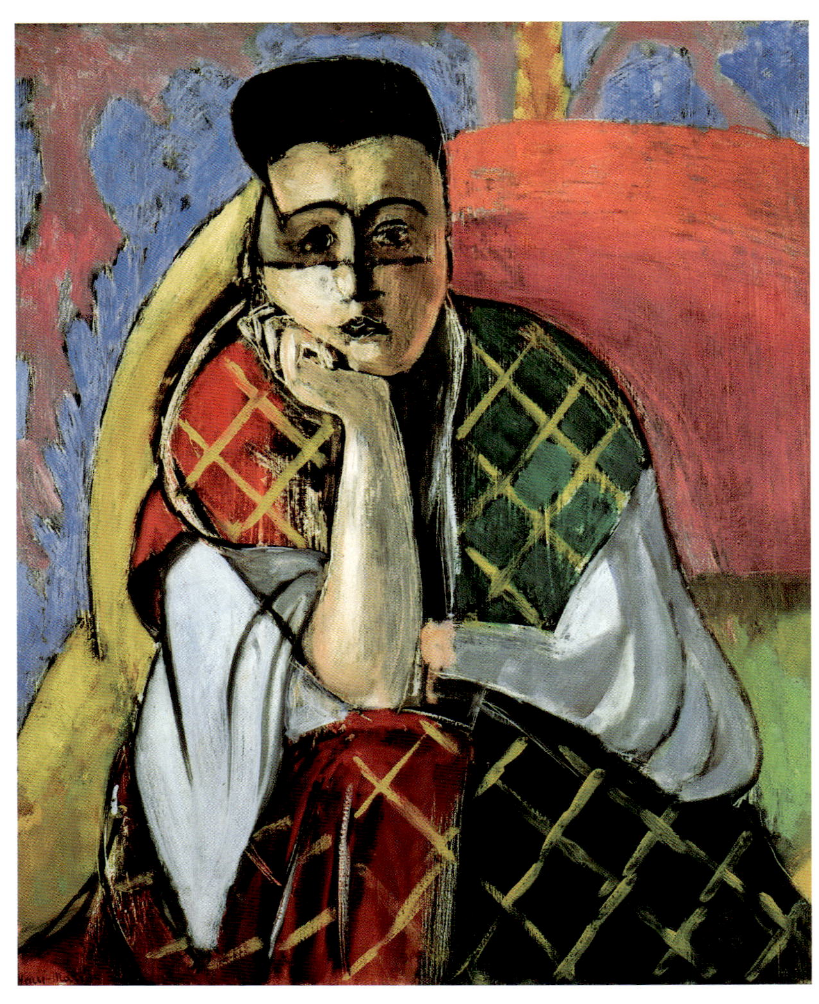

Woman with a Veil • 1927

The Museum of Modern Art, New York, The William S. Paley Collection

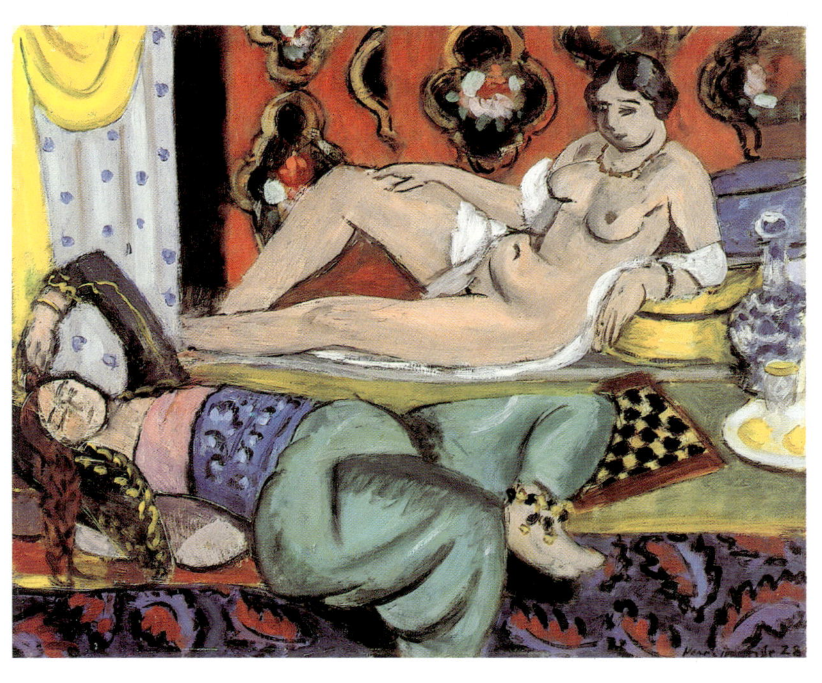

Two Odalisques • 1928
Moderna Museet, Stockholm

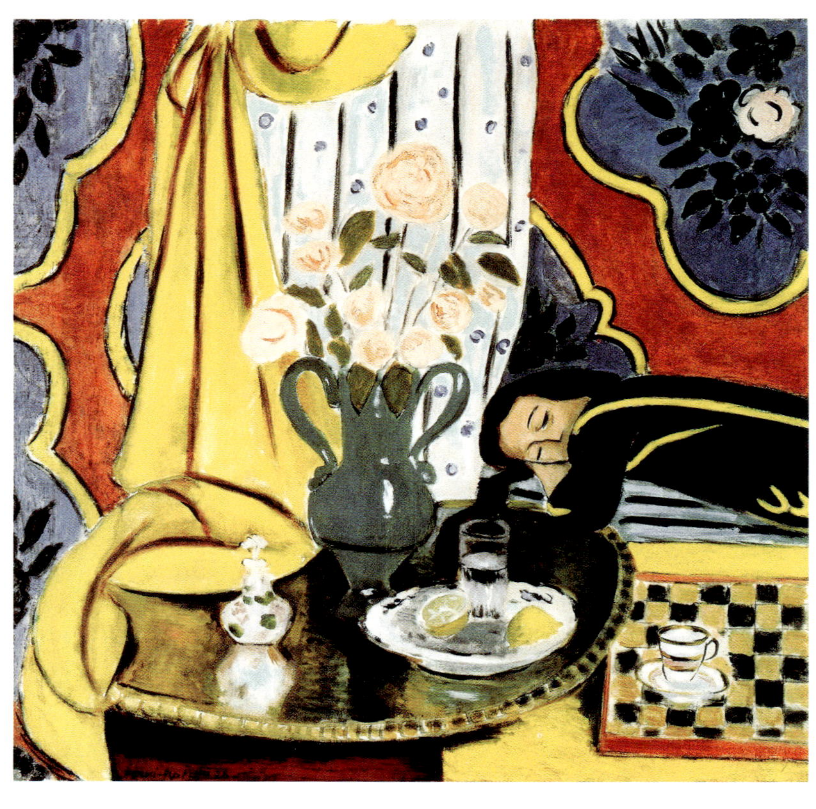

Harmony in Yellow • Summer 1928
Private collection

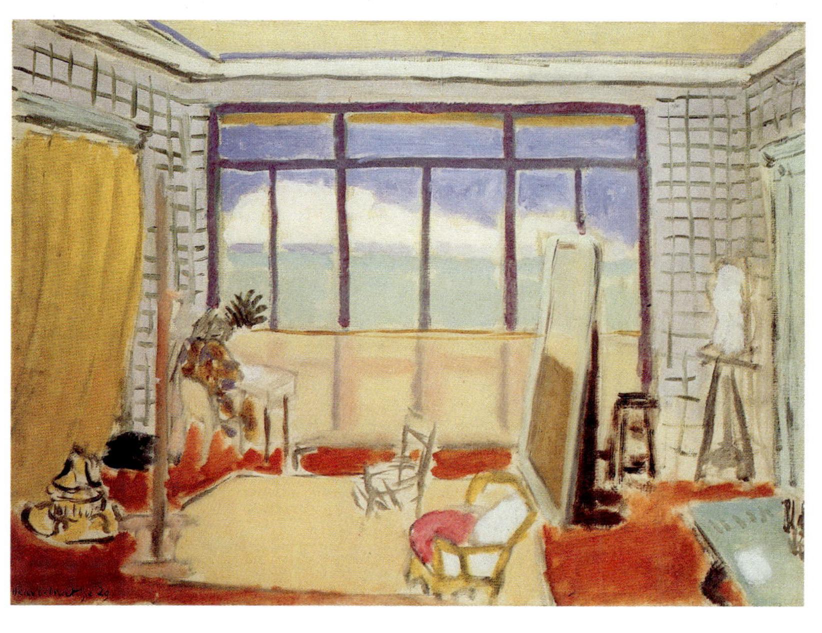

The Studio • 1929
Private collection

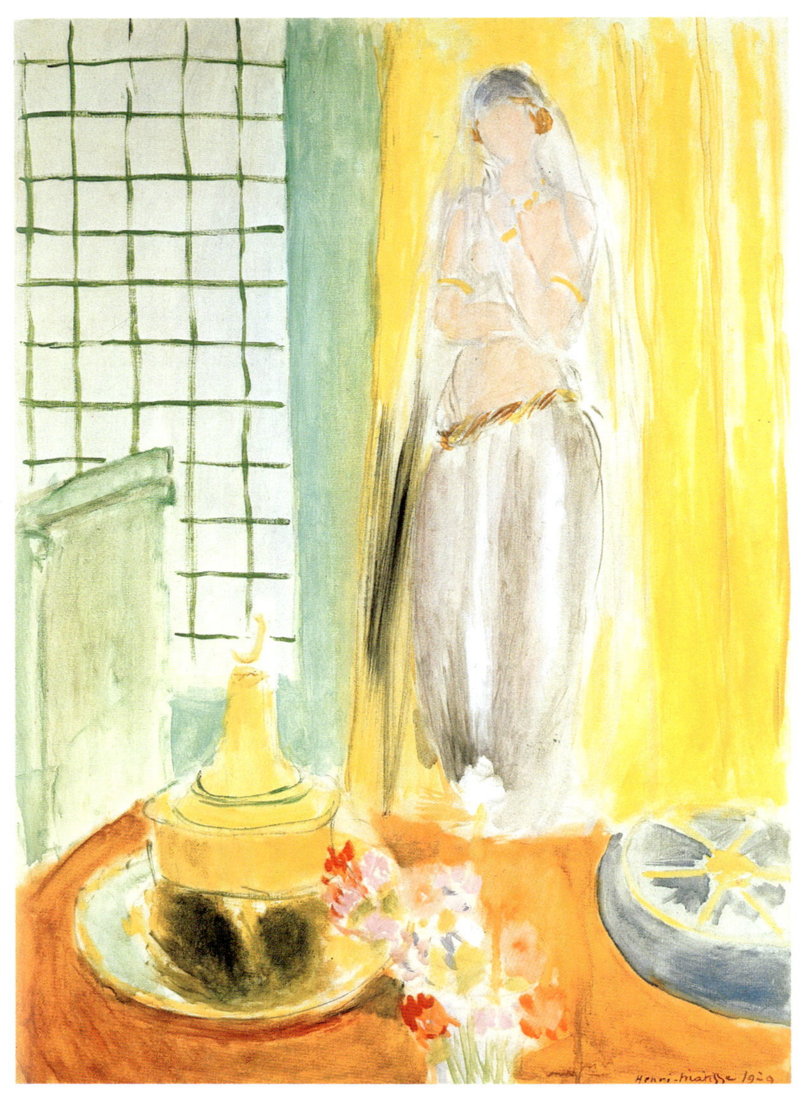

The Mauresque • 1929

Private collection

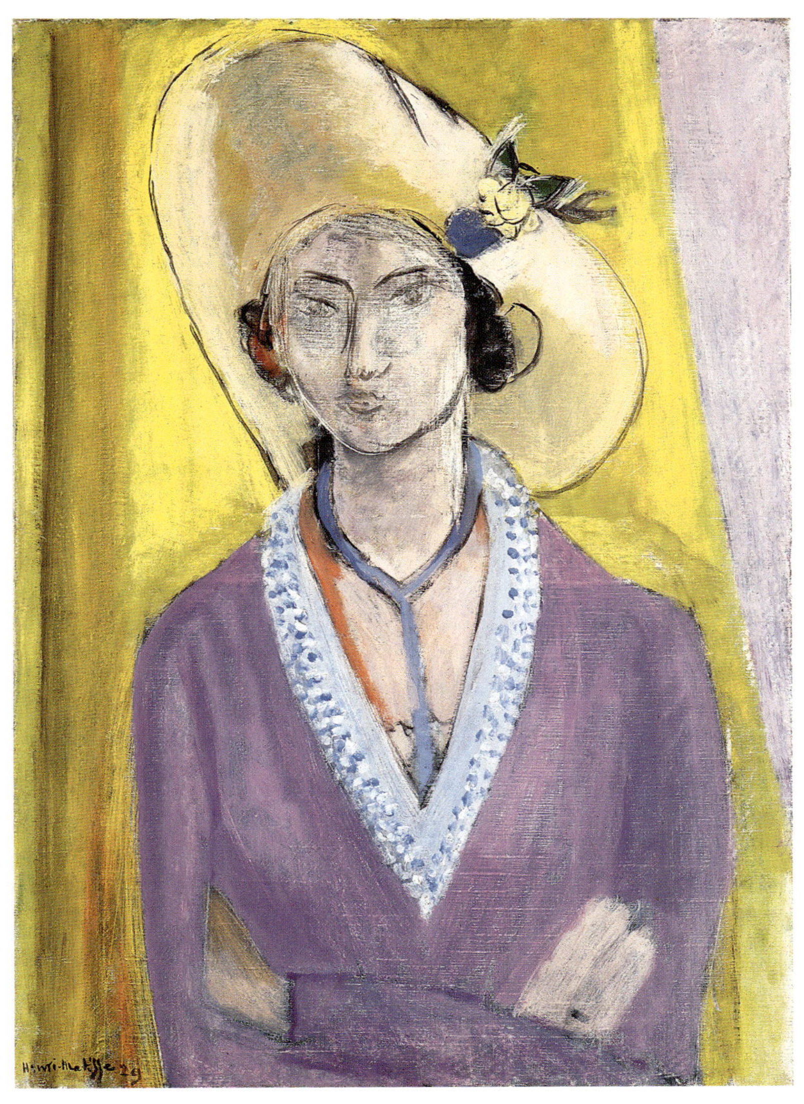

The Yellow Hat • 1929

Private collection

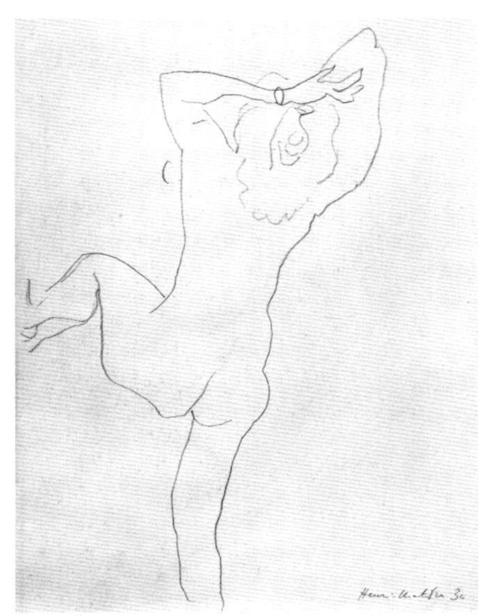

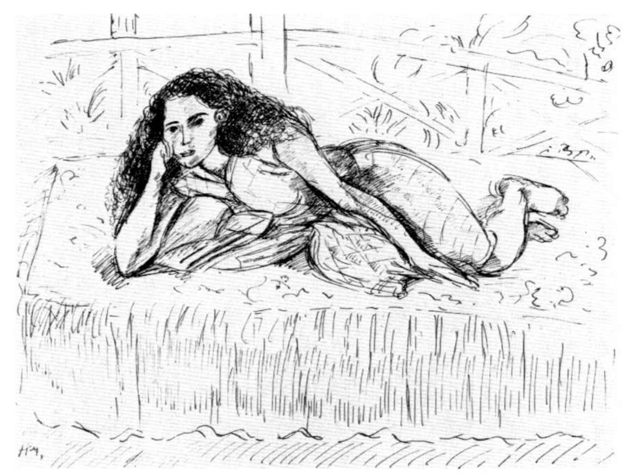

Dancer • 1930

Private collection

Tahitian Woman • 1930

Private collection

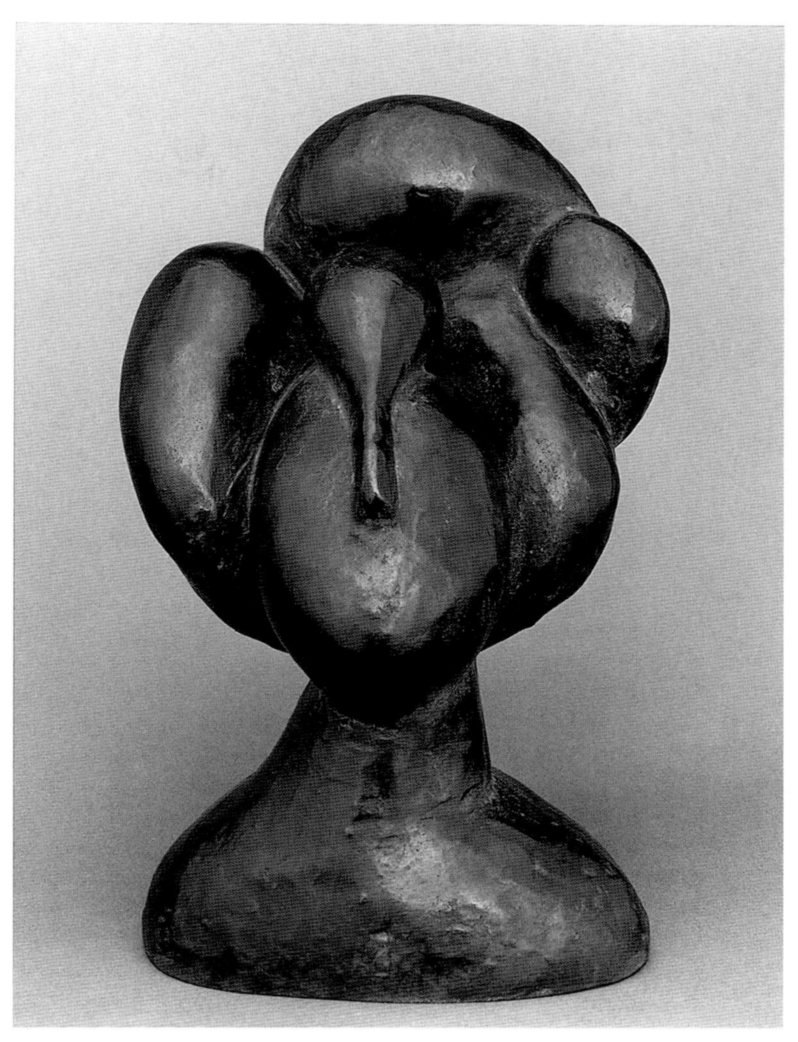

Tiaré • 1930
Private collection

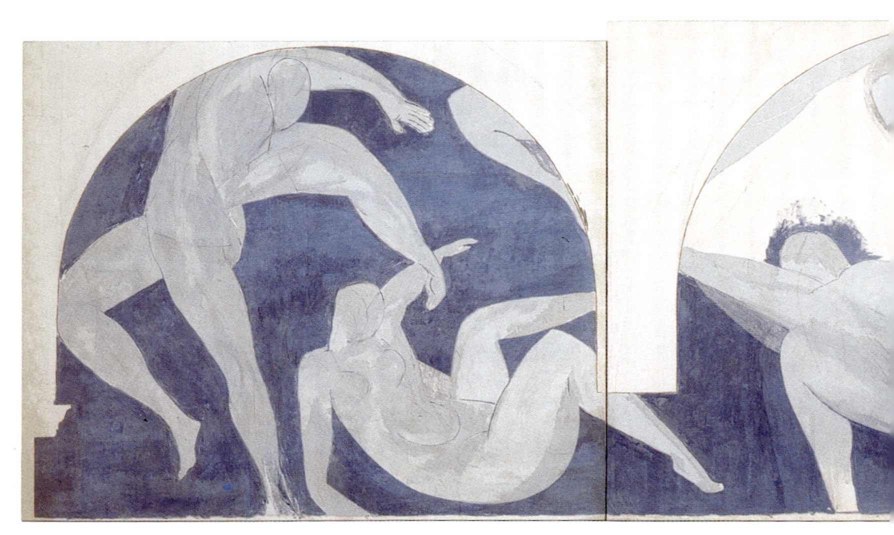

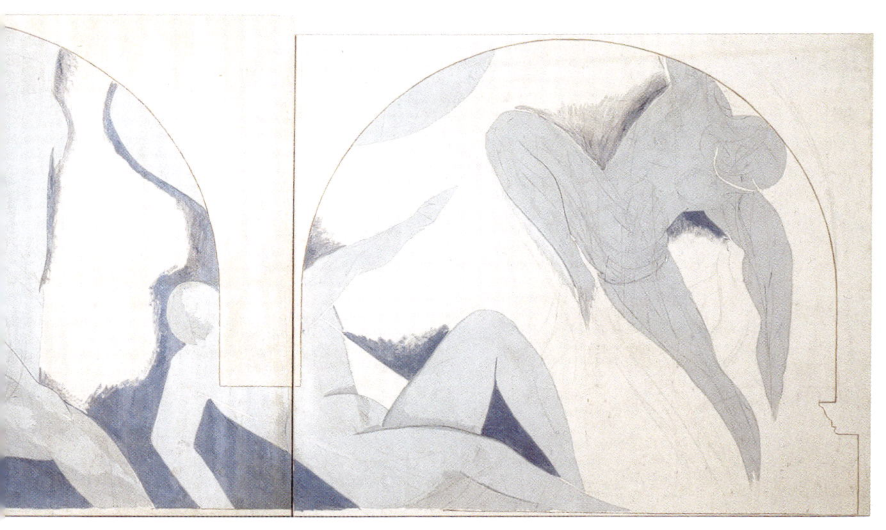

The Dance • 1931 • Musée national d'art moderne, Paris

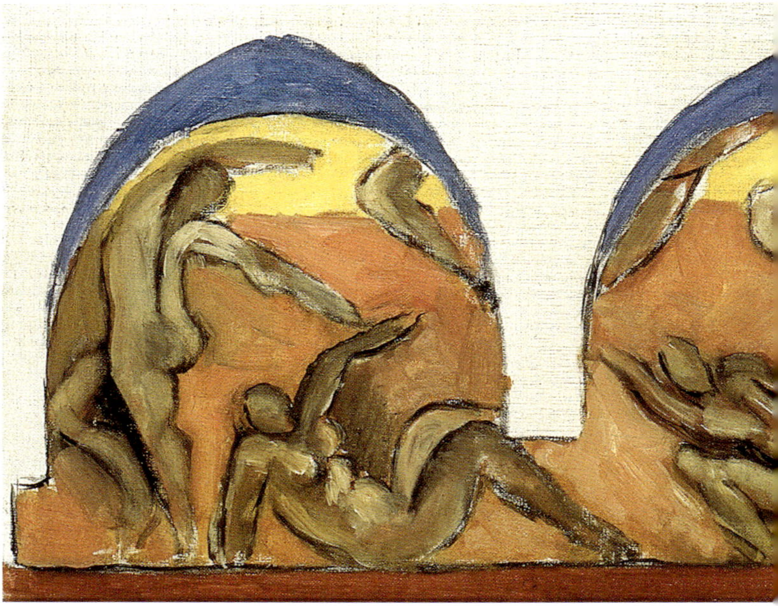

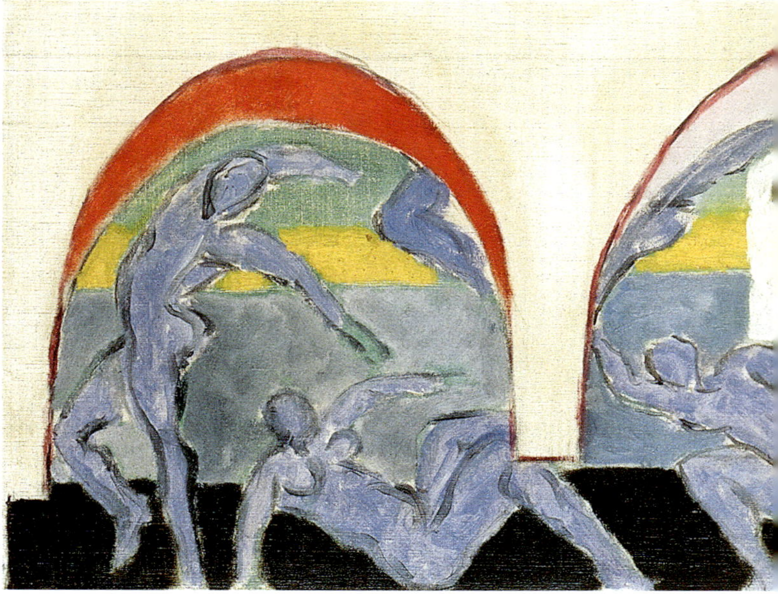

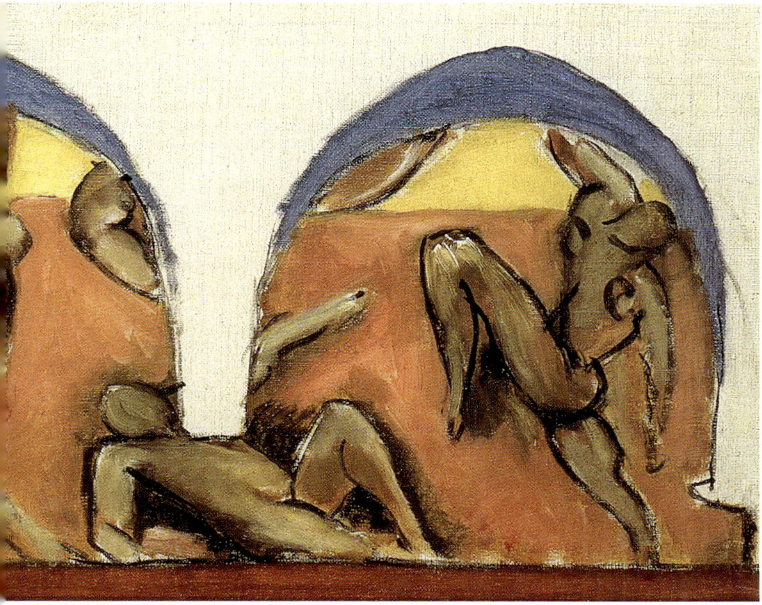

Study for "The Dance" (Ochre Harmony) • early 1931 • Musée Matisse, Nice

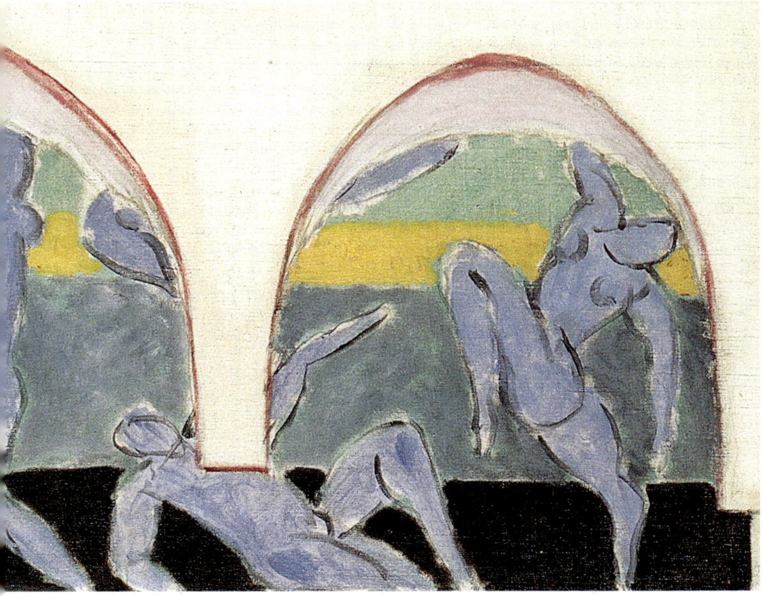

Study for "The Dance" (Blue Harmony) • early 1931 • Musée Matisse, Nice

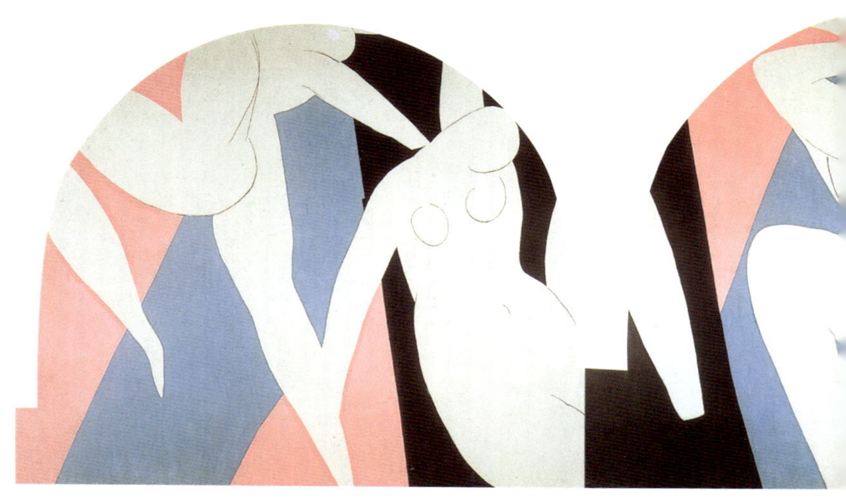

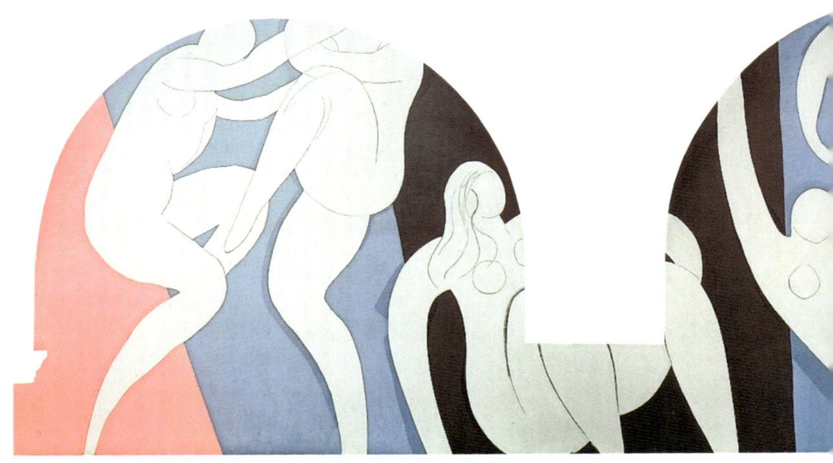

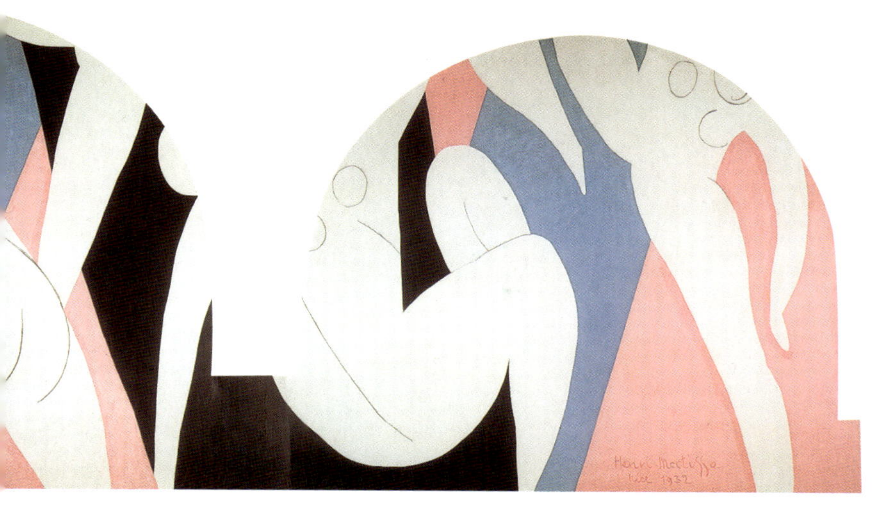

The Dance (first version) • 1931–1933 • Musée d'art moderne de la Ville de Paris

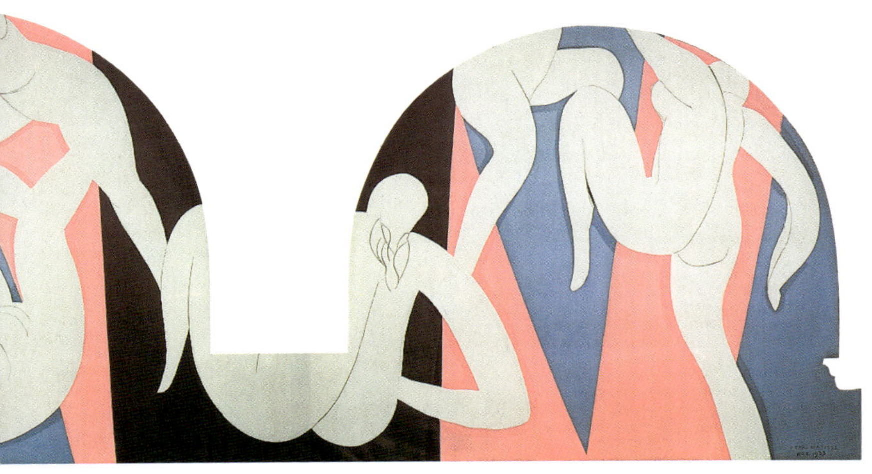

The Dance • 1932–1933 • The Barnes Foundation, Merion, Pennsylvania

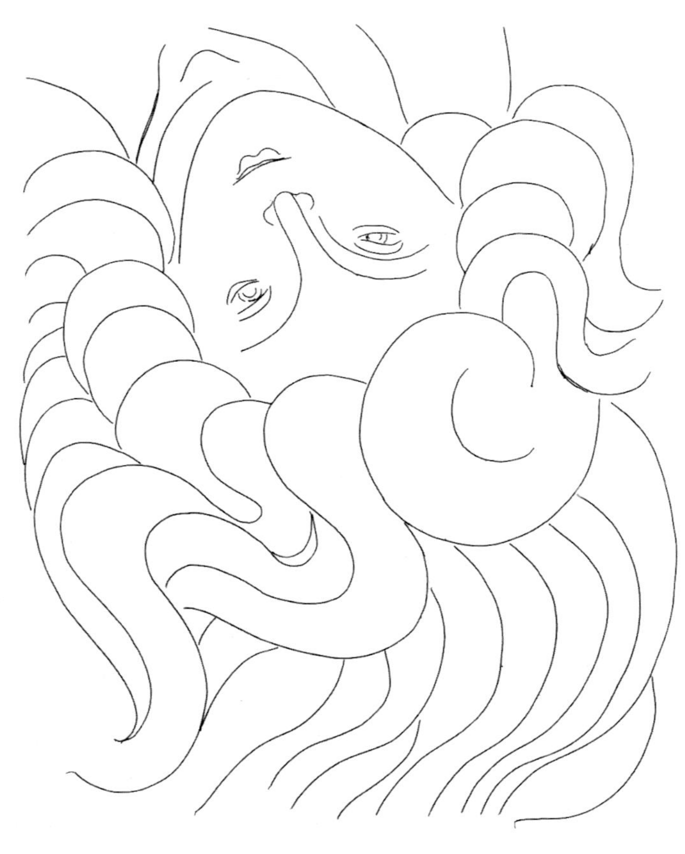

Hair, "Poésies de Mallarmé" (1932) · Summer 1931–Autumn 1932
Private collection

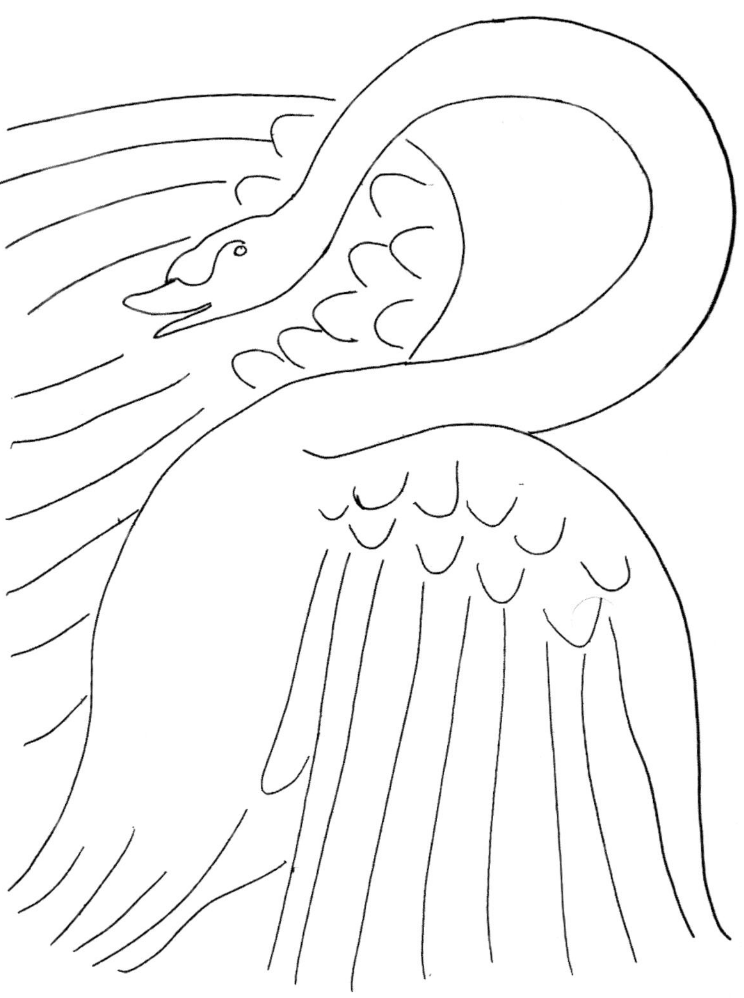

The Swan, "Poésies de Mallarmé" (1932) • Summer 1931–Autumn 1932
Private collection

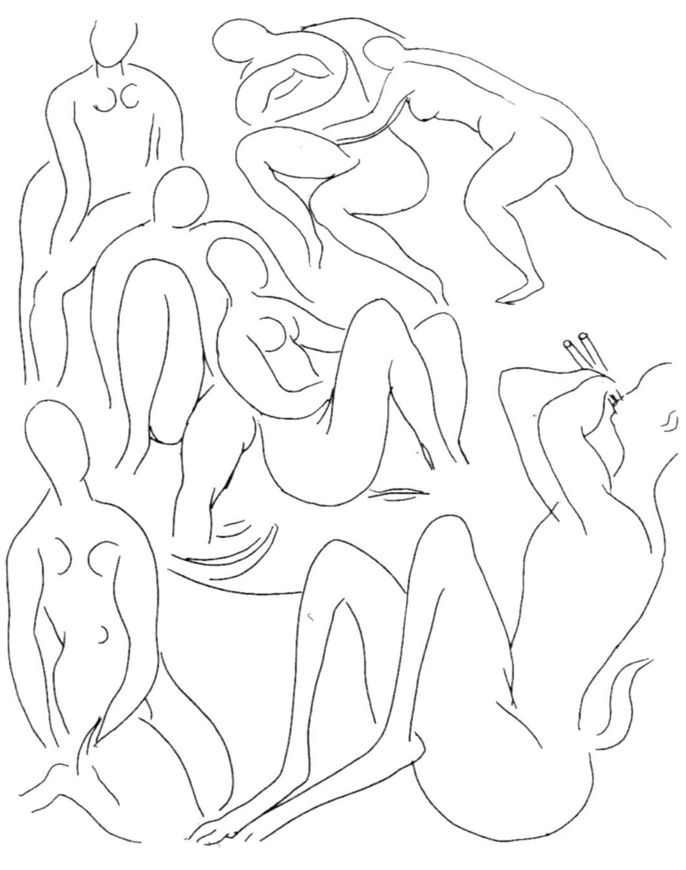

Nymphs and Faun, "Poésies de Mallarmé" (1932) · Summer 1931–Autumn 1932
Private collection

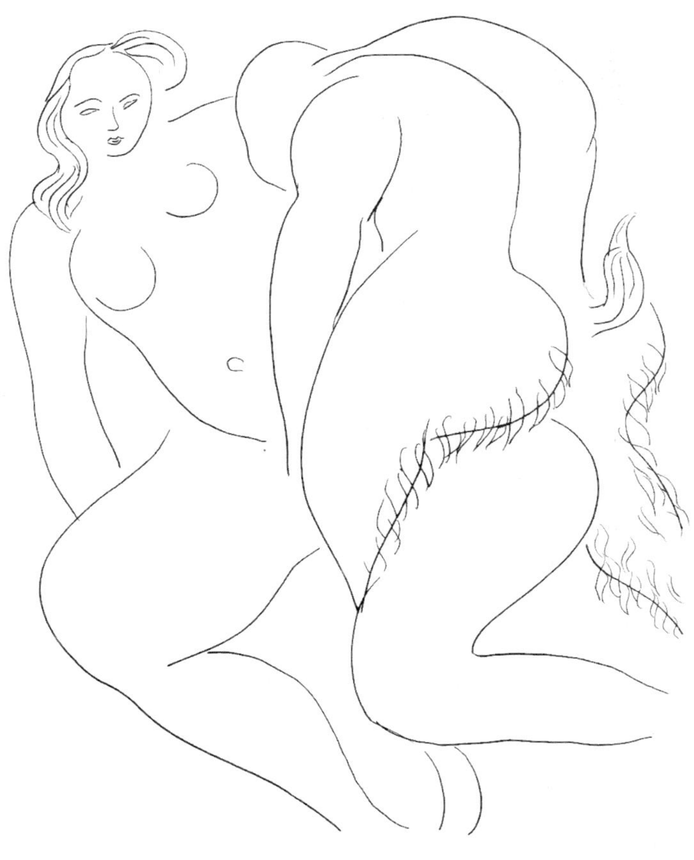

Nymph and Faun, "Poésies de Mallarmé" (1932) · Summer 1931–Autumn 1932
Private collection

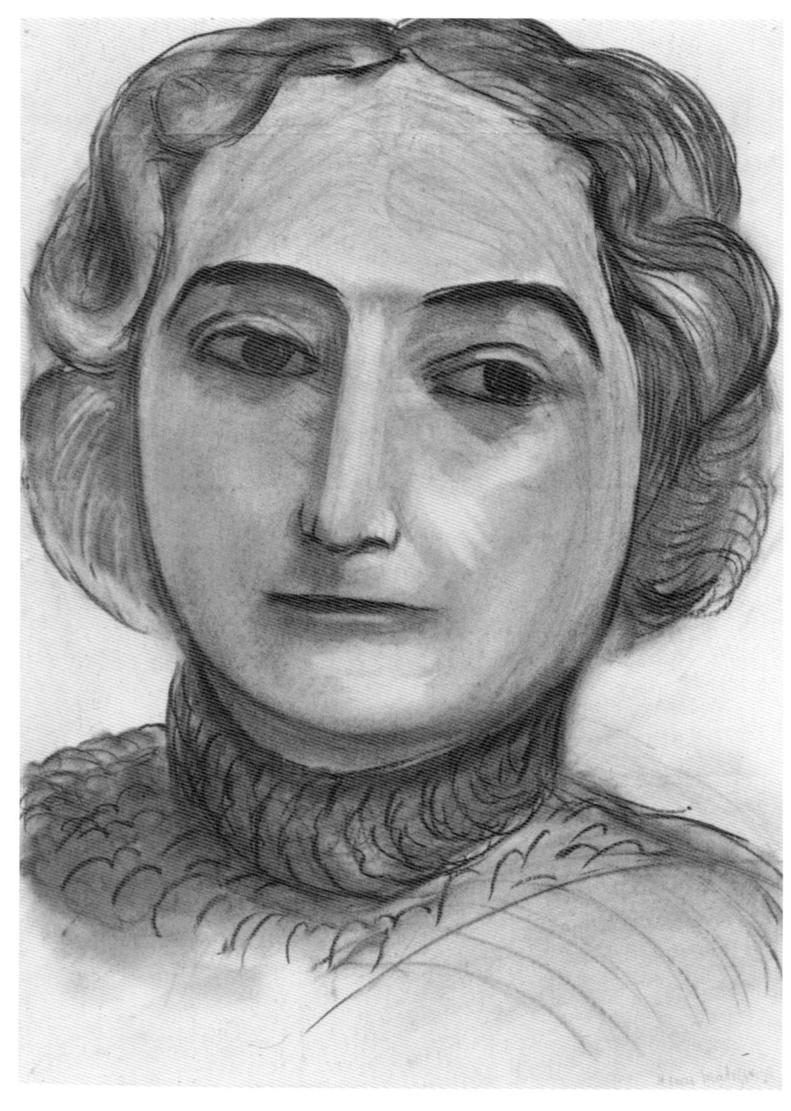

Portrait of Claribel Cone • 1933–1934
The Baltimore Museum of Art, The Cone Collection

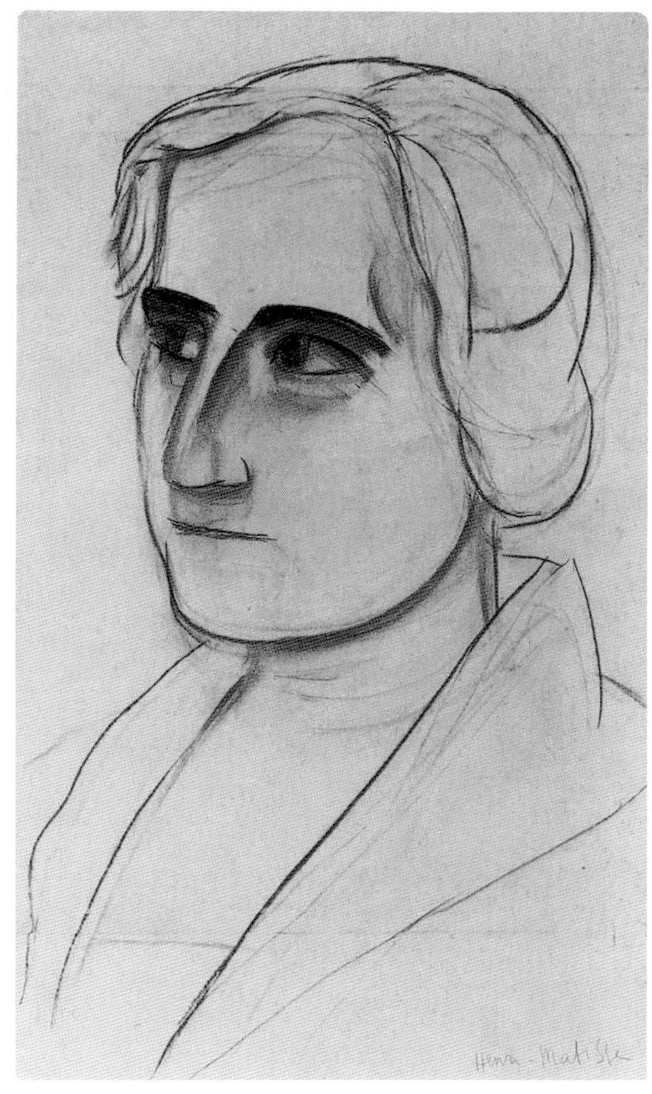

Portrait of Etta Cone • 1934
The Baltimore Museum of Art, The Cone Collection

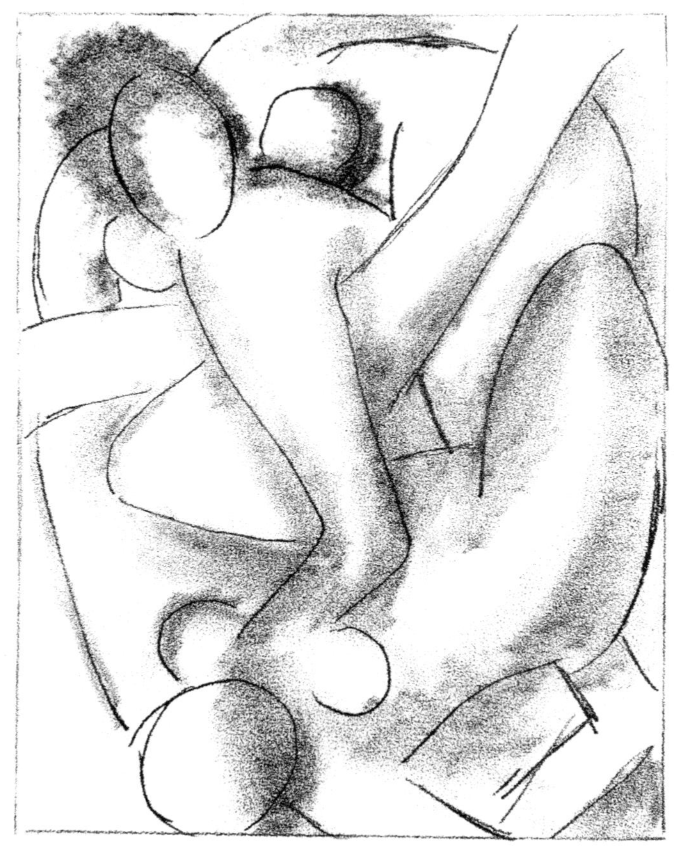

Calypso • 1934
Private collection

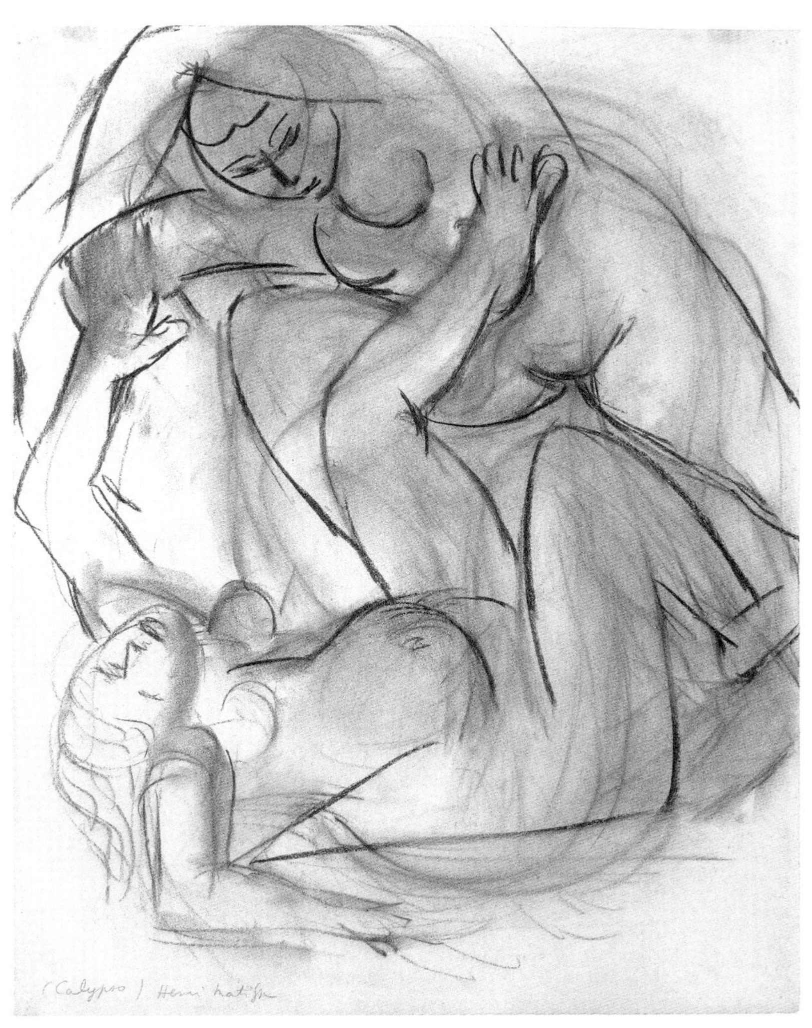

Study for "Calypso" · 1934
Private collection

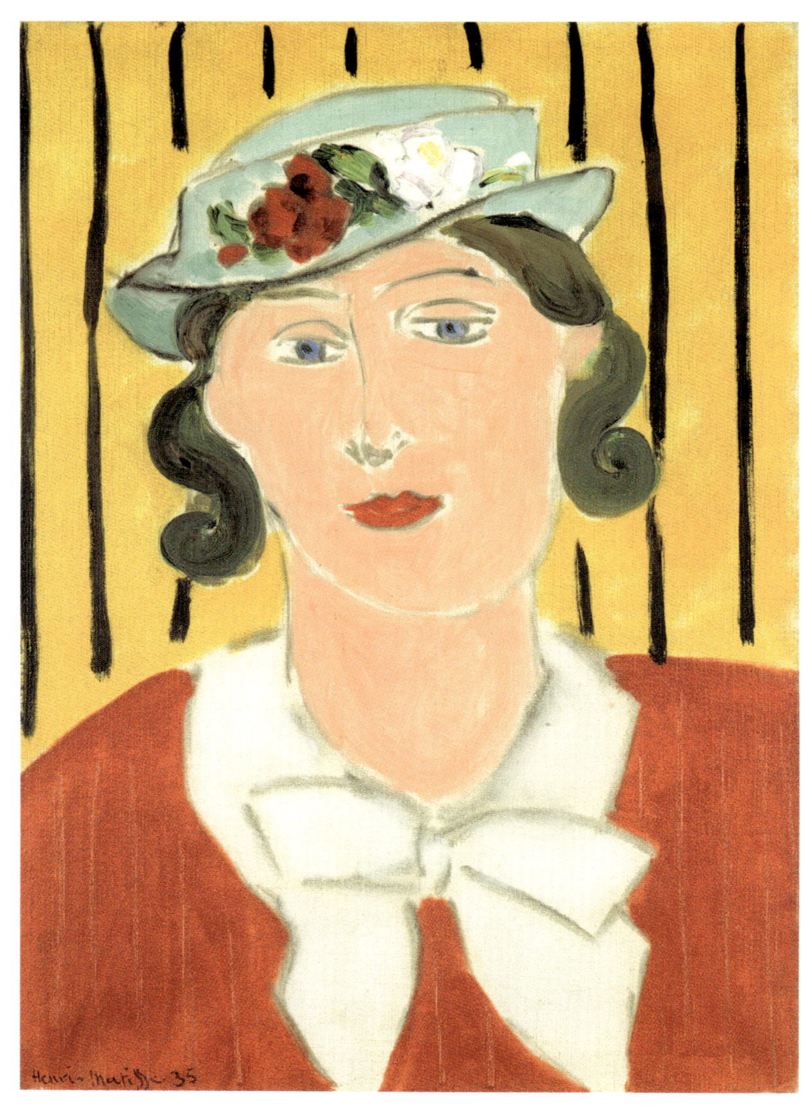

Hat with Roses • 1935

Private collection

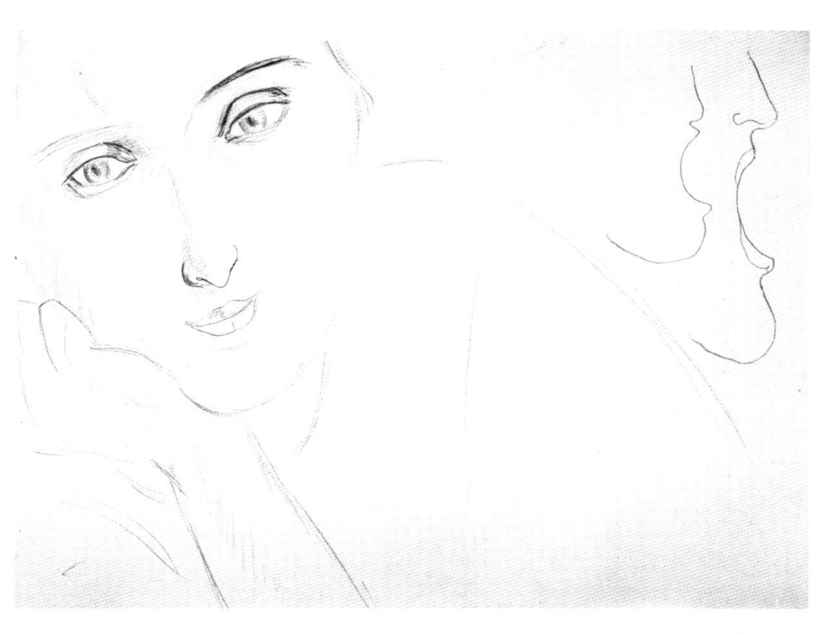

Dreaming Head • 1935
Private collection

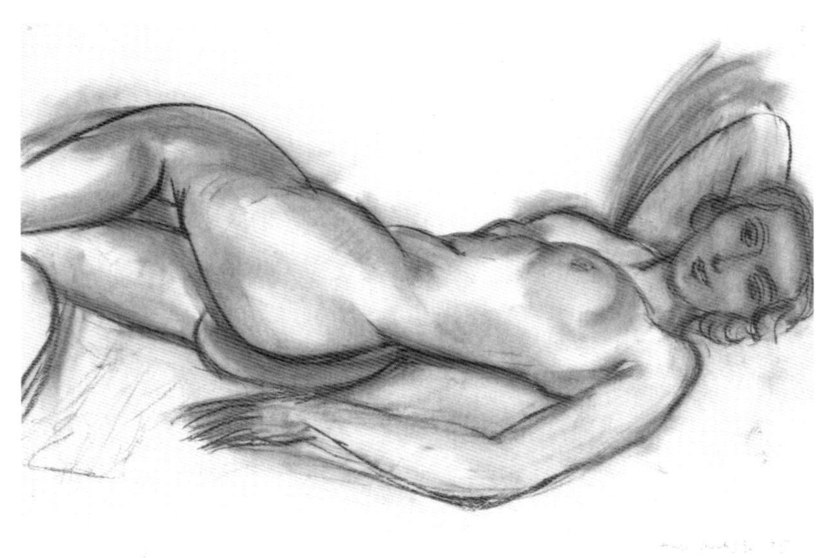

Reclining Nude · 1935
Private collection

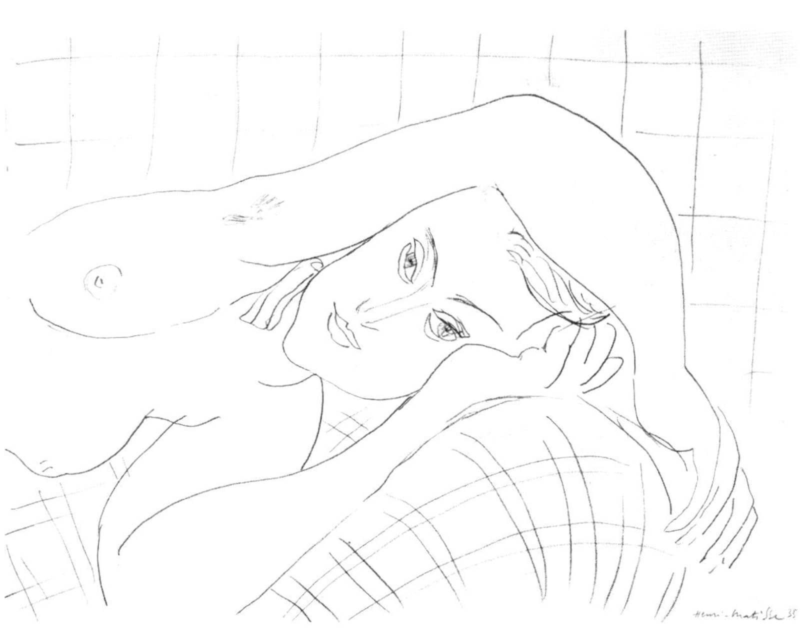

Reclining Nude • 1935
Private collection

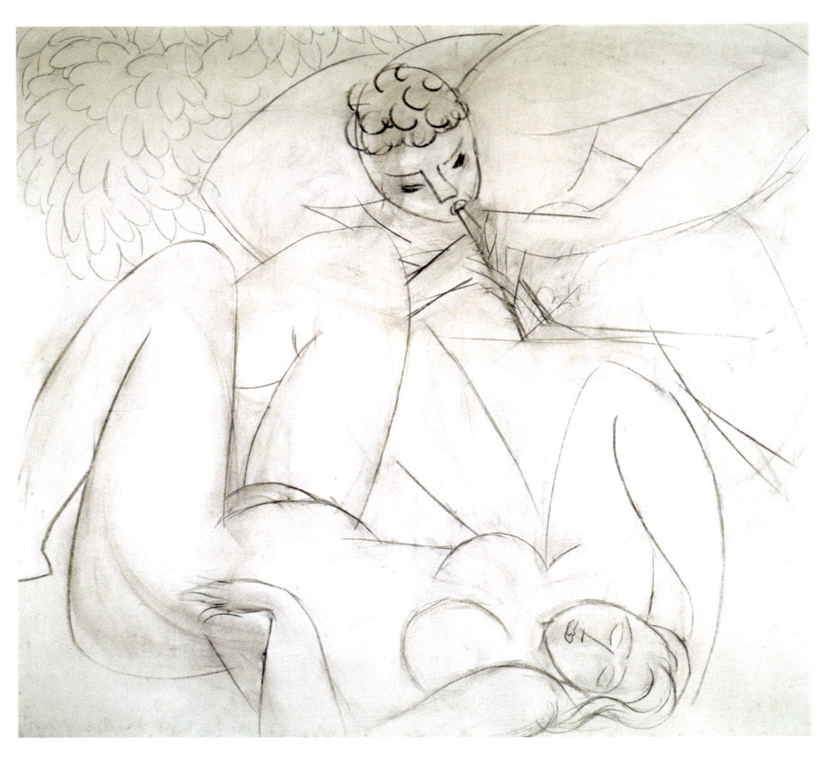

Faun Seducing a Sleeping Nymph · 1935
Musée national d'art moderne, Paris

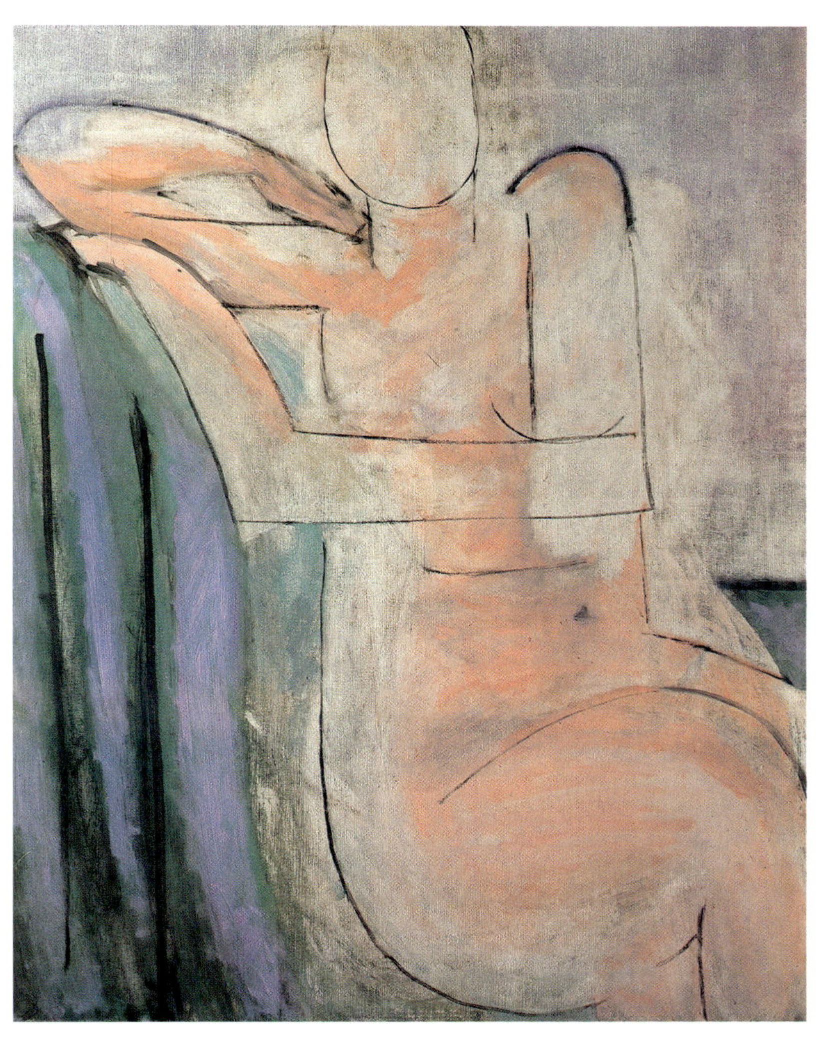

Seated Pink Nude • 1935–1936
Musée national d'art moderne, Paris

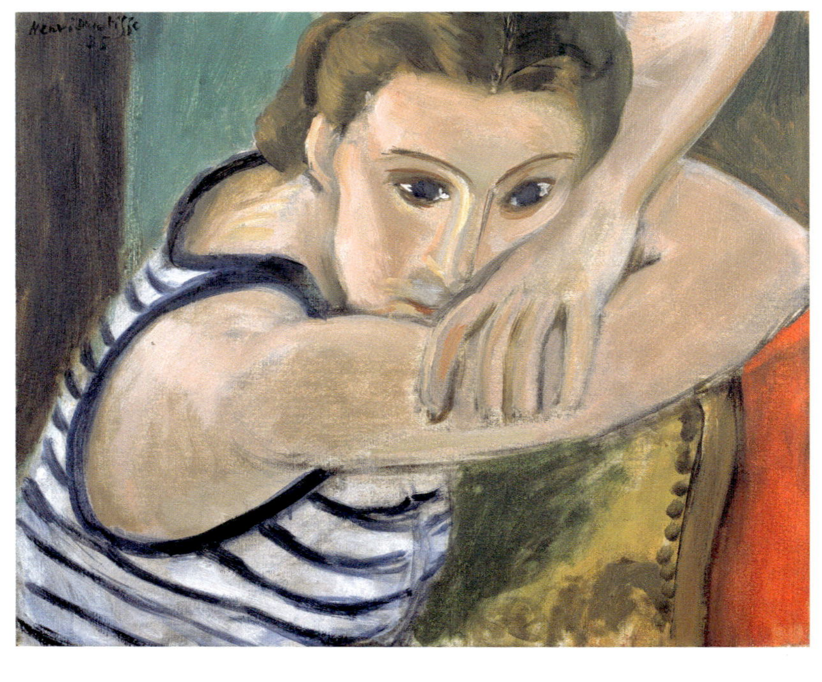

The Blue Eyes • 1935
The Baltimore Museum of Art, The Cone Collection

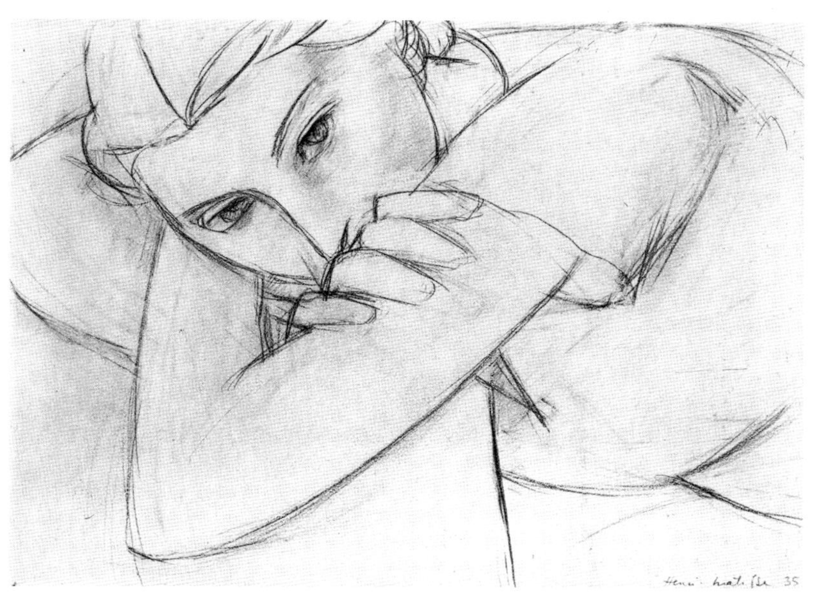

The Woman with Blue Eyes • 1935
Private collection
> **Large Reclining Nude / The Pink Nude** • 1935
The Baltimore Museum of Art, The Cone Collection

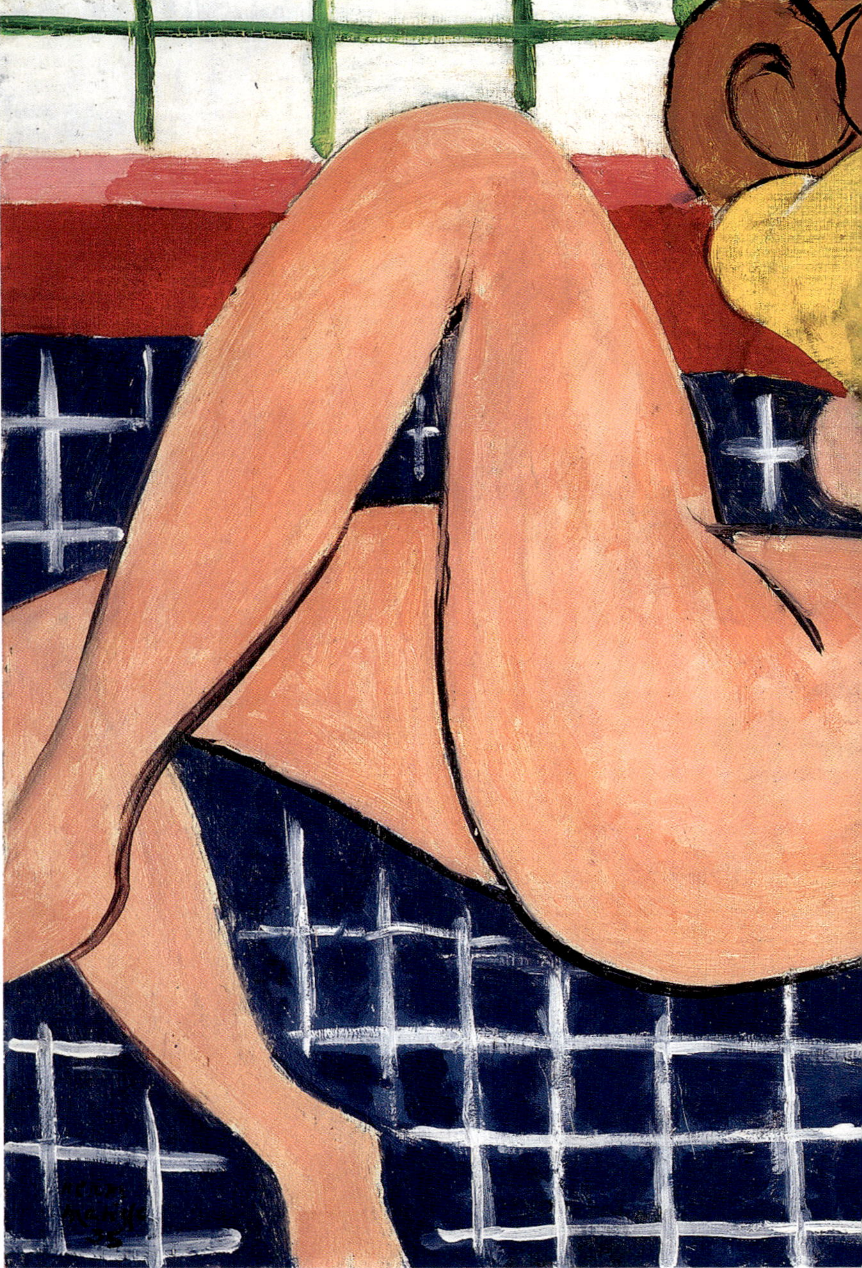

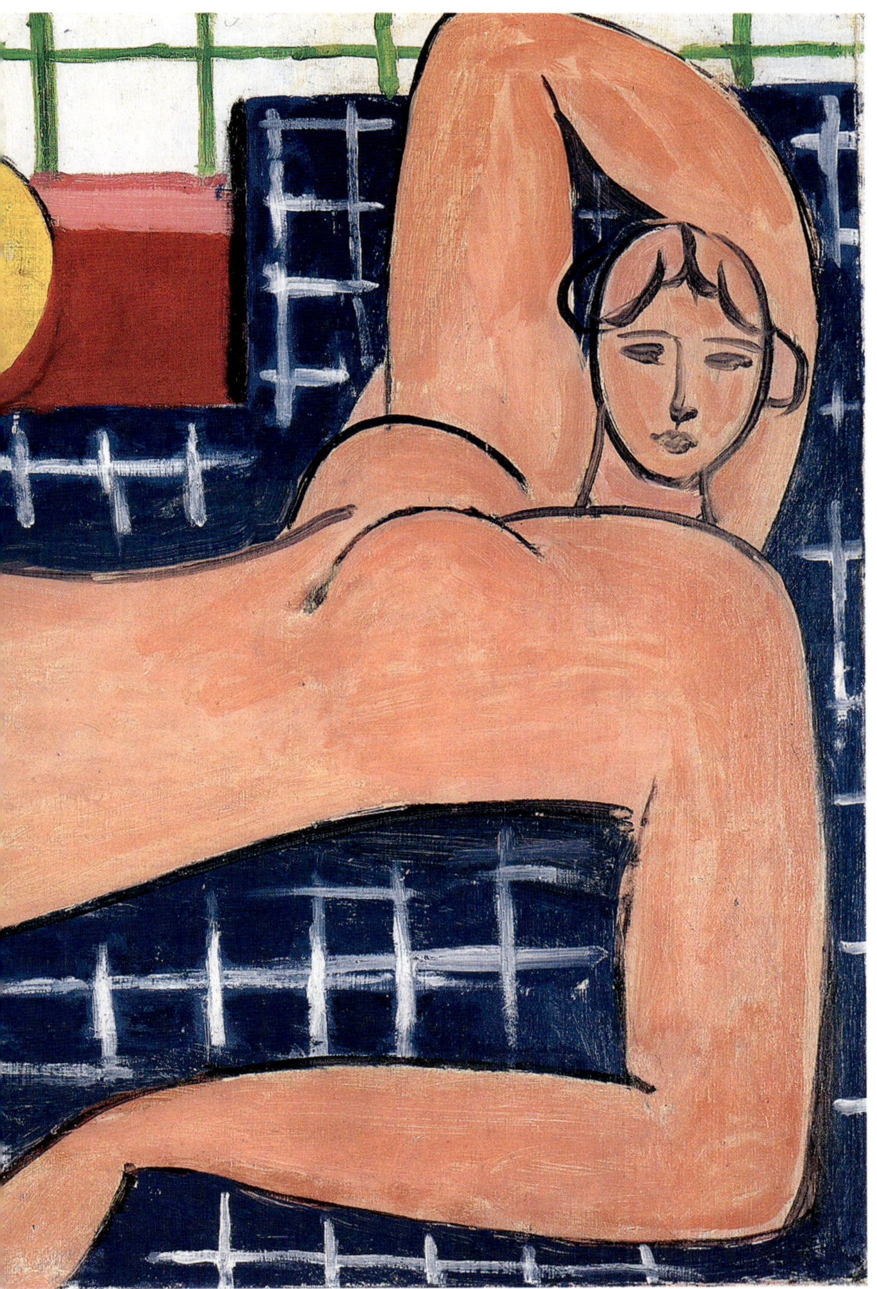

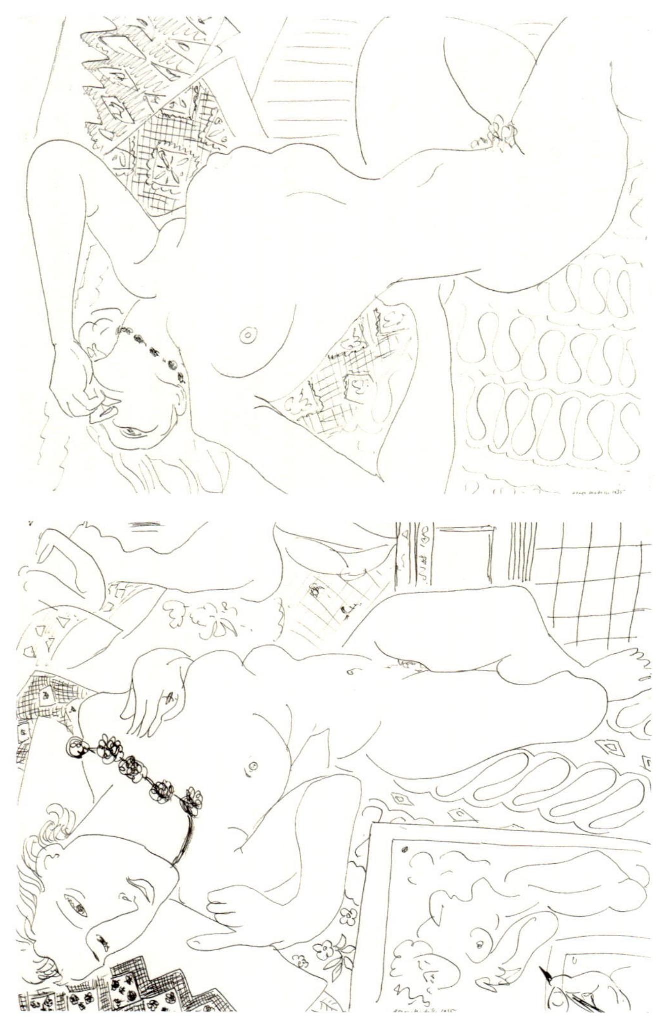

Reclining Nude · 1935

Collection of Dina Vierny

Reclining Nude in the Studio · 1935

Private collection

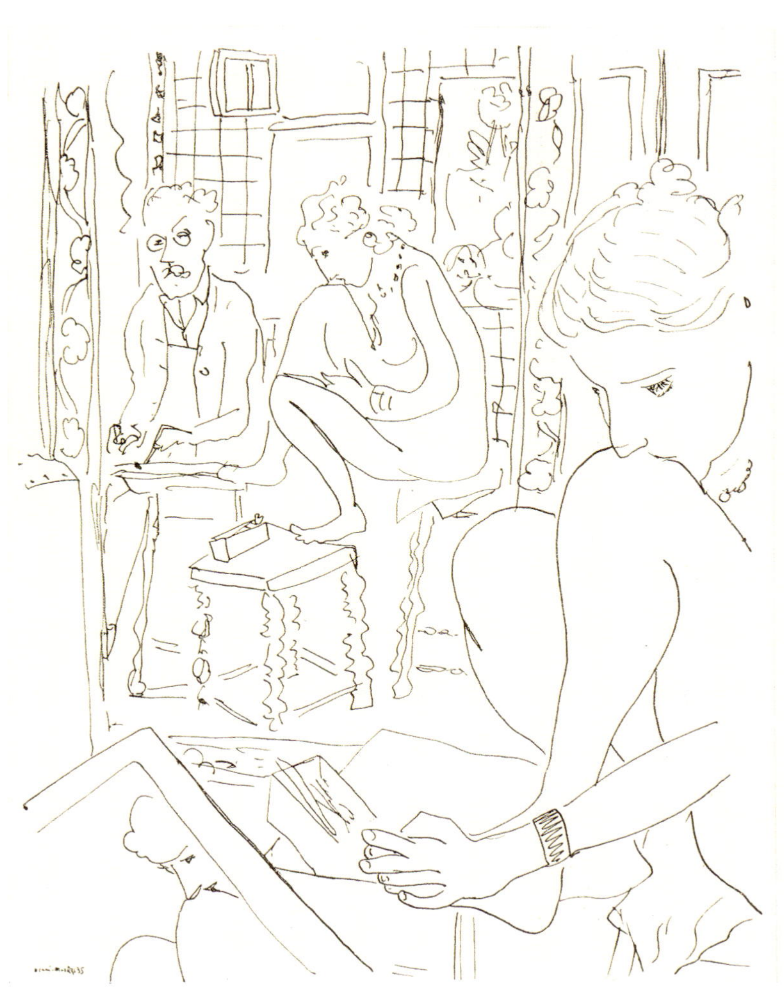

Artist and Model Reflected in a Mirror • 1935

Whereabouts unknown

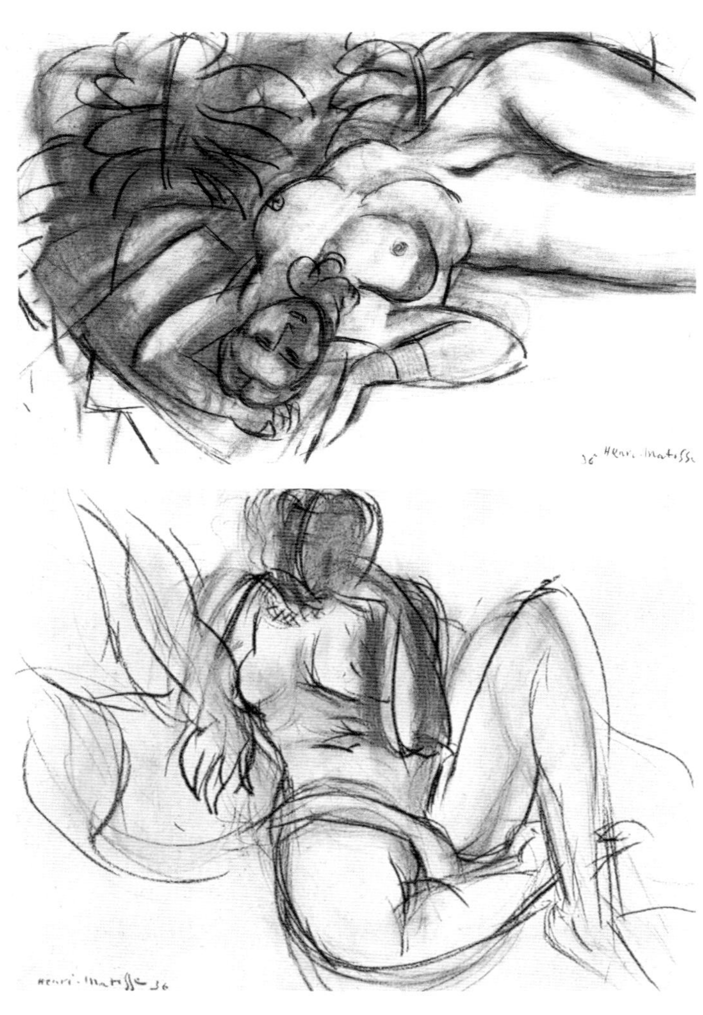

Reclining Nude · 1936
Musée Matisse, Nice
Crouching Nude · 1936
Whereabouts unknown

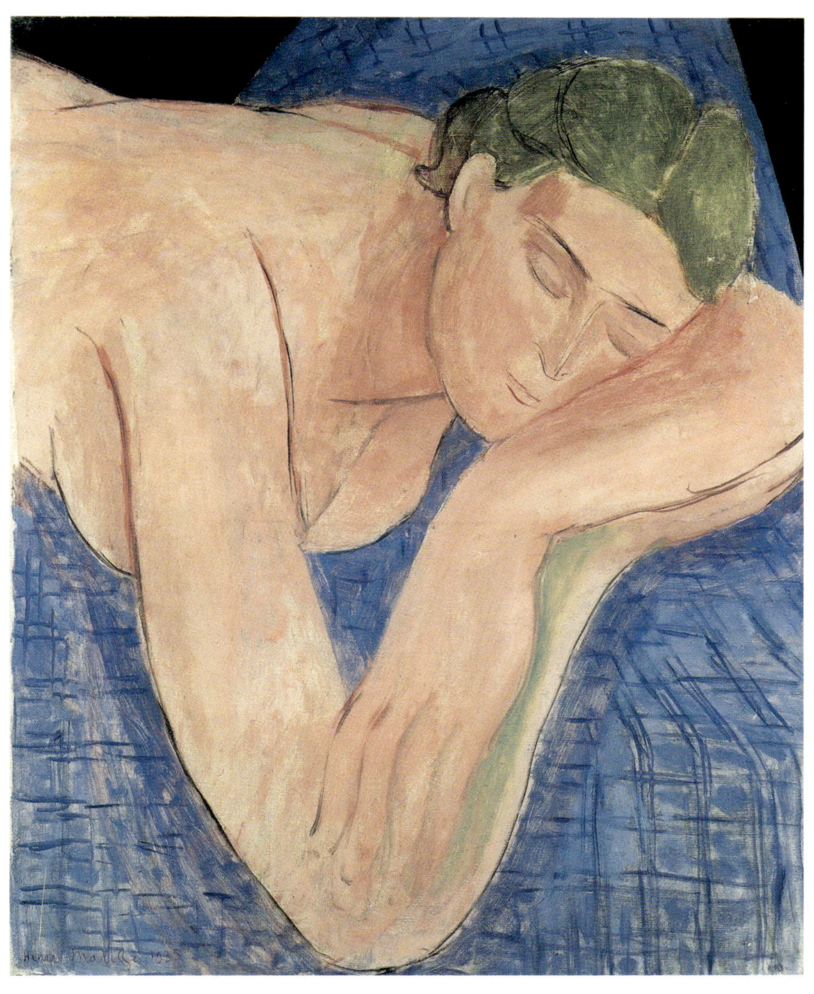

The Dream • April–May 1935
Musée national d'art moderne, Paris

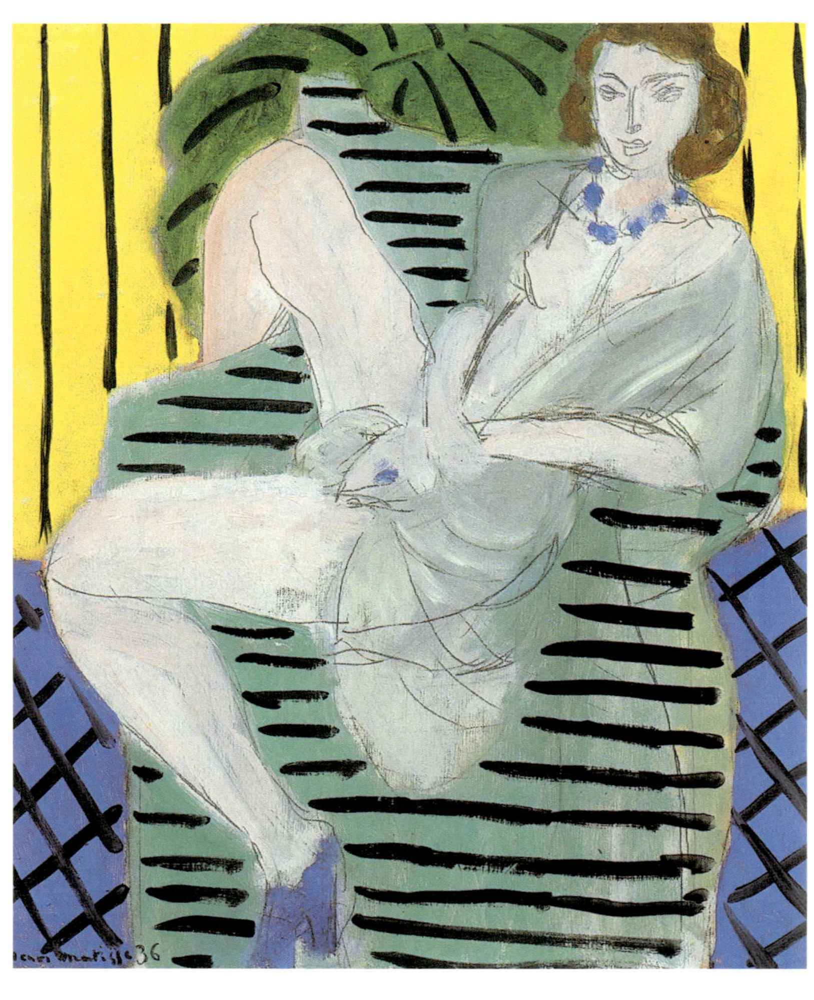

Woman in an Armchair on a Blue and Yellow Background • 1936

Private collection

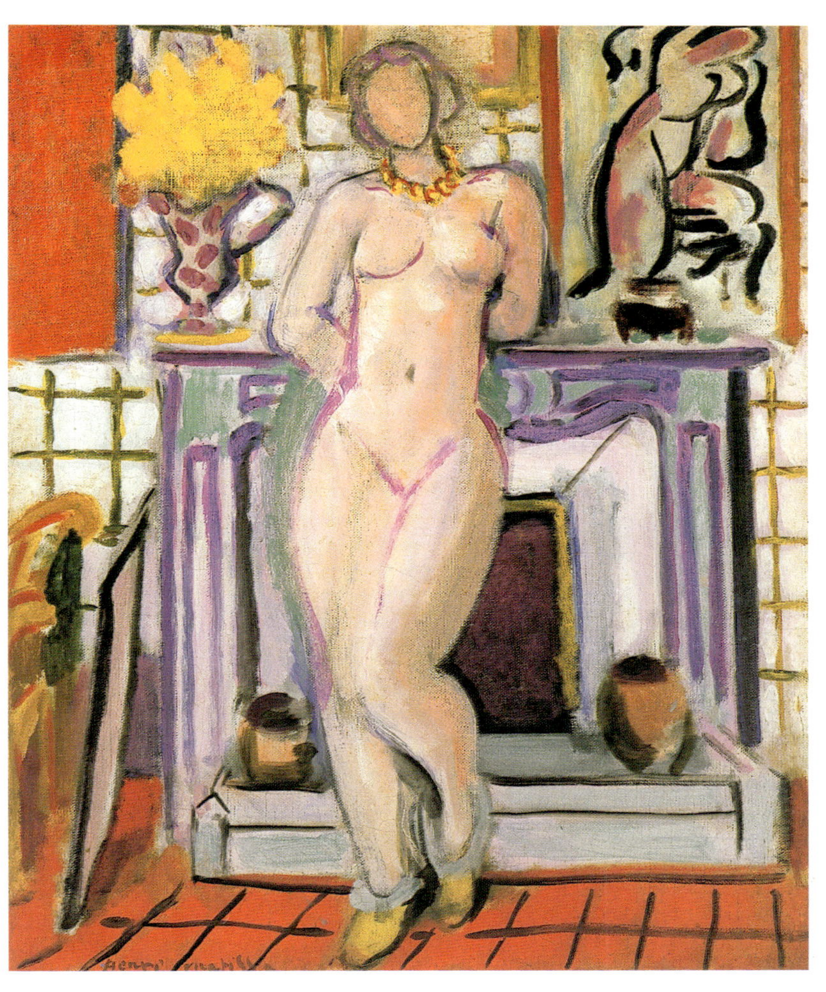

Nude beside a Fireplace · 1936

Private collection

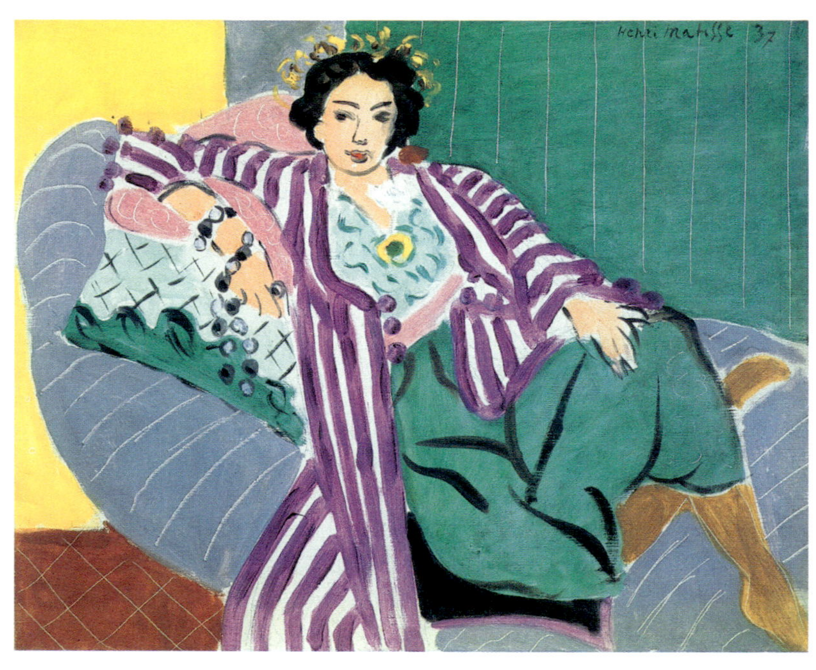

Small Odalisque in a Purple Robe · 1937

Private collection

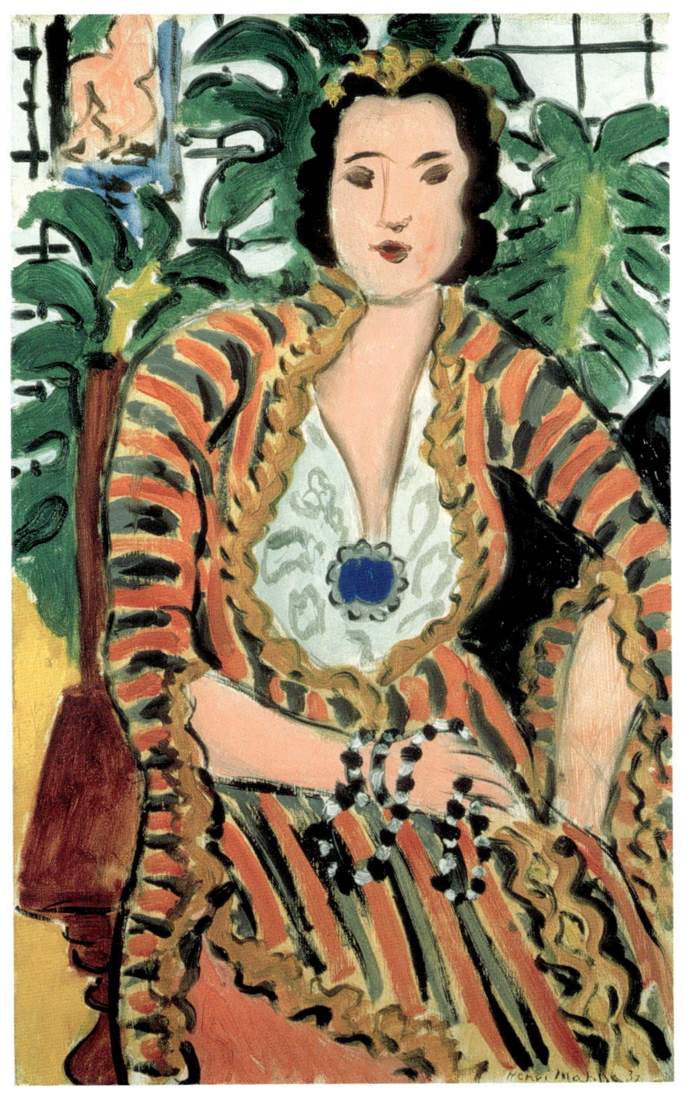

Portrait of Hélène Galitzine • 1937

Private collection

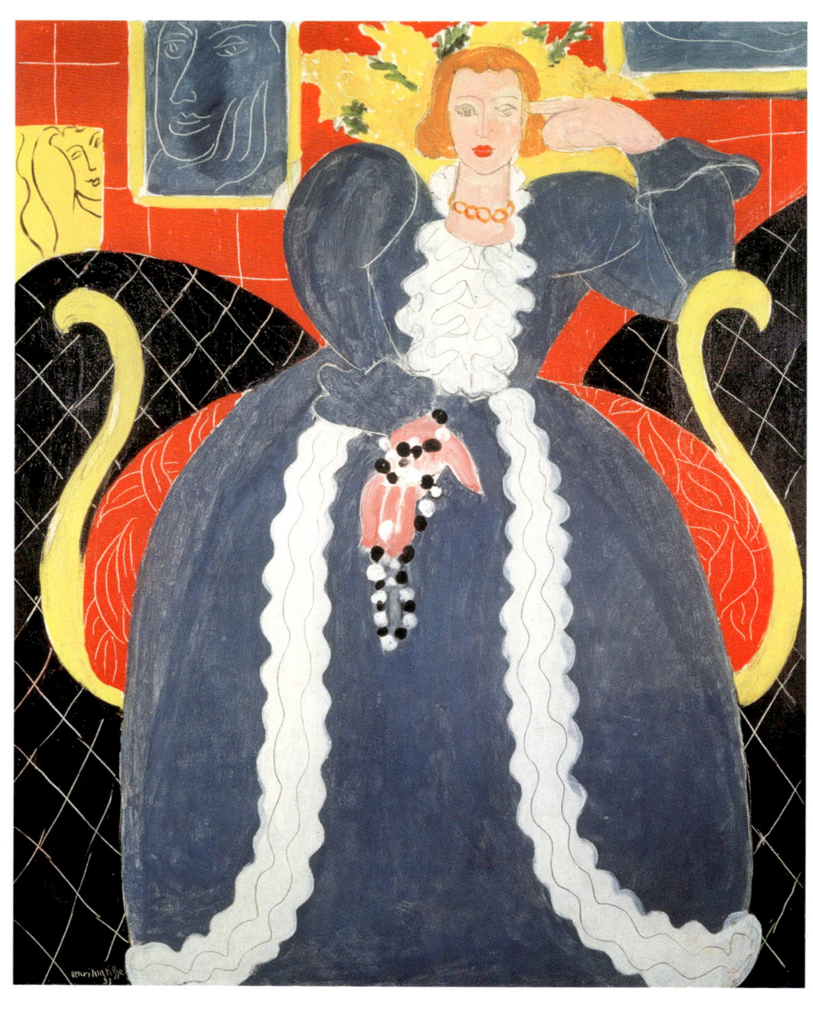

Woman in Blue / The Large Blue Robe and Mimosas • 1937
Philadelphia Museum of Art, gift of Mrs. John Wintersteen

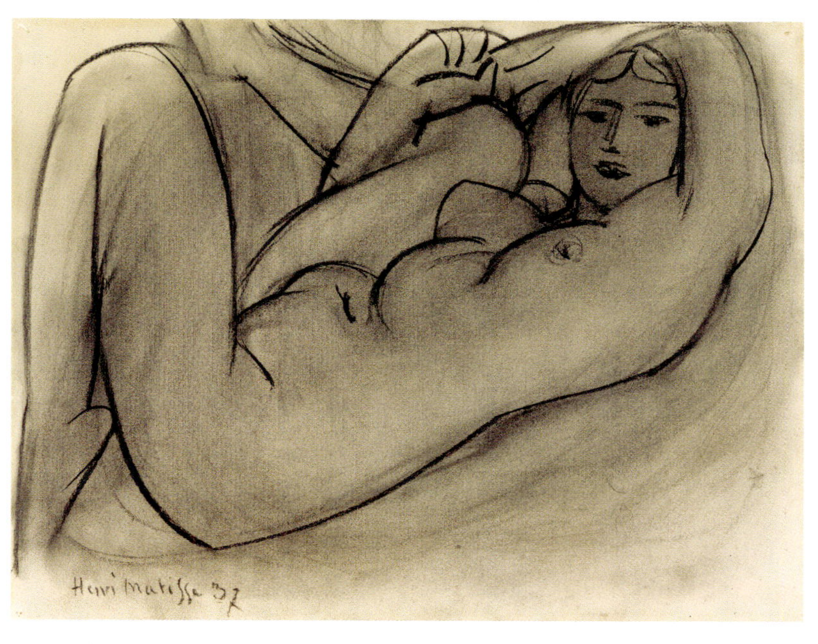

Reclining Nude with Arm behind Head • 1937

The Baltimore Museum of Art, The Cone Collection

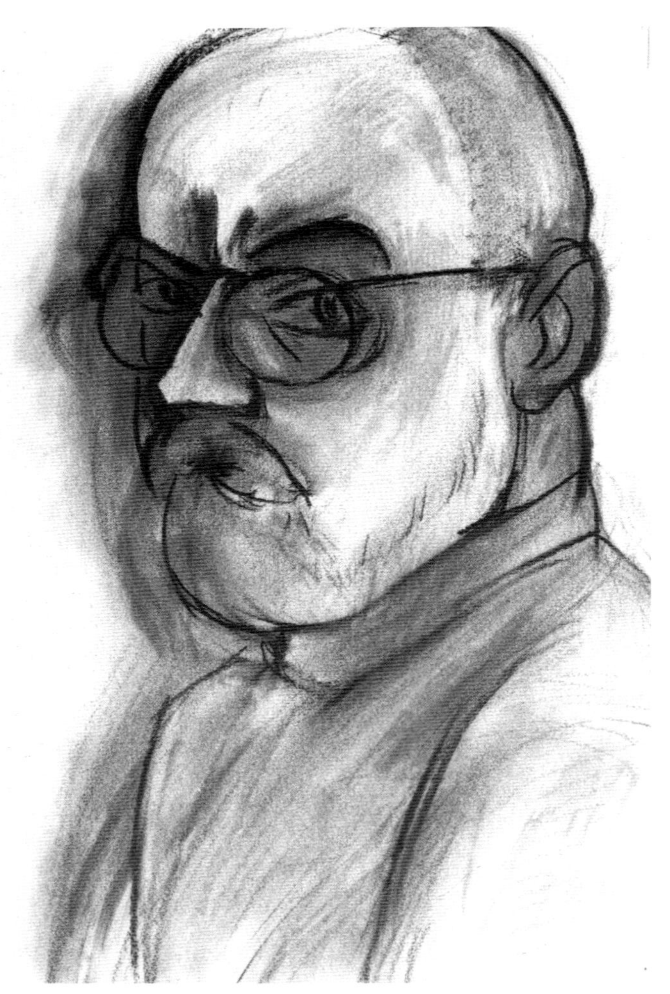

Self-Portrait • 1937

The Baltimore Museum of Art, The Cone Collection

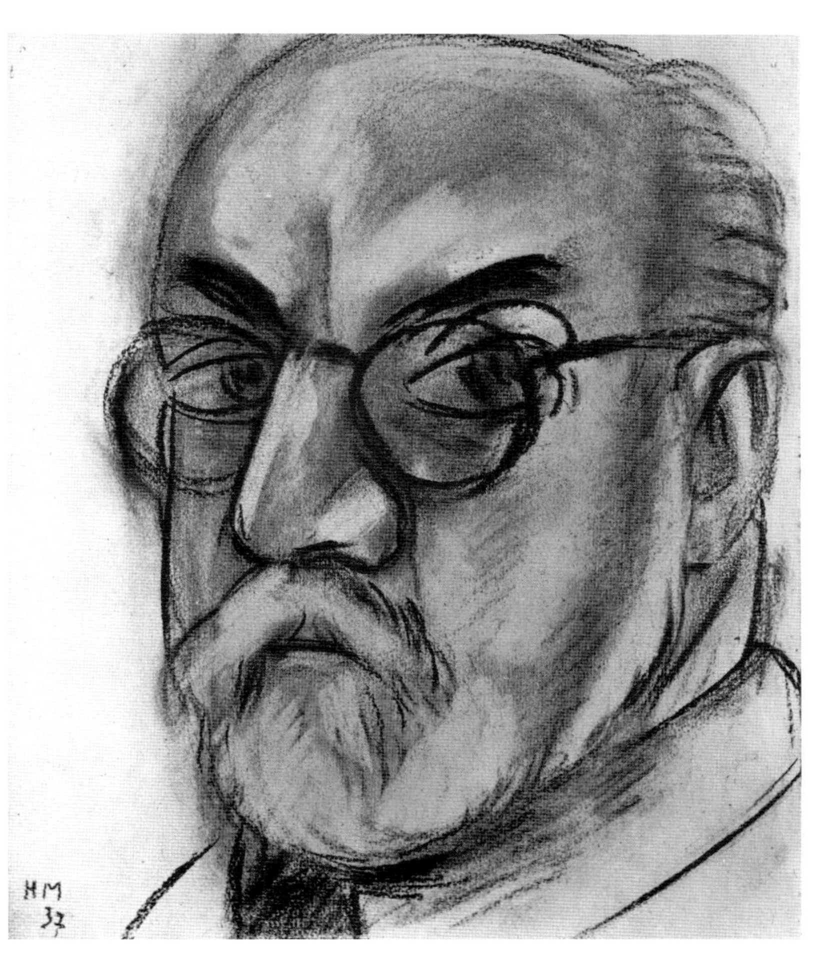

Self-Portrait • 1937

National Gallery of Art, Washington, Collection of Mr. and Mrs. Mellon

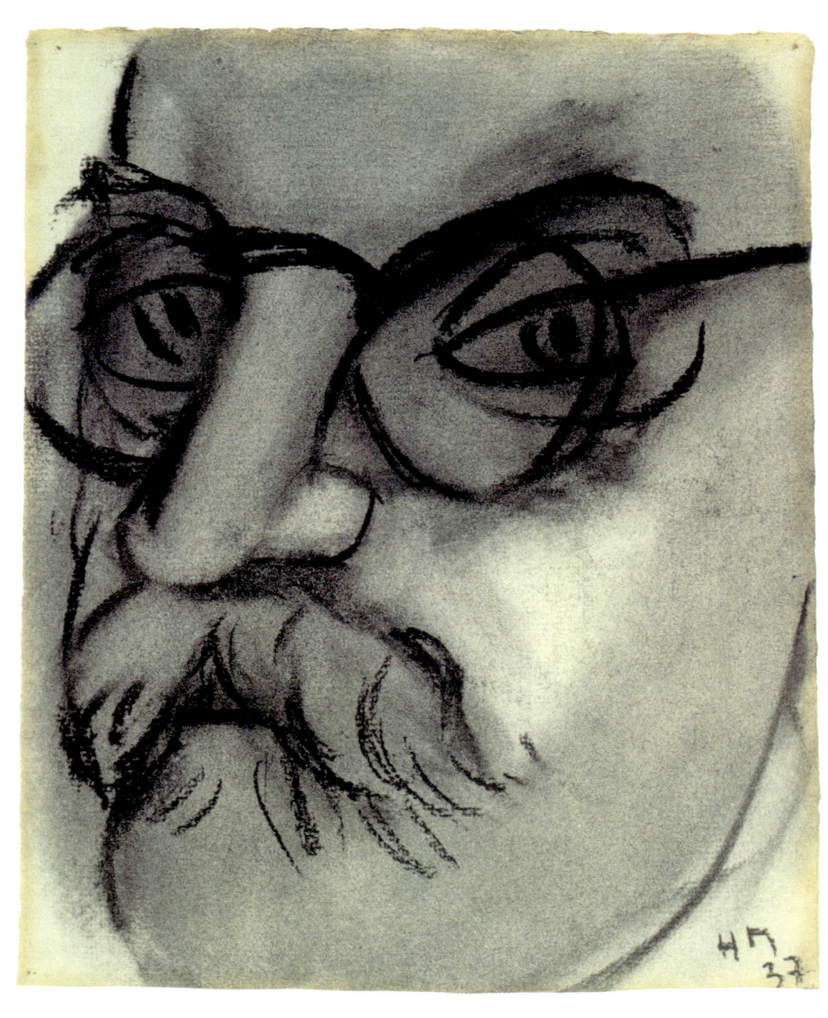

Self-Portrait · 1937
Musée national d'art moderne, Paris

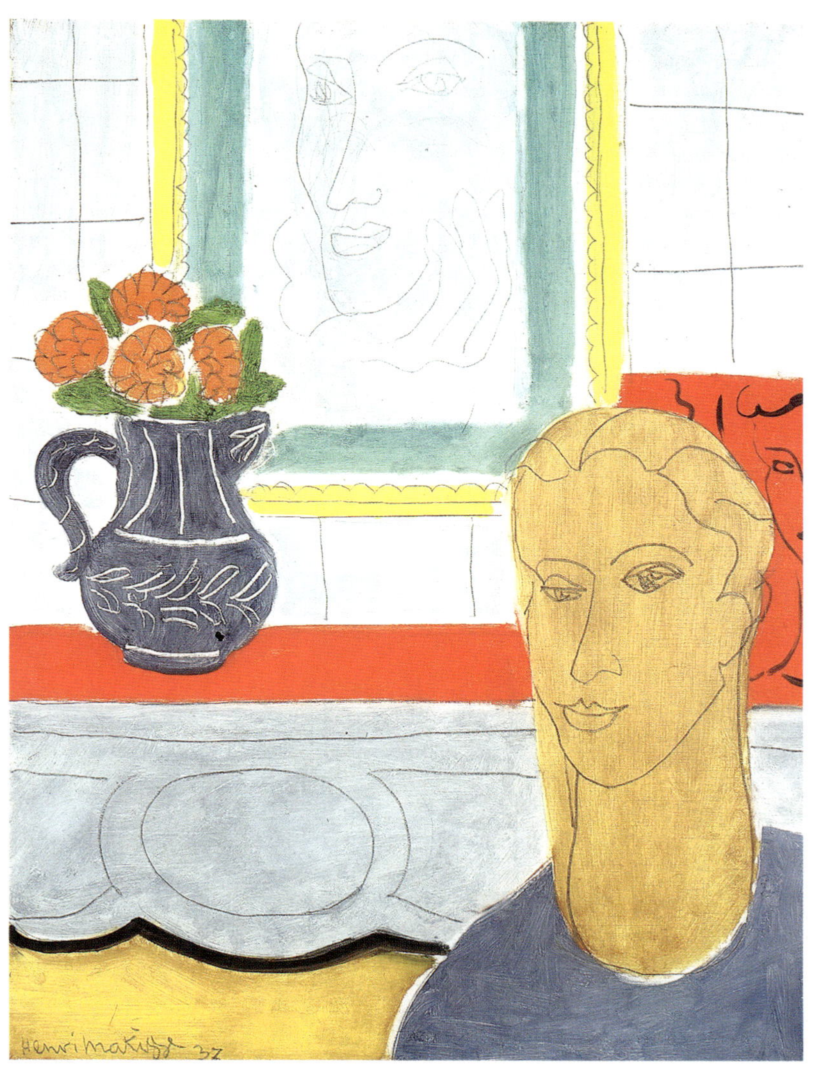

The Ochre Head • February 1937

Private collection

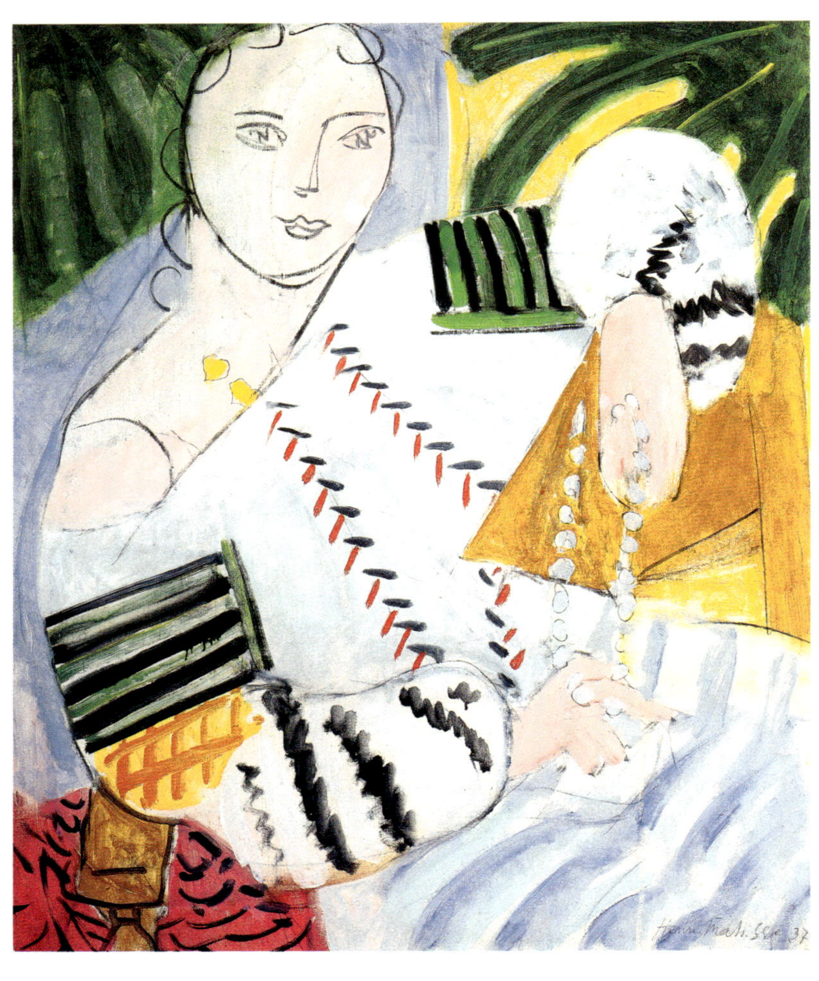

The Rumanian Blouse with Green Sleeves • March–April 1937

Cincinnati Art Museum, Mary E. Johnston Bequest

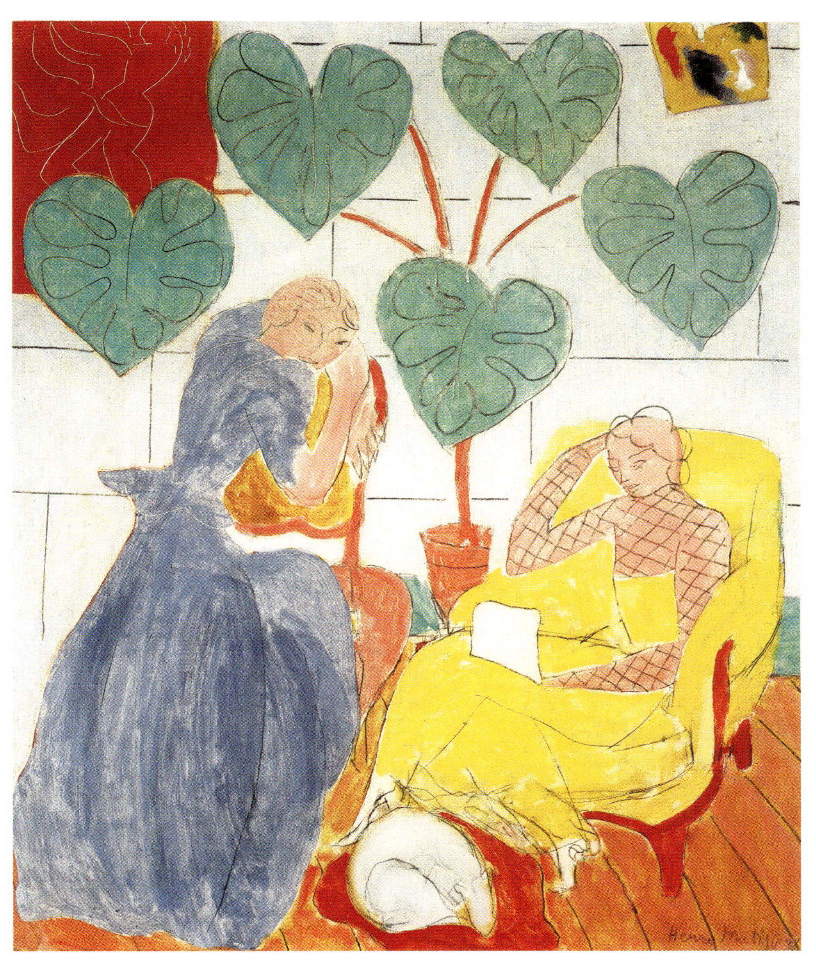

The Conservatory · November 1937–May 1938
Private collection

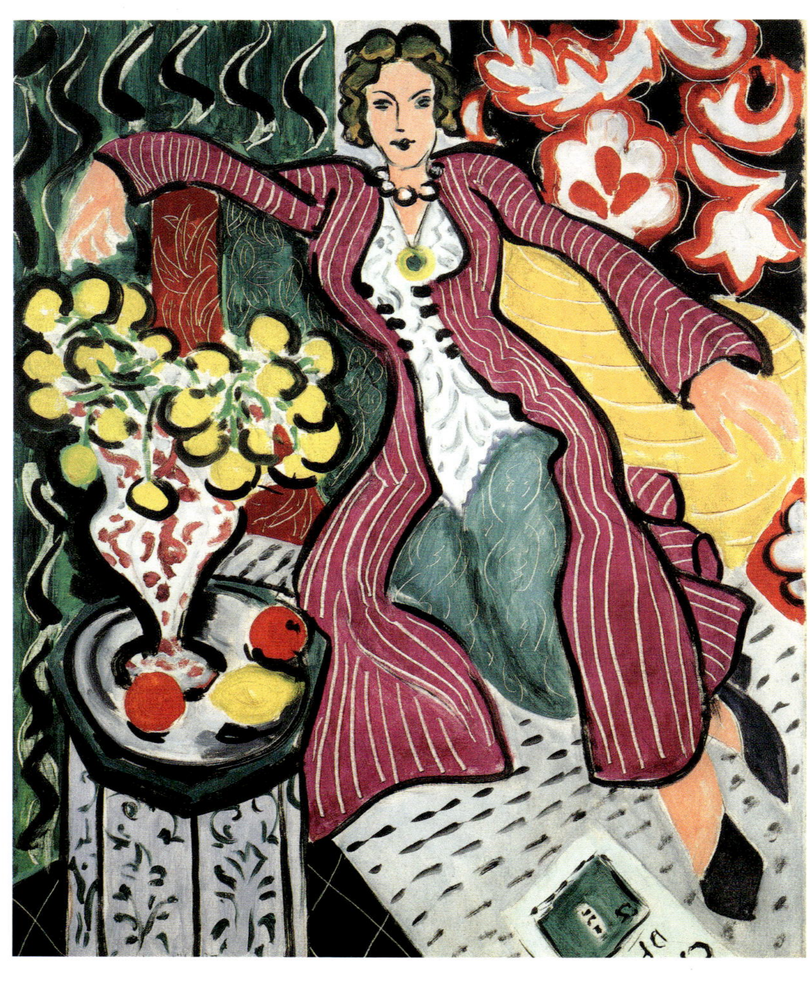

Woman in a Purple Robe with Ranunculi • February 1937
The Museum of Fine Arts, Houston, The John A. and Audrey Jones Beck Collection

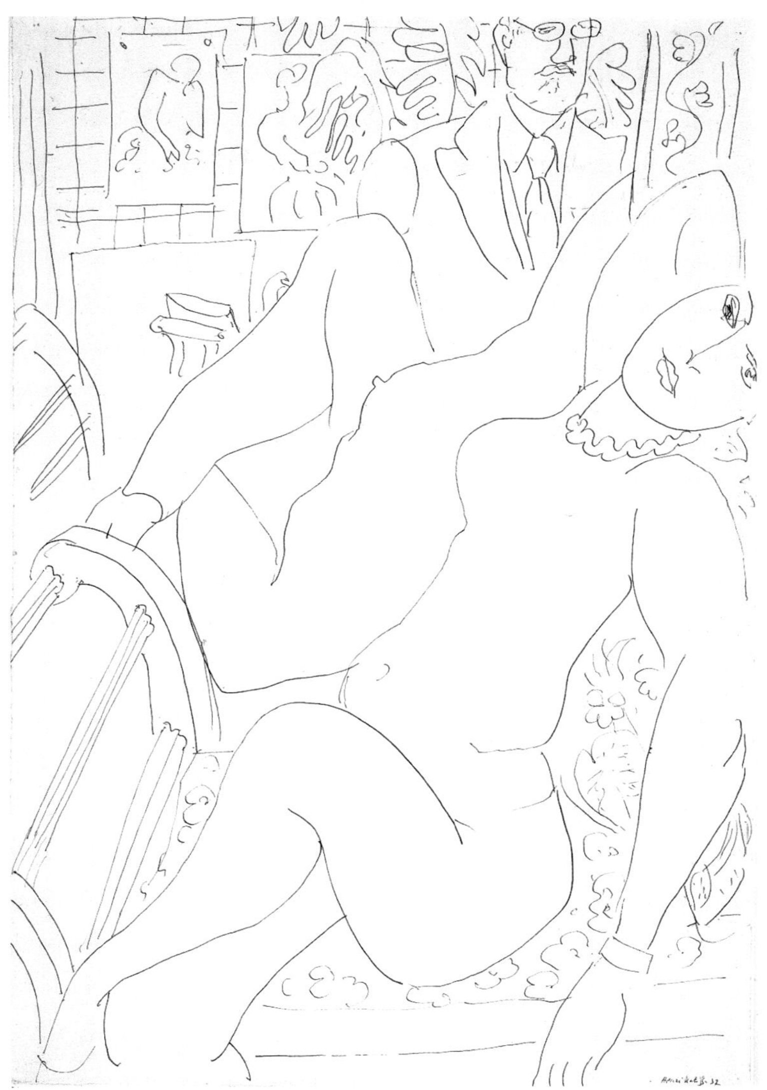

Artist and Model Reflected in a Mirror • 1937
The Baltimore Museum of Art, The Cone Collection

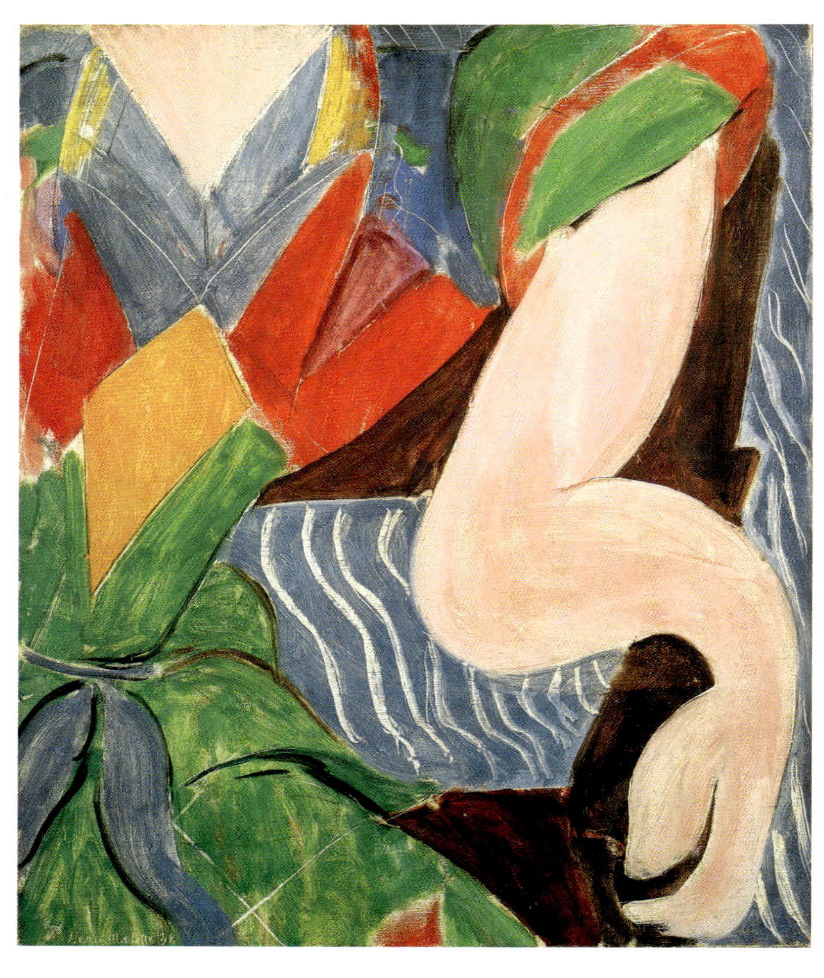

The Arm • January–June 1938

Private collection

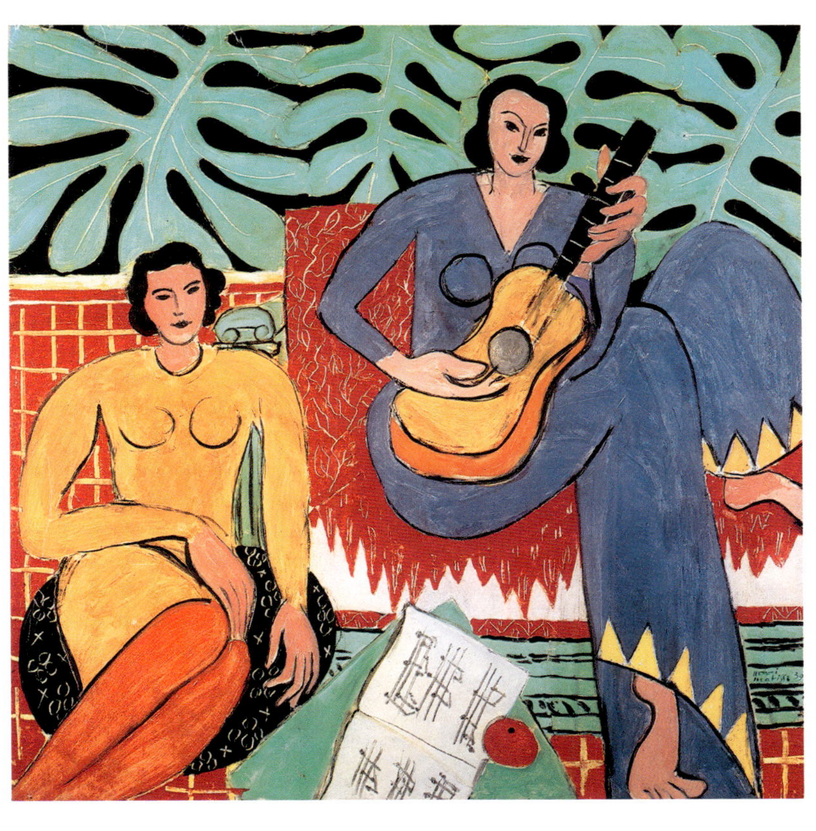

Music • 1939
Albright-Knox Art Gallery, Buffalo, New York

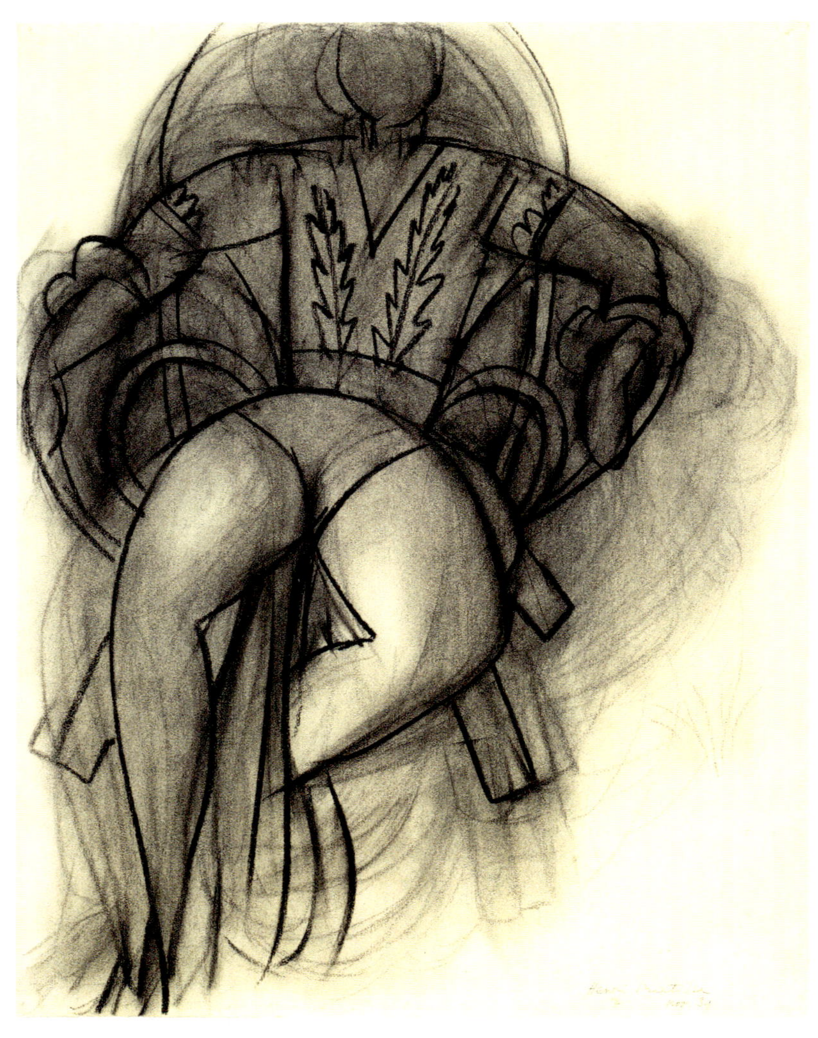

Dancer in Repose • 1939
Musée national d'art moderne, Paris

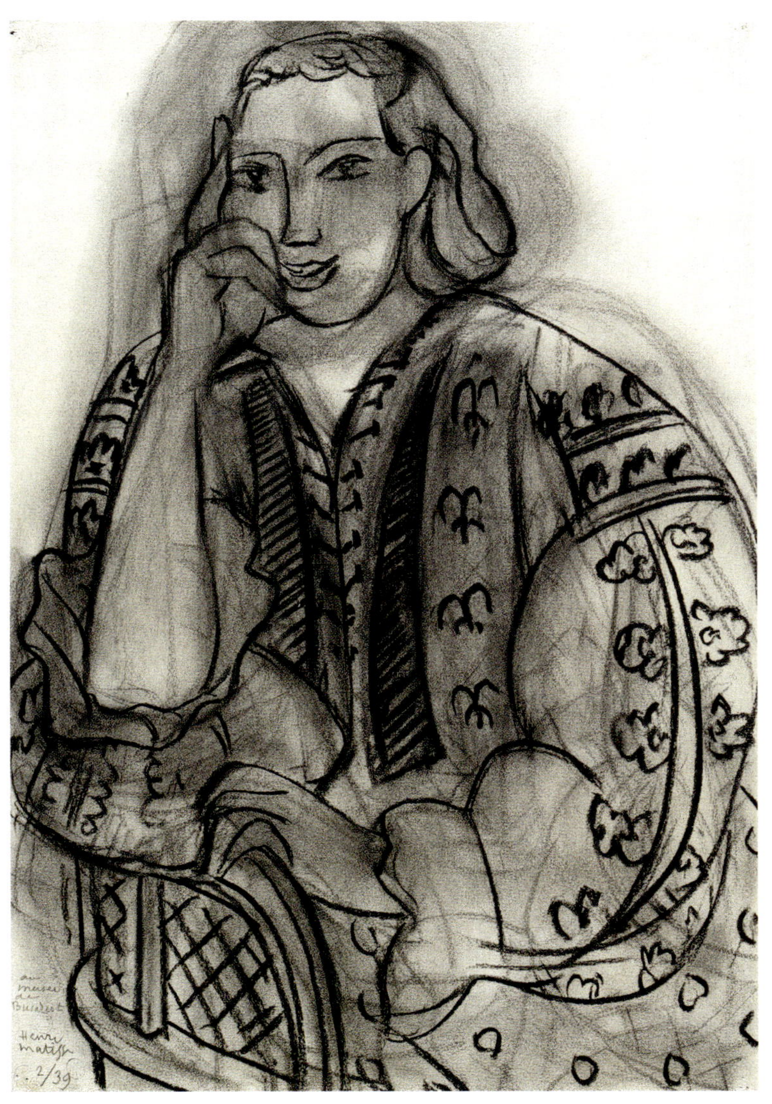

The Rumanian Blouse • 1939–1940
National Museum of Art, Bucharest

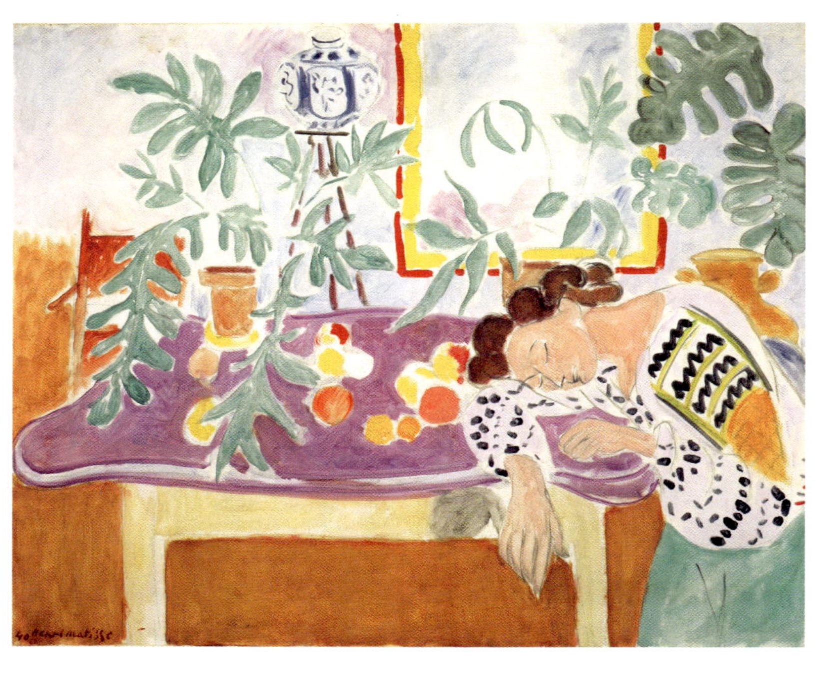

Still Life with a Sleeping Woman · late 1939–early 1940
National Gallery of Art, Washington, Collection of Mr. and Mrs. Mellon

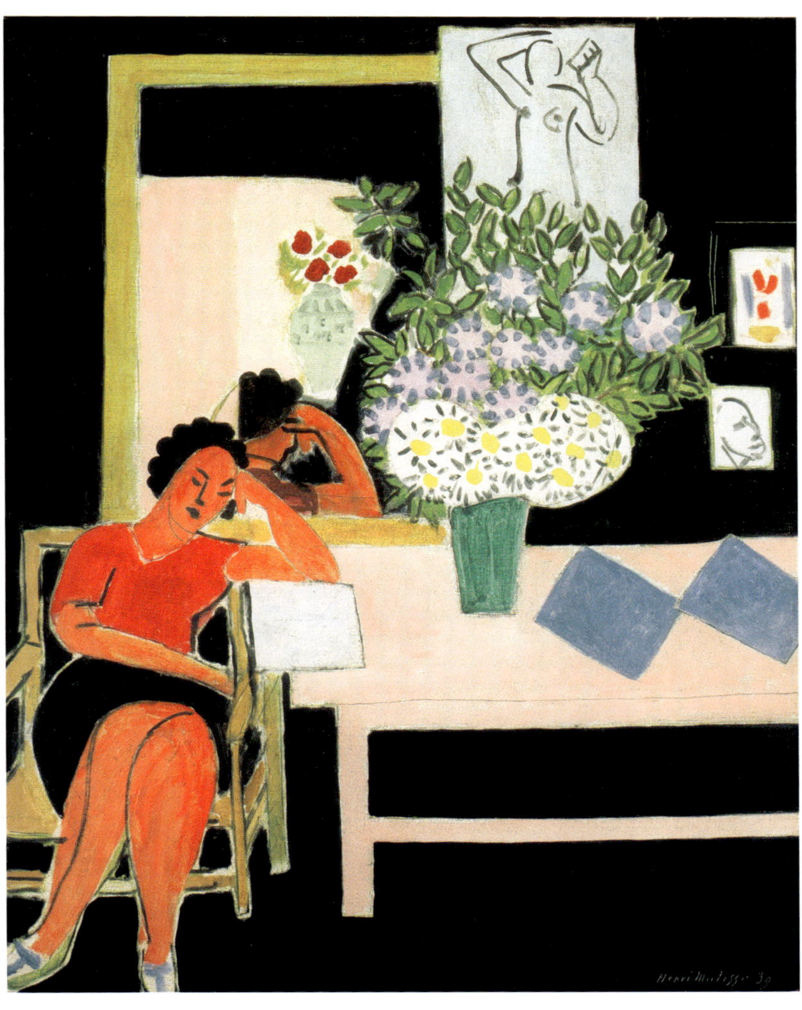

Woman Reading, on a Black Background • August 1939
Musée national d'art moderne, Paris

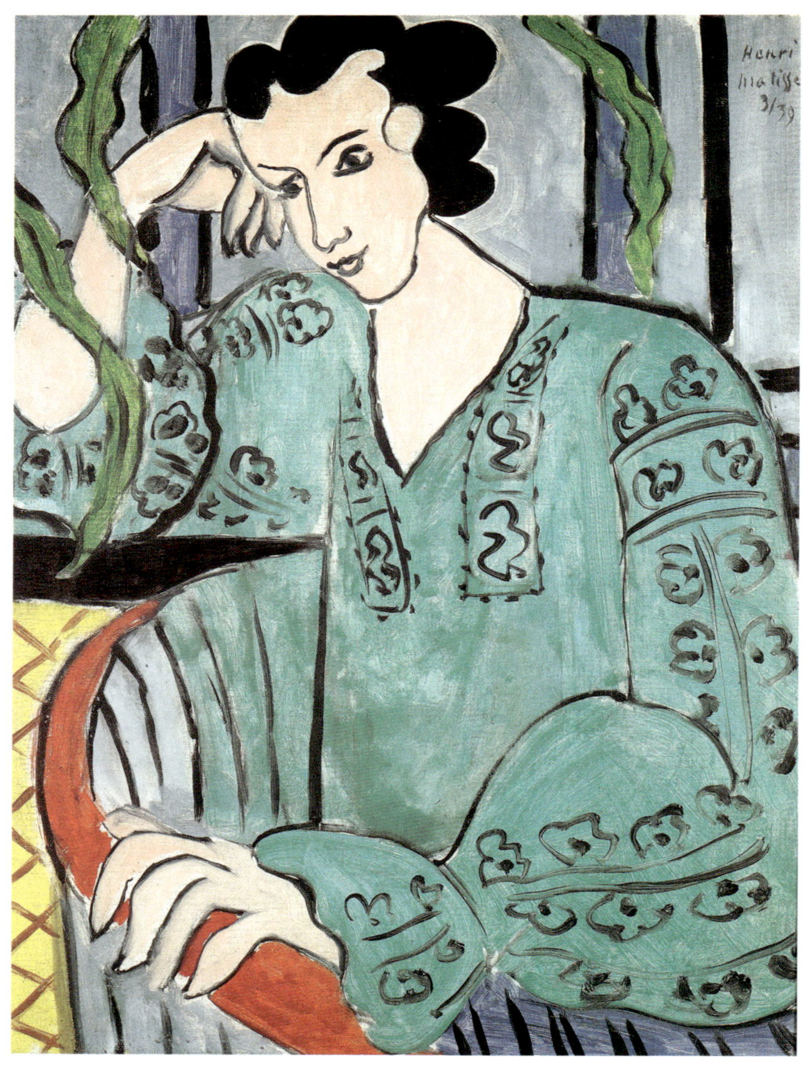

Green Rumanian Blouse · March 1939
Private collection

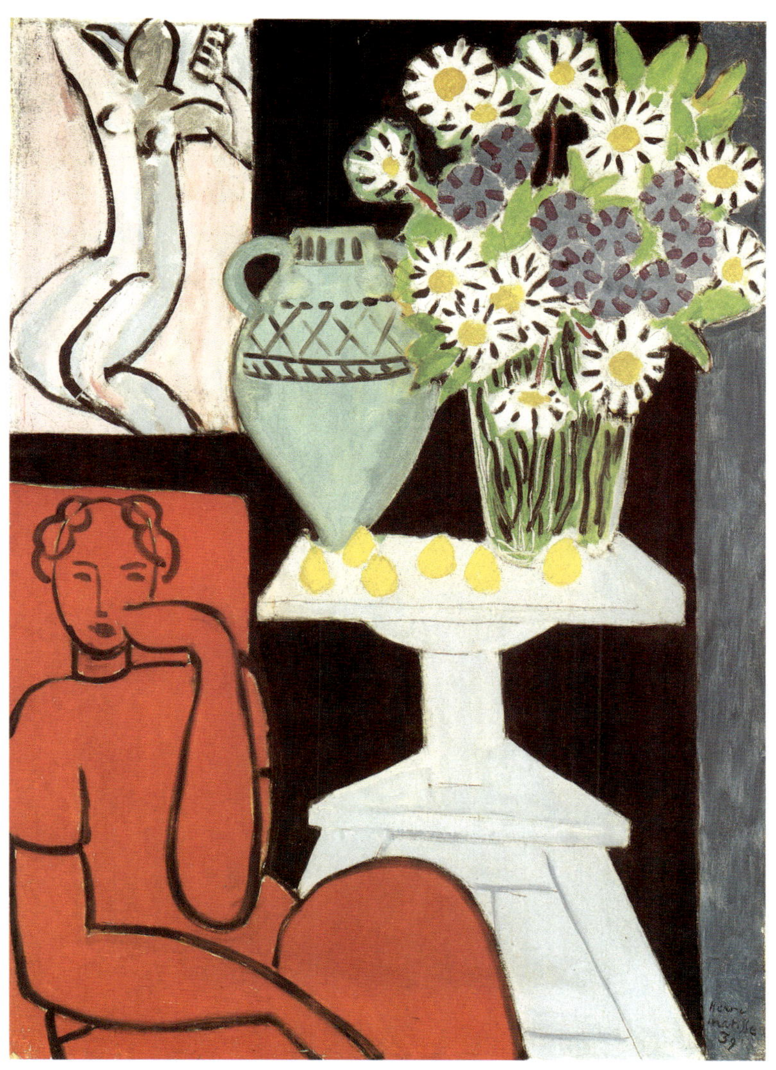

Daisies · July 1939
The Art Institute of Chicago, gift of Helen Pauling Donelly in memory of her parents, Mary Fredericka and Edward George Pauling

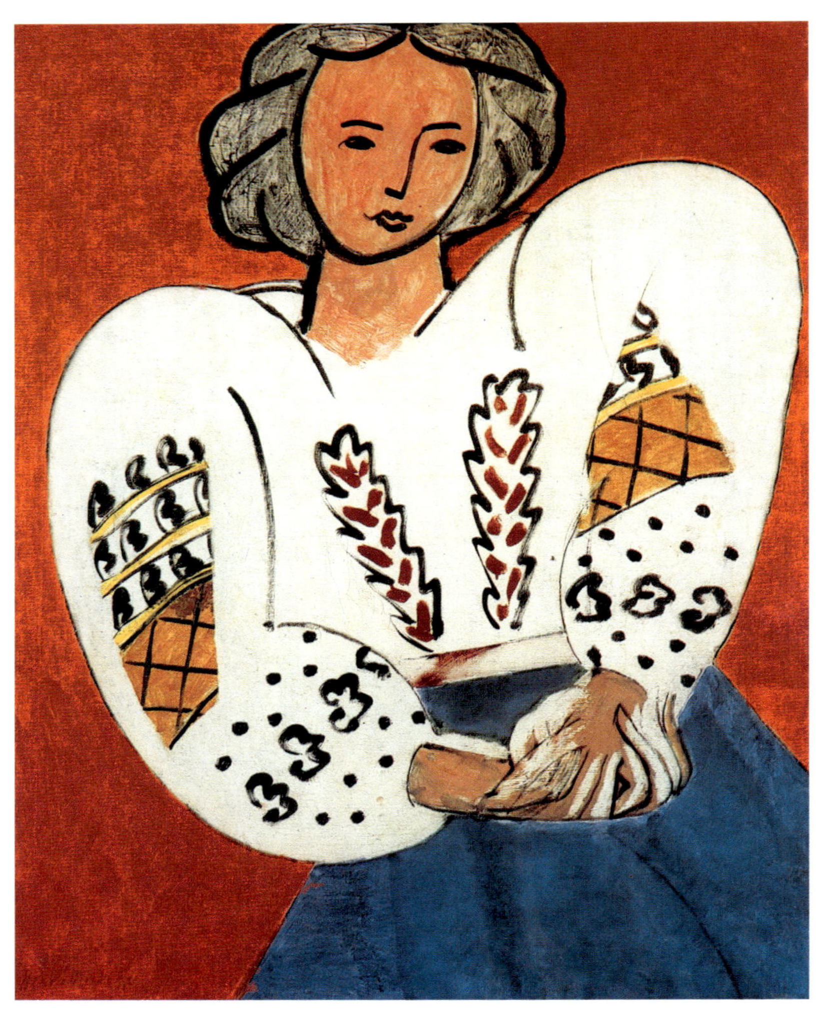

The Rumanian Blouse · December 1939–April 1940
Musée national d'art moderne, Paris

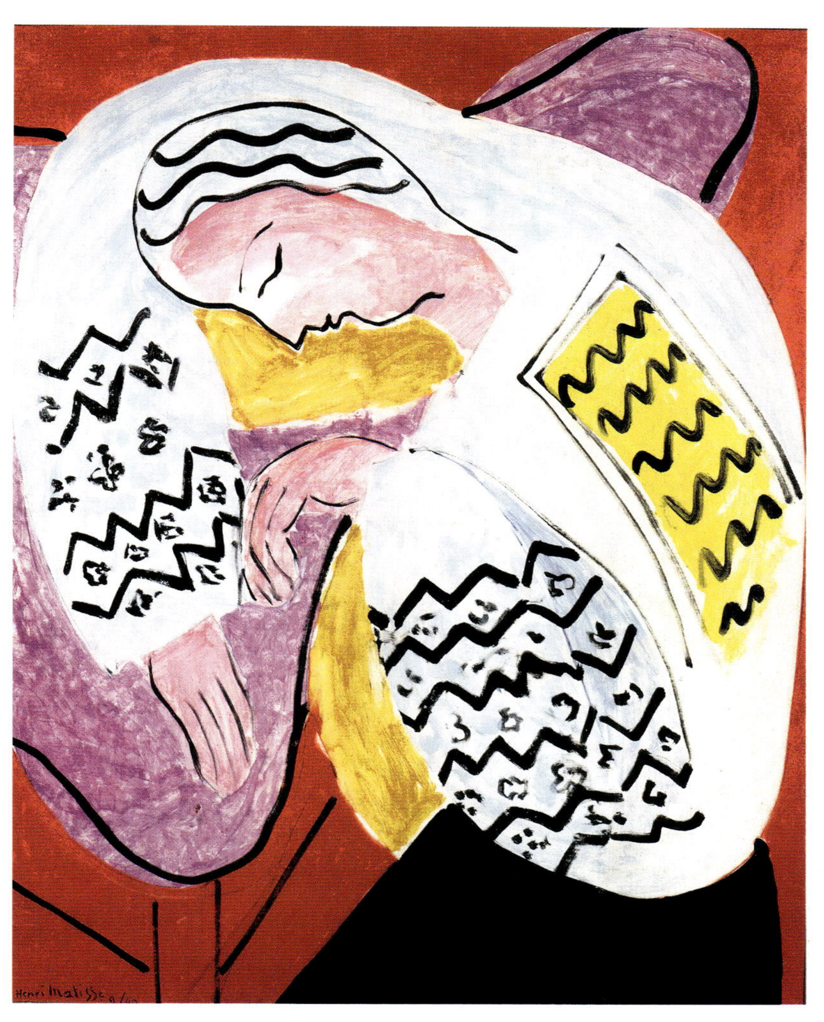

The Dream · January–October 1940

Private collection

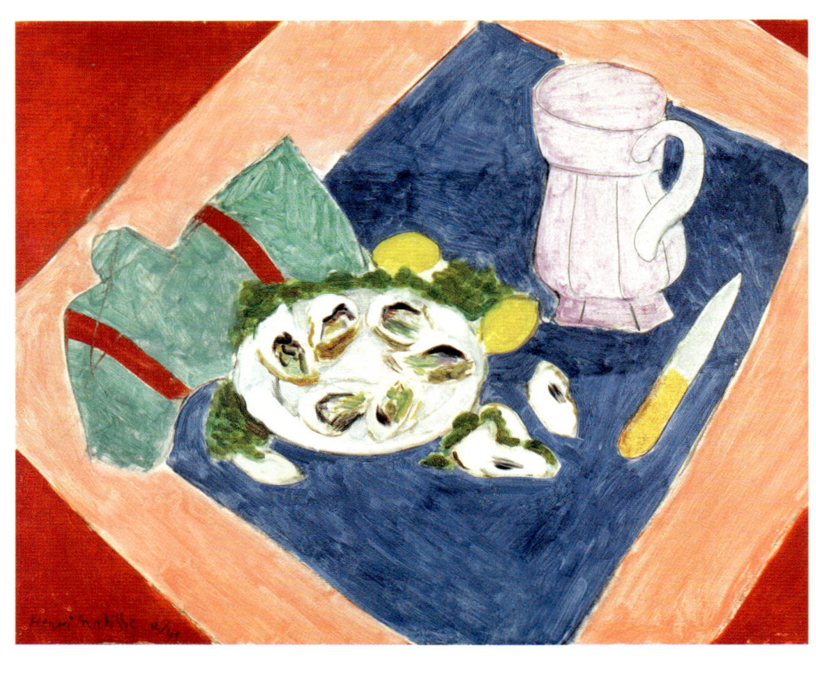

Still Life with Oysters • 1940

Kunstmuseum, Basel

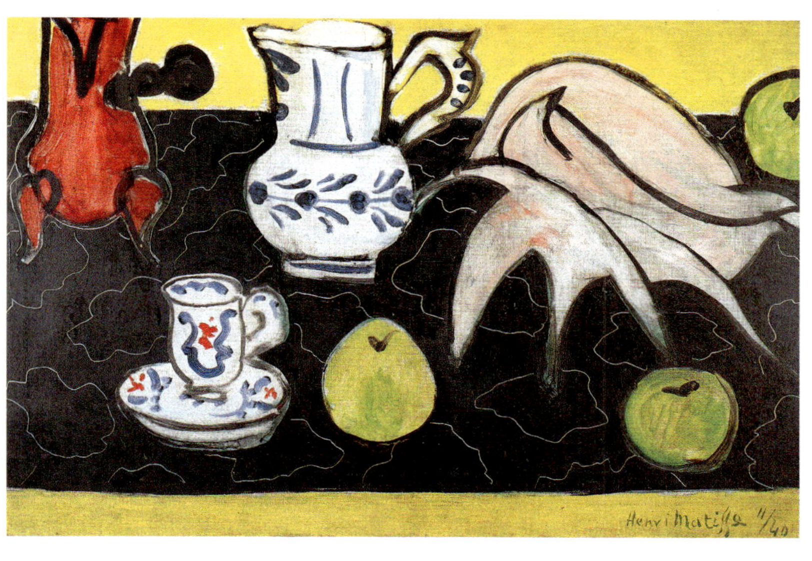

Still Life with Shell • September–December 1940
Pushkin Museum, Moscow
> **Still Life with Shell** • 1940
Private collection

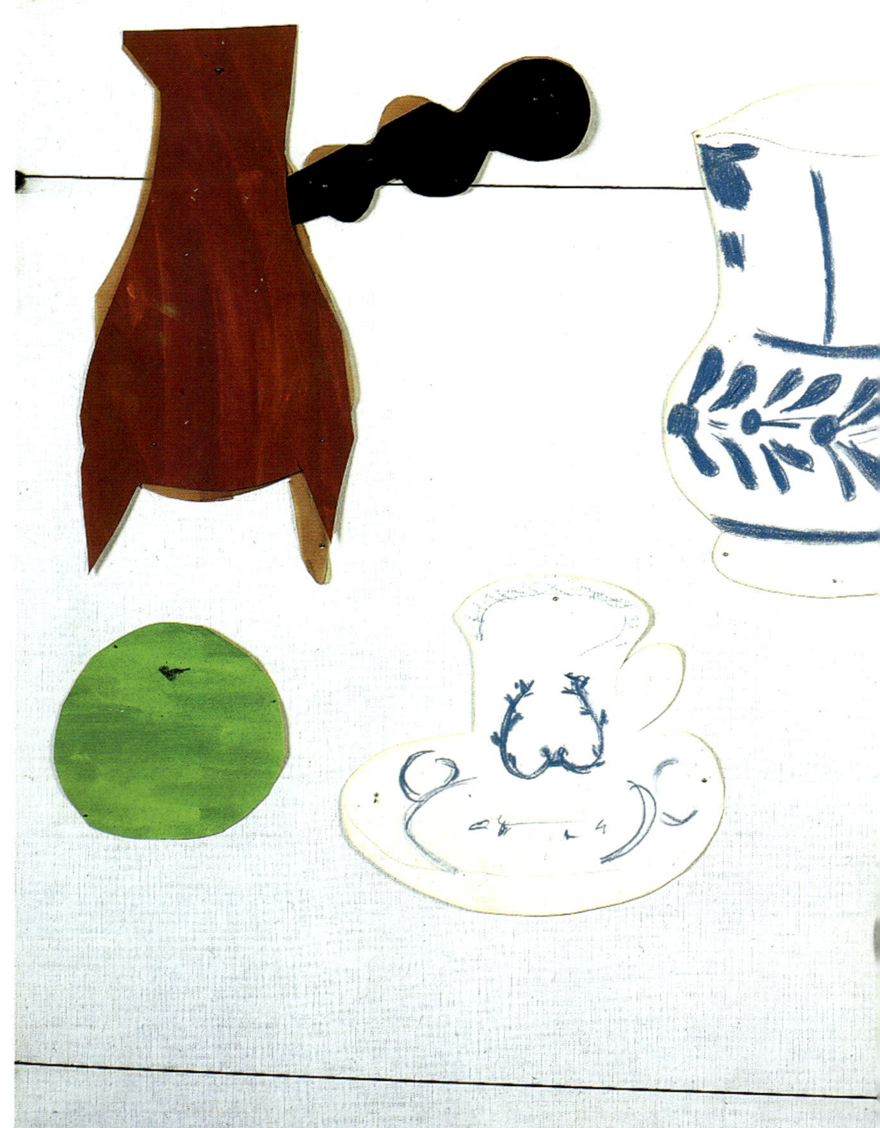

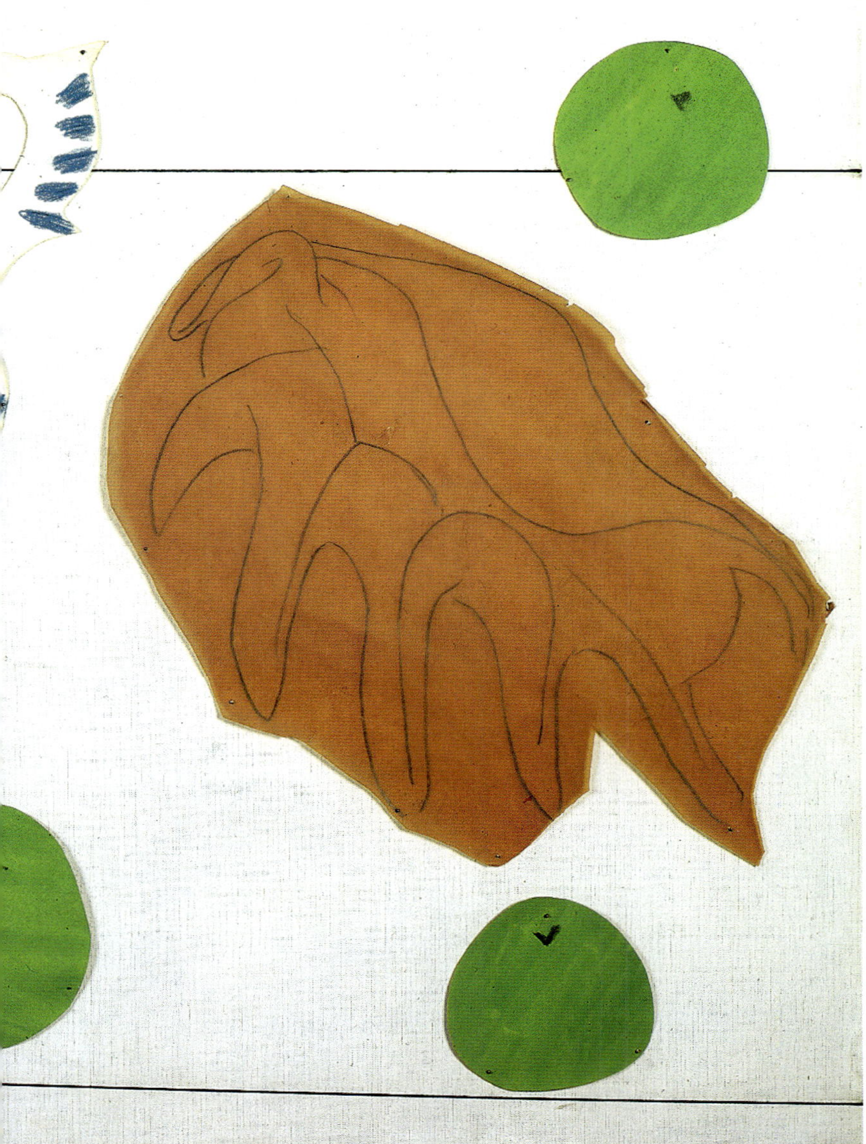

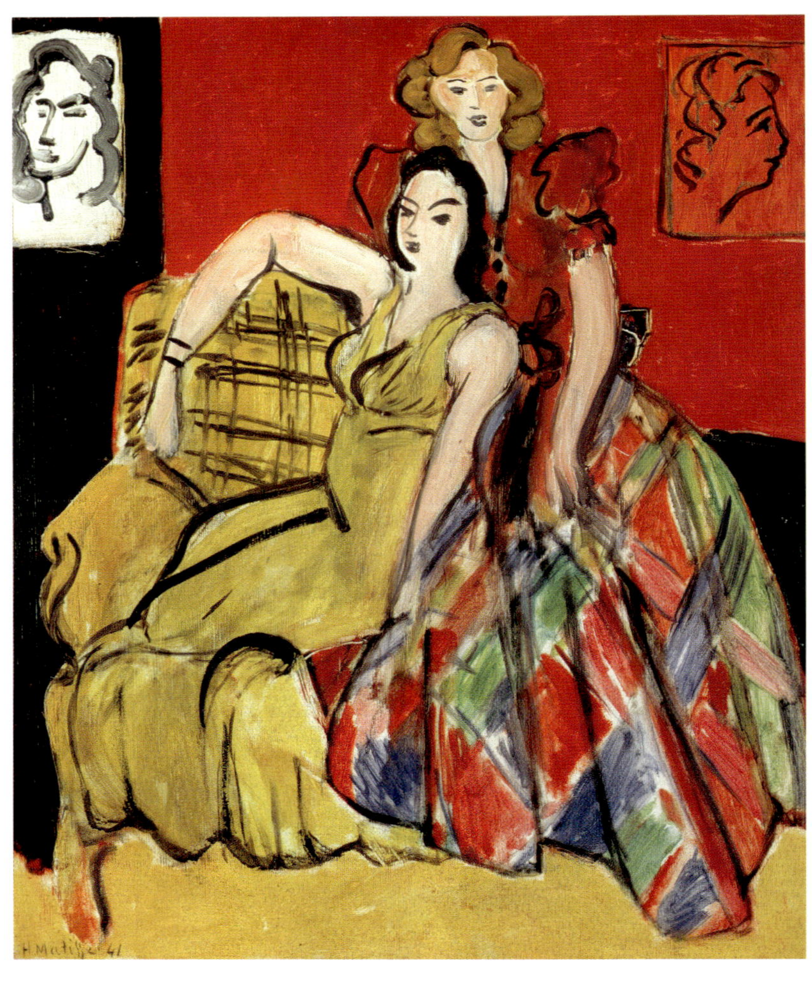

Two Girls, the Yellow and Plaid Skirt · November 1941

Musée national d'art moderne, Paris

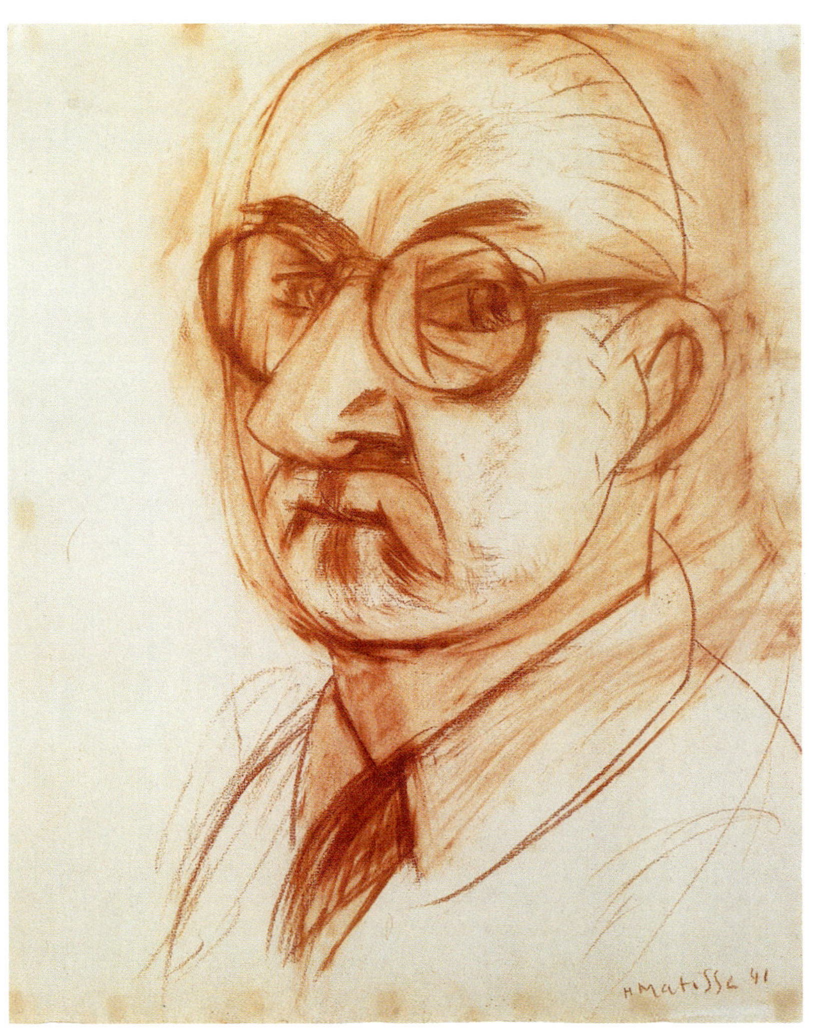

Self-Portrait • 1941
Private collection

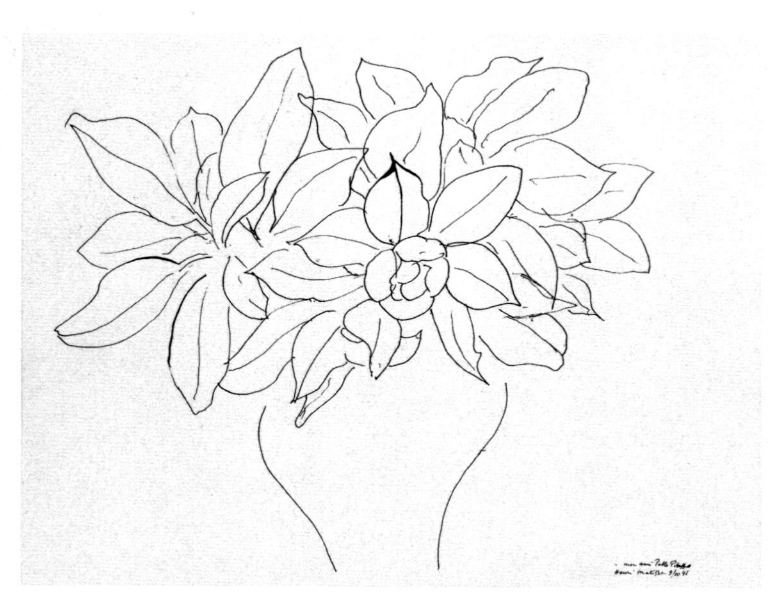

Still Life with a Magnolia · September 1941

Private collection

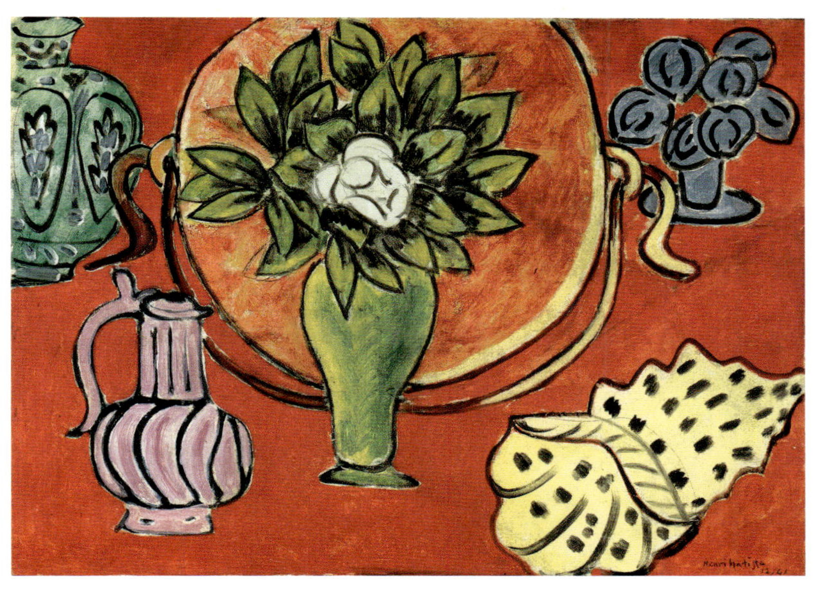

Still Life with a Magnolia · August–October 1941
Musée national d'art moderne, Paris

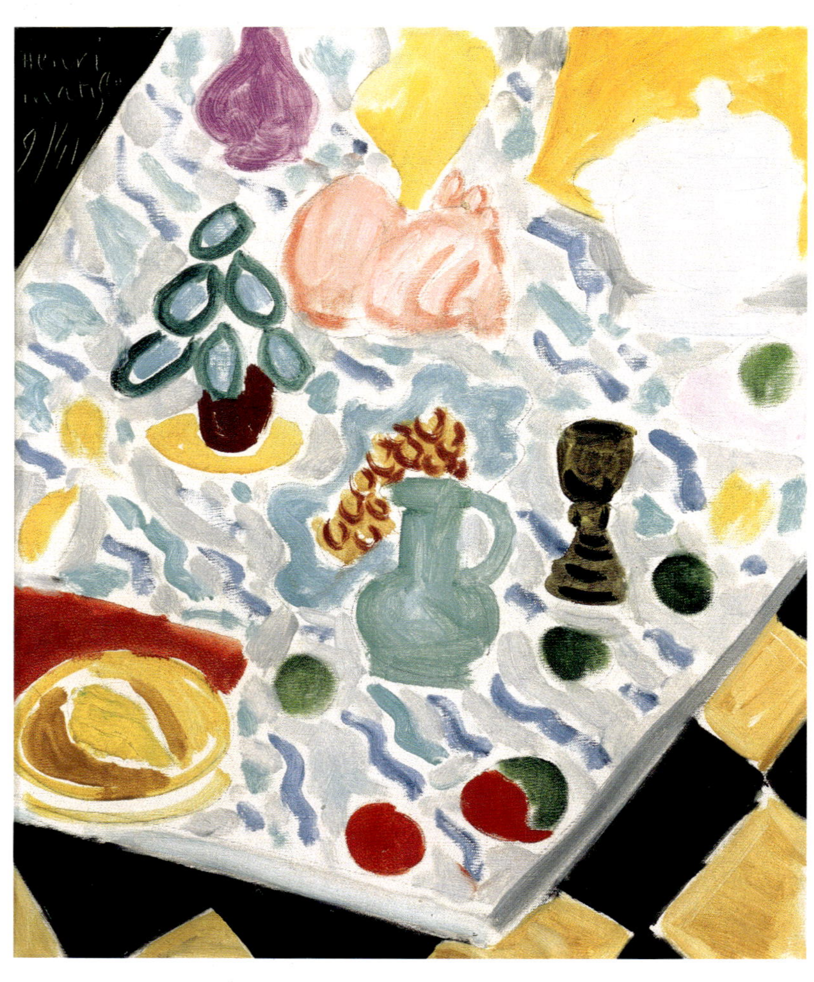

Still Life with Green Marble Table • 1941

Musée national d'art moderne, Paris

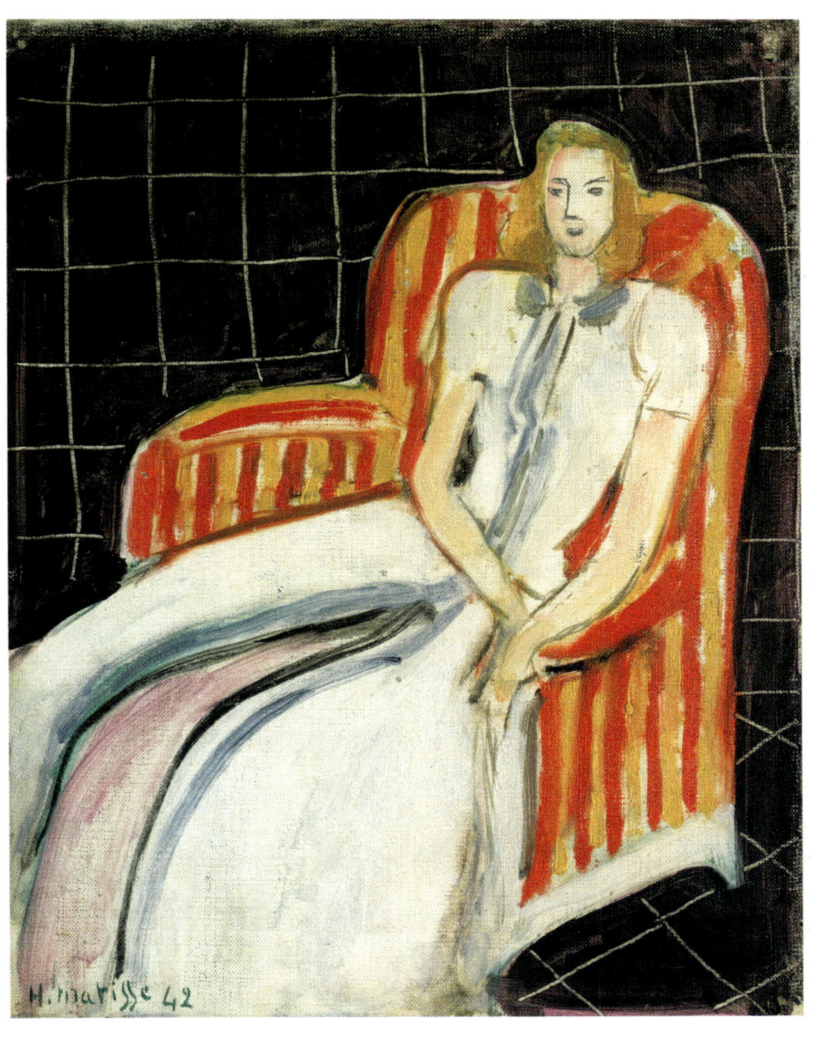

Simone in a Striped Armchair • 1942
Private collection

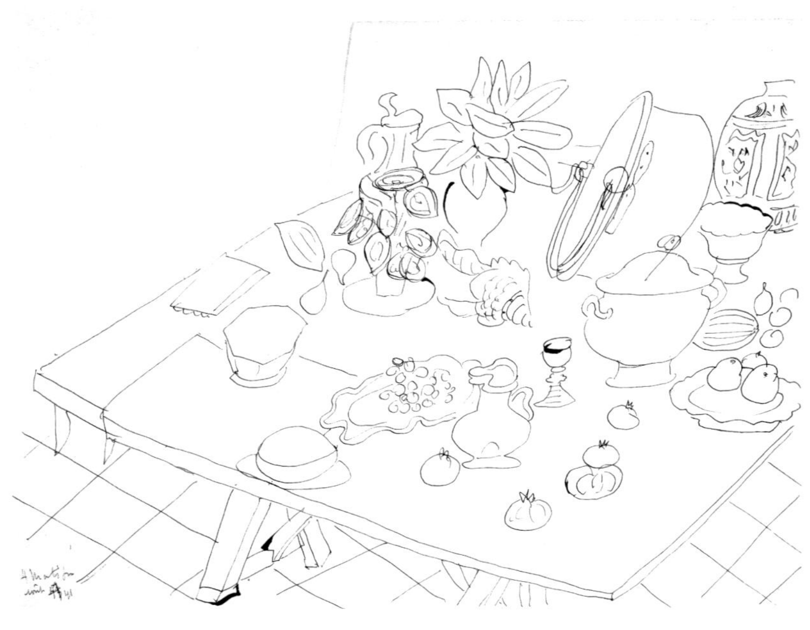

Still Life · 1941
Musée national d'art moderne, Paris

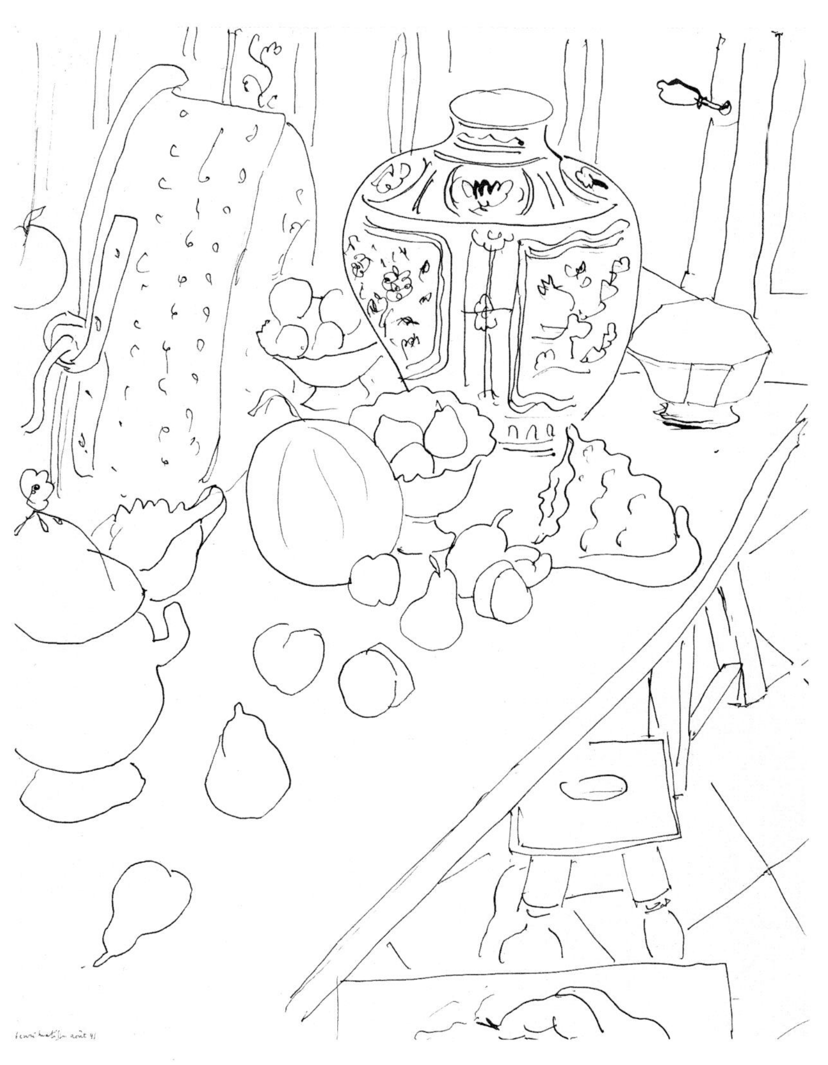

Still Life • August 1941
Musée national d'art moderne, Paris

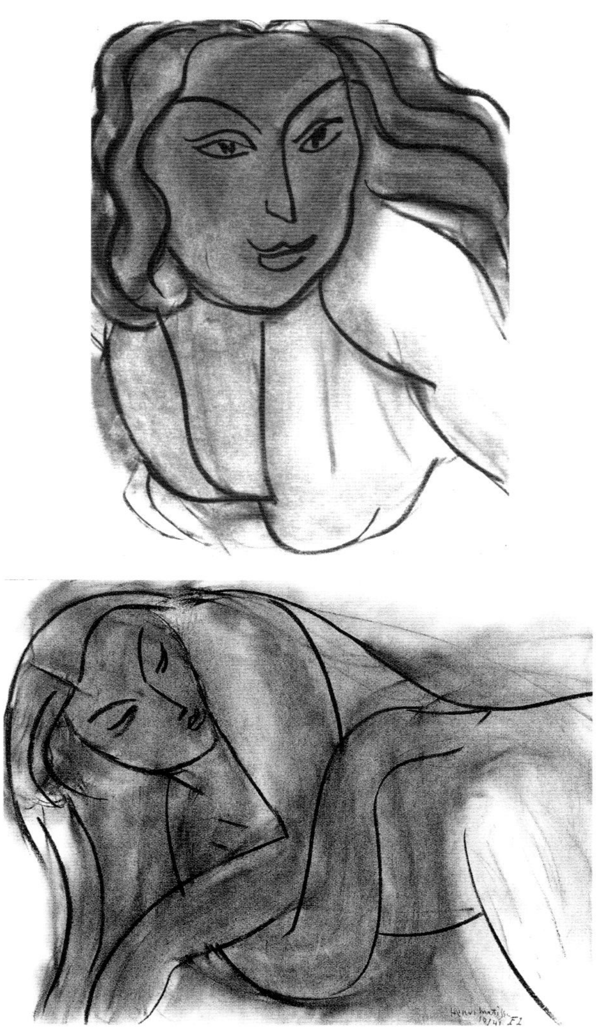

Themes and Variations. Series O, Theme Drawing · 1942
Musée Matisse, Nice
Themes and Variations. Series F, Theme · 1941
Musée de Grenoble

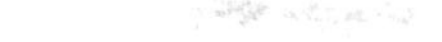

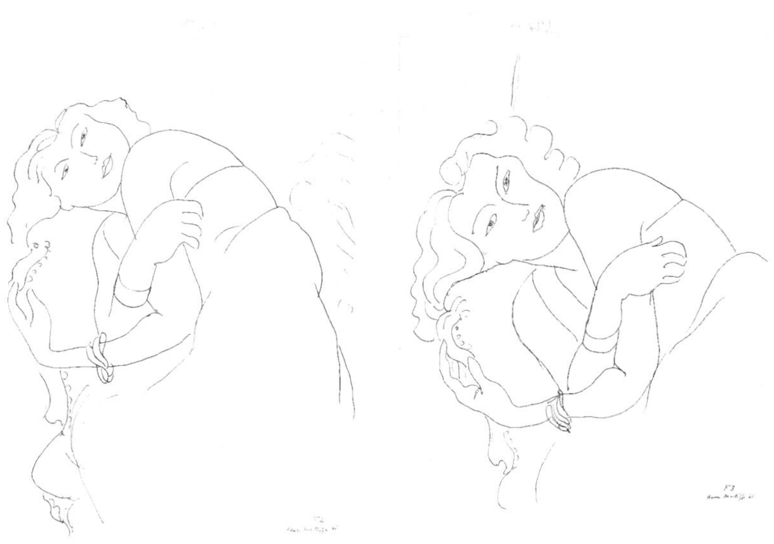

Themes and Variations, F2 • 1941
Musée de Grenoble
Themes and Variations, F3 • 1941
Musée de Grenoble

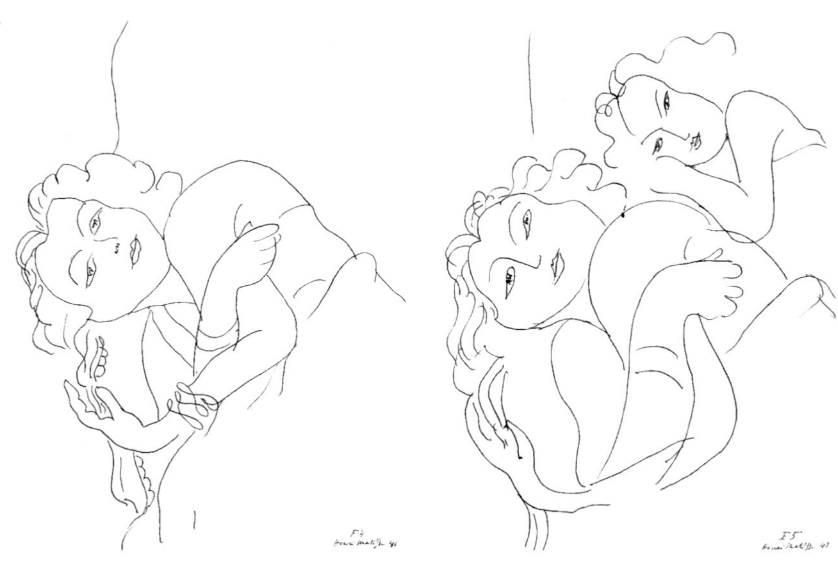

Themes and Variations, F4 · 1941
Musée de Grenoble
Themes and Variations, F5 · 1941
Musée de Grenoble

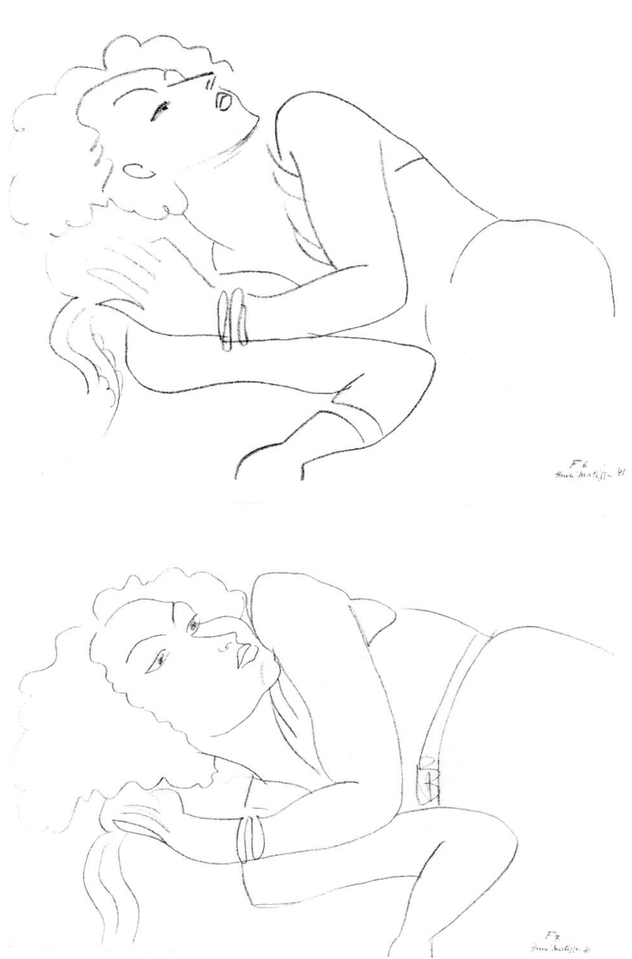

Themes and Variations, F6 · 1941
Musée de Grenoble
Themes and Variations, F7 · 1941
Musée de Grenoble

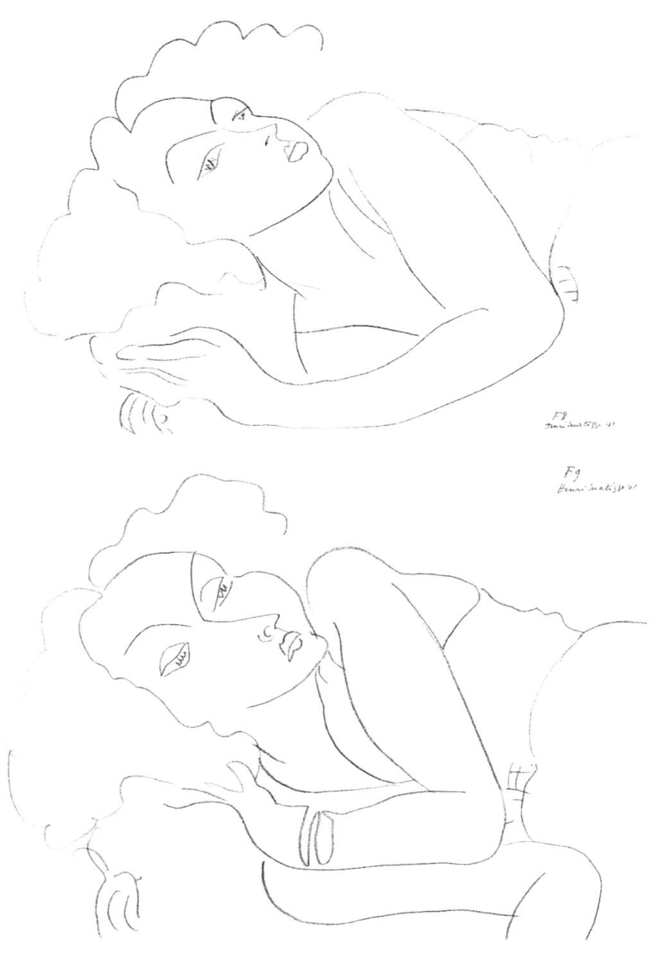

Themes and Variations, F8 · 1941
Musée de Grenoble
Themes and Variations, F9 · 1941
Musée de Grenoble

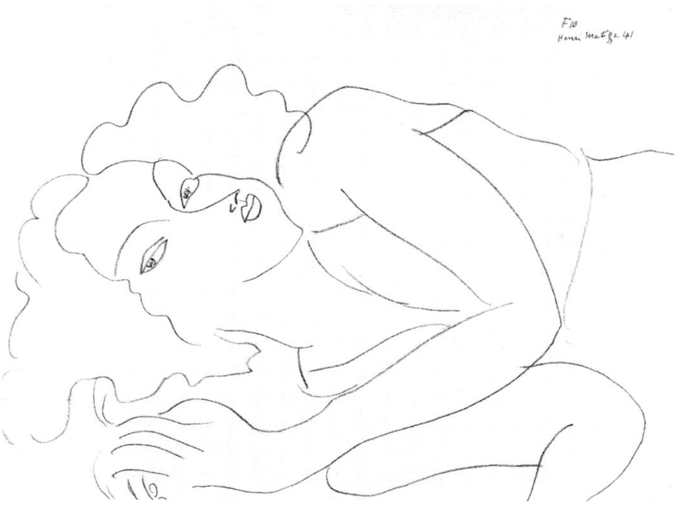

Themes and Variations, F10 · 1941

Musée de Grenoble

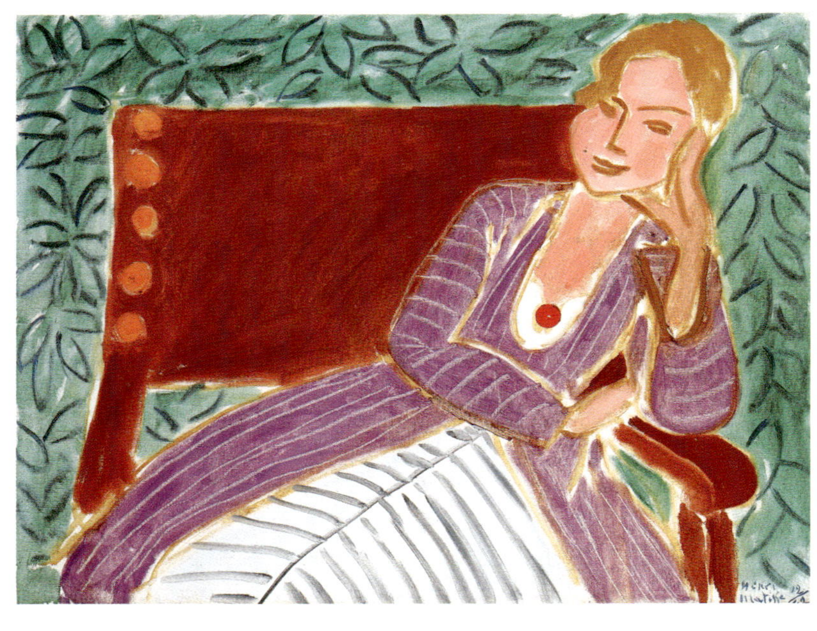

Seated Young Woman in a Persian Dress • December 1942

Musée Picasso, Paris

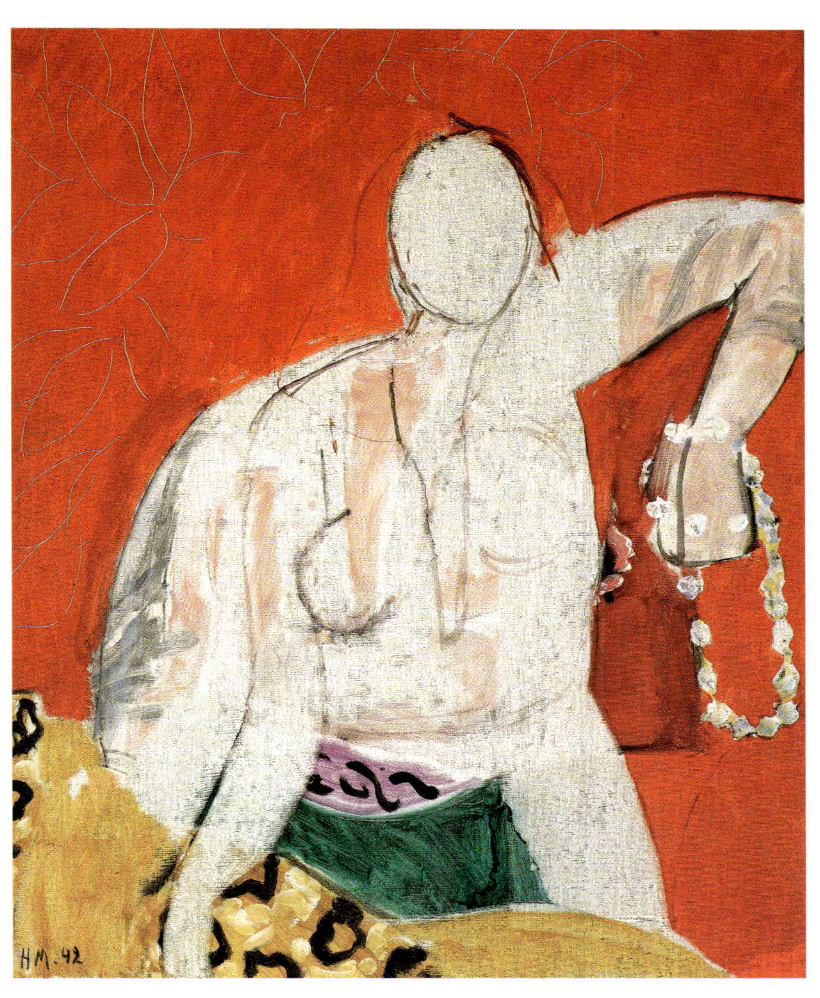

Woman with Pearl Necklace • 1942

Private collection

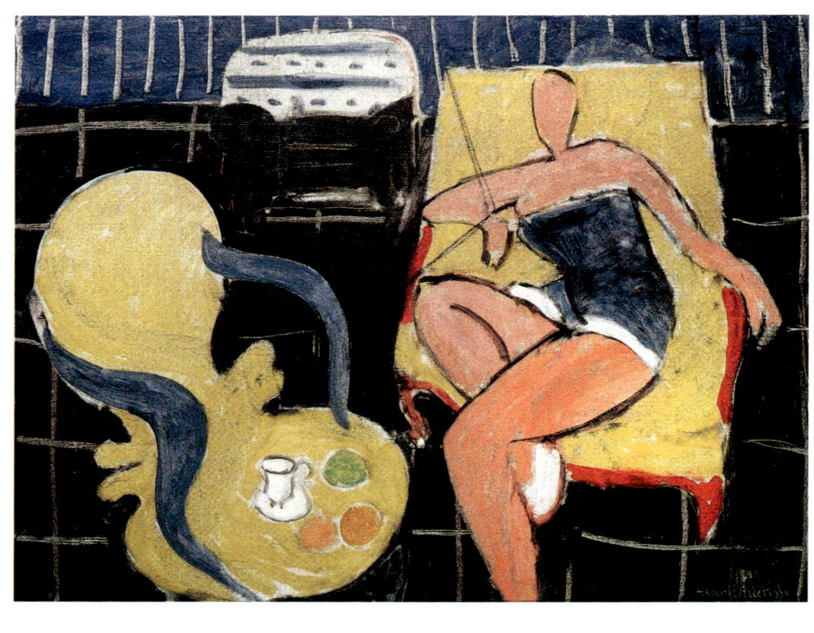

Dancer and Rocaille Armchair on a Black Background · September 1942

Private collection

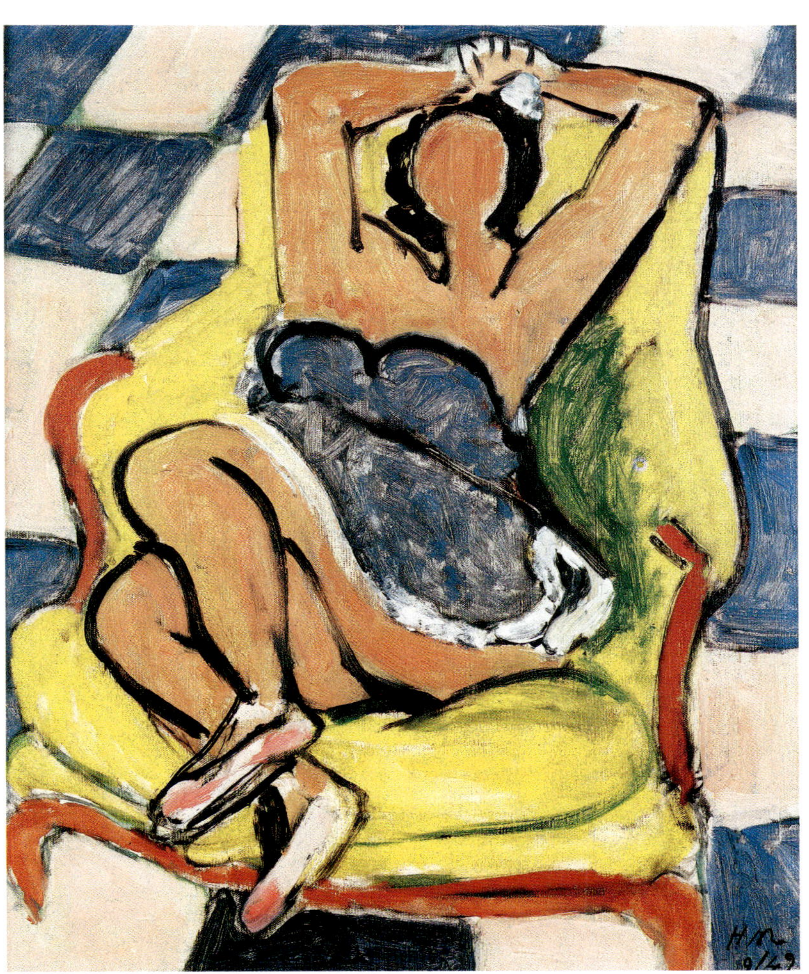

Dancer in Repose • August 1942
Private collection

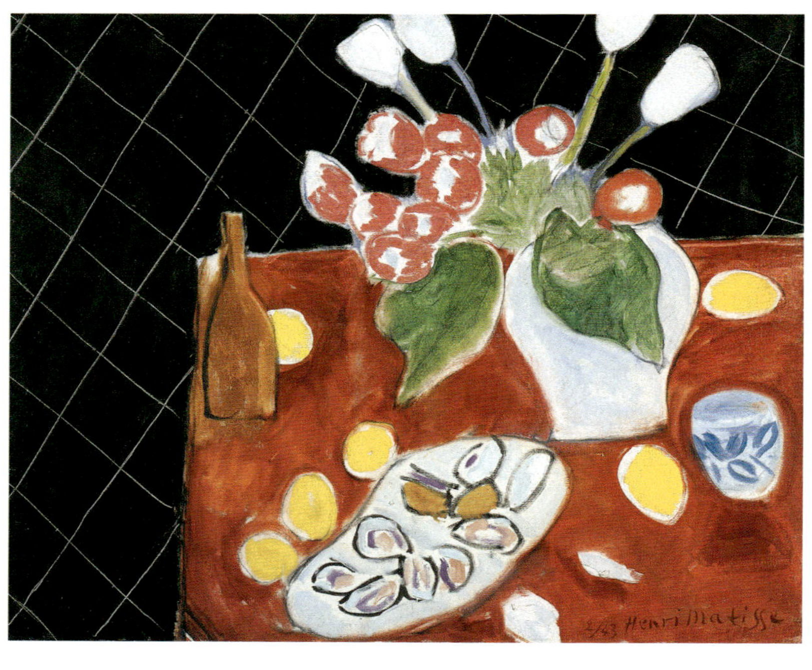

Tulips and Oysters on a Black Background • February 1943

Musée Picasso, Paris

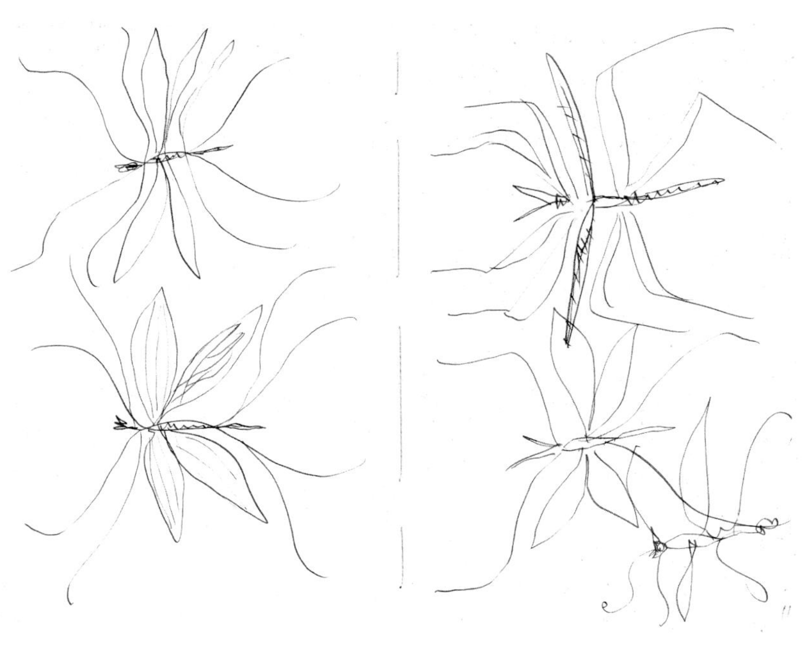

Mosquitos (Study for a vignette in "Florilège des Amours de Ronsard," 1948) · c. 1943

Private collection

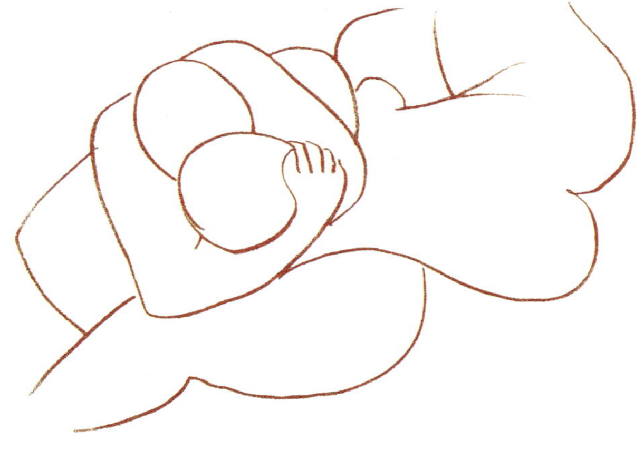

Embrace (Illustration for "Florilège des Amours de Ronsard," 1948) • c. 1943

Private collection

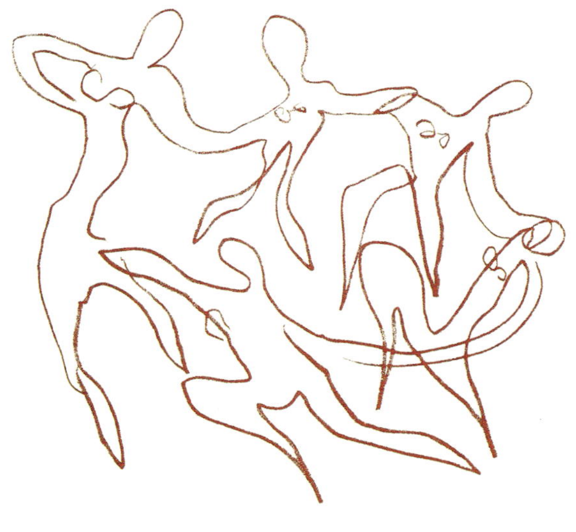

D'embas la troupe (Illustration for "Florilège des Amours de Ronsard," 1948) · c. 1943

Private collection

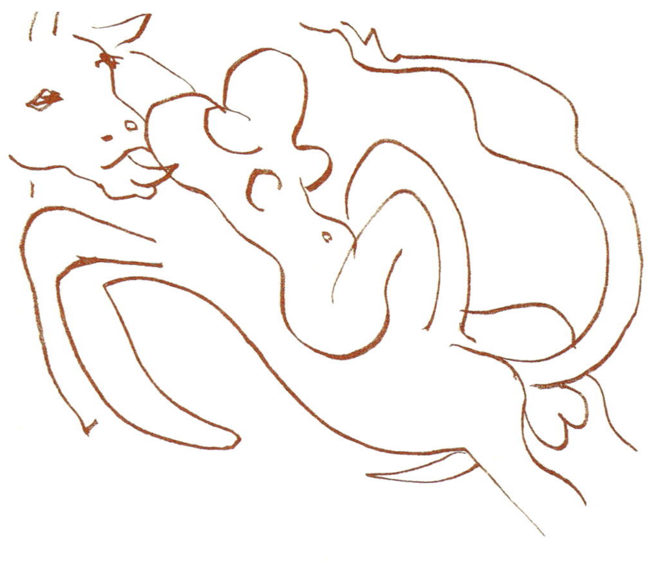

Jupiter and Europa (Illustration for "Florilège des Amours de Ronsard," 1948) • c. 1943

Private collection

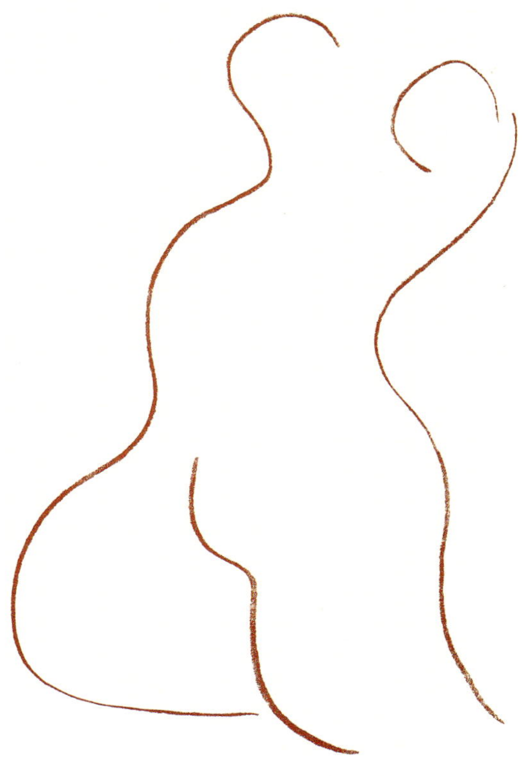

D'un orenger (Illustration for "Florilège des Amours de Ronsard," 1948) · c. 1943
Private collection

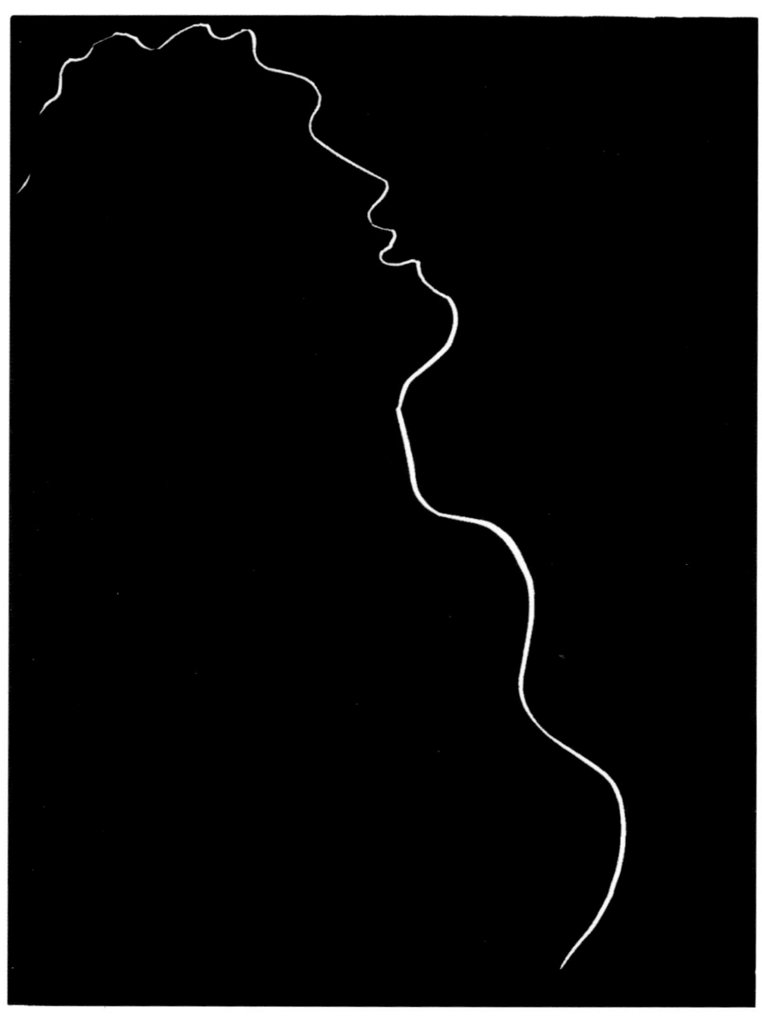

L'Angoisse qui s'amasse en frappant sous ta gorge
(Illustration for Henri de Montherlant's "Pasiphaé," 1944) · 1943
Private collection

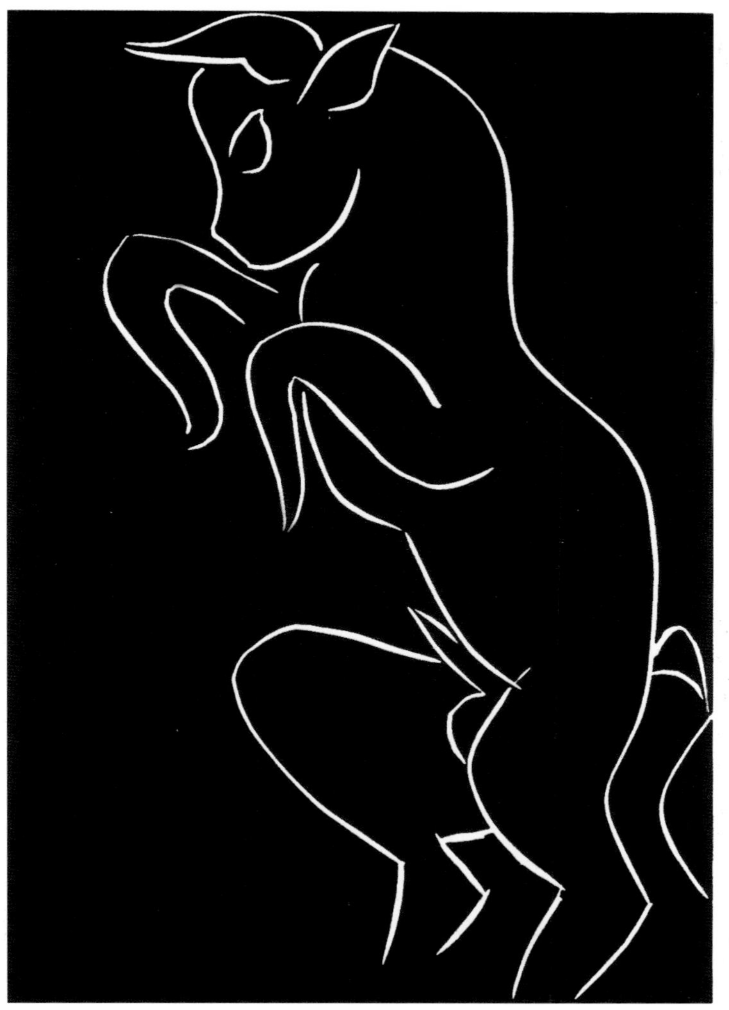

Un Meuglement différent des autres
(Illustration for Henri de Montherlant's "Pasiphaé," 1944) · 1943
Private collection
> **Polynesia, the Sky** · 1946
Musée national d'art moderne, Paris

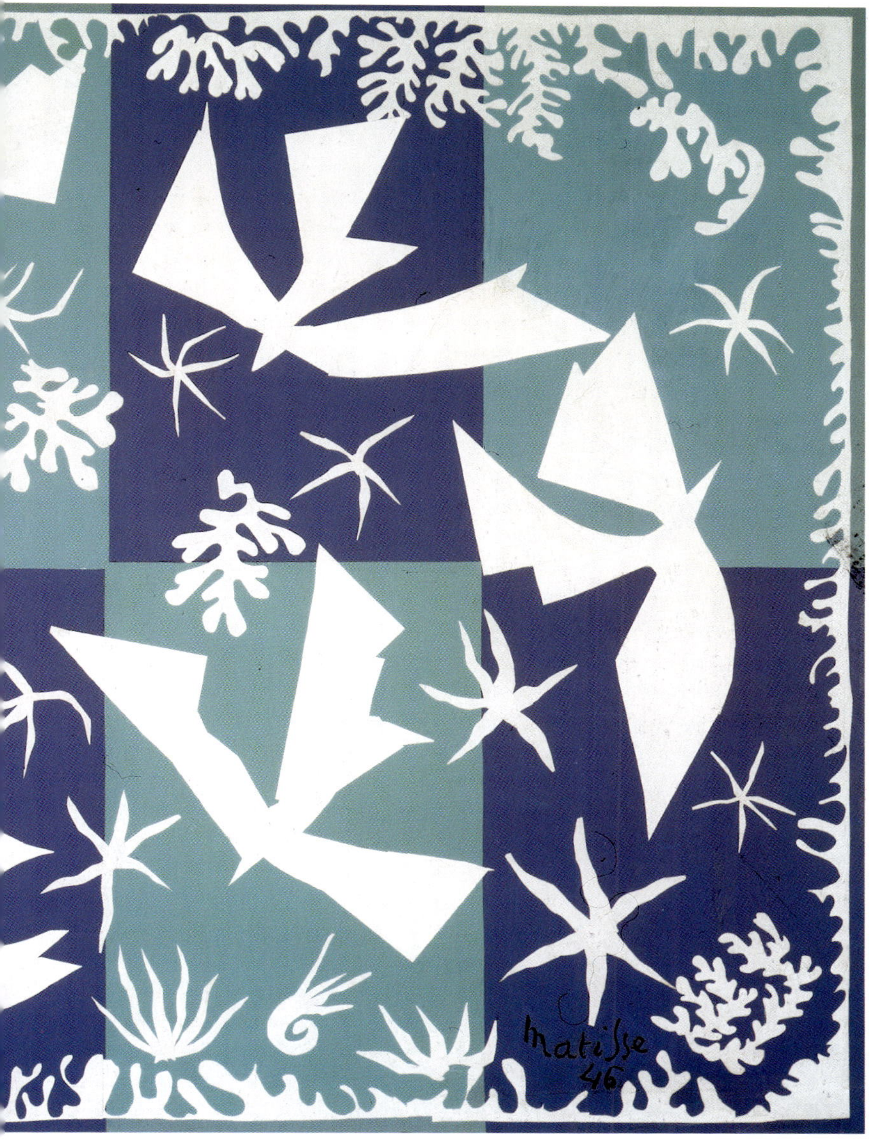
Matisse
46

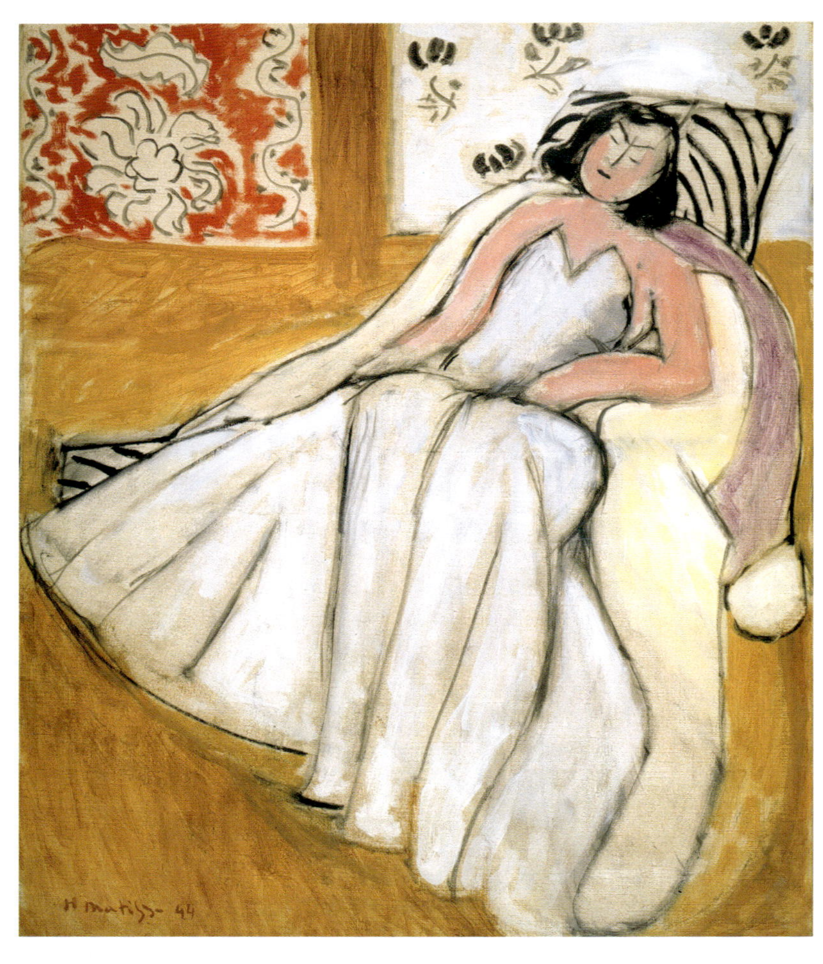

Young Woman with White Fur Coat · 1944

Musée national d'art moderne, Paris

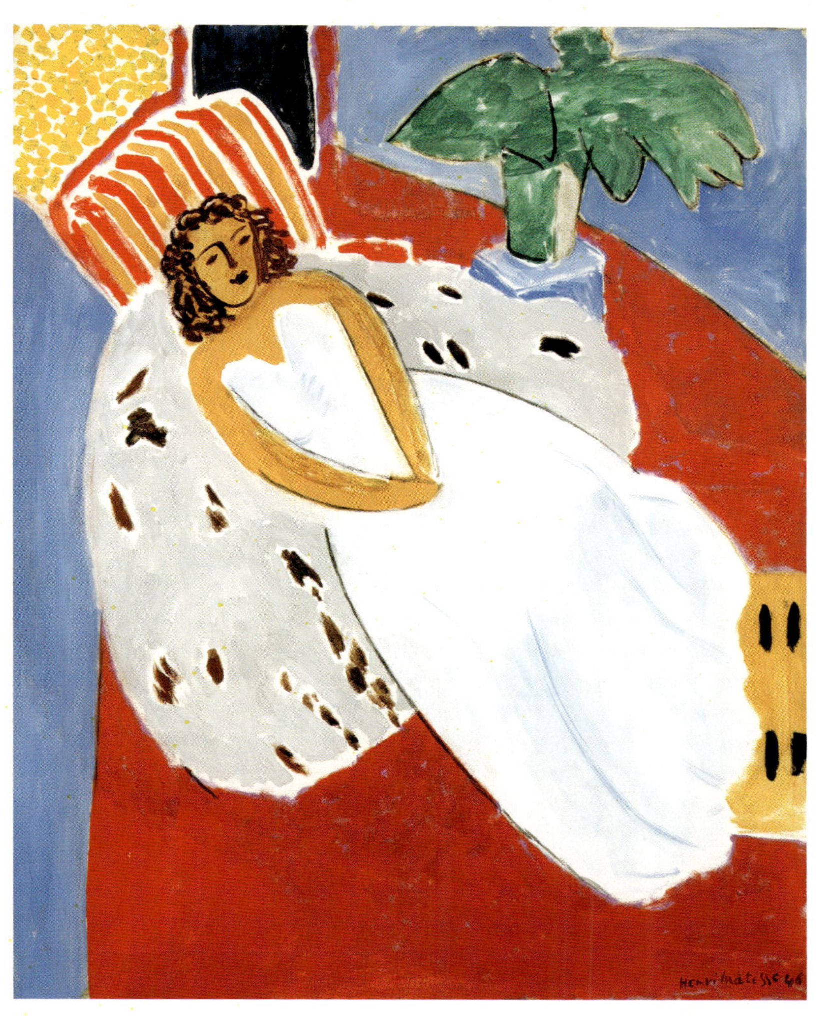

Young Woman in White, Red Background • 1946
Musée des Beaux-Arts, Lyons (housed at the Musée national d'art moderne, Paris)

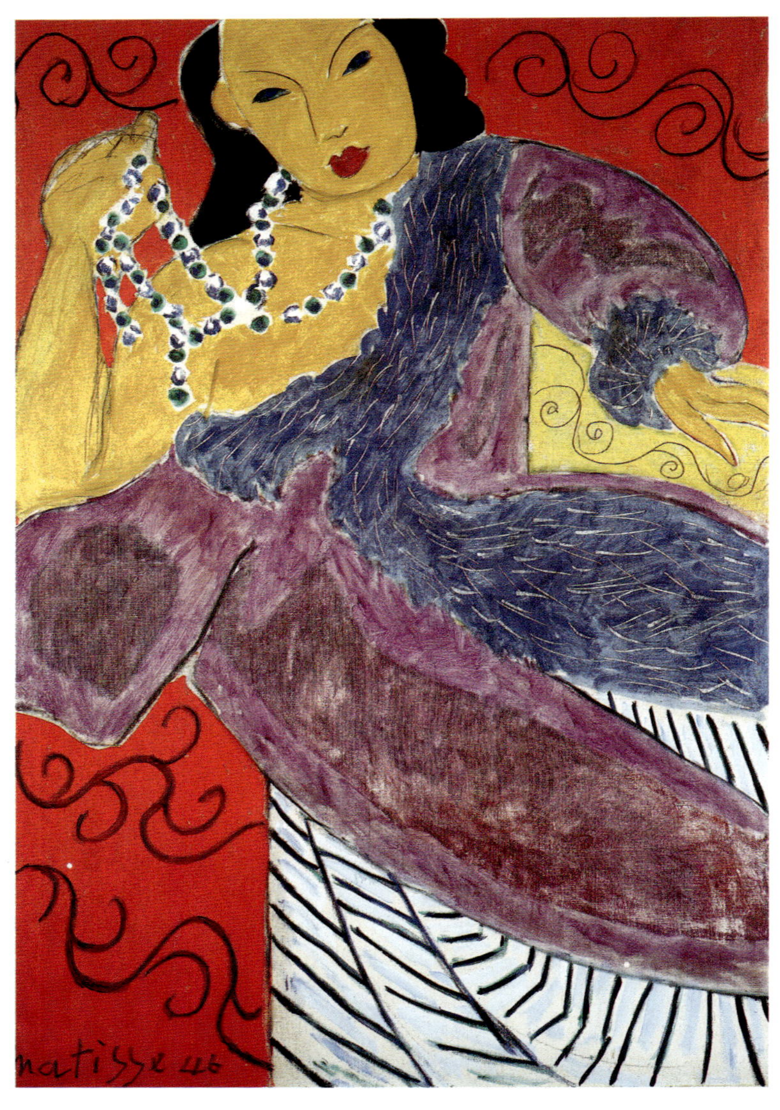

Asia • 1946

Kimbell Art Museum, Fort Worth, Texas

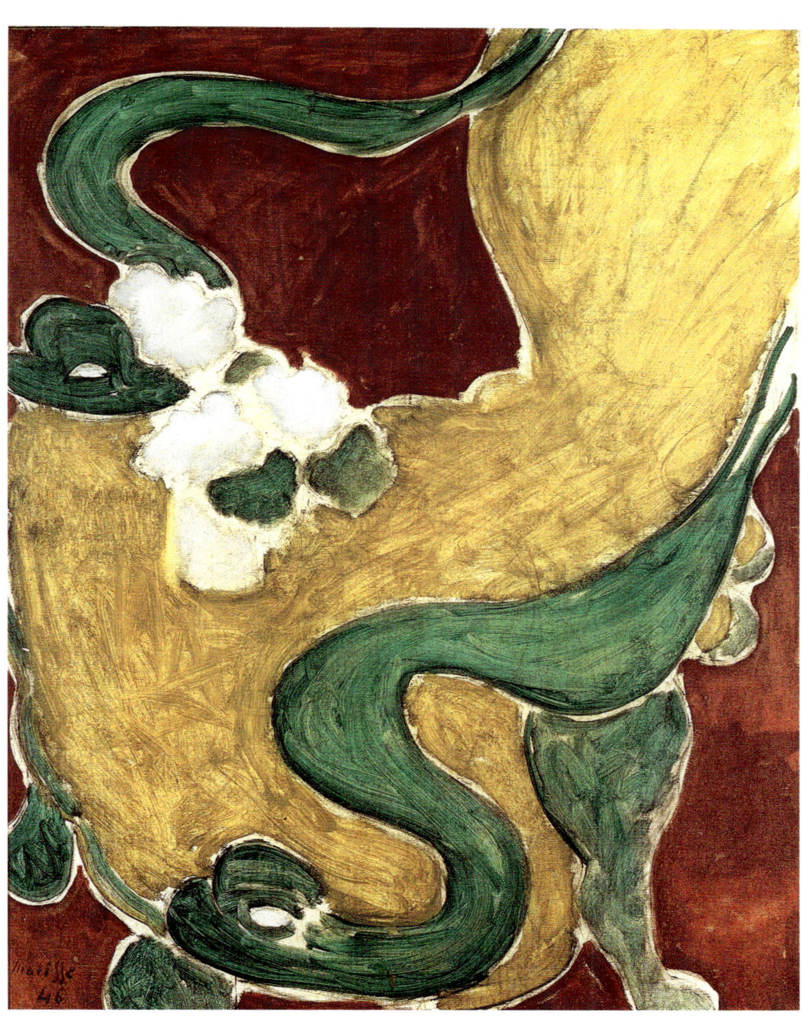

The Rocaille Armchair • 1946

Musée Matisse, Nice

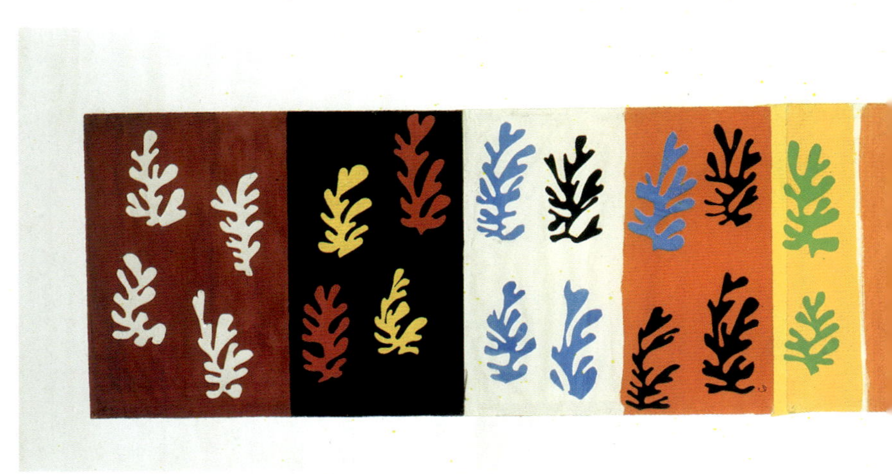

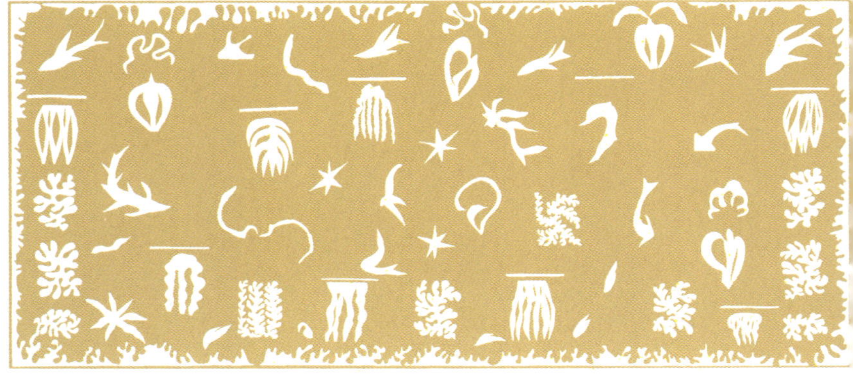

Oceania, the Sea • 1946 • National Gallery of Art, Washington, gift of Mr. and Mrs. Burton Tremai

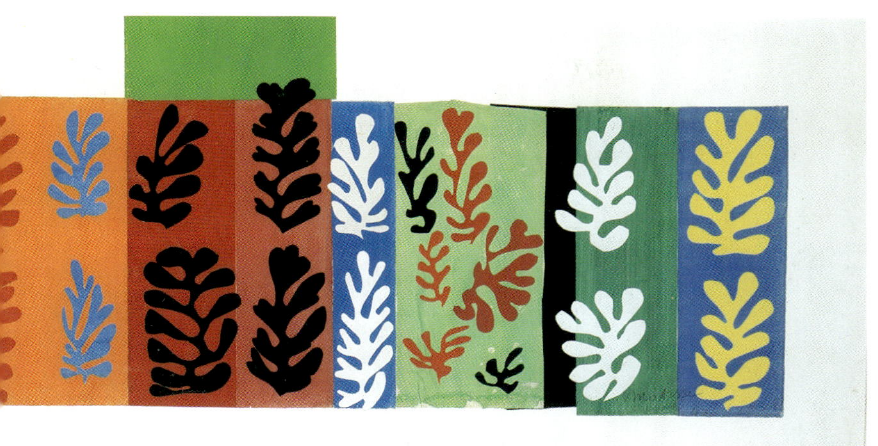

Composition • 1947 • Kunstmuseum, Basel

Oceania, the Sky • 1946 • Musée Matisse, Le Cateau-Cambrésis

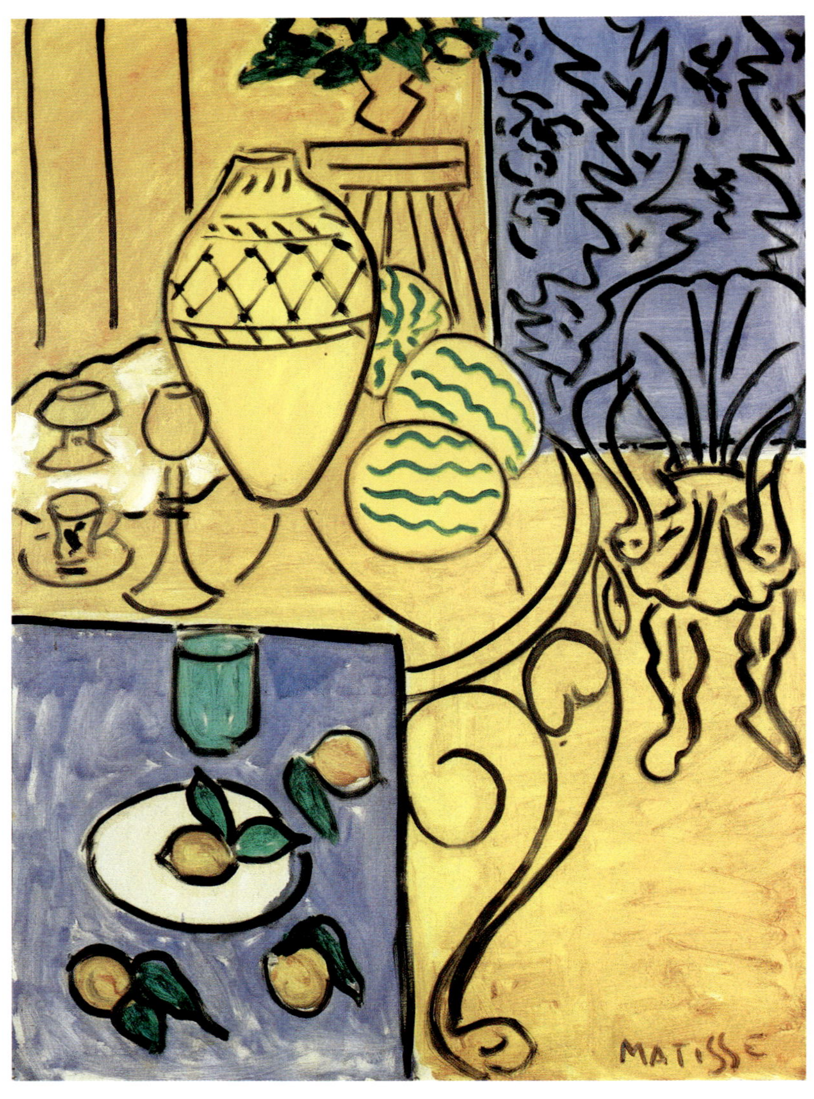

Interior in Yellow and Blue · 1946
Musée national d'art moderne, Paris

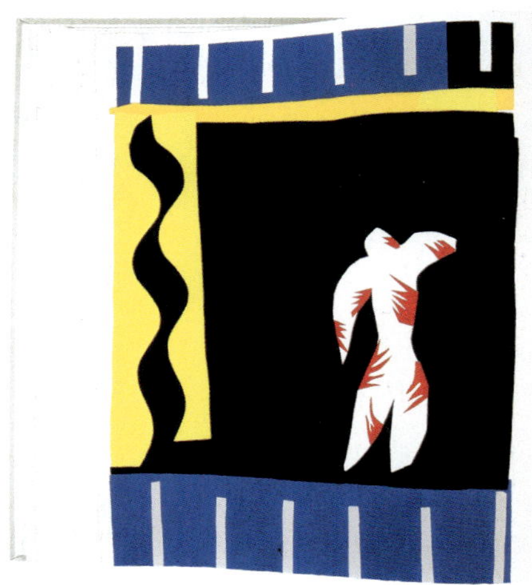

The Clown (plate I and title page, from "Jazz," published in 1947 by E. Tériade [Paris] in an edition of 280 copies) • 1947
Private collection

> **The Circus (plate II from "Jazz")** • 1947
Musée national d'art moderne, Paris

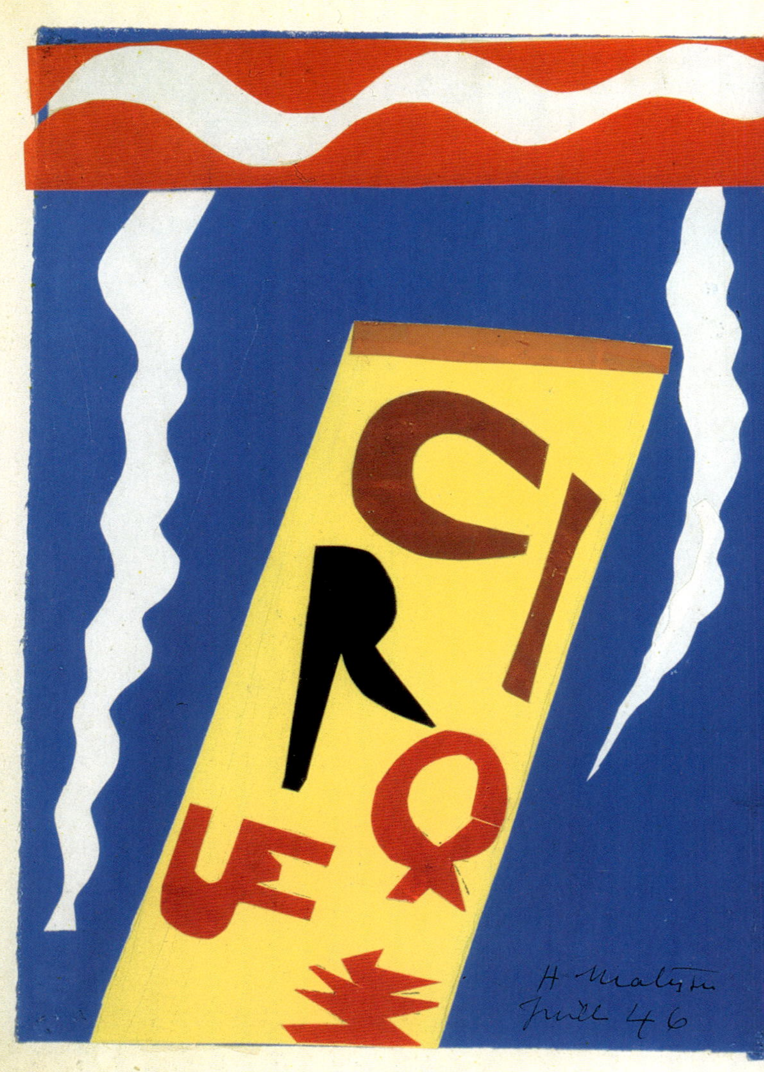
CIRQUE

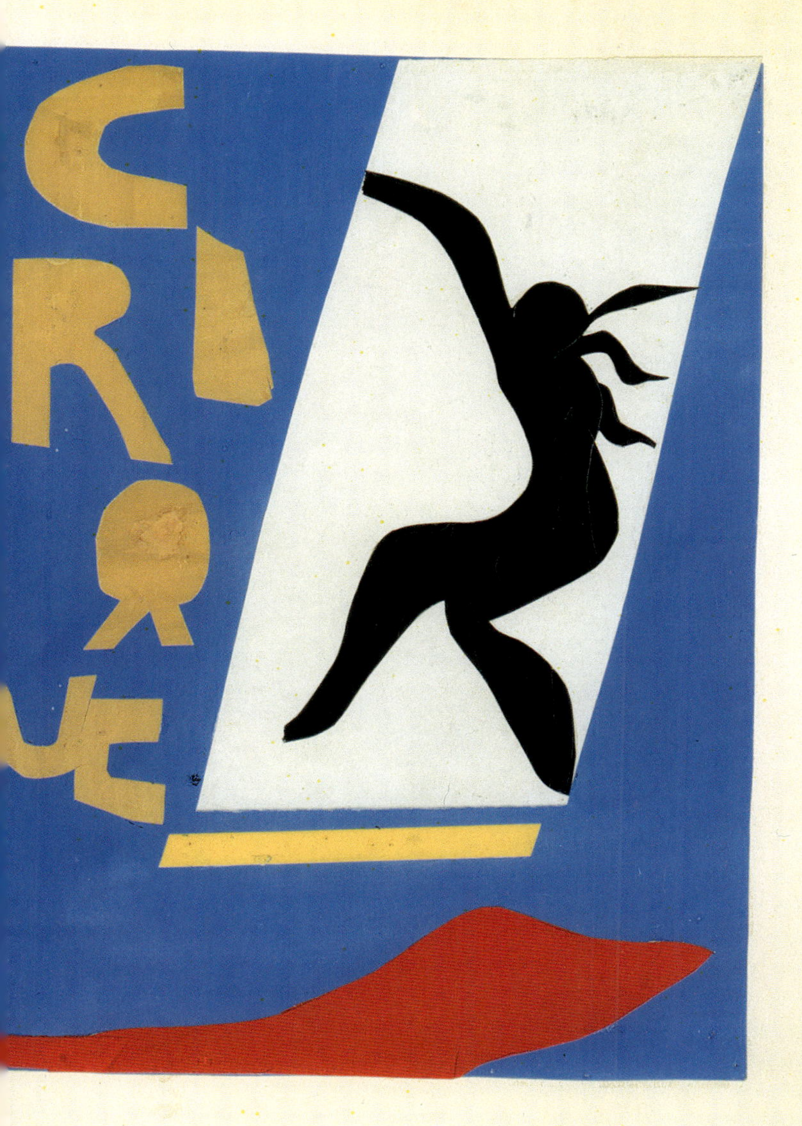

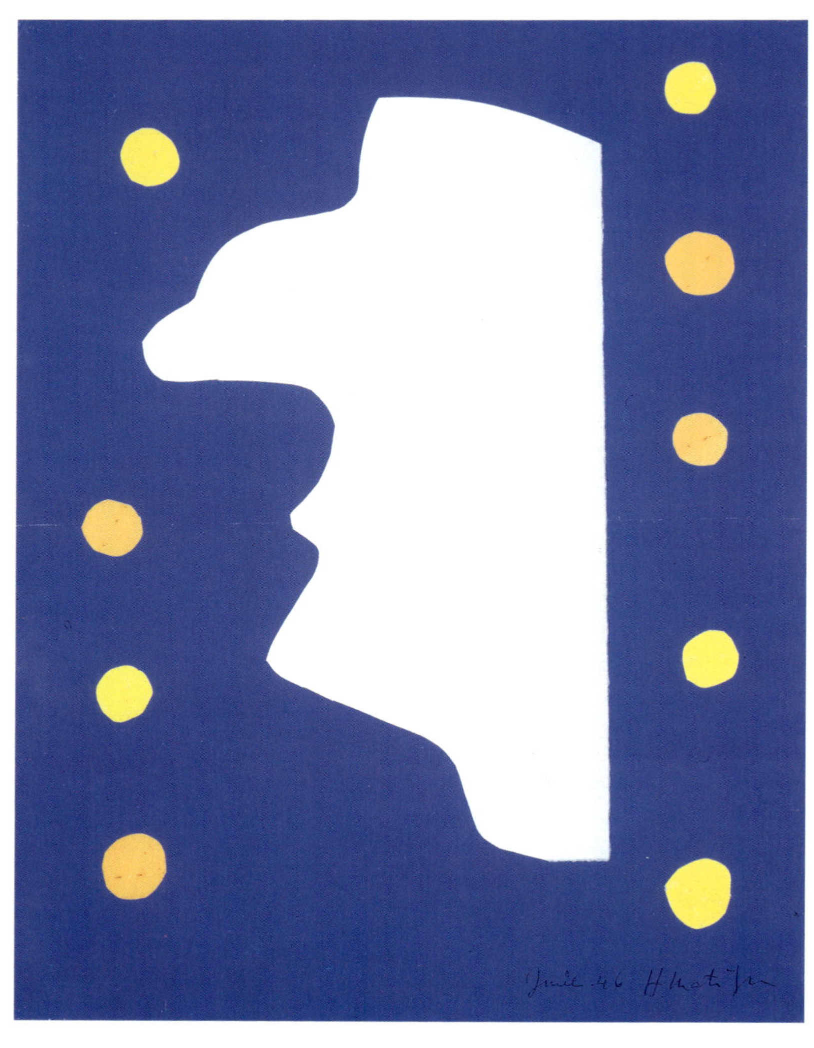

Monsieur Loyal (plate III from "Jazz") • 1947
Musée national d'art moderne, Paris

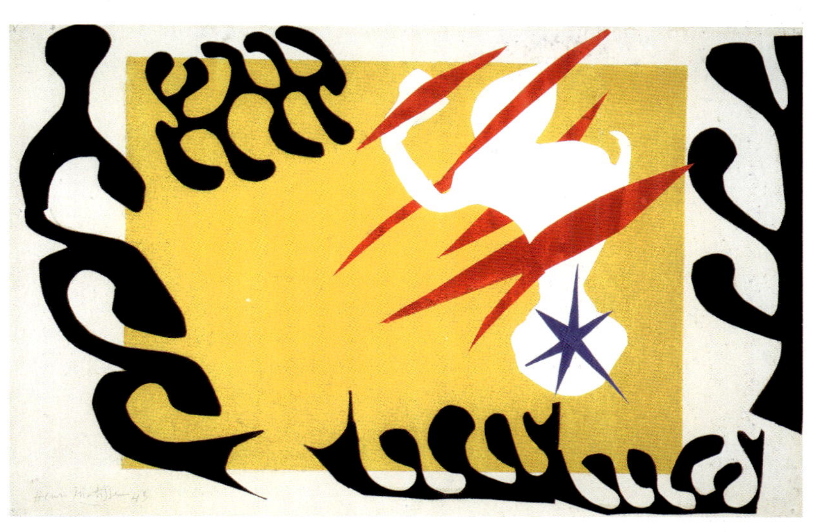

The Nightmare of the White Elephant (plate IV from "Jazz") • 1947
Musée national d'art moderne, Paris

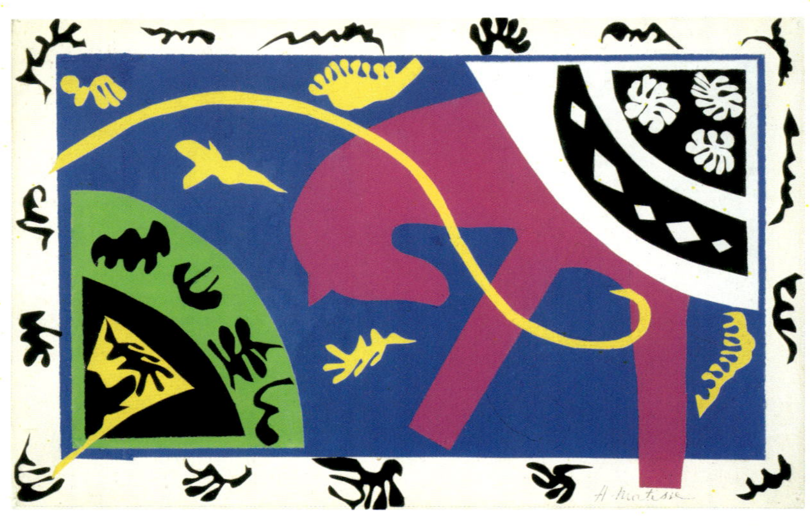

Horse, Rider and Clown (plate V from "Jazz") · 1947
Musée national d'art moderne, Paris

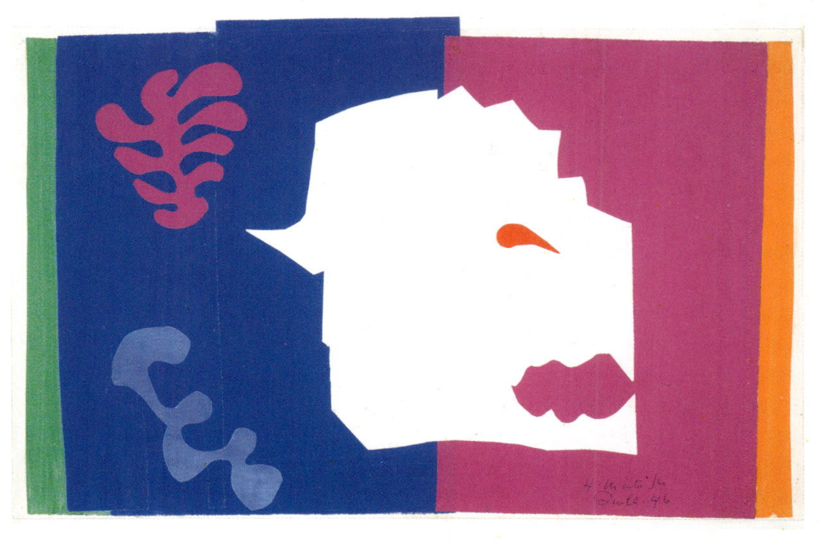

The Wolf (plate VI from "Jazz") • 1947
Musée national d'art moderne, Paris

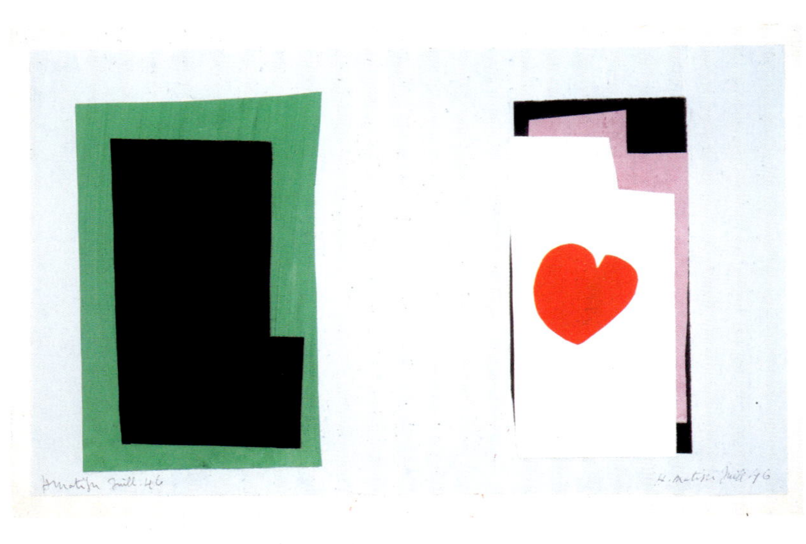

The Heart (plate VII from "Jazz") · 1947

Musée national d'art moderne, Paris

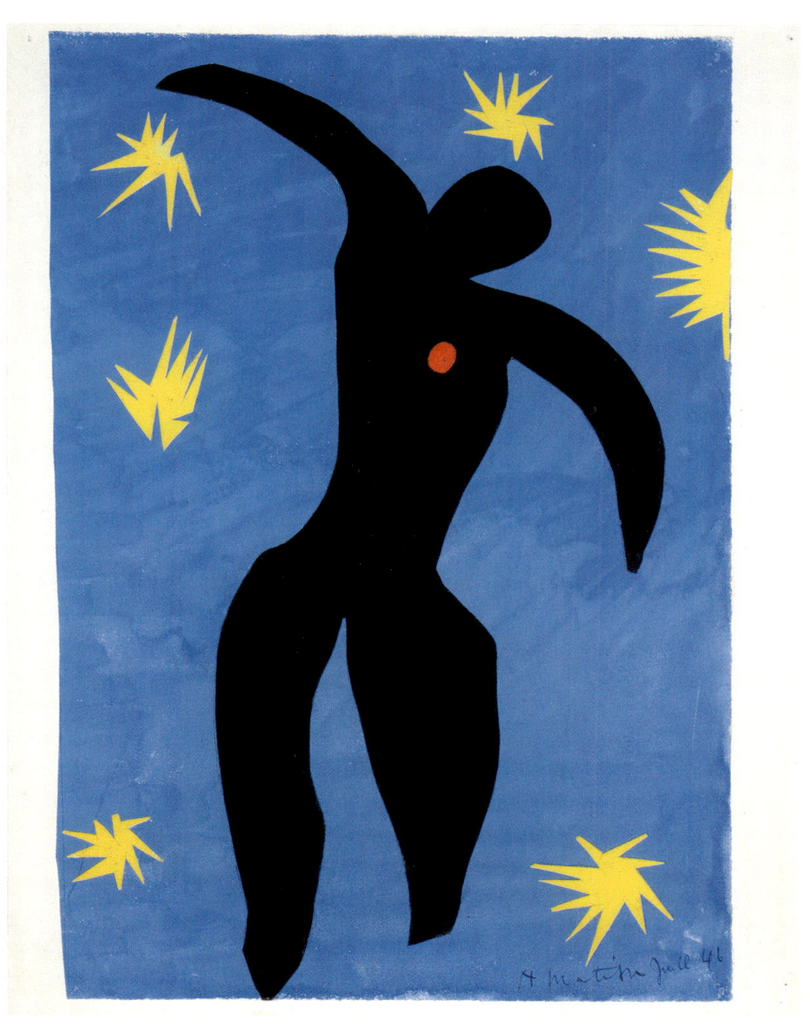

Icarus (plate VIII from "Jazz") · 1947
Musée national d'art moderne, Paris

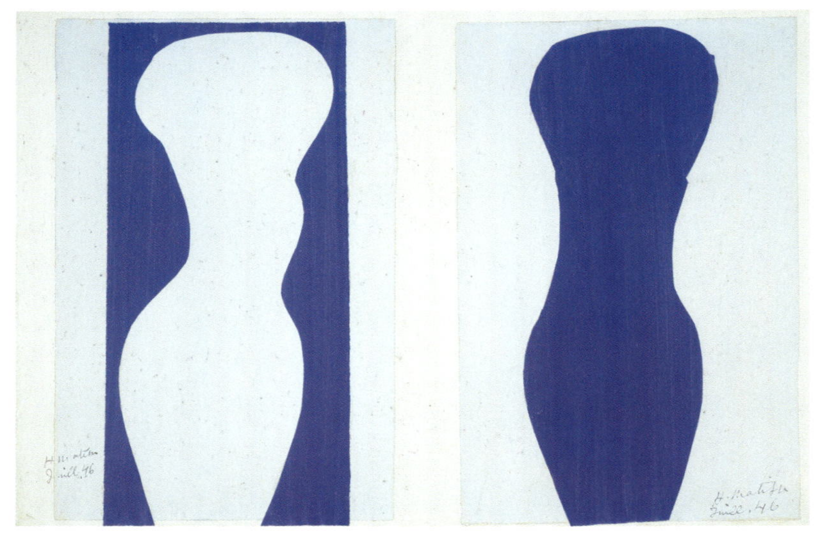

Forms (plate IX from "Jazz") · 1947
Musée national d'art moderne, Paris

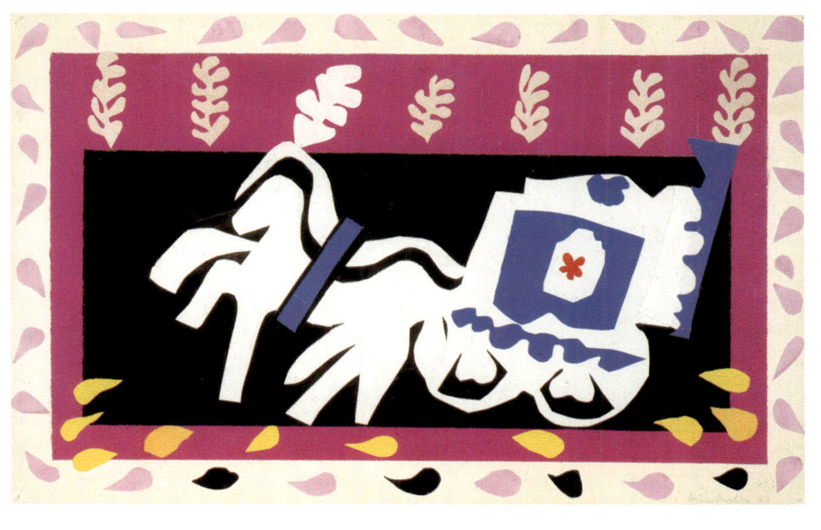

Pierrot's Funeral (plate X from "Jazz") · 1947
Musée national d'art moderne, Paris

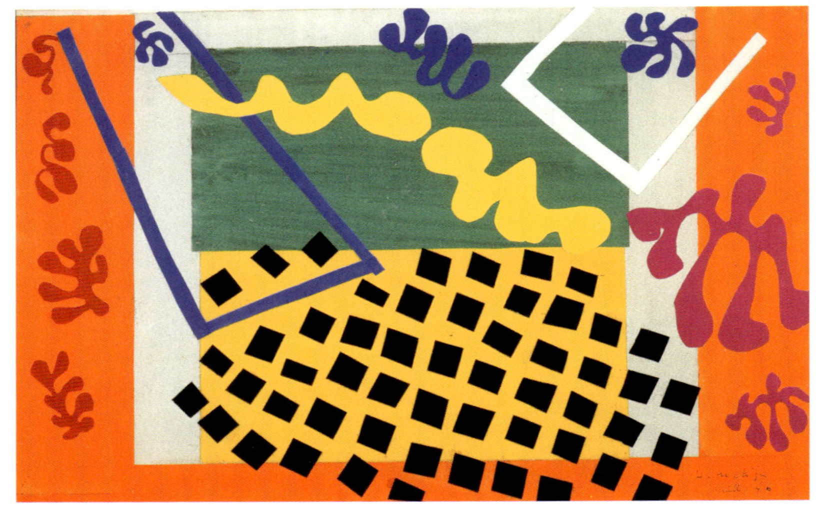

The Codomas (plate XI from "Jazz") • 1947
Musée national d'art moderne, Paris

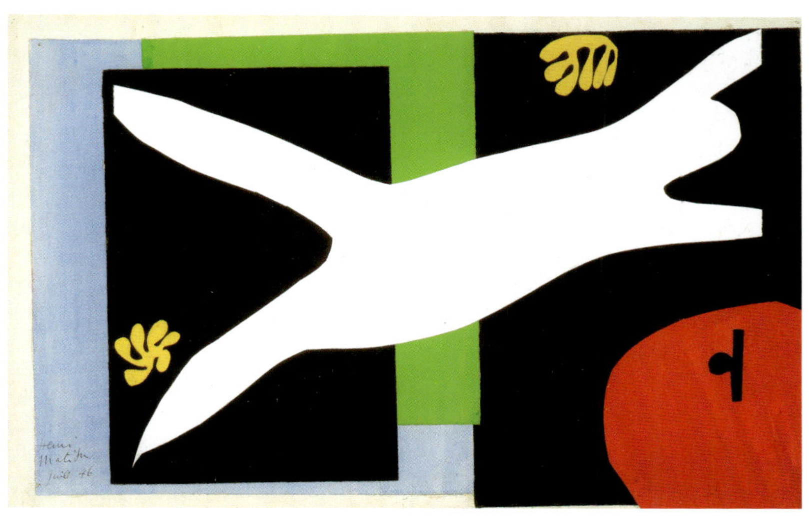

The Swimmer in the Tank (plate XII from "Jazz") · 1947
Musée national d'art moderne, Paris

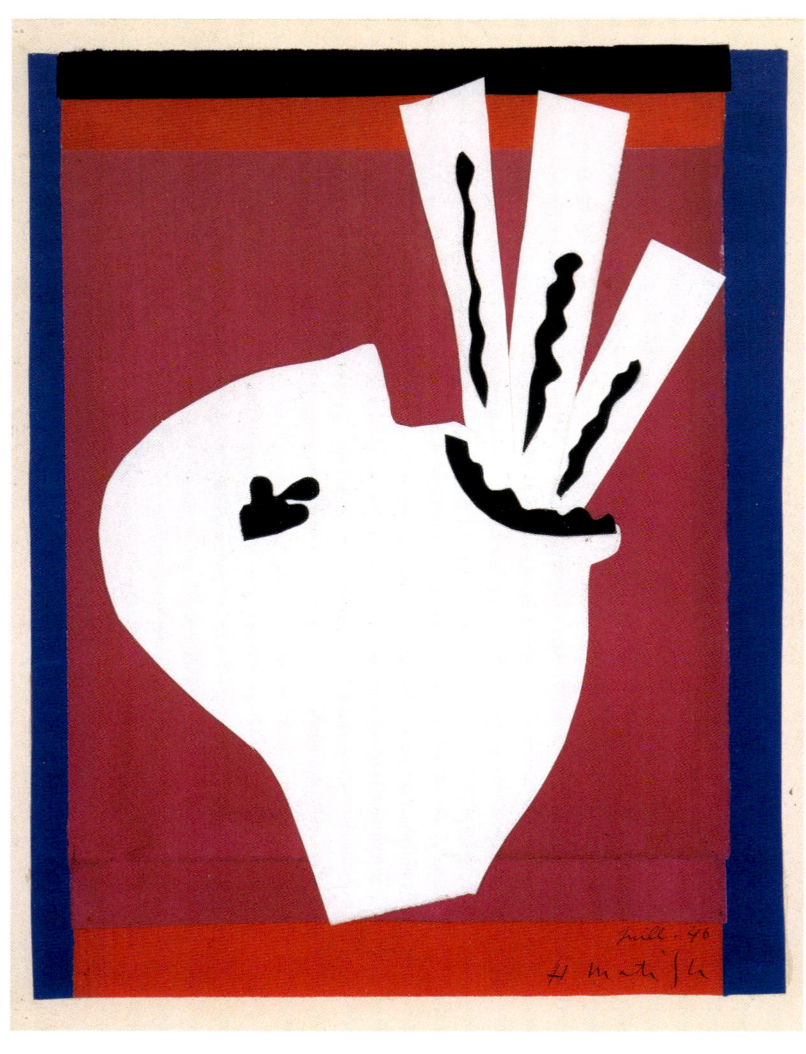

The Sword Swallower (plate XIII from "Jazz") • 1947
Musée national d'art moderne, Paris

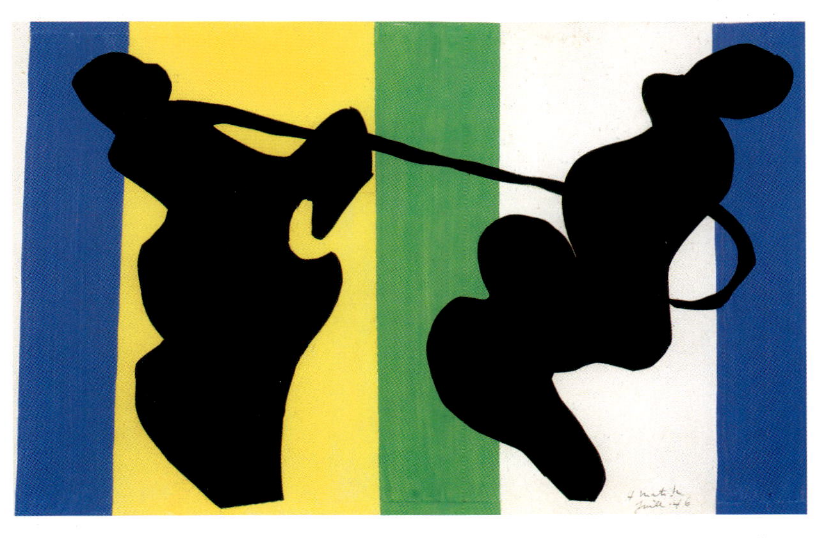

The Cowboy (plate XIV from "Jazz") · 1947

Musée national d'art moderne, Paris

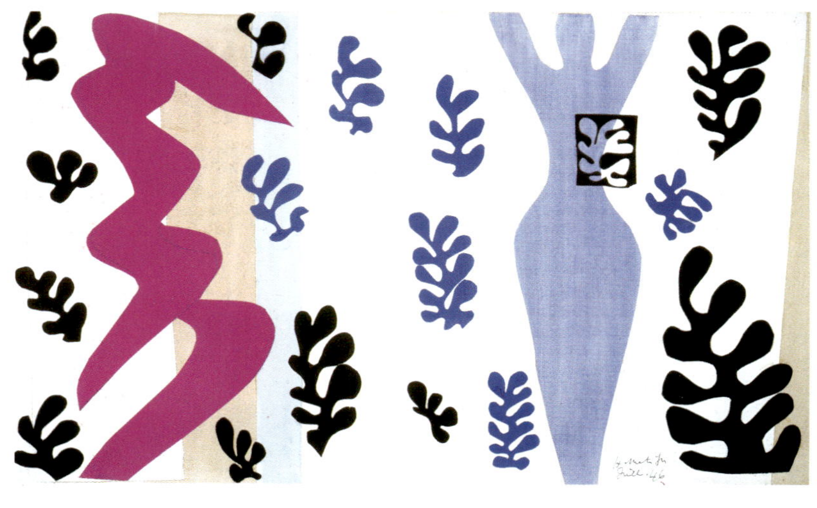

The Knife Thrower (plate XV from "Jazz") • 1947
Musée national d'art moderne, Paris

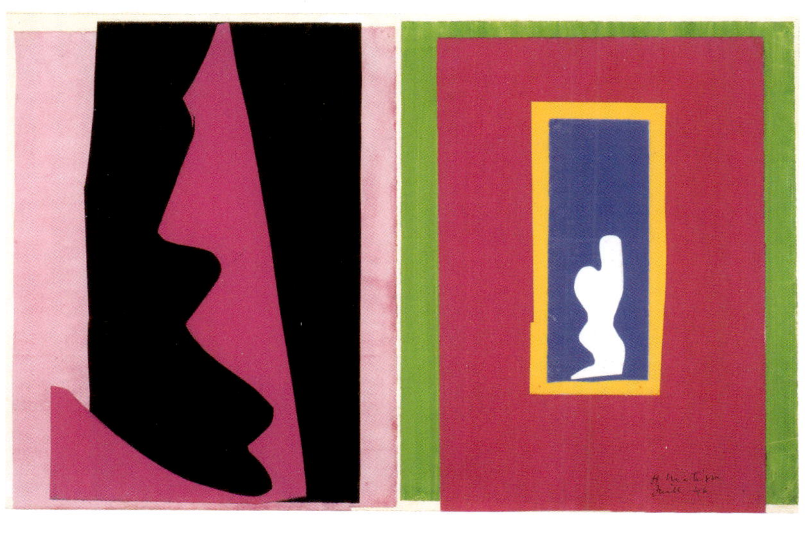

Destiny (plate XVI from "Jazz") · 1947

Musée national d'art moderne, Paris

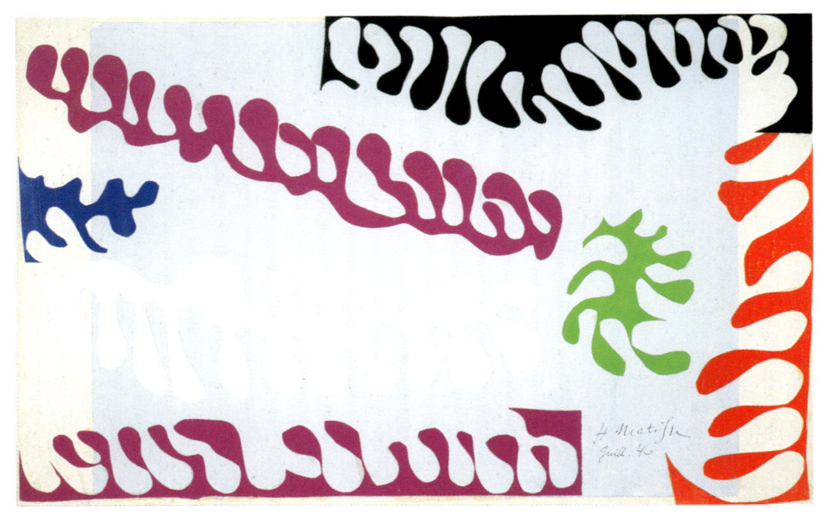

Lagoon (plate XVII from "Jazz") • 1947
Musée national d'art moderne, Paris

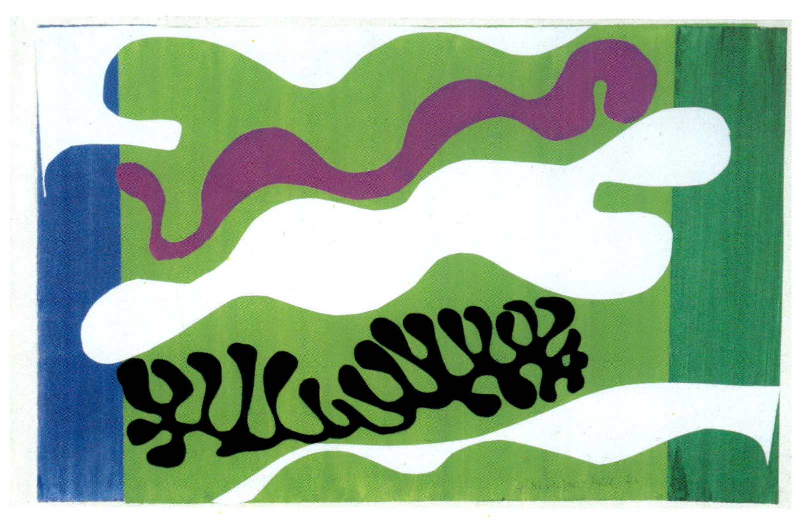

Lagoon (plate XVIII from "Jazz") · 1947
Musée national d'art moderne, Paris

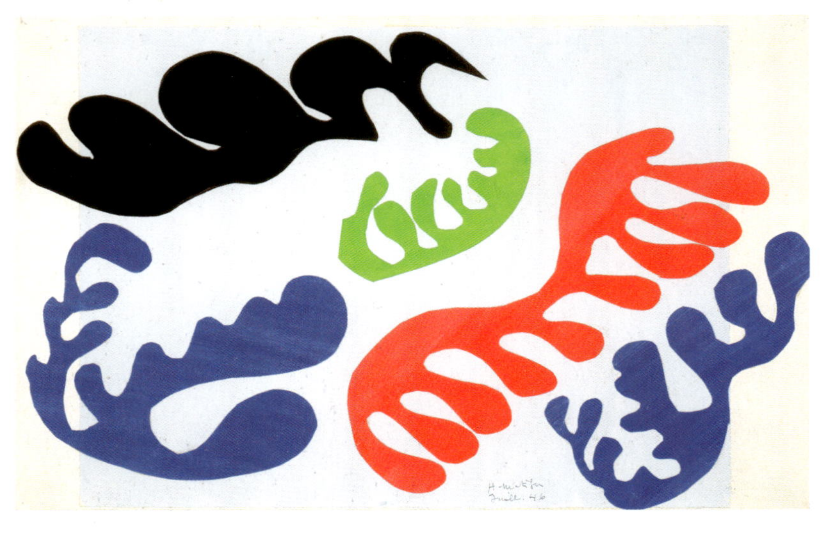

Lagoon (plate XIX from "Jazz") • 1947
Musée national d'art moderne, Paris

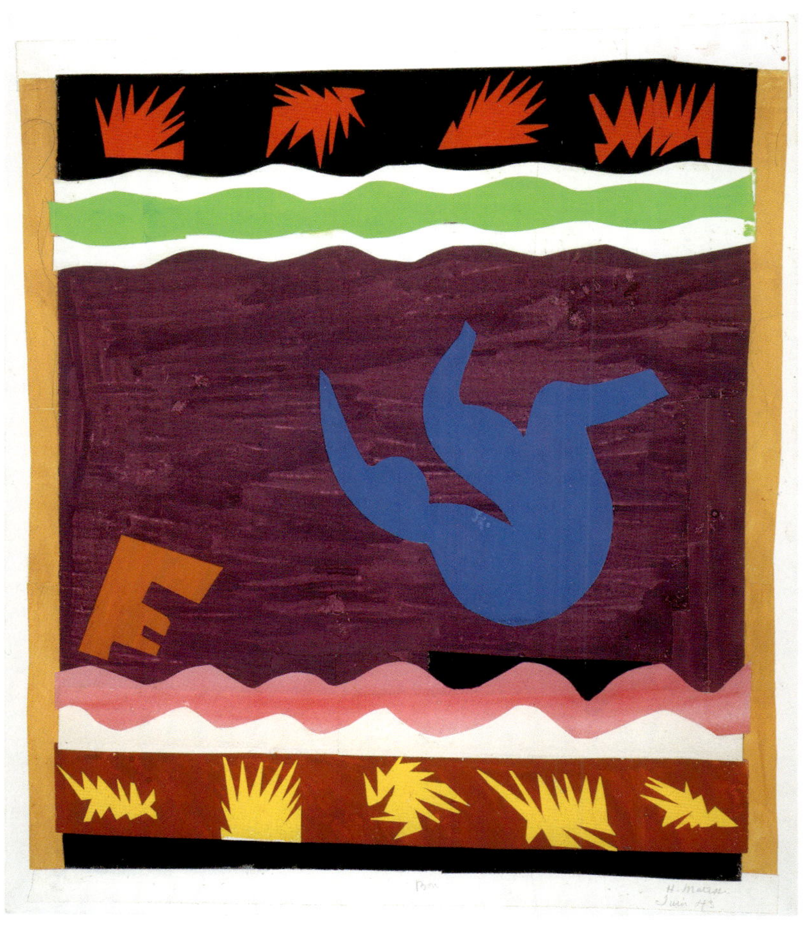

Toboggan (plate XX from "Jazz") · 1947
Musée national d'art moderne, Paris

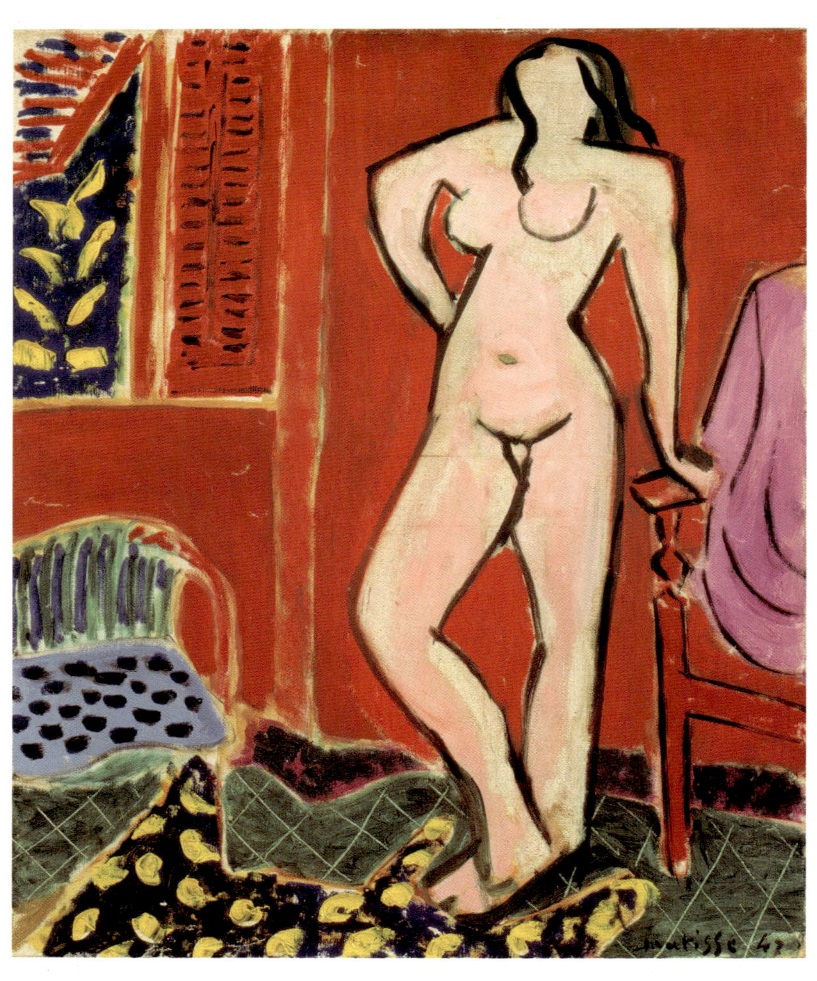

Standing Nude · 1947
Musée national d'art moderne, Paris

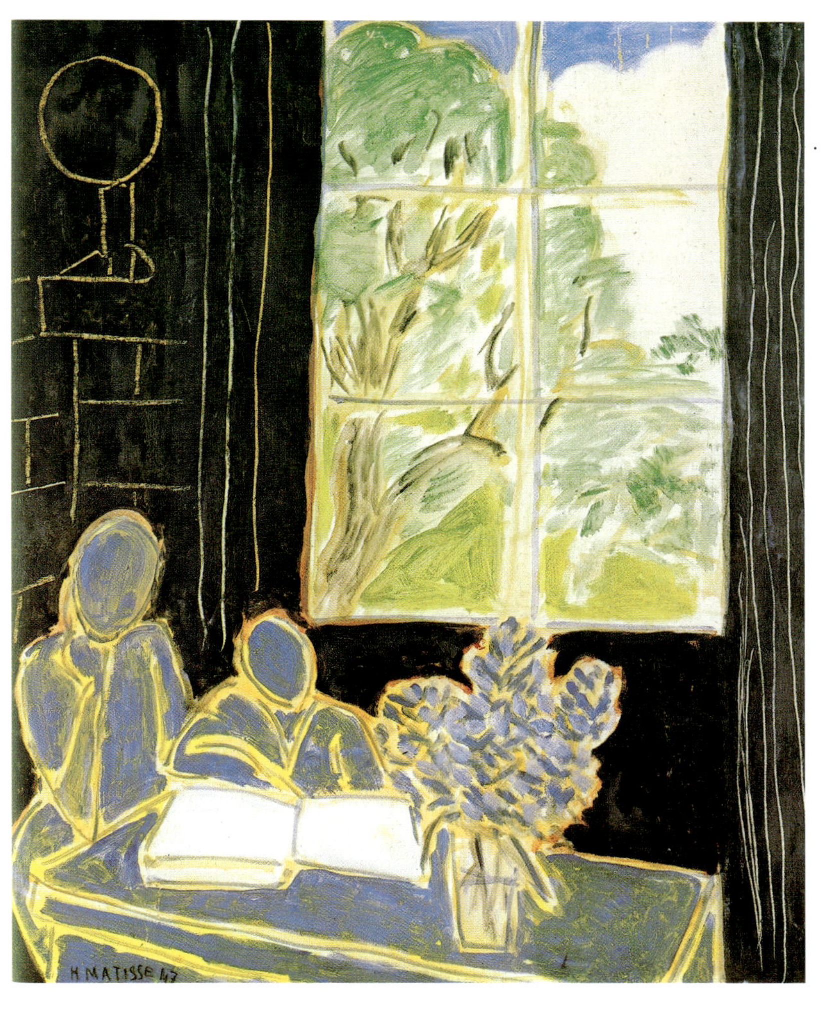

The Silence Living in Houses • 1947

Private collection

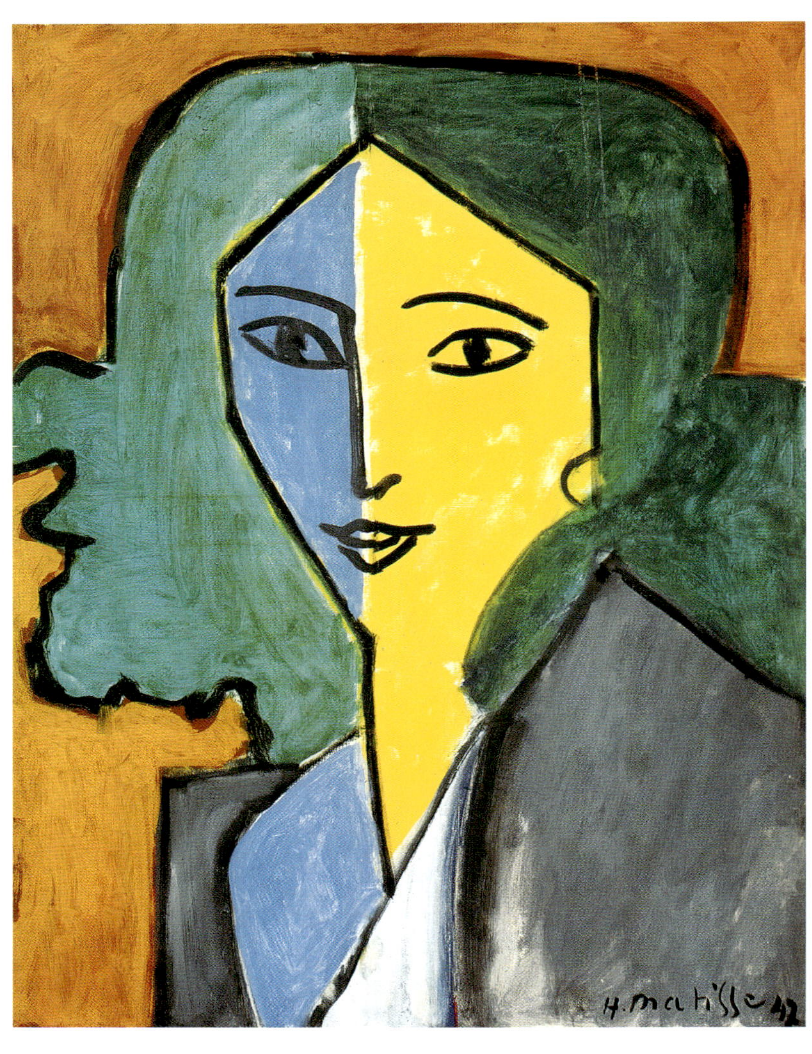

Portrait of Lydia Delectorskaya • 1947

Hermitage, Saint Petersburg

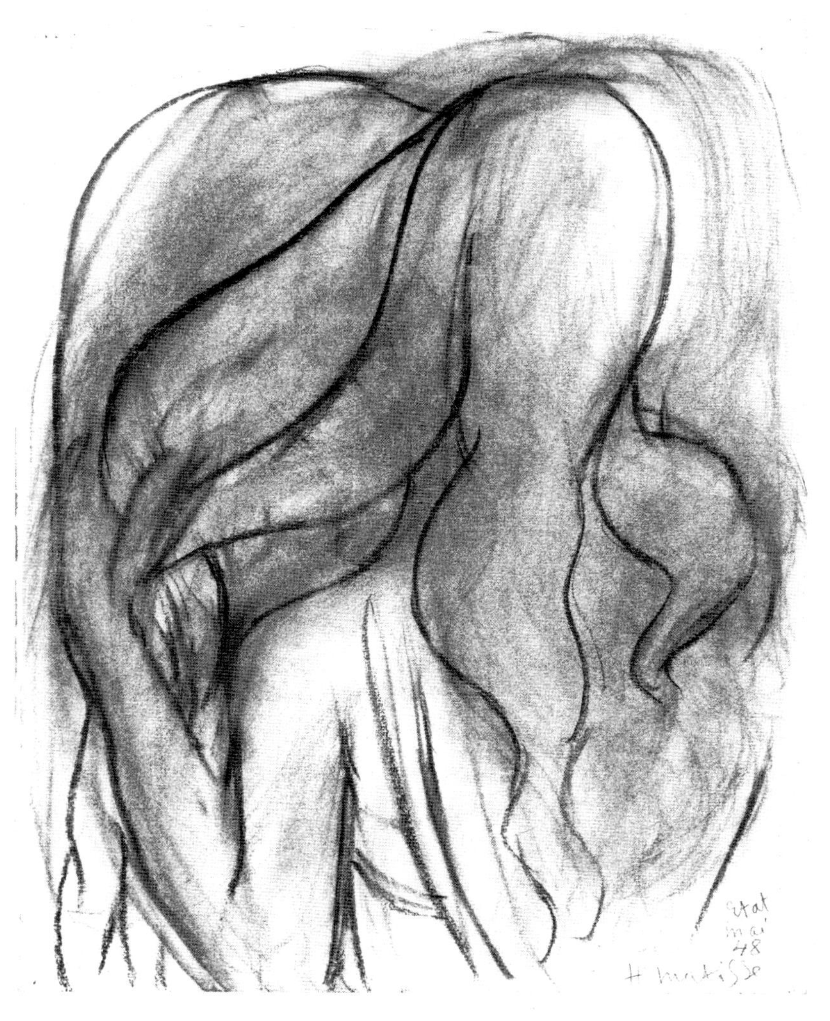

Hair • 1948
Private collection

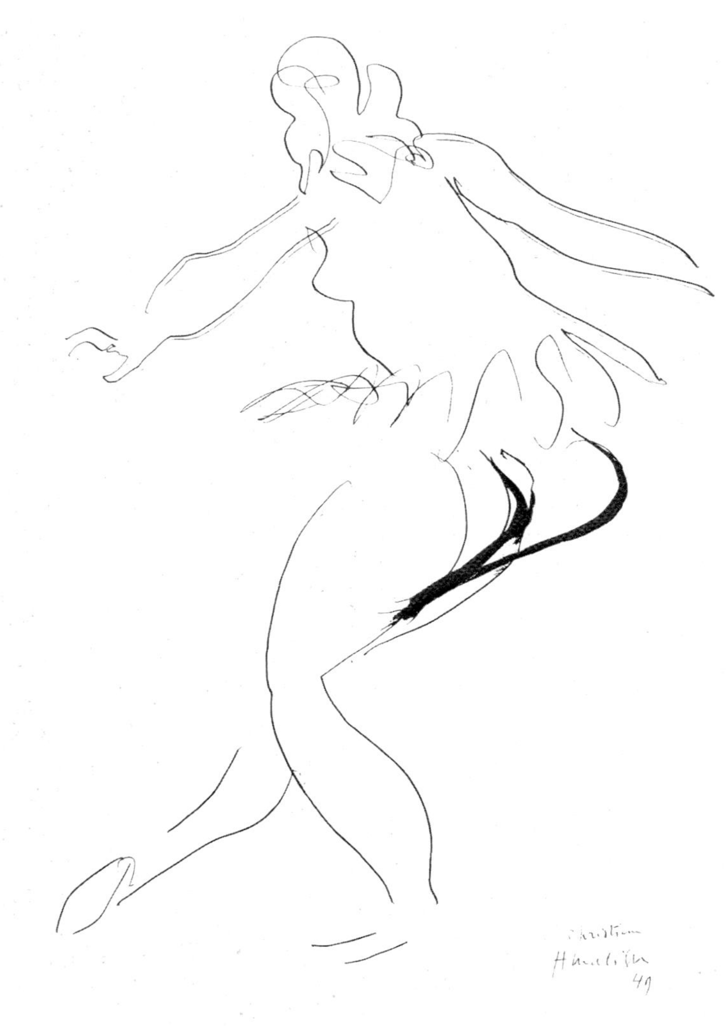

Dance Movement • 1949

Private collection

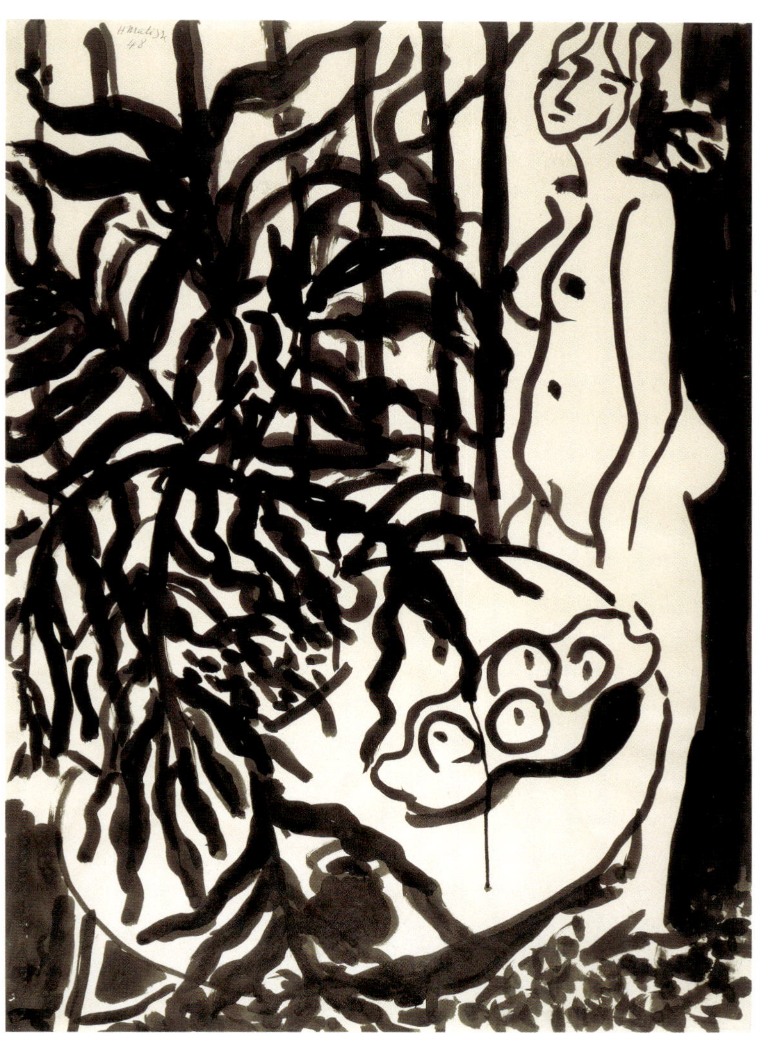

Composition with a Standing Nude and Black Fern · 1948
Musée national d'art moderne, Paris

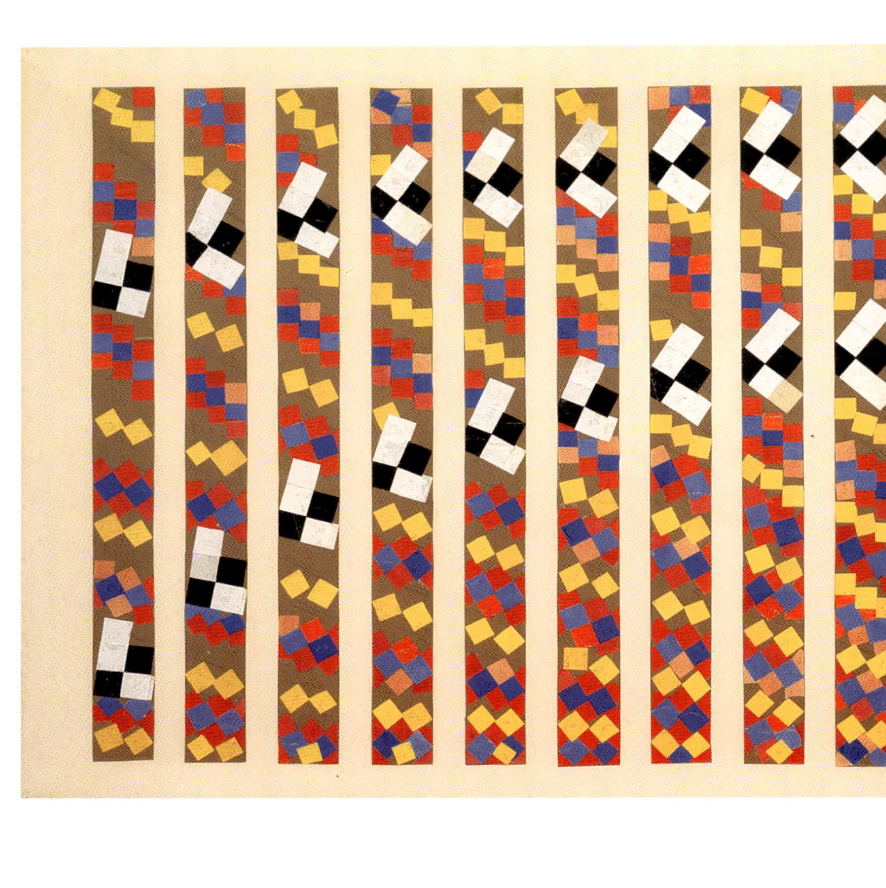

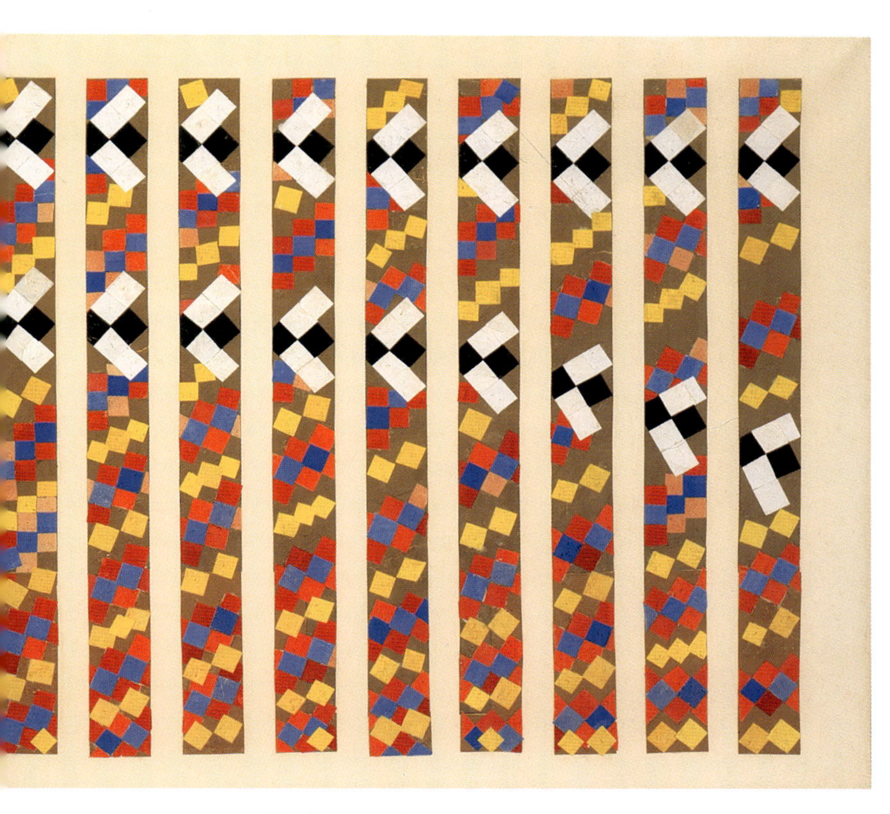

The Bees • 1948 • Musée Matisse, Nice

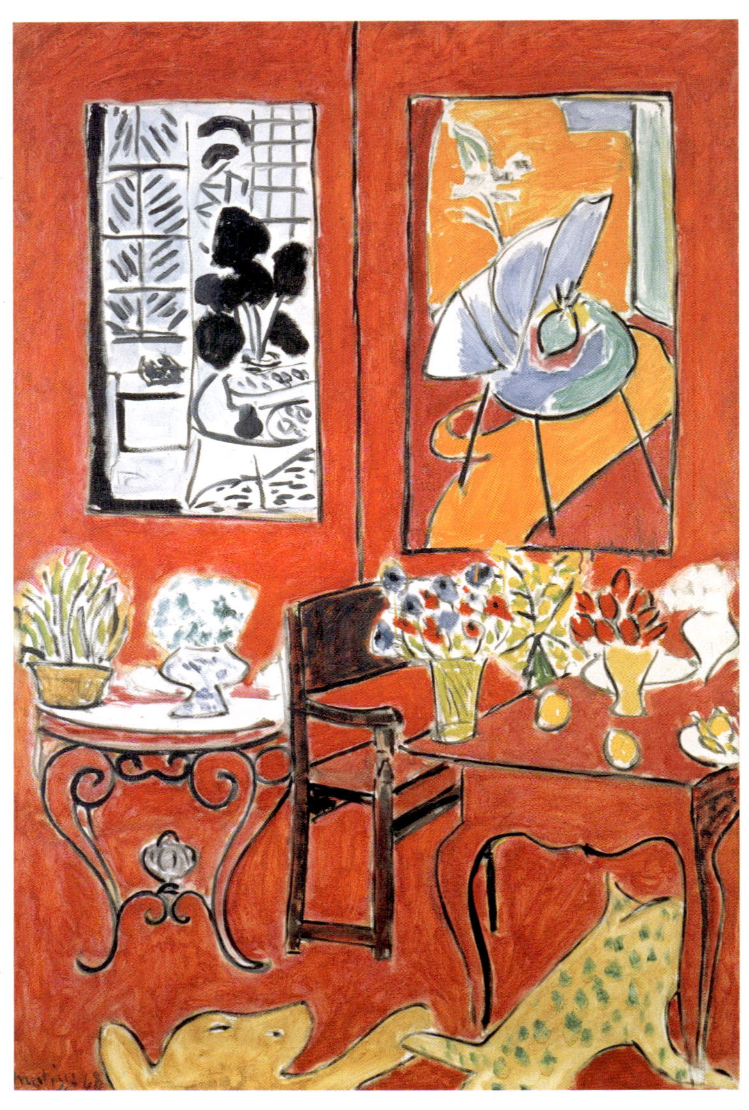

Large Red Interior • 1948
Musée national d'art moderne, Paris

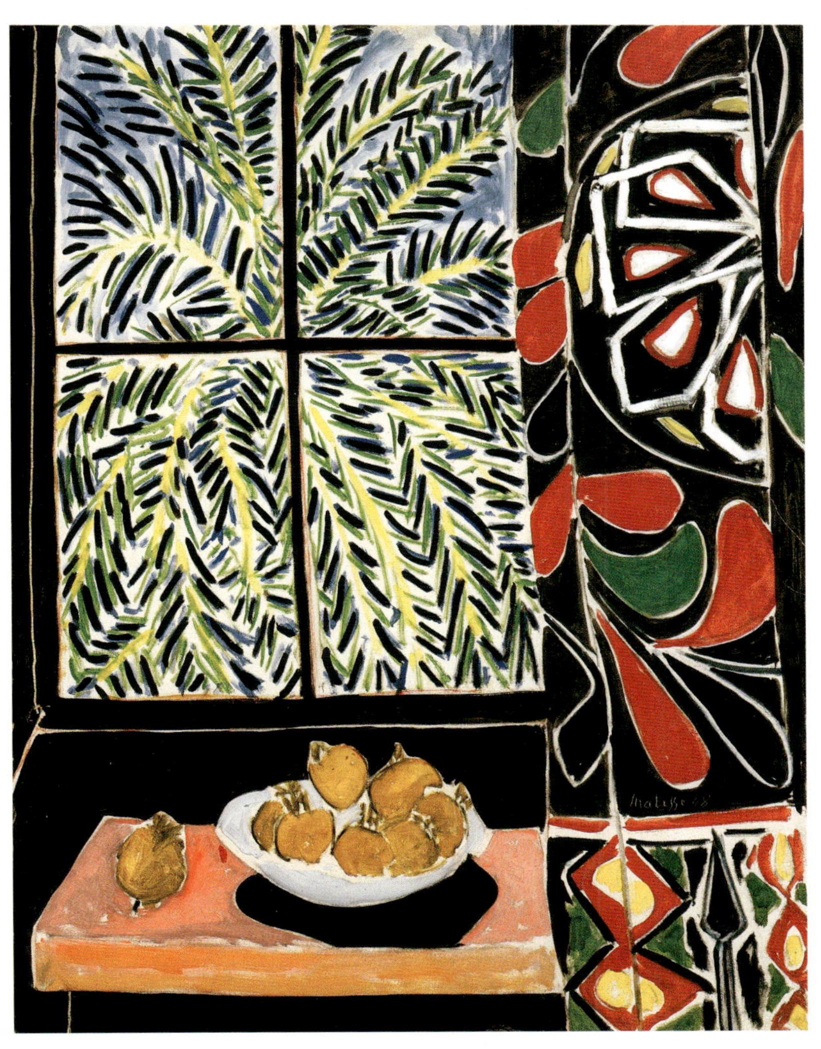

Interior with Egyptian Curtain • 1948
The Phillips Collection, Washington

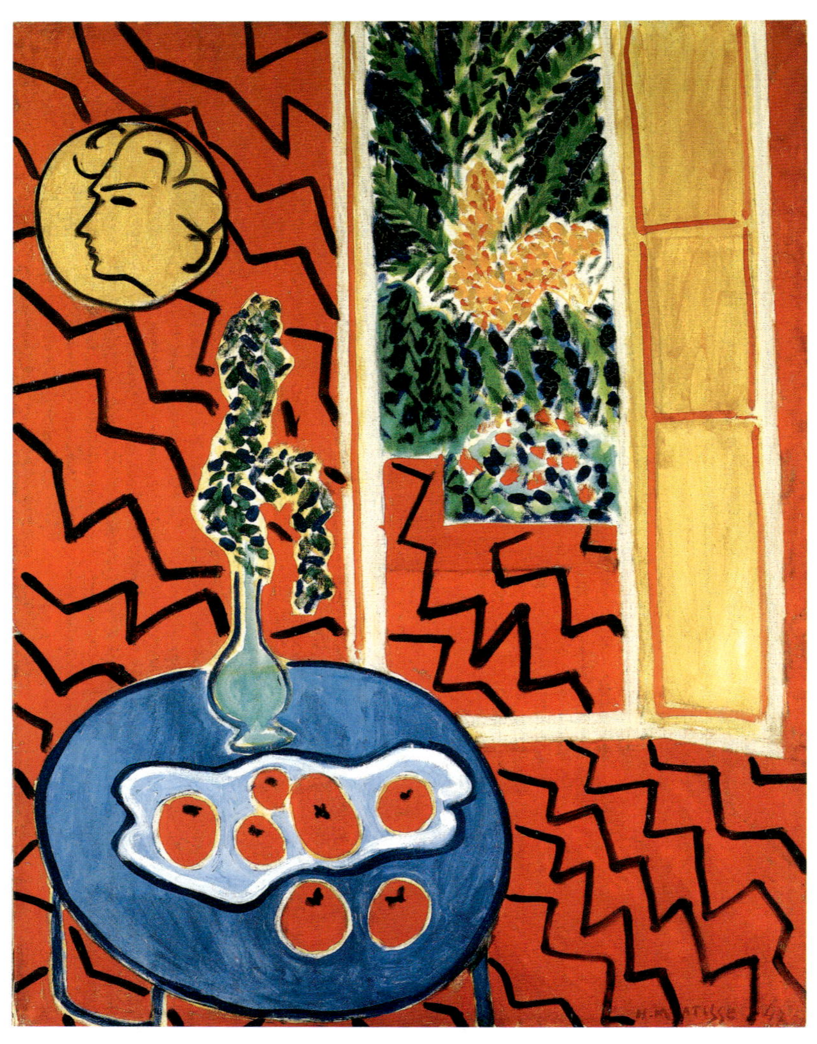

Red Interior / Still Life on a Blue Table · 1948
Kunstsammlung Nordrhein-Westfalen, Düsseldorf

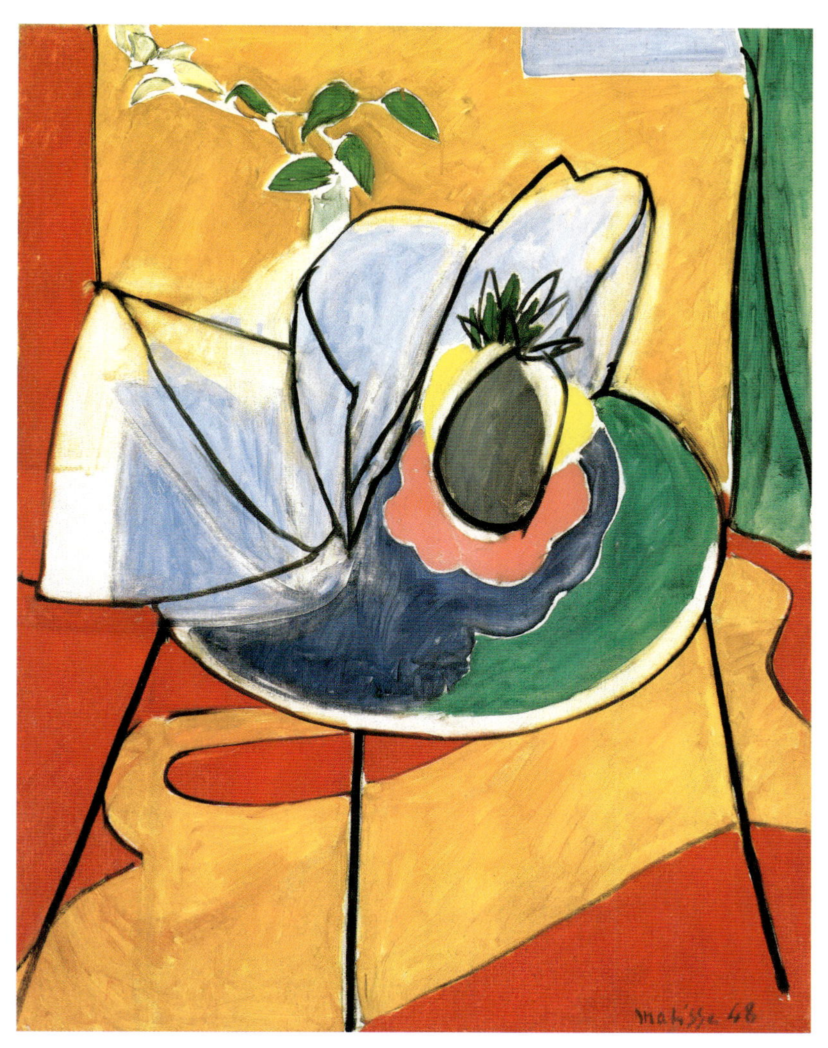

The Pineapple • 1948
The Metropolitan Museum of Art, New York, The Alex Hillman Family Foundation Collection

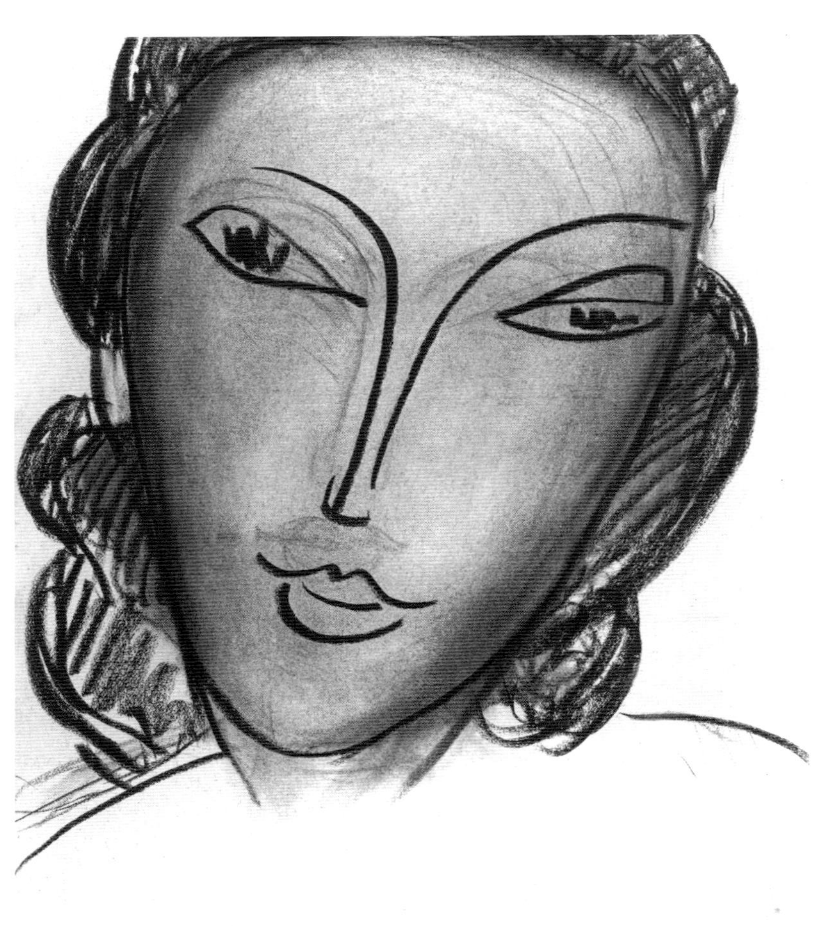

Head (Rosabianca Skira) • 1948
Private collection

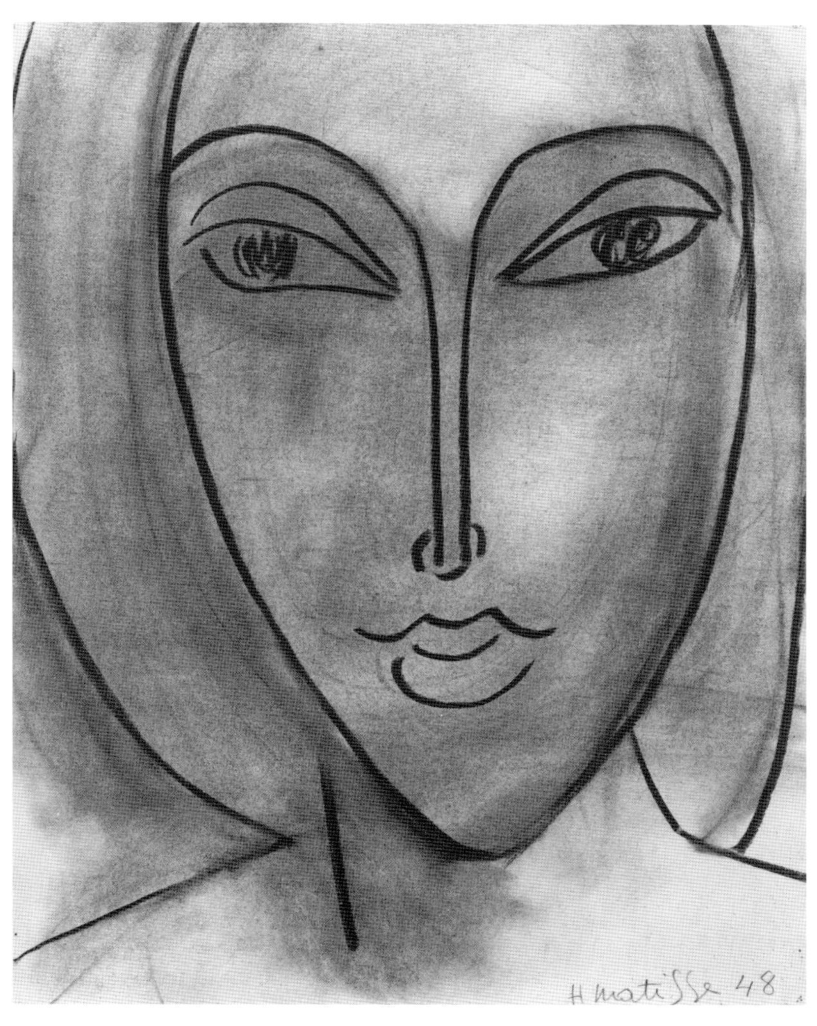

Head (Rosabianca Skira) · 1948
Private collection

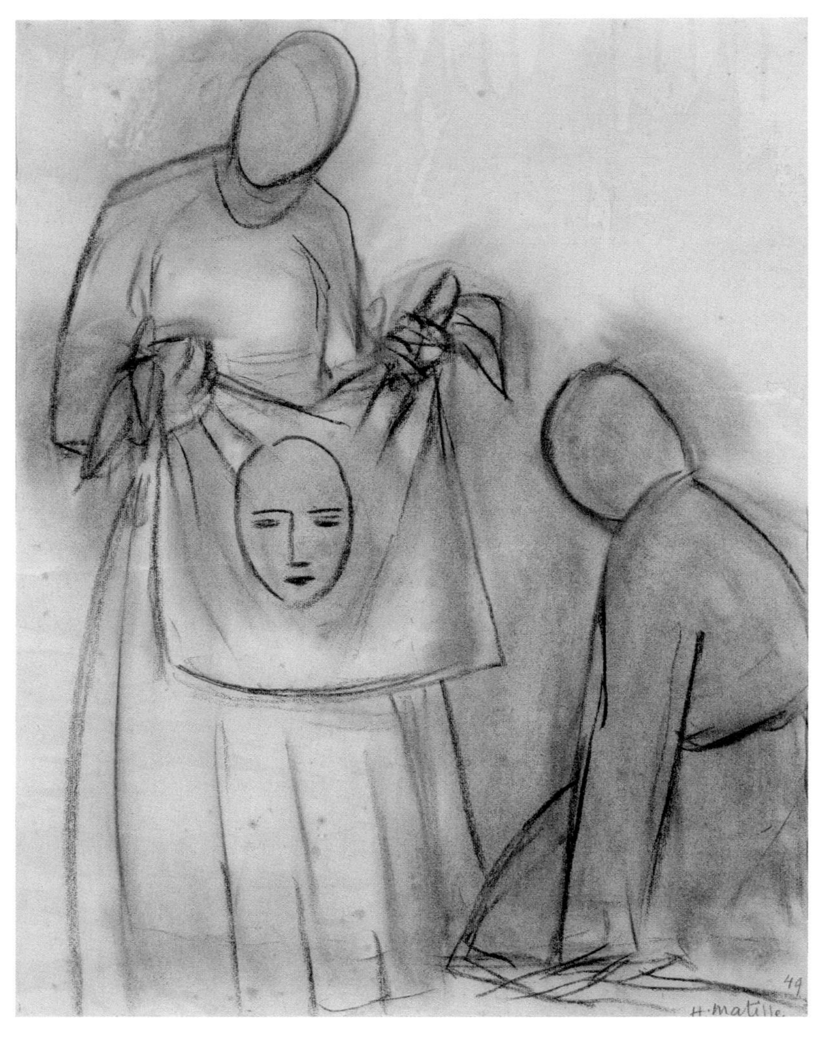

Study for the Sixth Station of the Cross · 1949
Château de Villeneuve, Vence

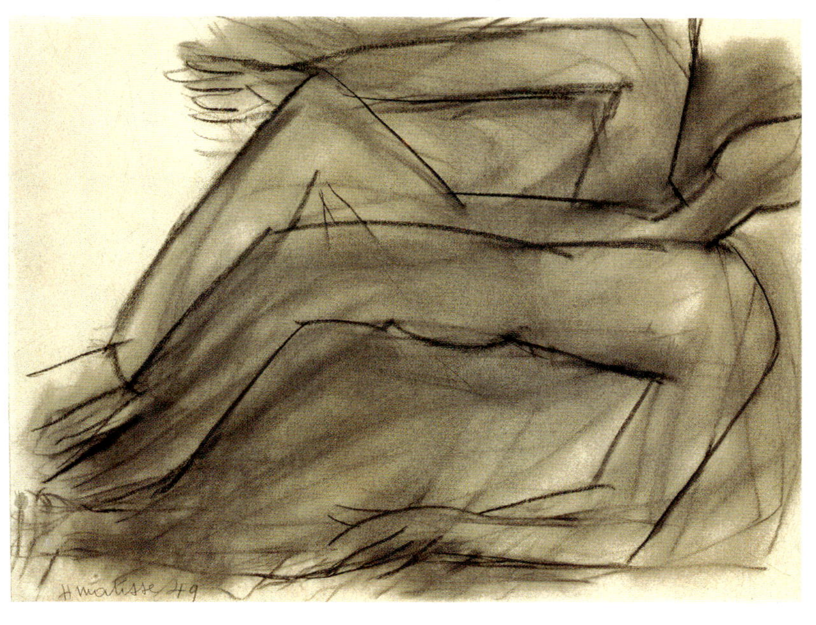

Study for the Ninth Station of the Cross • 1949

Musée Matisse, Nice

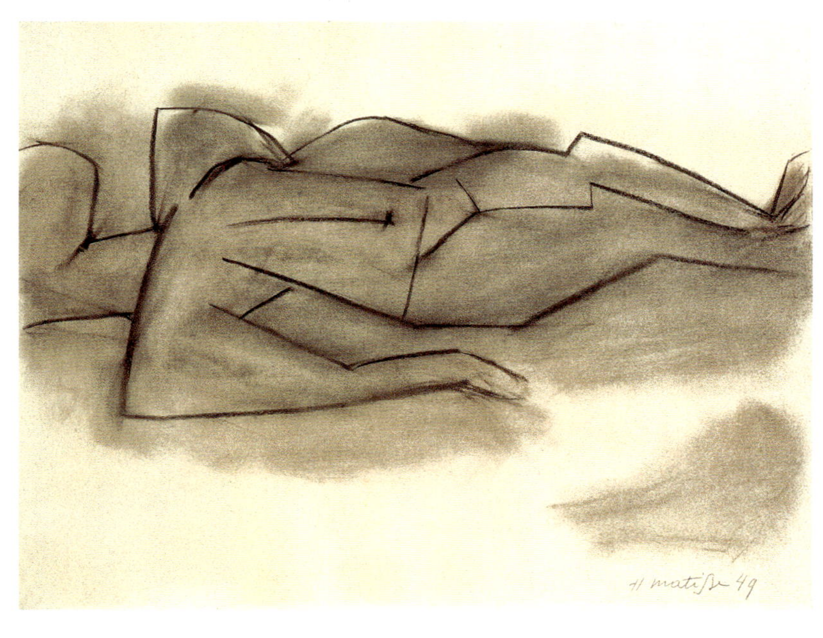

Study for the Fourteenth Station of the Cross · 1949

Musée Matisse, Nice

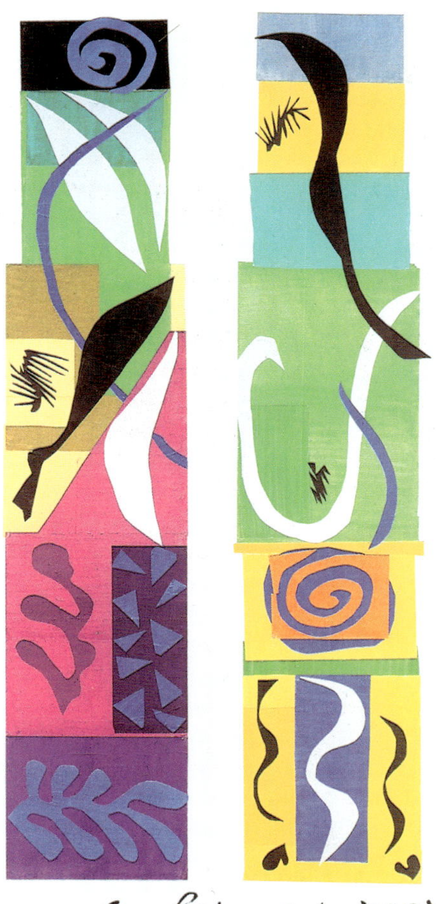

The Beasts of the Sea . . . • 1950
National Gallery of Art, Washington, Ailsa Mellon Bruce Fund
> **Cover for "Verve" (6, nos. 21–22) •** 1948
Private collection

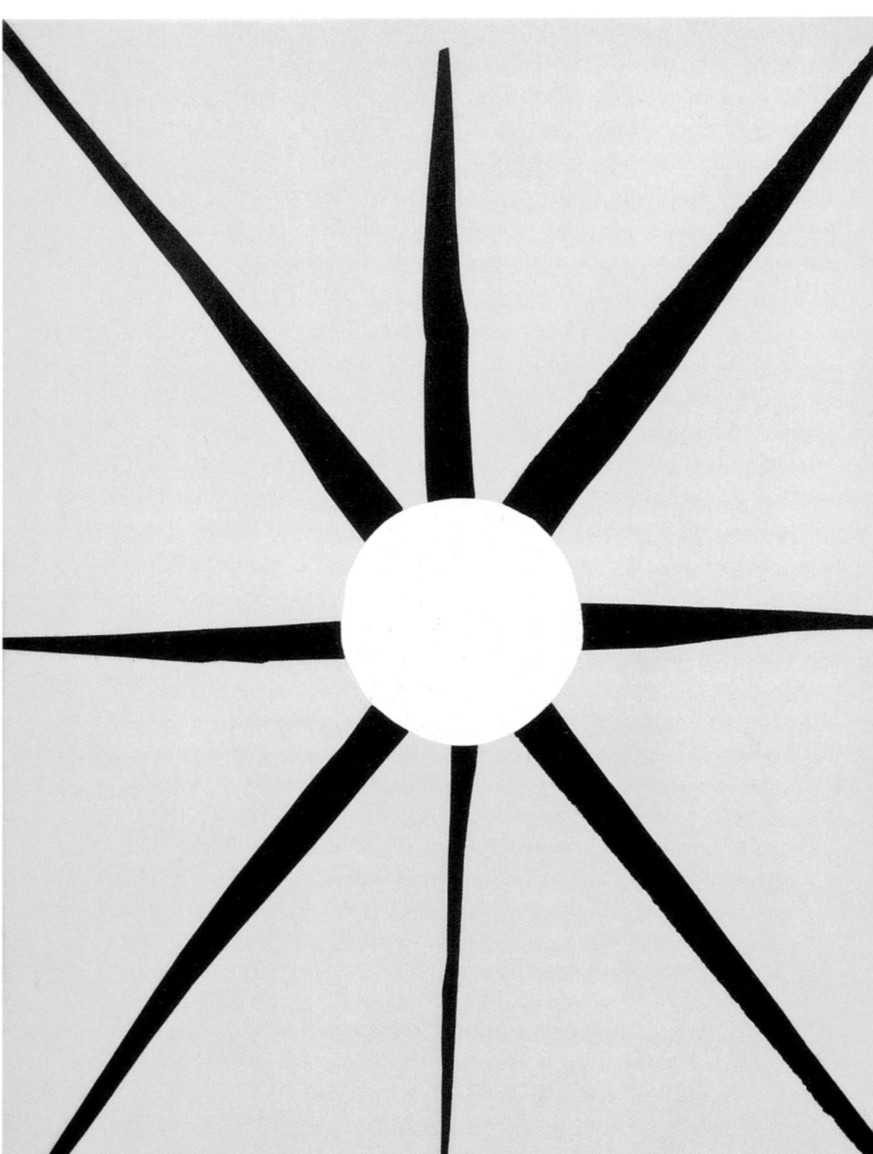

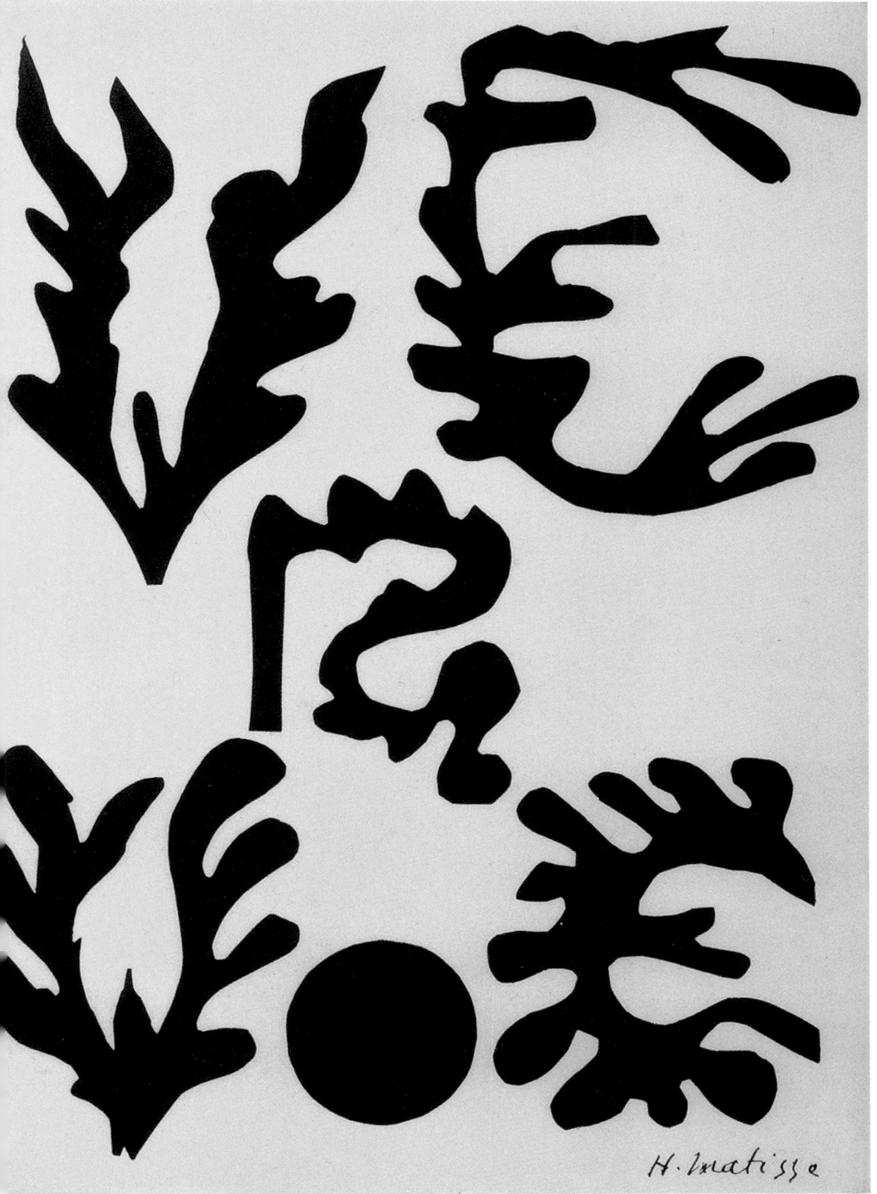
H. Matisse

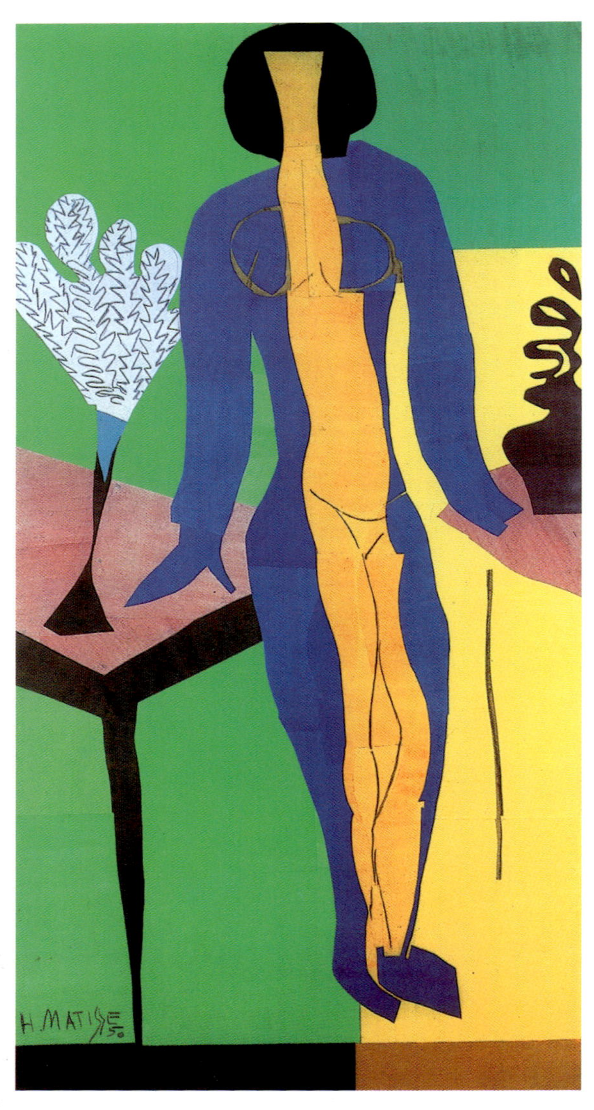

Zulma • 1950

Statens Museum for Kunst, Copenhagen

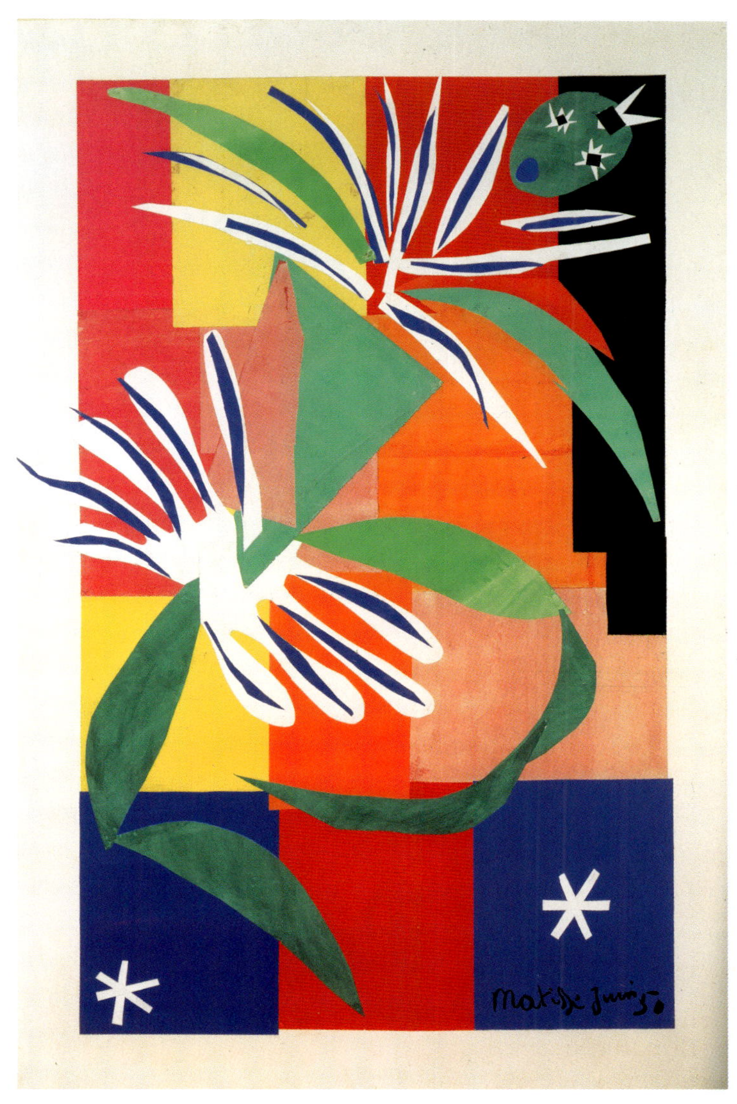

Creole Dancer • 1950

Musée Matisse, Nice

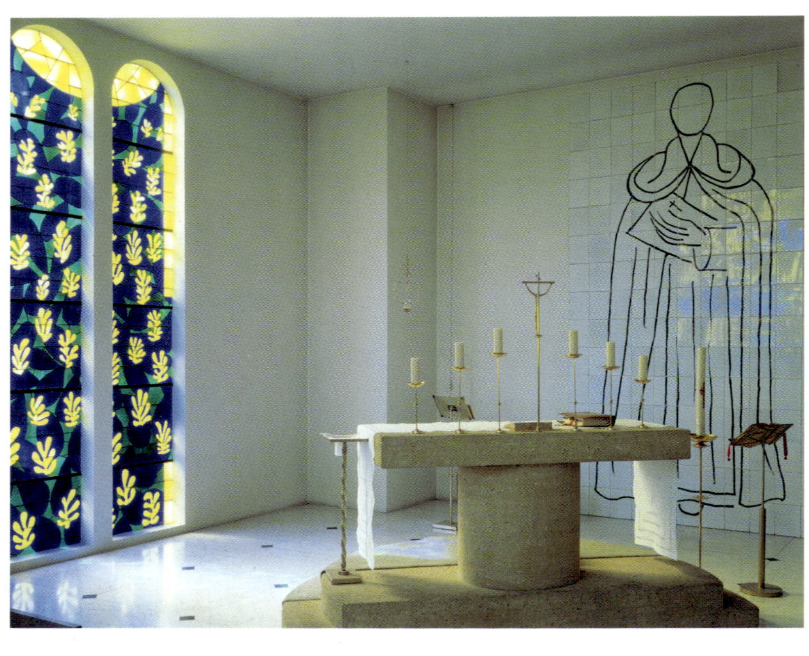

The Altar, Saint Dominic and the Tree of Life (apse window) • 1950

Chapelle du Rosaire, Vence

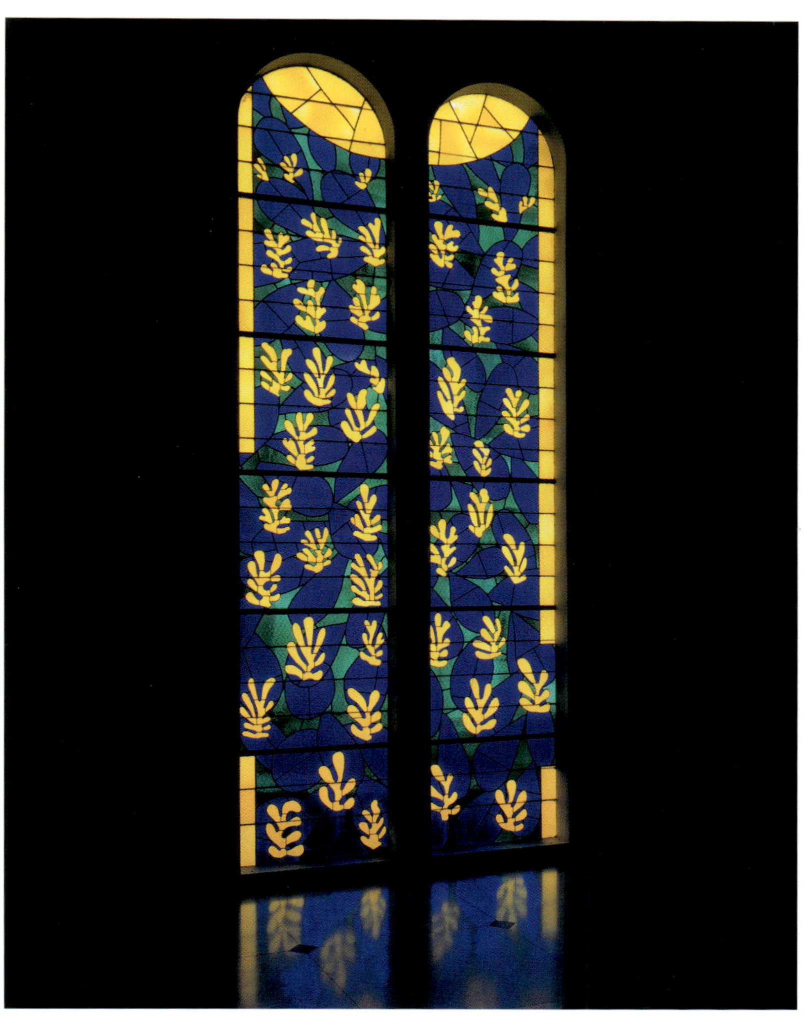

The Tree of Life (apse window) • 1950
Chapelle du Rosaire, Vence

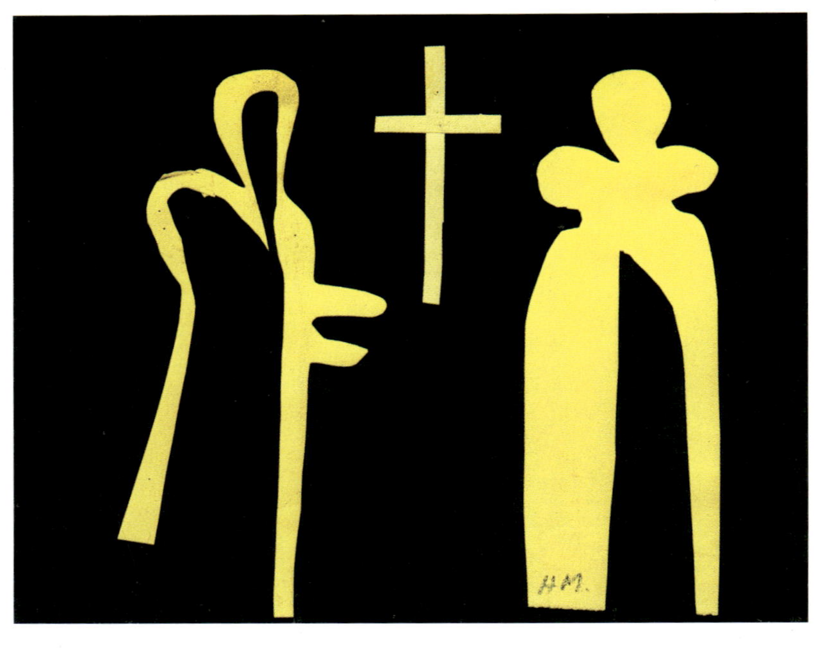

Study for the Tabernacle of the Chapelle du Rosaire, Vence • 1950

Private collection

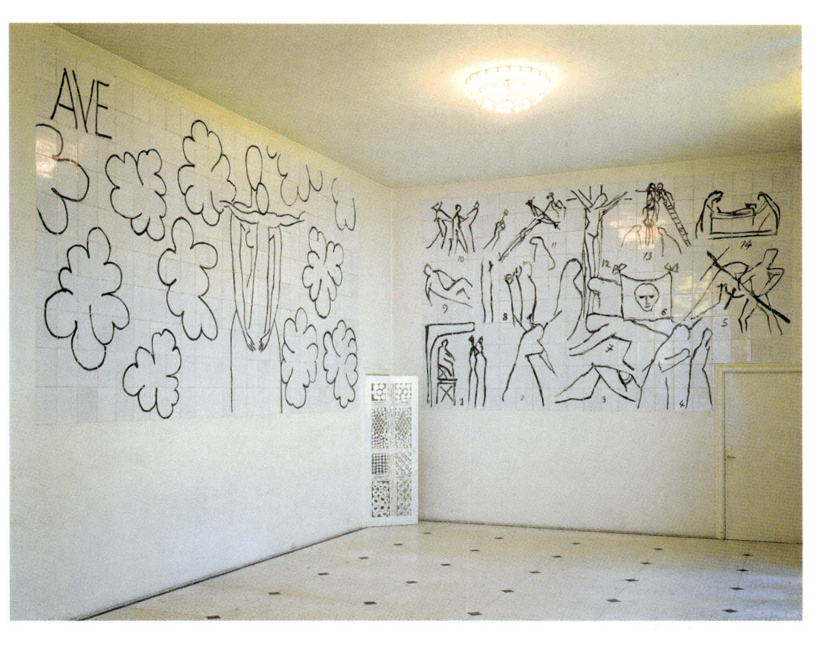

The Stations of the Cross · 1950

Chapelle du Rosaire, Vence

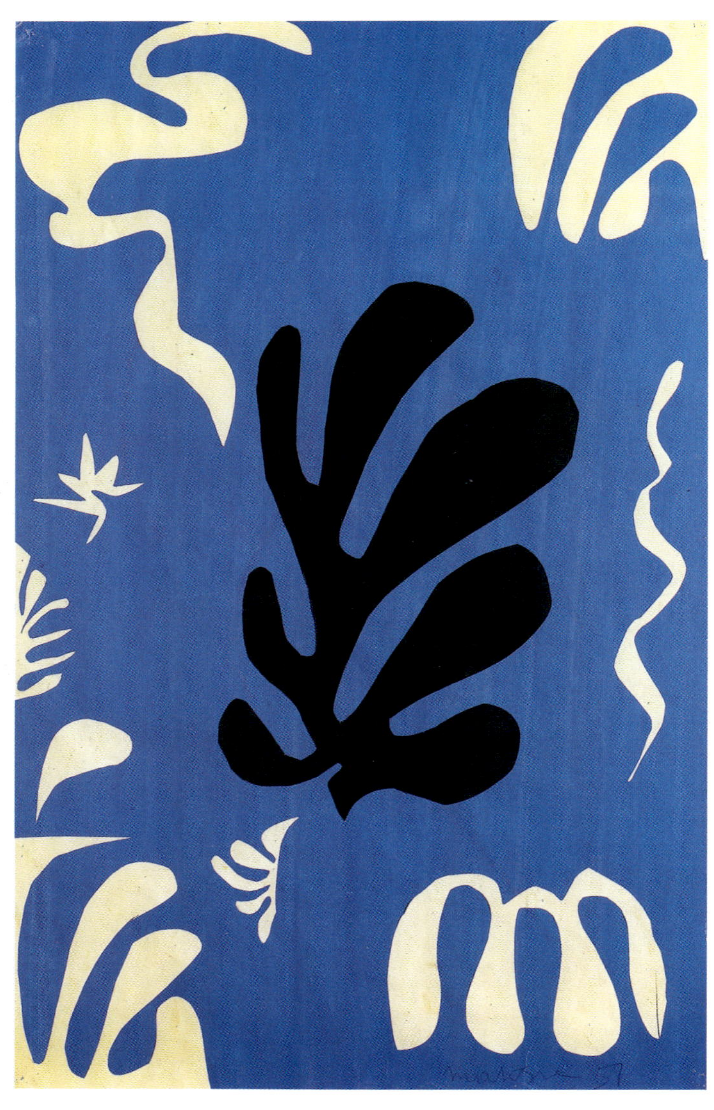

Composition • 1951
Private collection

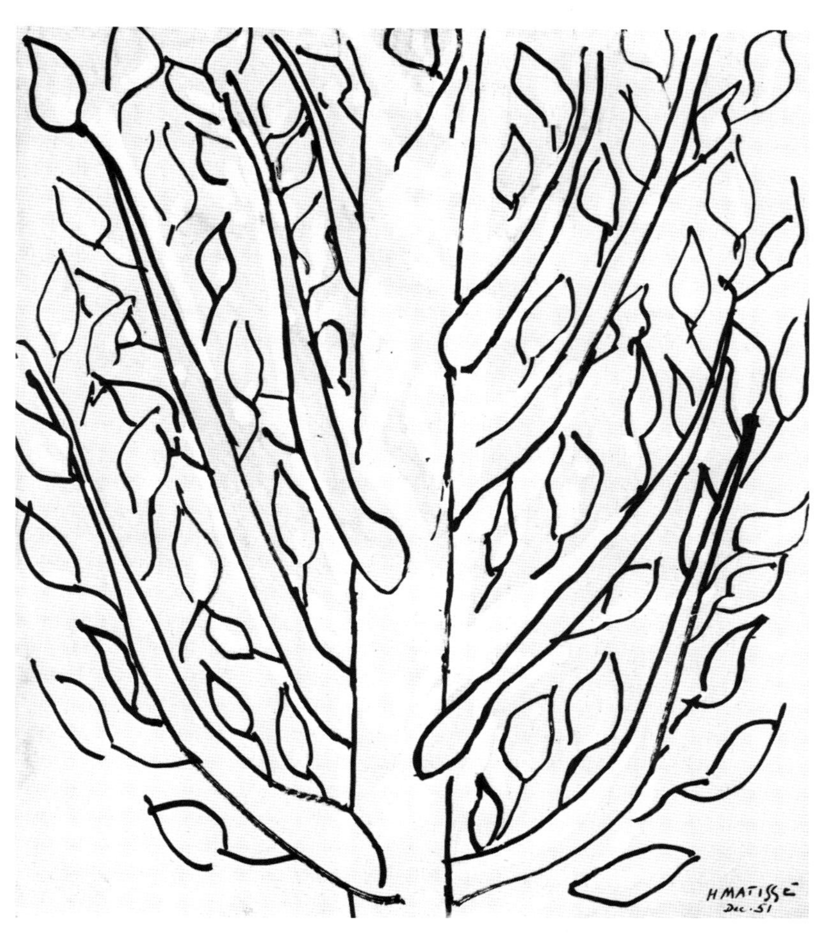

Plane-tree • 1951
Private collection

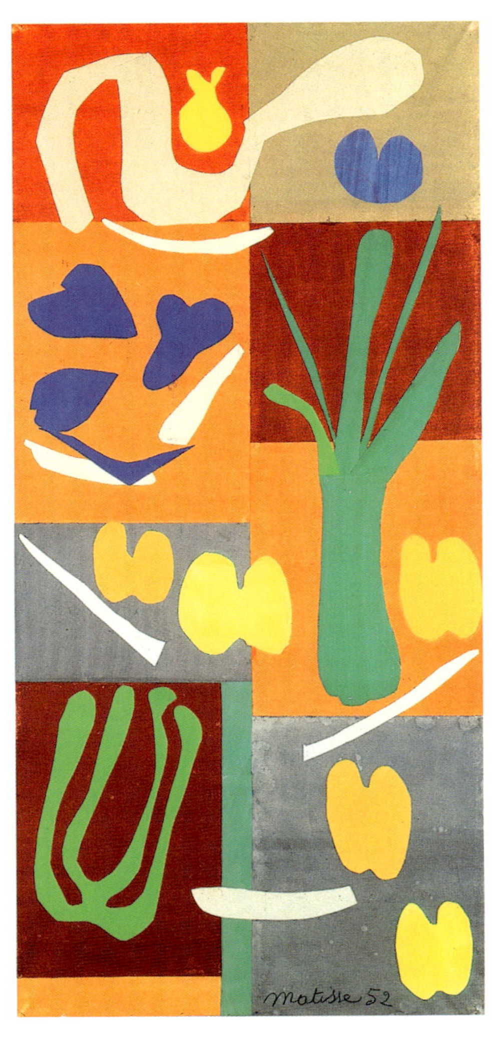

Vegetables • c. 1951
Private collection

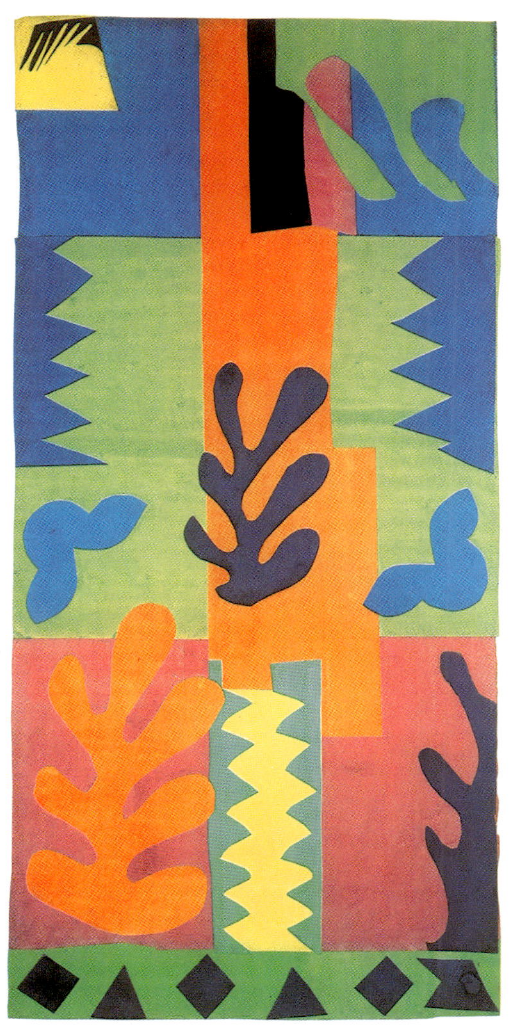

The Wine Press • c. 1951
Private collection
> **The Sorrow of the King** • 1952
Musée national d'art moderne, Paris

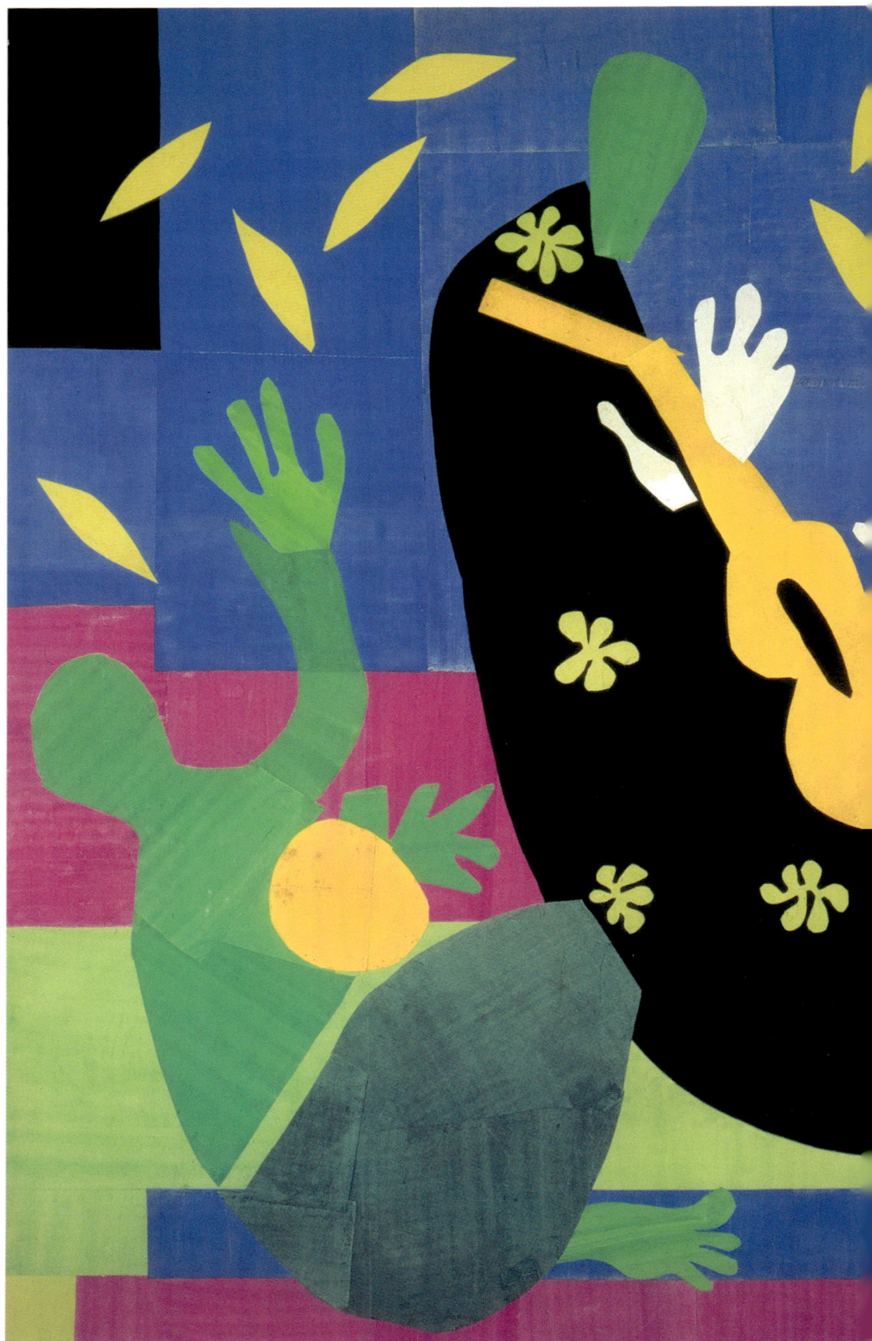

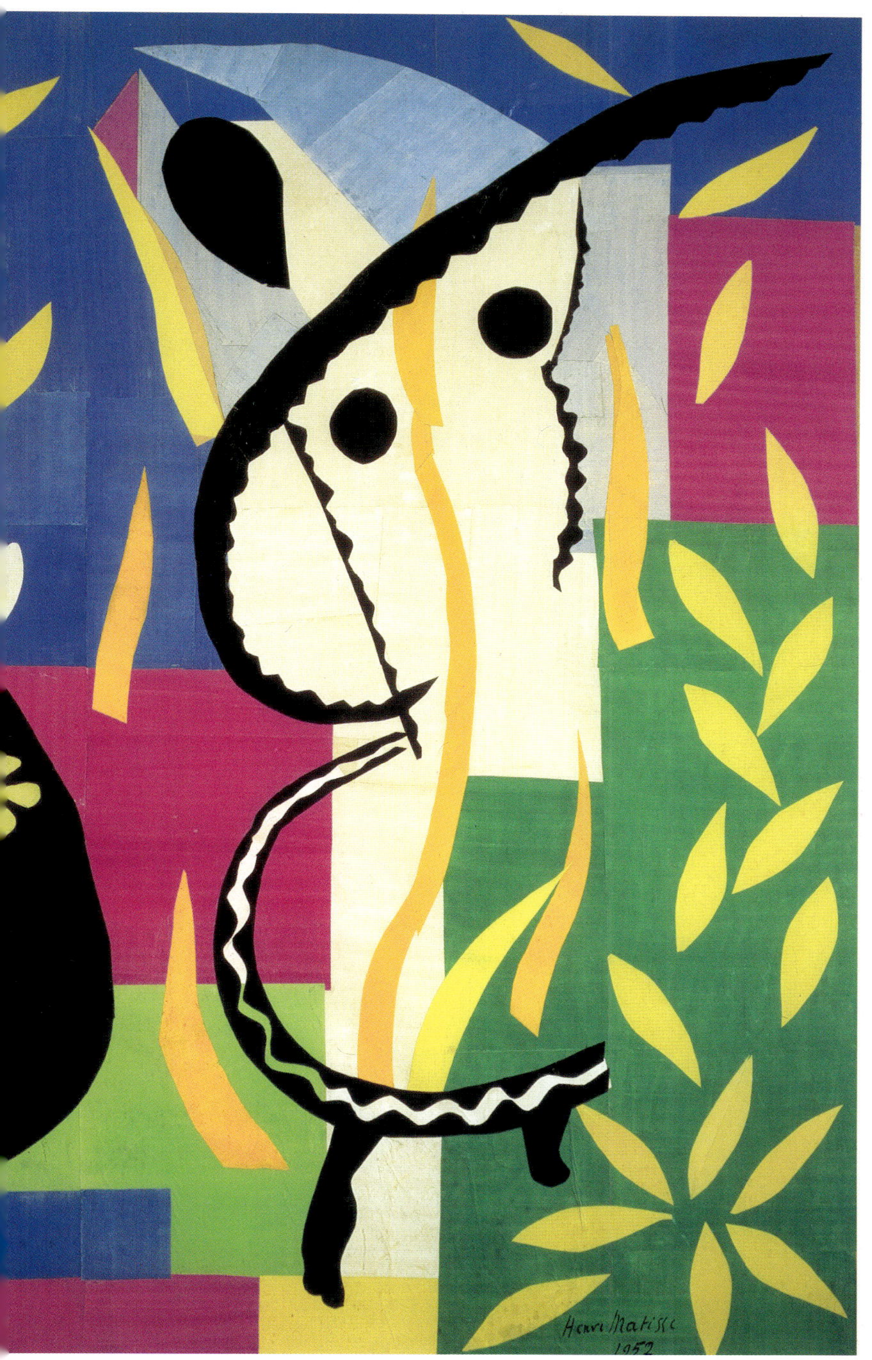
Henri Matisse
1952

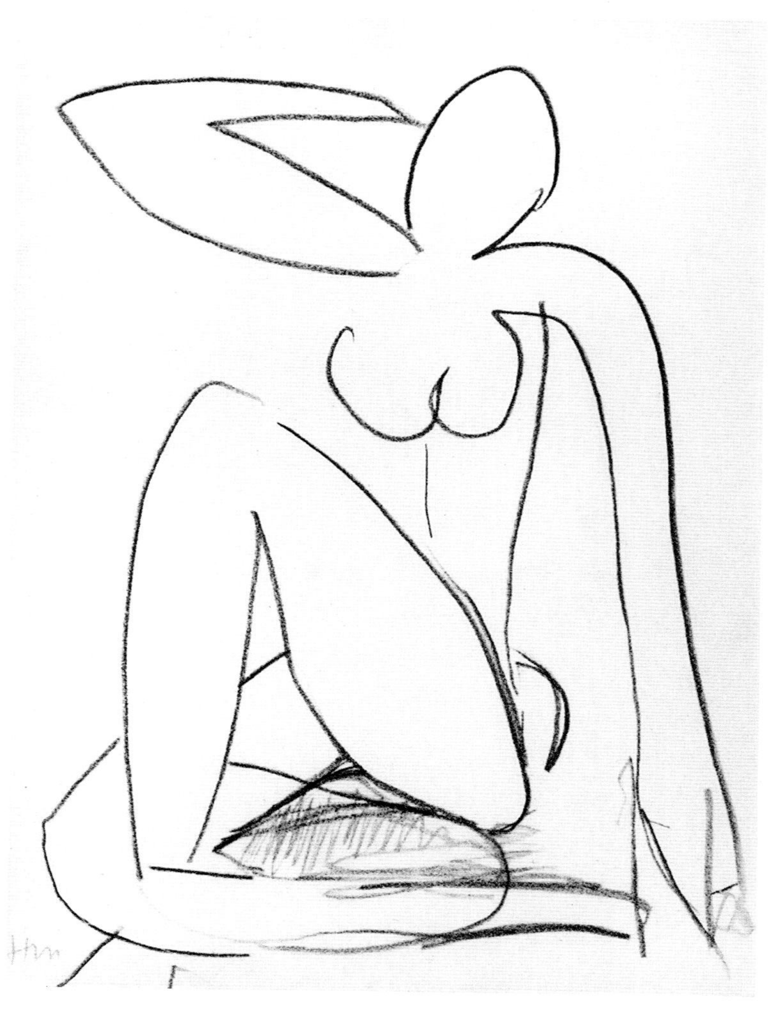

Sketch for the "Blue Nude" series • c. 1952

Whereabouts unknown

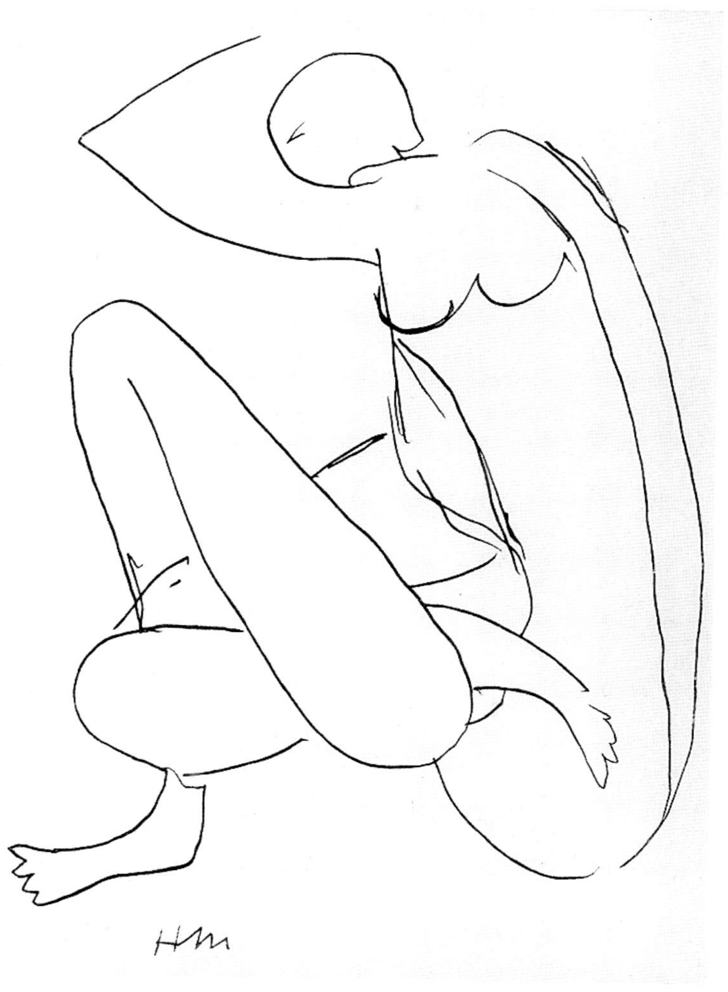

Sketch for the "Blue Nude" series • c. 1952

Whereabouts unknown

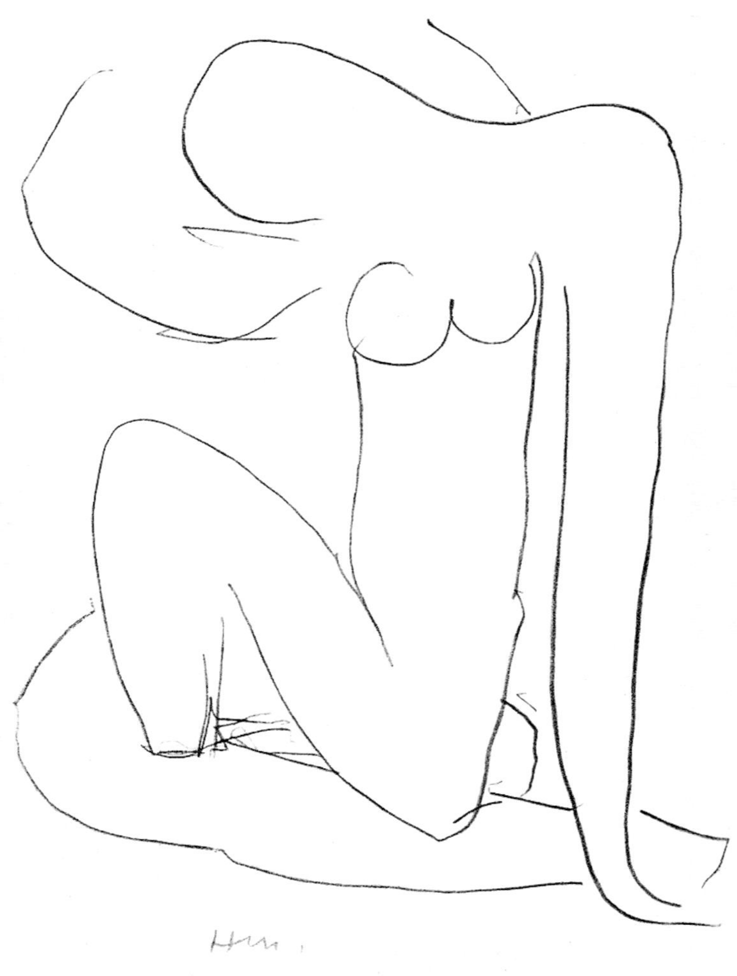

Sketch for the "Blue Nude" series · c. 1952
Whereabouts unknown

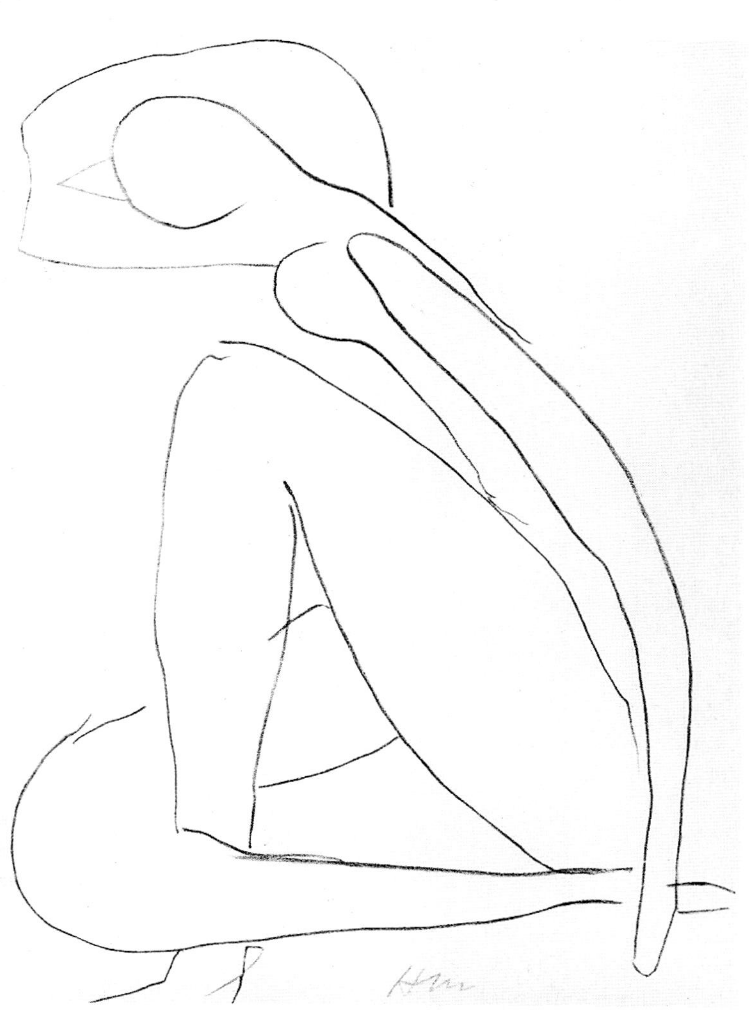

Sketch for the "Blue Nude" series · c. 1952
Whereabouts unknown

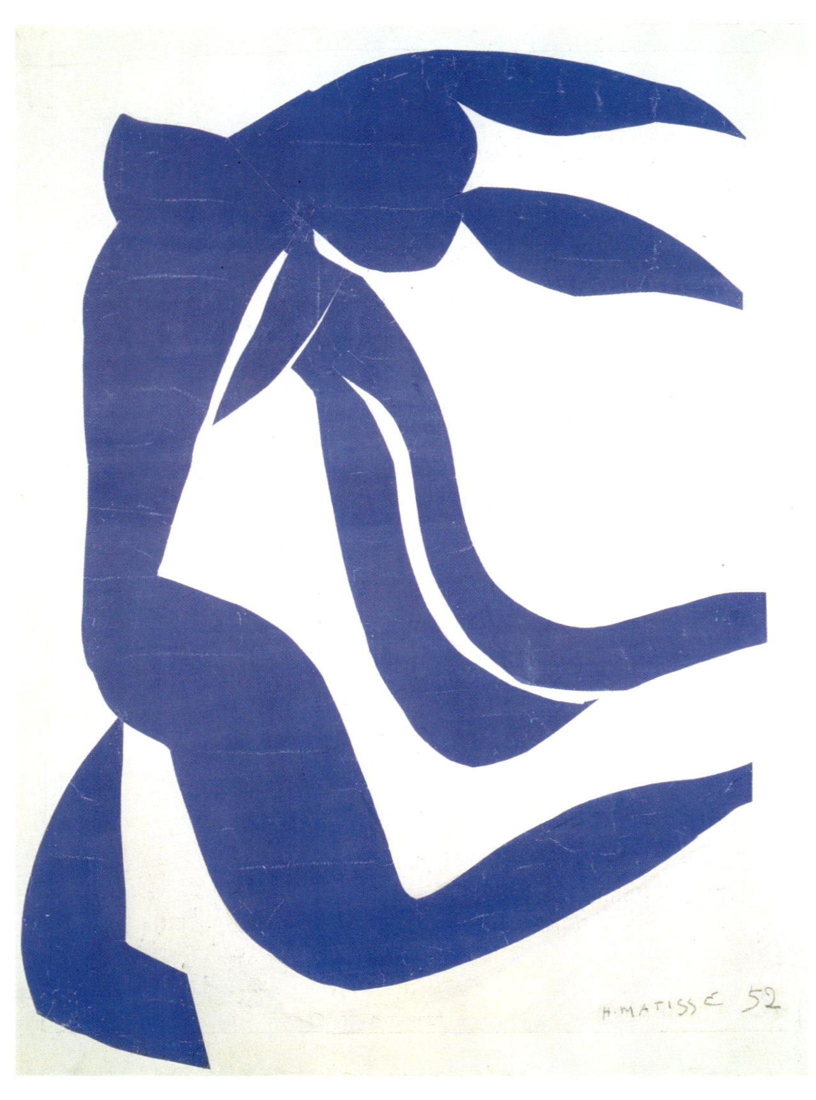

The Flowing Hair • 1952

Private collection

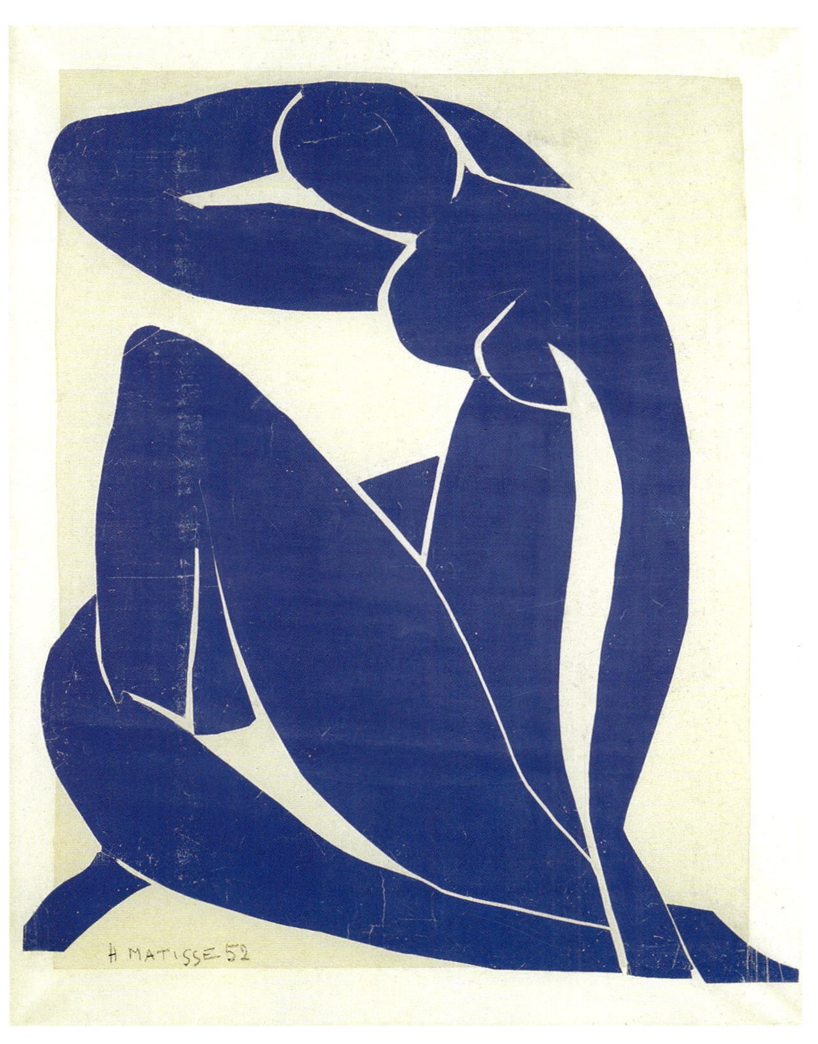

Blue Nude II • 1952
Musée national d'art moderne, Paris

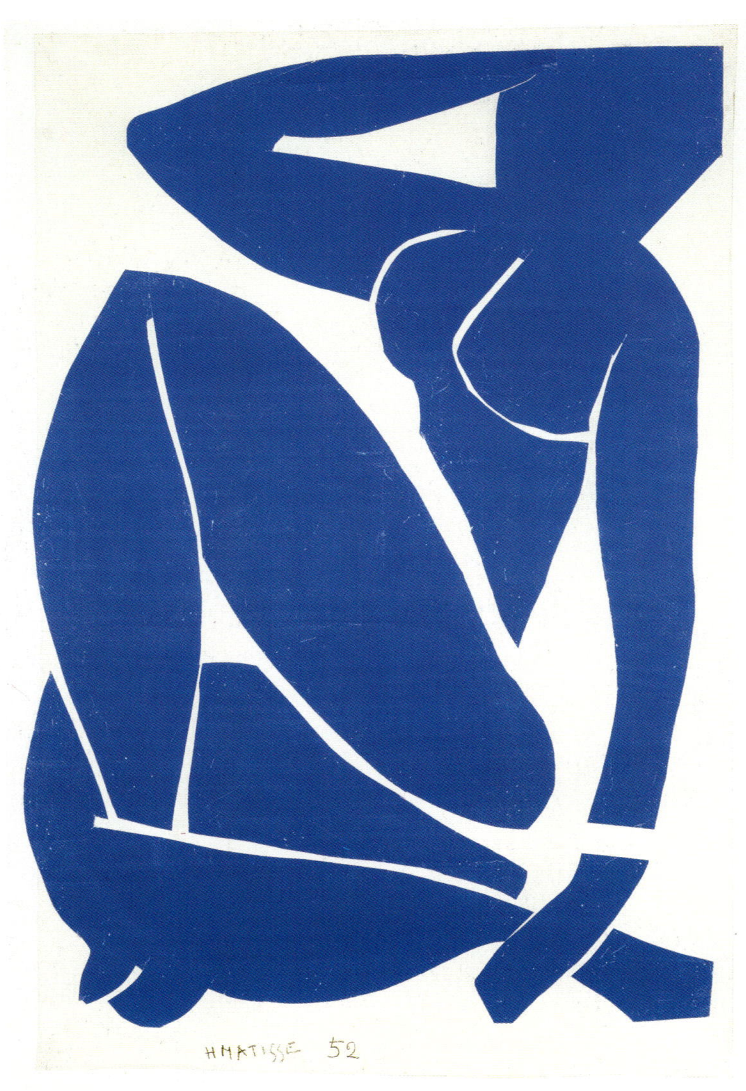

Blue Nude III • 1952
Musée national d'art moderne, Paris

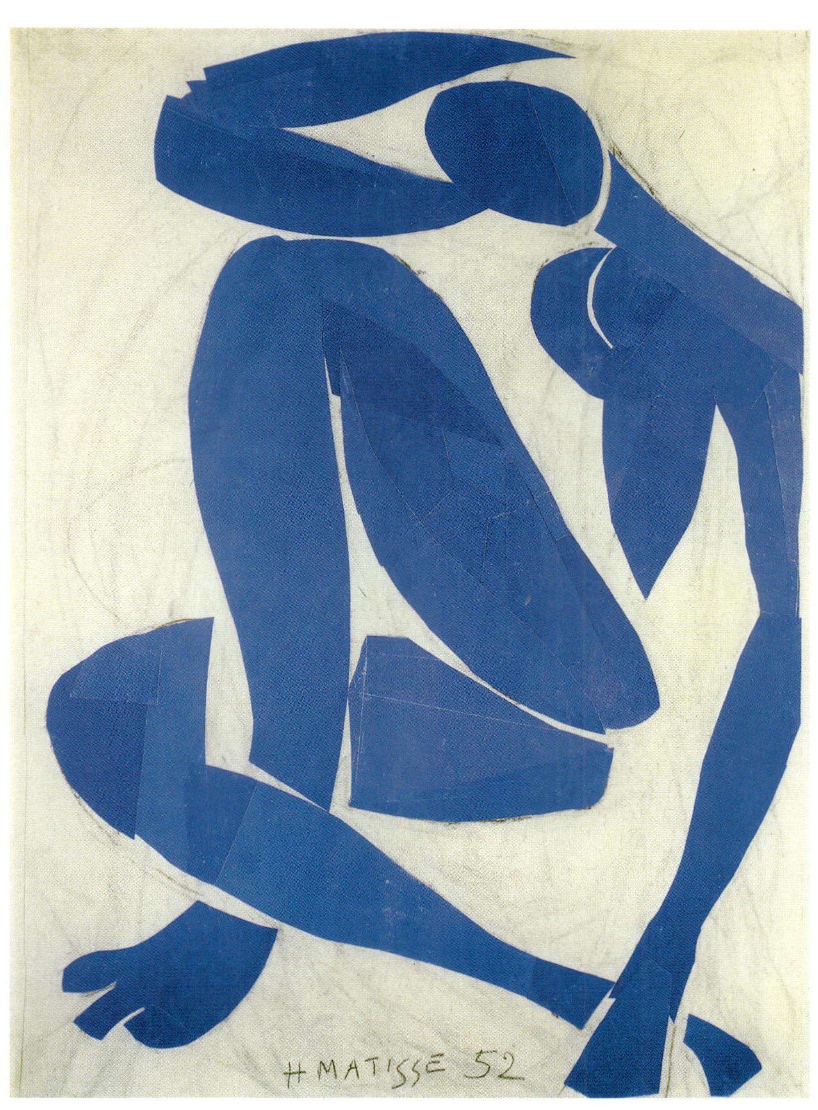

Blue Nude IV · 1952

Musée Matisse, Nice

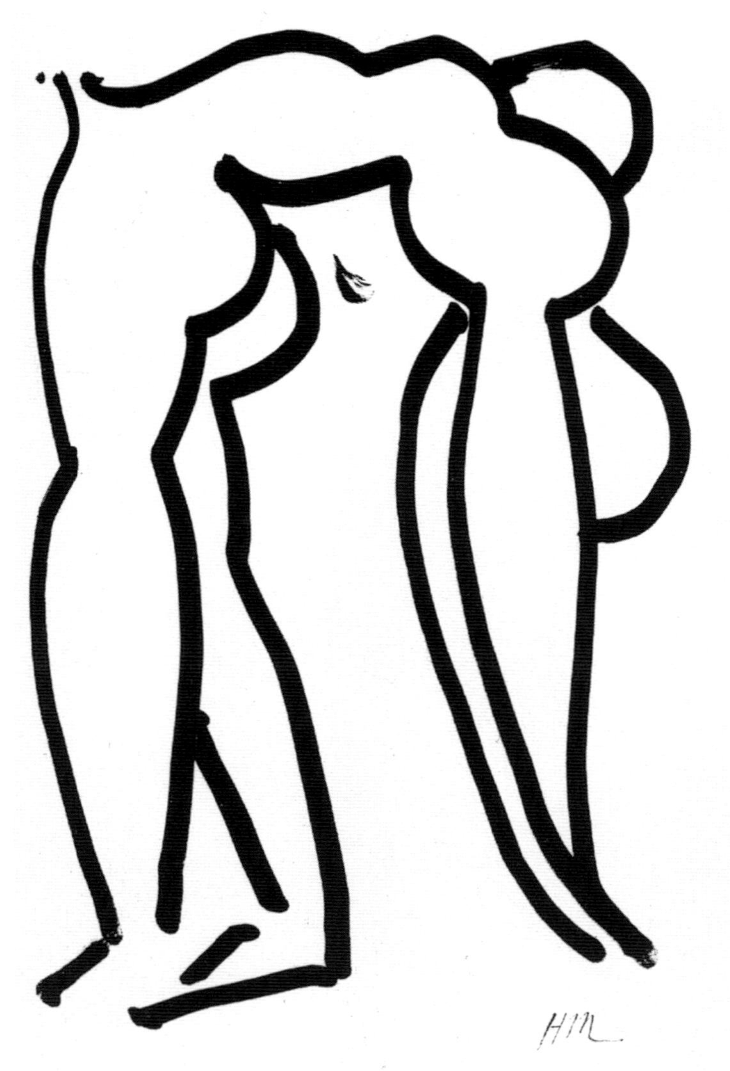

Acrobat • 1952
Musée national d'art moderne, Paris

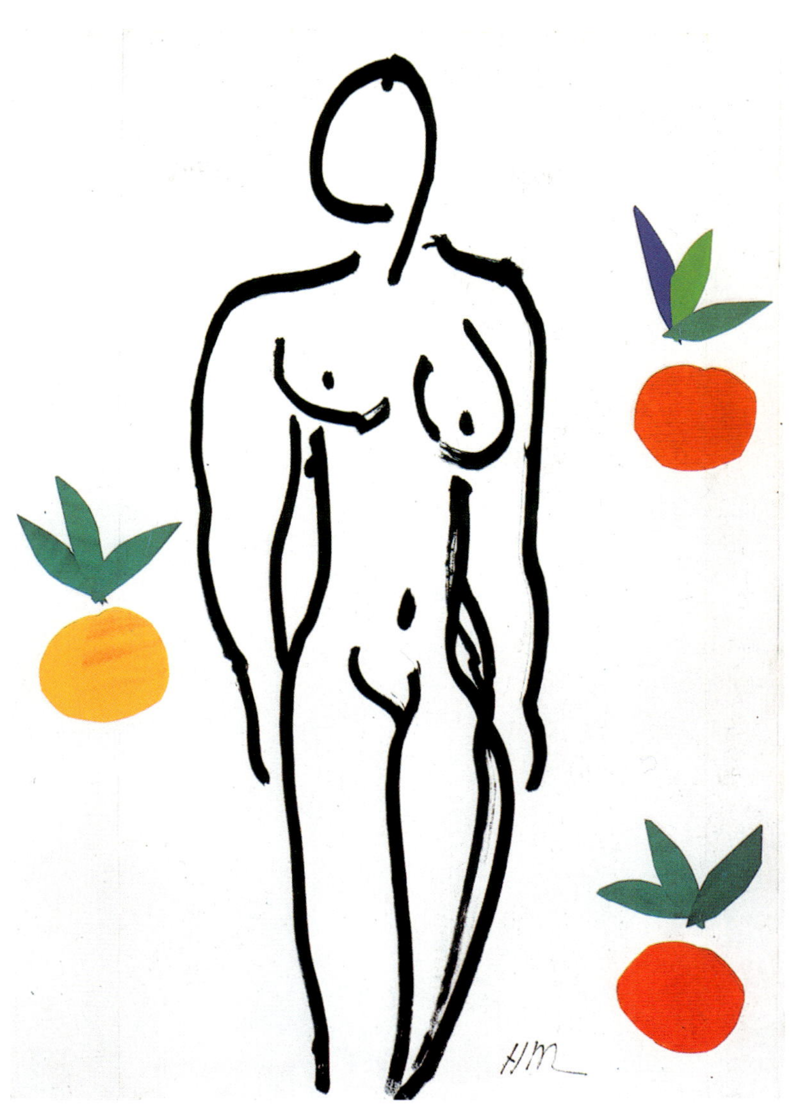

Nude with Oranges • 1952–1953
Musée national d'art moderne, Paris

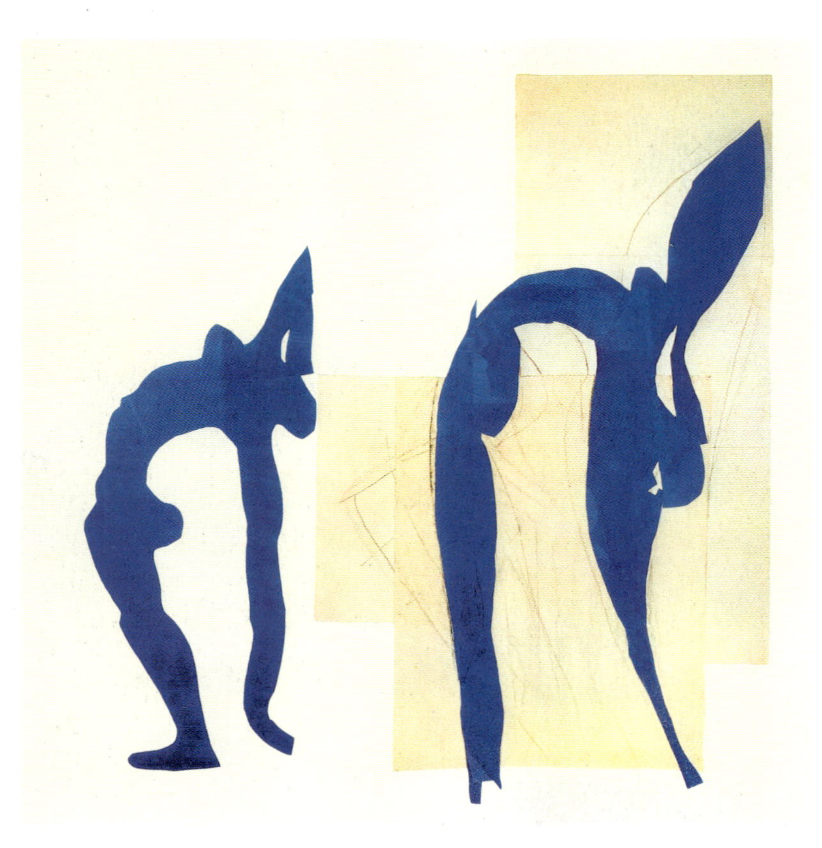

Acrobats • 1952
Private collection

The Sails · 1952
Private collection

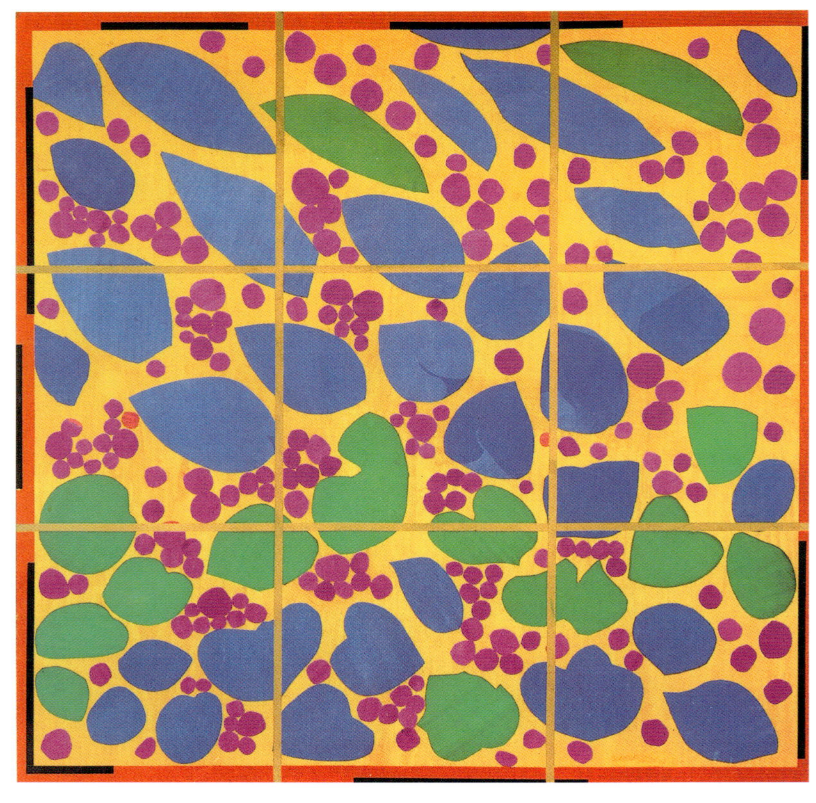

Ivy in Flower • 1953
Dallas Museum of Art, Foundation for the Arts Collection,
gift of the Albert and Mary Lasker Foundation

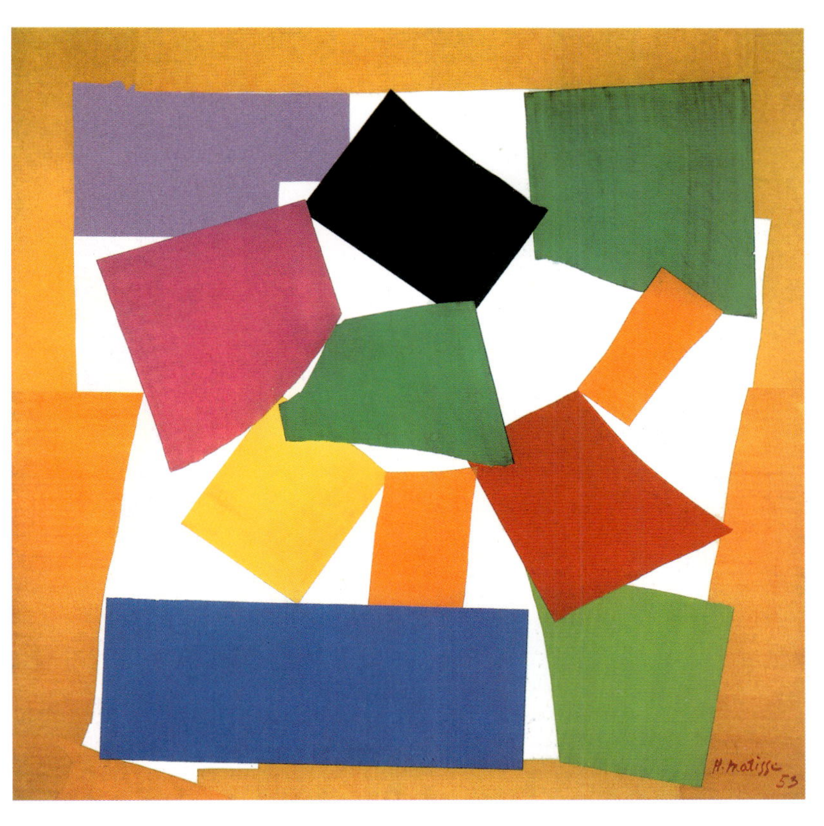

The Snail • 1953

Tate Gallery, London

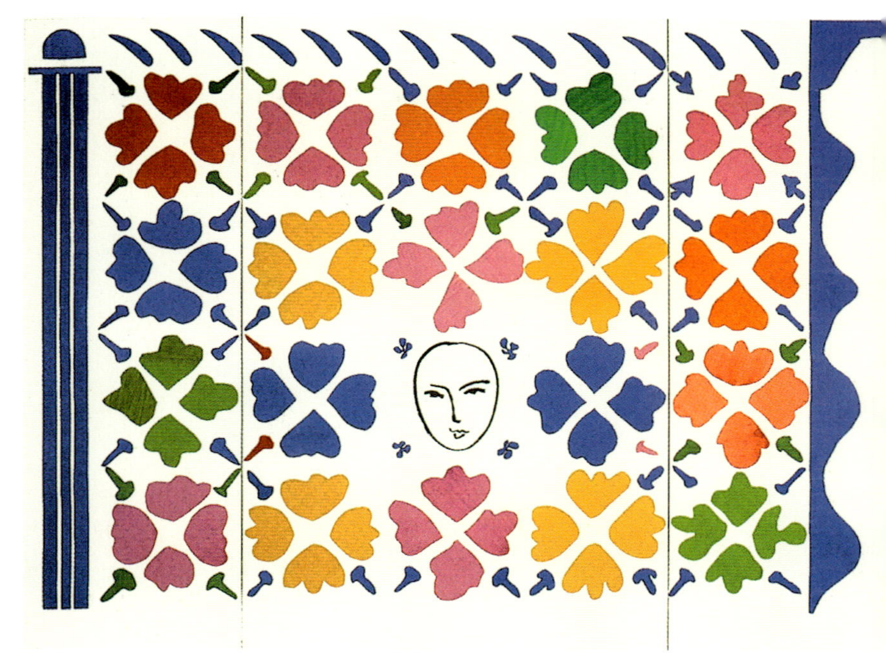

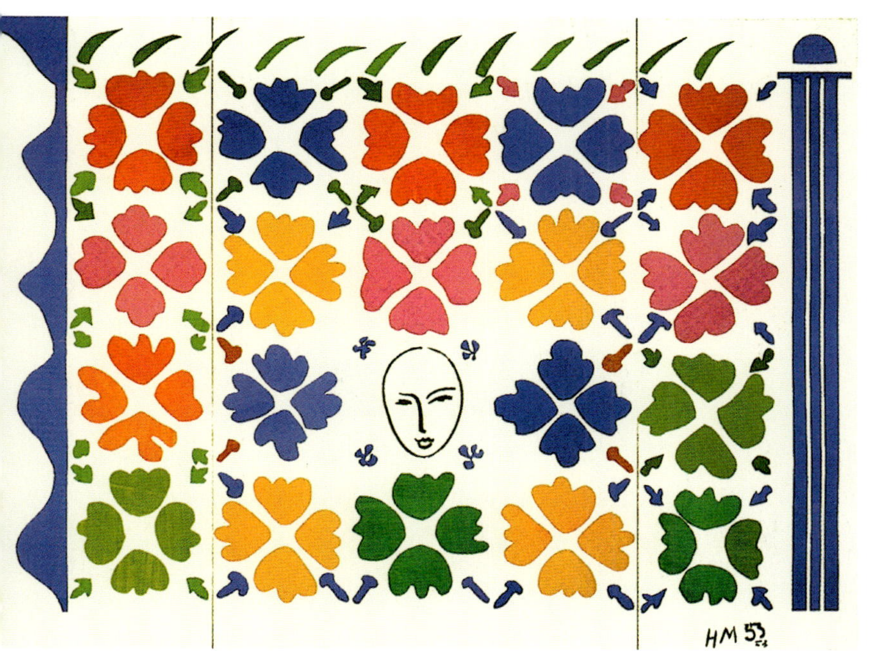

Large Decoration with Masks • 1953
National Gallery of Art, Washington, Ailsa Mellon Bruce Fund

Biographical Chronology

1869 Henri Emile Benoît Matisse is born on 31 December 1869 at Le Cateau-Cambrésis (in the Nord region of France). **1882–1889** Destined to follow in his father's footsteps running the family grain business, Henri attends the lycée in Saint-Quentin and then goes on to study law in Paris. In 1889, he is taken on as a solicitor's clerk in the Duconseil legal practice in Saint-Quentin. **1890** He is confined to bed for a year with appendicitis. His mother gives him a box of paints. He makes his first copies of paintings. He then wants to devote more of his time to painting and, when recovered, attends drawing lessons at the Ecole Quentin-de-La-Tour while continuing to work as a clerk. **1891–1895** His father reluctantly agrees to Henri following his new vocation and studying at the Académie Julian in Paris, where Bouguereau and Ferrier are among the staff. In 1892, he meets Gustave Moreau, who gives him access to his studio, where he meets Albert Marquet, Georges Rouault, and, a little later, Charles Camoin and Henri Manguin. In 1894, his daughter Marguerite is born. (He does not marry her mother Caroline Joblaud.) In 1895, he travels to Brittany, then moves into premises at 19, quai Saint-Michel, Paris. **1896** He successfully exhibits at the Salon de la Société Nationale des Beaux-Arts, of which is he an associate member: *Woman Reading* is bought by the State. During his second stay in Brittany, he meets the Australian collector, John Russel, a friend of van Gogh and Monet. **1897** *La Desserte* exhibited at the Salon de la Société Nationale is badly received. Russel introduces him to Auguste Rodin, a source of inspiration in his first sculptures, and to Camille Pissarro, who encourages him to study Impressionist painting. **1898** He marries Amélie-Noémie-Alexandrine Parayre, who bears him two sons, Jean and Pierre. The newlyweds spend their honeymoon in London, where Matisse discovers Turner. He then travels to Toulouse and Corsica, and experiences the Mediterranean for the first time. **1899** Deaths of Stéphane Mallarmé and Gustave Moreau. The Nabis exhibit at the Durand-Ruel gallery. Together with Marquet, Matisse paints pictures based on this style. He purchases Cézanne's painting *Three Bathers*, a Rodin plaster bust and a Gauguin painting from Ambrose Ambrose Vollard. **1900** Matisse experiences serious financial difficulties. He is forced to work with Marquet, painting decorations for the Grand Palais at the Exposition Universelle de Paris; his wife opens a fashion shop. Birth of his son, Pierre. **1901–1902** In 1901, he exhibits for the first time at the Salon des Indépendants. At the Van Gogh retrospective at the Bernheim-Jeune gallery, Derain introduces him to Vlaminck. The following year, he exhibits at the Berthe Weil gallery. **1903** Foundation of the Salon d'Automne, where he exhibits with Rouault and Derain. Gauguin dies this year and is entitled to a retrospective. Matisse makes his first etchings. **1904** A year of critical experiences. After having exhibited at the Vollard gallery in June (first one-man exhibition), Matisse spends the summer in Saint-Tropez close to Signac and Cross. He experiments with the Divisionist technique of the Neo-Impressionists. **1905** Signac buys *Luxury, Serenity and Pleasure* when it is exhibited at the Salon des Indépendants. The scandal of Les Fauves explodes at the Salon d'Automne. *The Woman with the Hat*, the standard-bearer of Les Fauves, is bought by Michael and Sarah Stein. **1906** In the year of Cézanne's death, *The Joy of Life* is exhibited at the Salon des Indépendants. Matisse visits Algeria. He becomes interested in African art and makes his first lithographs and woodcuts. **1907** He exchanges paintings with Picasso, who is working on *Les Demoiselles d'Avignon*. *Le Luxe I* is exhibited at the Salon d'Automne. He leaves for Italy, where he visits Padua, Florence, Arezzo, and Siena. **1908** In his studio in the rue de Sèvres, Paris, Matisse opens an academy, attended primarily by Americans, Germans, and Scandinavians. He exhibits in New York, Moscow, and Berlin. He paints *Harmony in Red / La Desserte*. In *La Grande Revue*, he publishes his *Notes d'un peintre*, critical to understanding his work. **1909** He moves to Issy-les-Moulineaux, where he has bought a house. Shchukin, the Moscow industrialist, commissions *Dance* and *Music* from Matisse. **1910** A retrospective exhibition is devoted to him at the Bernheim-Jeune gallery. Together with Marquet, he visits the Islamic art exhibition in Munich. He spends the winter in Andalusia, Spain. **1911–1912** He goes to Moscow to install *Dance* and *Music* and studies icons there. Together with Marquet and Camoin, he makes several trips to Tangier, Morocco. **1913** Bernheim-Jeune organizes an exhibition of his Moroccan paintings. Matisse exhibits in the Berlin Secession and the Armory Show in New York, Chicago, and Boston. **1914** The works exhibited in Berlin are seized. He meets Juan Gris, a refugee at Collioure, and helps him financially. He again takes a studio at 19, quai Saint-Michel, Paris. He paints *Notre-Dame* and *French Window at Collioure*. **1916** He exhibits in London and spends his first winter in Nice, where he will stay regularly from 1918. **1918** He meets Renoir at Cagnes and exhibits with Picasso at the Paul Guillaume gallery. Death of Apollinaire. **1919** He paints *The Black Table*. **1920** He designs the scenery and costumes of *Chant du Rossignol* for Diaghilev's Ballets Russes. He spends the summer in London, then at Etretat, Normandy, where he paints the cliffs. **1921** He divides his time between Etretat, Paris, and Nice. **1922** He paints the *Odalisque* series. **1924** Exhibition in New York, retrospective in Copenhagen. **1925** Travels in Italy. The *Decorative Figure on an Ornamental Ground* marks the start of a fresh study of monumental style and ornamental order. **1927** He receives the Carnegie Prize in Pittsburgh and exhibits in New York in a show organized by his son Pierre. **1930** Matisse travels to Tahiti via New York and San Francisco. In the autumn he returns to the United States, where he has been asked to sit on the panel of the Carnegie Prize in Pittsburgh. He then goes to Merion, Pennsylvania, where Dr. Barnes commissions a mural on the theme of *Dance*, a subject he had already tackled for Shchukin in 1910. For Albert Skira he makes etchings of the illustrations of Mallarmé's *Poèmes* (29 etchings in all). **1932–1933** He completes the second version of *Dance* and returns to Merion to install it. **1934–1935** Lydia Delektorskaya, his assistant, poses for the *The Large Reclining Nude / The Pink Nude*, of which he will go on to make twenty-two versions. **1937** He designs the scenery and costumes for *Scarlet and Black*, choreographed by the Monte Carlo Ballets Russes in 1939. He is given his own salon at "Les maîtres de l'art indépendant," an exhibition at the Petit Palais. Picasso paints Guernica. **1938** Moves to the Hôtel Régina in the Cimiez suburb of Nice. "Matisse-Picasso-Braque" exhibitions are held in Oslo, Copenhagen, and Stockholm. **1940** He decides to stay in France and separates from Amélie after forty years together. He paints *Rumanian Blouse* and *Dream*. **1941** Operated on for a serious intestinal complaint at Professor Leriche's clinic in Lyons. Illustrates Ronsard's *Florilège des Amours* and Montherlant's *Pasiphaé*. **1943** He moves to Vence, to the villa "Le Rêve," where he lives until 1948. **1944** He begins his series of paper cutouts that will form the illustrations for *Jazz*, published by Tériade in 1947. He works on illustrating Baudelaire's *Fleurs du mal*. Amélie is imprisoned and Marguerite deported for having been involved in the Resistance. **1945** Retrospective of his work at the Salon d'Automne. He exhibits with Picasso at the Victoria and Albert Museum in London. At the Maeght gallery, he exhibits his recent canvases with photographs of their interim stages. **1947** He is made commander of the Légion d'honneur. Deaths of Bonnard and Marquet. **1948** He devotes himself to decorating the Rosaire chapel in Vence. **1950** He receives the first prize for painting at the 25th Venice Biennale. **1951** The Rosaire chapel in Vence is consecrated. Exhibitions at the Museum of Modern Art in New York, Cleveland, Chicago, San Francisco, and Tokyo. **1952** Opening of a Matisse museum at Le Cateau-Cambrésis, his birthplace. He paints the series of *Blue Nudes*, his final, supreme homage to womankind. **1954** Matisse dies on 3 November in Nice and is laid to rest at Cimiez cemetery in a plot given by the City of Nice.

Bibliography

Marcel Sembat. "Henri Matisse" in *Les peintres français nouveaux*, Editions de la Nouvelle Revue Française, Paris, 1920. **Roger Fry.** *Henri Matisse*, E. Weyhe, New York, [1930]. **Albert C. Barnes & Violette de Mazia.** *The Art of Henri Matisse*, Scribners, New York & London, 1933. **Raymond Escholier.** *Henri Matisse*, Floury, Paris, 1937. **Pierre Courthion.** *Le visage de Matisse*, Jean Marguerat, Lausanne, 1942. **Alfred Barr.** *Matisse: His Art and His Public*, Museum of Modern Art, New York, 1951. **Louis Aragon.** *Henri Matisse: A Novel*, Harcourt Brace Jovanovich, New York, 1972. **Lawrence Gowing.** *Matisse*, Oxford University Press, New York & Toronto, 1979. **Luzi & Massimo Carrà.** *Tout l'œuvre peint de Matisse*, Flammarion, Paris, 1982. **Pierre Schneider.** *Matisse*, Rizzoli, New York, 1984. **Nicolas Watkins.** *Matisse*, Oxford University Press, New York, 1985. **Mario Jack D. Flam.** *Matisse: The Man and His Art 1869–1918*, Cornell University Press, Ithaca & London, 1986. **Isabelle Monod-Fontaine.** *Matisse: catalogue des œuvres de Henri Matisse (1869–1954)*, Centre Georges Pompidou, Paris, 1989. **John Elderfield.** *Henri Matisse. A Retrospective*, The Museum of Modern Art, New York, 1992. **John Klein.** *Matisse Portraits*, Yale University Press, New Haven & London, 2001.

Index of Works

mitage, Saint Petersburg. **Boy with a Butterfly Net (Allan Stein) 74,** 1907, oil on canvas, 177.2x115.1cm, The Minneapolis Institute of Arts, Ethel Morrison Van Derlip Fund. **Branch of Lilacs 143,** 1914, oil on canvas, 145x97cm, private collection. **The Breakfast 207,** late 1919–Spring 1920, oil on canvas, 64x74cm, Philadelphia Museum of Art, The Samuel S. White III and Vera White Collection. **Calla Lilies, Irises, and Mimosas 138,** early 1913, oil on canvas, 145.5x97cm, Pushkin Museum, Moscow. **Calypso 266,** 1934, soft-ground etching, 28.4x22.5cm, private collection. **Carmelina 38,** c.1903–1904, oil on canvas, 81.3x59cm, Museum of Fine Arts, Boston, Tompkins Collection. **The Casbah Gate 126,** 1912–1913, oil on canvas, 116x80cm, Pushkin Museum, Moscow. **The Circus (plate II from "Jazz") 346,** 1947, 42.5x65.5cm, Musée national d'art moderne, Paris. **Clearing in the Woods of Fontainebleau 91,** 1909, oil on canvas, 60x73.5cm, private collection. **The Clown (plate I and title page, from "Jazz," published in 1947 by E. Tériade [Paris] in an edition of 280 copies) 345,** 1947, 42.5x65.5cm, private collection. **The Codomas (plate XI from "Jazz") 356,** 1947, 42.5x65.5cm, Musée national d'art moderne, Paris. **La Coiffure 70,** 1907, oil on canvas, 116x89cm, Staatsgalerie, Stuttgart. **Collioure 44,** 1905, reed pen, black ink, 25x19cm, private collection. **Composition 342,** 1947, mixed media on canvas, 60x238cm, Kunstmuseum, Basel. **Composition 392,** 1951, gouache on paper, cut and pasted, on paper, 80x50cm, private collection. **Composition with a Standing Nude and Black Fern 371,** 1948, brush and ink on paper, 105x75cm, Musée national d'art moderne, Paris. **Compotier with Nutcracker 165,** 1916, oil on canvas, 61x49.5cm, Statens Museum for Kunst, Copenhagen. **The Conservatory 293,** November 1937–May 1938, oil on canvas, 71.8x59.7cm, private collection. **Conversation 130,** 1908–1912, oil on canvas, 177x217cm, Hermitage, Saint Petersburg. **The Courtyard of the Mill 23,** 1898, oil on canvas, 38x46cm, Musée Matisse, Nice. **Cover for "Verve" (6, nos. 21–22) 384,** 1948, 35.5x26.5cm, private collection. **The Cowboy (plate XIV from "Jazz") 359,** 1947, 42.5x65.5cm, Musée national d'art moderne, Paris. **Creole Dancer 387,** 1950, gouache on paper, cut and pasted, and crayon, 205x120cm, Musée Matisse, Nice. **Crouching Nude 280,** 1936, charcoal on paper, 50.6x66cm, whereabouts unknown. **Daisies 303,** July 1939, oil on canvas, 98x71.8cm, The Art Institute of Chicago, gift of Helen Pauling Donelly in memory of her parents, Mary Fredericka and Edward George Pauling. **The Dance (II) 96,** 1909–1910, oil on canvas, 260x391cm, Hermitage, Saint Petersburg. **The Dance 254,** 1931, oil on canvas, 398x344cm; 498x358cm; 398x344cm, Musée national d'art moderne, Paris. **The Dance 258,** 1932–1933, oil on canvas, 339.7x441.3cm; 355.9x503.2cm; 338x439.4cm, The Barnes Foundation, Merion, Pennsylvania. **The Dance (first version) 258,** 1931–1933, oil on canvas, 340x387cm; 355x498cm; 335x391cm, Musée d'art moderne de la Ville de Paris. **Dance Movement 370,** 1949, pen, brush, and ink on paper, 56.5x38cm, private collection. **Dancer 252,** 1930, pencil on paper, 38x28cm, private collection. **Dancer and Rocaille Armchair on a Black Background 326,** September 1942, oil on canvas, 50.8x64.8cm, private collection. **Dancer in Repose 298,** 1939, charcoal and estompe on paper, 65.5x50.5cm, Musée national d'art moderne, Paris. **Dancer in Repose 327,** August 1942, oil on canvas, 46x38cm, private collection. **Decorative Figure 86,** 1908, bronze, 72.1x51.4x31.1cm, Collection of Patsy R. and Raymond Nasher, Dallas. **Decorative Figure on an**

49.4cm, National Gallery of Art, Washington, Chester Dale Collection. **Life Study 37,** c.1903, pencil on paper, 29.5x23.5cm, private collection. **Le Luxe (I) 67,** Summer 1907, oil on canvas, 210x138cm, Musée national d'art moderne, Paris. **Le Luxe (II) 68,** Summer 1907–1908, casein on canvas, 209.5x138cm, Statens Museum for Kunst, Copenhagen. **Luxe, calme et volupté 42,** 1904–1905, oil on canvas, 98.5x118cm, Musée d'Orsay, Paris. **The Luxembourg Gardens 34,** c.1902, oil on canvas, 59.5x81.5cm, Hermitage, Saint Petersburg. **Male Model 28,** c.1900, oil on canvas, 99.3x72.7cm, The Museum of Modern Art, New York, Kay Sage Tanguy and Abby Aldrich Rockefeller Funds. **The Manila Shawl 120,** 1911, oil on canvas, 118x75.5cm, Rudolf Staechelin Family Foundation, Basel. **Marguerite 65,** 1906, oil on wooden panel, 71.1x53.3cm, private collection. **Marguerite 104,** 1907, oil on canvas, 65x54cm, Musée Picasso, Paris. **Marguerite 153,** 1915, crayon on paper, 22x 17.2cm, private collection. **Marguerite Reading 59,** Summer 1906, oil on canvas, 65x 81cm, Musée de Grenoble. **Marguerite with Hat with Roses 144,** 1914, oil on canvas, 112x 49cm, private collection. **The Mauresque 250,** 1929, oil on canvas, 92x65cm, private collection. **Meditation / After the Bath 204,** late 1920–Spring 1921, oil on canvas, 73x34cm, private collection. **Melchers 145,** 1914, charcoal on paper, 28x21.7cm, Musée Matisse, Nice. **Mme Matisse in a Japanese Robe 30,** c.1901, oil on canvas, 116.8x80cm, private collection. **Monsieur Loyal (plate III from "Jazz") 348,** 1947, 42.5x65.5cm, Musée national d'art moderne, Paris. **The Moorish Screen 210,** late 1921, oil on canvas, 90.8x74.3cm, Philadelphia Museum of Art, bequest of Lisa Norris Elkins. **Mosquitos (Study for a vignette in "Florilège des Amours de Ronsard," 1948) 329,** c.1943, pen and ink on paper, 29x38cm, private collection. **Mountains, Collioure 46,** 1905, watercolor, 20.6x26.2cm, private collection. **Music 94,** 1909–1910, oil on canvas, 260x389cm, Hermitage, Saint Petersburg. **Music 297,** 1939, oil on canvas, 115.2x115.2cm, Albright-Knox Art Gallery, Buffalo, New York. **The Music Lesson 182,** 1917, oil on canvas, 244.7x200.7cm, The Barnes Foundation, Merion, Pennsylvania. **My Room at the Beau-Rivage 175,** 1917–1918, oil on canvas, 73x61cm, Philadelphia Museum of Art, A.E.Gallatin Collection. **Nasturtiums with "Dance" (II) 129,** 1912, oil on canvas, 190.5x114cm, Pushkin Museum, Moscow. **The Night 219,** 1922, lithograph, 25.5x29.3cm, private collection. **The Nightmare of the White Elephant (plate IV from "Jazz") 349,** 1947, 42.5x65.5cm, Musée national d'art moderne, Paris. **Notre-Dame in the Late Afternoon 35,** 1902, oil on paper, mounted on canvas, 72.5x 54.5cm, Albright-Knox Art Gallery, Buffalo, New York, gift of Seymour H. Knox. **Nude beside a Fireplace 283,** 1936, oil on canvas, 46.3x38.2cm, private collection. **Nude with a Blue Cushion beside a Fireplace 232,** 1925, lithograph, 63.6x47.8cm, Bibliothèque nationale, Paris. **Nude with a White Scarf 103,** 1909, oil on canvas, 116.5x89cm, Statens Museum for Kunst, Copenhagen. **Nude with a White Towel 31,** 1902–1903, oil on canvas, 81x59.5cm, private collection. **Nude with Oranges 407,** 1952–1953, gouache on paper, cut and pasted, and brush and ink on white paper, 154.2x107.1cm, Musée national d'art moderne, Paris. **Nude, Black and Gold 83,** 1908, oil on canvas, 100x65 cm, Hermitage, Saint Petersburg. **Nymph and Faun, "Poésies de Mallarmé" (1932) 263,** Summer 1931–Autumn 1932, etching, 33x25cm, private collection. **Nymph and Satyr 81,** 1908–1909, oil on canvas, 89x117cm, Hermitage, Saint Petersburg. **Nymphs**

and Faun, "Poésies de Mallarmé" (1932) 262, Summer 1931–Autumn 1932, etching, 33 x 25 cm, private collection. **Oceania, the Sea 342,** 1946, gouache on paper, cut and pasted on paper mounted on canvas, 166 x 380 cm, National Gallery of Art, Washington, gift of Mr. and Mrs. Burton Tremaine. **Oceania, the Sky 343,** 1946, gouache on paper, cut and pasted on paper, mounted on canvas, 178.3 x 369.7 cm, Musée Matisse, Le Cateau-Cambrésis. **The Ochre Head 291,** February 1937, oil on canvas, 12.7 x 54 cm, private collection. **Odalisque or The White Slave 237,** date unknown, oil on canvas, 82 x 54 cm, Musée de l'Orangerie, Paris. **Odalisque with a Tambourine 223,** 1923, pencil on paper, 30 x 26 cm, private collection. **Odalisque with a Tambourine 238,** 1926, oil on canvas, 74.3 x 55.7 cm, The Museum of Modern Art, New York, The William S. Paley Collection. **Odalisque with a Turkish Chair 241,** late 1927–Summer 1928, oil on canvas, 60 x 73 cm, Musée d'art moderne de la Ville de Paris. **Odalisque with Gray Culottes 239,** late 1926–Spring 1927, oil on canvas, 54 x 65 cm, Musée de l'Orangerie, Paris. **Odalisque with Magnolias 222,** 1923 or 1924, oil on canvas, 65 x 81 cm, private collection. **Odalisque with Red Culottes 214,** Autumn 1921, oil on canvas, 65 x 90 cm, Musée national d'art moderne, Paris. **Odalisque with Red Culottes 224,** date unknown, oil on canvas, 50 x 61 cm, Musée de l'Orangerie, Paris. **Odalisque with Turkish Trousers 208,** 1920–1921, pen and ink on paper, 28 x 29 cm, Musée national d'art moderne, Paris. **The Olive Tree 22,** 1898, oil on canvas, 38 x 46 cm, private collection. **The Ostrich Feather Hat 187,** Autumn 1918, oil on canvas, 46 x 38 cm, Wadsworth Atheneum, Hartford, The Ella Gallup Sumner and Mary Catlin Sumner Collection. **The Painter and His Model / Studio Interior 193,** late 1918–Spring 1919 or late 1920–Spring 1921, oil on canvas, 60 x 73 cm, private collection. **The Painter in His Studio 162,** 1916, oil on canvas, 146.5 x 97 cm, Musée national d'art moderne, Paris. **The Painter's Family 118,** Spring 1911, oil on canvas, 143 x 194 cm, Hermitage, Saint Petersburg. **The Painting Session 190,** 1918–1919, oil on canvas, 74 x 93 cm, Scottish National Gallery of Modern Art, Edinburgh. **Pastoral 57,** Summer 1906, oil on canvas, 46 x 55 cm, Musée d'art moderne de la Ville de Paris. **The Pewter Jug 176,** c. 1917, oil on canvas, 92.1 x 65.1 cm, The Baltimore Museum of Art, The Cone Collection. **Pianist and Checker Players 228,** early 1924, oil on canvas, 73.7 x 92.1 cm, National Gallery of Art, Washington, Collection of Mr. and Mrs. Mellon. **The Piano Lesson 171,** Summer 1916, oil on canvas, 245.1 x 212.7 cm, The Museum of Modern Art, New York, Mrs. Simon Guggenheim Fund. **Pierre Matisse 105,** 1909, oil on canvas, 40.6 x 33 cm, private collection. **Pierrot's Funeral (plate X from "Jazz") 355,** 1947, 42.5 x 65.5 cm, Musée national d'art moderne, Paris. **The Pineapple 377,** 1948, oil on canvas, 116 x 89 cm, The Metropolitan Museum of Art, New York, The Alex Hillman Family Foundation Collection. **Pink Onions 63,** Summer 1906?, oil on canvas, 46 x 55 cm, Statens Museum for Kunst, Copenhagen. **The Pink Studio 114,** 1911, oil on canvas, 179.5 x 221 cm, Pushkin Museum, Moscow. **Plane-tree 393,** 1951, ink and white gouache on paper, 158 x 120 cm, private collection. **Plaster Figure, Bouquet of Flowers 200,** Summer 1919, oil on canvas, 113 x 87 cm, Museu de Arte, São Paulo. **Plate with Nude 76,** 1907, ceramics, diam.: 35 cm, private collection. **The Plumed Hat 196,** 1919, pencil on paper, 34.9 x 29.2 cm, private collection. **The Plumed Hat 197,** 1919, pencil on paper, 53 x 36.5 cm, The Detroit Institute of Arts, bequest of John S. Newberry.

The Plumed Hat 198, 1919, pencil on paper, 49x37cm, The Baltimore Museum of Art, The Cone Collection. **Polynesia, the Sky 336,** 1946, gouache on paper, cut and pasted, 200x314 cm, Musée national d'art moderne, Paris. **Pont Saint-Michel 25,** c.1900, oil on canvas, 58x71cm, Musée national d'art moderne, Paris. **Poppies 82,** 1908, oil on canvas, 110x 45cm, private collection. **Portrait of Auguste Pellerin (I) 160,** 1916, oil on canvas, 92.3x 78.5cm, private collection. **Portrait of Auguste Pellerin (II) 161,** 1917, oil on canvas, 150.2x96.2cm, Musée national d'art moderne, Paris. **Portrait of Baroness Gourgaud 229,** 1924, oil on canvas, 81x65cm, Musée national d'art moderne, Paris. **Portrait of Claribel Cone 264,** 1933–1934, charcoal on paper, 59x40.6cm, The Baltimore Museum of Art, The Cone Collection. **Portrait of Etta Cone 265,** 1934, charcoal on paper, 70.5x 40.6cm, The Baltimore Museum of Art, The Cone Collection. **Portrait of Greta Moll 84,** 1908, oil on canvas, 93x73.5cm, The National Gallery, London. **Portrait of Greta Prozor 163,** late 1916, oil on canvas, 146x96cm, Musée national d'art moderne, Paris. **Portrait of Hélène Galitzine 285,** 1937, oil on canvas, 55x33cm, private collection. **Portrait of Lydia Delectorskaya 368,** 1947, oil on canvas, 63.4x49.7cm, Hermitage, Saint Petersburg. **Portrait of Michael Stein 158,** Autumn 1916, oil on canvas, 67.3x50.5cm, San Francisco Museum of Modern Art, Michael and Sarah Stein Memorial Collection, gift of Nathan Cummings. **Portrait of Mlle Yvonne Landsberg 146,** 1914, oil on canvas, 147.3x97.5cm, Philadelphia Museum of Art, The Louise and Walter Arensberg Collection. **Portrait of Mme Matisse 140,** 1913, oil on canvas, 145x97cm, Hermitage, Saint Petersburg. **Portrait of Mme Matisse 152,** 1915, pencil on paper, 63x48cm, Musée Matisse, Nice. **Portrait of Mme Matisse / The Green Line 49,** 1905, oil on canvas, 40.5x32.5cm, Statens Museum for Kunst, Copenhagen. **Portrait of Olga Merson 122,** Summer 1911, oil on canvas, 100x 80.6cm, The Museum of Fine Arts, Houston. **Portrait of Sarah Stein 159,** Autumn 1916, oil on canvas, 72.4x56.5cm, San Francisco Museum of Modern Art, Michael and Sarah Stein Memorial Collection, gift of Elise S. Haas. **Reclining Laurette with a Cup of Coffee 173,** 1917, oil on canvas, 92x73cm, Kunstmuseum, Solothurn. **Reclining Nude 218,** 1922, ink, 22x31cm, private collection. **Reclining Nude 270,** 1935, charcoal on paper, 37.5x 56.5cm, private collection. **Reclining Nude 271,** 1935, pen, 26x32.3cm, private collection. **Reclining Nude 278,** 1935, pen and ink on paper, 45x56.5cm, Collection of Dina Vierny. **Reclining Nude 280,** 1936, charcoal on paper, 32.9x50.2cm, Musée Matisse, Nice. **Reclining Nude in the Studio 278,** 1935, pen and ink on paper, 45.1x56.8cm, private collection. **Reclining Nude Playing Pipes / Study for "Le bonheur de vivre" 45,** 1905–1906, pen and ink on paper, 45.8x60.4cm, private collection. **Reclining Nude Seen from the Back 244,** Summer 1927, oil on canvas, 66x92cm, private collection. **Reclining Nude with a Drape 234,** date unknown, oil on canvas, 39x61cm, Musée de l'Orangerie, Paris. **Reclining Nude with Arm behind Head 287,** 1937, charcoal and estompe on paper, 38x48.5cm, The Baltimore Museum of Art, The Cone Collection. **Red Interior / Still Life on a Blue Table 376,** 1948, oil on canvas, 116x81cm, Kunstsammlung Nordrhein-Westfalen, Düsseldorf. **The Red Jacket 181,** 1917, oil on canvas, 46.4x36.2cm, The Columbia Museum of Art, gift of Ferdinand Howald. **The Red Madras Headdress 75,** 1907, oil on canvas, 99.4x80.5cm, The Barnes Foundation, Merion, Pennsylvania. **The Red Studio 116,** Autumn 1911, oil on canvas, 181x219.1cm, The Museum of Modern Art, New York, Mrs. Simon Guggenheim Fund. **Road to Clamart 180,** 1917, oil on canvas, 33.4x46.5cm, Musée national d'art moderne, Paris. **The Rocaille Armchair 341,** 1946, oil on canvas, 92x73cm, Musée Matisse, Nice. **The Rumanian Blouse 299,** 1939–1940, charcoal and estompe on paper, 56.8x38.6cm, National Museum of Art, Bucharest. **The Rumanian Blouse 304,** December 1939–April 1940, oil on canvas, 92x73cm, Musée national d'art moderne, Paris. **The Rumanian Blouse with Green Sleeves 292,** March–April 1937, oil on canvas, 73x60cm, Cincinnati Art Museum, Mary E. Johnston Bequest. **The Sails 409,** 1952, gouache on paper, cut and pasted, 72x60cm, private collection. **Seated Nude 60,** early 1906, woodcut, 47.5x38cm, The Museum of Modern Art, New York, gift of Mr. and Mrs. R. Kirk Askew, Jr. **Seated Nude 61,** early 1906, woodcut, 46x28.4cm, The Museum of Modern Art, New York, Abby Aldrich Rockefeller Fund. **Seated Nude 69,** 1906, pastel and gouache on paper, 73x51cm, private collection. **Seated Nude, Arm behind the Back 99,** 1909, bronze, 32.3x23x18cm, Musée national d'art moderne, Paris. **Seated Nude (Olga) 101,** 1909–1910, bronze, 42.5x24.6x33.2cm, private collection. **Seated Nude on a Red Background 235,** 1925, oil on canvas, 74x61cm, Musée national d'art moderne, Paris. **Seated Pink Nude 273,** 1935–1936, oil on canvas, 92x73cm, Musée national d'art moderne, Paris. **Seated Young Woman 92,** 1909, oil on canvas, 41.5x33.5cm, Wallraf-Richartz Museum, Cologne. **Seated Young Woman in a Persian Dress 324,** December 1942, oil on canvas, 43x56cm, Musée Picasso, Paris. **Self-Portrait 64,** Summer 1906?, oil on canvas, 55x46cm, Statens Museum for Kunst, Copenhagen. **Self-Portrait 186,** 1918, oil on canvas, 65x54cm, Musée Matisse, Le Cateau-Cambrésis. **Self-Portrait 288,** 1937, charcoal and estompe on paper, 47.3x39.1cm, The Baltimore Museum of Art, The Cone Collection. **Self-Portrait 289,** 1937, charcoal on paper, 34x28.5cm, National Gallery of Art, Washington, Collection of Mr. and Mrs. Mellon. **Self-Portrait 290,** 1937, charcoal on paper, 25.4x 20.3cm, Musée national d'art moderne, Paris. **Self-Portrait 311,** 1941, sanguine chalk on paper, 48x37.5cm, private collection. **The Serpentine 100,** 1909, bronze, 54.6x29.2x19cm, private collection. **Seville Still Life 112,** 1910–1911, oil on canvas, 90x117cm, Hermitage, Saint Petersburg. **Shaft of Sunlight, the Woods of Trivaux 177,** 1917, oil on canvas, 91x 74cm, private collection. **Siesta, Interior at Nice 221,** 1922, oil on canvas, 66x54.5cm, Musée national d'art moderne, Paris. **The Silence Living in Houses 367,** 1947, oil on canvas, 61x50cm, private collection. **Simone in a Striped Armchair 315,** 1942, oil on canvas, 32x25cm, private collection. **Sketch for the "Blue Nude" series 398,** c. 1952, crayon on paper, 21x27cm, whereabouts unknown. **Sketch for the "Blue Nude" series 399,** c. 1952, crayon on paper, 21x27cm, whereabouts unknown. **Sketch for the "Blue Nude" series 400,** c. 1952, crayon on paper, 21x27cm, whereabouts unknown. **Sketch for the "Blue Nude" series 401,** c. 1952, crayon on paper, 21x27cm, whereabouts unknown. **Small Odalisque in a Purple Robe 284,** 1937, oil on canvas, 38x45,7cm, private collection. **The Snail 411,** 1953, gouache on paper, cut and pasted, on white paper, 287x288cm, Tate Gallery, London. **The Sorrow of the King 396,** 1952, gouache on paper, cut and pasted, on white paper, 292.7x386cm, Musée national d'art moderne, Paris. **Spanish Still Life 109,** 1910–1911, oil on canvas, 89x116cm, Hermitage, Saint Petersburg. **Spanish Woman with a**

Fan 226, 1923, charcoal and estompe on paper, 51x40.2cm, Musée national d'art moderne, Paris. **Spanish Woman with a Tambourine 89**, early 1909, oil on canvas, 92x73cm, Pushkin Museum, Moscow. **Standing Model / Nude Study in Blue 29**, Autumn 1900–Spring 1901, oil on canvas, 73x54cm, Tate Gallery, London. **Standing Nude 88**, late 1906–1907, oil on canvas, 92.1x64.8cm, Tate Gallery, London. **Standing Nude 366**, 1947, oil on canvas, 65x54.2cm, Musée national d'art moderne, Paris. **The Standing Riffian 135**, late 1912, oil on canvas, 146.5x97.7cm, Hermitage, Saint Petersburg. **The Stations of the Cross 391**, 1950, ceramic tiles, Chapelle du Rosaire, Vence. **Still Life 316**, 1941, pen and ink on paper, 40.6x52.2cm, Musée national d'art moderne, Paris. **Still Life 317**, August 1941, pen and ink on paper, 52x40cm, Musée national d'art moderne, Paris. **Still Life on a Green Sideboard 242**, 1928, oil on canvas, 81.5x100cm, Musée national d'art moderne, Paris. **Still Life with a Black Rug 58**, 1906, oil on canvas, 61x73cm, Hermitage, Saint Petersburg. **Still Life with a Geranium 62**, Summer 1906, oil on canvas, 97.9x80.2cm, The Art Institute of Chicago, Joseph Winterbotham Collection. **Still Life with a Magnolia 312**, September 1941, pen and ink on paper, 40x53cm, private collection. **Still Life with a Magnolia 313**, August–October 1941, oil on canvas, 74x101cm, Musée national d'art moderne, Paris. **Still Life with a Pewter Jug and Pink Statuette 110**, 1910, oil on canvas, 90x117cm, Hermitage, Saint Petersburg. **Still Life with a Plaster Bust 167**, Spring 1916, oil on canvas, 100x81cm, The Barnes Foundation, Merion, Pennsylvania. **Still Life with a Sleeping Woman 300**, late 1939–early 1940, oil on canvas, 81x100cm, National Gallery of Art, Washington, Collection of Mr. and Mrs. Mellon. **Still Life with Asphodels 73**, 1907, oil on canvas, 114x87cm, Museum Folkwang, Essen. **Still Life with Black Knives 20**, c. 1896, oil on canvas, 60x85cm, Fonds national d'art contemporain, on deposit at Musée Fabre, Montpellier. **Still Life with Black Statuette 90**, 1908–1909, oil on canvas, 105x70cm, private collection. **Still Life with Blue Tablecloth 26**, c. 1900–1902, oil on canvas, 73x92cm, Hermitage, Saint Petersburg. **Still Life with Fruit 106**, 1910, oil on canvas, 89x116.5cm, Pushkin Museum, Moscow. **Still Life with Geraniums 108**, 1910, oil on canvas, 93x115cm, Staatsgalerie moderner Kunst, Munich. **Still Life with Green Marble Table 314**, 1941, oil on canvas, 46x38.5cm, Musée national d'art moderne, Paris. **Still Life with Lemons and a Bottle 19**, 1896, oil on canvas, 31.2x29.3cm, The Museum of Modern Art, New York, gift of Mr. and Mrs. Warren Brandt. **Still Life with Oysters 306**, 1940, oil on canvas, 65.5x81.5cm, Kunstmuseum, Basel. **Still Life with Shell 307**, September–December 1940, oil on canvas, 54x82cm, Pushkin Museum, Moscow. **Still Life with Shell 308**, 1940, mixed media on canvas, 59x91.4cm, private collection. **Still Life with Two Bottles 18**, 1896, oil on canvas, 73x60cm, private collection. **Still Life: Pink Tablecloth, Vase of Anemones, Lemons and Pineapple 231**, 1925, oil on canvas, 80x100cm, private collection. **The Studio 249**, 1929, oil on canvas, 46x61cm, private collection. **Studio of the Picard Weaver 14**, 1895, oil on wooden panel, 40x54.5cm, Musée national d'art moderne, Paris. **Studio Under the Eaves 33**, 1901–1902, oil on canvas, 55x44.5cm, Fitzwilliam Museum, University of Cambridge. **Study for "Calypso" 267**, 1934, charcoal on paper, 52.5x40.5cm, private collection. **Study for "Le Luxe (I)" 66**, 1907, charcoal on paper, 225x137cm, Musée national d'art moderne, Paris. **Study for "The**

mitage, Saint Petersburg. **Vase with Two Handles 72,** 1907, oil on canvas, 74x61cm, Hermitage, Saint Petersburg. **Vegetables 394,** c.1951, gouache on paper, cut and pasted, 175x81cm, private collection. **View of Collioure 51,** Summer 1905, oil on canvas, 46x55cm, Musée Matisse, Le Cateau-Cambrésis. **View of Notre-Dame 148,** Spring 1914, oil on canvas, 147.3x94.3cm, The Museum of Modern Art, New York. **Village in Brittany 16,** 1896, oil on canvas, 59.5x73cm, Musée Matisse, Nice. **Violonist at the Window 189,** Spring 1918, oil on canvas, 150x98cm, Musée national d'art moderne, Paris. **The Waterfront 71,** 1907, oil on canvas, 73x60cm, Kunstmuseum, Basel. **White and Pink Head 147,** Autumn 1914, oil on canvas, 75x47cm, Musée national d'art moderne, Paris. **The White Plumes 199,** early 1919, oil on canvas, 73x60.3cm, The Minneapolis Institute of Arts, The William Hood Dunwoody Fund. **The Window 166,** Spring 1916, oil on canvas, 146x116.8cm, The Detroit Institute of Arts. **Window at Nice 174,** 1917–1918, pen on paper, 27.4x21.3cm, Musée national d'art moderne, Paris. **The Wine Press 395,** c.1951, gouache on paper, cut and pasted, on white paper, 175x82cm, private collection. **The Wolf (plate VI from "Jazz") 351,** 1947, 42.5x65.5cm, Musée national d'art moderne, Paris. **Woman Before an Aquarium 209,** late 1921 or 1923, oil on canvas, 81.3x100.3cm, The Art Institute of Chicago, Helen Birch Bartlett Memorial Collection. **Woman Bending Her Arm 240,** 1927, charcoal on paper, 38.7x28.8cm, private collection. **Woman in a Flowered Hat 192,** 1919, oil on canvas, 58.9x49.9cm, private collection. **Woman in a Purple Robe with Ranunculi 294,** February 1937, oil on canvas, 81x65cm, The Museum of Fine Arts, Houston, The John A. and Audrey Jones Beck Collection. **Woman in an Armchair on a Blue and Yellow Background 282,** 1936, oil on canvas, 46x38cm, private collection. **Woman in an Armchair, or Antoinette 194,** 1919, oil on canvas, 52.5x36cm, private collection. **Woman in Blue / The Large Blue Robe and Mimosas 286,** 1937, oil on canvas, 92.7x73.6cm, Philadelphia Museum of Art, gift of Mrs. John Wintersteen. **Woman on a Sofa 202,** late 1920–Spring 1921, oil on canvas, 60x70.3cm, Kunstmuseum, Basel. **Woman Reading 15,** 1895, oil on wooden panel, 61.5x48cm, Musée national d'art moderne, Paris. **Woman Reading 217,** c.1922, oil on canvas, 28x35cm, Musée d'art moderne, Troyes. **Woman Reading, on a Black Background 301,** August 1939, oil on canvas, 92x73.5cm, Musée national d'art moderne, Paris. **Woman with a Green Parasol on a Balcony 183,** Winter 1918–1919, oil on canvas, 66.5x47cm, private collection. **Woman with a Mandolin 220,** c.1922, oil on canvas, 47x40cm, Musée de l'Orangerie, Paris. **Woman with a Veil 246,** 1927, oil on canvas, 61.5x50.2cm, The Museum of Modern Art, New York, The William S. Paley Collection. **Woman with a Violin 212,** 1921, oil on canvas, 55x40cm, Musée de l'Orangerie, Paris. **The Woman with Blue Eyes 275,** 1935, crayon on paper, 28x38cm, private collection. **Woman with Pearl Necklace 325,** 1942, oil on canvas, 62x50cm, private collection. **The Woman with the Hat 48,** Autumn 1905, oil on canvas, 80.6x59.7cm, San Francisco Museum of Modern Art, bequest of Elise S. Haas. **The Yellow Hat 251,** 1929, oil on canvas, 65x45cm, private collection. **The Yellow Robe, Zorah 132,** 1912, oil on canvas, 89x63.5cm, Cowles Collection, Lake Forest, California. **Young Girl 155,** 1916–1917, charcoal on paper, 35.5x26.8cm, private collection. **The Young Sailor (I) 54,** 1906, oil on canvas, 100x82cm, private collection. **The Young Sailor (II) 55,** 1906, oil on canvas, 101x

83 cm, The Metropolitan Museum of Art, New York. **The Young Woman and the Vase of Flowers or The Pink Nude 213**, date unknown, oil on canvas, 60x73 cm, Musée de l'Orangerie, Paris. **Young Woman in White, Red Background 339**, 1946, oil on canvas, 92x73 cm, Musée des Beaux-Arts, Lyons (housed at the Musée national d'art moderne, Paris). **Young Woman with White Fur Coat 338**, 1944, oil on canvas, 73x60 cm, Musée national d'art moderne, Paris. **Zorah on the Terrace 127**, 1912–1913, oil on canvas, 115x100 cm, Pushkin Museum, Moscow. **Zorah Standing 133**, late 1912, oil on canvas, 146x61 cm, Hermitage, Saint Petersburg. **Zulma 386**, 1950, gouache on paper, cut and pasted, and crayon, 238x133 cm, Statens Museum for Kunst, Copenhagen.

First published in the United States of America in 2002
By UNIVERSE PUBLISHING
A Division of Rizzoli International Publications, Inc.
300 Park Avenue South
New York, NY 10010

Photo credits:
Albright-Knox Art Gallery, Buffalo, New York; The Art Institute of Chicago; Artothek, Weilheim; The Baltimore Museum of Art; Bridgeman Art Library, London; The Detroit Institute of Arts; Isabella Stewart Gardner Museum, Boston; Kunstsammlung Nordrhein-Westfalen, Düsseldorf; Musée d'art moderne de la Ville de Paris; Musée de l'Orangerie, Paris; Musée Matisse, Nice; Museum Folkwang, Essen; Museum of Fine Arts, Boston; National Gallery of Art, Washington; Philadelphia Museum of Art; Photo Archives Matisse, Paris; RMN Réunion des musées nationaux, Paris; The Saint Louis Art Museum; San Francisco Museum of Modern Art; Scottish National Gallery of Modern Art, Edinburgh; Städelsches Kunstinstitut und Städtische Galerie, Frankfurt am Main; Statens Museum for Kunst, Copenhagen; Tate Gallery, London; Wadsworth Atheneum, Hartford.

Designed by Griet Van Haute
Translation biography: Harriet Horsfield in association with First Edition Translations Ltd, Cambridge, UK

Cover: *Icarus (plate VIII from "Jazz")*, 1947, Musée national d'art moderne, Paris and *Blue Nude II*, 1952, Musée national d'art moderne, Paris
Frontispiece: *The Open Window, Collioure*, 1905, National Gallery of Art, Washington, Collection of Mr. and Mrs. John Hay Whitney.
Page 4: *Bathers with a Turtle*, 1908, The Saint Louis Art Museum, gift of Mr. and Mrs. Joseph Pulitzer, Jr.

Printed in China

Library of Congress Control Number: 2002108752

ISBN 0-7893-0843-6